The New Sabin

Cumulative Index
to Entries 1—13513

"The New Sabin;"
Books Described by Joseph Sabin and His
Successors, Now Described Again on the
Basis of Examination of Originals,
and Fully Indexed by Title, Subject,
Joint Authors, and Institutions and Agencies.

by

Lawrence S. Thompson

Cumulative Index
to Entries 1—13513

The Whitston Publishing Company
Troy, New York
1978

The New Sabin

Cumulative Index
to Entries 1—13513

of races, 977
Abolition Society of Paint
Valley, 3131, 3132
Abolitionists, 1043
Aborigines' Protection Society,
London, 5812, 5813
About the South, 3986
Abrahall, Chandos Hoskyns, 23
Abraham Lincoln, 5640, 5814
Abraham Lincoln Association,
Springfield, Ill., 5815,
5816, 5821
Abraham Lincoln Book Shop,
Chicago, 6586, 6667
Abraham Lincoln Centre and
All Souls Church, Chicago,
5817
Abraham Lincoln Foundation,
New York, 5818
Abraham Lincoln, his life in
Illinois, 6004
Abraham Lincoln in Great
Britain, 7073
Abraham Lincoln Memorial
Garden, Springfield, Ill.,
5819
Abraham Lincoln Memorial High-
way Association, 5820
Abraham Lincoln quarterly, 5821
Abraham Lincoln sees Peoria,
6653
Abraham Lincoln traveled this
way, 3907
Abraham Lincoln University,
5818, 5822
Abraham Lincoln's character,
11544
Abraham Lincoln's last case in
Chicago, 5823
Abraham Page, esq., 9907
Abram Lincoln and South Caro-
lina, 13212
Abramo Lincoln, 5824
Abreu de Galindo, Juan de, 24
An abridgement of the laws of
Jamaica, 13146
The absent Lord of Rochefort,
5616
Acacia, 2563

Academia de la historia,
Madrid, 7657
Academia nacional de la
historia, Caracas, 6956
Academia nacional de San
Carla, Mexico, 7401
Academia real das sciencias,
Lisbon, 11525
Académie d'agriculture de
France, Paris, 11983
Academy of natural sciences
of Philadelphia. Concho-
logical section, 259
Acadia, see Nova Scotia.
Acadia, 6487, 6575, 6951, 7268,
7865, 8045, 8984
Acadians, 3597, 7865, 8045
L'Acadie, 147
Accolon of Gaul, 2948
An accompaniment to Mitchell's
reference and distance map
of the U. S., 4488
Accompaniment to the map of
the emigrant road from
Independence to San Fran-
cisco, 4049
According to St. John, 11011
According to the law, 10808
Account of a journey through
northeastern Texas, 5191
An account of a journey to
Niagara, Montreal and
Quebec, 13117
An account of a voyage for
the discovery of a north-
west passage by Hudson's
Streights, 6624
An account of Abimelech
Coody, 1904
An account of Col. Crockett's
tour to the North and down
East, 3121
An account of East-Florida,
5291
Account of Mrs. Beecher Stowe
and her family, by an
Alabama man, 10910
An account of the conduct of the
war in the middle colonies,

12189

An account of the European settlements in America, 2857, 11615

Account of the expedition of Lieut. Gov. Hamilton, 3760

An account of the first discovery, and natural history of Florida, 4976

An account of the French settlements in North America, 25

An account of the gospel labours, 3001

An account of the great earthquakes, 4793

An account of the imprisonment and sufferings of Robert Fuller, 2359

An account of the late invasion of Georgia, 5324

An account of the life of that ancient servant of Jesus Christ, John Richardson, 4954

An account of the life, travels, and Christian experiences in the work of the ministry of Samuel Bownas, 2773

The account of the new invented Pennsylvanian fire places, 12162

An account of the origin, progress, doctrines... of the Methodist Episcopal Church in the United States, 12321

An account of the present state of Nova Scotia, 12853

An account of the province of Carolina in America, 5742

An account of the remarkable occurrences in the life and travels of Col. James Smith, 5199

An account of the Society for the encouragement of the British troops, 12659

An account of the Spanish settlements in America, 26

An account of the State prison, 2180

An account of the U. S. A., derived from actual observation, during a residence of four years in that republic, 3909

An account of the writings of Roger Williams, 12489

An account of Virginia, 3628

An account showing the progress of the colony of Georgia, 3590

Accounts of shipwreck and of other disasters at sea, 199

Acereto, Albino, 5825

Acevedo Escobedo, Antonio, 1909-, ed., 6273

Achenbach, Hermann, 27

Achenwall, Gottfried, 1719-1772, 28

The Acme Haversack's Lincoln memoranda, 5826

Acme publishing co., Chicago, pub., 7760

Acosta, Joaquin, 1799-1852, 29

Acosta, José de, 1539(ca.)-1600, 5827

Acrelius, Israel, 1714-1800, 30

Across America, 5044

Across Mexico in 1864-5, 6936

Across the Atlantic, 4270

Across the continent, 2772

Across the Everglades, 5731

Across the gulf, 9355

Across the plains in 1850, 5078

Across the street, 10841

Across the sub-Arctics of Canada, 8252

Acrostics, 6093

Acta in Commitiis Provincialibus Angelopolitanae Sancti Michaelis, 5828

Acta Provincialis, S. Michaelis Archāg and SS. Angelorum Provinciae Ordinis Praedicatorum, 5829

3

Actaeon, 9314
Active service, 9209
Acton, Me. - Hist., 2360
Actors - Correspondence,
  reminiscences, etc., 5211,
  5212, 5560, 11251
The actress of Padua, 10815
The acts of Dr. Bray's
  visitation, 1448
Acuña, Cristóbal de, b. 1597, 31
Adair, James, trader with
  the Indians, 32
Adalaska, 1248
Adam family (John Adam,
  1714-1802), 33
Adam Floyd, 10163
Adam, George, 2700
Adam Johnstone's son, 9219
Adam, Paul Auguste Marie,
  1862-1920, 2489
Adam W. Snyder and his period
  in Illinois history, 5225
Adam, William, b. 1799, 33
Adam y Arriaga, José,
  d. 1698, 5830
Adams, Abigail (Smith) 1744-
  1818, 62
Adams, Amos, 1728-1775, 34, 35
Adams, Charles Baker, 1814-
  1853, 36, 37, 12354
Adams, Charles Francis, 1807-
  1886, 38, 39, 40, 41, 42,
  62, 63
Adams, Charles Francis, 1835-
  1915, 5831
Adams co., Pa. - Hist. -
  Fiction, 8715
Adams, Daniel, 1773-1864, 43
Adams, Eliphalet, 1677-1753,
  44
Adams family (Henry Adams,
  d. 1646), 6836
Adams family (Stephen Olney
  Adams, 1620-1718), 5835
Adams family (William Adams,
  of Ipswich, Mass., d. 1661),
  418
Adams, Francis Colburn, 45,
  46, 47, 48

Adams, George Everett, 1840-,
  5832, 5833
Adams, George Washington,
  d. 1829, 49, 2221
Adams, Hannah, 1755-1831, 50,
  51, 52, 53, 54
Adams, Herbert Baxter, 1850-
  1901, 2490
Adams, Horace, 5834
Adams, James Capen, 2491, 3888
Adams, John, 1704-1740, 55
Adams, John, 1750?-1814, 64
Adams, John, 1760?-1829, 10698
Adams, John Greenleaf, 1810-
  1887, 65
Adams, John Gregory Bishop,
  1841-1900, 2492
Adams, John Merriman, 1834-,
  5835
Adams, John, pres. U.S.,
  1735-1826, 56, 57, 58, 59,
  60, 61, 62, 63, 1808, 6393,
  11480, 12179, 12197, 12207,
  12601
Adams, John Quincy, pres. U.S.,
  1767-1848, 66, 67, 68, 69,
  70, 71, 72, 73, 74, 75, 76,
  77, 78, 79, 80, 81, 12115,
  12401, 12527
Adams, Oscar Fay, 10283
Adams, Randolph Greenfield,
  1892-, 5836
Adams, Samuel, 1722-1803,
  60, 11385
Adams, Seth, defendant, 1912
Adams, W. L., 5837
Adams, William Edwin, 1832-,
  2493
Adams, William Henry Daven-
  port, 1828-1891, tr., 4935
Adams, Zabdiel, 1739-1801,
  2101
Adamson, Augustus Pitt,
  1844-, 2494
Adamson, John, 1787-1855, 82
Adamson, Thomas, 83
Adán y Arriaga, José. See
  Adam y Arriaga, José.
Added upon, 8537

4

5

Addresses and memorials,
5839
Addresses of the Chillicothe
Association for Promoting
Morality and Good Order,
2990
Addresses of the city of New
York to George Washington,
7577
Addums, Moses, pseud. of
George William Bagby,
2590, 2591
Adeler, Max, pseud., 9006
Adelman, David C., 5840
Adelung, Friedrich von,
1768-1843, 97
Adelung, Johann Christoph,
1732 - 1806, 97, 1589
Adet, Pierre-Auguste, 1763-
1834, 5841, 6774
Adger, John Bailey, 1810-
1899, 98
Adirondack iron and steel
company, New York, 99
Adirondack mountains, 10398,
12630
Adlam, Samuel, 1798-1880, 100
Adlard, George, 101
Administration dissected, 102
Administrative law - France,
952
The administratrix, 9286
Admiralty, 9918
Adolphus, John, 1768-1845, 103
Adrian, 10009
Adrift in Dixie, 3393
Adrift on an ice-pan, 6899
Adrift with a vengeance, 9172
Adsonville, 8481
Advance and retreat, 3922
Advance in the Antilles, 6907
Adventure and adventurers,
1450, 2616, 2987, 3786,
3890, 9007, 12562
The adventure of the missing
briefs, 6006
An adventure on a frozen lake,
9972
The adventurer, 8669

The adventurer of the northern
wilds, 9432
Adventures amidst the equatorial
forests and rivers of South
America, 5315
Adventures in Mexico and the
Rocky Mountains, 5053
Adventures in rebeldom, 3387
Adventures in search of a
living in Spanish America,
8289
Adventures in Texas, 4334
Adventures in the Apache
country, 2837
Adventures in the Camanche
country, 5651
Adventures in the Camanche
country in search of a gold
mine, 11115
Adventures in the far west,
2680, 2683
Adventures in the gold region,
10501
Adventures in the wilderness,
10398
Adventures in the wilds of
the U. S. and British American
provinces, 4215, 7240
Adventures of a consul abroad,
7523
The adventures of a French
captain, 3618
The adventures of a Georgian,
11031
The adventures of a New Bedford
boy on sea and land, 12562
The adventures of a night,
9294
The adventures of a wanderer,
10503
The adventures of a widow,
9499
Adventures of Alf. Wilson,
5737
The adventures of an enthu-
siast, 10330
The adventures of Big-Foot
Wallace, 3330
Adventures of Col. Gracchus

6

Vanderbomb,· 4109
Adventures of Elder Tripto-
lemus Tub, 10659
The adventures of Harry
Franco, 8845
The adventures of Hector
Wigler, 11222
The adventures of James
Sharan, 5128
The adventures of Miles
Wallingford, 9127
The adventures of my cousin
Smooth, 8456
The adventures of Search
for Life, 10313
The adventures of Sir Lyon
Bouse, 11144
Adventures of the first
settlers on the Oregon or
Columbia river, 5017
The adventures of three
Southerns, 2924
The adventures of Uncle Sam,
9507
Adventures on the Mosquito
shore, 8098, 13485
Advice and guide to emigrants,
4643
Advice to the officers of
the British army, 12460
AEnone, 10142
Aengemerckte voorvallen op
de vredens articulen met
Portugael, 104
Aeronautics - Flights, 7362
Affaires de l'Angleterre et
de l'Amérique, 105
Aflalo, Frederick George,
1870-1918, 2495
Afloat and ashore, 9127
Afoot and alone, 4843
Africa and the American flag,
12147
Africa - Colonization -
Negroes, 12783
Africa - Descr. & trav.,
4853, 5073, 13335
Africa - Disc. & explor.,
1081

Africa - Entomology, 4684
Africa - Hist., 11589
Africa, South - Descr. &
trav., 8106
Africa, West - Descr. &
trav., 12147
African colonization unveiled,
5039
African servitude, 106
The African squadron, 2265
After Dinner Club, Moline,
Ill., 5842, 5843
After freedom, 4839
After his kind, 10472
After many days, 5417
After the storm, 5174
After the war, 4927
Aftermath, 8511
Against human nature, 10539
Against the world, 11058
Agassiz, George Russell,
1862-, ed., 4321
Agassiz, Louis, 1807-1873,
107, 108, 109, 1404
Agatha Webb, 10661
Agave - Therapeutic use, 726
Ager, Carolus, jt. author,
9509
Agli Stati Uniti, il pericolo
americano, 4385
Agnes, 8555, 10525
Agnes Farriday, 9011
Agnes Goodmaid, 10713
Agnes Hilton, 9881
Agnes Stanhope, 10607
Agnes Wentworth, 10470
Agnew, John Holmes, 1804-
1865, 110
The agnostic, 4792
Agreda y Sánchez, José María
de, 1837-1916, tr., 6835
Agresti, Antonio, 1866-1927,
5844
Agricola, 3370
Agricultural chemistry,
13234, 13307
Agricultural editors asso-
ciation, 7584
Agricultural tour in the

7

United States and Upper
Canada, 2506
Agriculture, 1657, 4704
Agriculture - Addresses,
essays, lectures, 1253,
12296, 12962, 13124, 13265
Agriculture - Belgium, 12735
Agriculture - British Colum-
bia, 6177
Agriculture - Canada, 2506,
4078, 6271, 12372
Agriculture - Cuba, 613
Agriculture - Dictionaries,
11957, 13234
Agriculture - England, 12735
Agriculture - France, 12735
Agriculture - French Guiana,
1202, 1831
Agriculture - Georgia,
13307
Agriculture - Jamaica, 1035
Agriculture - Louisiana,
3231
Agriculture - Massachusetts,
1538
Agriculture - Mexico, 7262
Agriculture - Missouri, 4698
Agriculture - New Brunswick,
13274
Agriculture - North America,
5049
Agriculture - North Carolina,
5040
Agriculture - Societies, 1538
Agriculture - South Carolina,
13265
Agriculture - Southern States,
11368
Agriculture - Tropics, 11368
Agriculture - U. S., 2506,
3039, 4078
Agriculture - West Indies,
576, 1080
Aguas termales de Cartago,
Costa Rica, 5845
Agüero, Pedro de, 1821-, 111
Aguero y Sota, Baltasar de,
5846
Aguilar, Federico Cornelio,

1834-1887, 5847
Aguirre, José M., 5848
Aguirre, Juan Francisco,
d. 1811, 5849
Ahumada y Villalón, Agustín de,
marqués de las Amarillas,
viceroy of Mexico, d. 1760,
5807
Ahumada y Villalón, Agustín de.
marqués de las Amarillas,
viceroy of Mexico, d. 1760 -
Poetry, 5806
Ai; a social vision, 9324
The aid-de-camp, 4329
Aiken, John, 112
Aiken, Peter Freeland, 113
Aiken, Solomon, 1758-1833, 114
Aikin, John, 1747-1822, 115
Aikman, William, 1824-1909,
116, 117
Aimard, Gustave, 1818-1883,
2496
Aimée's marriage, 9190
Ainslie, Hew, 1792-1878, 2497
Ainsworth, William Harrison,
1805-1882, 118
Aislabie, John, 1670-1742, 119
Aked, Charles Frederic, 1864-,
5850
Akins, Thomas B., ed., 7599
The Alabama and Kearsarge,
12003
Alabama - Biography, 3576
Alabama (Confederate cruiser),
5123, 13405
Alabama - Descr. & trav., 3171,
3595, 3650, 4173, 4791, 5034,
5706, 5717
Alabama - Fiction, 3926
Alabama - Hist., 13456
Alabama infantry. 1st regt.,
1861-1865, 4369
Alabama infantry. 60th regt.,
1862-1865, 5130
Alabama (Privateer), 12003
Alabama - Soc. life & cust.,
707
Alachua county, Florida - Descr.
& trav., 5647

8

Alaman, Lucas, 1792-1853,
  defendant, 120
Alamance, 11164
The alarm bell, 121
Alas y garras, 6610
Alaska, 11941
Alaska - Antiq., 2231
Alaska - Bound. - Canada,
  6053, 6054, 6181
Alaska - Descr. & trav.,
  4750, 5915, 6162, 6192,
  6237, 6422, 7369, 7982,
  8410
Alaska - Descr. & trav. -
  Guide-books, 5978, 5979
Alaska - Yukon game-lands,
  7369
Alba, Raphael de, 7837
Alban, 9974
Albany Congress, 1754, 12898
Albany co., N. Y. - Biog.,
  11829
Albany co., N. Y. - Hist. -
  Civil war, 11829
Albany - Hist., 857, 858
Albany, N. Y. - Biog., 11829
Albany, N. Y. Dudley obser-
  vatory, 12331, 12332
Albemarle Sound, 3358
Albenino, Nicolao de, 1514?-,
  122
Alberdi, Juan Bautista,
  1810-1884, 123
Alberta - Descr. & trav.,
  6226, 7392, 7656, 8007,
  8074, 8126, 8383
Alberti, Leandro, 1479-1552,
  124
Albertus Magnus, bp. of
  Ratisbon, 126
Albion, Ill. - Hist., 2258
Albright, Philip, 8037
Albro, John Adams, 1799-1866,
  127
The album, 10197
Album de México monumental,
  6865
Album del Ferrocarril mexi-
  cano, 6815

Album gráfico de la Republica
  Mexicana, 6691
Album mexicano, 5851
Album of the Mexican railway,
  6815
Alcalá Galiano, Dionisio de,
  1760-1805, 5852
Alcazar y Zúñiga, Andres del,
  conde de la Marquina, 5853,
  5854
Alcedo, Antonio de, 1736-1812,
  128
Alcedo y Herrera, Dionisio de,
  1690-1777, 5855
The alchemist, 9486
Alchemy - Fiction, 8937
Alcocer, Ignacio, 7932
Alcocer y Sasinana, Baltasar
  de, 5856
Alcoforado, Francisco, 129
Alcott, Louisa May, 1832-1888,
  130, 131, 10163
Alcover y Beltran, Antonio
  Miguel, 1875-, 5857
Aldao, Carlos A., 1860-, 5858
Aldeane, 9837
Alden, Ebenezer, 1788-1881, 132
Alden, Joseph, 1807-1885, 133
Alden, Timothy, 1771-1839,
  134, 135, 136, 137, 138
Alderbrook, 10082
Aldrich, Julia Carter, 5859
Aldrich, Lewis Cass, 5860
Aldrich, Lorenzo D., 2498
Aldrich, Thomas Bailey, 1836-
  1907, jt. author, 10447
Aldridge, William, 1737-1797,
  4396
Aldunate Philips, Arturo,
  1902-, 2499
Alduvin, Ricardo D., 7451
Aleck and Pete, 8504
Alegre, Francisco Javier,
  1729-1788, 139
Alemán, Mateo, 1547-1614? 5861,
  5862
Alessio Robles, Vito, 1879-,
  ed., 7536, 7878
Alexander, Alexander, fl. 1825,

9

140
Alexander, Archibald, 1772-
1851, 141, 142, 148
Alexander, Caleb, 1755-
1828, 143
Alexander, Charles A., 144
Alexander, Charles W.,
Philadelphia, pub.,
8553, 10932
Alexander, Charles Wesley,
1837-1927, 2500, 2501
Alexander family, 757, 13013
Alexander, G. W., 2048
Alexander, George William,
1802-1890, 145, 146
Alexander, Sir James Edward,
1803-1885, 147, 1331,
2502, 5863
Alexander, James Waddell,
1804-1859, 148, 2503
Alexander, John Henry,
1812-1867, 149, 150
Alexander (Ship), 7912
Alexandria Co., Va. -
Hist., 151
Alexandria, Va., 4966
Alexandria, Va. Citizens,
151
Alexandria, Va. - Soc. life
& cust., 9761
Alexia, 8450
Alfaro, Francisco de, 16th
cent., 5864
Alfaro y Acevedo, José
Jorge, 6160
Alfieri, Vittorio, 1749-1803,
152
Alfonso, Pedro Antonio, 153
Alfonso V, el Magnánimo, king
of Aragon, d. 1458 - Poetry,
6118
Alford and Selina, 10673
Alfred, 9709
Algar, W. H., 2504
Alger, William Rounseville,
1822-1905, 154, 155, 156, 157
Algeria - Descr. & trav.,
7858, 8877, 11036, 11811
The Algerine captive, 11036

The Algerine spy in Pennsylvania,
10317
Algiers, Battle of, 1816, 12841
Algiers (City) - Descr., 1425
Algonquian language - Diction-
aries - English, 7224
Algonquian language - Diction-
aries - French, 13143
Algonquian language - Glossaries,
vocabularies, etc., 7223
The Alhambra, 9993
Alice Brand, 10617
Alice Gordon, 8490
Alice Mannering, 8451
Alice Murray, 9882
Alice of old Vincennes, 10961
Alice Singleton, 10816
Alice Tracy, 9282
Alice Waters, 9863
Alice (Yacht), 3950
Alida, 2006, 9086
Alien Americans, 5102
Alien and sedition laws, 1798,
4400, 13500
The alienigenae of the United
States, 1308
The aliens, 4400
Alif-Laila, 9678
Alina Derlay, 10195
All about Texas, 3362
All for her, 8506
All for him, 8507
All for love, 9441
All my sad captains, 10038
All's well that ends well, 10882
Allan, Dorothy Carter, 1896-,
5865
Allan-Olney, Mary, 2505
Allan, William, 1837-1889,
jt. author, 12924
Allardice, Robert Barclay,
1779-1854, 2506
Alleghany mountains, 4217,
4694
Alleghany river - Descr., 2561
Alleghany Roughs, 3493
Allegheny college, Meadville,
Pa., 159
Allegheny co., Pa., - Biog.,

7455
The Allegheny magazine, 158
Allegiance, 12480
Allegories of life, 8464
Allemagne, d', 2507
Allen, Miss A. J., comp.,
 2508
Allen, Andrew, 1740-1825, 160
Allen, Andrew, 1740-1825 -
 Claims vs. U. S., 160
Allen, Bird, d. 1841, 7917
Allen, Ethan, 1738-1789,
 161, 162, 163, 164, 165,
 166, 167, 168, 169, 170,
 171, 5866
Allen, George, 1792-1883,
 172, 173
Allen, Harrison, 1841-1897,
 174
Allen, Ira, 1751-1814, 175,
 176, 177, 178
Allen, James, 1739-1808,
 179
Allen, James, 1809-1837, 180
Allen, James Lane, 1849-1925,
 2509, 7385, 8219, 8221,
 8222
Allen, John, fl. 1764,
 supposed author, 181
Allen, John, 1763-1812, 182
Allen, John, of Hackney, ed.,
 1721
Allen, Joseph, 1772-1806,
 183
Allen, Joseph, 1790-1873,
 184
Allen, Joseph, 1810?-1864,
 185, 186
Allen, Joseph Henry, 1820-
 1898, 187, 188
Allen, Lewis Leonidas, 189,
 190
Allen, Lyman Whitney, 1854-
 1930, 5867, 5868, 5869
Allen, Myron Oliver, 191
Allen, Obridge, 2510
Allen, Paul, 1775-1826, 192,
 193, 194, 4272, 13385
Allen, Richard, bp., 1760-1831,

13284
Allen, Richard L., 1808-1873,
 195
Allen, Robert, late of Peru,
 196
Allen, Solomon Metcalf, 1789-
 1817, 12570
Allen, Wilkes, 1775-1845, 197
Allen, William, 1780-1873, 198
Allen, William, 1784-1868, 199,
 200, 201, 202, 203, 204
Allen, William, 1803-1879, 205
Allen, William G., 206
Allen, William Henry, 1808-1882,
 207, 208
Allen, William Joshua, 1828-
 1901, 209
Alley, John Bassett, 1817-1896,
 210
Allgemeine histoire der reisen
 zu wasser und lande, 211
Allibone, Samuel Austin, 1816-
 1889, 212
Allin, John, 1596-1671, 213
Alling, Jeremiah, 214
Allison, Joseph, 1819-1896,
 215
Allison, Patrick, 1740-1802,
 216
Alloza, Juan de, 1598-1666,
 5870
Allsop, Robert, ed., 217
Allsop, Thomas, 1795-1880, 217
Allston, Robert Francis Withers,
 1801-1864, 218, 5871
Allston, Washington, 1779-1843,
 2511, 2512, 2513, 2514,
 3469
Alltag in USA, 5661
Allworth abbey, 10829
Allyn, John, 1767-1833, 219,
 220
Almanach intéressant dans les
 circonstances présentes,
 2804
Almanacs, American, 239, 326,
 1876
Almanacs. Nova Scotia, 5872,
 5873

11

Almanacs, Spanish, 8436
Almbert, Alfred d', 1813-
  1887, 221
Almon, John, 1737-1805, 222,
  223, 224, 225, 226, 11748
Almost a priest, 11210
Almost persuaded, 3773
The alms-house, 10760
Almshouses - New England,
  9475
Alnomuc, 8533
Alnwick castle, 12585
Alone, 10934
Alone in a great city, 8788
Along Alaska's great river,
  7982
Alonso de San Juan, 5874
Alphabet, 2351
Alphonsine, 10197
Alpine club of Canada, 6317
Alpizar Caire, Ramón, 5875
Alsinet, José, 227
Alsop, George, 1638-, 2515
Alsop, Richard, 1761-1815,
  228, 229
Alstead, N. H. - Hist., 479
Altamira, Juan Rodríguez de
  Albuerne, marques de,
  5876
Altamirano, Diego, 5877
Altars of sacrifice, 11185
Alter und verbesserter schreib-
  kalender, 5427
Altes und neues aus der
  Neuen welt, 4280
Althea Vernon, 10194
Alton, Ill. - Riot, 1837, 1051
Altowan, 5278
Altsheler, Joseph Alexander,
  1862-1919, 2516-2522
Alva y Astorga, Pedro de,
  d. 1667, 5878, 5879
Alvarado Pinto, Carlos Román,
  5880
Alvarado Tezozomoc, Fernando,
  fl. 1598, 5881
Alvarez de Prado, Simón, 6851
Alvarez de Vega, Nicolás,
  6381

Alvarez de Velasco, Gabriel,
  fl. 1650, 5882, 5883
Alvarez, Francisco, Asturian,
  230
Alvarez, José Justo, 1821-1897,
  5884
Alvarez, José María, 1777-1820,
  231
Alvin, Juan, 5885
Alvord, Benjamin, 1813-1884, 232
Alvord, Clarence Walworth, 1868-,
  ed., 2523
Alvord family (Alexander Alvord,
  1620?-1683), 1426
Alvord, John Watson, 1807-1880,
  233
Alzate y Ramírez, José Antonio,
  1738-1845, 6400, 6401
Amabel, 10167
Amador de los Rios, José, 1818-
  1878, ed., 7657
Amanda, 8849
Amanda and love, 9575
Amanda Willson, 8891
Amaru, Severino, pseud., 7516
Amat y Junient, Manuel de,
  viceroy of Peru, 18th cent.,
  5886
Amati, Giacinto, 1778-1850, 234
Amazon river, 31, 577, 1670,
  5939, 7218, 11259
Amazon valley, 961
The Amazonian republic, 10707
The ambassador in spite of
  himself, 10298
The ambassadors, 7115
Amberglow of Abraham Lincoln
  and Joshua Speed, 6831
The ambiguities, 10347
An ambitious man, 11163
The ambitious wasp, 10046
An ambitious woman, 9500
Ambrose, Daniel Leib, 2524
Ambrosio de Letinez, 9597
Amcham guide to Mexico, 8101
L'âme américaine, 4587
Amelia, pseud., 5669
Amelia Sherwood, 8527
America, 235, 236, 1974, 4363,

12105
America: a four years'
residence in the U. S.
and Canada, 6200
America after sixty years,
4858
America and American Method-
ism, 4061
America and Europe, 3721
America and other poems, 5236
America, and the American
church, 2943
America and the American
people, 4898
America and the Americans,
2645, 3109, 6104
America and the Americans
from a French point of
view, 3053
America - Antiq., 249, 1081,
1100, 1443, 11498, 13298
America as I found it, 3319
America at home, 4307
America - Bibl., 2476
America - Biog., 1238
America by river and rail,
3434
America - Comm. - France,
11711
America compared with England,
2525
America - Descr. & trav.,
321, 971, 1557, 1852, 2857,
3653, 4392, 4507, 4900,
5316, 5319, 5793, 6674,
7040, 7629, 8124, 11408,
11586, 11615, 12994
America - Descr. & trav. -
Gazetteers, 128, 251
America - Disc. & explor.,
311, 582, 765, 1081,
1101, 1261, 1598, 2484,
2857, 6623, 6832, 7034,
7035, 7209, 7221, 7657,
7825, 8083, 8160, 8169,
8401, 11523, 11615, 12112
America - Disc. & explor. -
Basque, 7567
America - Disc. & explor. -

English, 1479, 6925
America - Disc. & explor. -
French, 1827, 4144, 6396,
7268, 11715
America - Disc. & explor. -
Irish, 1005
America - Disc. & explor. -
Norse, 1005, 1026, 1322
America - Disc. & explor. -
Phenician, 13298
America - Disc. & explor. -
Pre-Columbian, 610
America - Disc. & explor. -
Poetry, 13293
America - Disc. & explor. -
Spanish, 26, 3547, 4631,
6430, 7393, 7567, 7649,
11708, 12448, 13109
America - Disc. & explor. -
Spanish - Poetry, 794
America - Disc. & explor. -
Welsh, 1692
America during and after the
war, 3433
America - Early accounts to
1600, 29, 373, 374, 375, 376,
406, 407, 794, 1186, 1187,
4631, 5827, 5909, 5920, 8168
America - Early works to
1600, 7657
América (estudios históricos
y filológicos), 7305
America - Geography, 6125
America - Hist., 1112, 1598,
2420, 5793, 11589
America - Hist. - Period., 321
America - Hist. - Poetry,
809, 819
The America I saw in 1916-1918,
5230
America in 1876, 4251
America, its realities and
resources, 5782
L'America libera, 152
America - Maps, 128
America - Politics, 12105
America revisited, 4376, 5063
L'America, ricerca della
felicità, 5070

13

America saved, 1550
L'America vittoriosa, 4642
American, 1262, 7116
American academy of arts
    and sciences, Boston, 238
The American alarm, 181
The American almanac and
    repository of useful
    knowledge, 239
The American annual, 3334
The American annual encyclo-
    paedia and register of
    important events, 240
The American annual register,
    241
American antiquarian society,
    Worcester, Mass., 242, 243,
    244, 12748, 13204
American anti-slavery
    society, 1339, 8181, 13184
American archives, 11844
American association for the
    advancement of science, 245
American Atlantic and Pacific
    Ship Canal Company, 1897
American Autograph Shop,
    Merion Station, Pa., 5887
American ballads and songs,
    302, 12250
The American bee, 246
An American biographical and
    historical dictionary,
    201, 202, 203
American biographical publish-
    ing company, pub., 8260
The American boy's life of
    Washington, 13057
American bureau of mines,
    New York, 247
The American cardinal, 10175
The American church and the
    American union, 11694
The American churches, 2718
An American citizen, 411,
    11774
The American citizen's manual
    of reference, 12520
The American claimant, 9024
The American coast pilot,

2526, 2527
American coin, 8528
American colonization society,
    639, 1699, 5254, 6429, 11563,
    11565, 12618, 12692, 12827,
    13184
The American commonwealth, 1630
American cottage library, 2315
The American cotton industry,
    5792
American criminal trials, 11719
The American crisis, 4763
The American cruiser, 10223
American destiny, 248
American education, 4739
American Education Society, 289
American Education Society.
    Quarterly register, 289
American Education Society.
    Quarterly register and
    journal, 289
The American Egypt, 5932
American enterprise, 2528
American entomology, 5079
American essays, 13513
American estates and gardens,
    3435
American Ethnological Society,
    249
American evening entertainments,
    8934
American family antiquity,
    8365
An American family in Germany,
    8877
The American family Robinson,
    2664
The American female poets, 4424
American fiction (Collections),
    10122, 10675
The American gazette, 250
The American gazetteer, 251
American genealogy, 12847
The American geography, 4539
The American gift book, 252
An American girl abroad, 10157
An American girl in Mexico,
    7364
American hazard, 4884

14

The American hero, 11688
American herpetology, 12683
American highways, 5127
The American historical
  magazine, 254
American historical society,
  Washington, D. C., 255
The American idea, and what
  grows out of it, 11729
The American in Algiers, 256
The American Indian, 630
American institute of instruct-
  ion, 257
American Institute of Mining,
  Metallurgical, and
  Petroleum Engineers, 5888
American international relief
  committee, for the suffer-
  ing operatives of Great
  Britain, 258
American journal of concho-
  logy, 259
The American journal of
  education, 260
The American journal of
  education and college
  review, 261
The American journal of
  improvements in the use-
  ful arts, 262
The American kalendar, 263
The American keepsake, 264
The American laborer, 11226
American life, 5028
American life at home, 8950
American literary gazette and
  publishers' circular, 265
American literature -
  Addresses, essays, lectures,
  4433
American literature -
  Bibl., 212
American literature -
  Bibl. - Early, 11697
American literature -
  Bibl. - Period., 265
American literature
  (collections), 3699, 10154
American literature - Hist.

and criticism, 3332, 3803,
  5165, 11759
American literature - Kentucky,
  5446
American literature - Maryland,
  3077, 5264
American literature - 19th
  cent., 8612
American literature - Ohio
  Valley, 5566
American literature - Period.,
  277, 3857, 5678, 5679
American literature (Selections,
  extracts, etc.), 8626, 9517,
  9616, 11605, 13483
American literature - Southern
  states, 2632, 3183, 3536,
  4408, 5346, 10357
American literature - The West,
  1984, 3043, 3563
The American lounger, 3996
American loyalists, 160, 2383,
  3336, 3418, 11689, 11923,
  11967, 12190, 12602, 12799
American loyalists - Pennsylva-
  nia, 1370
American loyalists - South
  Carolina, 11614
American lyrics, 13293
The American magazine, 266
The American magazine and
  monthly chronicle for the
  British colonies, 267
The American magazine of wit,
  268
The American mariners, 3188
American mechanics' magazine,
  269
American medical botany, 1267
The American melodies, 11886
The American military pocket
  atlas, 5082
American mind, 1461
The American mineralogical
  journal, 270
American missionary memorial,
  4794
The American monthly magazine
  and critical review, 271

15

The American monthly review,
272, 1935
The American museum, 273
The American musical mis-
cellany, 274
American naval battles,
275, 276
American naval biography,
656
American neutrality, 1141,
12668
American newspapers -
Hist., 1640
American newspapers - New
Hampshire, 137
American nights' entertain-
ments, 9658
An American nobleman, 8547
American notes, 5325
American notes and pictures
from Italy, 6588, 6589
American notes and queries,
277, 5889
American notes for general
circulation, 3243
American numismatic society,
278
American orations, 279,
7005, 11671
American oratory, 279
American party, 2194, 5083,
11677
American peace society,
1815, 11370
American periodicals - Hist.,
1640
American Pharmaceutical
Association, 281
American philosophical
society, Philadelphia,
282, 283, 284, 285, 286,
13084
American photographs, 5485
An American physician, 11042
The American pioneer, 287
American poetry (Collections)
3258, 3701, 4294, 4424,
5264
American poetry - Early

19th cent. - Hist. & crit.,
10560
American poetry - Hist. & crit.,
2788
American poetry - Kentucky, 3245
American poetry - The West, 2376
An American politician, 6491
American politics, 12649
The American prejudice against
color, 206
American principles, 69
The American privateer, 9040
American prose literature,
3702, 3802
The American quarterly observer,
288
The American quarterly register,
289
The American querist, 11721
The American question, 290, 291,
2483
American railway guide, 292, 3035
The American register, 293, 294
American rejected addresses,
1268
The American remembrancer, 295,
12673
American republics, 7482
American republics - For. rel. -
League of nations, 8270
American resistance inde-
fensible, 296
American resorts, 4039
The American review, 297, 317
American revolution society,
Charleston, S. C., 11448,
12391, 12445, 12611
American satire, 2800, 5475
The American scene, 4040
American scenery, 5729
American scenes and Christian
slavery, 3185
American sketches, 298
American society, 5443
American society for promoting
national unity, 299
American society for the
encouragement of domestic
manufactures, 300

16

bieten, 5306
Amerikanische lebensbilder, 4190
Amerikanische reisebilder mit besonderer berücksichtigung der dermaligen religiösen, 4766
Amerikanische streiflichter, 2659
Das amerikanische volk, 5172
Amerikanisches, 4182
Amerikanisches magazin, 322
Amerikanisches wanderbuch, 6074
Amerikas wichtigste charakteristik nach land und leuten, 11586
L'Amérique au XXe siècle, 4279
L'Amérique protestante, 4937
Ames, Fisher, 1758-1808, 69, 323, 324, 5890
Ames, Julius Rubens, 1801-1850, 325
Ames, Mrs. Mary (Clemmer) Hudson, 1839-1884, 2530-2532, 2931
Ames, Nathaniel, 1708-1764, 326
Ames, Pelham Warren, 1839-, ed., 5890
Ames, Samuel, 1806-1865, plaintiff, 1399
Amherst college, 327, 328, 329, 8667
Amherst college. Library, 330
Amherst college - Registers, 329
Amherst, Jeffrey Amherst, 1st baron, 1717-1797, 331
Amherst's expedition against Ticonderoga and Crown point, 1759, 331
Amicus reipublicae, pseud., 332
Amis et fortune, 3217
Amistad (Schooner), 70, 789
The amnesty again, 8146

Amnesty question, 8147
Among the Americans, 3920
Among the corn-rows, 9606
Among the guerrillas, 9621
Among the pines, 3610
Among the Selkirk glaciers, 6890
Amory, Charles Bean, 1841-, 2533
Amory, Thomas Coffin, 1812-1889, 333
Amos, Andrew, 1791-1860, ed., 334
Ampère, Jean Jacques Antoine, 1800-1864, 335, 336, 5891
Amphlett, William, 337
Ampzing, Samuel, 1591?-1632, 338
Amsterdams dam-praetje, 339
Amsterdams tafel-praetje, 340
The amulet, 341
Amunátegui, Gregorio Victor, 1830-1899, jt. author, 5893
Amunátegui, Miguel Luis, 1828-1888, 5892, 5893
Amusing and thrilling adventures of a California artist, 4118
Amy Denbrook, 11122
Anahuac, 8159, 8251
The Analectic magazine, 342
Ananias, 9745
Anania, Giovanni Lorenzo d', 343
Anastasio's revenge, 9254
Anburey, Thomas, 344, 345, 346, 347, 5894, 5895
The ancestors of Peter Atherly, 9793
Anchieta, José de, 1534-1579, 1189
The anchoret reclaimed, 10983
Les anciennes villes du Nouveau monde, 6406
The ancient cities of the new world, 6407
Ancient history, 4881
The ancient right of the English nation to the American

Anecdotes of the life of the
Right Hon. William Pitt,
222
Anecdotes secrètes sur la
révolution du 18 fructidor,
366
Anecdotes - U. S., 13450
Anent the North American
continent, 367
Anent the United States and
Confederate States of
North America, 368
The angel and the demon, 8556
The angel child, 9216
Angelis, Pedro de, 1784-1859,
369, 370, 371, 372, 432
Angelo, C. Aubrey, 2548
Angels, 13049
Angels - Art, 11108
Angels in art, 11108
Anghiera, Pietro Martire d',
1455-1526, 373, 374, 375,
376, 5909, 5920
Angier, Joseph, 377
Angina maligna, 2119
Angle, Paul McClelland, 1900-,
5910, 5911, 7280, 7282
An angler's reminiscences,
3758
Anglo-American literature
and manners, 11759
Anglo-Californian, pseud.,
378
Anglo-Dutch war, 1780-1784,
13281
Anglo-French war, 1755-1763,
650
Anglo-French war, 1778-1783,
13281
Anglo-Norman dialect -
Dictionaries, 11425
Anglo-Saxon race, 2534
The Anglo-Saxons historic
and romantic America, 6463
Anglo-Saxons, onward! 9332
Anglo-Spanish war, 1718-1720,
1221
Anglo-Spanish war, 1779-1783,
13281

The anglomaniacs, 9758
Angulos de México, 7400
Animal magnetism, 1406
Ann Ellsworth, 9702
Ann Rutledge, 5912
Anna Clayton, 9401
Annaes maritimos e coloniaes,
379
The annals of administration,
380
The annals of Jamaica, 1499
The annals of Salem, 2243
Annals of the aristocracy, 11168
Annals of the City of Kansas,
5233
Annals of the Fifty-seventh
regiment Indiana volunteers,
4164
Annals of the town of Keene,
2455
Annals of the West, 4752
Annapolis, 12652
Annapolis - Hist., 169
Annapolis. St. Ann's parish,
169
Anne, 9355
Anne, queen consort of Louis
XIII, king of France, 1601-
1666 - Fiction, 10931
Anneke, Fritz, 381
Annetta, 9965
Annette, 11057
Annie Grayson, 10166
Annie Kilburn, 9938
Annie Reilly, 10271
Annie Tousey's little game,
9916
Annina, 11198
An anniversary discourse, on
the state and prospects of the
Western museum society, 3285
Anniversary suggestions, 12590
Annual discourse, delivered
before the Ohio historical
and philosophical society,
5602
The annual register of the
Baptist denomination, 506
Annuttaliga Hammock, Fla., 3486

Año espiritual, 7666
An anonymous letter, 9358
Anschauungen und erfahrungen in Nordamerika, 2767
Ansermo of the crag, 8847
Der ansiedler im Missouri-staate, 970
Anson, George Anson, baron, 1697-1762, 885
Anspach, Frederick Rinehart, 1815-1867, 382
Anspach, Lewis Amadeus, 383, 384, 385
Ansted, David Thomas, 1814-1880, 386, 387
The answer and pleas of Samuel Chase, 11757
The answer at large to Mr. P--tt's speech, 11227
An answer to an anonymous libel, 12606
An answer to the Declaration of the American Congress, 13387
Antartic regions, 4678, 13200
Ante bellum, 9103
Anthoine de Saint-Joseph, Arthur, baron, b. 1829, ed., 388
Anthoine de Saint-Joseph, Fortuné, 1794-1853, 388
Anthon, George Christian, 1820-1877, 389
Anthon, Henry, 1795-1861, 390, 391
Anthon, John, 1784-1863, 392
Anthony, Elliott, 1827-1898, 393
Anthracite coal - Pennsyl-vania, 8376
Anthropo-geography - U. S., 8003
An anti-abolitionist, 13168
Anticipation continued, 394
Anticipation of marginal notes on the declaration of government, 395
Anticosti island, 6511, 6512
An antidote to John Wood's poison, 11768
Antidote to the merino-mania now progressing through the United States, 396
Anti-duelling association of New York, 1063
Antigua and the Antiguans, 397
Antigua - Descr. & trav., 397, 5808, 8181
Antigua - Hist., 397, 5808, 12172
Antigüedades americanas, 610
Anti-Jackson Convention, Richmond, Va., 5913
Antilles, Lesser - Descr. & trav., 4998, 5569, 7204
Anti-masonic convention, Middle-bury, Vt., 1830, 780
Antimasonic party, 173, 458, 780, 10384, 11257, 11562, 12166, 12181, 12203, 12399, 12587
Antiquarian researches, 12970
Antiquities of the southern Indians, 4102
Antiquities of the West, 3002
Anti-rent troubles, New York, 1839-1846, 12334
Anti-rent troubles, New York, 1839-1846 - Fiction, 9129, 9149
Anti-Van Buren members of the General Assembly of Virginia, 5914
Antoine, Antoine, de Saint-Gervais, 1776-1836, 398
Antologia nacional, 6692
L'Antoniade, 5024
Antonio de Ciudad Real, supposed joint author, 5874
Antonio, Nicolás, 1617-1684, 399, 400
Antonita, the female contra-bandista, 10251
Antony Brade, 10247
Antrobus, Benjamin, d. 1715, 401
Antúnez y Acevedo, Rafael, 402
Anville, Jean Baptiste Bourgignon d', 1697-1789, 2549
Apache country, 2837

21

Apache Indians, 5299
Apalachicola land company, 1413
Aparicio, Sebastián de, 1502-1600, 6384
Aperçus sur les institutions et les moeurs des Américains, 4478
Apes, William, b. 1798, 403, 404, 405
Aphorisms and reflections, 5237
Apianus, Petrus, 1495-1552, 406, 407
Apolla, Arnaldo, 1879-, 5915
Apollonius, Levinus, 16th cent., 408
An apology, 358
An apology for the times, 409
The apology of patriots, 566
Apostolic succession, 12156
Appalachia - Fiction, 3366, 4561, 4563, 4567, 8758, 9867, 10592
Appalachian region - Descr. & trav., 2997, 3261, 3626, 4559, 5798
Appalachian region - Soc. cond., 3769
Appalachian region - Soc. life & cust., 3522
The apparition, 9702
The appeal for suffering genius, 1617
An appeal from the madness of disunion, 11861
An appeal from the misrepresentations of James Hall, 2869
An appeal in favor of that class of Americans called Africans, 1888
Appeal of Cassius M. Clay to Kentucky and the world, 3021
An appeal to the conservative men of all parties, 410
An appeal to the government

and Congress of the United States, 411
An appeal to the justice and interests of the people of Great Britain, 13376
An appeal to the people of the North, 412
L'appel du Chibougamou, 8393
Appendix, 10338
Appendix to a late Essay, 413
Apples Blossoms, 11191
Appleton, E. H., 8597
Appleton family (Samuel Appleton, 1586-1670), 13222
Appleton, firm, publishers, New York, 6318
Appleton, Jesse, 1772-1819, 414, 415, 416, 417
Appleton, Nathan, 1779-1861, supposed author, 754
Appleton, William Sumner, 1840-1903, 418
Appleton's general guide to the U. S. & Canada, 2550, 2551
Appleton's guide to Mexico, 6454, 6455
Appleton's handbook of American travel, 2552, 5916, 5917
Appleton's illustrated handbook of American travel, 5918
Appleton's new and complete U. S. guide-book for travellers, 8388
Appleton's railroad and steamboat companion, 5724, 8389
Appleton's southern and western travellers' guide, 5725
April hopes, 9939
April's sowing, 8883
Apthorp, East, 1732 or 3-1816, 419
Apuntes para la historia del gobierno del general D. Antonio Lopez de Santa Anna, 1758
An aquatic expedition from Gibraltar to Barcelona, 10916
Aquidneck, 1575

22

The Arab wife, 8542
Arabesques, 9660
Arabs in Spain - Bio-bibl.,
400
Arago, Dominique François
Jean, 1786-1853, 423
Arago, Jacques Étienne
Victor, 1790-1855, 420,
421, 422, 423
Arango y Nuñez del Castillo,
José de, 1765-1851, 424,
612
Arango y Nuñez del Castillo,
José de, 1765-1851. Inde-
pendencia de la isla de
Cuba, 424
Araoz de la Madrid, Gregorio,
1795-1857, 5919
The Arapahoe halfbreed, 4972
La Araucana, 6677, 6678, 6679,
6680, 6681, 6682, 6683,
6684, 6685, 6686, 6687,
6688
Araucania - Hist. - Poetry,
6680, 6681, 6682, 6683,
6684, 6685, 6686, 6688
Araucanian Indians, 8291,
10574
Araucanian Indians - Wars,
8309
Arauco, Chile (Province) -
Descr. & trav., 2108
Araujo e Silva, Domingos de,
1834-, 425
Arbella (ship), 6810
Arber, Edward, 1836-1912,
ed., 5920
Arbitrary arrests in the
South, 5372
Arbitration, International,
8270
Arc measures, 11403
Arce, Francisco de, 5921
Archaeologiae americanae
telluris collectanea et
specimina, 928
Archaeological sites in
Mexico, 6715
The archbishop, 8770

The archbishop's unguarded
moment and other stories,
8473
Archdale, John, 1642?-1717,
426, 2553
Archenholz, Johann Wilhelm von,
1743-1812, 427, 428
Archer, Armstrong, 429
Archer, William Segar, 1789-1855,
430, 431
Archery, 5400
Archibald, A., 6315
Architecture, Domestic - U. S.,
3435
Architecture - Mexico, 7711
Archives - Maryland, 149
Archives - U. S., 919
Archivo americano y espiritu
de la prensa del mundo, 432
Arctic enterprise, 23
The Arctic expedition, 1910,
6303
Arctic miscellanies, 433
The Arctic prairies, 8007
Arctic regions, 433, 614, 615,
883, 1066, 1067, 1116, 1117,
2213, 2428, 2585, 3528, 3529,
4678, 5169, 6048, 6058, 6303,
6449, 6623, 6870, 7591, 7652,
7695, 7696, 8050, 8123, 8134,
11238, 11582, 12560, 13428
Arctic regions - Disc. &
explor., 4175, 4880
Arctic regions - Maps, 7109
Arctic regions - Poetry, 23,
1376
Arctic rewards and their
claimants, 434
Arctic rovings, 12562
Arctic (steamship), 6303
An arctic voyage to Baffin's
bay, 6870
Arcturus, 435
Arcturus, Selections from,
10326
Are the southern privateersmen
pirates? 11950
Arébalo, Nicolás de, 6754
Arenales, José Alvarez de,

23

1798-1862, 436, 437
Arenales, José Alvarez de,
1798-1862. Memoria
historica sobre las opera-
ciones... de la division
libertadora... a la Sierra
del Perú, 369
Arenales, Juan Antonio
Alvarez de, b. 1770, 369,
436
Arey, Henry W., 438
Areytos, 5155
Arfwedson, Carl David, 1806-
1881, 439, 440, 441
La Argentina, 794
Argentine literature -
Period., 5961, 6244
Argentine republic, 1719
Argentine republic - Biog.,
12510
Argentine republic -
Bound., 372
Argentine republic - Bound. -
Bolivia, 7953
Argentine republic. Congreso.
Cámara de senadores, 7953
Argentine republic - Consti-
tutional law, 123
Argentine republic - Descr.
& trav., 359, 592, 1023,
1028, 1380, 1431, 7977,
11964, 12249, 12497, 12498,
12519, 12529, 13054
Argentine republic - Econ.
cond., 697, 12519, 13054
Argentine republic - Emig.
& immig., 437
Argentine republic - For.
rel. - Mexico, 7792
Argentine republic - For.
rel. - Uruguay, 1764
Argentine republic - Hist.,
1588, 12249
Argentine republic - Hist. -
1535-1617 - Poetry, 794
Argentine republic - Hist. -
1776-1810, 596
Argentine republic - Hist. -
To 1810, 592, 594

Argentine republic - Hist. -
1810-, 7708
Argentine republic - Hist. -
1817-1860, 432, 1023, 1764,
7943
Argentine republic - Hist. -
Period., 6244
Argentine republic - Hist. -
Sources, 370
Argentine republic - Hist. -
War of independence, 1810-
1817, 7708, 7762, 7943
Argentine republic - Hist. -
War of independence, 1810-
1817 - Sources, 1662
Argentine republic - Period.,
5961
Argentine republic - Pol. &
govt., 123
Argentine republic - Pol. &
govt. - 1810-1817, 7943,
8026
Argentine republic - Pol. &
govt. - 1817-1860, 7943,
8026
Argentine republic - Soc. life
& cust., 7977
The Argonauts of North Liberty,
9776
Argow, Wendelin Waldermar
Wieland, 1891-, 5922
Arguedas, Alcides, 1879-1946,
5923, 7752
Argyll, John George Edward Henry
Douglas Sutherland Campbell,
9th duke of, 1845-1914, 5924,
5925, 5926, 5927, 5928,
5929, 7970
Arid regions, 7468
The Arikara Indian fight, 2554
Arikara Indians, 2554, 4942
Aristides, pseud., 12652, 12653
Aristocracy, 807, 808, 11169,
11232
Aristocracy in America, 3711
The aristocrat, 8799
L'aristocratie en Amérique,
3558
Aristodemus, pseud., 1516

24

Arizona, 4545
Arizona - Descr. & trav.,
  2575, 2837, 3113, 4341,
  4544, 4922, 5539, 6087,
  6088, 6139, 6165
Arizona - Hist., 3113
Arizona: its resources and
  prospects, 4341
Arizona - Pol. & govt., 4545
Ark (sailing vessel), 7374
Arkansas, 5100
Arkansas - Biog., 1350
Arkansas - Descr. & trav.,
  2739, 3304, 3425, 3479,
  3594, 3790, 4173, 4411,
  4480, 4632, 4799, 4973,
  5062, 5098
Arkansas - Fiction, 4902
Arkansas - Hist., 4825
Arkansas - Hist. - Civil
  war, 1350, 1351, 11244
An Arkansas planter, 4902
Arkansas - Pol. & govt. -
  Civil war, 4800
Arkansas River, 4632
Arkwright, Sir Richard,
  1732-1792, 12483
Arlach, H. de T. d', 442
The arm-chair of Tustenuggee,
  10783
Armand, pseud., 5306
Armendáriz, José de. See Castel-
  fuerte, José de Armendáriz,
  marques de, Viceroy of Peru.
Armes, Elizabeth Marie, 5930
Armijo, Antonio, 2555
Armistead family, 6812
Armistead, Wilson, 1819?-1868,
  443, 444, 445, 496
Armitage, John, 1807-1856, 446
Armitage, Thomas, 1819-1896,
  447
Armor-plate, 1219
Armored vessels, 1219
Armour, 8534
Armroyd, George, 448
Arms and the man, 3928
Armstrong, Sir Alexander,
  1818-1899, 449

Armstrong, Edward, 450, 1651
Armstrong, George Dodd, 1813-
  1899, 451, 452
Armstrong, John, 1758-1843,
  455, 1917, 2364, 13100
Armstrong, John J., 453, 454
Armstrong, Kosciuszko, 455
Armstrong, Lebbeus, 1775-1860,
  456, 457, 458
Armstrong, Mrs. Louise (Van
  Voorhis) 1889-, 5931
Armstrong, Robert, 459
Armstrong, Robert G., 460
Armstrong, William, 461
Army and Navy chronicle, 11228
The Army and Navy chronicle and
  scientific repository, 462
The Army and navy official
  gazette, 463
The army chaplain's manual,
  12628
The army hymn book, 464
Army letters, 4622
Army letters from an officer's
  wife, 5004
Army life, 3592, 4399
Army life in a black regiment,
  3864
Army life of an Illinois soldier,
  5732
The army ration, 12907
Army regulations adopted for use
  of the Army of the Confederate
  States, 2067
An army wife, 10109
Arnaud, Achille, 1826-, 465
Arnold at Saratoga, 10510
Arnold, Benedict, 1741-1801,
  354, 355, 466, 467
Arnold, Benedict, 1741-1801 -
  Fiction, 8785, 8967, 10510,
  10513
Arnold, Channing, 5932
Arnold, Charles Henry, 468
Arnold, George, 1834-1865, 8597
Arnold, Isaac Newton, 1815-1884,
  469, 470, 471, 472, 473,
  5933, 5934, 5935, 6415, 7279
Arnold, Josias Lyndon, 1768-1796,

474

Arnold, Matthew, 1822-1888, 2556

Arnold, Samuel, 1838(ca.)-1906, defendant, 1305

Arnold, Samuel George, 1806-1891, 475, 476

Arnold, Samuel Greene, 1821-1880, 477, 478

Arnold, Seth S., 479

Arnold, William E., comp., 2557

Arnott, George Arnott Walker, 1799-1868, jt. author, 12883

Arnould, Ambroise Marie, 1750?-1812, 480

Aroostook, The lady of the, 9946

Aroostook River and Valley - Descr. & trav., 12868

Around and around, 2640

Around the Caribbean and across Panama, 7583

Around the U. S. by bicycle, 4568

Arredondo, Antonio de, 2558

Arredondo's historical proof of Spain's title to Georgia, 2558

Arriaga, Miguel, 5936

Arriaga, Pablo José de, 1564-, 5937

Arricivita, Juan Domingo, 2559

Arrington, Alfred W., 1810-1867, 481

Arriola, Juan de, b. 1698, 5938

L'arrivée des pères capucins, 1899

Arróniz, Marcos, d. 1858 or 9, 482, 483

The arrows of love, 9315

Arrowsmith, Aaron, 1750-1823, 128

Art, 825

Art - Addresses, essays, lectures, 2511

Art and industry, 12373

Art and morals, 825, 5388

Art - Anecdotes, facetiae, satire, etc., 10186

Art, Byzantine, 727

Art culture, 825

Art - Mexico, 6940

The art of living, 9637

The art of mettals, 773

The art of war, 2015

Art - U. S., 1227

Art - U. S. - Hist., 2135

Arte de construcción, 7436

Arte de el idioma maya, 1136

Arte de la lengua mexicana, 583

Artemus Ward, 8874

Artemus Ward in London, 8875

Artemus Ward on his visit to Abe Lincoln, 6201

Artemus Ward's panorama, 8876

Arthur Bonnicastle, 9886

Arthur, Richard, 5939

Arthur, Samuel John, 5940

Arthur, Timothy Shay, 1809-1885, 484, 485, 486, 487, 11673

Arthur Woodleigh, 9649

Arthus, Gotthard, 1570-1630? 488

Articles of agreement, 489

Artie, 8475

Artigue, Jean d', 5941

Artillery, Coast, 837

Artist-life in Italy, 9659

The artist of the beautiful, 9823

The artist's bride, 2670

The artist's dream, 11047

The artist's love, 10830

An artist's tour, 4196

An artistic necessity, 10283

Artists, American, 2135

Artists - Fiction, 10301

Artrip, Fullen, jt. author, 5942

Artrip, Louise, 5942

Arts of design in the United States, 2135

As a medicine, 10700

As by fire, 4325

As common mortals, 9126
As good as a comedy, 5156
As it is, 5217
As it is to be, 9325
As one woman to another, 10896
As the light led, 2633
"As we went marching on", 9924
Asaph, 9123
Asbury, Francis, 1745-1816,
490, 5302
Asceticism - Catholic church,
7673
Ascutney street, 11151
Asgill, Sir Charles, 1762-
1823, 13008
Ash, Thomas, fl. 1682,
supposed author, 491
Ashe, E. M., illustr., 2546
Ashe, Samuel A'Court, 1840-
1938, 5943
Ashe, Thomas, supposed author,
fl. 1682, 2560
Ashe, Thomas, 1770-1835, 492,
493, 494, 2561
Asher, Adolf, 1800-1853, 495
Asher, Jeremiah, b. 1812, 496
Ashes and incense, 2609
The ashes of southern homes,
4736
Ashley, Chester, 1790-1848,
497
Ashley, James Monroe, 1824-
1896, 498, 499, 5944, 5945,
5946
Ashley, John, d. 1751, 500,
501
Ashley, William Henry, 2554,
4942
Ashmead, A. S., 5947
Ashmun, George, 1804-1870,
502
Ashmun, Jehudi, 1794-1828,
503, 12508
Ashworth, Henry, 1794-1880,
2562
Así es México, 7485
Asia - Descr. & trav., 4853
Asia - Hist., 11589
Askaros Kassis, 9380

Asleep, 9667
Asmodeus, 8889
Asociación mexicana automovilís-
tica, 7990
Asociación mexicana de turismo,
5948, 5949
The aspect of the times, 504
Aspendale, 10565
The Aspern papers, 7117
Asphodel, 9515
Aspinall, Sir Algernon Edward,
1871-, 5950, 5951
Aspinwall, Thomas, 1786-1876,
505
Asplund, John, d. 1807, 506
Assall, Friedrich Wilhelm, 507
The assassination and history
of the conspiracy, 508
The assay office and the proposed
mint at New Westminster, 7822
Assaying - Tables, calculations,
etc., 6702
L'Assemblée des noirs, 5952
Assiniboia (District) 1836-1870.
Council, 7641
Assiniboine river, 3878
Assistance (Ship), 433, 6058
Associaçao maritima e colonial,
Lisbon, 379
Associates of Doctor Thomas
Bray for founding clerical
libraries and supporting
negro schools, 958, 1006,
1610, 11260, 11635, 12161
Association of American geolo-
gists and naturalists, 509
Association of Franklin medal
scholars, Boston, 510
Association of Friends for the
diffusion of religious and
useful knowledge, 1158
Assollant, Alfred, i.e. Jean
Baptiste Alfred, 1827-1886,
2563
Asters and disasters of society,
10419
Asti, Felice, 511
Astié, Jean Frédéric, 1822-1894,
512

Astley, Thomas, 211
Aston, Anthony, 2564
"Astonished at America", 5799
The astonishing adventure
    of James Botello, 10338
Astor, John Jacob, 1763-1848,
    5017
Astor library, New York,
    513, 514, 515, 516, 517,
    518
Astoria, 3971, 4026
Astoria, Or., 4026, 5017
Astounding disclosures! 13018
The astrologer of the nine-
    teenth century, 10693
Astrology, 6480, 7418, 7419
The astronomical diary, 326
Astronomy - Addresses,
    essays, lectures, 81
Astronomy - Early works to
    1800, 6728
Astronomy - Observations,
    993, 7092
At a winter house-party, 9768
At anchor, 2565
At eve, 10899
At home and abroad, 4153
At last, 10935
At last: a Christmas in the
    West Indies, 7194, 7195
At love's extremes, 5387
At midnight and other poems,
    5197
At the end of his rope,
    10448
At the end of the trail,
    5953
At the evening hour, 5622
At the foot of the Rockies,
    3638
At the holy well, 4770
At the Maison Dobbe, 11198
At the mission of San Carmel,
    9788
At the sign of the savage,
    9943
At the station, 9355
At you-all's house, 2634
Atala, La nouvelle, 5026

Atcheson, Nathaniel, 1771-1825,
    519, 520
Atchinson city directory, 2566
Atchinson, Kansas - Directories,
    2566
Atchinson, David Rice, 1807-
    1886, 521
Aten, Henry J., 1841-, comp.,
    2567
Ateneo de Costa Rica, 5954
Ateneo de Honduras, 5955
El Ateneo de Lima, 5956
Athabasca and Peace River treaty
    exhibition, 1899, 7392
Athaliah, 9655
Athalie, 3272
Athenaeum association, New York,
    5957
Athol, Mass. First church,
    11848
Athol, Mass. - Hist., 11848
Atkins, John, 1685-1757, 522
Atkins, John, d. 1834, 1411
Atkins, Smith Dykins, 1836-1913,
    5958
Atkinson, Archibald, 1792-1872,
    523
Atkinson, C. F., jt. author,
    4301
Atkinson, Christopher William,
    524
Atkinson, Edward, 1827-1905,
    525, 526
Atkinson, Mrs. Eleanor (Stack-
    house) 1863-, 5959,5960
Atkinson, John, 527
Atkinson, William King, 528
Atlanta campaign, 1864, 2945,
    3075, 3830, 4077, 4749
Atlantic City - Hist., 11666
The Atlantic club-book, 529
Atlantic coast - Descr. & trav.,
    27, 2724, 4620, 12852
Atlantic coast - Descr. & trav.,
    Guide-books, 12567
The Atlantic navigator, 530
Atlantic states - Descr. &
    trav., 1992, 2506, 2944,
    3446, 3449, 3553, 3632,

28

3734, 3975, 4022, 4040,
4137, 4197, 4263, 4410,
4574, 4584, 5151, 5341,
5405, 5634, 6104, 6547,
6548, 7172, 7345, 7346,
7347, 7549, 11948
Atlantic states - Descr. &
trav. - Guide-books, 8388
The Atlantic telegraph, 532
Atlantic telegraph company,
London, 531
Atlantida, 5961
Atlantis, 533, 1443, 5157
Atlas metódico para la
enseñanza de la geografía
de la República Mexicana,
6816
Atlas of Muskingum Co., Ohio,
1068
Atlases, 1111
Atlee, Edwin Pitt, 1799-1836,
534
Atlee, Washington Lemuel,
1808-1878, 535
Atonement, 2896
Atson, William, 536
An attempt to elucidate the
pernicious consequences of
a deviation from the prin-
ciples of the Orders in
council, 537
An attempt to murder, 10310
Atterbury, John Guest, 1811-
1887, 538
Attleborough, Mass. - Hist.,
11936
Attmore, William, 2568
Attorneys, 554
The attractions of New Haven,
Connecticut, 12030
Attraverso gli Stati Uniti,
4427
Atwater, Caleb, 1778-1867,
507, 539, 540, 541, 542,
2569, 11229
Atwater, Jesse, 543
Atwood, Edward Sumner, 1833-
1888, 544
Atwood, Thomas, d. 1793, 545

Atwood, William, d. 1705?, 546
Atzerodt, George A., 1835-1865,
defendant, 1305
Au Mexique, 5962
Au pays de "la vie intense",
4185
Au pilori, 5963
Aubert Dubayet, 3582
Aubert du Bayet, Jean Baptiste
Annibal, 1759-1797 - Fiction,
3582
Aubert, Georges, 5964
Aubertin, John James, 1818-1900,
2570, 5965
Aubin, Joseph Marius Alexis,
b. 1802, 6105
Aubin, Nicolas, b. ca. 1655,
tr., 1435
Aucaigne, Félix, d. 1914, 547
Auchinleck, Gilbert, 548
Audouard, Olympe, 2571
Audré, John, 1751-1780 - Fiction,
10513
Audry, François Xavier, d. 1854,
3723
Audubon, John James, 1785-1851,
549, 2572, 2573, 2574, 4924,
8217
Audubon, John Woodhouse, 1812-
1862, 2575, 2576, 5966
Audubon's western journal, 2575
Auf alten wegen in Mexiko und
Guatemala, 7996
Auf forschungsreisen in Mexiko,
7997
Auf schiffen, schienen, pneus,
7740, 7741
Aufenthalt und reisen in Mexico
in den jahren 1825 bis 1834,
6254
Auger, Edouard, 550
Aughey, John Hill, b. 1828, 551
Augusta, Ga. - Hist., 4105
Augustinians, 7843
Augustinians in Chile, 8056
Aulnay-Charnisay, Charles de
Menou, sieur d', 1605-1650 -
Fiction, 8953, 8984
Aunt Becky's army-life, 4693

Aunt Caroline's present,
9676
Aunt Charlotte, 10669
Aunt Cynthia Dallett,
10042
Aunt Jane's hero, 10561
Aunt Leanna, 5003
Aunt Mary, 10904
Aunt Patty's scrap-bag, 3840
Aunt Phillis's cabin, 9457
Aunt Randy, 10790
Aurand, Ammon Monroe, 1895-,
tr., 7412
Aureola, 10289
Aurifodina, 10501
Aurora and Pennsylvania
gazette, Philadelphia,
12080
Aurora de Chile, 5967
La aurora en Copacabana,
6274
The auroraphone, 9069
Aus Amerika, alte und neue
heimat, 3548
Aus Amerika. Erfahrungen,
reisen und studien, 3549
Aus Mexico, 7807
Aussichten für gebildete
Deutsche in Nordamerika,
4289
Austin, Arthur Williams,
1807-1884, 552
Austin, Benjamin, 1752-
1820, 553, 554
Austin, David, 1760-1831,
555, 556
Austin, Mrs. Jane (Goodwin)
1831-1894, 10283
Austin, Sir Horatio Thomas,
1800 or 1-1865, 433
Austin, Ivers James, 1808-
1889, 557, 558, 559
Austin, J. P., 2577
Austin, James Trecothick,
1784-1870, 560, 561,
562, 563
Austin, Moses, 1761-1821, 564
Austin, Samuel, 1760-1830,
565, 566, 567

Austin, Stephen Fuller, 1793-
1836, 568, 5968
Austin, William, 1778-1841, 569
Australia - Descr. & trav.,
3977, 3991, 4636, 7556
Austrian succession, War of,
1740-1748, 11265
Des auswanderers handbuch, 5020
Das Auswanderungs buch, 2705
Auszüge aus briefen aus Nord-
Amerika, 2578
An authentic historical memoir
of the Schuylkil fishing
company of the state in
Schuylkil, 13435
An authentic journal of the siege
of the Havana, 570
The authentic life of Billy,
the kid, 3575
The authentic life of Mrs. Mary
Ann Bickford, 1247
An authentic narrative of facts
relating to the exchange of
prisoners taken at the Cedars,
571
Authentic papers from America,
572
Authentic papers relating to the
expedition against Carthagena,
573
Authentic papers relative to the
expedition against the Charibbs,
574
An authentic register of the
British successes, 575
The author turned critic, 11978
Authors, American - Autographs,
8612
Authors, American - New York
(State), 1904
Authors, American - Portraits,
10154
An author's reading and its
consequences, 9762
Authorship, 10406
Autobiographical sketches and
recollections, 3006
An autobiography, 9427
The autobiography and ministerial

Azerbaijan - Relations
(general) with Cuba, 7189
Azlor, Joseph de, marqués
de San Miguel de Aguayo,
4742
Azores, 7017
Azores - Descr. & trav.,
4571, 6961
Aztec land, 5991
Aztec language, 583
Aztec language - Texts, 2011,
7932
Aztecs, 1236, 7932
Azara, Felix de, 1746-1821,
589, 590, 591, 592, 593,
594, 595, 596, 597, 598
Azarian, 10853
Azile, 9250

B. B., 1920
B. C., 1887, 7259
B. T., 8763
Babbidge, Charles, 599
Babbitt, Benjamin B., 600
Babbitt, Elijah, 1796-
1887, 601, 602
Babcock, Mrs. Bernie
(Smade) 1868-, 5974
Babcock, George R., d.
1876, 603
Babcock, Rufus, 1798-1875,
4728
Babcock, Samuel Brazer,
1807-1873, 604
Babson, John James, 1809-
1886, 605
Babylon's fall in Maryland,
5305
Bach, Moriz, 606
Bache, Alexander Dallas,
1806-1867, 607
Bache, Franklin, 1792-1864,
608
Bache, Rene, illustr.,
10253
Bache, William, 1811-, 609
Bachelder, John Badger,
1825-1894, 2583

Bachelor Ben, 10681
A bachelor maid, 9759
The bachelor's Christmas,
9639, 10770
A bachelor's story, 8893
A bachelor's ward, 8935
Bachelors and butterflies,
8552
Bachiller y Morales, Antonio,
1812-1889, 610, 611, 612, 613
Bachmann, Ida, 2584
Back, Sir George, 1796-1878,
614, 615, 2585
Backman, Daniel And., 11231
The backslider, 10183
Backus, Azel, 1765-1817, 616
Backus, Isaac, 1724-1806, 617,
618, 619, 620, 621, 622
Backus, Joseph, b. 1667, 623
Backus, Simon, 624
Backwoods and prairies, 4919
The backwoods of Canada, 8225
The backwoodsman, 4720, 5772
Back-yard grangers, 10792
Bacon, Alvin Q., d. 1863, 2586
Bacon, Anthony, 625
Bacon, Delia Salter, 1811-1859
Bacon, Edward, 1830-1901, 2587
Bacon, Mrs. Eliza Ann (Munroe),
626
Bacon, George Washington,
1830-1921, 627, 628, 629,
5975
Bacon, Henry, 1813-1856, 626
Bacon, James, fl. 1795, 630
Bacon, John, 1738-1820, 631, 632
Bacon, Leonard, 1802-1881, 633,
634, 635, 636, 637, 638, 639,
640, 641, 642
Bacon, Leonard Woolsey, 1830-
1907, 643
Bacon, Mrs. Lydia B. (Stetson)
1786-1853, 644
Bacon, Oliver N., 645
Bacon, Thomas, 1700(ca.)-1768,
646
Bacon's rebellion, 1676, 3662,
5297
Bacon's rebellion, 1676 -

Fiction, 8784, 9592, 10885, 5478

Bacourt, Adolphe Fourier de, 1801-1865, 2588

Bacqueville de la Potherie, Claude Charles Le Roy, 1668-1738, 647

Baddeck, 8343

Baden, Mrs. Francis (Henshaw) d. 1911, 10830, 10834, 10844

Badger, George Edmund, 1795-1866, 648

Badger, Henry Clay, 1832-1894, 5976

Badger, William Whittlesey, 649

Badia, Marco Antonio, 650

Badillo, Luisa Bernardi de, 5977

Badin, Stephen Theodore, 1768-1853, 651

Baedeker, Karl, firm, publishers, Leipzig, 5978, 5979, 5980, 5981

Baers, Johannes, d. 1653, 652, 653

Baffin's Bay, 7912, 8134

Baffin's Bay - Descr., 7930

Baffled schemes, 8637

Bagby, George William, 1828-1883, 2589, 2590, 2591

Bagg, Lyman Hotchkiss, 1846-1911, 2592

Bagot, Lewis, bp. of St. Asaph, 1740-1802, 654

Bahamas - Descr. & trav., 5101, 9774

Bahia, Brazil (State) - Descr. & trav., 577

Bahr, Max, 1863-, 2593

Baides, Marqués de, 8291

Bailey, Goldsmith F., 1823-1862, 655

Bailey, Isaac, d. 1824, 656

Bailey, Jacob, 1731-1808, 923

Bailey, John J., d. 1873, 657

Bailey, John W., 658

Bailey, Philip James, 1816-1902, 659

Bailey, Robert, b. 1773, 660

Bailey, Silas, 1809-1874, 661

Bailey, Wilfred Ormrod, 5982

Bailey, William, 662

Baillie-Grohman, Mrs. Florence (Nickalls), 5983

Baillie-Grohman, William Adolph, 1851-, 5983

Baillie, Hugh, 663

Baily, Francis, 1774-1844, 2594

Baily, John, fl. 1811-1850, 664, 13342

Bainbridge, William, 1774-1833, 12711

Baines, Edward, 1774-1848, 665

Baird, Henry Carey, 1825-1912, 666

Baird, Robert, 1798-1863, 667, 668, 669, 670, 671, 672, 673, 2595

Baird, Robert, 1798-1863. A letter to Lord Brougham, on the subject of American slavery, 12344

Baird, Samuel John, 1817-1893, comp., 674

Baird, Spencer Fullerton, 1823-1887, 675, 676, 677, 678, 679, 5255

Bajon, fl. 1763, 680

The baked head, 8647

Baked meats of the funeral, 9713

Baker, Charles T., 5984

Baker, Daniel, fl. 1650-1660, 681

Baker, Daniel, 1791-1857, 2599

Baker, David Charles, 5985

Baker, DeWitt Clinton, 1832-1881, comp., 2596

Baker, Edward Dickinson, 1811-1861, 682

Baker, Frank Collins, 1867-, 5986

Baker, George E., ed., 683

Baker, George Melville, 1832-

34

Baltimore - Hist. - Revo-
lution, 2423, 11560
Bambuk - Descr. & trav.,
344
Bame, H. D., illustr.,
8630
Banchero, Giuseppe, ed.,
727
Banco Nacional de Mexico,
5994
Bancroft, Aaron, 1755-1839,
728, 729, 730, 731, 732
Bancroft, Edward, 1744-1821,
733, 734
Bancroft, Edward Nathaniel,
1772 - 1842, 735
Bancroft, George, 1800-1891,
736, 737, 738, 739, 740,
741, 742, 743, 744, 5995,
11917
Bancroft, George, 1800-1891.
History of the United
States. v. 9, 12395
Bancroft, Hubert Howe,
1832-1918, 5996
Bandanna ballads, 5659
Bandelier, Adolphe Francis
Alphonse, 1840-1914, ed.,
4631
Bandelier, Mrs. Fanny R.,
tr., 4631
The bandit of Austria, 11183
The bandit of the ocean,
8698
The bandits of the Osage,
2671
The banditti of the Rocky
mountains, 2607
Bangor, Me. Ordinances,
etc., 745
Bangs, Edward, 1756-1818,
746, 747
Bangs, Edward Dillingham,
1790-1838, 748
Bangs, Nathan, 1778-1862,
749, 750
Banister, Thomas, fl. 1715,
751, 752
Banister, William Bostwick,

1773-1853, 753
Bank bills or paper currency,
754
Bank-notes, 12886
Bank of Maryland, Baltimore,
13256
Bank of North America, Phila-
delphia, 11843
Bank of the United States,
1791-1811, 543, 11843, 13488
Bank of the United States,
1816-1836, 11843, 12133,
12270
Bank of the United States,
1816-1836 - Speeches in
Congress, 1315
Bank of Virginia, 756
Bank robbers and the detectives,
10526
Banking law - South Carolina,
11877
Bankruptcy - Massachusetts,
11926
Bankruptcy - U. S., 11797
Banks and banking, 2001
Banks and banking - Canada,
6309
Banks and banking - Direct.,
11804
Banks and banking - Hist., 2422
Banks and banking - Massachu-
setts, 754
Banks and banking - U. S., 543,
685, 1900, 2378, 2379,
2422, 12326, 12682
Banks and banking - U. S. -
Hist., 11843, 12327
Banks and banking - Virginia,
756
Banks, Henry, fl. 1781-1826,
755, 756
Banks, John, d. 1784, 755
Banks, Mrs. Nancy Houston,
1850-, 2608
Banks, Nathaniel Prentice,
1816-1894, 1328
Banks, Thomas Christopher,
1765-1854, 757, 758
Bannister, Saxe, 1790-1877,

759, 760, 761
Banta, Richard Elwell, ed.,
3693
Banvard, John, 1815-1891,
762
Banvard, Joseph, 1810-1887,
763, 764, 765, 766, 767,
768, 769
Banville, Théodore de, 7544
Baptism - Early works to
1800, 11979
The Baptist denomination,
12758
Baptists, 506, 1406, 4728,
12758
Baptists - Doctrinal and
controversial works, 619
Baptists - Hist., 1146
Baptists - Missions, 4344
Baptists - New England,
621, 767
Baptists - New Hampshire,
11899
Baptists - Ohio - Miami
association, 2137
Baptists - Rhode Island,
100
Baptists - South Carolina,
10446
Bar Association of the City
of Boston, 5997
Bar Harbor days, 9760
Bar Harbor tales, 9773
The bar-rooms at Brantley,
8557
Baraga, Friedrich, bp.,
1797-1868, 770, 771
Baralt, Rafael María,
1810-1860, 772
Barba, Alvaro Alonso,
b. 1569, 773, 5998
Barba de Coronado, Juan,
5999
The Barbadoes packet, 774
Barbados - Descr. & trav.,
8181
Barbados - Hist., 11876
Barbados - Pol. & govt.,
774

Barbaroux, Charles Ogé, 1792-
1867, 775
Barbe, Waitman, 1864-1924,
2609, 2610
Barbé-Marbois, François,
marquis de, 1745-1837, 776,
777, 778, 1831, 7938, 7939,
7941
Barbee, David Rankin, 1874-,
6000
Barber, Daniel, 1756-1834,
779
Barber, Edward Downing, 1806-
1855, 780
Barber, Elizabeth G., jt.
author, 786
Barber, John Warner, 1798-
1885, 781, 782, 783, 784,
785, 786, 787, 788, 789,
790, 791, 792
Barber, Lucius W., 1839-1872,
2611
Barbeu-Dubourg, Jacques, 1709-
1779, 793
Barbosa, Joseph, 6001
Barbour, George M., 2612
Barbour, James, 1775-1842,
6002
Barbour, Ralph Henry, 1870-,
jt. author, 8797
Barclay Compton, 10196
Barclay, Peter. A persuasive
to the people of Scotland,
12156
The Barclays of Boston, 10456
Barco Centenera, Martin del,
b. 1535, 794
Bard, Samuel A., pseud., 13485
Bard, William, 1777-1853, 795
Barère de Vieuzac, Bertrand,
1755-1841, 6003.
Barham, William, 796
Barhydt, David Parish, d. 1908,
797
Baril, V. L. comte de la
Hure, 798
Barinetti, Carlo, 799
Barker, David, 1797-1834, 800
Barker, George Payson,

1807-1848, 1620
Barker, Harry Ellsworth,
1862-, 6004
Barker, James Nelson,
1784-1858. The Indian
princess, 1447
Barker, Jacob, 1779-1871,
801, 802
Barker, Joseph, 1751-1815,
803, 804
Barker, Robert, b. 1729,
805
Barker´s luck, 6971
Barley Wood, 10474
Barlow, Edward, 1639-1719,
806
Barlow, Joel, 1754-1812,
807, 808, 809, 810, 811,
812, 813, 814, 815, 816,
817, 818, 819, 6005,
11232
Barlow, Joel, 1754-1812.
The Columbiad, 12419
Barnard, Daniel Dewey,
1797-1861, 820, 821,
822, 823, 824
Barnard, Frederick Augustus
Porter, 1809-1889, 825,
826, 827
Barnard, George N., 828
Barnard, Henry, 1811-1900,
260, 261, 829, 830, 831
Barnard, John, 1681-1770,
832
Barnard, John Gross, 1815-
1882, 833, 834, 835, 836,
837, 838, 839
Barnard, Thomas, 1716-1776,
841, 843
Barnard, Thomas, 1748-1814,
840, 842
Barnave, Antoine-Pierre-
Joseph-Marie, 1761-1793,
7507
Barnes, Albert, 1798-1870,
844, 845, 846, 847, 848,
849, 850, 13357
Barnes, David, 1731-1811,
851

Barnes, David M., 852
Barnes, George Owen, 1827-,
4860
Barnes, Isaac O., 853
Barnes, Joseph, 854, 855
Barnes, Thomas, 1749-1816,
plaintiff, 856
Barnes, William, 1824-1913,
857, 858
Barnes, William Horatio, 859,
11233
Barnet, James, ed., 860
Barnett, Mrs. Evelyn Scott
(Snead), 2613, 2614
Barnett, Francis, b. 1785, 861
Barney, C., 2615
Barnum, E. M., 862
Barnum, H. L., 863
Barnum, James Harvey, 2616
Barnum, Phineas Taylor, 1810-
1891, 864, 11234
Barnum's Parnassus, 1773
Barnwell, Stephen Elliott,
6632
Baron Montez of Panama and
Paris, 9672
The Baron of Cherubusco, 10675
Barondess, Benjamin, 1891-,
6006
Baronia anglica concentrata,
758
Barr, James, 2617
Barr, John, 4589
Barr, Knut August, 1871-1929,
2618
Barr, Lockwood Anderson, 1883-,
13214
Barr, Thomas Hughes, 1807-1877,
865
Barrage, Joseph Perrin, 1842-
1863, 1791
Barrande, Joachim, 1799-1883,
866
Barras, Louis, comte de, d. 1788,
13473
Barre academy, Barre, Vt., 867
Barré de Saint-Venant, Jean,
1737-1810, 11235
Barre, W. L., 868, 869, 4401

Barreda, Francisco de,
6007
Barreda, Roque de la, 8272
Barrell, Joseph, d. 1804,
13341
Barrenechea, Juan de, 6008
Barrère, Pierre, 1690-1755,
870
Barrett, Benjamin Fiske, 1808-
1892, 871
Barrett, Frank William
Zelotes, 1867-, 6009
Barrett, Joseph Hartwell,
1824-1910, 872, 873, 874
Barrette, J. E. T., 6010
Barrientos, Felipe Santiago,
6011
Barrillon, François Guillaume,
875
Barringer, Daniel Moreau,
1806-1873, 876
Barrington, Daines, 1727-
1800, 877, 878
Barrington, Shute, bp. of
Durham, 1734-1826, 11236
Barrington, William Wildman
Barrington, 2d vis-
count, 1717-1793, 11236
Barrio, Paulino del, 879
Barrios, Juan de, fl. 1590-
1610, 6012
Barron, James, 1769-1851,
defendant, 880
Barron, Samuel Benton,
1834-1912, 2619
Barros, André de, 881
Barros Arana, Diego,
1830-1907, 8112
Barros, João de, 1496-
1570, 882
Barrow, Sir John, bart.,
1764-1848, 883, 884,
885, 886, 11237, 11238
Barrow, John, 1808-1898,
ed., 1924
Barrow, Robert, 3247
Barrow Straits, 8134
Barrow, Washington, 1817-
1866, 887

Barrows, Elijah Porter, 1807-
1888, 888
Barrows, William, 1815-1891,
889
Barruel-Beauvert, Philippe
Auguste de, 890
Barry, Charles, 6013
Barry, Etheldred B., illustr.,
2613
Barry, Henry, 1750-1822,
11239
Barry, John Stetson, 1819-1872,
891, 892
Barry, Patrick, 893
Barry, Thomas, 2620
Barry, William Farquhar, 1818-
1879, jt. author, 839
Barry, William Taylor, 1785-
1835, 894
Barstow, Benjamin, 895, 896
Barstow, George, 1812-1883,
897, 898
Bart Ridgeley, 10618
A bartered birthright, 10304
Barthe, Joseph Guillaume,
1818-, 899
Barthelmess, Richard, 900
Bartholow, Otho F., 6014, 6015
Bartleby, 10346
Bartletson, John, 2621
Bartlett, David Vandewater
Golden, 1828-1912, 901, 902
Bartlett, Elisha, 1804-1855,
903, 904, 905, 2622, 2623,
7093
Bartlett, John Russell, 1805-
1886, 906, 907, 908, 909,
2624
Bartlett, John Sherren, 1790-
1863, 910
Bartlett, Joseph, 1686-1754,
1972
Bartlett, Joseph, 1763-1827,
911
Bartlett, Josiah, 1759-1820,
912, 913, 914, 915, 916
Bartlett, Josiah, 1768-1838,
917
Bartlett, Josiah, 1803-1853,

917
Bartlett, Montgomery Robert,
918
Bartlett, Napier, 1836-1877,
2625
Bartlett, Richard, 1794-
1837, 919
Bartlett, Samuel Ripley,
1837-, 920
Bartlett, Washington Allen,
1820-1871, 921
Bartlett, William Francis,
1840-1876, 4683
Bartlett, William Henry,
1809-1854, 922, 5729
Bartlett, William Stoodley,
1809-1883, 923
Bartley, James Avis, 1830-,
924
Bartol, Cyrus Augustus,
1813-1900, 925
Barton, Andrew, pseud.?
926
Barton, Benjamin Smith,
1766-1815, 927, 928,
929, 930, 931, 932, 933
Barton, Charles Crillon,
d. 1851, 934
Barton, Cyrus, d. 1855,
935, 936
Barton, David, 1783-1837,
937, 11240
Barton, Edward H., d. 1859,
938
Barton, Harry Scott, 1862-,
2626
Barton, Ira Moore, 1796-
1867, 636
Barton, James L., d. 1869,
939, 940
Barton, Mary, 6016
Barton, Robert S., 6017,
6018, 6019
Barton, Thomas H., 1828-,
2627
Barton, William, 1754-1817,
941
Barton, William Eleazar,
1861-1930, 2628, 2629,

2630, 6020, 6021, 6022,
6023
Barton, William Paul Crillon,
1786-1856, 942, 943, 944,
11241
Barton, William Sumner, 1824-
1899, 945
Bartram, John, 1699-1777,
5291, 11242
Bartram, William, 1739-1823,
946, 2631
Basalenque, Diego, 1577-1651,
947
Bascom family (Thomas Bascom,
d. 1682), 12701
Bascom, Henry Bidleman, bp.,
1796-1850, 948, 3835
Bascom, Jonathan, 949
Baskervill, William Malone,
1850-1899, 2632
Baskett, James Newton, 1849-,
2633
Basque language, 97
Bassols Batalla, Angel, ed.,
7488
The bastard, 9546
Basterot, Florimond Jacques,
comte de, 950
The bastiles of the North,
2479
Batalla de Yanacocha, 951
Batbie, Anselme Polycarpe,
1828-1887, 952
Batch, Thomas, 1821-1877, ed.,
2731
Batchelder, Eugene, 1822-1878,
953, 954
Batchelder, John Putnam,
1784-1868, 955
Batchelder, Samuel, 1784-1879,
956
Batchelder, Samuel, 1830-1888,
957
Bateman, Edmund, 958
Bateman, Newton, 1822-1897,
6024
Bates, Barnabas, 1785-1853,
959
Bates, David Homer, 1843-1926,

6025
Bates, Edward, 1793-1869,
  960
Bates, Elisha, 1779 or 80-
  1861, 2636, 2637, 2638
Bates, Emily Katharine,
  2639
Bates, Finis Langdon, 6026
Bates, Henry Walter, 1825-
  1892, 961
Bates, Isaac Chapman,
  1780-1845, 962
Bates, James Hale, 1826-
  1901, 6027
Bates, Joshua, 1776-1854,
  963, 964
Bates, Katharine Lee, 1859-
  1929? 8969
Bates, Lindon Wallace, jr.,
  1883-, 6028
Bates, Mary, 965
Baths, 1089
Bathurst, Henry Bathurst,
  3rd earl of, 1762-1834,
  6029, 13512
Baton Rouge, La. - Hist. -
  Civil war, 3199
Batres, Leopoldo, 7490, 7491
Bats, 174
Batten, John Mullin, 1837-
  1916, 2640
Battle echoes, 13063
Battle field and prison
  pen, 5555
The battle forest, 5745
Battle, Kemp Plummer,
  1831-1919, ed., 4486
The battle of Bunker Hill,
  3382, 11481
The battle of Chancellors-
  ville and the Eleventh
  army corps, 966
The battle of Coney Island,
  8652
The battle of Fort Sumter
  and first victory of the
  southern troops, 11243
The battle of freedom, 3503
Battle of Lake Erie monu-

ment association, 967
The battle of Lexington, 10670
The battle of Monmouth, 10921
The battle of Monterey, 4407
The battle of Tippecanoe, 5603
The battle-fields of the
  republic, 12715
Battle-fields of the South, 968
The battlefields of our fathers,
  11006
The battle-fields of Virginia,
  12924
Battles of the British navy,
  185
Battles - U. S., 12715
Batwell, Daniel, 969
Baudissin, Adelbert Heinrich,
  graf von, 1820-1871, 970
Baudry des Lozières, Louis
  Narcisse, 1761-1841, 2641
Bauerle, Charles, illustr.,
  4283
Baumann, Felix, 1868-, 2642
Baumann, Ludwig Adolph, 1734?-
  1802, 971
Baumbach, Ludwig Carl Wilhelm
  von, 1799-1883, 2643
Baumgartner, Andreas, 1844-
  1936, 2644
Baxter, James Phinney, 1831-
  1921, 6030, 6031
Baxter, Joseph, 1676-1745,
  972
Baxter, Perceval P., 6031
Baxter, Sylvester, 1850-,
  6032
Baxter, U. J., 3537
Baxter, William, 11244
Baxter, William Edward, 1825-
  1890, 2645
Bayard, Ferdinand Marie,
  1768-, 2646
Bayard, James, 973
Bayard, James Asheton, 1767-
  1815, 974, 975, 976, 978,
  12244
Bayard, James Asheton, 1799-
  1880, 977, 978
Bayard, Lewis Pintard, 1791-

40

1840, 979
Bayard, Nicolas, 1644?-1707,
546, 980, 981
Bayard, Samuel, 1767-1840,
982
Bayard, William, 1764?-1826,
983
Bayfield, Lake Superior, 984
Bayfield, Wis., 984
Bayley, Daniel, d. 1792,
comp., 985
Bayley, Frederic William
Naylor, 1808-1853, 986
Bayley, James Roosevelt,
abp., 1814-1877, 987
Bayley, Richard, 1745-1801,
comp., 988
Baylies, Francis, 1783-1852,
989, 990, 991, 992, 2647
Baylor, Orval W., 6033,
6034, 6035
Bayly, William, 1737-1810, 993
Bayman, Mrs. A. Phelps, 994
Bayne, Charles Joseph,
1870-, 2648
Bayne, Peter, 1830-1896,
995
Baz, Gustavo Adolfo, 1852-
1904, 6036, 6037
Bazancourt, César Lecat,
baron de, 1810-1865, 996
Bazile, L., 997
Bazin, René, 1853-1932,
2649
Beach, David, 998
Beach, Lewis, 1835-1886,
999
Beach, Samuel B., 1000
Beach, Thomas Miller,
1841-1894, 6038
Beadle, Charles, 2650
Beadle, Delos White, 1001
Beadle, John Hanson, 1840-
1897, 2651
The beads of Tasmer, 8720
Beal, John Yates, 1835-
1865, 4311
Beale, Charles T., 3122
Beale, Edward Fitzgerald,

1822-1893, 2652, 2653, 3826
Beale, George William, 1842-
2654
Beale, Joseph H., 2655
Beale, Richard Lee Tuberville,
1819-1893, 2656
Beall, John Yates, 1835-1865,
1002, 7410
Beals, James, 1844?-, 3076
Beaman, Fernando C., 1814-1882,
1003, 1004
Beamish, North Ludlow, 1797-
1872, 1005
Bean, Robert, 3111
Beanlands, Arthur John, 1857-
1918, comp., 6178
Bearcroft, Philip, 1697-1761,
1006, 1007
Beard, W. L., 10448
Beardslee, George W., 1008
Beardsley, Eben Edwards, 1808-
1891, 1009, 1010
Beardsley family (William
Beardsley, 1605?-1661), 1010
Beardsley, Levi, 1785-1857,
1011
Bearing arms in the Twenty-
seventh Massachusetts regiment
of volunteers infantry during
the civil war, 3235
Beatrix, Randolph, 9805
Beatson, Robert, 1742-1818, 1012
Beatty, Charles, 1715?-1772,
1013, 1014
Beatty, John, 1828-1914, 2657
Beauchamp, Alphonse de,
1767-1832, 1015, 1016, 1017
Beauchampe, 10766
The Beauforts, 8794
Beaufoy, Mark, 1764-1827, 878,
1018
Beaugrand, Honoré, 6039
Beauharnais family - Fiction,
9532
Beaujour, Louis Auguste Félix,
baron de, 1763-1836, 1019,
1020
Beaumarchais, Pierre Augustin
Caron de, 1732-1799, 1868

41

Beaumont, Arthur, J.,
1021, 1022
Beaumont, J. A. B., 1023
Beaumont, Pablo de la
Purísima Concepcion,
6040
Beaumont de La Bonninière,
Gustave Auguste de,
1802-1866, 2658
Beauregard, George, 6041
Beauregard, Pierre Gustave
Toutant, 1818-1893, 2037
Beauseincourt, The romance
of, 5618
Beautés de l'histoire du
Canada, 11760
The beauties and celebrities
of the nation, 12020
The beauties of Washington
Irving, 9994
The beautiful Jewess Rachel
Mendoza, 8763
The beautiful star, 2994
The beautiful widow, 8558
The beauty of a well cul-
tivated heart, 9486
Beauvallet, Léon, 1829-1885,
1024
Beaven, James, 1025
Beauvois, Eugène, 1835-,
1026
Becerra, Ricardo, 1836-1905,
6042
Becher, Carl Christian,
6043, 6044, 6045
Becher, Henry C. R., 6046
Bechtel, Johannes, 1690-
1777, ed., 1027
Beck, Carl, 1856-1911, 2659
Beck, John Brodhead, 1794-
1851, 1029
Beck, Lewis Caleb, 1798-1853,
1030, 1031, 1032, 11245
Beck, Paul, 1760?-1844, 1033
Beck-Bernard, Mme. Lina
(Bernard), 1028
Beck, Theodoric Romeyn, 1791-
1855, 12608
Becker, John H., 2660

Becket, John J. à, 10283
Beckett, Sylvester Breakmore,
1812-1882, 1034
Beckford, William, d. 1799,
1035
Beckley, Hosea, 1036
Beckman, Ernst, 1850-1924,
2661
Beckwith, Edward Griffin,
5519, 5523
Beckwith, George Cone, 1800-
1870, 1037, 11370
Bedford, Cornelia E., illustr.,
9268
Bedford, Gunning S., 1038, 1039
Bedford, John Russell, 4th
duke of, 1710-1771, 1040
Bedford, N. H. - Hist., 853
Bedford, N. Y. St. Matthew's
church, 13177
Bedinger, Daniel, 1041
Bed-time stories (More), 10392
Bee culture - U. S., 13436
The bee hunter, 5412, 9140
Beech Bluff, 11092
The beechen tree, 5378
Beechenbrook, 4854
Beecher, Catherine Esther, 1800-
1878, 1042, 1043, 1044, 1045,
1046, 1047, 1052
Beecher, Charles, 1815-1900,
1048, 1049, 1050, 1059
Beecher, Edward, 1803-1895,
1051
Beecher, Eunice White (Bullard),
2662
Beecher, George, 1809-1843,
1052
Beecher, Henry Ward, 1813-1887,
1053, 1054, 1055, 1056, 1057,
1058, 6047, 7039
Beecher, Henry Ward, 1813-1887.
Norwood, 11773, 11949
Beecher, Lyman, 1775-1863,
1059, 1060, 1061, 1062, 1063,
1064, 1065, 11246, 11247,
12469
Beechey, Frederick William,
1796-1856, 1066, 1067,

6048, 12883
Beers, Mrs. Fannie A., 2663
Beers, Frederick W., 1068
Beers, William Pitt, 1766-
1810, 1069
Bees, 9046, 1081, 12733,
13436
Bees - Cuba, 11343
Beesly, Edward Spencer,
1831-, 13104
Beeson, John, b. 1803, 1070
Beetles - Mexico, 1871
Beets and beet sugar -
France, 11970
Befo' de war, 3643
Before and after marriage,
8580
Before and behind the
curtain, 10623
Before the dawn, 2516, 10507
Before the Hon. Philip F.
Thomas, commissioner of
patents, 7076
Begbie, Matthew Baille, 6183
Begg, Alexander, 1839-1897,
6049, 6050, 6051, 6052,
6053, 6054, 6055, 6056,
7384
The beggar on horseback,
10705
Beginnings of literary culture
in the Ohio Valley, 5566
Begonias - Therapeutic use,
726
Behaim, Martin, 1459?-1506,
1081
Behemoth, 10322, 10326
Behind a bugler, 10598
Behind closed doors, 10662
Behind plastered walls, 9171
Behind the Blue Ridge, 8758
Behind the curtain, 8769
Behind the scenes, 11208
Behind the seams, 7177
Beker, Ana, 6057
Beknopte en zakelyle besch-
ryving der voornaamste
engelsche volkplantingen,
1071

'Bel of Prairie Eden, 10211
Belaúnde, Victor Andres,
1883-, ed., 7464
Belcher, Edward, 6058, 6059
Belcher, Jonathan, 1681-1757,
1780
Belcher, Jonathan, 1710-1776,
1780
Belcher, Joseph, 1669-1723,
1072, 1073
Belcher, Joseph, 1794-1859,
1074, 1075
Belcher, Mrs. Mary (Partridge)
1685-1736, 1780
Belcourt, George Antoine,
1803-1874, 11353
Belden, David, 1832-, 6060
Belden, Elizur, 1763-1786,
12812
Belden, Ezekiel Porter, 1823-
1911, 1076, 1077
Beleña, Eusebio Buenaventura,
1736-1794, 1078
Belew, Pascal Perry, 1894-,
6061
Belfast, Ireland, 11248
Belgians in Virginia, 2242
Die belgische neutralität,
1079
Belgium - Neutrality, 1079
Belgrano, Manuel, 1770-1820,
7708
Belgrove, William, 1080
Belhaven tales, 9761
Belice, tierra nuestra, 6803
Belisle, David W., 2664
Belknap, Jeremy, 1744-1798,
1081, 1082, 1083, 1084
Bell, Agrippa Nelson, 1820-,
1085
Bell, Andrew, of Southampton,
fl. 1838-1866, 1086
Bell, Benjamin, 1752-1836,
11249
Bell, Charles Napier, 6062,
6225
Bell, Hiram, 1808-1855, 1087
Bell, James Stanislaus, ed.,
8164

43

Bell, John, 1796-1872,
1088, 1089
Bell, John, 1797-1869,
1090, 1091, 11250
Bell, John Thomas, 1842-,
2665
Bell, Joshua Fry, 1811-1870,
1092
Bell, Landon C., 6063
Bell, Louis, 1837-1865,
11415
Bell, Luther Vose, 1806-
1862, 1093, 12054
Bell Martin, 8559
Bell, Orelia Key, 1864-,
2666
Bell, Robert, fl. 1570,
1094
Bell, Rev. William, 1095
The bell-ringer of Angel's,
6963
Bell Smith abroad, 10520
The bell-tower, 10346
Bella, 8796
"Bella Vista", Agua Caliente,
Costa Rica, 5845
Bellamy, B. W., 9769
Bellamy, George Anne,
1731?-1788, 11251
Bellamy, Joseph, 1719-1790,
1096, 1097, 1098
Bellardi, Luigi, 1818-1889,
1099
The belle and the bleu,
9702
Belle Boyd in camp and prison,
11455
Belle Brittan on a tour, 2357
The belle of Bayou Luie, 9579
A belle of Canada City, 6969
Belle Scott, 10055
Bellecombe, André Ursule
Casse de, 1822-1897, 1100
Bellegarde, Dantes, 1877-,
6064
Bellegarde, Jean Baptiste
Morvan de, 1648-1734, 1101
Bellegarrigue, A., 1102
Bellemare, Gabriel de,

1846-, 1104
Bellemare, Louis, i.e. Eugène
Louis Gabriel de, 1809-1852,
1103, 1104, 1105, 1106, 1107,
1108, 6065
Bellers, John, 1654-1725, 8165
Belligerency, 1142, 12668, 12669
Bellin, Jacques Nicolas,
1703-1772, 1109, 1110, 1111,
2667
Belloc, Hippolyte, 1112
Bellomont, Charles Coote, earl
of, 1738?-1800, 1113
Bellon de Saint Quentin, J.,
1114
Belloro, Tommaso, 1741-1821,
1115
Bellot, Joseph René, 1826-1853,
1116, 1117
Bellows family (Benjamin Bellows,
1712-1777), 1119
Bellows, Henry Whitney, 1814-
1882, 1118, 1119, 1120, 1121,
1122
Belloy, Auguste, marquis de,
1815-1871, 1123
Belly, Félix, 1816-1886, 1124,
1125
Belmar, Francisco, 1859-, 6066
Belmont, Mass. - Hist., 558
Belmonte, Benjamin Elie Colaço,
1126, 1127
Belot, Charles, 1128
Belot, Gustave de, 1129
Below, Ernst, 1845-1910, 6067
Below the salt, 4983
Belsham, Jacobus, 1130
Belsham, Thomas, 1750-1829,
11252
Belsham, W. J., 1131
Belt, Edward W., 1132
Beltrami, Giacomo Constantino,
1779-1855, 1133, 1134, 1135,
6068
Beltrán de Beltrán y Barnuevo,
Luis, 6160
Beltran, Pedro, fl. 1742, 1136
Beman, Nathan Sidney Smith,
1785-1871, 1137, 1138

44

Bembo, Pietro, cardinal, 1470-1547, 1139, 1140
Bemis, George, 1816-1878, 1141, 1142, 1143
Benavente, Diego José, 1789-1867, 1144
Benavides, Alonso de, fl. 1630, 1145
Benavides y de la Cueva, Diego de, 6069
Ben-Bear, 8801
The bench and bar of Georgia, 13434
Benedict, David, 1779-1874, 1146, 1147
Benedict, Erastus Cornelius, 1800-1880, 1148
Benedict, George Grenville, 1826-1907, 1149
Benedict, Kirby, 1810-1874, 1150
Benedict, Lewis, 1785-1862, 12576
Benedict, Mrs. Susan (Stafford), 1790-1869, 12576
Benedict, William B.? ed., 10315
The Benedictines, 9132
Benezet, Anthony, 1713-1784, 1151, 1152, 1153, 1154, 1155, 1156, 1157, 1158
Benham, Asahel, 1159
Benítez, José R., 6070
Benito Cereno, 10346
El Benjamin de la ss.ma trinidad, 5853
Benjamin, Israel Joseph, 1818-1864, 2668
Benjamin, Judah Philip, 1811-1884, 1160, 1161, 1162, 1163, 1164, 1165, 1166
Benjamin, L. N., comp., 1167
Benjamin, Samuel Greene Wheeler, 1837-1914, 1168
Bennett, Andrew J., b. 1841

or 2, 2669
Bennett, Daniel K., 1830-1897, 1169
Bennett, Edmund Hatch, 1824-1898, ed., 1378
Bennett, Emerson, 1822-1905, 1170, 2670-2685
Bennett, Emily Thacher B., 1171
Bennett, Frederick Debell, 1172
Bennett, William Wallace, 1821-1887, 2686
Bennie Ben Cree, 9082
Bennington, Vt. First church, 13206
Bennington, Vt. - Hist., 13206
Benny, 4165
Benoist, Pierre Vincent, comte, 1758-1834, tr., 946
Bensley: a story of today, 8894
Benson, Alfred G., 1173
Benson, Alfred G. - Claims vs. U. S., 1173
Benson, Egbert, 1746-1833, 1174, 1175, 1176, 1177
The Benson family, 8550
Benson family (William Benson, 1718-1755), 2412
Benson, Henry Clark, b. 1815, 1178
Bent, St. Vrain, & co., 5503
Bent's Fort - Fiction, 2672
Bentham, Edward, 1707-1776, 1179
Bentham, Jeremy, 1748-1832, 1180, 1181, 11253
Bentley, William, 1759-1819, 1182
Bentley, William H., 2687
Bentom, Clark, 11254
Benton, Nathaniel Soley, 1183
Benton, Thomas Hart, 1782-1858, 1184, 1185, 2688, 2689, 2690, 5508, 11255
Benton's policy of selling and developing the mineral lands, 2079
Benwell, J., 2691
Benzoni, Girolamo, b. 1519, 1186, 1187

45

Bera Cerxcada, Antonio,
6071
Berard, Augusta Blanche,
1824-1901, 1188
Berard's history of the
United States, 1188
The Berber, 10336
Berbers, 10336
Berbice river, 1193
Berchmans, Jean, Saint,
1599-1621, 1189
Berea College, Berea, Ky.,
3427
Berdan's United States
sharpshooters in the
Army of the Potomac, 5267
Berenice, 9386
Berettari, Sebastiano,
1543-1622, 1189
Berg, Joseph Frederick,
1812-1871, 1190
Berger, Friedrich Ludwig
von, 1701-1735, 1191
Berger, Martin Luther,
1839-1906, 6655
Bergh, Henry, 1811-1888,
1192
Berghaus, Erwin, 1894-,
ed., 2692
Berghaus, Heinrich Karl
Wilhelm, 1797-1884, tr.,
1836
Berghes, Carlos de, 2186
Berghoff, Stephan, 1891-,
2693
Bering Strait, 7209
Berkel, Adriaan van, 1193
Berkeley co., S. C., 4023
Berkeley, George, bp. of
Cloyne, 1685-1753, 1194,
1195, 1196, 11256
Berkeley, George Charles
Grantley Fitzhardinge,
1800-1881, 1197
Berkeley, Sir William,
1608?-1677, 1198
The Berkeleys and their
neighbors, 5114
Berkshire association of

Congregational ministers,
Berkshire co., Mass., 2251
Berkshire co., Mass., 2251,
12279
Berkshire co., Mass. - Hist.,
2251
Berlandier, Luis, d. 1851, 7480
Berlandier, Luis, d. 1851 -
Bibl., 8049
Bermuda - Fiction, 3998
Bermuda islands, 2426, 4947
Bermuda islands - Descr. & trav.,
1110, 12680
Bermuda islands - Descr. & trav. -
Guide-books, 7616, 7617, 8102
Bermuda islands - Religious and
ecclesiastical institutions,
1195
Bermudez, José Manuel, 1764-1830,
1199
The Bermudian, 13491
Bernáldez, Andres, d. 1513?
1200
Bernard, Mrs. Bayle, ed., 2695
Bernard, David, 1798-1876,
11257
Bernard, Sir Francis, bart.,
1712?-1779, 11258
Bernard, Jean Frédéric, d. 1752,
ed., 1201, 2694
Bernard, John, 1756-1828, 2695
Bernard Lile, 9020
Bernard, Louis, b. 1781, 1202,
1203
Bernard, Mountague, 1820-1882,
1204, 1205
Bernard, Sir Thomas, bart.,
1750-1818, 686
Bernard's American journal of
education, 260
Bernardo de Quirós, Alvaro,
7644
Bernath, Ursula, 7440, 7441,
7442
Bernedo, Vicente, 1562-1619,
7453
Bernhard, Karl, duke of Saxe-
Weimar-Eisenach, 1792-1862,
2696

46

Bernicia, 8721
Bernier, Joseph Elzear, 6303
Bernstorff, J. H. von, Graf, 4607
Berquin-Duvallon, 1206
Berredo, Bernardo Pereira de, d. 1748, 11259
Berrian, Richard, 1207
Berrian, Samuel, 1208
Berrian, William, 1787-1862, 1209, 1210, 1211
Berriman, William, 11260
Berrios, Héctor H., 1922-, 7747
Berry, C. B., 1812-1900, 2697
Berry, Harrison, b. 1816, 1212
Berry, Henry, 1213
Berry, Philip, 1214, 1215
Berry, Robert Taylor, 1812-1877, 1216
Berry, Thomas Franklin, 1832-, 2698
Berryer, Pierre Antoine, 1790-1868, 1217
Besançon's annual register of the state of Mississippi, 2699
Beschke, William, 1218, 1219, 2700
Beschreibung des Brittischen Amerika zur esparung der englischen karten, 4248
Beschreibung einer reise durch die Vereinigten Staaten von Nord-Amerika in den jahren 1838 bis 1840, 3595
Beschryving der colonien van Groot-Britanje in Noord-Amerika, 2701
Bessau, Oscar, illustr., 4215
Beste, John Richard Digby, 1806-1885, 1220
Betagh, William, 1221
Bertha, 10760
Bertha and her baptism, 8470

Bertha the beauty, 11156
Bertha's engagement, 10865
Bessie Wilmerton, 11125
Bessie's fortune, 9891
Bethune, George Washington, 1805-1862, 1222, 1223, 1224, 1225, 1226, 1227
Bethune, Mrs. Joanna (Graham) 1770-1849, 1225
The betrayed, 10580
Bettendorf, João Filippe, b. 1626?, 1228
Better days, 9521
The better element, 9533
The better part, 9709
The better way, 10841
Bettridge, William Craddock, 1791-1879, 1229
Betts, Alexander Davis, 1832-, 2702
Betts, Craven Langstroth, jt. author, 9460
Betts, William Archibald, ed., 2702
Betty, 11167
Betty Alden: the first born daughter of the Pilgrims, 8600
Between Mass and Vespers, 10041
Between showers in Dort, 10808
Between the crusts, 9743
Between the lines, 10110
Between two fires, 10417
Between two oceans, 3777
Beukma, K. Jz., 1230
Bevens, W. E., 2703
Beveridge, Albert Jeremiah, 1892-1927, 6000
Beverley, Robert, ca. 1673-ca. 1722, 1231, 1232
Beverly, 11061
The Beverly family, 8968
Bewick, Thomas, 1753-1828, illustr., 82
The bewildered querists and other nonsense, 9248
Beyer, Edward, 1820?-1865, 2704
Beyer, Moritz, 1807-1854, 1233,

Bigelow, Abijah, 1264
Bigelow, Burton, 6080
Bigelow, Erastus Brigham,
1814-1879, 1265, 1266
Bigelow, Jacob, 1787-1879,
1267, 1268, 1269, 1270,
1271
Bigelow, John, 1817-1911,
1272, 1273, 2712, 6081,
11263
Bigelow, John Flavel,
1818-1884, 11264
Bigelow, John Reynolds, 1274
Bigelow, Timothy, 1767-1821,
1275, 1276
Bigelow, Tyler, 1277
Biggs, James, 1278, 1279
Biggs, William, 11265
Bigland, John, 1750-1832,
1280, 11266
Bigler, John, 2891
Bigler, William, 1814-1880,
1281, 1282
Biglow, William, 1773-1844,
1283, 1284, 1285, 1286
Bigney, Mark Frederick,
1817-1886, 1287
Bigot, Jacques, 1644-1711,
1288, 1289, 1290
Bigsby, John Jeremiah, 1291
Bilder aus dem gesellschaft-
lichen leben der Nord-
Amerikaner, 2713
Bill Arp, so called, 5186
Bill Arp's peace papers,
5187
Bill Drock's investment,
8975
Bill family (John Bill,
d. 1638), 1292
Bill, Ledyard, 1836-1907,
1292, 2714, 11267
Billardon de Sauvigny, Edmé
Louis, 1293
Billaud-Varenne, Jacques
Nicolas, 1756-1819, 1294
Billecocq, Jean Baptiste
Louis Joseph, 1765-1829,
tr., 5423, 13397

Billerica, Mass., 11268
Billerica, Mass. First Con-
gregational church, 11892
Billerica, Mass. - Hist.,
11268
Billings, Mrs. Eliza (Allen)
b. 1826, 1295
Billings, John Davis, 1842-,
2715
Billington's valentine, 10465
Billtry, 9318
Billy Buck's visit, with his
master, to England, 10861
Billy the kid, 3575
Biloxi - Descr., 3597
Bingham, Hiram, 1789-1869,
1296, 1297
Bingham, Joel Foote, 1827-
1914, 1298, 1299, 1300, 1301
Bingham, John Armor, 1815-1900,
1302, 1303, 1304, 1305,
11269
Bingham, J. C., 1306
Bingham, Kinsley Scott, 1808-
1861, 1307
Bingley, William, 1774-1823,
2716
Binney, Horace, 1780-1875,
1308, 1309, 1310, 1311,
1312, 1313, 1314, 1315,
6082, 11270, 11271
Binney, Horace, 1780-1875.
An eulogium upon the Hon.
William Tilghman, 12296
Binney, Horace, 1780-1875.
The privilege of the writ of
habeas corpus under the
Constitution, 1676, 11272,
12461, 13134
Binney, William, 1316, 7783
Binney, William Greene,
1833-, 1317, 1318
Binns, John, 1772-1860, 1319,
1320
Binns, William, 1321
Biographia americana, 12171
Biographical and historical
memoirs of the early pioneer
settlers in Ohio, 3868

The biographical annual,
12455
A biographical dictionary,
1397, 12007
Biographical, literary, and
political anecdotes, of
several of the most eminent
persons of the present
age, 223
The biographical remains of
Rev. George Beecher, 1052
A biographical romance, 8800
Biographical sketch of Hon.
Charles Fenton Mercer,
6826
A biographical sketch of the
life of the late Capt.
Michael Cresap, 13138
Biographical sketch of
Thomas Singularity,
10434
Biographical sketches,
2905
Biographical sketches of
General Nathaniel Massie,
General Duncan McArthur,
Captain William Wells,
and General Simon
Kenton, 4347
Biography, 1525, 12296,
12890
Biography - Dictionaries,
700, 1397
Biography - Juvenile
literature, 1954
The biography of elder
David Purviance, 4866
Biological investigations
in Mexico, 6862
Biondelli, Bernardino,
1804-1886, 1322
Bionne, Henri, d. 1881,
1323
Biot, Jean Baptiste,
1774-1862, 1324
Birch, Edmund Pendleton,
1824-1883, 1325
Birch, James H., 1804-1878,
11273

Birch, Thomas Ledlie, d. 1808,
1326
Bird family, 1330
Bird, Francis William, 1809-
1894, 1327, 1328, 11274, 11275
Bird, Henry Merttins, 1329
Bird, Isaac, 1793-1876, 1330
Bird, James, 1788-1839, 1331
Bird, Mark Baker, 1807-1880,
6083
Bird, Robert Montgomery,
1806-1854, 1332, 1333, 2717
Bird-song, 5398
Bird, William A., 1796-1878,
1334
Birds - Arctic regions, 6302
Birds - Argentine Republic, 589
Birds - Classification, 549
Birds - Eggs and nests, 1486
Birds - Europe, 11349
Birds - Geographical distri-
bution, 11349
Birds - Jamaica, 12324
Birds - Minnesota, 4664
Birds - New Hampshire, 6111
Birds - North America, 549,
675, 676, 1486, 11349
Birds - Nova Scotia, 6111
Birds - Paraguay, 589, 598
Birds - Pennsylvania, 931
Birds - Pictorial works, 5735
Birds - Rocky Mountains, 5524
Birds - U. S., 5735
Birds - Wisconsin, 4664
Birdseye, George W., 1844-,
11276
Birkbeck, Morris, 1764-1825,
1335, 1336, 1337, 3487
Birkbeck, Morris, 1764-1825.
Letters from Illinois, 3039,
3424, 13233
Birkbeck, Morris, 1764-1825.
Notes on a journey in
America, 3039, 3424
Birkinbine, Henry E., 6084
Birkinbine, John, 1844-,
6084
Birkinshaw, Maria Louisa, 1338
Birney, James Gillespie,

1792-1857, 1339, 1340,
1341, 1342, 2718, 2719,
2720
Biron, Armand Louis de
Gontaut, duc de Lauzun,
1747-1793, 2721
The birthday gifts, 8807
A birthday present for
Lincoln, 5865
The birth-mark, 9823
Bisbie, D. T., 1343
Bishop, Abraham, 1763-1844,
1344, 1345, 1346, 1347,
1348, 1349
Bishop, Albert Webb, 1832-
1901, 1350, 1351
The bishop and Nannette,
9668
Bishop, Mrs. Anna (Rivière)
1814-1884, 6085, 8230
Bishop, Mrs. Harriet E.,
1817-1883, 1352
Bishop, Isabella Lucy (Bird)
"Mrs. J. F. Bishop",
1831-1904, 2722, 6086
Bishop, Joel Prentiss,
1814-1901, 1353, 1354,
1355
Bishop, John Leander, 1820-
1868, 1356
Bishop, John Soast, 1834-
1915, 11277
Bishop, Joseph, b. 1770,
3668
Bishop, Judson Wade, 1831-
1917, 11278
Bishop, Matthew, fl. 1701-
1744, 1357
Bishop, Nathaniel Holmes,
1837-1902, 2723, 2724
Bishop, Putnam P., 1358
Bishop, Robert Hamilton,
1777-1855, 1359
Bishop, Samuel G., 11279
Bishop, William Henry,
6087, 6088
The bishop's conversion,
10333
The bishop's ghost and the

printer's baby, 10896
The bishop's son, 8946
Bisset, George, d. 1788, 1360
Bisset, Robert, 1759-1805,
1361, 1362, 1363
Bits of blarney, 10291
The bivouac and the battle-
field, 4630
Bixby, O. H., 2725
Le bizco, 1235
Björck, Tobias Er., 1364
Black and white, 4221
Black blood and white, 10787
The black book, 5033
The black brigade of Cincinnati,
11826
The black crook, 8808
The black cross, 10668
Black diamonds, 10198
Black diamonds gathered in the
darkey homes of the South,
4813
The black gauntlet, 10715
Black Hawk, Sauk chief, 1767-
1838, 1365, 1366, 3282
Black Hawk war, 1832, 1366,
3081, 5596, 9585, 12148
Black Hills - Fiction, 3373
Black Hills, S. D. - Hist.,
5201
Black ice, 10988
Black, Jeremiah Sullivan,
1810-1883, 1367, 1368, 1369
Black list, 1370
The black plume rifles, 9936
Black Ralph, the forest fiend!
4990
Black Republican imposture
exposed! 1371
The Black Riders of Congaree,
10775
Black, Robert, 6089
The black sheep, 10289
Black spirits and white, 9204
Black, William Harman,
1868-, 6090, 6091
The black wolf's breed, 9400
Blackbeard, 8699
Blackburn, Colin Blackburn,

51

baron, 1813-1896, 2199

Blackburn, James Knox Polk, 1837-1923, 2726

Blackburn, William Maxwell, 1828-1898, 1372

Blackford, Charles Minor, 1833-1903, 2727

Blackford, Dominique de, 1373

Blackford, Mrs. Susan Leigh (Colston) 1835-1903, comp., 2727

Blackie, Walter Graham, 1816-1906, 1374

Blackley, Frederick Rogers, 1375

Blackmore, Richard Doddridge, 1825-1900, 1376

Blacknall, O. W., 6092

Blackstone, Sir William, 1723-1780. Commentaries, 1181

The Blackwater chronicle, 4157

Blackwell, Robert, 6093

Blackwell, Robert S., 1823-1863, 1377, 1378

Blackwell, Sarah Ellen, 1828-, 6094

Bladensburg, Battle of, 1814 - Poetry, 1379

The Bladensburg races, 1379

Blades o' bluegrass, 3245

Bladh, Carl Edvard, 1790-1851, 1380

Blagden, George Washington, 1802-1884, 1381

Blaine, James Gillespie, 1830-1893, 1382, 8261

Blair, Francis Preston, 1791-1876, 6095

Blair, Francis Preston, 1821-1875, 1383, 2728

Blair, James, 1656-1743, 1384, 3805

Blair, John Durbarrow, 1759-1823, 1385

Blair, Montgomery, 1813-1883, 1386, 6096, 6097, 11280

Blair, Samuel, 1741-1818, 1387, 1388

Blake, Dominick T., d. 1839, 1389

Blake family (Samuel Blake, 1715-1754), 1401

Blake family (William Blake, 1594-1663), 1401

Blake, Francis, 1774-1817, 1390, 11281

Blake, George, 1768?-1841, 1391, 1392, 12681

Blake, Harrison Gray, 1818-1876, 1393, 6098

Blake, Henry Nichols, 1838-, 1394

Blake, James, 1688-1753, 1395

Blake, John Lauris, 1788-1857, 1396, 1397, 1398

Blake, Joseph M., 1809-1879, 1399

Blake, Mrs. Mary Elizabeth, 1840-1907, 6099

Blake, Mortimer, 1813-1884, 1400

Blake, Samuel, 1797-1867, 1401

Blake, William J., 1402

Blake, William O., 1403

Blake, William Phipps, 1826-, 1404, 11282, 11283

Blakeslee, Bernard F., 2729

Blakiston, Thomas Wright, 1832-1891, 2730

Blakman, Learner, 1781?-1815, 2818

Blakslee, Solomon, 1762-1835, 1405

Blanc, Hippolyte, b. 1820, 1406

Blanchard, Amos, of Cincinnati, 1407, 1408

Blanchard, Calvin, 1409

Blanchard, Charles, 1410

Blanchard, Claude, 1742-1802, 2731

Blanchard, Ira Henry Thomas, d. 1845, 1411

Blanchard, Joshua Pollard, 1782-1868, 1412

Blanchard, P., 2732

Blanche Gilroy, 9926

Blanche of Brandywine, 10212
Blanche Talbot, 3997
Blanchelande, royal lieute-
  nant in Haiti, 7828
Blanco-Fombona, Rufino,
  1874-, 6109, 6814, 7245,
  7635, 7637, 8009, 8267
Bland, Thomas, 1809-1885,
  jt. author, 1318
Blandford, Mass. - Hist.,
  12236
Blanding, Stephen F., 2733
Blane, William Newnham,
  1800-1825, 2734
Blanton, Lindsay Hughes,
  8192
Blatchford, John, 1762(ca.)-
  1794(ca.), 11284
Blatchford, Richard M.,
  1413
Blatchford, Samuel, 1767-
  1828, 1414
Blatchford, Thomas Windeatt,
  1794-1866, 1415
Blauvelt, 1416
Blauvelt, Charles Clare, 6100
Bledsoe, A. J., 6101
Bledsoe, Albert Taylor,
  1809-1877, 2735, 2736
Blccker, Leonard, 1417
The Blemmertons, 10423
The blessed bees, 9046
Blessington, Joseph P., 2737
Blitchfeldt, Emil Harry,
  1874-, 6102
Blind, 11443
Blind - Education, 7181
Blind leaders of the blind,
  9054
The blind sisters, 11173
A blindman's offering,
  11443
The blindman's world, 8773
Bliss, Edward, 1822-1877,
  2738
Bliss, George, 1764-1830,
  1418
Bliss, George, 1793-1873,
  1419, 1420

Bliss, Henry, 1797?-1873, 1421
Bliss, Leonard, 1811-1842, 11285
Bliss, Philemon, 1814-1889,
  1422
Bliss, Sylvester, 11286
The Blithedale romance, 9818
Blocher, W. D., 2739
Blocher's Arkansas land-guide,
  2739
Blockade, 12222
A blockaded family, 3728
The blockheads, 1423
Blockley and Merion agricultural
  ·society, Pa., 1455
Blodget, Lorin, 1823-1901,
  1424, 11287
Blodget, Samuel, 1757-1814,
  11288
Blois, John T., 11289
Blom, Frans Ferdinand, 1893-,
  ed., 8212
Blome, Richard, d. 1705, 1425
Blondel, Georges, 1856-, 2740
Blood - Circulation, 535
Blood, Henry Ames, 1838-1901?
  11290
The blood of the Mohawk! 10158
Blood, William, 11291
Bloodgood, Simeon De Witt,
  1799-1866, 11292, 11293
Bloody Brook, Battle of, 1675,
  12110
The bloody chasm, 9369
The bloody junto, 3134
The bloody week, 11294
Bloomfield, Me. - Hist., 12657
Bloomington, Ind. - Soc. life
  & cust., 9705
Blooms of the berry, 2949
Bloor, Alfred Janson, d. 1917,
  11295
Blossom (Ship), 1066, 6048,
  12883
Blouet, Guillaume Abel, 1795-
  1853, 3229
Blouët, Paul, i.e., Léon Paul,
  1848-1903, 2741
Blount, William, 1747-1800,
  defendant, 11296

53

Blow, Henry Taylor, 1817-1875, 11297
Blowe, Daniel, 2742
The Bloxhams, 10196
The blue and the gray, 2577
The blue cotton umbrella, 10194
Blue, Daniel, 2743
Blue-grass and rhododendron, 3522
A blue grass Penelope, 9788
The blue-grass region of Kentucky, 2509, 5432
The Blue guide to Cuba, 6103
Blue Licks, Battle of the, 7376
Blue ribbons, 10200
Blue Ridge Mountains - Fiction, 8758
Blumenthal, Ida (Gawell) 1869-, 2744
Blundell, Bezer, 11298
Blunt, Joseph, 1792-1860, ed., 241, 11299
Blyth, Joseph, 11300
Board of agents for the American loyalists, 12190
Board of aid to land owner- ship, Boston, 2745
The boarding school, 9548
Boarding-school scenes, 10953
Boardman, George Dana, 1828-1903, 11301
Boardman, George Nye, 1825-1915, 11302
Boardman, Henry Augustus, 1808-1880, 11303, 11304, 11305, 11306, 11307, 11308, 11309, 11310, 11311, 11312, 11313
Boardman, James, 6104
Boards of trade, 12788
The boarwolf, 10693
Bob Rutherford and his wife, 10372
Boban, Eugène, 6105
"Bobbie", 8821
The bobolink minstrel, 1677

Het bock der landverhuizers, 1234
Bockett, Elias, 11314
Bocock, John Holmes, 1813-1872, 2746
Boddily, John, 1755-1802, 11315
Bodenstedt, Friedrich Martin von, 1819-1892, 2747
Boesnier, 11316
Bogart, David Schuyler, 1770-1839, 11317
Bogart, William Henry, 1810-1888, 2748, 11318
Bogen, Frederick W., 11319
Boggs, Edward Brenton, 1821-1895, 13177
Boggs, Samuel S., 2749
Boggs, William Robertson, 1829-1911, 2750
Bogle, Robert, 1258
Bohemia invaded, 9533
The Bohemian, 11320
Bohemian days in San Francisco, 6978
The Bohemian girl, 9740
Bohn, Henry George, 1796-1884, tr., 13004
Bohun, Edmund, 1645-1699, 11321
Bohun family 11321
Boies, Andrew J., 2751
The boiler explosion of the Martin boiler on board the U. S. "double-ender" Chenango, 11322
Boimare, A. L., 11323
The Bois Brûlé, 10827
Boisgilbert, Edmund, pseud., 9412
Boislecomte, André Olivier Ernest Sain de, b. 1799, 11324
Boker, George Henry, 1823-1890, 11325, 11326
Bokum, Hermann, 1807-1878, 2752, 11327, 11328, 11329
Bolanyo, 10593
Bold works at the bridge, 10042
Bolduc, Jean-Baptiste-Zacharie, 2753, 6106
Boletín histórico de Puerto Rico,

6107
Bolivar en el Perú, 6250
Bolivar, Fernando S., 2754
Bolivar, Simón, 1783-1830,
  6028, 6108, 6109, 6110,
  6250, 6476, 6794, 6866,
  7015, 7053, 7245, 7635,
  7636, 7637, 7761, 8026
Bolivia, 13272
Bolivia - Bound. - Argentine
  republic, 7953
Bolivia. Constitution,
  12513
Bolivia - Descr. & trav.,
  11964
Bolivia - Hist. - 1825-,
  7752
Bolivia - Hist. - Wars of
  independence, 1809-1825,
  5923, 7752
Bollaert, William, 1807-
  1876, 11330
Bollan, William, d. 1776,
  11331, 11332, 11333, 11334,
  11335, 11336
Bolles family (Joseph Bolles,
  1608-1678), 11338
Bolles, Frank, 1856-1894,
  6111
Bolles, James Aaron, 1810-
  1894, 11337
Bolles, John Augustus,
  1809-1878, 11338, 11339
Bolles, Lucius, 1779-1884,
  11340
Bollmann, Erich, 1769-1821,
  11341, 11342
Boloix, Pablo, 11343
Bolton, Charles Edward,
  1841-1901, 2755
Bolton, Edward Chichester,
  11344
Bolton, Eng. (Lancashire)
  Mechanics' institution,
  2562
Bolton, Robert, 1814-1877,
  11345, 11346
Bolzius, Reverend, 4908
Bombardement de Valparaiso,

11347
Bombardement et entière des-
  truction de Grey-town, 890
Bona, Félix de, 1821?-1889,
  11348
Bonaparte, Charles Lucien Jules
  Laurent, prince de Canino,
  1803-1857, 11349
Bonaparte, Roland Napoléon,
  prince, 1858-1924, 7494
Bonar, Lewis J., 6112
Bond, Alvan, 1793-1882, 11350,
  11351
Bond, Beverly Waugh, 1882-, 5229
Bond, Christiana, 6113
Bond, John Wesley, 1825-1903,
  11352, 11353
Bond, Samuel R., 5535
Bond, William Cranch, 1789-1859,
  11354
Bond, William Key, d. 1864,
  11355, 11356
Bondage a moral institution,
  11357
Bonduel, Florimond J., 11358
Bone, John Herbert A., 1830-
  1906, 2756, 11359
A bone to gnaw, 1931, 1932
Boner, John Henry, 1845-1903,
  2757
Bonfield, 3998
Bonilla, Policarpo, pres. Honduras,
  1858-1926, 7451
Bonneau, Alexandre, 1820-, 11360
Bonnefoux, L., 11361
Bonnefoy, Antoine, 2758
Bonnell, George William, 2759
Bonnell, Joseph Gatch, ed., 5215
Bonner, John, 1828-1899, 11362
Bonnet, Stede, d. 1718,
  defendant, 11363
Bonneville, Benjamin Louis
  Eulalie de, ca. 1795-1878,
  4028
Bonneville, Zacharie de Pazzi de,
  11364
Bonney, William H., 1859-1881,
  3575, 7755
Bonny Kate, 5418

Bonnycastle, Sir Richard
Henry, 1791-1847, 11365,
11366, 11367
Bonpland, Aimé Jacques
Alexandre Goujaud, called,
1773-1858, 7092
Bonrepos, Chevalier de, 2760
Bonynge, Francis, 11368
Book collecting, 8186
Book collecting - U. S.,
7001
A book for an hour, 9025
Book of anecdotes, 6114
The book of bubbles, 11369
The book of four and twenty
chapters, 9477
A book of gold, 4771
A book of martyrs, 9084
The book of my lady, 10767
The book of peace, 11370
The book of Saint Nicholas,
10480
The book of the colonies,
12173
The book of the continuation
of foreign passages, 11371
A book of the heart, 10362
A book of the Hudson, 9995
The book of the navy, 12174
Book of the prophet, Stephen,
son of Douglas, 6115
The book of the signers, 1590
Book verse, 684
A book without a title, 11035
Bookbinding, 8186
Bookbinding - U. S., 8188
Booksellers and bookselling -
U. S., 7001
Boole, William H., 11372
The boom in the "Calaveras
Clarion", 6972
The boom of a western city,
9124
The booming of Acre Hill,
8674
Boone, Daniel, 1734-1820,
2748, 3445, 12730, 13199
Boone, Daniel, 1734-1820 -
Fiction, 4621

Boone, Daniel, 1734-1820 - Poetry,
2844
Boone Island, Me., 2089
Boorjes de Oropesa, Ambrosio,
8275
Boorn, Jesse, 12761
The Boot on the other leg, 11373
Booth, Benjamin F., 1837?-,
2761
Booth, George Wilson, 1844-1914,
2762
Booth, John Wilkes, 1838-1865,
5987, 6026, 6116, 6293, 6580.
6827, 7163, 8218
Booth, John Wilkes, 1838-1865 -
Fiction, 3134
Booth, Mary Louise, 1831-1889,
tr., 2413, 11374, 12199
Booth, Robert Russell, 11375
Booth, Sherman M., 11376
Boott, John Wright, 1788 or 9-
1845, 1577
Booty, James Horatio, 2763
Borcke, Heros von, 1835-1895,
2764
Bordeaux, Albert François
Joseph, 1865-, 6117
Borden, Nathaniel B., 1801-1865,
11377
Borden, William, 1689-1748, 2765
Border adventures, 953
Border and bastille, 4230
Border beagles, 10768
The border rover, 2672
The border ruffian, 9202
The border ruffian code in
Kansas, 11378
A border shepherdess, 8722
The border states, 4154
Border states of Mexico, 6942,
6943
Border war, 4110
Borgia, Cesare, 1476?-1507 -
Fiction, 8590
Borja, Francisco de, príncipe
de Esquilache, 1582-1658,
6118, 6119, 6120
Borland, Solon, 1808-1864,
11379

Borragán, María Teresa,
6121, 6122
Borrett, George Tuthill,
11380
Bory de Saint-Vincent,
Jean Baptiste Genevieve
Marcellin, baron, 1778-
1846, 2213, 11381
Bosbyshell, Oliver Christian,
1839-, 2766
Bosch, Gerardus-Balthasar,
1794-1839, 11382
Bosch, Leonard Eduard,
1792-1865, ed., 11382
Bosch-Spencer, Guillaume
Henri, 1802-1873, 11383
The bosom serpent, 3848
Bosshard, Heinrich, 2767
Bossi, Bartolomé, 1812-
1891, 11384
Bossu, Jean Barnard,
1720-1792, 2768
Boston, 12009
Boston. An appeal to the
world, 11385
Boston and Providence
railroad, 11935
Boston and Worcester
railroad, 12494
Boston before the revo-
lution, 8994
Boston. Board of trade,
526
Boston. Channing home,
10978
Boston. City Council,
6123, 6124, 12330
Boston. Common council,
12242
The Boston conspiracy,
10632
Boston daily times, 1951
Boston - Descr., 2092,
12542
Boston - Descr. - Guide-
books, 11442, 13427
Boston - Direct., 1756
Boston dispensary, 1970
Boston - Fiction, 5037

Boston - Fire, 1872, 2345
Boston. First church, 2306,
12060
Boston. First church, Jamaica
Plain, 12363
Boston Franklin association,
1693
Boston - Geneal, 1505, 1506
Boston - Harbor, 12330
Boston - Hist., 2092, 11683
Boston - Hist., Colonial period -
Fiction, 8994
Boston - Hist. - Chronology,
11442
Boston - Hist. - Fiction, 9980
Boston - Hist. - Revolution -
Fiction, 9136, 9137, 10632,
10633
Boston. King's chapel, 2266,
12415
Boston - King's Chapel burial
ground, 1505
Boston massacre, 1770, 179, 11571,
11790, 13373,
Boston. Mercantile library
association, 684, 1383
Boston. Municipal court, 1951,
11607
Boston. National peace jubilee
and musical festival, 1869,
12267
Boston neighbors in town and out,
10546
Boston. New North church, 2358
Boston - Police, 333
Boston - Pol. & govt. - Colonial
period, 1496
Boston - Pol. & govt. - Revolu-
tion, 11385
Boston - Public works, 12338
Boston. St. Paul's church,
13170
Boston - Sanit. aff., 11921
Boston - Siege, 1775-1776, 698
Boston - Soc. life & cust.,
10151, 10205, 12538
The Boston spy, 10205
Boston. Tremont house, 12011
Boston two hundred years ago,

8822, 10179
Boston - Water supply,
710, 2177, 2179
Boston - Water supply -
Mystic lakes, 12908
Boston - Wharves, 11436
The Bostonian prophet,
11386
Bostwick, David, 1721-1763,
11387
Bostwick, Henry, 1787-
1836 or 7, 11388
Botany - Arctic regions,
6302
Botany Bay, 10790
Botany - District of
Columbia, 1480
Botany, Economic, 4827
Botany - Georgia, 12041
Botany - Mackenzie district,
8252
Botany - Massachusetts,
12807
Botany, Medical, 1267,
4827, 11803
Botany - Mexico, 7019,
7969, 12883
Botany - Minnesota, 4664
Botany - Missouri Valley,
2784
Botany - Morphology,
13004
Botany - New York (State),
1911
Botany - North America,
942
Botany - Oceanica, 12883
Botany of the northern
and middle states, 11245
Botany - Rocky Mountains,
5524
Botany - South America,
7092, 12883
Botany - South Carolina,
12041
Botany - Southern states,
4827
Botany - Southwest, New,
5513

Botany - U. S., 1031, 1267,
2462, 2940, 11245, 11620,
11803, 12355
Botany - Virginia, 930, 3703
Botany - West Indies, 11620
Botany - Wisconsin, 4664
Boteler, Alexander Robinson,
1815-1892, 11389
Botero, Giovanni, 1540-1617,
6125
Botocudo Indians - Language,
13282
Botta, Anne Charlotte (Lynch)
1815-1891, tr., 6902
Botta, Carlo Giuseppe Guglielmo,
1766-1837, 11390
Botts, John Minor, 1802-1869,
11391
Botume, Elizabeth Hyde, 2769
Boturini Benaducci, Lorenzo,
1702-1751, 11392
Boucarut, Alcide, b. 1825,
11393
Bouchacourt, Charles, 11394
Boucher de la Bruère, fils,
11396
Boucher, Jonathan, 1738-1804,
11395
Boucher, Pierre, sieur de
Boucherville, 1620?-1717, 6126
Bouchette, Joseph, 1774-1841,
6127, 6128
Bouchot, Auguste, 11397
Boudinot, Elias, 1740-1821,
11400, 11401, 11402
Boudinot, Elias, d. 1839, 11398,
11399
Bouguer, Pierre, 1698-1758,
11403
Bouillé, René, marquis de,
1802-1882, 11404
Bouillé, François Claude Amour,
marquis de, 1739-1800, 11404
Bouis, Amédée Théodore, 11405
Boulanger, Nicolas Antoine,
1722-1759, 11406
Boulter, Hugh, abp. of Armagh,
1672-1742, 11407
Boulton, Charles Arkoll,

58

b. 1841, 6129
Bound down, 9519
Bounties, Military - U. S.,
12131
Bounty (Ship), 884, 10698,
12609
Bourdon, Louis Gabriel,
1741-1795, 11408
Bourgeois, Léon Victor
Auguste, 1851-1925,
7494
Bourget, Paul-Charles-Joseph,
1852-1935, 2770
Bourinot, Sir John George,
1837-1902, 6130-6133
Bourne, Benjamin Franklin,
11409
Bourne, Edward Emerson,
11410
Bourne, George, 1780-1845,
11411, 13483
Bourne, Henry Richard Fox,
1837-1909, 11412
Bourne, William Oland, 11413
Boutelle, John Alonzo, 1426
Bouton, Jacques, 1592-1658,
11414
Bouton, John Bell, 1830-1902,
11415
Bouton, Nathaniel, 1799-1878,
11416, 11417, 11418,
11419, 11420
Bouturini-Benaduci, Lorenzo,
ca. 1702-1750, 6105
Boutwell, George Sewall,
1818-1905, 6134, 11421,
11422, 11647
Bouvet de Cressé, Auguste
Jean Baptiste, 1772-1839,
11423, 11424
Bouvier, John, 1787-1851,
11425
Bowditch, Charles Pickering,
1842 - 1921, 6135
Bowditch, Henry Ingersoll,
1808-1892, 11426, 11427,
11428, 11429, 11430
Bowditch, Nathaniel, 1773-
1838, 11431, 11434

Bowditch, Nathaniel, 1839-1863,
11430
Bowditch, Nathaniel Ingersoll,
1805-1861, 11432, 11433, 11434,
11435, 11436
Bowditch, William Ingersoll,
1819-1909, 11437, 11438, 11439
Bowdler, Thomas, 1754-1825,
11440
Bowdoin college, 414, 6136, 11441
Bowdoin, James, 1752-1811, 1644
Bowdoin port-folio, 11441
The bowels of a battle-ship,
10608
Bowen, Abel, 1790-1850, 11442
Bowen, B. F., Logansport, Ind.,
pub., 6559
Bowen, Benjamin B., 1819-1905,
11443
Bowen, Eli, 1824-, 2771, 11444
Bowen, Francis, 1811-1890,
239, 11445, 11446
Bowen, Henry L., 1810-1865,
11447
Bowen, Nathaniel, 1779-1839,
11448
Bowen, Noel Hill, d. 1872, 11449
Bowers, A. Herbert, jt. author,
8596
Bowers, Claude Gernade, 1878-1958,
6137
Bowker, J., 11450
Bowles, Charles S. P., ed., 11451
Bowles, Leonard C., Boston pub.,
3098
Bowles, Samuel, 2772
Bowling, William King, 1808-1885,
11452, 11453
Bowlsby, Alice Augusta, d. 1871,
9648
Bowman, Samuel Millard, 1815-
1885, 11454
Bownas, Samuel, 1676-1753,
2773, 12655
Box, Henry W., ed., 6138
Box, Michael James, 6139
The boy in the cloth cap, 10808
The boy inventor, 1669
The boy of Mount Rhigi, 10722

The boy orator of Zepata
City, 9358
The boy spy, 4163
The boy travellers in Mexico,
7202
Boyce family, 7433
Boyce, J. R., 6140
Boyce, Neith, 1872-, 8969
Boyce, William Dickson,
1848-1929, 6141
Boyd, Andrew, 6142
Boyd, Belle, 1844-1900,
11455
Boyd, Daniel French, 1834-,
6915
Boyd, Hugh, 1746-1794, 11456
Boyd, John, 11457
Boyd, John Parker, 1764-1830,
11458
Boyd, Samuel Stillman,
1807-1867, 11459
Boyd, William, d. 1800,
11460
Boyd, William Kenneth,
1879-, ed., 2750
Boyle Co., Ky., 4812
Boyle, Frederick, b. 1841,
11461
Boyle, Henry, 11462
Boyle, Robert, 1627-1691,
11463
Boyle, Mrs. Virginia
(Frazer) 1863-, 2774,
2775
Boylston, Peter, pseud.,
9268
Boylston, Thomas, 1720-
1798, 11464
Boylston, Ward Nicholas,
1749-1828, 11464
Boylston, Zabdiel, 1679-
1766, 11465
Boynton, Charles Brandon,
1806-1883, 2776, 11466,
11467, 11468, 11469
Boynton, Edward Carlisle,
1824-1893, 11470
The boys and girls stories
of the war, 11471

The boys in blue, 12835
The boys in blue of 1861-1865,
4255
The boys in white, 3537
Boys, stay at home, 3651
Bozman, John Leeds, 1757-1823,
11472
Brabant, Augustin Joseph,
1845-1912, 6143
Brace, Charles Loring, 1826-1890,
11473
A brace of boys, 10250
Bracebridge Hall, 9996
Bracht, Victor, 1819-1886, 2777
Brackenridge, Henry Marie,
1786-1871, 2778, 2779, 11474,
11475, 11476, 11477, 11478,
11479, 11480
Brackenridge, Hugh Henry,
1748-1871, 2780, 2781, 2782,
11481, 11482, 11483, 11484
Brackett, Albert Gallatin,
1829-1896, 2783, 6144
Brackett, Edward Augustus,
1818-1908, 11485
Brackett, Joseph Warren,
1775-1826, 11486
Bradburn, George, 1806-1880,
11487
Bradbury, Charles, 1798-1864,
11488
Bradbury, James Ware, 1802-1901,
11489, 11490
Bradbury, John, fl. 1809, 2784
Braddock's campaign, 1755, 3404,
5072
Bradford, Alden, 1765-1843,
11491, 11492, 11493, 11494,
11495, 11496, 11497
Bradford, Alexander Warfield,
1815-1867, 11498, 11499
Bradford, Annie Chambers,
pseud., 10098
Bradford, Benjamin Chambers,
d. 1867, 4165
Bradford, Ebenezer, 1746-1801,
11500, 11501
Bradford, Ephraim Putnam,
1776-1845, 11502

Bradford, George W., 1796-
1883, 11503
Bradford, James Morgan,
d. 1837, 7885
Bradford, John, 1749-1830,
6445, 7885
Bradford, Mary F., 6145
Bradford, Moses, 1765-1838,
11504
Bradford, Samuel Dexter,
11505
Bradford, Samuel Fisher,
1776-1837, 1427
Bradford, Thomas Gamaliel,
tr., 1867
Bradford, William John
Alden, 1791-1858, 11506
Bradley, Arthur Granville,
1850-1943, 2785, 2786,
6146, 6147, 6148, 6149
Bradley family, 6150
Bradley, George S., 2787
Bradley, John C., 6150
Bradley, Thomas H., 6151
Bradshaw, Sidney Ernest,
1869-, 2788
Brady, William, 2789
Bragg, Braxton, 1817-1876,
2039
Brainerd, C. N., 11507
Brainerd, Cephas, 1831-
1910, 7283
Brainerd, David, 1718-
1747, 6152
Brains, 10394
Braintree, Mass. - Hist., 39
Bramantip, Bocardo, pseud.,
6243
Branagan, Thomas, b. 1774,
1428, 1429, 1941
A branch of May, 4916
A branch road, 9606
Branch, William, jr., 1430
Brand, Charles, 1431
The branded hand, 10270
Brandegee, Augustus, 1828-,
1432
Brandes, Karl, 1433
Brandin, Abel Victorino, 1434

Brandon, 10977
Brandt, Geeraert, 1626-1685,
1435
Brandywine, Battle of, 1777 -
Fiction, 10212
Brannan, John, comp., 1436
Brannan, William Penn, 1825-
1866, 1437
Brant, Joseph, Mohawk chief,
1742-1807 - Fiction, 10396
Brantly, William Theophilus,
1787-1845, 1438
Brashears, Noah, 1439
Brasseur de Bourbourg, Charles
Étienne, 1814-1874, 1440, 1441,
1442, 1443, 1444, 6153
Brassey, Annie (Allnutt) baroness,
1839-1887, 6154
Brattle family (Thomas Brattle,
1624?-1683), 12700
Brauns, Frederick William,
1830-1895, 1445
Brave hearts, 10591
A brave little Quakeress, 10653
The bravo, 9128
Bravo en 1812, 7407
Bravo, Nicolás, 7407
The bravo's daughter, 9433
Braxton, Carter M., 1446
Braxton's bar, 9307
Bray, John, 1782-1822, 1447
Bray, Thomas, 1656-1730,
1448, 1449, 2790
Brayman, James O., 1815-1887,
ed., 1450
Brayton, Matthew, 2756
Brazen gates, 10805
Brazer, John, 1787-1846, 1451
Brazer, Samuel, 1785-1823, 1452
Brazer, Samuel, jr. 1453
Brazil, 798, 2138, 3401, 6881
Brazil and the river Plate in
1868, 12519
Brazil - Bibl., 11636
Brazil - Bound. - Paraguay,
591, 596
Brazil - Comm. - Hist., 1526
Brazil - Comm. - U. S., 691
Brazil - Descr. & trav., 31,

492, 578, 798, 1720,
3401, 4389, 5454, 5849,
7218, 7339, 7757, 8024,
11230, 11636, 11811, 12518,
12519, 12906
Brazil - Econ. cond., 492,
798, 12518, 12519
Brazil - Emig. & immig.,
2138
Brazil - For. rel., 1017
Brazil - Hist., 7640, 12648
Brazil - Hist. - 1549-1762,
1543
Brazil - Hist. - 1763-1821,
446
Brazil - Hist. - To 1821,
1016, 1542, 1551, 6881,
11259, 11530
Brazil - Hist. - 1822-1889,
446, 6640
Brazil - Hist. - Dutch
conquest, 1624-1654, 104,
339, 340, 653, 1526,
1542, 8323
Brazil - Nationality, 7640
Brazil - Neutrality, 2051
Brazil - Pol. & govt. -
1822-1869, 798
Brazil - Pol. & govt. -
1822-1889, 1017
Brazil - Soc. life & cust.,
3401
Brazil, the home for
southerners, 2138
Brazil, the river Plate, and
the Falkland islands,
12518
Brazos River, 5532
The bread-winners, 9828,
10424
Breazeale, J. W. M., 11508
Breck, Robert L., 1454
Breck, Samuel, 1771-1862,
1455, 1456, 1457, 1458,
13093
Breckinridge County, Ky.,
5953
Breckinridge Co., Ky. -
Hist., 2795

Breckinridge, John Cabell,
1821-1875, 3417
Breckinridge, John Cabell,
1821-1875. Speech on executive
usurpation, 6351
Breckinridge, Robert Jefferson,
1880-1871, 1459, 1460, 1461,
1462, 1463, 1464, 1466, 1467,
2791, 2792, 2793, 2794, 5698
Breckinridge, William Campbell
Preston, 1837-1904, 2795
Breech-loaders versus muzzle-
loaders, 11989
Breed, William Pratt, 1816-1889,
1468, 1469, 1470
Breen, Henry Hegart, 11509
Breese, Sidney, 1800-1878, 1471,
1472
Brehme, Hugo, 6155, 6156
Bremer, Fredrika, 1801-1865,
1473, 6157
Brenchley, Julius Lucius,
1816-1873, 4931
Brent, Henry Johnson, 1811-
1880, 1474
Brent, John Carroll, 1475
Brent, Linda, pseud., 10008
Brenton, Edward Pelham, 1774-
1839, 1476, 1477
Brents, John A., 1478
Brereton, John A., 1480
Brereton, John, fl. 1603, 1479
Brerewood, Edward, 1565?-1613,
11510
Bressani, Francesco Giuseppe,
1612-1672, 1481, 1482
Bressant, 6992
Brett, William Henry, 1818-
1886, 1483, 11511
Breugel, Gaspard Philippe
Charles van, 1798-1888, 1484
Breuíssima relación de la des-
truycion de las Indias, 6358
Breve descripcion de la fabrica,
y adornos del Templo de la
Compañia de Jesus de Zacatecas,
5803
Breve descripcion de los sucesos
festivos con que la ciudad de

A brief and perfect journal
of the late proceedings
and success of the English
army in the West Indies,
1507
A brief and true narrative
of the hostile conduct of
the barbarous natives
towards the Dutch nation,
11518
A brief answer to two
papers, 1650
A brief consideration of the
important services, and
distinguished virtues
and talents..., 12197
A brief examination of the
expediency of repealing
the naturalization laws,
1508
A brief examination of the
plan and conduct of the
northern expedition in
America, in 1777, 11519
A brief extract... in support
of the supremacy of the
British legislature,
1509
A brief historical, statistical, and descriptive
review of East Tennessee,
5198
A brief history of the mail
service, 2801
A brief history of the
Mississippi territory,
3741
Brief history of the
Thirtieth Georgia regi-
ment, 2494
A brief journal of the life,
travels and labours of
love in the work of the
ministry of... Thomas
Wilson, 5744
A brief outline of the rise,
progress, and failure of
the revolutionary scheme
of the nineteen Van Buren

electors of the Senate of
Maryland, 1510
A brief popular account of all
the financial panics and
commercial revulsions in the
United States, 1511
Brief remarks on the slave
registry bill, 1512
A brief review of the rise and
progress, services and
sufferings, of New England,
1513
A brief sketch of the life,
character, and writings of
William Charles Wells, 2622
A brief sketch of the political
importance of the British
colonies, 1514
A brief view of constitutional
powers, 13082
Briefe aus den Vereinigten Staaten
von Nord-Amerika, 4123
Briefe in die heimath, 7207
Briet, Philippe, 1601-1668, 1515
Brieven over het bestuur der
colonien Essequebo en Demerary,
1516
Brieven uit en over Amerika,
3593
Brieven uit en over de Vereenigde
Staten van Noord-Amerika, 4098
The brigand, 2674
Briggs, Charles Frederick,
1804-1877, 11520
Briggs, George Ware, 1810-1895,
1517, 1518
Briggs, Henry, 1561-1630, 5632
Briggs, John, 1519
Briggs, Lloyd Vernon, 1863-,
6165
Briggs, Nathan M., defendant,
12403
Brigham, Amariah, 1798-1849,
12302
Brigham, William, 1806-1869,
1520
Brigham, William Tufts, 1841-
1926, 6166
Bright days in the old plantation

time, 8691
Bright extremes in human
life, 11041
Bright family, 1523
Bright family (Henry Bright,
bapt. 1602), 1523
Bright, Jesse David, 1812-
1875, 1521, 13231
Bright, John, 1811-1889,
1522, 1946
Bright, Jonathan Brown,
1800-1879, 1523
The bright side of prison
life, 5329
Bright skies and dark
shadows, 3441
Bright, William, jt.
author, 5775
Brightly's orphan, 11194
Brighton, John George, 1524
Brighton, Mass. - Direct.,
1566
Brightwell, Cecilia Lucy,
1811-1875, 1525
Bril-gesicht voor de ver-
blinde eyghen baetsuchtige
handelaers op Brasil,
1526
Brimblecomb, Nicholas, pseud.,
1527
Brine, Lindesay, 1834-1906,
6167
Brininstool, Earl Alonzo,
1870-, 7755
Brink, McCormick, & co.,
publishers, 6168
Brink (W. R.) and company,
6169
Brinsley, John, fl. 1633,
1528
Brinson, Lessie Brannen,
6170
Brinton, Daniel Garrison,
1837-1899, 1529, 2802
Brinton, John Hill, 1832-
1907, 2803
Brion de la Tour, Louis,
2804
Brisbane, Albert, 1809-

1890, 1530
Brisbin, James Sanks, 1837-
1892, 1531
Brisée, 8850
Brissot [de Warville] Anacharsis,
6171, 11522
Brissot de Warville, Jean Pierre,
1754-1793, 1532, 2805, 6172,
11521, 11522
Bristed, Charles Astor, 1820-
1874, 1533, 1534, 1535
Bristed, John, 1778-1855, 1536,
1537, 2806
Bristoe station, Va., Battle of,
1863, 2073
Bristol academy, Taunton, Mass.,
2249
Bristol County (Mass.) agricul-
tural society, 1538
Bristol, Pa., 609
Britain and her colonies, 13040
Britannia, 12368
Britannia major, 1539
Britannia triumphant, 1540
British America, 7367, 12825
British America - Descr. & trav.,
1425
British America - Descr. & trav. -
Guide-books, 5724
British association for the
advancement of science, 6551
British colonization society,
12827
British Columbia, 5837, 6013,
6178, 6198, 6769, 7363
British Columbia and Vancouver's
Island, 6173
British Columbia. Bureau of
Mines, 6174
British Columbia. Bureau of
Provincial Information, 6175
British Columbia, Canada's
most westerly province, 6176
British Columbia. Department
of Agriculture, 6177
British Columbia - Descr. &
trav., 2730, 2753, 4481, 5839,
5896, 5897, 5983, 6106, 6173,
6176, 6179, 6180, 6192, 6198,

6226, 6237, 6555, 6600, 6890,
7063, 7259, 7324, 7360, 7460,
7579, 7656, 8074, 8126, 8284,
8285, 8286, 8372, 8383, 8420,
11662
British Columbia - Exploring
expeditions, 6179
British Columbia - Forestry,
6182
British Columbia - Gold
discoveries, 5898, 6173
British Columbia - Hist.,
5839, 6051, 7539, 12774
British Columbia, its present
resources and future
possibilities, 6178
British Columbia. Lands
and Works Dept., 6179
British Columbia. Lands
Dept., 6180
British Columbia - Maps,
5593
British Columbia, Northern
Interior, 7539
British Columbia - Pol.
& govt., 8284, 8285,
8286
British Columbia - Popu-
lation, 6175
British Columbia. Porcupine
District Commission, 6181
British Columbia - Public
lands, 6180
British Columbia. Royal
Commission of Inquiry
on Timber and Forestry,
6182
British Columbia. Royal
Commission on Acquisition
of Texada Island, 6183
British emigrant society,
Susquehanna Co., Pa.,
13233
British Guiana, 12641,
13449, 13475
British Guiana - Descr. &
trav., 2502, 5319, 12589
British Guiana - Hist. -
To 1803, 1516

British Honduras, 2353, 6803
12704, 13485
British Honduras - Bound. -
Guatemala, 8298
British Honduras - Bound. -
Mexico, 8433
British Honduras - Descr. &
trav., 7623
British Honduras - Econ. cond.,
7623
British Honduras - Hist., 8298
British Honduras question,
8433
British in Mexico, 7065
The British in Philadelphia,
10066
British in Spain, 7065
British North America, 1541,
3877
The British sailor's discovery,
11523
British temperance emigration
society and saving fund,
11524
The British worthies, 12286
Brito Freire, Francisco de,
1542, 1543
Brito, Paulo José Miguel de,
d. 1832, 11525
Brittan, Samuel Byron, 12590
Britten, Mrs. Emma (Hardinge)
d. 1899, 6184
Britton, James B., 2807
Britton, John, 1771-1857,
1544
Britton, Wiley, 2808
"Bro", 11207
Broad, Amos, defendant, 11526
Broad, Mrs. Demis, defendant,
11526
Broad River valley, Ga., 12263
Broaderick, Cephas, pseud.,
9613
The Broadway, 11527
Broadway pneumatic underground
railway, 13068
Brock, Charles E., illustr.,
11159
Brock, Sir Isaac, 1769-1812,

7613
Brock, R. A., ed., 3662
Brockett, Linus Pierpont,
1820-1893, 1545, 1546,
1547, 1548, 11528
Brocklehurst, Thomas Unett,
6185
Brockley Moor, 10171
Brockway, Diodate, 1776-
1849, 1549
Brockway, Thomas, 1745-
1807, 1550, 2809, 12087
Brockwell, Charles, 1551
Brode, Gertrude, 10899
Brodhead, Mrs. Eva Wilder
(McGlasson) 1870-1915,
2810, 2811, 2812
Brodhead, John Romeyn,
1814-1873, 1552, 1553,
11529
Brodie, Walter, 1554
Brodigan, Thomas, 1555
Broeck, Matheus van den,
11530
Broke family, 1524
Broke, Hezekiah, 2813
Broke, Sir Philip Bowes
Vere, 1776-1841, 1524
The broken engagement,
10832
Broken idols, 10899
A broken looking-glass,
9740
The broken seal, 12399
Brokenburne, 2774
Brokesby, Francis, 1637-
1714, 1556
Bromley, Clara Fitzroy
(Kelly), 1557
Bromley, Walter, 1558,
1559, 11531
Bromme, Traugott, 1802-1866,
1560, 1561, 1562, 2814,
6186, 11532
Bromwell, William, 1563
Bromwell, William Jeremy,
1834-1874, 11533
Bronner, Milton, ed., 3827
Bronson, Francis S., 2815

Bronson, Henry, 1804-1893,
11534, 11535
Bronson's travelers' directory,
2815
The bronze Buddha, 9326
The bronzed beauty of Paris,
10835
Brook, Benjamin, 1776-1848,
11536
Brooke, Francis Taliaferro,
1763-1851, 11537
Brooke, Henry, 1703?-1783, 1564
Brooke, John T., 11538
Brooke, Rupert, 1887-1915, 6187
Brookes, Richard, fl. 1750,
1565, 2816
Brookfield, Mass. - Hist., 6392
Brookline directory, 1566
Brookline, Mass. - Direct., 1566
The Brooklyn city and Kings
county record: a budget of
general information, 11541
Brooklyn city library, 11542
Brooklyn, N. Y., 11539, 13262
Brooklyn, N. Y. Charters,
1568, 1569, 11541
Brooklyn, N. Y. Ordinances,
etc., 1569, 1570, 11540
Brooklyn, N. Y. - Pol. & govt.,
11539
Brooklyn, N. Y. - Registers, 11541
Brooklyn, N. Y. - Water supply,
1571, 1729
Brooklyn, N. Y. - Water works,
1571
Brooks, Abbie M., 2817
Brooks, Charles, 1795-1872,
1572, 1573, 1574
Brooks, Charles Timothy, 1813-
1883, 1575, 11543
Brooks, David, 1744-1802, 1576
Brooks, Edward, 1784-1859, 1577
Brooks, Geraldine, 1875-,
6188
Brooks, James, 1810-1873, 6189
Brooks, John, 1752-1825, 1578
Brooks, John, 1792-, 2818
Brooks, Nathan Covington,
1809-1898, 1579, 1580

Brooks, Noah, 1830-1903,
6190, 6191
Brooks, Phillips, bp.,
1835-1893, 1581, 1582
Brooksmith, 7122
Broom, Jacob, 1808-1864,
1583
Broom, Walter William,
1584, 11544
Broomall, John Martin,
1816-1894, 1585
Broome, Mary Ann (Stewart)
Barker, lady, d. 1911,
2819
Bross, William, 1813-1890,
1586, 1587, 8431
Brossard, Alfred de, 1588
Brosses, Charles de,
1709-1777, 1589
Brother Jonathan's welcome
to Kossuth, 954
Brother Jonathan's wife,
11545
Brother Mason, the circuit
rider, 8854
A brother to dragons, 5465
The brother's revenge,
9855
Brotherhead, William, 1590,
1591, 11546
Brotherhood, 9266
The brothers, 9841
The brothers in arms, 9842
Brothers, Thomas, 1592
Brotherton, Mrs. Alice
(Williams) 2820
Brough, John, 1811-1865,
1593, 7565
Brougham and Vaux, Henry
Peter Brougham, 1st
baron, 1778-1868,
1594, 1595, 1596, 1597,
11547, 11548
Broughton, Thomas, 11549
Broughton, William Robert,
6192
Browder, Earl Russell,
1891-, 6193
Brower, Arier C., jt.

author, 2881
Brown, Aaron Venable, 1795-
1859, 11550, 11551
Brown, Albert Gallatin, 1813-
1880, 11552
Brown, Alexander Enos, d. 1865,
11553
Brown, Andrew, 1748-1813, 11554
Brown, Augustus Cleveland,
1839-, 2821
Brown, Charles Brockden, 1771-
1810, 293, 297, 11555
Brown, David, 1786-1875, 2822
Brown, David L., 2823
Brown, David Paul, 1795-1872,
11556
Brown, Edmund Randolph, 1845-,
2824
Brown family, 11554
Brown, Francis, 1784-1820, 11557
Brown, Francis Henry, 1835-
1917, comp., 12737
Brown, Frederick Thomas, 1822-
1893, 11558, 11559
Brown, George Stayley, 6194
Brown, George William, 1812-
1891, 11560
Brown, Henry, 1789-1849, 11561,
11562
Brown, Isaac Van Arsdale, 1784-
1861, 11563, 11564, 11565
Brown, J. Robert, 2825
Brown, John, 1722-1787, 11566
Brown, John, 1757-1837, 7276
Brown, John, 1800-1859, 6417,
13386
Brown, John, 1800-1859 - Fiction,
9960, 10007
Brown, John, fl. 1858, 6195
Brown, John Henry, 1820-1895,
2826, 2827, 2828
Brown, John Howard, 1840-, 7227
Brown, John Mason, 1837-1890,
2829
Brown, John Mathias, 1745-1838,
11567
Brown, John Walker, 1814-1849,
ed., 979
Brown, Jonathan, M. D., 11568

68

Brown, Leonard, 1837-1914, 11569

Brown, Lloyd Arnold, ed., 3205

Brown, Marcus Monroe, 1854-, 6196

Brown, Mary Edwards, 6197

Brown, Mason, 1799-1867, jt. ed., 13363

Brown, Orlando, 13452

Brown, Peter, 1784-1863, 11570

Brown, Philip Francis, 1842-, 2830

Brown, R. C. Lundon, 6198

Brown, Mrs. Rebecca Warren, 11571

Brown, Samuel, 1768-1805, 11572

Brown, Samuel Gilman, 1813-1885, 11573

Brown, Samuel R., 1775-1817, 2831, 11574, 11575

Brown, Sarah Poseg, 1859-, 6199

Brown, Tarleton, 1757-1846, 2832

Brown university - Biog., 2425

Brown university. Class of 1802, 12284

Brown unversity - Hist., 12490, 12492

Brown, Virginia Stuart, illustr., 5816

Brown, W. P., 10125

Brown, William Linn, supposed author, 11109

Brown, William, of Leeds, 6200

Brown, William Perry, 10125

Brown, William Wells, b. 1814, 2833, 2834, 2835

Brown's revenge, 10863

Browne, Charles Farrar, 1834-1867, 6201

Browne, Dunn, pseud., 3457

Browne, Edith A., 1874-, 6202

Browne, Francis Fisher, 1843-1913, ed., 2836

Browne, John Ross, 1821-1875, 2837, 2838, 11576

Browne, Junius Henri, 1833-1902, 2839

Browne, Nathaniel Borodaille, 1819-1875, 11577

Browne, Patrick, 1720?-1790, 11578

Browne, Peter Arrell, 1782-1860, 11579, 11580

Browne, Sir Thomas, 1605-1682, 11581

Browne, Thomas M., 3044

Browne, William Hand, jt. author, 4080

Browne, William Henry James, 11582

Brownell, Charles De Wolf, 1822-, 11583

Brownell, Henry Howard, 1820-1872, 1598, 1599, 1600, 11584

Brownell, Thomas, d. 1872, 1601

Brownell, Thomas Church, bp., 1779-1865, 1602

Browning, Charles, b. 1765, 1603

Browning, Charles Henry, 6203, 6204, 6205

Browning, Meshach, b. 1781, 11585

Browning, Orville Hickman, 1806-1881, 7279

Browning, Orville Hickman, 1806-1881 - Addresses, sermons, etc., 5934

Browning, Robert, 1812-1889, 7119

Browning, Samuel, 1604

Brownlow, William Gannaway, 1805-1877, 1605, 2840

Brownson, Orestes Augustus, 1803-1876, 1606, 1607

Brownstown, Mich., Battle of, Aug. 5, 1812, 11944

Bruce, Archibald, 1777-1818, ed., 270

Bruce, Eli, 1793-1832, 4531

Bruce, George A., 6206
Bruce, Hamilton, comp.,
1608
Bruce, James C., 1609
Bruce, [Miss] John Jessie,
2841
Bruce, Lewis, 1610
Bruce, Peter Henry, 1692-
1757, 1611, 1612
Bruchesi, Jean, 1901-,
6207
Brückner, G., 11586
Brüder über dem meer,
3653
Bruges, Roger, graf von,
6208
Brundle, John, 1882-,
6209, 6210
Brunson, Alfred, 1793-
1882, 1613
Brunswick canal and railroad
company, 709
Brunswick, Georgia -
Descr., 5207
Brunt, Jonathan, b. 1760,
1614
Brush, John C., 1615
Brush, Samuel, 1616
Brutus, Lucius Junius,
pseud., 11587
Bruun, Ellen (Raon) 1892-,
2842
Bruyas, Jacques, 1635-1712,
11588
Bruzen de La Martinière,
Antoine Augustin, 1662-1746,
11589
Bryan, Claude Glennon,
1876-, jt. author, 7687
Bryan, Daniel, 1795-1866,
1617, 1618, 1619, 2843,
2844
Bryan, Francis Theodore,
2845, 5547
Bryan, George J., 1620
Bryan, Hugh, 1699-1753,
1621
Bryan, James, 1810-1881,
1622, 1623

Bryan, Mrs. Mary (Baird),
1861-, 6211
Bryan Station, Kentucky, 4891
Bryan, Thomas Barbour, 1828-
1906, 11590
Bryan, William Jennings,
1860-1925, 6211, 7263
Bryan, William Smith, 1846-,
ed., 7639
Bryant, Charles S., 1624
Bryant, Edwin, 1805-1869, 2846
The Bryant homestead-book,
12742
Bryant, James Ray M'Corkle,
1802-1866, 1625
Bryant, Joseph, 1742-1807,
7429
Bryant, Wilbur Franklin, 6212
Bryant, William Cullen, 1794-
1878, 1626, 1627, 1628,
1629, 6213, 6214, 11591,
11592, 12742
Bryce, George, 1844-1931,
6215-6236
Bryce, James Bryce, viscount,
1838-1922, 1630
Brydges, Harold, pseud., 2800
Brydges, Sir Samuel Egerton,
bart., 1762-1837, 1631
Bryner, Byron Cloyd, 1849-,
2847
Buache, J. N., 6237
Buache, Philippe, 6238, 7109
Bubbles of fiction, 8747
Los bucaneros de las Indias
occidentales, 6956
The buccaneer, 12552
The buccaneer of King's bridge,
9636
Buccaneers, 427, 428, 1730,
6256, 6956, 9962, 9963,
10074
Buchan, David, b. 1780, 1067
Buchan, David Stewart Erskine,
11th earl of, 1742-1829, 1632
Buchan, Susan (Grosvenor),
1882-, 6239
Buchanan, Archibald, 11593
Buchanan, Isaac, 1810-1883, 1633

Buchanan, James A., of
Baltimore, 12133
Buchanan, James, British
consul at New York,
11594
Buchanan, James, pres. U. S.,
1791-1868, 1634, 2848,
6586
Buchanan, Joseph Rodes,
1814-1899, 11595
Buchanan, Thompson, 1877-
1937, 2849
Buchanan, William B., 11596
Buck, Edward, 1635
Buck, Edward, of Boston,
11597
Buck, William Joseph, 1825-,
1636, 1637
Buckalew, Charles R.,
1821-1899, 2076
Bucke, Charles, 1781-1846,
11598
Buckholtz, L. von, 1638
Buckingham, Henry A., 1639
Buckingham, James Silk,
1786-1855, 2850, 11599,
11600, 11601, 11602, 11603
Buckingham, John Edward,
1828-1909, 6240
Buckingham, Joseph H., 1806-
1880, 11604
Buckingham, Joseph Tinker,
1779-1861, 1640, 11605,
11606, 11607
Buckingham, Samuel Giles,
1641
Buckler, Thomas Hepburn,
1812-1901, 1642
Buckley, Kate, ed., 6241,
6242
The Buckley Lady, 9578
Buckley, Michael Bernard,
1831-1872, 6241, 6242
Buckminster, Joseph, 1751-
1812, 1643, 11608
Buckminster, Joseph Stevens,
1784-1812, 1644, 1645,
1646
Buckminster, Lydia Nelson

(Hastings), b. 1818, 11609
Buckner, Aylett, 1828-1864,
1647
Buckner, Henry F., 1818-1882,
ed., 1648
"Buckra" land, 11174
Bucks co., Pa. - Biog., 1636
Bucks co., Pa. - Hist., 1636
Buckskin Mose, 10508
Budan, A., 1649
Budd, Thomas, d. 1698, 1650,
1651, 1652
Budington, William Ives,
1815-1879, 1653, 1654
Buds and bird-voices, 9823
Buds and blossoms of piety,
401
Buechler, Johann Ulrich, 2851
Buel, Alexander Woodruff, 1813-
1868, 1655
Buel, David, 1784-1860, 1656
Buel, Jesse, 1778-1839, 1657
Buel, Oliver Prince, 1838-1899,
6243
Buell, Don Carlos, 1818-1898,
1658
Buell, P. L., 1659
Buell, Samuel, 1716-1798, 1660,
1661
Buell, Samuel, 1771-1787, 1660
Buena Vista, 3149
Buenos Aires, 1662
Buenos Aires - Descr., 12518
Buenos Aires. Junta provisional
gubernativa. 1810, 1662
Buenos Aires (Province). Consti-
tution, 123
Buenos Aires (Province) - Descr.
& trav., 594
Buenos Ayres and Argentine
gleanings, 13054
Buenos Ayres and Chile, Sketches
of, 12529
Buff and blue, 10880
Buffalo Bill, 7712
Buffalo, Chamber of commerce,
1663
Buffalo. Charters, 1664
Buffalo. Common council, 11610

71

Buffalo. First Presbyterian
church, 11850
Buffalo - Harbor, 11610
Buffalo historical society,
1334
Buffalo - Hist., 11850
Buffalo. Ordinances, etc.,
1664
Buffalo society of natural
sciences, 1911
Bugle echoes, 2836
Buhle, M., 1665
Buhoup, Jonathan W., 1666
Building laws - Washington,
D. C., 1686
Building on the rock, 10474
Buist, George, 1770-1808,
1667
Buitrago de Santiago,
Zayda, 7747
Bulfinch, Benjamin S.,
1668
Bulfinch, Thomas, 1796-
1867, 1669, 1670
Bulger's reputation, 6971
Bulkeley, Peter, 1583-
1659, 1671
Bulkley, Charles Henry
Augustus, 1819-1893,
1672, 1673
Bulkley, Edwin Adolphus,
1826-1905, 1674
The bull-fight, 10909
Bull, Jerome Case, 10283
Bull Run, 1st battle,
1861, 833, 11640, 12042
Bull Run, 2d battle,
1862, 7325, 8373
Bull-us, Hector, pseud.,
10482
Bullard, Frederic Lauriston,
1873-, ed., 6586
Bullard, Henry Adams, 1788-
1851, 1675
Buller, Charles, 1806-1848,
6647, 6648
Bullet and shell, 5715
Bullitt, John Christian,
1824-1902, 1676

Bullock, Alexander Hamilton,
1816-1882, 6245
Bullock, William, fl. 1649,
2852
Bullock, William, fl. 1808-
1828, 2853, 6246, 6247, 6248
Bulnes, Francisco, 1848-, 6249
Búlnes, Gonzalo, 1851-, 6250
Bülow, Dietrich, i.e., Adam
Heinrich Dietrich, freiherr
von, 1757-1807, 2854
Bunce, Oliver Bell, 1828-1890,
6214, 11611
Buncombe Co., N. C. - Descr. &
trav., 3603
Buncombe Co., N. C. - Fiction,
10543
Bungay, George Washington,
1818-1892, 1677, 1678, 1679,
13050
Bungener, Laurence Louis Felix,
1814-1874, 6251
Bunker-Hill, 1707
Bunker Hill, Battle of, 1775,
569, 1882, 2349, 11491, 11839,
12055, 12982,
Bunker Hill, Battle of, 1775 -
Drama, 11481
Bunker Hill, Battle of, 1775 -
Poetry, 3382
Bunker Hill declaration, 1680
Bunn, Alfred, 1796?-1860, 1681
Bunn, Matthew, b. 1772? 2855
Bunnell, David C., b. 1793,
1682
Bunner, E., 1683
The Bunsby papers, 8856
Bunte briefe aus Amerika, 5795
Buntline, Ned, pseud., 10078-
10081
Bunyan, Mary, b. 1650 - Fiction,
3506
Burbank, Addison, 1895-, 6252
Burbank, Caleb, 1761-1849,
defendant, 1684, 1685
Burbridge, Stephen Gano,
1831-1894, 13318
Burch, George W., 6253
Burch, Samuel, 1686

Burchard, Jedediah, 1687
Burchard, Samuel Dickinson, 1812-1891, 1688
Burchell, Thomas, 1799-1846, 1689
Burchell, William Fitzer, 1689
Burchett, Josiah, 1666?-1746, 1690, 1691
The burden of Christopher, 9096
The burden of the South, 1710
Burder, George, 1752-1832, 1692
Burdett, Charles, 1815-, 2856
Burdick, William, 1693
Burdon, William, 1764-1818, tr., 12145
Burford, Robert, 1791-1861, 1694
Burge, William, 1787-1849, 1695
Burges, Bartholomew, 1696
Burges, Tristam, 1770-1853, 1697, 11447
Burgess, Chalon, 1817-1903, 1698
Burgess, Ebenezer, 1790-1870, 1699, 1700
Burgess family (Thomas Burgess, d. 1685), 1700
Burgess, George, bp., 1809-1866, 1701
The burglar who moved paradise, 11080
The burglar's fate and the detectives, 10527
Burgoa, Francisco de, 1605-1681, 1702
Burgoyne, John, 1722-1792, 1703, 1704, 1705, 11519, 11612, 11688
Burgoyne, Sir John Fox, bart., 1782-1871, 1706
Burgoyne's invasion, 1777, 345, 346, 347, 1704, 1705, 4960, 5894, 5895,

11519, 11612
Burgoyne's invasion, 1777 - Fiction, 2522
A burial among the mountains, 10747
Burk, John Daly, d. 1808, 1707, 11613, 11658
Burk, John Junius, 1800?-1866, 11658
Burkart, Josef, 1798-1874, 6254
Burke, Aedanus, 1743?-1802?, 11614
Burke, Arthur Meredyth, 6255
Burke, Edmund, 1729?-1797, 1363, 1708, 1709, 2857, 11615, 11616, 11617, 11618
Burke, Edmund, 1729?-1797. A letter from Edmund Burke... 22
Burke family (Richard Burke, of Sudbury, Mass., 1640?-1693 or 4), 1426
Burke, John, d. 1873, 1710, 1711
Burke, William, 1714, 2858
Burke, William, 1752-1836, 1712
Burke, William, d. 1798, 2857, 11615
Burke, William, fl. 1805-1810, 1713
Burke, William Alvord, 1811-1887, 1426
Burkitt, Lemuel, 11619
Burleigh, Joseph Bartlett, 1715
Burleigh, Walter Atwood, 1820-1896, 1716
Burleigh, William Henry, 1812-1871, 1717, 12590
Burlend, Edward, d. 1875, 2859
Burlend, Mrs. Rebecca, 1793-1872, 2859
Burlingame, Anson, 1820-1870, 1718
Burlington co., N. J., 8445
Burman, Ben Lucien, 1895-, 2860
Burmann, Johannes, 1646-1764, 11620

Burmeister, Hermann, 1807-
1892, 1719, 1720
Burn, Andrew, 1742-1814,
1721
Burnaby, Andrew, 1734?-1812,
2861, 11621
Burnap, George Washington,
1802-1859, 11622, 11746
Burnap, Uzziah Cicero, 1794-
1854, 1722
A Burne-Jones head, 10669
Burnet, Mrs. Ann, 1754?-
1789, 1725
Burnet, Jacob, 1770-1853,
1723, 12084
Burnet, Matthias, 1749-
1806, 1724, 1725
Burnett, Alfred, b. 1823
or 4, 1726
Burnett, Henry Clay,
1825-1866, 1727
Burnett, Peter Hardeman,
1807-1895, 1728
Burnett, Ward B., 1729
Burney, James, 1750-1821,
1730, 6256, 11623, 11624
Burnham, Benjamin Franklin,
1830-1898, 6257
Burnham, George P., jt.
author, 9453
Burnham, George Pickering,
1814-1902, 1731
Burnham, Richard, 1711-
1752, 1732
Burning of Havre de Grace,
10310
The burning of the convent,
10070
The burning of the St.
Louis theatre, 5863
Burns, Jabez, 1805-1876,
2862
Burns, James, R., 11625
Burns, Robert, 1759-1796,
1733
Burnside, Samuel McGregore,
1783-1850, 1734
Burnyeat, John, 1631-1690,
1735

Burr, Aaron, 1716-1757,
11626
Burr, Aaron, 1756-1836, 9022,
11627, 11628, 11770, 12068,
13365, 13497
Burr, Charles Chauncey, 1817-
1883, 1736, 1737
Burr conspiracy, 1805-1807,
11627, 11628, 13511
Burr conspiracy, 1805-1807 -
Fiction, 10929
Burr, Fearing, 11629
Burr, Samuel Jones, 11630
Burr, William, 1738
Burrill Coleman, colored, 9081
Burrill, George Rawson, 1770-
1818, 1739, 11631
Burrill, James, 1772-1820, ed.,
474
Burriss, Charles Walker, 1860-,
6258
Burritt, Elihu, 1810-1879,
2863, 11632
Burroughes, Jeremiah, 1599-1646,
jt. author, 12308
Burroughs, Charles, 1787-1868,
1740, 11633
Burroughs, Stephen, 1765-1840,
11634
Burrows, E. J., 1741
Burrows, John Lansing, 1814-
1893, 1742, 1743
Burson, William, 1833-, 2864
Burt, John S. G., 13081
Burton, 3999
Burton, Elijah P., 2865
Burton, John, 1696-1771, 11635
Burton, Sir Richard Francis,
1821-1890, 1744, 11636
Burton, Warren, 1800-1866,
1745, 1746, 11637
Burton, William Evans, 1802-1860,
1747
Burtschi, Joseph Charles, 1874-,
jt. author, 7980
Burus, Anthony, 1834-1862,
11438
Burwell, William MacCreary,
1809-1888, 1748, 1749, 11638

74

Bury, Viscount, 6259
Busch, Moritz, 1821-1899, 2866
Bush, Celeste E., ed., 1188
Bushnell, Charles Ira, 1826-1883, 1176, 1750, 1751, 1752, 1753, 1754, 1966, 2832, 11284, 12753
Bushnell, Horace, 1802-1876, 1755, 11640, 11641, 11642
The bushwhackers, 4553
Business directory of the principal southern cities, 1756
Business ethics, 2105
Busk, Hans, 1815-1882, 1757
Bussierre, Marie Théodore Renouard, vicomte de, 1802-1865, 11643
Bustamantc, Anastasio, pres. Mexico, 1780-1853, 120
Bustamante, Carlos Maria de, 1774-1848, 139, 1758, 1759, 1760, 1761, 1762, 1763
Bustamante, José Luis, 1799-1857, 1764
Busteed, Richard, 1822-1898, 11644, 11645
Busy moments of an idle woman, 8827
A busy time in Mexico, 7758
Butel-Dumont, Georges Marie, 1725-1788, 2867, 6260, 6261
Butler, Benjamin Franklin, 1795-1858, 11646, 13412
Butler, Benjamin Franklin, 1818-1893, 1765, 11647, 12986
Butler, Caleb, 1776-1854, 1766, 1767
Butler, Clement Moore, 1810-1890, 1768, 1769, 11648
Butler, Edward C., 6262

Butler family (John Butler, 1677-1759), 1767
Butler, George B., 11690
Butler, George Bernard, 1809-1886, 11649
Butler, Henry E., 11650
Butler, James Davie, 1815-1905, 1770
Butler, Jay Caldwell, 1844-1885, 2868
Butler, John, bp., 1717-1802, 1771, 11651
Butler, Mann, 1784-1852, 1772, 2869
Butler, Rector Laphan, 3329
Butler, Watson Hubbard, 1878-, ed., 2868
Butler, William Allen, 1825-1902, 1773, 1774, 1775
Butler, Sir William Francis, 1838-1910, 6263, 6264, 6265
Butler, William Orlando, 1793-1880, 2728
Butterfield, Carlos, 11652
Butterfield, Consul Willshire, 1824-1899, 11653
Butterfield, Horatio Quincy, 1822-1894, 1776
Les butterfly, 2563
Butterneggs, 10790
Butterworth, Hezekiah, 1839-1905, 2870, 2871
Büttner, Johann Carl, 1754-, 2872
Büttner, Johann Gottfried, 2873
Button's inn, 10990
The Buttonwoods, 8922
Buttrick, Tilly, b. 1783, 1777, 2874
Buzeta, Pedro Antonio, 6364
Buzhardt, Beaufort Simpson, 1838-1862, 2875
By canoe and dog-train among the Cree and Salteaux Indians, 8428
By dint of valor, 10709
By hook or crook, 9639
By Parna's grave, 11198
By shore and sedge, 9777

By the morning boat, 10043
By way of the wilderness,
8488
Byam, George, 11654, 11655
Byepaths of biography, 1525
Byerley, Sir John, 6246,
6247
Byerley, Thomas, 1788-1826,
comp., 13450
Byers, Samuel Hawkins
Marshall, 1838-1933, 2876
Byers, William Newton,
1831-1903, 2877
Byles, Mather, 1707-1788,
1778, 1779, 1780
Byrd, William, 1674-1744,
2878, 11656
Byrdsall, Fitzwilliam, 1781
Byrne, Bernard M., 1782
Byrnes, Thomas F., 1847?-,
9815
The Byrnes of Glengoulah,
10426
Bywater, John, 2784
Byxbee, O. F., 6266

C., A., 8259
C., J., 401, 8259
The C. S. A. and the battle
of Bull Run, 833
C., T., 401
C., T. E., 968
ça ira, 11009
Caballero, Francisco José,
5803
Caballero, Manuel, jt.
author, 7532
Caballero y Góngora,
Antonio, Cardinal, 1723-
1796, 8204
Cabañas, Trinidad, pres.
Honduras, d. 1871, 12877
Cabell, Mrs. Julia (Mayo),
1783
Cabin and gondola, 11198
The cabin and parlor, 10509
The cabin book, 10717
The cabinet, 1784

The cabinet organ, 9581
Cable, George Washington,
1844-1925, 3417
Cable, George Washington,
1844-1925. The Grandissimes,
5025
Cables, Submarine - Atlantic,
531, 532, 11520
Cabot, James Elliot, 1821-1903,
108, 1785, 6267
Cabot, John, d. 1498, 1261
Cabot, Sebastian, ca. 1474-1557,
1261
Cabrera, Luis, 6268
Cabrera, Miguel, 1695-1768,
1786
Cabrera y Quintero, Cayetano,
d. 1775, 1787, 6269
Caccia, Antonio, 1788
Cachet, 9723
Cacoethes scribendi, 10730
Caddell, Cecilia Mary, d. 1877,
1789
Caddy, Alice, illustr., 2860
Cadet days, 10111
Cadet life at West Point, 2481
Cadillac, Antoine de la Mothe,
1656(ca.)-1730? - Fiction,
6520
Cadiz, Diego José de, 1743-1801,
6270
Cadogan, George, 2879
Cadwalader, John, 1742-1786,
1790
Cadwell, Charles K., 2880
Cady, Daniel Reed, 1813-1879,
1791
Caesar's column, 9412
Cahaba, Ala. Military prison,
3812
Cahoone, Sarah S., 1792
Cain against Abel, 2298
Cain, Joseph, 2881
Caines, George, 1771-1825, 1793
Caird, Sir James, 1816-1892,
6271
Cairnes, John Elliott, 1823-
1875, 1794
Cairo city property, Cairo,

Ill., 1795
Cairo, Ill., 1795
Cakes and ale at Woodbine,
1975
Calamy, Edmund, 1671-1732,
1796
Calatayud y Borda, Cipriano
Gerónimo, 1735-1814,
1797
Calavar, 1332
Calderon de la Barca, Frances
Erskine (Inglis), 1804-
1882, 1798, 6272, 6273
Calderón de la Barca, Pedro,
1600-1681, 6274
Calderón, Fray Francisco
Santiago, bp., d. 1736,
6275
Calderón, Jacinto, 6276
Calderón, Juan Alonso, 6277
The Calderwood secret,
10045
Caldwell, Charles, 1772-
1853, 1799, 1800, 2882,
2883, 2884, 2885, 2886,
2887, 2888
Caldwell, James Fitz James,
2889
Caldwell, John Edwards,
1769-1819, 2890
Caldwell, Joseph Blake,
d. 1811, 1801
Caldwell, Samuel Lunt,
1820-1887, 1802
Caleb Krinkle, 9057
Caleb West, master diver,
5192
Calef, John, 1725-1812,
1803
Calendar, Maya, 6135
Calendar, Mexican, 6644,
7932
Calendar of Maryland state-
papers, Index to, 149
Calendrier de Philadelphie,
793
Calero Y Moreira, Jacinto,
ed., 7463
Calhoun, John Caldwell,

1782-1850, 499, 965, 3720,
5946, 8232, 12444, 12610,
12626
Calico, 11075
California, 2486, 11394, 13261
California and its gold mines,
217
The California and Oregon trail,
4705
California. Constitution,
1804
California - Descr. & trav.,
550, 2132, 2491, 2498, 2555,
2575, 2576, 2597, 2624,
2668, 2711, 2846, 2891,
3018, 3047, 3105, 3117,
3420, 3459, 3515, 3541,
3631, 3730, 3740, 3772,
3955, 4068, 4139, 4213,
4372, 4398, 4715, 4756,
4922, 4931, 5060, 5125,
5145, 5301, 5336, 5351,
5410, 5492, 5588, 6027,
6400, 6401, 7057, 7256,
7371, 7913, 8038, 8157,
8158, 8175, 8406, 8407,
10355, 11834
California - Descr. & trav. -
Guide-books, 3735
California - Fiction, 4499
California - Gold discoveries,
550, 2132, 3220, 3730, 3740,
4372, 5078, 5351, 5410,
5758, 8157, 8158, 10501,
11394, 13261
California. Governor, 1851-
1855 (John Bigler), 2891
California, Gulf of, 2003,
6955
California - Hist., 5406,
6101, 7842
California - Hist. - To 1846,
3420
California - Hist. - 1846-1850,
3151, 3962, 11842
California in 1850, 5301
California. Legislature.
Senate. Committee on Internal
Improvements, 2892

California, Lower - Descr.
& trav., 7174
The California overland
express, 5336
California - Pol. & govt.,
11552, 11692, 12362
California - Pol. & govt. -
Civil war, 1685
California (ship), 6624
California sketches, 3459
California - Soc. life &
cust., 8878, 10501, 12841
California, Southern -
Descr. & trav., 6087, 6088
California. State board of
agriculture, 11282
California. State library,
Sacramento. Sutro branch,
San Francisco, 6278
California - Surveys, 3541
California three hundred
and fifty years ago, 9068
The Californian Crusoe,
4948
Call, Richard Ellsworth,
1856-1917, jt. author,
3949
A call to the unfaithful
professors of truth,
12083
Calla-Lilies and Hannah,
9575
Callan, John F., comp.,
1805
Callcott, Maria (Dundas)
Graham, lady, 1785-
1842, 6279
La calle de San Francisco,
6473
Calleja, Felix Maria,
conde de Calderon,
viceroy of Mexico,
b. 1750, 1759
Callender, James Thomson,
1758-1803, 1806, 1807,
1808, 1809, 1810, 1811,
11757
Callender, James Thomson,
1758-1803. The history

of the United States for
1796, 12604
Callender, James Thomson,
1758-1803. Political progress
of Great Britain, 1932
Callender, John, 1706-1748,
1812
Callender, John, 1772-1833,
1813
Callicot, Theophilus Carey,
b. 1826, 1814
Caloya, 10783
The Calumet, 1815
Calvert family, 1603
Calvert, George Henry, 1803-
1889, 1816
Calvert, Henry Murray, 2893
Calvert of Strathore, 3639
Calvin, George, 1875-1928,
6461
Calvinism, 11896
Calvo, Joaquín Bernardo,
1857-1915, 6280
Camacho Roldán, Salvador,
1827-1900, 2894, 6281
Camacho y Palma, José, 6160
Camargo, Jerónimo de, 6282
Camargo, Juan, 8008
Cambreleng, Churchill Caldom,
1786-1862, 1817
Cambridge, Mass. - Hist.,
12864
Camden, 4336
The camel hunt, 9488
Camelback mountain, 10052
Cameron, Agnes Deans, 6283
Cameron, Allan, 1818
Cameron, Archibald, 1771-
1836, 2895, 2896
Cameron, Mrs. Charlotte (Wales-
Almy), 6284
Cameron, Donald Roderick,
1834-, tr., 8148
Cameron, Edward Robert, 1857-,
6285
Cameron hall, 9269
Cameron, Kenneth Walter,
1908-, 6286
Cameron, Rebecca, ed., 5148

Canada - Descr. & trav. -
Guide-books, 2147,
2550, 2551, 4614, 5726,
5916, 5917, 5918, 5978,
5978, 5979, 6090, 6091,
6130, 6308, 6318, 6551,
6675, 7267, 7748, 8388,
8389, 12092, 12846, 12852
Canada - Descr. & trav. -
Maps, 6807, 7764
Canada - Descr. & trav. -
Maps - Bibl., 6296,
8210
Canada - Descr. & trav. -
Period., 6307
Canada - Descr. & trav. -
Views, 3733, 6207, 7597
Canada - Econ. cond., 519,
1240, 2195, 3641, 6310,
7078, 7428, 8022
Canada - Emig. & immig.,
1095, 1291, 2195, 4847,
6132, 7367, 7979, 8091,
8240, 8370, 11601, 12092,
12350, 12372
Canada - Emig. & immig. -
Hist., 7158
Canada - Exploring expeditions, 3200, 3878, 4685,
6302, 6303, 6312
Le Canada français, 6307
Canada (French colony),
11882
Canada - Geneal. - Dictionaries, 8153
Canada - General sources,
8129
Canada. Geological survey,
6308
Canada - Hist., 1441, 1978,
6130, 6131, 6146, 6231,
6239, 6278, 6825, 6829,
6903, 7062, 7193, 7361,
7367, 7550, 7593, 7808,
7809, 7841, 8023, 8224,
11760, 12826 ˇ
Canada - Hist. - To 1763
(New France), 25, 647,
1239, 2972, 3597, 3990,

4051, 6126, 6396, 6443, 6599,
6649, 6703, 6735, 6737, 7197,
7222, 7223, 7224, 7692, 7767,
8129, 8197, 8338, 8401, 13046
Canada - Hist. - To 1763 (New
France) - Fiction, 1858, 1859,
6520, 6622, 7467, 7688
Canada - Hist. - 1755-1763,
6148, 6397, 8412, 8413, 8414
Canada - Hist. - 1763-1867,
1242, 6149, 7613, 8333,
11396
Canada - Hist. - 1763-1867 -
Sources, 6297
Canada - Hist. - 1841-, 6574
Canada - Hist. - 1867-, 7776
Canada - Hist. - 19th cent.,
6532
Canada - Hist. - Addresses,
Essays, lectures, 7525
Canada - Hist. - Fenian inva-
sions, 1866-1870, 6038
Canada - Hist. - Fiction,
6379, 8955, 9972
Canada - Hist. - Period., 6307
Canada - Hist. - Rebellion,
1837-1838, 2202, 6647, 6996,
6997, 8333, 9972, 10915,
12031, 12784
Canada - Hist. - Sources, 7149
Canada in the twentieth
century, 6147
Canada - Intellectual life,
1240, 6133
Canada. Laws, statutes, etc.,
6309
Canada - Mail, 6555
Canada. National development
bureau, 6306
Canada. Northern Co-ordination
and Research Centre, 7328
Canada. Parliament. House of
commons. Select standing
committee on banking and
commerce, 6309
Canada. Parliament. Senate.
Select committee on resources
of territory between Labrador
and the Rocky Mountains, 6310

Candia, N. H. - Hist.,
12000
Candidius, Georgius, 12067
Candler, Isaac, 2906
Cañedo, Estanislao, 1825
Canigonet, merchant in
Haiti, 6326
Canisius, Theodor, 6327
Cañizares, José de, 1676-
1750, 6328
Cannabis, indica, 10249
Cannabis sativa, 8516
Canning, George, 1770-
1827, 2420, 12115
Cannon, J. P., 2907
Cannon, Joseph Gurney,
1836-1926, 7530
Cannon, Mrs. Lucretia P.
(Hanly), 10405
Cano, Juan, 6329
Cano, Juan Sebastien del,
1526, 7567
The canoe and the saddle,
8403
The canoe Aurora, 4583
A canoe voyage up the
Minnay Sotor, 2237
Canoes, 1898
Canoes and canoeing, 11636
Canolles: the fortunes of
a partisan of '81, 9104
Canon family, 7435
Canon law, 7732
Canonge, Louis Placide,
1822-1893, 2908
Canova, Andrew P., 2909
Cansinos Assens, Raphael,
1883-, 7893
Cant, 4275
Cap and bells, 4730
Cap sheaf, 9872
Cape Breton, 11336
Cape Breton - Descr. & trav. -
Maps, 11707
Cape Cod and all along
shore, 10427
Cape Cod - Descr. & trav.,
2328
Cap Polonio, 6939

Capers, Henry Dickson, 1835-
1910, 2910
Capital punishment, 456
Capsadell, Lou, pseud., 9726
Captain Blake, 10113
Captain Brand, of the "Centipede",
11195
Captain Close, 10114
Captain Dreams, 10115
Captain Eli's best ear, 10896
Captain Gray's company, 3322
Captain Hall in America, 1260
Capt. James Box's adventures
and explorations in new and
old Mexico, 6139
Captain Jim's friend, 6970
Captain Jinks, 10863
Captain John Baptiste Saucier
at Fort Chartres in the
Illinois, 5226
Captain Kidd's money, 10909
Captain Kyd, 9979, 4000
Captain Santa Claus, 10112
Captain Tom: a resurrection,
10427
Captain Velasco; and the young
lieutenant, 9988
The captain's romance, 4903,
10598
The captain's story, 5447,
10338
The captive, 10827
The captive boy in Terra del
Fuego, 12637
The captive boys of Rensselaer-
ville, 10570
The captive in Patagonia, 11409
A captive of war, 3983
The captivity in Babylon, 1902
Capture and escape, 4142
Capture at sea, 12667, 12669
The capture, death and burial
of J. Wilkes Booth, 5987
The capture, the prison pen,
and the escape, 3621
The captured dream, 9580
Captured in escaping, 9251
Capturing a locomotive, 4805
Capuchins, 5809

84

Capuchins in Brazil, 1899
Capuchins - Missions, 1899
Caraway, Thaddeus Horatius,
 1871-1931, 5834
Carbutt, Mary (Rhodes) lady,
 "Mrs. E. H. Carbutt",
 6330
The Carcellini emerald,
 9762
Carden, Allen D., fl. 1837,
 comp., 2911
Cárdenas, Pedro de, 6677,
 6678, 6679, 6687
The cardinal's daughter,
 5611
The cardinal's snuff box,
 9739
Cardona, Adalberto de,
 6331, 6332
Cardozo, Jacob Newton,
 11659
Care, Henry, 1646-1688,
 11660
Carew, Bampfylde-Moore,
 1693-1758, 2912, 4275
Carey, Mathew, 1760-1839,
 273, 295, 2913, 11661,
 13496
Carey, Mathew, 1760-1839.
 The olive branch, 11373
Carey, Mathew, 1760-1839.
 A short account of the
 malignant fever, lately
 prevalent in Philadelphia,
 13284
Carey's American pocket
 atlas, 2913
Carib Indians, 397, 574,
 11414
Carib language - Diction-
 aries, 4998
Caribbean Commission, 6333
Caribbean sea, 7533, 7917
Caribbean sea - Maps, 7995
Caribbean tourist trade,
 6333
Cariboo, the ... gold fields
 of British Columbia,
 11662

Caricatures and cartoons,
 7537
Caring for no man, 10550
Carita, 4744
Caritat, H., ed., 1244
Carl Werner, 10769
Carlé, Erwin, 1876-1923, 2914
Carles, Rubén Dario, 6334
Carleton, 11175
Carleton, Clifford, illustr.,
 9581
Carleton, James Henry, 1814-
 1873, 2915, 2916, 6335
Carlier, Auguste, 1803-1890,
 1826, 11663
Carlile, Thomas, 1792-1824,
 11664
Carlin, Thomas, defendant,
 13288
Carlisle, George William
 Frederick Howard, 7th earl of,
 1802-1864, 2917
Carlos IV, king of Spain,
 1748-1819 - Poetry, 7626
Carlotina and the Sanfedesti,
 9497
Carlotta's intended, 5310
Carlton, Robert, pseud., 12554
Carlyle, Thomas, 1795-1881,
 11665
Carman, Louis Dale, 1860-,
 6336, 6337, 6338
Carmela, 10966
Carmelites, Discalced, 7520
Carmen's inheritance, 5419
Carmichael, Mrs. A. C., 6339
Carmichael, Sarah E., 6340
Carnahan, David Todd, 1820-
 1901, 6341
Carnahan, James, 1775-1859,
 ed., 13275
Carnegie, James, 1827-1905,
 Earl of Southesk, 6342
Carneiro Leão, Antonio, 1887-,
 2918
Carnesworthe, pseud., 11666
Carnochan, Janet, 6532
Carochi, Horacio, d. 1662,
 7667

Carolana, 3103
Carolina, 491, 2560
Carolina chronicle, 4075
Carolina constitution, 3860
Carolina described more
fully than heretofore,
2919
Carolina - Descr. & trav.,
4629
Carolina sports, 3369
Carolina sports by land
and water, 12048
Caroline Nichols, 10310
Carpenter, Francis Bicknell,
1830-1900, 6343
Carpenter, George W.,
1802-1860, 11667
Carpenter, Hugh S[mith],
11668
Carpenter, Matthew Hale,
1824-1881, 11669
Carpenter, Philip Pearsall,
1819-1877, 11670
Carpenter, Stephen Cullen,
d. ca. 1820, 11671
Carpenter, Thomas, 2337
Carpenter, William Henry,
1813-1899, 484, 485,
486, 11672, 11673
Carpenter, William W.,
6344
The carpetbagger, 4904
Carr, Clark Ezra, 1836-
1919, 6345, 6346
Carr, John, 11674
Carr, Julian Shakespeare,
1845-1924, 6347
Carr, Spencer, 1811-1880,
11675
Carranza, Venustiano, pres.
Mexico, 1859-1920, 6268
Carreño, Alberto María,
1875-, ed., 6835
Carreño, Teresa, 8292
Carriage friends, 9802
The carriage-lamps, 9216
Carried by storm, 9523
Carrillo, Alonso, 6348
Carrillo, Crescencio, 7836

Carrillo de Córdoba, Fernando,
6011
Carrillo de Córdoba, Hernán,
6011
Carillo, José, 6349
Carrillo Laso de la Vega,
Alonso, 1582-1647, 5998
Carrillo, Mariano, 6350
Carrington, John W., 11676
Carrión, Alonso, 6354
Carrión, Antonio, 8441
Carroll, Anna Ella, 1815-1894,
6094, 6351, 11677, 11678,
11679
Carroll, Charles, 1737-1832,
5030, 11680
Carroll O'Donoghue, 9491
Carson, Christopher, 1809-1868,
2581, 2796, 2856, 2920, 4759
Carta misiva de lo acaecido
al navio San Martin, 6352
Cartagena, Colombia - Siege,
1741, 573, 13334
Cartago, Costa Rica, 5845
Cartas de Bolivar, 6109
Cartas, escritas en el interior
de Cuba, 5810
Cartas sobre Mexico, 6043
Carter, Abdiel, 3747
Carter, Clarence Edwin, ed.,
2523
Carter, Howell, 2921
Carter Quarterman, 8653
Carter, Robert, pub., New York,
2212
Carthage - Colonies, 13425
Cartier, Jacques, 1827
Cartier to Frontenac, 8401
Cartwright, Peter, 1785-1872,
2922
Caruthers, William Alexander,
1802-1846, 2923, 2924, 2925
Carvalho, S. N., 2926
Carver, Jonathan, 1710-1780,
2927, 11681, 11682
Carver, Jonathan, 1732-1780,
3429, 5457
Carver, Robin, 11683
Carver, William F., 1840-, 6353

Cary, Alice, 1820-1871,
2531, 2928, 2929, 2930,
2931, 2932
Cary, Lott, 1780-1828,
12508
Cary, Phoebe, 1824-1871,
2531, 2928, 2931, 2933
Cary, Thomas Greaves,
1791-1859, 11684,
11685, 11686
Casa Braccio, 6492
Casa Calderón, Angel Ventura
Calderón, marqués de,
8277
Casahonda, Jorge, jt.
author, 7320
Casalbón y Geli, Rafael,
1729-1787, 399
Casanate, Luis de, 6354
Casares, Manuel José,
6160
Casas, Bartolomé de las,
bp., 1474-1566, 6355,
6356, 6357, 6358, 6359,
6360, 6361, 6362, 6363
Casas, Felipe de las,
d. 1732, 6378
Casas Mota y Flores, Lucas
de las, 6364
Casco Bay, Me., 6030
The case and claim of the
American loyalists...
considered, 11689
Case, Charles, b. 1817,
11687
Case, Francis M., 3255
A case in point, 10669
Case, J. I., threshing
machine co., Racine,
Wis., 9078
The case of Great Britain
and America, 11690
The case of the Episcopal
churches in the U. S.,
13510
The case of the planters
of tobacco in Va., 11691
The case of the Whigs who
loaned their money, 11905

The case of William Atwood,
esq., 546
Case, Wheeler, d. 1793, 11688
Casement, Gray, 1870-, tr.,
6724
Cases of personal identity,
13445
Casey, Charles, 2934
Casey, Joseph, 1814-1879,
11692
Casket of reminiscences, 3496
Caskoden, Edwin, pseud., 10309
Casler, John Overton, 1838-,
2935
Casler, Melyer, 2936
Caspipina's letters, 11992
Cass, Lewis, 1787-1866,
5693, 6450
Casseday, Benjamin, 2937
Cassell, John, 1817-, 2938
Cassin, John, 1813-1869, 675
Cassini, Jean Dominique,
comte de, 1748-1845, 6400, 6401
Cassius Marcellus Clay, 2898
Cast adrift, 8560
Castaigne, A., illustr., 6492
Castaneyra, Isidro Alphonso de,
6365
Castelar y Ripoll, Emilio,
1832-1899, 7794
Castelfuerte, José de Armendáriz,
marques de, viceroy of Peru,
6366, 6367, 6368
Castellanos de Losada, Basilio
Sebastian, 1807-1891, ed.,
592, 596
Castellanos García, Gerardo,
1879-, 6369
Castelman, Richard, 2986
Castelnau, Francis, comte de,
1812-1880, 2939, 11693
Castéra, Jean Henri, b. ca. 1755,
tr., 13411
Castiglioni, Luigi, conte,
1756 or 1757-1832, 2940
Castillero, Andrés, appellee,
1166
Castillo, Benjamin E. del,
2941

Castillo de Herrera, Alonso de, 6370
Castillo, F., 6371, 6372
Castillo, Martín del, d. 1680, 6373, 6374
Castillo, Pedro del, 17th century, 6276
Castillo y Piña, José, 6375
Castine, 8632
The casting away of Mrs. Leeks and Mrs. Aleshine, 10887
Castle Dismal, 10770
Castle Nowhere, 11205
Castle Thunder (Confederate prison), 2048
Castler Crosier, 8843
Castles in the air, 9059, 10554
Castles near Spain, 9740
Castorena y Ursúa, Juan Ignacio de, 1668-1733, 6754
Castrillo, Hernando, 1586-1667, 6376
Castro, Casimiro, 6815
Castro, Henry, 1786-1865, 2942
Castro Leal, Antonio, ed., 7891
Castro, Lorenzo, 6377
Castro, Luis de, 6378
Caswall, Henry, 1810-1870, 2943, 2944, 11694, 11695
Caswell, Alexis, 1799-1877, 11696
Catalogs, Booksellers' - U. S., 11697
Catalogs, Library, 12727
A catalogue of all the books, printed in the U. S., 11697
Catalogue of books on the Masonic institution, 2415
A catalogue of plants, 12916
Catalogue of works in refutation of Methodism, 1847
Catalogus provinciae mexicanae Societatis Jesu, 7151
The catastrophe, 8951

Catcott, Alexander, 11698
Cate, Wirt Armistead, ed., 1900-, 2945
Catecismo de geografía de la República Mexicana, 5977
Catesby, Mark, 1683-1749, 1828, 2946
Catfish catching squirrels, 10310
Catharine, 8471
Cathcart, Almira, d. 1869? 8553
Cathcart, John, 1829
A cathedral courtship, 11157
Catherwood, Frederic, 1830
Catherwood, Mary (Hartwell) 1847-1902, 6379
The Catholic chapter in the history of the U. S., 12990
Catholic church - Biog., 7770
Catholic church - Clergy, 7993
Catholic church - Collected works, 7733
Catholic church. Congregatio sacrorum rituum, 6380
Catholic church - Dictionaries, 5870
Catholic church - Doctrinal and controversial works - Catholic authors, 5870
Catholic church - Education - U. S., 2000
Catholic church in Canada, 1441
Catholic church in Ireland, 11256
Catholic church in Kentucky - Missions, 5250
Catholic church in Mexico, 5973, 6275, 12480
Catholic church in New York (City) - Hist., 987
Catholic church in Peru, 7770
Catholic church in South America, 2473
Catholic church in Spain, 7731
Catholic church in Spanish America, 6432, 8443
Catholic church in the U. S., 5067, 7351, 10579, 11677, 11679
Catholic church. Liturgy and

ritual, 7863
Catholic church. Liturgy
and ritual, Mercedarian,
6365
Catholic church. Liturgy
and ritual. Ritual, 6381
Catholic church, Mexico.
Archbishop, 6382
Catholic church - Missions,
651, 2366, 5227, 6796,
6799, 7718, 8171
Catholic church - Pastoral
letters and charges, 7326,
7327, 7895, 7948
Catholic church. Pope,
1644-1655, 6383
Catholic church. Pope,
1644-1655 (Innocentius X)
Cum sicuti accepimus
(14 May 1648), 7669
Catholic church. Pope,
1740-1758 (Benedictus XIV),
7013
Catholic church - Prayer-
books and devotions -
Spanish, 7668, 8297
Catholic church. Sacra
Rituum Congregatio,
6384, 6385
Catholic church - Sermons,
1797, 7031
The Catholic emigrants,
9416
The Catholic Iroquois,
10730
Catholic literature, 10675
The catholic man, 11027
Catholic University of
America, 5235
Catholics in Maryland,
170, 2088
Catholics in New York
(City), 987, 12991
Catholics in Spanish
America, 7674
Catholics in Texas, 5368
Catholics in the U. S.,
121, 12990
Catineau-Laroche, Pierre

Marie Sébastien, 1772-1828,
1831
Catlin, George, 1796-1872, 1832,
1833, 1834, 1835, 1836,
1837, 1838
Caton, John Dean, 1812-1895,
1410
Catskill association, 1839
Catskill, N. Y., 1839
Cattle, 4704
Cattle industry - Texas, 5942
Catto, William T., 1840
Cauchon, Joseph, 1841
Caucuses of 1860, 6938
Caudevilla y Escudero, Joaquín,
6386
Caughnawaga Indians, 5199
Caught on the ebb-tide, 10653
Caulkins, Frances Manwaring,
1795-1869, 1842, 1843
Cause and contrast, 13414
The cause of it, 9330
Causten, James H., 1844
A caution to sinners against
abusing the patience of God,
2259
Cautla Morclos, 7313
Cauvin, R. S., 6730
Cavada, Frederick Fernandez,
1832-1871, 1845
The cavaliers of England, 9842
The cavaliers of the Cross,
9543
The cavaliers of Virginia, 2923
A caveat against unreasonable
and unscriptural separations,
11699
Cavelier, Jean, 1846
Cavender, Curtis H., 1847
Caverly, Abiel Moore, 1817-
1879, 11700
Caverly, Robert Boodey, 1806-
1887, 11701
The cavern of death, 10693
Cavling, Henrik, 1859-, 2947
Cawein, Madison Julius,
1865-1914, 2948, 2949, 2950,
2951, 2952, 2953, 2954,
2955, 2956

Caxton Club, Chicago, 7282
Caxton, Laura, pseud., 9088
Caylus, Ernest, 11702
Cazeaux, Pierre Euryale,
  tr., 615
Cazneau, Mrs. William
  Leslie, 2957
Cecil Dreeme, 11192
Cecil, E., pseud.? 11703
Cedar, 7693
Cedarholm, Rev. A., 1822-
  1867, 6387
Cedarholm, Caroline, tr.,
  6387
Celebra la muy noble, 7478
The celebrated jumping frog
  of Calaveras County,
  9026
Celebration of the eighty-
  sixth anniversary of the
  independence of the
  United States, 1874
Celebration of the ninetieth
  anniversary of American
  independance [!] 12205
The celebrity, 9002
Celeste, the pirate's
  daughter, 9443
The celestial railroad, 9823
Celio, 9544
Cemeteries - East Attleborough,
  Mass., 11935
'Cension, 8611
Censoria lictoria, 9471
Censoria lictoria of facts
  and folks, 9472
Censures, Ecclesiastical,
  5971
Cent-vingt jours de service
  actif, 6542
The centenary of Abraham
  Lincoln's birth, 7633
The centennial celebration
  at Cherry Valley, 11778
Centennial history of the
  city of Washington, 6514
Centeola, 10957
Central America, 442, 664,
  1124, 7521, 7675, 8097,

13484
Central America and its
  problems, 7675
Central America - Antiq., 1830,
  7439
Central America - Bibl., 6166
Central America - Descr. & trav.,
  1957, 1958, 2366, 4196, 4213,
  4967, 5492, 6057, 6258, 6440,
  6545, 6776, 6784, 6796, 6798,
  6799, 6800, 6840, 6961, 7228,
  7343, 7534, 7541, 7583, 7623,
  7751, 7878, 7883, 7913, 7917,
  7952, 8168, 8239, 8243, 8336,
  11655, 13165
Central America - Descr. & trav. -
  Guide-books, 7653
Central America - Econ. cond.,
  7623
Central America - Hist., 6789,
  8281, 13342
Central America - Politics,
  5848
Central America - Stat., 8336
The central gold region, 3615
Central railroad of New Jersey,
  12486
Century association, New York,
  11704
Cerisier, Antoine Marie, d. 1828,
  11705
Cerro Mercado, Mexico, 6708
Cervantes de Salazar, Francisco,
  ca. 1514-1575, 6388, 6389
Cesnola, Luigi Palma di, 1832-
  1904, 11706
Ceylon - Descr. & trav., 11456
Chabert de Cogolin, Joseph
  Bernard, marquis de, 1724-1805,
  11707
Chabrand, Émile, 6390
Chaco Austral, Argentine republic,
  13144
Chaco, El Gran, 437, 595
Chafee, George D., 6391
Chaffin, William Ladd, 1837-
  1922, 2958
Chahtima, pseud. of Adrien
  Emmanuel Rouquette.

90

The chainbearer, 9129
The chained mother, 3782
The chairman chastised,
   12468
Chaix, Paul Georges Gabriel,
   1808-1901, 11708
Chalk marks of overland travel
   Pike's Peak-wards, 4712
Chalkley, Thomas, 1675-1741,
   2959
Challenger (ship), 2108
Chalmers, George, 1742-1825,
   11709
Chalmers, Lionel, 1715-1777,
   2960
Chamberlain, Daniel Henry,
   1835-190-? 6392
Chamberlain, Leander Trow-
   bridge, 1837-1913, 6392
Chamberlain, Mellen, 1821-
   1900, 6393
Chamberlain, Nathan Henry,
   6394
Chamberlaine, William W.,
   1836?-, 2961
Chamberlayne, Churchill
   Gibson, 1876-, ed., 2962
Chamberlayne, John Hampden,
   1838-1882, 2962
Chambers, Ernest John,
   1862-1925, 6310
Chambers, William, 1800-
   1883, 2963, 2964, 11710
Chambersburg, Pa. - Hist.,
   2410
Chambon, fl. 1775, 11711
Chambon, Ludovic, 6395
The Chameleon, 8967
Champ d'Asile, Tex., 5032
Champagny, Jean Baptiste
   Nompère de, duc de
   Cadore, 1756-1834, 11712
Champigny, Jean, chevalier
   de, 1717-1787?, 2965,
   2966
Champion, Richard, 1743-
   1791, 11713
The champions of freedom,
   11204

Champlain, N. Y., 12724
Champlain, Samuel de, 1567-
   1635, 6396, 6443, 6599,
   11714, 11715
Champlin, James, 1821-, 2967
Champney, E. W., 10163
Champney, J. Wells, illustr.,
   4173
A chance shot, 10669
Chancellor, Richard, d. 1556,
   12192
Chancellorsville, Battle of,
   1863, 966, 2034, 4335, 12924
Chandler, Adoniram, 11716
Chandler, Charles Frederick,
   1836-1925, 11717
Chandler, Daniel, supposed
   author, 409
Chandler, Elizabeth Margaret,
   1807-1834, 2968, 2969
Chandler, James, 1706-1789,
   11718
Chandler, James, 1706-1789.
   A sermon preached at Newbury-
   port, June 25, 1767, 11718
Chandler, Joseph Ripley, 179?-
   1880, 12276
Chandler, Peleg Whitman, 1816-
   1889, 11719, 11720
Chandler, Samuel, 1713-1775, 605
Chandler, Thomas Bradbury,
   1726-1790, 11721, 11722
Chandler, Thomas Bradbury,
   1726-1790. A friendly address
   to all reasonable Americans...
   13379, 13394
Chandless, William, 2970
A change of the luck, 9533
The changed brides, 10833
Channing, Edward Tyrrel, 1790-
   1856, 11723
Channing, Henry, 1760?-1840,
   11724
Channing, Walter, 1786-1876,
   11725
Channing, William Ellery,
   1780-1842, 1118
Channing, William Ellery,
   1780-1842. Slavery, 563

91

Channing, William Francis, 1820-, 11726
Channing, William Henry, 1810-1884, 11727
Chanticleer, 10324
Chap-books, 805
Chapais, Thomas, 1858-1946, 6397
The chapel of St. Mary, 10955
The chaperone, 7126
Chapin, Alonzo Bowen, 1808-1858, 11728
Chapin, Edwin Hubbell, 1814-1880, 11729
Chapin family (Samuel Chapin, d. 1675), 11730, 11732
The Chapin gathering, 11732
Chapin, Orange, b. 1790, 11730
Chapin, Stephen, 1778-1845, 11731
The chaplains and clergy of the revolution, 12775
A chaplain's campaign with Gen. Butler, 12986
Chapleau, J. A., 8231
Chapleau, Joseph Adolphe, 6398, 6399
Chaplin, Charles, 1889-, 6562
Chapman, Henry Samuel, 1803-1881, 11733
Chapman, Isaac A., 11734
Chapman, J. Linton, illustr., 11196
Chapman, John Gadsby, 1808-1889, 11735
Chapman, Mrs. Maria (Weston) 1806-1885, 11736, 11737
Chapman, Nathaniel, 1780-1853, ed. Select speeches... 11671
Chapman, Robert D., 1839-, 2971
Chapman, Silas, 11738
Chappaqua, N. Y., 9036
Chappe d'Auteroche, Jean, 1728-1769, 6400, 6401
Chappelsmith, John, 11739
A chapter in the life of a city pastor, 10515
A chapter of American history, 11740
Chapters from the unwritten history of the war between the states, 3056
The character of Abraham Lincoln, 7702
The character of Rev. John Eliot, D. D., 12168
A character of the province of Maryland, 2515
Characteristics, 10366
Characters, 11741
Charcoal sketches, 10414
Chardon, Daniel Marc Antoine, 1730-1795? 11742
Charette, 10691
Charity, 1998
Charity - Addresses, essays, lectures, 11340
The charity "boom", 9056
Charity Green, 9795
Charity's reward, 9844
Charlecote, 11183
Charles, Cecil, 6402
Charles Elwood, 8886
Charles Hess, 10827
Charles Hopewell, 4713
Charless, Joseph, 1772-1834, 7380
Charleston, S. C., 8237
Charleston, S. C. - Census, 1848, 11744
Charleston, S. C. City Council, 11744
Charleston, S. C. City Council. Committee on ways and means, 11745
Charleston, S. C. - Descr., 4146, 4178
Charleston, S. C. - Descr. - Guide-books, 4428
Charleston, S. C. - Direct., 1756
Charleston, S. C. - Fire, 1861,

92

12959
Charleston, S. C. - Hist., 3530
Charleston, S. C. - Hist. - Revolution - Fiction, 10774
Charleston, S. C.   Magnolia cemetery, 5158
Charleston, S. C. - Siege, 1780, 5493, 12932
Charleston, S. C. - Siege, 1863, 2037, 4650
Charleston, S. C.   Unitarian church, 11746
Charlestown, Mass.   City council, 704
Charlestown, Mass.   First church, 1653, 1654
Charlestown, Mass. - Hist., 914, 2350
Charlestown, Mass.   McLean asylum for the insane, 2359
Charlestown, Mass.   Ursuline convent, 9586, 10070
Charlestown, Mass. - Water supply, 704
Charlevoix, Pierre François Xavier de, 1682-1761, 25, 2972, 6403, 6404
Charlie Whittler's Christmas party, 10465
Charlotte Temple, 10676
Charlotte's daughter, 10677
Charlton, Edwin Azro, 1828-1896, 11747
Charlton, William Henry, 2973
Charmingfare, 12000
Charnay, Désiré, 1828-1915, 6405, 6406, 6407, 6408, 6409
Charpenne, Pierre, 6410
Charrney, Theodore S., 6411
The charter of the corporation of Trinity church defended, 12817
The charter of the rector and inhabitants of the

city of New York, 12817
Charteris, 10341
The Charters of the British colonies in America, 11748
Charton, Édouard Thomas, 1807-1890, ed., 11749
The chase, 9134
Chase, C. Thurston, b. 1819, 11750
Chase, Ezra B., 11751
Chase, Francis, 11752
Chase, George Wingate, 1826-1867, 11753, 12943
Chase, Henry, 11754
Chase, Henry B., 2218
Chase, Horace, 1788-1875, ed., 11755
Chase, Loring, 10197
Chase, Lucien Bonaparte, 1817-1864, 2974
Chase, Philander, bp., 1775-1852, 2975, 2976, 2977
Chase, Pliny Earle, 1820-1886, 11756
Chase, Salmon Portland, 1808-1873, 2978, 6698
Chase, Samuel, 1741-1811, defendant, 11757
Chase, Thomas, 1827-1892, 6412
Chase, Warren, 1813-1891, 11758
Chasles, Philarète, 1798-1878, 11759, 11760
Chastellux, François Jean, marquis de, 1734-1788, 2979, 13009
Chastellux, François Jean, marquis de, 1734-1788. Voyage dans l'Amérique Septentrionale, 11521
Chateau d'Or, 9892
Chateaugay region, 12630
The chatelaine of Burnt Ridge, 6973
The chatelaine of La Trinité, 9590
Chatham (ship), 8283
Chattanooga, 10056
Chattanooga railroad expedition, 1862, 3417, 4805, 5737

Chatterjee, Sudhananda,
1912-, 6413
Chaudron, Mrs. Adelaide de
Vendel, 11761
Chaudron's spelling book,
11761
Chaumonot, Pierre Joseph
Marie, 1611-1693, 11762
Chauncey, Charles, 1777-
1849, 1314, 11307
Chauncey, Nathaniel, 1789-
1865, 2294
Chauncy, Charles, 1705-
1787, 11763, 11764
Chauncy, Charles, 1705-
1787. A letter...
containing remarks on...
a sermon preached by...
John. lord bishop of
Landaff, 13098
Chautard, Léon, 11765
Chauveau, Pierre Joseph
Olivier, 1820-1890, 6414
Chauveton, Urbain, 16th
cent., tr., 1187
Chauvin, dit Joyeuse, 2758
Chavarría, Agustín Bernardo
de, 6694, 6695
Chavero, Alfredo, 1841-1906,
7873
Chávez, Nabor, ed., 8209
Chazotte, Peter Stephen,
ca. 1770-ca. 1849, 11766,
11767
Che! wah! wah! 8122
Cheadle, Walter Butler, 1835-
1910, jt. author, 4481
Cheap cotton by free labor,
525
Cheap, healthy and happy
homes in West Virginia,
3104
Chee-ho-carte, 3919
Cheek, Philip, 1841-, 2980
Cheetham, James, 1772-1810,
11768, 11769, 11770,
11771
Cheetham, James, 1772-1810.
A view of the political

conduct of Aaron Burr, 13497
Cheever, Ezekiel, 1614-1708,
829
Cheever, George Barrell, 1807-
1890, 11772
Cheever, Henry Theodore, 1814-
1897, ed., 2074
Chelmsford, Mass. - Hist., 197
Chelonia, 107
Cheltnam, Charles Smith, tr.,
12497
Chenango (Gunboat), 11322
Cheney, J., illustr., 2513
Cheney, S. W., illustr., 2513
Cher, Henry W. B., pseud., 11773
Cherault, Mrs. Inez Bateman,
1886-, jt. author, 7182
Cheraw Indians, 12416
Les chercheurs d'or au Mexique,
6755
The Cherokee embassage, 10769
Cherokee Hills, Stories of the,
5397
Cherokee Indians, 1090, 2237,
3342, 4217, 4396, 5423,
5723, 11398, 11775, 11776,
12263, 13448
Cherokee Indians - Government
relations, 11399, 11774
Cherokee Indians - Treaties,
12104
Cherokee Indians - Wars, 1759-
1761 - Fiction, 4565
Cherokee language - Texts, 11777
Cherokee nation, 11774, 11775
Cherokee nation. Constitution,
11776
Cherokee nation. Laws,
statutes, etc., 11776
Cherokee primer, 11777
Cherrycote, 9764
Cherry Valley, N. Y., 11778
Cherry Valley, N. Y. - Hist.,
11778
Chervin, Nicolas, 1783-1843,
11779
Chesapeake and Delaware canal,
12271
Chesapeake and Ohio canal company,

11780
Chesapeake Bay, 4136
Chesapeake-Leopard affair,
1807, 413, 880
Chesebro', Caroline, 1825-
1873, 8597, 9769
Cheshire co., N. H. - Biog.,
7094
Cheshire co., N. H. - Hist.,
7094
Cheshire library association,
Cheshire, Mass., 1848
Cheshire school, Cheshire,
Conn., 1009
Chesney, Charles Cornwallis,
1826-1876, 1849, 1850
Chesnutt, Charles Waddell,
1858-1932, 2981, 2982
Chessman, Daniel, 1787-
1839, 1851
Chest - Diseases, 6466
Chester, Albert Tracy,
1812-1892, 11850
Chester, Anson G., 4140
Chester, Anthony, 2983
Chester, Charles Anderson,
d. 1849, 10204
Chester, Clarence Lyon,
1877-, jt. author, 6928
The Chester family, 9584
Chester, Greville John,
1830-1892, 1852
Chester, John, 1785-1829,
1853
Chester, John, 1832-1910,
1854
Chester, Joseph Lemuel,
1821-1882, 1855, 1856,
1857
Chesterman, William Dallas,
1845-1904, 2984, 2985
Chetwood, William Rufus,
d. 1766, 2986, 2987
Chevalier, Henri Émile,
1828-1879, 1858, 1859
Chevalier, Michel, 1806-
1879, 1860, 1861, 1862,
1863, 1864, 1865, 1866,
1867, 2988

The Chevalier Saint Agar, 11018
Chevallie, P. J., 1868
Cheves, Mrs. Elizabeth Washington
(Foote), 1869
Cheves, Langdon, 1776-1857, 1870
Chevrolat, Auguste, 1871
Chew, John H., 1872
Cheyenne Indians, 3398, 5776
Chiabrera, Gabriello, 1552-1638,
1873
Chiapas, Mexico - Antiq., 1830
Chiapas, Mexico - Descr. & trav.,
7996
Chibougamou, Quebec - Descr.,
8393
Chicago, 1874
The Chicago almanac and adver-
tiser, 1876
Chicago bar association, 6415
Chicago. Board of education,
1875
Chicago - Comm., 12512
The Chicago Copperhead Convention,
6416
Chicago - Descr., 3894, 4696
Chicago - Descr. - Guide-books,
12484
Chicago - Descr. - Views, 1877
Chicago - Direct., 1876
Chicago. Douglas monument,
2109
Chicago - Fire, 1871 - Fiction,
10643
Chicago - Hist., 716, 1878,
8431, 10141
Chicago illustrated, 1877
Chicago magazine, 1878
Chicago - Manuf., 12512
Chicago. Mechanics' institute,
1878
Chicago Tribune, 6417
Chicago. World's Columbian
exposition, 1893 - Jamaica,
7114
Chickamauga, Battle of, 1863,
2039, 5483
Chickering, Jesse, 1797-1855,
1879
Chicora, 3671

Chicóra and other regions of
the conquerors and the
conquered, 11996
Chidlaw, Benjamin Williams,
1811-1892, 1880
The chief, 5218
The chieftain of Churubusco,
9716
Chihuahua, Mexico (State) -
Descr. & trav., 2624, 7837,
8122
The child and the man, 12590
Child, Andrew, 2989
The child captives, 12922
Child, David Lee, 1794-1874,
1881, 1882, 1883, 1884,
1885
Child, John, 1886
Child, Mrs. Lydia Maria
(Francis) 1802-1880,
1887, 1888, 1889, 1890,
1891, 1892, 1893, 1894,
1895, 10008
The child of the bay, 9050
The child of the islands,
9650
Child, Robert, 1613-1654,
12735
The child's funeral, 10747
A child's history of the
United States, 11362
The child's mother, 9376
Children, 10910
Children - Biog., 13159
Children - Charities,
protection, etc., 11473
Children - Employment -
South Carolina, 5562, 5563
Children of destiny, 5115
The children of light, 8985
The children of the border,
4992
The children of the king,
6493
The children out-of-doors,
4772
Children's aid society, New
York, 11473
Children's literature -

Confederate States of America,
11471
Childs, Henry Halsey, 1783-1868,
1896
Childs, Orville Whitmore, 1803-
1870, 1897
Chile - Antiq., 11330
Chile - Bibl. - Period., 7846
Chile. Congreso. Redactor de
las sesiones, 7275
Chile. Congreso. Redactor
extraordinario, 7275
Chile - Descr. & trav., 420,
6279, 6929, 6930, 7050,
8319, 10574, 11654, 12529,
13277
Chile - Econ. cond., 7651
Chile - Hist., 6734, 8291
Chile - Hist. - Period., 7848,
7851, 7852
Chile - Hist. - War of inde-
pendence, 1810-1824, 1144,
5892, 5893, 5967, 6279,
6640, 7631, 12841, 13277
Chile - Hist. - War with Spain,
1865-1866, 11347
Chile. Ministerio de hacienda,
879
Chile - Pol. & govt., 7651
Chile - Pol. & govt. - 1810-
1824, 5967
Chile - Pol. & govt. - 1810-
1824 - Period., 7275
Chile - Soc. cond., 7651
Chile - Soc. life & cust., 1245
Chilean literature - Period.,
7851
Chilean periodicals, 7275
Chillicothe Association for
Promoting Morality and Good
Order, 2990
Chiloe, Chile (Province),
2436
Chilton, Edward, fl. 1710-1727,
3805
Chim: his Washington winter,
9308
"Chimmie Fadden", 10997
The chimney-corner, 10902

China - For. rel., 7913
Chinard, Gilbert, 1881-,
ed., 7222
Chiniquy, Charles Paschal
Telesphore, 1809-1899,
6418
Chinook jargon, 5307
Chinook jargon - Dictionaries,
5898
Chinook jargon - Glossaries,
vocabularies, etc., 4690,
5017, 7360, 8403, 12233
The chip boy of the dry
dock, 8938
Chipman, Nathaniel, 1752-1843,
11781
Chippewa Indians, 5343, 8428,
13313, 13314, 13360
Chippewa language, 12967
Chippewa language - Diction-
aries - English, 770
Chippewa language - Grammar,
771
Chippewa language - Texts,
2375, 2381, 13312
Chips from the workshop,
13115
Chisholm, Daniel Fore,
1866-, 5942
Chisholm Trail, 5942
Chita, 9832
The chivalric sailor, 10730
Chivers, Thomas Holley,
1809-1858, 2991, 2992,
2993, 2994
Chivington, John Milton,
2995
Chivington massacre of the
Cheyenne Indians, 5776
Chocolate, 6480
Choctaw Indians, 1178
A choice, 10283
The choice of Paris, 8783
The choir invisible, 8513
Choirs (Music), 9620
Choisy, 10901
Cholera, Asiatic - Baltimore,
1849, 1642
Cholera, Asiatic - U. S., 156

The cholera at Quebec, 11173
Choses d'Amerique, 4234
Chovel, Rafael, 7480
Christ in the camp, 4119
Christ rejected, 9858
Christian art and symbolism,
11108
Christian biography, 1732,
11566
Christian citizenship and
honest legislation, 13031
The Christian Indian, 8999
Christian life, 995, 9119,
11081, 13159
Christian life - Catholic
authors, 7032, 7033
Christian memorials of the
war, 12516
A Christian merchant, 1742
Christian patriotism, 12179
The Christian retrospect and
register, 667
The Christian, the student,
and pastor, exemplified, 11566
The Christian traveller, 4913
Christianity - Apologetic works -
19th cent., 8886
Christie, Robert, 1788-1856,
11782
Christie, Thomas, 2996
Christine, 10311
Christmas, 10910
The Christmas banquet, 9823
Christmas carillons, 4166
The Christmas club, 9463
A Christmas dream, 8839
Christmas eve in war times,
10653
Christmas eve on Lonesome, 9553
A Christmas-eve suit, 10653
Christmas evening legends, 10841
Christmas greetings, 6419
The Christmas guest, 10278,
10834
The Christmas holly, 10936
A Christmas in the West
Indies, 7194, 7195
Christmas Jenny, 9575
The Christmas mummers, 9916

Christmas stories, 3910,
6589, 11101
A Christmas story, 9559
A Christmas surprise, 9254
Christopher, 8723
Christy, David, b. 1802,
11783, 11784
Christy, Howard Chandler,
illustr., 3639, 9360
Chronander, Gustav, 11785
Chronica de la provincia de
San Joseph de los
descalços, 7166
The chronicle of Bearn
island, 9995
A chronicle of Louisiana,
9000
A chronicle of the conquest
of Granada, 9997
Chronicles of a Kentucky
settlement, 5642
The chronicles of Aunt
Minervy Ann, 9746
The chronicles of Bellevue,
11057
Chronicles of border war-
fare, 5754
Chronicles of Carter
barracks, 10122
The chronicles of Gotham,
11145
Chronicles of Pineville,
5403
Chronicles of the city of
Gotham, 10481
Chronicles of the late war,
10300
Chronicles of the town of
Easthampton, 2395
Chronicles of Turkeytown,
10824
Chronological account of
remarkable occurrences,
11786
Chronology, Historical,
6431, 8436, 11462
Chronology, Mexican, 7231
Chu Chu, 6963, 6971
Chuck, 10863

Chumillas, Julian, d. 1696.
Memorial jurídico y legal,
5885
Chunn, Ida F., 2997
Church and education, 13139
Church and education in the
U. S., 2024
Church and state, 622, 624, 13043
Church and state in Massachusetts,
12052
Church and state in Mexico,
12480
Church and state in New England,
1349
Church and state in the U. S.,
2000
Church, Benjamin, 1639-1718,
11787, 11788, 11789, 11790
Church dedication sermons,
5803, 8311, 11746
Church discipline, 4120
Church, George Earl, 1835-1910,
11791
Church history - 19th cent., 667
Church history - Primitive
and early church - Fiction,
10138
Church, Jeremiah, 2998
Church, John Hubbard, 1772-1840,
11792
A church mouse, 9575
Church music - New England,
12879
Church music - U. S., 12336
Church of England in America,
1449, 2790
Church of England in America -
Government, 1556
Church of England in America -
Sermons, 1384
Church of England in Canada,
2536
Church of England in Maryland,
1448
Church of England in Maryland -
Fiction, 10859
Church of England in the West
Indies, 2790
Church of England - Sermons,

654, 1007, 1196, 11407, 11651, 13391
Church of Jesus Christ of Latter-Day Saints, 2999, 3000, 4846, 8044
Church, R. S. H., 11793
Church, Thomas, 1674-1746, 11787
Church union, Boston, 600
The churches and sects of the United States, 12320
Churchill, Charles, 11794
Churchill, Winston, 1871-1947, 6420
Churchman, John, 1705-1775, 3001
Chydenius, Anders, 1898
Cibola, 8293, 8294, 11474
Cifuentes, Domingo de, fl. 1673, 6421
A cigarette from Carcinto, 10125
A cigarette-maker's romance, 9220
Cinchona, 511
Cincinnati, 3284
Cincinnati. Black brigade, 11826
Cincinnati. Board of Education, et al., defendants, 13439
Cincinnati - Descr., 3289, 3290, 11795
Cincinnati - Fiction, 9495
Cincinnati. Great western sanitary fair, 1863, 11468
Cincinnati - Hist., 4384
The Cincinnati miscellany, 3002
Cincinnati Southern Railway, 3798
Cincinnati. Superior Court, 13439
Cincinnati. University. Observatory, 81
Los cinco errores capitales de la intervencion anglo-francesa en el Plata, 1764
Cinderella, 9356
Cinquante nouvelles lettres

du R. P. de Smet, 5178
Cipher, 8601
Cipolla, Arnaldo, 1879-, 6422
A circle in the sand, 10073
The circle of a century, 9763
Circled by fire, 11211
The circuit rider, 9462
A circuit rider in early Indiana, 6423
The circular study, 10663
Circumstantial evidence, 8696
Cist, Charles, 1792-1868, 3002, 11795
Cités et ruines americaines, 6408
Cities and towns, 12009
Cities and towns - Canada, 6858
Cities and towns, Ruined, extinct, etc., 6408, 6715
Cities and towns - U. S., 6858
A citizen of Maryland, 4888, 13003
A citizen of Massachusetts, 11917
A citizen of New York, 96, 1784
A citizen of Ohio, 11229
A citizen of Philadelphia, 13101
A citizen of the United States, 12105
The citizen-soldier, 2657
Citizenship, 1955, 1999, 11920
Citizenship - U. S., 960
City and country life, 10987
The City of Endeavor, 9345
The city of the Mormons, 11695
The city of the saints, 1744
The city of the silent, 5158
The city urchin and the chaste villagers, 9216
Civil government an ordinance of God, 11922, 12050
Civil law, 388
Civil law - France, 388
Civil procedure - New York (State), 12065
Civil prudence, 11796
A civil servant, 9678
Civil service - Gt. Brit. - Examinations, 2013
Civil service in the departments,

99

9038
Civil service - U. S.,
12530
Civil service - U. S. -
Speeches in Congress,
11356
Civil war letters and docu-
ments, 4740
Civilization, Christian,
13151
Civilization in the United
States, 2556
Civilization of the Indian
natives, 13125
Civilized America, 3663
Civis, pseud., 11797
Claas Schlaschenschlinger,
10480
Claggett, William, 1790-
1870, 11798
Claiborne the rebel, 8942
The claim for interest on
the advances of Massa-
chusetts, 11799
The claim of the American
loyalists reviewed, 2383
The claim of the colonies to
an exemption, 13368
The claims of citizens of
the United States of
America, 12111
The claims of God to
recognition in the assas-
sination of President
Lincoln, 6705
Clairborne, John Francis
Hamtramck, 1809-1854,
3003, 3004
La clarière du bois des
Hogues, 1108
Clallam language -
Glossaries, vocabularies,
etc., 12232
The clan of No-name, 9217
The clandestine marriage,
9444
Clap, Thomas, 1703-1767,
11800, 11801, 11802
Clapp, Asahel, 11803

Clapp, Charles B., comp.,
11804
Clapp, Henry Austin, 1841-1904,
ed., 11203
Clapp, John T., 3005
Clapp, Theodore, 1792-1866,
3006
Clara Moreland, 1170
Clare, Mrs. Josephine, 3007
Claremont, 9005
Clarence, 6964, 10723
Claretie, Jules, 1840-1913,
7494
Clarière, Etienne, 1735-1793,
2805
Clarimonde: a tale of New
Orleans life, 8752
Clark, Aaron, 11805
Clark, Alonso Howard, 1850-
1918, ed., 8076
Clark, Benjamin Franklin,
1808-1879, 11806
Clark, Charles, d. 1881, 11807,
11808, 11809
Clark, Charles Eugene, 6424
Clark, Charles M., 1834-, 3008
Clark, Christopher, 3009
Clark, D. W., ed., 3452
Clark, Daniel, 1809-1891,
6425
Clark, Daniel Atkinson, 1779-
1840, 328, 11810
Clark family, 3386
Clark, George, 1841-, 3010
Clark, George Rogers, 1752-
1818, 3017, 3386
Clark, Hamlet, 1823-1867, 11811
Clark, Henry, 1829-1899, 11812
Clark, Hiram C., 11813
Clark, Horace Francis, 1815-
1873, 11814
Clark, Sir James, bart., 1788-
1870, 11815
Clark, James H., 1842-, 3011
Clark, James Samuel, 1841-,
3012
Clark, Joel W., 11816
Clark, John, 1745-1809? 13183
Clark, John Alonso, 1801-, 3013

Clark, Jonas, 1730-1805,
11817
Clark, Jonathan, 11818
Clark, Joseph, 1751-1813,
11819
Clark, Joseph G., 11820
Clark, Joseph Sylvester,
1800-1861, 11821
Clark, Joshua Victor Hopkins,
1803-1869, 11822
Clark, Lewis Garrard, 1812-
1897, 3014
Clark, Lewis Gaylord, 1808-
1873, 9012, 10154
Clark, Lincoln, 1800-1886,
11823
Clark, Mary, 1792?-1841,
11824
Clark, Mary, of Washington
co., Va., 2045
Clark, Milton, 1817?-1901,
3014
Clark, Peter, 1694-1768,
11825
Clark, Peter H., 11826
Clark, Rufus Wheelwright,
1813-1886, 11827, 11828,
11829, 11830
Clark, Thomas, 1787-1860,
11831
Clark, Thomas March, bp.,
1812-1903, 3015, 11832
Clark, Thomas S., 2587
Clark, William, 3017
Clark, William, 1770-1838,
4272, 5457, 13385
Clark, William Adolphus,
1825-1906, 11833
Clark, William Jared, 1854?-
1922, 6426
Clark, Willis Gaylord, 1808-
1841, 9012
Clark's expedition against
Detroit, 1781, 3386
Clark's expedition to the
Illinois, 1778-1779,
3386, 3760
Clark's grant, 3386
Clarke, A. B. of Westfield,

Mass., 11834
Clarke, A. S., 10448
Clarke, Abraham Lynsen, 1768?-
1810, 11835
Clarke, Asa Bement, 3018
Clarke, Edward, 1810-1891,
11836
Clarke, Sir Edward George,
1841-, 11837
Clarke, Edward Hammond, 1820-
1877, ed., 11845
Clarke, Frank Wigglesworth,
1847-, 11838
Clarke, George, 1676-1760,
3019
Clarke, John, lieutenant of
marines, 11839
Clarke, John, 1755-1798, 11841
Clarke, John Hopkins, 1789-
1870, 11842
Clarke, John, of Philadelphia,
11840
Clarke, Mrs. Mary Jones (Stimson)
1785-1866, 11845
Clarke, Matthew St. Clair, 11843,
11844
Clarke, Pitt, 1763-1835, 11845
Clarke, Samuel, 1599-1682, 11846
Clarke, Samuel Clarke, b. 1806,
11847
Clarke, Samuel Fulton, 1818-
1861, 11848
Clarke, Thomas Curtis, 1827-
1901, 11849
Clarke, Walter, 1812-1871, 11850
Clarkson, Matthew, 3020
Clarkson, Thomas, 1760-1846,
11851, 11852, 11853, 11854,
11855, 12625
Clarkson, Thomas Streatfeild,
11856
Clary, Dexter, 11857
Clary, Timothy Farrar, 1817-
1912, 11858
Clason, Isaac Starr, 1789?-
1834, 11859
Classical education, 2400
Claude d'Abbeville, father,
d. 1632, 1899

101

Claude Melnotte as a
detective, 10528
Claudia Hyde, 8759
Claussen, Pierre, chevalier,
1818
Claver, Pedro, Saint,
1580(ca.)-1654, 6725
Clavijero, Francisco Javier,
1731-1787, 6427
Clay, Cassius Marcellus,
1810-1903, 2898, 3021,
3022, 3023, 3024, 3025,
3026, 3884
Clay, Henry, 1777-1852,
382, 708, 1605, 2284,
3720, 5426, 6428, 6429,
7900, 12146
The Clay minstrel, 13392
Clayton, William, 1814-1879,
3027
The clean face, 10197
Cleland, Thomas, 1778-1858,
3028
Clemens, Samuel Langhorne,
1835-1910, 3029
Clement Falconer, 10567
Clemente, Claudio, 1594?-
1642 or 3, 6430, 6431,
6432
Cleopatra's daughter, 8548
Clergy, 11980
Clergy - Gt. Brit., 13450
Clergy in Maryland of the
Protestant Episcopal church,
167
Clergy - Maryland, 167
Clergy - New Hampshire, 11416
Clericus, esculapius, and
scepticus, vs. Col. M.
Jewett, and his chemical
preparations, 3854
Clermont, N. Y., 11856
Cleugh, James, tr., 6057
The Cleveland family, 10803
Cleveland, Grover, pres.
U. S., 1837-1908, 6433,
6869
Cleveland, Henry, 3030
Cleveland, John F., jt.

author, 6888
Clibborn, Edward, 1900
The Cliff Dwellers, 6921
The Clifford family, 11860
Clifford, Jeronimy, d. 1737,
2026
Clifford Troup, 11127
Cliffton, William, 1772-1799,
1901
The Clifton picture, 9178
The climate of the United
States and its endemic
influences, 12149
Climatology, Medical, 1434,
11578, 11815, 12791
Climatology of Florida, 4161
Climbs & exploration in the
Canadian Rockies, 8126
Clinch, Joseph Hart, d. 1884,
1902
Cline, A. J., 11861
Clinedinst, V. West, illustr.,
9637
Clingman, Thomas Lanier, 1812-
1897, 1903
Clinton Bradshaw, 5379
Clinton, Charles A., supposed
author, 3031
Clinton, De Witt, 1769-1828,
1904, 1905, 1906, 1907,
1908, 1909, 1910, 2078,
11862, 13023
Clinton, George, 1739-1812, 94
Clinton, George William,
1807-1885, 1911
Clinton, Sir Henry, 1738?-
1795, 13473
Clinton, Henry Lauren, 1820-
1889, 1912
Clipperton, John, 1221
Clippings from the California
press, 1913
Clock and watch making, 11374
Clock and watch making - U. S.,
11374, 13214
Clocks and watches, 6401
Clopper, Jonas, 1914
The close of the late rebellion,
in Rhode-Island, 13220

102

Closson, H. W., 10122
Clotelle, 2833
'A cloud of witness' against slavery and oppression, 443
A cloud on the mountain, 9529
Cloud pictures, 5495
The cloud with a golden border, 9830
The clouds of the mind, 10009
Clough, Simon, 1915
Cloverly, 9862
Clovernook, 2930, 8947
Club of Odd Volumes, Boston, 2573, 2574
Clubb, Henry Stephen, b. 1827, 1916
Clubb, Stephen, b. 1762, 1917
Cluny, Alexander, 3032, 6434, 6435
Cluseret, Gustave Paul, 1823-1900, 1918
Clutterbuck, Walter J., jt. author, 7259
The Clyde, 10172
Clyde Wardleigh's promise, 10635
Clymer, George, d. 1881, 1919
Coahuila, Mexico - Descr., 4314, 7219, 7837
Coahuila, Mexico - Hist., 7219
Coal, 11444, 13263
Coal and coal oil, 11444
Coal mines and mining - Chile - Coronel, 879
Coal mines and mining - Chile - Lota, 879
Coal mines and mining - Pennsylvania, 8376
Coal - Rhode Island, 12066
Coal-tar products, 12075, 12220
Coal trade, 13263
Coal - U. S., 13264

Coale, Charles B., 3033
Coann, Pearl Clement, jt. author, 10425
Coast defenses, 837
The coast of Bohemia, 9940
The coast survey, 1920
Coasts - Cuba, 8438
Coates, Benjamin, 1921
Coates, Benjamin Hornor, 1922
Coates, Reynell, 1802-1886, 1923
Coats, William, 1924
Coatzacualcos, Mexico - Descr., 6410
Cobb, Alfred, 3034
Cobb, Alvan, 1925
Cobb, Charles, comp., 292, 3035
Cobb, Darius, 1834-1919, jt. author, 9049
Cobb family, 8103
Cobb family (Henry Cobb, d. 1679) 1928
Cobb, Howell, 1815-1868, 1926
Cobb, Irvin Shrewsbury, 1876-1944, 7155
Cobb, Joseph Beckham, 1819-1858, 3036, 3037
Cobb, Lyman, 1800-1864, 1927
Cobb, Sylvanus, 1798-1866, 1928
Cobb, Sylvanus, 1823-1887, 1928
Cobb, Thomas Read Rootes, 1823-1862, 3038
Cobbe, Frances Power, 1822-1904, 1929
Cobbett, Griffith Owen, 6436
Cobbett, James Paul, 1930
Cobbett, William, 1763-1835, 1931, 1932, 1933, 1934, 1935, 1936, 1937, 1938, 1939, 1940, 1941, 1942, 1943, 1944, 1945, 2478, 3039, 3965, 11863
Cobbett, William, 1763-1835. The life and adventures of Peter Porcupine, 1427
Cobbett, William, 1763-1835. The scare-crow, 1427
Cobden, Richard, 1804-1865, 1865, 1946, 1947, 1948, 1949
Cobleigh, Nelson E., 1950

Cobos y Luna, Manuel de los,
  marqués de Camarasa, 7920
Coburn, Edward Otis, b. 1830,
  defendant, 1951
Cobus Yerks, 10480
Cochin, Augustin, 1823-1872,
  2414
Cochran, Clara C., d. 1853,
  10089
Cochrane, Clark Betton,
  1815-1867, 1952
Cochrane, John, 1813-
  1898, 1953
Cock Robin, 10434
Cockayne, M. S., 1954
Cockburn, Sir Alexander
  James Edmund, 1802-1880,
  1955
Cockburn, G. F., 1956
Cockburn, John, mariner,
  1957, 1958
Cockburn, John, mariner.
  Diario del viaje, 8303
Cocke, Richard Ivanhoe,
  1959
Cocke, William Archer,
  1960
Cocke, Zitella, 1848?,
  3040
Cockrell, Thomas J.,
  photographer, 7477
Coclenterata - U. S., 107
Cocos Island - Descr. &
  trav., 8303
Cod-fisheries, 6401, 6575
Codding, Milo Defonz, 1961
Coddington, David Smith,
  1823-1865, 1962, 6437
Code des noirs, 8053
Code noir, 13147
The code of laws for the
  government of the negro
  slaves in the island of
  Jamaica, 13147
Codex Chimalpopocatl, 1442
Codex Fejerváry-Mayer, 6438
Codex Gondra, 1442
Codice diplomatico colombo-
  americano, 727

Codman, John, 1782-1847, 1963
Cody, John Sherwin, 8425
Cody, Sherwin, 1868-, 6439
Cody, William Frederick, 1845-
  1917, 7712
Coe, David Benton, 1814-1895,
  1964
Coe family (Robert Coe, b. 1596),
  1964
Coe, Fanny E., 6440
Coffee and repartee, 8675
Coffey, W. A., 1965
Coffin, Alexander, 1765?-1836,
  1966
Coffin, Alfred Oscar, 6441
Coffin, Charles Carleton, 1823-
  1896, 1967, 3041, 11864
Coffin, Ebenezer, 1769-1816,
  1968
Coffin, Frederick M., illustr.,
  10476
Coffin, James Henry, 1806-1873,
  1969
Coffin, John Gorham, 1770-1829,
  1970
Coffin, Joshua, 1792-1864, 1971,
  1972, 1973
Coffin, Mrs. Kezia (Folger)
  1723-1798, 9775
Coffin, Levi, 1798-1877, 3042
Coffin, Nathaniel Wheeler,
  1815-1869, 1974
Coffin, Robert Barry, 1826-1886,
  1975
Coffin, Robert Stevenson,
  1797-1827, 1617, 1976, 1977
Coffin, Thomas Edward, 1838-,
  12637
Coffin, William Foster, 1808-
  1878, 1978
Coggeshall, George, 1784-1861,
  1979, 1980, 1981
Coggeshall, William Turner,
  1824-1867, 1982, 1983, 1984,
  1985, 3043
Coggins, James Caswell, 1865-,
  6442
Coghill, Howard, 1858-, jt.
  author, 8931

Coghlan, Mrs. Margaret
(Moncrieffe), 1986
Cogley, Thomas Sydenham,
1840-, 3044
Cogswell, Elliott Colby,
1814-1887, 1987, 1988
Cogswell, Joseph Green,
1786-1871, comp., 514,
515, 516
Cogswell, Nathaniel, 1773-
1813, 1989
Cohen, Ernest Julius, 1869-,
3045
Cohen, Myer M., 1990, 3046
Cohn, Alfons Fedor, 1878-,
tr., 7191
Cohoes, N. Y. Charters,
1991
Cohoes, N. Y. Ordinances,
etc., 1991
A Cohutta Valley shooting
match, 10125
Coinage, International, 150
Coinage - Peru, 8312
Coins, 2173
Coit, Thomas Winthrop, 1803-
1885, 11865
Coke, Edward Thomas, 1807-
1888, 1992
Coke, Henry John, 1827-1916,
3047
Coke, Thomas, bp., 1747-1814,
1993, 1994, 1995, 3048,
11866
Colby, Charles William,
1867-, 6443
Colby, John, 1787-1817, 3049
Cole, Jacob Henry, 1847-, 3050
Cole, jt. author, 4727
Cole, Thomas, 1801-1848, 1627
Colección Chimalistac de
libros y documentos acerca
de la Nueva España, 6444
Colección de documentos
inéditos para la historia
de Ibero-América, 7524
Colección de ducomentos [!]
relativos a la conducta,
12480

Colección de itinerarios para
diferentes puntos de la
República Mexicana, 7489
Colección de itinerarios y
leguarios formada por la Sección
de estadística militar, 7487
Colección linguística americana,
6076
Coleman, Ann Mary Butler (Crittenden) "Mrs. Chapman Coleman,"
1813-1891, 3051
Coleman, John Winston, 1898-,
6445, 6446
Coleman, William, 1766-1829,
supposed author, 412, 11587
Coleman, William Macon, 1838-,
6447
Coleraine, George Hanger,
4th baron, 1751?-1824, 3052
Colhoun, James Edward, 13360
Coll y Toste, Cayetano, 1850-
1930, ed., 6107
Collaboration, 10020
Collection linguistique Américaine,
6076
A collection of college words
and customs, 12558
A collection of interesting,
authentic papers, relative
to the dispute between Great
Britain and America, 224
A collection of poems, 3929
A collection of the epistles and
works of Benjamin Holme, 3905
College of physicians of
Philadelphia, 535
College of William and Mary,
Williamsburg, Va., 3805
The college, the market, and
the court, 11939
College verse - Dartmouth, 9734
Colleges and universities -
New York, 12619
Collie, John Norman, 1859-,
jt. author, 8126
Collier, Price, 1860-1913,
3053
Collins, Clarissa W., 6448
Collins, Elizabeth, 3054

Collins, Emma (Gowdy)
"Mrs. William Leslie
Collins", 3055
Collins, John, jr.,
plaintiff, 13288
Collins, R. M., 3056
Collins, S. H., 3057
Collins steamship line,
648
Collins, Stephen Foster,
1826-1864, 7365
Collinson, Richard, 6449
Collinson, T. B., ed.,
6449
Collyer, Robert H., 3058
Colman, Samuel, pub.,
4743
Colmer, J. G., 8106
Colombia - Antiq., 11330
Colombia - Descr. & trav.,
7264, 7583, 8168, 8319,
12569, 13451
Colombia - For. rel. - U. S.,
7859, 12716
Colombia - Hist. - To 1810,
29
Colombia - Hist. - 1822-
1832, 7761, 8267
Colombia - Hist. - 1832-
1886, 7761
Colombia - Hist. - Period.,
7545, 7847, 7956
Colombia - Hist. - War of
independence, 1810-1822,
7322, 7762, 7897, 8009,
8267, 8268
Colombia: its present state,
in respect of climate,
soil, 12569
Colombia - Period., 7683
Colombian literature -
Period., 7545, 7847
Colombo, Cristoforo, 1446-
1506, 13, 234, 311, 727,
1081, 1123, 1544, 6331,
7305, 7567, 8083
Colombo, Cristoforo. Codice
diplomatico colombo-ameri-
cano, 727

Colombo, Cristoforo - Drama,
1493
Colombo, Cristoforo, 1446-1506 -
Iconography, 8083
Colombo, Cristoforo - Poetry,
809, 819
Colombo family, 1115
Colón de Córdova Bocanegra y
Pacheco, Carlos, 5877
Colón de Córdova y Bocanegra,
Francisco, marqués de Villa-
mayor, 6850
Colón de Portugal, Alvaro, 5877
Colón de Portugal, Ana Francisca,
6850
Colón de Portugal, Pedro, 6850
Colón de Toledo, Alvaro, 5877
Colón de Toledo y Larreatigui,
Diego, 6850
Colon family, 7567
Colón, Panama - Descr., 6334
The colonel, 3038
Colonel Carter of Cartersville,
10807
Col. Clipsham's calendar, 9677
Colonel Dunwoddie, millionaire,
8654
Colonel Eph's shoe-buckles,
10909
Colonel Floyd's wards, 5358,
10940
Colonel Hungerford's daughter,
8466
Col. Judson of Alabama, 8762
Colonel Starbottle's client,
6965
The colonel's Christmas dinner,
10116
The colonel's daughter, 10117
The colonel's diary, 4036
Coloniae anglicanae illustratae,
11332
Colonial families of the
U. S. A., 7374
The colonial history of
Vincennes, 4229
Colonial records of Spanish
Florida, 3066
A colonial wooing, 8445

Colonies, 11809
Les colonies anglaises de
1574 à 1660, 2242
Colonization and Christian-
ity, 12965
Colonization - Period.,
379
The color-guard, 3944
Color in man, 1081
Color studies, 10025
Colorado - Descr. & trav.,
2738, 2743, 2877, 3008,
3063, 3551, 3677, 3715,
3717, 3987, 4529, 4549,
4707, 5000, 5421, 5455,
5695, 7868, 11134
Colorado - Descr. & trav. -
Guide-books, 3735
Colorado - Gold discoveries,
3616, 3717, 4594, 4707,
4708, 5421
Colorado - Gold mines, 5573
Colorado - Hist., 2995, 3398
Colorado: its mineral and
agricultural resources,
5000
Colorado - Maps, 3255
Colorado River, 4996, 5517,
5524
A colored man's reminiscences
of James Madison, 13209
The colossus, 10594
Colt, Mrs. Mirian (Davis)
b. 1817, 3059
Colton, George Hooker,
1818-1847, ed., 317
Colton, Joseph Hutchins,
1800-1893, 3060
Colton's traveler and
tourist guide book, 3060
Columbia river, 1670, 3100,
3578, 3971, 4272, 5017,
5526
Columbia, S. C. Asylum
prison, 5058
Columbia, S. C., Burning of,
1865, 5163
Columbia, S. C. Camp
Sorghum, 2876

Columbia university, 13174
The Columbiad, 809
Columbian association, New
York, 248
The Columbian naval songster,
12250
The Columbian traveller, and
statistical register, 12763
Columbia's wreath, 1439
Colvil, Edward, pseud., 10581
Colvin, John B., 1996
Colvin, Russell, 12761
Colvocoresses, George Musalas,
1816-1872, 11867
Colwell, Stephen, 1800-1871,
1997, 1998, 1999, 2000,
2001
Colyar, Arthur St. Clair,
1818-1907, 2047
Colyer, Vincent, 1825-1888,
2002
Comanche Indians, 3945, 4577,
5533, 12698
Comanche Indians - Fiction,
5651, 10081
The Comanche's dream, 10081
Combe, George, 1788-1858,
3061
Combe, William, 1741-1823,
ed., 3052, 4362
Combier, Cyprien, b. 1805,
2003
Combs, Leslie, 1793-1881,
2004
Come forth! 11069
A comedy of elopement, 10967
Comets, 1696
Comettant, Jean Pierre Oscar,
1819-1898, 2005
Comfield, Mrs. Amelia Stratton,
2006
Comfort, Benjamin Freeman,
6450
The comic history of the
United States, 10753
Coming down the Pike, 5581
The coming empire, 4346
Coming from the front, 10899
The coming of Theodora, 11137

Comitatus, Zedekiah, pseud.,
11868
Comité colonial, Paris,
6326
Commencement, 1283
Commerce, 893, 2001, 7913
Commerce - Addresses, essays,
lectures, 12878
Commerce - Hist., 480, 1979
Commerce of the American
States, 13477
Commercial associations,
12788
Commercial convention,
Detroit, 1865, 2007
Commercial Cuba, 6426
Commercial directory, 2008
Commercial law - Newfound-
land, 385
Commercial law - Spain, 402
Commercial law - U. S.,
1001, 1494, 1793
Commercial products - Asia,
13154
Commercial products -
Spanish America, 11383
A commercial rip-snorter,
10598
A commercial view, and
geographical sketch, of
the Brasils in South
America, 492
Commissary Wilson's orderly
book, 331
Commissioner Hume, 8697
The Commonwealth, Boston,
11740
Communion sermons, 11746
Communipaw, 9995
Communism, 1530, 5050
Communism - Mexico, 6001
Communism - U. S., 6193
Como me lo contaron te lo
cuento por la Calle de
Juarez, 6070
Compagnie des Indes dans
les País-Bas autrichiens,
1191
Compagnie des Indes

Orientales, 1201
The companion, 11869
"Co. Aytch", Maury Grays, 5635
Comparative law, 388
A comparison between the
British sugar colonies and
New England, 2009
Compedio de la historia de los
Estados Unidos de America,
2010
Compedio del confesionario en
mexicano y castellano, 2011
Compendio della guerra nata per
confini in America tra la
Francia e l'Inghilterra, 650
Compendio elemental de geografía
y estadística de la República
mejicana, 7018
Compendio historico del descu-
brimiento y colonizacion de
la Nueva Granada, 29
A compedious description of the
thirteen colonies, 3062
A complaint to the --- of ---
against a pamphlet, 2012
A complete descriptive and
statistical gazetteer of the
U. S., 3806
A complete 1859 guide to the
gold mines in Kansas and
Nebraska, 3063
Complete guide to the new gold
regions, 5386
A complete practical guide to
Her Majesty's civil service,
2013
Complete report of the trial
of Edward O. Coburn and
Benjamin F. Dalton, 1951
A compressed view of the points
to be discussed, 520
Compromise of 1850, 1091, 1655,
1903, 3672, 8331, 11692
Comstock, Samuel, 1802-1824,
9090
Comunicaciones, entre el señor
Carlos Biddle, 1250
Conant, Abigail (Huntington)
Frink, 1731-1759, 2016

Conant, Gaius, 1776-1862, 2014
Conant, Helen Peters (Stevens) 1839-1899, jt. tr., 6407
Conant, Sylvanus, 1720-1777, 2015, 2016
Concealed weapons, 9916
Conciliator, pseud., 2017
A concise answer, to the general inquiry, who, or what are the Shakers, 4373
A concise description of the English and French possessions in North America, 4682
A concise historical account of all the British colonies in North America, 2018
Concklin, Seth, 1802-1851, 10521
Conclusiones in repetitione agitandae, 5846
Concord, Battle of, 1775, 11817, 13418
Concord, Battle of, 1775 - Poetry, 920
Concord fight, 920
Concord, N. H. - Geneal, 11417
Concord, N. H. - Hist., 11417
Concordance entre les codes civils étrangers et le Code Napoléon, 388
Conde y Oquendo, Francisco Xavier, 1733-1799, 6451
Conder, John, 1714-1781, ed., 1621
Conder, Josiah, 1789-1855, 2019, 3064, 6452
Condiciones comunes de las contratas celebradas con los cosecheros de tabaco, 6481
Condict, Ira, 1764-1811, 2020
Condie, David Francis,

1796-1875, 2021
Condie, Thomas, 1775?-1814, 2022
Condit, Jonathan Bailey, 1808-1876, 2023, 2024
Condorcet, Marie Jean Antoine Nicolas Caritat, marquis de, 1743-1794, 2025
The conduct of General Washington, 13008
Conduct of life, 1224, 1489, 5237, 10986, 12892, 13348
The conduct of the administration, 12106
The conduct of the Dutch relating to their breach of treaties with England, 2026
The conduct of the French, with regard to Nova Scotia, 13191
The conduct of the ministry impartially examined, 2027
The conduct of the two b-rs vindicated, 2028
Condy, Jeremiah, d. 1768, 2029
Cone, Andrew, 2030
Cone, David D., 2031, 2032
Cone, Edward Winfield, 1814-1871, 11870
Cone, Spencer Houghton, 1785-1855, 11870
Cone, Spencer Wallace, 1819-1888, jt. author, 11870
Conestoga Indians, 2317
The Confederate flag on the ocean, 4733
Confederate General Ben Hardin Helm, 7381
A Confederate girl's diary, 3199
Confederate hand-book, 5759
A Confederate idyl, 10163
Confederate Power Works, Augusta, Ga., 4885
Confederate States of America, 3140, 3222, 3539, 3617, 3934, 4869, 5759
Confederate States of America - Army, 2686

109

Confederate States of America.
Army - Artillery, 2961
Confederate States of America.
Army. Dept. of Mississippi
and east Louisiana, 2033
Confederate States of America.
Army. Dept. of Northern
Virginia, 2034, 2035, 2036
Confederate States of America.
Army. Dept. of South
Carolina, Georgia and
Florida, 2037
Confederate States of America.
Army. Dept. of southwestern
Virginia, 2038
Confederate States of America.
Army. Dept. of Tennessee,
2039
Confederate States of America.
Army - Negro troops, 12223
Confederate States of America.
Army - Recruiting, enlist-
ment, etc., 2044, 2053
Confederate States of America.
Army - Regulations, 2067
Confederate States of America.
Army. Trans-Mississippi
dept., 2040
Confederate States of America.
Army - Transportation, 2059
Confederate States of America.
Bureau of exchange, 2041
Confederate States of America.
Bureau of printing, 2054
Confederate States of America -
Claims, 2045
Confederate States of America.
Congress, 2042, 2043, 2069,
2070
Confederate States of America.
Congress. Conference
committees, 2044
Confederate States of America.
Congress. House of
representatives. Committee
on claims, 2045
Confederate States of America.
Congress. House of repre-
sentatives. Committee on

Quartermaster and Commissary
departments, 2046
Confederate States of America.
Congress. House of repre-
sentatives. Committee on
ways and means, 2047
Confederate States of America.
Congress. House of repre-
sentatives. Committee to
enquire into the treatment of
prisoners at Castle Thunder,
2048
Confederate States of America.
Congress. House of repre-
sentatives. Roanoke island
investigation committee, 2049
Confederate States of America.
Congress. House of repre-
sentatives. Special committee
on the recent military
disasters, 2050
Confederate States of America.
Congress. Senate. Committee
on finance, 11871
Confederate States of America.
Congress. Senate. Committee
on foreign relations, 2051
Confederate States of America.
Congress. Senate. Committee
on the judiciary, 2052
Confederate States of America.
Congress. Senate. Select
committee on a portion of the
Message of the president of
the 13th instant [March, 1865],
2053
Confederate States of America.
Constitution, 2063, 11872,
12212
Confederate States of America.
Dept. of justice, 2054, 2055
Confederate States of America.
District courts. Alabama,
2056
Confederate States of America.
Executive departments, 2052
Confederate States of America -
For. rel. - France, 2712
Confederate States of America -

For. rel. - Gt. Brit.,
4763, 12231
Confederate States of America -
Hist., 2900, 3202, 3301
Confederate States of America -
Hist., Military, 2035, 2036,
2040, 2050, 2068, 2069,
2070, 2071, 3195, 3828,
4610, 11875
Confederate States of America -
Hist. - Sources, 4814
Confederate States of America.
Laws, statutes, etc., 2057,
2058, 2059, 2060, 2061,
2062, 2063, 2064, 11872
Confederate States of America -
Navy, 2712, 5085, 5123,
11950
Confederate States of America.
Navy dept., 2065
Confederate States of America.
Navy dept. Office of
ordnance and hydrography,
2066
Confederate States of America -
Navy - Hist., 4035
Confederate States of America -
Navy - Registers, 2065
Confederate States of America -
Officials and employees,
2052
Confederate States of America -
Officials and employees -
Salaries, allowances, etc.,
2058
Confederate States of America -
Pol. & govt., 2042, 3187,
4817, 5344, 6063, 9876,
11874, 12264
Confederate States of America.
Post-office dept., 11873
Confederate States of America.
President, 3065, 11874
Confederate States of America -
Secret service, 7410, 11455
Confederate States of America -
Soc. cond., 8656
Confederate States of America -
Soc. life & cust., 2544,

3610, 4523, 8634
Confederate States of America.
Treasury dept., 2060
Confederate States of America.
Treaties, etc., 2063
Confederate States of America.
War dept., 2034, 2037, 2046,
2068, 2069, 2070, 2071,
2072, 2073, 11875
Confession, 2011, 6357
The confession of a house-
breaker, 10040
The confessions of a bank
officer, 8474
The confessions of a frivolous
girl, 9640
The confessions of a husband,
4207
The confessions of a magdalen,
8820
The confessions of a minister,
10192
Confessions of a poet, 10451
The confessions of a society
man, 9160
The confessions of Emilia
Harrington, 11184
The confessors of Connaught,
10339
Confidence, 10010
The confidence-man, 10343
A confident tomorrow, 10327
Congar, Obadiah, 1768-1848,
2074
Congdon, Charles Taber,
1821-1891, 2075
A congratulatory letter from
a gentleman in the West,
12819
Congregational board of
publication, 11821, 13064
Congregational churches -
Collected works, 1098
Congregational churches -
Discipline, 631
Congregational churches -
Doctrinal and controversial
works, 11801
Congregational churches -

112

Colonial period, 635, 12183

Connecticut - Pol. & govt. - 1775-1865, 12844, 12947

Connecticut republicanism, 1344, 1345

Connecticut - Soc. life & cust., 10761

Connell, Mrs. Mary, 12834

Connor, Charlotte Reeve, 6457

Connor, Mrs. Jeannette M. (Thurber) ed. & tr., 3066, 5228

Connor, Selden, 1839-, 6458

Conover, Charlotte Reeve, 6459

Conover, James F., 3067

Conquered, 9265

Conquering the wilderness, 5460

The conquest of California and New Mexico, 3151

The conquest of Canada, 8338

The conquest of Constantinople, 9279

The conquest of Quebec, 12771, 12948

The conquest of Santa Fe and subjugation of New Mexico, 3068

Conrad, David Holmes, 7386

Conrad, Harrison, 1869-, 3069, 3070

Conrad, John, ed., 316

Conrad, Timothy Abbot, 1803-1877, 1404

Conrad Weickhoff, 10769

Conrotte, Manuel, 6460

Conroy, Kitty, 6461

Conscientious objectors - U. S., 7967

A conscript's Christmas, 9745

The conscription act vindicated, 12794

Le conseil des colons de Saint-Domingue, 997

Conser, Solomon L. M., 1812-, 3071

Consideraciones generales sobre la geografía, meteorología y climatología de la zona inter-tropical de la República Mexicana, 7309

Considérant, Victor Prosper, 1808-1893, 3072

Consideration of the claims and conduct of the United States respecting their north eastern boundary, 1421

Considerations on certain political transactions, 13383

Considerations on the appointment of a justice of the Supreme court of the United States, 11459

Considerations on the institution and conduct of the Society for the propagation of the gospel in foreign parts, 419

Considerations on the present situation of Great Britain and the U. S., 11713

Considerations on the provisional treaty with America, 13364

Considerations on the slavery question, 8046

Considerations relative to the North American colonies, 2288

Considerations upon the present state of our affairs, at home and abroad, 13408

A consolation for our grammar schooles, 1528

The conspiracy in the North case, 10371

The conspiracy of kings, 810

The conspiracy of Mrs. Bunker, 9791

The conspiracy unveiled, 3969

The conspirators, 8963

Constance Allerton, 10197

Constance and Calbot's rival, 9806

Constance Beverly, 9563

Constantinople - Siege,
1453 - Fiction, 9279
Constantius and Pulchera,
9878
The constituents of climate
with special reference
to the climate of Florida,
4253
The constitution and laws
of the Cherokee nation,
11776
Constitution (Frigate),
2136
The constitution shown to
be consistent with a new
election, 3534
The constitution upheld
and maintained, 6957
Constitutional history,
4946
Constitutional republicanism,
553
A constitutionalist, 121
Constitutions, State, 1274,
12198
Constitutions, State -
U. S., 253
Construyendo México, 1910-
1946, 7315
Consumption - New England,
11428
Contagion and contagious
diseases - Prevention,
12757
Contemporáneos, 6462
Contempt of court, 1256
The contest between
Christianity and
political Romanism,
11677
The contest between three
Indians and one white
man, 10570
The Continent, 3073
The continental dragoon,
10877
Continental system of
Napoleon, 13113
A continuation of the

state of New England, 11876
Continued corruption, 11333
Continuous voyages (International
law), 12667
Contostavlos, Alexander. A
narrative of the material
facts in relation to the
building of two Greek frigates,
983
Contraband of war, 12222
The contrast, 10184
Contrasted lives, 10553
Contribution among terre-tenants,
1254
Contributions to a history
of the Richmond howitzer
battalion, 5575
Contributions to conchology,
37
Contributions to the early
history of the Northwest,
3869
The controversy touching the
old stone mill, in... Newport,
Rhode Island, 11543
The convalescence of Jack Hamlin,
6977
The convent and the manse,
8972
Convention of banks of the
city of Charleston, 1841, 11877
The convention vindicated from
the misrepresentations of the
enemies of our peace, 13505
Convents and nunneries - Peru,
8296
The convent's doom, 9586
A conversational tour in
America, 8356
Conversations around the
campfire, 4924
Conversations on slavery, 10059
A convert of the mission, 6971
Convict labor, 4934
Conway, Cornelius, 3074
Conway, George Robert Graham,
1873-, 7064
Conway, Moncure Daniel, 1832-
1907, 8327

Conyngham, David Power,
1840-1883, 3075
Conyngham, Dane, pseud.,
9278
Conyngham Foxe and the
charity ball, 10122
Cook, Benjamin F., b.
1835 or 6, 3076
Cook, Ebenezer, fl. 1708-
1732, 3077
Cook, Ebenezer. The sot-
weed factor, 5264
Cook, Ebenezer. Sot-weed
redivivus, 5264
Cook, George Cram, 1873-
1924, jt. author, 8690
Cook, James, 1728-1779,
993
Cook, Joel, 1842-1910,
3078, 6463
Cooke, Mrs. Grace (MacGowan)
1863-, jt. author, 10274
Cooke, John, fl. 1794,
6464
Cooke, John Henry, 1791-1884,
3079
Cooke, Philip Pendleton,
1816-1850, 3080
Cooke, Philip St. George,
1809-1895, 3081
Cooke, R. T., 10163
Cooke, Mrs. Rose (Terry)
1827-1892, 8597
Cookman, George Grimston,
1800-1841, 1619
Cookson, Sir Charles Alfred,
1829-1906, 13104
Coolidge, Calvin, pres.
U. S., 1872-1933, 8353
The coon dog, 10042
Cooper, Alonzo, 3082
Cooper, Colin Campbell, jr.,
10737
Cooper, Isaac, supposed
author, 4504
Cooper, James Fenimore,
1789-1851, 3083
Cooper, James Fenimore,
1789-1851. The spy, 863

Cooper, Myers Young, 1873-,
6465
Cooper river, South Carolina,
4023
Cooper, Samuel, 1725-1783, 11841
Cooper, Samuel Williams,
1860-, 10737
Cooper, Thomas, 1759-1839,
3084, 10051, 11878, 11879
Cooper union for the advancement
of science and art, New York,
11880
Cooper, William, 1720-1809,
· supposed author, 11385
The Coopers, 9800
Copias a la letra, 1078
Copley, John M., 3085
Copp, Elbridge J., 1844-, 3086
Copp's hill burial ground,
Boston, 1503
Copper-distilled, 10863
The Copperhead, 6931, 9567
Copperhead Convention (The
Chicago), 6416
Copyright, International, 83
Copyrights, 4946
The coquette, 9549, 9550
Coquille, Jean Baptiste Victor,
1820-1891, 6710
Cora Glencoe, 8840
Cora O'Kane, 11190
The coral lady, 10835
Coral reefs and islands, 12909
Coranna, 9340
Corbella y Fondebila, Antonio,
6466
The Corbet chronicles, 9671
Corbett, Griffith Owen, 6467
Corby, William, 1833-1897,
3087
Corcoran, Michael, 1827-1863,
3088
Córdoba y Salinas, Diego de,
6468, 6469, 6470
Corleone, a tale of Sicily,
9221
Corlett, William Thomas,
1854-, 6471
Corndeau, 9254

Cornejo Franco, José, 6473
Cornelius, Elias, 1794-
1832, 3089, 3342
Cornell, Sarah Maria,
1802-1832, 11170, 12688
Corning, Howard, 1867-,
ed., 2573, 2574
Cornish, Louis Craig, 6474
Cornish, Louis Henry,
1855-1918, comp., 8076
Cornwallis, Charles Corn-
wallis, 1st marquis,
1738-1805, 13473
Cornwallis, Kinahan, 1839-
1917, 3090
Corografia brazilica, 11230
Corona mexicana, 7546
Corona of the Nantahalas,
4745
Coronado, Nicolás, ed.,
6478
The coronal, 8990
Corporal, pseud., 3729
Corporal punishment, 1927
The corporal's trousers,
9460
Corporation for promoting
and propagating the
gospel of Jesus Christ
in New England, London,
12006
The corps of observation,
10682
Correa, Luis, ed., 6476
Corrêa, Virgilio, 1887-,
6475
A correct and authentic
narrative of the Indian
war in Florida, 2617
Corrected proofs, 11116
Correo del Orinoco,
6476
Correspondance secrète des
députés de Saint-
Domingue avec les comités
de cette isle, 6477
Correspondence between Dr.
Charles Caldwell, of
the Medical school of

Transylvania University, and
Dr. James Fishback, pastor
of the First Baptist church
of Lexington, 2884
Correspondence between James G.
Birney, of Kentucky, and
several individuals of the
Society of Friends, 2719
Correspondence, orders, etc.,
between Major-General David
Hunter, 13024
Corresponsal en La Habana, 6745
Corsan, W. C., 3091
Cortambert, Louis Richard,
1808?-1881, 3092
The Cortelyou feud, 9538
Cortés, Hernando, 1485-1547,
11, 1544, 6478, 6863, 6864,
7387, 7774, 7775
Cortés, José Domingo, 1839-
1884, 6479
Cortijo Herraiz, Tomás, 6480
Cortina, José Antonio,
1852-1884, ed., 7849
Cortland county and the border
wars of New York, 12307
Cortland co., N. Y. - Hist.,
12307
Corwin, Thomas, 1794-1865,
3093
Cory, Charles Barney, 3094,
3095
Cos - Poetry, 3820
Cosa, Juan de la, d. 1510,
8083
Las cosas más considerables,
vistas en la Nueva España,
6835
Cosio, Pedro Antonio de,
6481, 6482
Cosmographia, 406, 407
Cosmography, 406, 407
Cosmopolite, 3277
Cosmopolite, pseud., 10172
Cost and standard of living,
9637, 10786
Costa Rica, 6280, 7795
Costa Rica - Descr. & trav.,
5845, 7517, 7620, 8303,

116

8324, 11461
Costa Rica - Hist., 6723
Costa Rica - Hist. -
Period., 5954
Costa Rican literature -
Period., 5954
Coste d'Arnobat, Charles
Pierre, b. 1732, 344
Costumbres yankees, 5068
Costume - New England,
2244
The cottage by the sea,
9048
The cottage on the cliff,
9102
Cottage piety exemplified,
9177
Cottages, 11750
Cotter, Joseph Seamon,
1861-, 3096, 7165
Cotton, Catherine B.,
d. 1853, 10089
Cotton culture and the
south considered with
reference to emigration,
4301
Cotton famine, 1861-1864,
258
Cotton growing and manu-
facture, 13149
Cotton growing and manu-
facture - Africa, 1921
Cotton growing and manu-
facture - Gt. Brit.,
12483
Cotton growing and manu-
facture - Louisiana,
4192
Cotton growing and manu-
facture - Lowell, Mass.,
11686
Cotton growing and manu-
facture - South Caro-
lina, 12418
Cotton growing and manu-
facture - Southern
states, 4301
Cotton growing and manu-
facture - U. S., 525,

526, 5792
Cotton is king, 3361
Cotton machinery, 12202
Cotton manufacture, 12202
Cotton manufacture - U. S., 956
Cotton, Nathaniel, 1697-1729,
1072
Cotton planters' convention of
Georgia, 13307
The cotton states in the spring
and summer of 1875, 4612
Cotton stealing, 3097
Coues, Elliott, 1842-1899,
6813, 7009
Coulter, Ellis Merton, 1890-,
6483
Council for New England, 12747
Counsel, 9802
The counterfeiter, 10957
The counterfeiters, 10434
The Countess Ida, 9504
The country cousin, 10730
A country doctor, 10034
A country girl, 9170
Country life, 5720, 10671
Country life - Texas, 7140
Country lodgings, 10197
Country margins and rambles
of a journalist, 9727
The country neighborhood, 9445
The country of the pointed
firs, 10035
The country v. the company,
8140
Coup d'oeil historique et
statistique sur le Texas,
2292
Coup d'oeil sur la situation
agricole de la Guiane
française, 1202
Coupon bonds, 11015
Cournand, Antoine de, abbé,
1747-1814, 6484
The court circles of the
republic, 12020
Court-martialled, 9460
Court records, 12890
The courting of Sister Wisby,
10037

Courts - Confederate States of America, 2054, 2055
Courts-martial and courts of inquiry - U. S., 354, 13253
Courts - Texas, 12939
Courts - U. S., 976, 11305, 12244
Courtship and marriage, 3841
Cousin Franck's household, 10496
Cousin William, 10904
The cousins' journey, 3098
Couto, Diogo do, 1542-1616, continuator, 882
Covenants (Theology), 1671
Coventry, Charles B., 1801-1875, 955
Covering end, 7131
The cow chace, 351, 352
Cowan, John F., 3099
The coward, 10379
The cowards' convention, 1533
Cowen, Benjamin Rush, 1831-1908, 6485
Cowper, Pulaski, comp., 3697
Cox, Earnest Sevier, 6486
Cox, Edward Travers, 1821-, jt. author, 4665
Cox, Ross, 3100
Cox, Sandford C., 3101, 3102
Coxe, Daniel, 1673-1739, 3103
Coxe, Tench, 1755-1824, 3084
Coyner, David H., 3104, 3105
Coyotes, 10863
Cozzens, Frederick Swartwout, 1818-1869, 6487, 11704
Craddock, Charles Egbert, pseud. of Mary Noailles Murfree.
The cradle of liberty, 8796
The cradle of the new world, 10492
Cradlebaugh, John, 11881

Crafford, John, 3106
Craft, David, 1832-1908, 3107
Crafts, William, 1787-1826, 3108
Crafts, William Augustus, 1819-, jt. author, 10980
Crafty, illustr., 4381
Crag-nest, 9381
Craib, Alexander, 3109
Craig, James, 3110
Craig, Wheelock, 1824-1868, 6488
Craigie, Christopher, 9070
Craik, James, 1730?-1814, 6842
Crakes, Sylvester, jr., 3112
Cram, Thomas Jefferson, 1807?-1883, 3113
Crambe, pseud., 4887
Cranch, William, 1769-1855, supposed author, 11587
Crane, Cephas Bennett, 1833-, 6489
Crane, James Campbell, 1803-1856, 1742
Crary, Charles, d. 1863, 11329
Crawford, Cora Hayward, 6490
Crawford family 7992
Crawford, Francis Marion, 1854-1909, 6491, 6492, 6493, 6494, 6495, 6496, 6497, 6498, 6499, 6500, 6501, 6502, 6503, 6504, 6505, 6506, 6507, 6508, 6509
Crawford, George Washington, 1798-1872, 12212
Crawford, J. Marshall, 3114
Crawford, John Wallace, 1847-1917, 5201
Crawford, Medorem, 5538
Crawford, William, 1788-1847, 3115
Crawford, William Harris, 1772-1834, 11879
Crawford's Indian campaign, 1782, 2781
Crayon, Geoffrey, pseud., 9996, 10001, 10002
The Crayon miscellany, 4027

La creación de Bolivia, 7752

The creamery man, 9606

Crease, Henry Pering Pellew, 1823-1905, 6183

The creation of Manitoba, 6049

Credit, 2001, 2373

Cree Indians, 8428

Cree language - Glossaries, vocabularies, etc., 5457

Cree language - Grammar, 12967

Creek Indians, 4104, 4824, 12752

Creek Indians - Government relations, 12130

Creek language - Texts, 1648

Creek war, 1813-1814, 3004, 13456

Creek war, 1836 - Fiction, 9880

The creole, 3036

Creole life, A story of, 8926

The Creole orphans, 10495

Creoles, 4276

Crequy, Charles de Blanche-fort, duc de, 1573-1638, 8323

Cresap, Michael, 1742-1775, 13138

Crescent-shine, 12227

Crespel, Emmanuel, 6511, 6512

Crespel, Louis, ed., 6512

Crespo y Martinez, Gilberto, 1853-, 6513

Cresswell, Nicholas, 1750-1804, 3116

Cressy, 6966

Creuzbaur, Robert, 3117

Crèvecoeur, Michel Guillaume St. Jean de, called Saint John de Crèvecoeur, 1735-1813, 3118, 9387

Crèvecoeur, Michel Guillaume St. Jean de, called Saint John de Crèvecoeur, 1735-1813. Letters from an American farmer, 588

Crew, Harvey W., ed., 6514

The cricket's friends, 10046

Crim, (Miss) Matt, 3119, 3120

Crime and criminals, 3764, 3781, 4934, 12300

Crime and criminals - France, 11765, 13358

Crime and criminals - Gt. Brit., 10861

Crime and criminals - Identification, 13445

Crime and criminals - New York (State), 1965

Crime and criminals - North Carolina, 5444

Crime and criminals - Ohio - Cincinnati, 11963

Crime and criminals - Southwest, Old, 9931

Crime and criminals - U. S., 2642, 4129, 11719

Crime and its consequences, 8998

Crime and punishment, 2279

Crime and retribution, 9451, 9498

The crime of Henry Vane, 10884

Crimean war, 1853-1856, 1706

The crimes committed by our government against the maroons, 12238

Criminal law - Mexico, 1078

Criminal law - Spain, 7242

Criminal law - U. S., 1353, 4129

Criminal trials, 11719

The criminal's career, 10960

Crimora, 9403

The crimson hand, 4052

El cris celeste de las católicas, 7789

Crisfield, John Woodland, 1808-1897, 6515

A crisis, 10163

Crisis americana, 7271

The crisis and the man, 6437

A crisis chapter on government,

1409
Criss-cross journeys,
5409
Critical dialogue between
Aboo and Caboo on a
new book, 5025
The critical moment, 13160
A criticism of Mr. Wm. B.
Reed's aspersions, 13245
Crittenden, John Jordan,
1787-1863, 3051
Crocker, Samuel Leonard,
1804-1883, 6516
Crockett, David, 1786-1836,
3121, 3122, 3123, 3372,
8206
Croffut, William Augustus,
1835-, 6517
Crofutt, George A., pub.,
12371
Croghan, George, d. 1782,
3124
Croghan, John, 3125
Croix, Carlos Francisco de
Croix, marques de, 1699-
1786, 6518
Croix, Teodoro de, 1730-
1791, 6519
Cromwell, 9843
Cromwell, Oliver, 1599-1658,
2091, 11523
Cromwell, Oliver - Fiction,
9843
Crónica de la orden N.
Serafico P. S. Francisco,
7811
Crónica mexicana, 5881
Crónica seráfica y apostólica
del Colegio de propagande
fide de la Santa Cruz de
Querétaro en la Nueva
España, 2559
Crónica social 1901, 7102
Cronin, David Edward,
1839-, 3126
Crooks, Ramsay, 2528
Croom, Wendell D., 3127
Croome, William, illustr.,
12174

Cropper, James, 1778-1840.
A letter to Thomas Clarkson,
639
Croquis de viaje, 8382
Croquis et impressions d'Amérique,
3629
Crosby, Daniel, 1799-1843, 12392
Crosby, Enoch, 1750-1835, 863
Crosby, James, d. 1834, 13331
Crosby, Margaret, 9769
Crosly, Oliver Martin, 3128
Cross, Osborne, 1803-1876, 3129
Cross purposes, 9382
Crossby, Peter Alfred, 1842-,
comp., 7331
Crossley, William J., 3130
Croswell, Andrew, 1709-1785.
A letter to Reverend Alexander
Cumming, 11896
Crothers, Samuel, 1783-1856,
3131, 3132
Croton aqueduct, 13215
The Crow captive, 3908
Crowe, Eyre, 1824-, 3133
Crowfield, Christopher, pseud.,
10902
Crowley, Mary Catherine, d. 1920,
6520
The crown and the cloister,
9417
A crown from the spear, 10022
The crown of duty, 9420
Crowther and the thirsk, 8723
Crozat, Antoine, marquis du
Châtel, 1655-1738, 1201
Crozer, Hiram P., 6521
Crozier, Robert Haskins, 3134,
3135
Cruel as the grave, 10836
A cruel revenge, 10203
Cruelty disarmed, 10950
Cruise of a guineaman, 10916
Cruikshank, Isaac Robert,
1789-1850, illustr., 4806
The cruise of a land yacht,
6032
The cruise of the Kaiserin,
6655
The cruise of the Montauk to

120

Bermuda, 4375
Cruise of the Neptune,
6302
The cruise of the Sea-
Slipper, 4001
The cruise of the Tomas
Barrera, 7007
The cruiser of the capes,
4014
Cruisings, afloat and
ashore, 10078
Crusade bulls, 7731
The crusade of the Excel-
sior, 6967
Crusades - Second, 1147-
1149 - Fiction, 9235
Crusades - Third, 1189-
1192 - Fiction, 10285
Crusoe in New York, 9678
Crosue's island, 8878
Crutchfield, William,
1775?-1812, 2818
Cruz, Ernesto de la, ed.,
7631
The cry of the children,
5562
Cryptobranchus, 932
Crystalina, 3785
Crystalline, 10746
Cuadro geográfico, esta-
dístico, descriptivo é
histórico de los
Estados Unidos Mexicanos,
6817
Cuadros de la historia
militar y civil de
Venezuela, 6629
Cuauhtemoc, emperor of
Mexico, 1495?-1525, 13213
Cuba, 365, 5992, 6524, 6556,
6563, 7176, 13285
Cuba - Biog., 611
Cuba - Civilization, 6563
Cuba - Climate, 5049
Cuba contemporánea, 6522,
6523
Cuba - Descr. & trav., 8,
14, 189, 335, 336, 724,
1024, 1473, 1628, 2502,

2562, 2957, 4221, 4227, 4309,
4569, 4571, 4756, 4769, 4964,
5006, 5454, 5716, 5747, 5810,
5891, 6157, 6208, 6213, 6426,
6540, 6556, 6561, 6563, 6661,
6699, 6745, 6904, 6907, 7007,
7049, 7083, 7086, 7112, 7137,
7189, 7191, 7212, 7217, 7264,
7370, 7541, 7557, 7558, 7589,
7639, 7819, 8043, 8104, 8108,
8161, 8178, 8302, 8421, 8438,
12226, 12956, 13041
Cuba - Descr. & trav. - Guide-
books, 6103, 6912
Cuba - Econ. cond., 4961, 6426,
12981
Cuba - Fiction, 4744
Cuba for invalids, 12226
Cuba - Hist., 724, 6556, 6563
Cuba - Hist. - Insurrection,
1849-1851, 13285
Cuba - Hist. - Insurrection,
1868-1878 - Fiction, 8696,
9379
Cuba - Hist. - Revolution,
1895-1898, 6750
Cuba. Oficina del censo,
6524
Cuba past and present, 8302
Cuba - Pol. & govt., 424, 11348
Cuba - Pol. & govt., 1959-,
6745
Cuba - Relations (general)
with Azerbaijan, 7189
Cuba - Soc. life & cust.,
6699
Cuba - Statistics, 12981
Cuban literature - Bibl., 611
Cuban literature - Hist. &
crit., 611
Cuban literature - Period.,
7845, 7849, 7850
Cuban question - To 1895, 1164
Cuban sketches, 8104
Cubero Sebastián, Pedro,
1640-ca. 1696, 6525, 6526,
6527
Cudworth, Warren Handel,
d. 1883, 3136, 6528

Cyclopaedia of American
literature, 3332, 12456
Cymon, pseud., 10828
The Cymry of '76, 13286
The Cynick, 11933
Cynthia Wakeham's money,
10664
Czeika, pseud., 5594

D., W. J., ed., 10259
Da Asia de João de Barros
e de Diogo de Couto,
882
Dabadie, F., 11934
Dabney, Richard, 1787?-
1825, 3152
Dabney, Robert Lewis,
1820-1898, 3153, 3154,
3155
Dabney, V., 10125
Dabney, Virginius, 1835-
1894, 3156, 3157, 10125
The Dabney will, 8629
Dacus, Joseph A., 3158
Dade's battle, 1835, 232
Daggett, David, 1764-1851,
supposed author, 12844
Daggett, John, 1805-1885,
11935, 11936
Daggett, Oliver Ellsworth,
1810-1880, 6537
Dagnall, John Malone,
1818-1917, 11937
The Dagon of Calvinism,
3159
Dagverhaal van eene reis
naar Paramaribo, 1484
Dahcotah, 2163
Daily bread, 9683
Daisy, 11093
Daisy Dare, and Baby Power,
4053
Daisy Swain, the flower
of Shenandoah, 11937
Daisy Thornton and Jessie
Graham, 9893
Daisy's necklace: and
what came of it, 8497

Dake, Orsamus Charles, 11938
Dakota Indians, 2163, 3147,
13360
Dakota Indians - Wars, 1862-
1865, 1624, 12776
Dakota language - Glossaries,
vocabularies, etc., 541
Dale, E. I., 6538
Dale, J. S. of, pseud. of
Frederic Jesup Stimson, 9641
Dale, Robert William, 1829-1895,
3160
Dale, Samuel, 1772-1841, 3004
Dall, Caroline [Wells] (Healey),
"Mrs. C. H. A. Dall",
1822-1912, 11939, 11940
Dall, William Healey, 1845-1927,
11941
Dallas, George Mifflin, 1792-
1864, 1252, 11942
Dallas, Robert Charles, 1754-
1824, 11943
Dalliba, James, 11944
Dally, 10540
Dalrymple, Alexander, 1737-
1808, 2476, 11945, 11946
Dalrymple, Sir John, bart.,
1726-1810, 11947
Dalton, Benjamin Franklin,
jt. defendant, 1951
Dalton, John Call, 1795-1864,
12382
Dalton, William, of Crackenthorpe,
Westmoreland, 11948
Daly, Augustin, 1838-1899,
11949
Daly, Charles Patrick, 1816-
1899, 11950
The Dalys of Dalystown, 10438
Dame Fortune smiled, 8714
Dame, William Meade, 1844 or 5-,
3161
Dames and daughters of the
young republic, 6188
A damsel errant, 11012
The damsel of Darien, 10771
Dan Briordy's gitaway shadder,
9533
Dan to Beersheba, 11951

Dana, Charles Anderson,
1819-1897, 3162, 6539
Dana, Edmund, 3163
Dana, James, 1735-1812,
11952, 11953
Dana, James Dwight, 1813-
1895, 11954, 11955
Dana, James Freeman,
1793-1827, 11956
Dana, Richard Henry,
1815-1882, 2511, 5831,
6540, 11723
Dana, Samuel Luther,
1795-1868, jt. author,
11956
Danbury, Conn., 8642
The dancing feather, 4001
Dandolo, Vincenzo, conte,
1758-1819, 511
Dandridge, Mrs. Danske
(Bedinger) 1858-1914,
3164, 3165
Danes in Canada, 7314
Danes in the U. S., 7314
Danger, 8561
Danger in the dark, 10091
The danger of being too
thorough, 10465
The danger of desertion,
12882
The dangerous condition
of the country, 13254
The dangerous ford, 10310
The dangers and sufferings
of Robert Eastburn, 11994
Daniel Boone, 2748
Daniel, Frederick S., 3166
Daniel, John Moncure,
1825-1865, 2589
Danielson, J. A., 6541
Danities - Fiction, 10352
The Danities in the
Sierras, 10352
Dansville, N. Y., 11816
D'Antin, Luis, tr., 7532
Danvers, Mass. - Hist.,
12658
The Danville quarterly
review, 3167

Danville, Va. Military prison,
4593, 4867
Daoust, Charles R., 6542
The dapper gentleman's story,
10172
Darby, George W., 3168
Darby, William, 1775-1854,
3169, 3170, 3171, 3172,
3173, 3174
Darien, 7567, 11887
Darien canal, 11887, 12278
Darien - Descr. & trav., 12278
Darien. Scot's colony, 11887
"Dark and bloody ground," a
romance of the, 4621
Dark and bloody ground, A tale
of the, 2682
Dark and terrible deeds of
George Lathrop, 9328
Dark days of the rebellion,
2761
A dark lantern, 4984
The dark maid of Illinois, 3754
Darley, Felix Octavius Carr,
1822-1888, illustr., 1747,
3840, 4832, 4833, 5403, 5405,
5411, 5460, 9453, 10000, 10361,
10964, 11101
Darlington, William M., ed.,
3620, 4425
Darryll Gap, 11007
Dartmoor prison, 356, 11107
Dartmouth college, 9734, 12535
Dartmouth college - Hist.,
2134
Dartmouth college. Society of
the alumni, 11573
Dartmouth college. A vindication
of the official conduct of
the trustees, 2134
D'Arusmont, William E. Guthrie,
6543
Dashed against the rock, 9083
Dashes at life with a free
pencil, 11176
Daubeny, Charles Giles Bridle,
1795-1867, 3176
Dauchy, George Kellogg, 1829-
1912, tr., 5461

The daughter of a
Republican, 8621
The daughter of a stoic,
9085
A daughter of New
France, 6520
A daughter's trials, 8901
Daughters of charity of
St. Vincent de Paul,
Emmitsburg, Md., 8896
Daughters of the revolution
and their times, 9058
Dauzats, Adria, 1804-
1868, jt. author, 2732
Dávalos, Balbino, tr.,
7340
Dave Summers, 10598
Davenport, Alfred, 3177
Davenport, Bishop, 3178
Davenport, Montague, 3179
Dave's wife, 10163
David Aldens' daughter,
8602
David Harum, 11124
David, Michael, 3180
David Swan, 9827
Davidson, Henry M.,
d. 1900, 3181, 4031
Davidson, James Wood,
1829-1905, 3182, 3183
Davidson, Robert, 1808-
1876, 3184
Davies, Ebenezer, 1808-
1882, 3185
Davila, Enrico Caterino,
1576-1631. Historia
della guerre civil de
Francia, 59
Dávila, Martin, 7397
Dávila Solera, José, tr.,
8324
Dávila, Vicente, 1874-,
6544
Davis, Charles E.,
b. 1842 or 3-1915, 3186
Davis, Dick, 1838?-1864,
3044
Davis, George, 1820-1896,
2055

Davis, George Lynn-Lachlan,
2088
Davis, Jefferson, pres. C.S.A.,
1808-1887, 2736, 3187, 4817,
6848, 7925, 7926, 8232, 8287
Davis, John, 1774-1854, 3188,
3189, 3191
Davis, John, 1788-1878, 6546
Davis, Mrs. Mary Evelyn (Moore)
1852-1909, 3191, 3192,
3193, 3194
Davis, Nicholas A., 3195
Davis, R. H., 10163
Davis, Mrs. Rebecca Harding,
1831-, 8597
Davis, Richard Harding, 1864-
1916, 6545
Davis, Stephen, 3196
Davis, Thomas Osborne, 6310
Davis, William J., ed., 4063
Davis, William Watts Hart,
1820-1910, 3197, 6546
Davison, Gideon Miner, 1791?-
1869, 6547, 6548
Dawes, Rufus R., 1838-1899, 3198
Dawley, Thomas Robinson, 1832-
1904, pub., 13075
Dawn, 8463
Daws doings, 10099
Dawson, Aeneas MacDonell,
1810-1894, 6549
Dawson, Henry Barton, 1821-
1889, 12352, 12943, 13178
Dawson, J. L., 11744
Dawson, James Lowes, 1801-1879,
6824
Dawson, S. J., 7922
Dawson, Samuel Edward, 1833-
1916, 6550, 6551
Dawson, Mrs. Sarah (Morgan)
3199
Dawson, Simon James, 3200,
6552
A day at Laguerre's and other
days, 5193
Day-dreams, 8519
Day, Francis, illustr., 9534
A day in the wilderness, 9565
Day, Lewis W., b. 1839 or 40,

126

128

supposed author, 2986
De Fontaine, Felix Gregory,
1832-1896, 2094
De Forest, Bartholomew S.,
3211
Degollado, Santos, 1813-
1861, 1825
Degoulet, Urbain, 3633
De Groot, Henry, 3212
De Hass, Wills, 1818?-1910,
3213
Dehay, Timothée, 1794-1851,
11970
Dehon, Theodore, bp., 1776-
1817, 11971, 11972
Deiler, John Hanno, 1849-
1909, 3214, 3215
Deitz family, 11513
Dejligt at Amerika ikke
ligger langt herfra,
2485
De Kay, James Ellsworth,
1792-1851, 11973
Del Gran Cairo al Grijalva,
6349
Del país gigante, 4299
Del Plata al Niagara, 3709
Delacroix, Jacques Vincent,
1743-1832, 11974
Delafield, Edward, 1794-
1875, 11975
Delafield, John, 1812-
1865 or 6, 3216, 11976
De la Houssaye, Mme. S.,
3217, 3218
De Lancey, William Heathcote,
bp., 1797-1865, 11977
De Land, Charles Victor,
1826-, 6559
Deland, Clyde O., illustr.,
2982, 6520
Deland, Mrs. Margaret
Wade (Campbell) 1857-, 3219
Delano, Alonzo, 1806-1874,
3220
Delaplaine, 11062
Delaplaine, Edward Schley,
1893-, 6560
Delaplaine, Joseph, 1777-

1824, 11978
Delaplaine, Joseph, 1777-1824.
Delaplaine's repository...
11978
De Lara, 3842
Delaware breakwater, 13322
Delaware co., N. Y. - Hist.,
12334
Delaware - Descr. & trav.,
3490, 5147
Delaware - Hist., 2264
Delaware - Hist. - Colonial
period, 3221
Delaware Indians, 12804
Delaware Indians - Fiction,
9840
Delaware Indians - Legends,
6153
Delaware language, 13169
Delaware river, 13321
De La Warr, Thomas West, 3d lord,
1577-1618, 3221
De Leon, Thomas Cooper,
1839-1914, 3222, 3223, 3224,
3225, 3226, 3227
Delgado, José María, 6561
Delia's doctors, 9239
The delight makers, 8673
Delius, Eduard, 3228
Dell, William, d. 1664, 11979,
11980
Delluc, Louis, 1890-1924, 6562
Del Mar, Alexander, 1836-,
11981
Deluge, 11698
Demagny, René, 1930-, 6563
Demarest, James, 1832-, 11982
Demerara (Colony) - Hist.,
1516
Demersay, Alfred, d. 1891,
11983, 11984
Demetz, Frédéric-Auguste,
1796-1873, 3229
Demeunier, Jean Nicolas,
1741-1814, 11985
Deming, Henry Champion,
1815-1872, 6564
Democracy, 5050, 5429, 8465,
11622, 11665, 12304, 12443

Democracy unveiled, 12143
Democrates segundo, 8004
Democratic party, 553, 1160,
1781, 2076, 12253, 13325
Democratic party - Hist.,
1307
Democratic party. National
committee, 1852-1856,
3230
Democratic party. National
committee, 1860-1864,
6565
Democratic party. National
committee, 1864-1868,
6566, 6567, 6568, 6569,
6570, 6571, 6572
Democratic party - New
England, 895
Democratic party. New
York (State), 11931
Democratic party. Penn-
sylvania. Philadelphia.
Committee of corres-
pondence, 2211
De Molai: the last of the
military grand masters
of the order of Templar
Knights, 3466
Demonology, 13049
Demonstración legal en
defensa de d. Joseph del
Pozo y Honesto, 7768
De Morgan, Augustus, 1806-
1871, ed., 2594
Den Ny verden, 4058
Denegri Luna, Félix, 6794
Denmark - Descr. & trav.,
7223, 7224
Dennett, Daniel, 3231
The Dennings and their
beaux, 10195
Denny, Ebenezer, 1761-
1822, 3232
Denominational colleges -
U. S., 2024
De Normandie, James,
1836-1924, 6573
Denslow, W. W., illustr.,
4902

Dent, John Charles, 1841-
1888, 6574
Denys, Nicolas, 1598-1688,
6575
Depredations and massacre by
the Snake River Indians,
5509
Derby, James Cephas, 1818-1892,
3234
Derby, William P., 3235
De Ros, John Frederick Fitzgerald,
1804-1861, 6576, 6577
Derrotero de la expedicion
en la provincia de los Texas,
4742
Derry, Joseph Tyrone, 1841-,
3236
The dervise of Alfouran, 10693
Des crises commerciales et
de leur retour, 13349
Desaché, Gaetán, 6578
De Saussure family (Henry de
Saussure, fl. 1631), 12695
De Saussure, Henry William,
1763-1839, 11744, 12695
Desborough connections, 6975
Descendants of Richard Gardner,
of Woburn, 12412
Descourtilz, Michel-Étienne,
1775-1835, 3237
Descripción de la nueva provincia
de Otuquis en Bolivia, 606
Descripción de las Indias
Occidentales de Antonio de
Herrera, 7034
Descripción de todas las
provincias y reynos del mvndo,
6125
Descripción historial de la
provincia y archipielago de
Chiloe, 2436
Description de la Louisiane,
3836
Description des anciennes
possessions méxicaines du
nord, 6913
Description des débouquemens
qui sont au nord de l'isle
de Saint-Domingue, 1109

Description du Mississippi,
2760
Description géographique
des isles Antilles,
1110
A description of Georgia,
2996
A description of Pitcairn's
island and its inha-
bitants, 884
A description of plants
found in the United
States, 11245
A description of South
Carolina, 3627
A description of Texas,
4974
A description of the
British possessions in
North America, 7454
A description of the
canals and railroads
of the U. S., 5340
Description of the
Cincinnati southern
railway, 3798
A description of the
eastern coast of the
county of Barnstable,
2328
A description of the
last voyage to
Bermudas, 12680
A description of the
plants found in the
United States, north
of Virginia, 11245
A description of the
present state of
that country, 2560
A description of Tremont
house, 12011
A description of Wier's
cave, 4100
Descriptions of terres-
trial shells of North
America, 5080
Descriptive and other
poems, 5605

Descriptive illustrated guide-
book to North Carolina
mountains, 2997
A descriptive reading on
picturesque Mexico, 6603
Descrizione geografica di parte
dell' America settentrionale,
3238
Desde Salamanca, España, hasta
Ciudad Real, Chiapas, 8212
Desengaños sobre las preocupa-
ciones del dia, 6579
Deserts, 3266
The deserter, 9565, 10118, 10670
The deserter's daughter, 9856
Des Essarts, Alfred Stanislaus
Langlois, 1811-1893, 2095
Deshler & Deshler, 10088
The despot of Broomsedge Cove,
4554
Despotic doctrines declared
by the United States Senate
exposed, 12947
Despotism, 11406
The despotism of freedom, 1881
Destiny, 10397
The destiny of the races of
this continent, 1383
Destructive consequences of
dissipation, 10245
Desultoria, 9394
A detail of some particular
services performed in
America, 2096
Détail sur la navigation aux
côtes de Saint-Domingue,
13464
A detection of the proceedings
and practices of the directors
of the Royal African company
of England, 2097
Detective stories, 10529
Detectives - Fiction, 10530
The dethroned heiress, 9446
Detroit - Hist. - Fiction,
6520
Detroit. Public library, 2098
Detroit - Surrender to the
British, 1812, 12741, 12998,

12999, 13000, 13504
Detroit young men's
   society. Library,
   2099, 2100
Der deutsche lausbub in
   Amerika, 2914
Der deutsche Pionier, 3233
Deutschland am Mississippi,
   4187
Les deux Ameriques, 3406
Deux ans au Mexique, 6710
Deux-Ponts, Guillaume,
   comte de, 1745-, 3239
De Vane, 9875
Devens, Samuel Adams, 2101
Devere, Paul, 6580
The devil and Tom Walker,
   9998
The devil in Mexico, 7540
Devil's Ford, 9786
The devil's visit to
   "Old Abe", 1325
De Voe, Thomas Farrington,
   1811-1892, 2102
Devol, George H., 1829-,
   3240
Devot, supposed author,
   12289
The devoted, 10827
The devotion of Enriquez,
   6971
Devotional literature,
   7666, 7668, 7670, 7671,
   7672
Dew, Thomas Roderick, 1802-
   1846, 2103
Dewees, William B., 3241
Dewey, Chester, 1784-1867,
   2251
Dewey, Dellon Marcus,
   11986
Dewey, John, 1859-1952,
   6581
The De Willoughby claim,
   8905
De Witt, Robert M., 13386
Dexter, Flavius Lucius,
   fl. 395, 400
Dexter, Franklin, 1793-1857,

2104
Dexter, Henry Martyn, 1821-
   1890, 6582, 11787
Dexter, John Haven, 1791-1876,
   2105
Dexter, Orrando Perry, 1854-
   1903, 7971
Dey, Peter A., 3255
Deye, Thomas Cockey, 13417
Dhormoys, Paul, 1829-, 6583
Diálogo político, 6584
Dialogue between a one thousand
   dollar clerk and a member
   of Congress, 2106
A dialogue, between a southern
   delegate, and his spouse,
   2107
A dialogue between the confession
   of faith in the Presbyterian
   church, and a preacher in that
   society, 2896
Dialogue on slavery, 3906
Dialogues curieux entre l'auteur
   et un sauvage, 7222
The diamond cross, 10519
Diamond leaves from the lives
   of the Dimond family, 8761
Diamond mines and mining -
   Brazil, 11636
The diamond necklace, 9864
The diamond ring vs. the gold
   ring, 10267
Diana Victrix, 9097
Diaries on the road to Santa Fe,
   7080
Diario de la navegacion y
   reconocimiento del rio Tebi-
   cuari, 593
El Diario, Mexico, 6585
Diario que formo yo el ciudadano
   Antonio Armijo, 2555
Diario y derrotero de lo caminado,
   visto y observado en el
   discurso de la visita general
   de precidios, 4967
The diary of a man of fifty,
   10011
The diary of a milliner, 11202
The diary of a pawnbroker, 9397

The diary of a public man,
6586
Diary of a southern refugee,
4354
Diary of a tour in America,
6241, 6242
Diary of a visit to the
U. S. A. in the year
1883, 5045
The diary of Barton Griffith,
3693
Diary of E. P. Burton, 2865
Diary of the Rev. Solomon
Spittle, 10701
A diary of the wreck of
His Majesty's ship
Challenger, 2108
Diary west of the Alle-
ghanies, 3020
Díaz de Guytián, José,
6536, 7929
Díaz de Léon, Francisco,
1837-1903, ed., 7834
Díaz de Ortega, Felipe,
7535
Diaz Pimienta, Francisco,
8291
Díaz, Ramon, jt. author,
772
Díaz y Díaz, Jesús, 6587
Diccionario biográfico
de historia antigua
de Mejico, 6821
Diccionario historico
e geographico da
provincia de S.
Pedro, 425
Dicey, Edward, 1832-
1911, 3242
Dick Boyle's business
card, 6977
Dick Sands, convict,
10808
Dick Spindler's family
Christmas, 6972
Dickens, Charles, 1812-
1870, 2623, 3243, 6588,
6589, 6590, 6591
Dickens, Charles, 1812-

1870. American notes, 11685
Dickert, D. Augustus, 3244
Dickey, Mrs. Fannie Porter,
comp., 3245
Dickinson, Daniel Stevens,
1800-1866, 6592
Dickinson, James, 1659-1741,
3246
Dickinson, John, 1732-1808,
13509
Dickinson, John R., 6592
Dickinson, Jonathan, 1663-
1722, 3247
Dickinson, Lydia (Knapp) "Mrs.
D. S. Dickinson", 6592
La dictadura de O'Higgins, 5892
A dictionary of all officers,
2402
A dictionary of all religions
and religious donominations,
50
A dictionary of Congregational
usages and principles, 11900
Did he take the prince to ride?
9683
The diddler, 10736
Didimus, H., pseud., 3327
Diehl, Louis, 3248
Dicner, Frau Mietze (Glanz),
6593
Diez De La Calle, Juan,
fl. 1646, 6594
A difference in clay, 10283
Digby: chess professor, 8716
A digest of tropical Mexico,
7823
Dilke, Sir Charles Wentworth,
bart., 1843-1911, 3249
Dillon, Arthur, abbé, 8054
Dimitrios and Irene, 9279
Dimitry, Charles Patton, 1837-
1910, 3250
Dimock, Anthony Weston,
1842-1918, 3251
The dinner horn, 3316
A dinner in poverty flat, 9533
Dinner speaking, 9683
Dinwiddie, William, 1867-1934,
6595

133

Diomed, 11196
Dionysius the weaver's
heart's dearest, 10947
Diphtheria - Boston,
1735-1736, 2119
A diplomat's diary, 9257
Diplomatic code of the
United States of
America, 12027
Diplomatic memoirs, 6766
Diptera - Mexico, 1099
The disappearance syndicate
and Senator Stanley's
story, 9238
The disappointed cater-
pillar, 10046
Disappointed love, 10089
The disappointment, 926
The discarded wife, 9447
Disciples of Christ,
3977, 5288, 7378
Disciples of Christ -
Ky., 4866
Discours en vers, adressé
aux officiers, 13009
A discourse and view of
Virginia, 1198
A discourse occasioned
by the death of Brigadier-
General John M'Pherson,
1667
Discourse of Dr. Breckin-
ridge, 2791
A discourse on the aborigines
of the Ohio Valley, 3797
A discourse on the first
centennial celebration of
the birthday of Washington,
2885
A discourse on the genius
and character of the
Rev. Horace Holley 2886
A discourse on the life,
character, and services
of Daniel Drake, M. D.,
3706
A discourse upon the good
work, 12643
Discourses and proceedings

at the dedication of the...
Unitarian church in Charleston,
S. C., 11746
Discourses delivered by appoint-
ment, before the Cincinnati
medical library association,
3286
Discourses on Davila, 59
A discovered pearl, 9575
Discoveries (in geography),
1081, 1979, 7657, 11332
Discoveries (in geography) -
French, 12082
Discoveries (in geography) -
Portuguese, 882
Discoveries (in geography) -
Russian, 11623
The discoveries of John Lederer,
4236
Discovery and exploration, 6431
Discovery and settlement of
the valley of the Mississippi,
4502
Discovery of the sources of
the Mississippi, 1135
Discovery (ship), 8283
Discurso apologético, médico
astronómico, 6480
Disenthralled, 9455
A disillusioned occultist, 8717
Disney, Daniel, 6596
Dissection, 2081
Dissertatio graduallis de
plantatione ecclesiae svecanae,
1364
A dissertation on the freedom
of navigation and maritime
commerce, 941
Dissertation sur la traite et
le commerce des Nègres, 1114
A dissertation upon the consti-
tutional freedom of the press,
11987
Distances - Tables, etc., 4491
District of Columbia, 12028
District of Columbia - Area, 151
District of Columbia cavalry.
1st regt., 1863-1864, 4458
District of Columbia infantry,

134

the late war, 11458
Dodd, Stephen, ed., 11688
Dodds, James, 6605
Dodge, Grenville Mellen,
1831-1916, 5686
Dodge, Jacob Richards,
1823-1902, 2113
Dodge, Mary Abigail, 1833-
1896, 2114, 3262, 8597
Dodge, Paul Hunter, ed.,
7287
Dodge, Robert, 1820-1899,
2115
Dodge, William, 1811-1875,
2397
Dodge, William Castle,
1827-1914, 11989
Dodge, William Earl,
1805-1883, 2116
Dodge, William Sumner, 3263
Doesticks, K. Philander,
pseud., 11038
Dog and gun, 3924
Dogs - Legends and stories,
11196
Dohla, Johann Conrad,
1750-1820, 3264
Doing Mexico with James,
7047
Doings in Maryland, 10258
Dollars and cents, 11085
Dollero, Adolfo, 6606
The Dolly dialogues, 9804
Dolly Dillenbeck, 9534
Dolores, 10193, 10631
Dolph, Eliza, 2221
Dolph Heyliger, 9995
Domenech, Emmanuel Henri
Dieudonné, 1826-1886,
3265, 3266, 6607, 6608,
6609
The domestic and profes-
sional life of Ann
Preston, 9331
Domestic committee, 3267
Domestic economy, 9617,
10786
Domestic explosives and
other sixth column

fancies, 8492
Domestic manners of the
Americans, 5463
Domestic service illustrated,
10726
Domestic sketches, 8624
Domingo de Guzman, Saint,
1170-1221, 7271
Domingo, Marcelino, 1884-,
6610
Domínguez, Josefina, 6611
Dominica, 545
Dominican republic - Descr. &
trav., 2201, 6583, 6726,
9489
Dominican republic - Econ.
cond., 6726
Dominican republic - Hist.,
11348
Dominicans in Mexico, 1762,
6276, 7860, 8212
Dominion government expedition
to Hudson Bay and the Arctic
Islands, 6302
The Dominion of Canada with
Newfoundland and an excursion
to Alaska, 5979
Don Balasco of Key West, 9673
Don Bullebulle, 6612
Don Miff, 3157
Don Orsino, 6494, 9223
Don Santiago Kirker the Indian
fighter, 3268
Don Sebastian, 10338
Donald Marcy, 11070
Donaldson, Mrs. Nanna
(Smithwick), comp., 5223
Donaldson, Sir Stuart Alexander,
1812-1867, 6613
Donaldson, Thomas, 1815-1877,
2117
Doneghy, George W., 3269
Donelson, Fort, Battle of,
1862, 2050
Doniphan, Alexander William,
4957, 4989
Doniphan's expedition,
1846-1847, 3068, 3343, 3962,
4989, 5753, 8408

136

Donnavan, Corydon, 6614,
6615
Donnelly, Eleanor Cecilia,
1838-1917, 10675
Doolittle, James Rood,
1815-1897, 6616
The doom of the Rebel
guard, 11190
The doom of the tory's
guard, 9293
The doomed chief, 10958
Dora Norton, 10580
Dora Raymond, 8806
Dorchester, Mass. - Hist.,
1395
Doré, Gustave, 1832-1883,
illustr., 7396
A Doric reed, 3040
Dörnberg, Karl Ludwig,
freiherr von, 1749-1819,
3270
Dornblaser, Thomas Franklin,
1841-, 3271
Dorothea (Ship), 1067
Dorothy, 10163
Dorr, J. C. R., 10163
Dorr rebellion, 1842,
11917, 13220
Dorsey, Mrs. Anna Hanson
(McKenney) 1815-1896,
10675
Dorsey, Ella Loraine,
1853-1935, 10675
Dorsey, Mrs. Sarah Anne
(Ellis) 1829-1879,
3272, 3273, 3274
Dos Américas, 2941
Dottings by the wayside,
10423
Dottings on the roadside,
7750
The double suicide, 9419
The double veil, 10298
A double wedding, 5612
Dougall, Allan H., 6617
Dougherty, John, 5503
Dougherty, Michael, 3275
Dougherty, Peter, 1805-
1894, tr., 2375

Douglas Camp, Ill., 3085
Douglas, Dana, of Georgia,
5335
Douglas, David, 3923
Douglas, James, 5839
Douglas, John, surgeon in
British army, 2118
Douglas, Stephen Arnold,
1813-1861, 2109, 5933,
5935, 6021, 6115, 6346,
6738, 7036, 7175, 7284,
7383, 7416, 11590
Douglas, Stephen Arnold,
1813-1861. Popular
sovereignty in the terri-
tories, 1368, 11916
Douglas, Stephen, pseud., 6115
Douglass, Adam, supposed
author, 9991
Douglass, Frederick, 1817-
1895, 6618
Douglass, William, 1691-1752,
2119, 3276
Dove (Sailing vessel), 7374
Dovecoat, 9873
Dow, Lorenzo, 1777-1834, 2120,
3277
Dow, Neal, 1804-1897, 1916
Dow, Mrs. Peggy (Holcombe)
1780-1820, 3278
Dowdell, James Ferguson,
1818-1871, 2121
Dowling, Joseph A., reporter,
12834
Dowling, Morgan E., 3279
Down among the Crackers,
8997
Down by the sea, 10899
The Down-easters, 10407
Down in Tennessee, 3611
Down memory's lane, 6199
Down north on the Labrador,
6900
Down South, 3202, 3779
Down the great river, 3622
Down the ravine, 4555
Down the river, 9910
The down-trodden, 10787
Downey, Edgar, 6619, 6620

137

Downing, Andrew Jackson,
1815-1852, 2122, 11990
Downing, Clement, 2123
Downing, Jack, pseud.,
10818-10822
Dowse, Thomas, 1772-1856,
6621, 12114
Dox, Peter Myndert,
1813-1891, 2124
Doyle, Sir Arthur Conan,
1859-1930, 6622
Doyle, William, 6623
Dozier, Orion Theophilus,
1848-1925, 3280
Draft riot, 1863, 117,
852, 2347, 11294
Drage, Theodore Swaine,
6624
Dragoon campaigns to the
Rocky Mountains, 3867
Dragoon expedition, 3281
Dragut, the corsair,
10338
Drake, Benjamin, 1794-
1841, 3282, 3283, 3284
Drake, Daniel, 1785-1852,
3285, 3286, 3287, 3288,
3289, 3290, 3291, 3292,
3293, 3706
Drake, James Madison,
1837-1913, 3294
Drake, Samuel Adams, 1833-
1905, 3295, 3296, 3297
Drake, Samuel Gardner,
1798-1875, 991, 2125,
11279, 11991
The drama in Pokerville,
9514
The drama of an evening,
10135
Dramatic persons and
moods, 4780
Dramatic sketch, 10172
Draper, John William,
1811-1882, 2126
Draper, Lyman Copeland,
1815-1891, 2127, 3509,
5754
Drascomb, Alfred Brooks,

1837-1894, 6625
Drax, Henry, 1080
Draxy Miller's dowry, 10006
Drayton, 5149
Drayton, John, 1766-1822,
3298
The dreadful sufferings and
thrilling adventures of an
overland party of emigrants
to California, 2700
Dream life, 10360
The dream of a loafer, 9486
The dreamers, 8676
Dreams and realities in the life
of a pastor and teacher,
9474
Dred, 10903
Dreer, Ferdinand Julius,
1812-, 11546
Drees, Ada M. C., ed., 6626
Drees, Charles William, 6626
Drei Jahre in Amerika, 2668
Drescher, Emil, ed., 5773
Dressed to death, 10672
Drew, C. S., 3299
A drift from Redwood Camp, 9789
Drift from two shores, 9779
The drift of the war, 11597
"Drifting about", 10321
Driggs, George W., 3300
Dring, Thomas, 1758-1825,
2128
Drinkwater, D. F., 2129
Drinkwater, John, 1882-1937,
5995
Driven from the path, 10799
Le droit des neutres sur mer,
12222
Droop Mountain, W. Va., Battle
of, Nov. 6, 1863, 2038
Drowne's wooden image, 9823
Drummond, Sir Gordon, 1772-
1854, 11782
Drummond, Josiah H., 3592,
6627
The drunkard, 10492
Duane, James, 1733-1797, 13316
Duane, Richard Bache,
1824?-1875, 6628

Duane, W. N., 11657
Duane, William, 1807-
1882, 2130, 2731
Duarte Level, Lino,
6629
Du Barry, Edmund L.,
tr., 7767
Du Bois, Coert, 1881-,
6333
Dubois, Marcel, i.e.
Edmond Marcel, 1856-,
7736
Du Bois, William Ewing,
1801-1881, jt. author,
2173
Du Bose, John Witherspoon,
1836-1918, 3301
Duché, Jacob, 1737-1798,
11992
The duchess and Sancho,
10197
The Duchess of Baden,
9532
Du Chilleau, Marie-
Charles, marquis,
7941
Duclós-Salinas, Adolfo,
6630
Duden, Gottfried, 3302
Dudley, Ethelbert,
1818-1862, 7737
Dudley family, 101
Dudley family (Thomas
Dudley, 1576-1653),
101
Dudley, John, 1805-1898,
2131
Dudley, John Langdon,
1812-1894, 6631
Dudley, Mass. - Hist.,
963
Dudley, Thomas Underwood,
6632
Dudley's defeat, 1813,
2004
Due south, 5992
Dueling, 1063, 2807, 9910
Dueñas Bolante, Fernando
de, 6633

Duff, Louis Blake, 1878-.
Portage Road, 8201
Duffels, 9463
Dufferin and Ava, Hariot
Georgina (Hamilton), 6634
Duffield, George, 1794-1868,
3303, 3304
Dufour, Auguste Henri, 1798-
1865, 7396
Dufur, Simon Miltimore, 1843-,
3305
Dugan, James, 3306
Duganne, Augustine Joseph
Hickey, 1823-1884, 3307,
11993
Dugard, Marie, 1862-, 3308
Dugas, George, 1833-, 6635
Dugué, Charles Oscar, 1821-,
3309, 3310, 3311
Du Halde, Jean Baptiste, 1674-
1743, 2466
Duke, Basil Wilson, 1838-1916,
3312, 3417
Duke, John K., 1844-, 3313
The Duke of Stockbridge, 8774
The duke's chase, 10267
Dukes co., Mass. - Hist. -
Sources, 12931
Dulac, George, pseud., 10507
Dulieu, Marie Henri Joseph,
1815-, 3314
Duluth, 4191
Dumas, Alex T., ed., 3122
Dumas, Alexandre, 1802-1870,
2132
Dumas, Alexandre (père) 1802-
1870. Le comte de Monte-
Cristo (sequels) 3467
Dumas, Mathieu, comte, 1753-
1807, 3315
Dumas, William Thomas, 1858-,
3316
The dumb girl, 10492
Dummer. Fort, 13051
Dumont de Montigny, Lieutenant,
3317
Dumont, Mary Wolfe, jt. author,
4941
Dunant, Jean Henri, 1828-, 2133

Dunbar, Edward E., 6636
Dunbar family, 6637
Dunbar, John, 3318
Dunbar, M., 6637
Dunbar, Seymour, 6638
Duncan Adair, 9251
Duncan, Mrs. Mary (Grey)
  Lundie, 3319
Duncan, John Morison,
  6639
Duncan, Thomas D., 3320
Dunckel, Johann Daniel,
  8037
Dundass, Samuel Ruther-
  ford, 3321
Dundonald, Thomas Cochrane,
  10th earl of, 1775-1860,
  6640, 8112
Dunham, Josiah, 1769-1844,
  2134
Duniway, Mrs. Abigail
  (Scott) 1834-1915, 3322
Dunkley & Woodman, New
  York, pub., 1756
Dunlap, William, 1766-1839,
  2135, 2136
Dunlevy, A. H., 2137
Dunn, Ballard S.,
  1829-1897, 2138
Dunn, John, 3323
Dunn, Thomas, 1761?-1833,
  2139
A Dunnet shepherdess, 10042
Dunning, Homer N., 1827-,
  2140
Dunraven, Windham Thomas
  Wyndham-Quin, 4th earl
  of, 1841-1926, 6641
Dunshee, Henry Webb, 2141
Dunstable, Mass. - Hist.,
  2297
Dunton, Larkin, 1828-1899,
  ed., 6440
Dupin de Sainte-André,
  1840-1921, 6642
Du Ponceau, Peter Stephen,
  1760-1844. Eulogium in
  commemoration of the
  Honorable William Tilghman,

12296
Dupont, Chevalier de, 8320,
  8321
Du Pont, Henry Algernon,
  1838-1926, 3324
Du Pont, Samuel Francis, 2142
Dupré, Joseph, 1742-1823, 6643
Duquesne, Fort - Hist. -
  Fiction, 10293, 10443
Durán, Diego, d. 1588? 6644
Duran, Rafael, jt. author, 5884
Durand, John, 1822-1908, 6645
Durand, Luz María, 6646
Durand, of Dauphiné, 3325
Dureau, Baptiste, 1820-, 3326
Durell, Edward Henry, 1810-,
  3327
Durham, John George Lambton,
  1st earl of, 1792-1840, 6647,
  6648
The Durket sperret, 3363
Du Roi, August Wilhelm, 3328
Du Ru, Paul, 1666-1741, 3329
Duryée's brigade, 1862, 12926
Dussieux, Louis Étienne, 1815-
  1894, 6649
Dust, 9807
The Dutch dominie of the
  Catskills, 10396
Dutch Guiana - Descr. & trav.,
  1193, 1484, 5319, 11382
Dutch in Brazil, 339
Dutch in Indiana, 1230
Dutch in New York (City) -
  Poetry, 12904
Dutch in the U. S., 1234, 11327
The Dutch pilgrim fathers,
  ˙12904
Dutcher, Salem, jt. author,
  4105
Dutchess Co., N. Y. - Hist.,
  1402
The Dutchman's fireside,
  10483, 10484
Dutrône la Couture, Jacques-
  François, 6650
Dutton, George, 2143
The duty of American women
  to their country, 1042

The duty of living for the good of posterity, 11731
Duval, John Crittenden, 1816-1897, 3330
Duvergier de Hauranne, Ernest, i.e. Louis Prosper Ernest, 1843-, 3331
Duychinck, Evert Augustus, 1816-1878, 435, 3332
Duyckinck, Evert Augustus, 1816-1878. Cyclopaedia of American literature, 12456
Duycinck, George L., jt. ed., 3332
Dwars door het land van Roosevelt, 4189
Dwellers in Gotham, 10053
Dwight, Edward Strong, 1820-1890, 2144
Dwight, Theodore, 1764-1846, 229, 2145, 2146, 2147
Dwight, Theodore, jr., 3173
Dwight, Timothy, 1752-1817, 2148
Dwight, William, 1831-1888, 2587
Dyar, C. W., jt. author, 10371
Dye, John Smith, 2149
Dyer, David, 2150
Dyer, George, 1755-1841, ed., 13489
Dyer, John Percy, 6651
Dyer, John Will, 3333
Dyer, Olive, 3657
The dying confession of Joseph Hare, 3781
Dymock, Cressy, 12735
Dymond, Jonathan, 1796-1828, 2151
Dyson, Howard F., 6652
Dyspepsy, 10492
Dzhalagoniĭa, Valeriĭ Pavlovich, jt. author, 7189

The eagle of the Mohawks, 10744
Eagle Pass, Tex., 8958
The eagle's heart, 9603
Earl, J. C., illustr., 8516
Earl Rupert, 10403
Earle, Pliny, 1809-1892, 2152
Early American orations, 7005
Early biography, travels and adventures of Rev. James Champlin, 2967
Early days in Arkansas, 4825
Early days of the Yukon, 7630
The early history of the southern states, 12754
Early, Jubal Anderson, 1816-1894, 2153
Early Maryland poetry, 3077, 5264
Early narratives of the Northwest, 4144
Early times in the Massachusetts, 10724
Early travels in the Tennessee country, 5723
Early years in the far west, 12559
An earnest address to such of the people called Quakers, 2154
Earthly care, a heavenly discipline, 10910
Earthquakes, 2303, 6008, 12800
Earthquakes - Jamaica, 12208
Earthquakes - New England, 2303
Earthquakes - The West, 4793
Earthquakes - Venezuela, 2396
Earth's holocaust, 9823
East and west, 5380, 10032
The east coast of Florida, 3813
East, Ernest Edward, 1885-, 6653
East (Far East) - Descr. & trav., 6413
East (Far East) - Hist., 882
East Hampton, N. Y. - Church history, 1660
East Hampton, N. Y. - Descr.,

2395
East Hampton, N. Y. - Hist.,
1064, 2395
East Haven, Conn. Congre-
gational church, 2155
East Indies - Descr. &
trav., 488, 4900
East, Melville A., 7715
East Tennessee relief asso-
ciation at Knoxville, 2156
Eastburn, James Wallis, 1797-
1819, 2157
Eastburn, Joseph, 1748-1828,
12377
Eastburn, Robert, 1710-1778,
2158, 11994
An Easter king, 9330
The Easter of La Mercedes,
10448
Eastern question (Balkan),
11466, 11467
Eastern question (Far East),
7913
Eastern states - Descr. &
trav., 2101
Eastford, 10255
Eastman, Charles Gamage,
1816-1860, 1687
Eastman family (Roger
Eastman, 1611-1694),
2161
Eastman, Francis Smith,
1803-1846 or 7, 11995
Eastman, Hubbard, d. 1891,
2159
Eastman, John Robie,
1836-1913, 2160
Eastman, Lucius Root,
1809-1892, 2161
Eastman, Mary F., 6654
Eastman, Mrs. Mary
(Henderson) 1818-, 2162,
2163, 3334, 11996
Eastman, Samuel Coffin,
2164
Eastman, Seth, 1808-1875,
illustr., 2163, 11996
Easton, Hosea, 2165
Easton, James, 2166

Easton, John, 1617-1705, 2167
Easton, Mass. - Hist., 2958
Easton, Pa. Library company,
11997
Easy Warren and his contemporaries,
9063
Eat not thy heart, 9258
Eaton, Amos, 1776-1842, 2168
Eaton, Arthur Wentworth, ed.,
4074
Eaton, Asahel K., 1571
Eaton, B. A., 11998
Eaton, Edward Byrom, 11999
Eaton, Francis Brown, 1825-1904,
12000
Eaton, H. M., illustr., 5392
Eaton, Horace, 1810-1883, 12001
Eaton, Jacob, 2169
Eaton, John Henry, 1790-1856,
4996, 12002
Eaton, Rebecca, 2170
Eaton, Samuel John Mills, 1820-
1889, 2171
Eaton, Thomas Treadwell, 1845-
1907, 6655
Eaton, William, 1764-1811, 2172
Eaves, Catherine, pseud., 6656
Ebb-tide, 10968
Ebeling, Christoph Daniel,
1741-1817, ed., 322
Eben Holden, 8627
Eby, Henry Harrison, 1841-, 3335
Ecce femina, 10498, 10499
Eccentric characters, 10291,
10310
Ecclesiastical law - Massa-
chusetts, 856, 1635
Ecclesiastical reminiscences of
the U. S., 5643
Echave y Roxas, Pedro Antonio
de, 6368
Echezárraga, Juan de, 6657
An echo, 9916
Echoes from Dartmouth, 9734
Echoes from the backwoods,
4266
Echoes from the south, 4814
Echoes of a belle, 10740
Echoes of the past, 4355

142

Echols, John, 2038
Echo's aus den Urwäldern, 7272
Eckfeldt, Jacob Reese, 1803-1872, 2173
Eckley, Joseph, 1750-1811, 2174
Eckman, James, 6658
The eclipse, 2175
Economic conditions, 1947
Economics, 11446
Ecuador - Antiq., 6868, 11330
Ecuador - Descr. & trav., 7946, 8168, 8299
Ecuador - Hist., 6370, 6868
Ecuador - Hist. - Wars of independence, 1809-1830, 7322
Ecuador - Pol. & govt. - To 1809, 7946
Eddis, William, 1745?-, 3336
Eddowes, Ralph, 1751-1833, 2176
Eddy, Caleb, 2177
Eddy, Daniel Clarke, 1823-1896, 2178
Eddy, Richard, 1828-1906, 3337, 6659
Eddy, Robert Henry, 1812-1887, 2179
Eddy, Thomas, 1758-1827, 2180
An edelweiss of the Sierras, 9764
Eden, John, 2181
The Eden of the South, 5647
Eden, Richard, 1521?-1576, 373, 5920
Eden, Robert C., d. 1907, 3338
Edes, Richard Sullivan, 1810-1877, 4425
Edgar County Historical Society, Paris, Illinois, 6660

Edgar Co., Ill., 6660
Edgar Huntly, 8859
Edge, Frederick Milnes, 12003
Edge-hill, 9836
Edgerton, A. P., 2978
Edisto rifles, 4033
Edith, 9339
Edith Lyle, 3911
Edith Moreton, 8892
Edith Vernon, 9451
Edmond Dantes, 3467
Edmonds, Francis William, 1806-1863, 2182
Edmonds, S. Emma E., 3339
Edmund Dawn, 8765
Edmundson, William, 1627-1712, 3340
Edna Browning, 3912, 9895
Education, 2280, 2569, 2797, 5241, 5247, 5248
Education - Addresses, essays, lectures, 1044, 2249, 2888, 3742, 5780, 11595
Education and society, 1222
Education and state, 1222
Education at the West, 2024
Education - Congresses, 13340
Education - Cuba, 611
Education, Higher, 12707, 13340
Education - Ireland, 1528
Education - Manitoba-Winnipeg, 6217
Education - Maryland, 8316
Education - New England, 829, 8919, 11637
Education - New Hampshire - Hist., 11418
Education - New York (State) - Hist., 8697
Education of women, 1045, 9548, 11939
Education of women - U. S., 1046
Education - Ohio - Cincinnati, 2267
Education - Pennsylvania, 2319
Education - Period., 260, 261, 289
Education - Poetry, 1618

Eisenberg, Maurice, jt. author, 8664

Eisenschiml, Otto, 1800-, 6667

Ekins, Sir Charles, 1768-1855, 2187

El Salvador - Descr. & trav., 7974

El Salvador - Period., 7951

Ela, Jacob Hart, 1820-1884, 2188

Elder, William, 1806-1885, 2189, 12005

Elder William Brewster and the Brewster family of Portsmouth, New Hampshire, 6163

The elder's wife, 10006

The eldest sister, 10730

El Dorado, 1670, 5351, 8157, 8158

Eleanor, 9240

Eleanor Cuyler, 9363

Election law - Massachusetts, 1264

The election of president of the United States, 2190

Election sermons - Connecticut, 1097, 1549, 1602, 1724, 12040, 12303, 13033

Election sermons - Massachusetts, 157, 220, 417, 832, 841, 1182, 1963, 2335, 2451, 11516, 11806, 13031, 13407

Election sermons - New Hampshire, 11420, 11502, 11504, 11792, 12050, 12361, 12551

Election (Theology), 619

Elections - Otsego Co., N. Y., 13072

Elections - Pennsylvania - Corrupt practices, 13101

Elegant Tom Dillar, 10298

Elegiac epistles on the calamities of love and war, 2191

An elegiac ode, 3930

An elegy on the late Honorable Titus Hosmer, esq., 811

The elements of national greatness, 11772

Elemjay, Louise, 3357

Elephants, Fossil, 928

An elephant's track, 3191

L'élevation et la chute de l'empereur Maximilien, 7188

Elfreide of Guldal, 4390

Elgin, Ill. - Hist., 7052

Elinor Fulton, 10185

Eliot, John, 1604-1690, 12006, 13141

Eliot, John, 1754-1813, 12007, 12168

Eliot, Jonathan, 1784-1846, 12008

Eliot, Samuel, 1821-1898, 12009

Eliot, Samuel Atkins, 1798-1862, 2104

Eliot, Thomas Dawes, 1808-1870, 12010

Eliot, William Harvard, 1796-1831, 12011

Elisabeth, princess of France, 1764-1794, 11440

Elivas, Knarf, pseud., 10709

The elixir of gold, 5614

The elixir of life, 9825

Eliza Farnharm, 10195

Elizabeth, Christian scientist, 9241

Elizaga, Domingo de, 7910

Elizaga, Lorenzo, 12012

Elizaga, Manuel Cayetano de, 7910

Elizalde, Matias, 8278

Elkanah Brewster's temptation, 10427

Elkins, Hervey, 12013

Elkswatawa, 3545

Ellen, 3782

Ellen Durand, 8711

Ellen Grafton, the lily of Lexington, 8700

Ellen Parry, 8846
Ellet, Charles, 1810-1862,
  12014, 12015, 12016, 12017,
  12018, 12019
Ellet, Mrs. Elizabeth Fries
  (Lummis) 1818-1877, 3358,
  3359, 12020, 12021, 12022,
  12023
Ellice, Edward, 6668
Ellicott, Andrew, 1754-
  1820, 3360, 12024
Ellicott, Thomas, 1738-
  1799, 12100
Ellie, 9106
Ellington, George, pseud.,
  12025
Elliot, Jonathan, 1784-
  1846, comp., 12026,
  12027, 12028
Elliot, Samuel, 1777-
  1845, 12029
Elliot, Samuel Hayes,
  1809-1869, 12030
Elliot, Sir Thomas
  Frederick, 1808-1880,
  12031
Elliot, William, 12032,
  12033
Elliott, Benjamin, 1786-
  1836, 12034
Elliott, Charles, 1792-
  1869, 12035, 12036
Elliott, Charles Wyllys,
  1817-1883, 12037
Elliott, E. N., ed.,
  3361
Elliott, Franklin Reuben,
  1817-1878, 12038
Elliott, Jesse Duncan,
  1782-1845, 934, 1697,
  12039
Elliott, John, 1768-1824,
  12040
Elliott, John F., 3362
Elliott, Sarah Barnwell,
  1848-1928, 3363, 3364,
  3365, 3366, 3367, 3368
Elliott society of natural
  history, Charleston,

S. C., 12049
Elliott, Stephen, 1771-1830,
  12041
Elliott, Stephen, bp., 1806-
  1866, 12042, 12043, 12044,
  12045, 12046, 12047
Elliott, William, 1788-1863,
  3369, 3370, 12048
Ellis, Charles Mayo, 1818-1878,
  6669
Ellis, Daniel, 1827-, 3371
Ellis, Edward Sylvester, 1840-
  1916, 3372, 3373
Ellis, Ferdinand, 1780-1858,
  12050
Ellis, G. A., 12051
Ellis, George Edward, 1814-1894,
  12052, 12053, 12054, 12055,
  12056
Ellis, George W., 12057
Ellis, Henry, 6670
Ellis, Henry, 1721-1806, 12058
Ellis, James Tandy, 1868-1942,
  3374
Ellis, John B., 12059
Ellis, Mina (Benson) Hubbard,
  6671
Ellis, Rufus, 1819-1885,
  12060
Ellis, Thomas T., 3375
Ellsworth, Ephraim Elmer, 7888
Elmore, Franklin Harper, 1799-
  1850, 1339
Elmore, James Buchanan, 1857-
  1942, 3376, 3377
Elocution, 2400
Eloge de M. Franklin, 2025
Elsie Magoon, 3556
Elsie Venner, 9905
Elsket, 10460
Elson, George, 6671
Elton, Romeo, 1790-1870, 12061
Elvas, Gentleman of, 5469, 7825
Elwyn, Thomas, 2192
Ely, Alfred, 1815-1892, 3378
Ely, Mrs. Hary Harris (Monteith),
  1824-1849, 12465
Elze, Karl, i.e. Friedrich Karl,
  1821-1889, ed., 533

146

Emancipate your colonies, 1180
Emancipation in the West Indies, 5385, 8181
Emancipation proclamation, 2276, 6669, 7258, 7335, 7466, 7781, 13237
Emancipation proclamation - Bibl., 5836
The embargo, 1626
Embargo, 1807-1809, 75, 974, 1626, 11281, 11555, 13088
Embarrassments, 7118, 10012
Embiotocidae, 109
The embroidered handkerchief, 10194
Emch, Arnold, 1871-, 3379
Emch, Hermann, jt. author, 3379
Emerson, Gouverneur, 1796-1874, 13234
Emerson, Joseph, 1777-1833. Letter to the members of the Genessee consociation, 12203
Emerson, Ralph Waldo, 1803-1882, 6267, 8175
Emerson, William, 1769-1811, 1645
Emery, Joshua, jr., 1807-1882, 2193
The emigrant, 5381, 6996
The emigrant's and traveler's guide to the West, 2595
The emigrant's friend, 4107
The emigrant's guide, 1933, 3350, 3380
The emigrant's guide to and description of the U. S. A., 3057
The emigrant's guide to California, 5345
Emigrant's guide to the gold mines of Upper California, 5125
The emigrant's guide to the new republic, 5369

The emigrant's guide to the United States of America, 12846
The emigrant's guide to the western and southwestern states, 3169
The emigrant's guide to the western states of America, 4919
The emigrant's handbook, and guide to Wisconsin, 12169
The emigrant's mother, 8623
Emigranternas land, 4194
The emigrants, 10921
Emigration and immigration, 1562
Emigration and immigration law - Canada, 7967
Emigration and immigration law - U. S., 11533
Emigration, emigrants and know-nothings, 2194
Emigration or no emigration, 4789
Emigration. Practical advice to emigrants, 2195
Emigration to Texas, 5365
Emigration to Virginia, 4596
Émigrés, 398, 777
Emily Chester, 10732
Emily Mayland, 9194
Emma Walton, 9448
Emmanuel; the story of the Messiah, 9125
Emmerich-Högen, Ferdinand, 1858-, 6672
Emmerton, James Arthur, 3381
Emmons, Richard, 1788-, 2196, 2197, 3382, 3383, 3384
Emory, William Hensley, 1811-1887, 5513, 5516
Empresa editora, s.a., 6673
The Empress of the ocean, 9721
The empty heart, 10938
En Amérique; de New York à la Nouvelle-Orléans, 3975
En camino hacia la democracia, 7682
En courant, le monde, 4751

En deux CV chez les
primitifs, 7310
En los Estados Unidos,
4402
En México y Cuba, 6513
En resa til Norra
America, 7170
En tierra yankee, 5150
En visite chez l'Oncle
Sam, 4381
The Encantadas, 10346
The enchanted babyhouse,
10046
The enchanted beauty,
9470
An enchanted castle, 4781
The enchanted typewriter,
8677
Enciso, Martín Fernandez
de, 6674
Encyclopedias and diction-
aries, 240, 2315
The end of a coil, 11094
The end of earth, 10224
The end of the vendetta,
9355
The end of the world, 9464
Endeavor doin's down to
the Corners, 9189
An enemy to the king,
10878
Engels, L., 12062
England - Descr. & trav.,
1832, 1834, 7170, 7207,
11923
England from a back-window,
8641
Der engländischen pflanz-
stadte in Nord-America,
6260
Engleheart, Sir John
Gardner Dillman, 1823-
1923, 3385
The English-American, his
travail by sea and land,
2366
An English combatant, 968
English, Henry, 1803-1855,
12063

English in Illinois, 2258
The English in the West Indies,
6786
English invasion, 1806-1807,
12249
The English lady, 10310
English language - Dialects,
Negro, 3643
English language - Dictionaries -
Algonquian, 7224
English language - Dictionaries -
Chippewa, 770
English language - Dictionaries -
Maya, 7590
English language - Rhetoric,
11723
English liberties, 11660
English literature - Bibl., 212
English literature (Collections),
1631
English literature - Early modern
(to 1700) - Bibl., 1631
English literature (Selections:
Extracts, etc.), 9517, 9616
English neutrality, 13405
The English orphans, 3913
The English practice, 12065
English satire, 5799
English serfdom and American
slavery, 2974
The English sportsman in the
western prairies, 1197
English West Indian Expedition,
1759, 2399
English West Indian Expedition,
1654-1655, 1507, 12368
English West Indian Expedition,
1739-1742, 311, 1829, 13339
English West Indian Expedition,
1759, 12209
English, William Hayden, 1822-
1896, 3386, 12064
The Englishman deceived, 13474
An Englishman in America, 6922
An Englishman's answer, to the
address, from the delegates
to the people of Great-Britain,
13388
The Englishman's guide book to

1504
Epitaphs - Northampton,
Mass., 1504
Epitaphs - U. S., 136
Epitaphs - Worcester,
Mass., 945
Epitoma de legis hvmane,
5883
Epping, Charlotte, S. J.,
ed., 3328
Equality, 8775, 11769
Equity pleading and pro-
cedure, 11480
Equity pleading and pro-
cedure - New York (State),
1389
Erasmus, Desiderius,
d. 1536, 12072
Erato, 3560
Ercilla y Zúñiga, Alonso de,
1533-1594, 6677, 6678,
6679, 6680, 6681, 6682,
6683, 6684, 6685, 6686,
6687, 6688
Erie Indians - Poetry,
5692
Erie, Lake, Battle of, 1813,
967, 1682, 1697, 1816,
12039
Erie railroad, 12696
Erinnerungen aus Amerika,
2644
Erinnerungen aus Süd-Amerika,
1245
Ermatinger, Edward, 1797-
1876, 12073, 12074
Ernest Carroll, 9659
Ernest Grey, 10334
Ernest Linwood, 9839
Ernest Quest, 3504
Erni, Henry, 12075
Eros, 9316
Eros and Anteros, 8935
An errand to the South
in the summer of 1862,
4379
An errant wooing, 9765
Erring, yet noble, 10602
The errors of education,

9890
Erwin, Milo, 3389
Esbozo de la historia de los
primeros diez años de la
revolución agraria de México,
7515
Escalala, 1000
Escalante Fontaneda, Hernando d',
3390
Escalera, Evaristo, 6689
The escape, 11010
The escape of Cowley and
Sawyer from the Indians, 10570
The escape of McKean's scouting
party in Otsego county, 10570
Escapes from Cayenne, 11765
L'esclavage aux Etats-Unis, 12237
Les esclaves, 2433
Escobar, Alonso de, 7917
Escobar, Jerónimo de, 8168
Escobar, Manuel de, 6690
Escobedo, Federico, 1874-, tr.,
7233, 7234
The escorted lady, 10197
Escritor, pseud., 9068
Escudo de armas de Mexico, 1787
La escultura de Palenque, 6788
La esfinge mestiza, 7824
Eskimo language - Glossaries,
vocabularies, etc., 8252
Eskimos, 2464, 6302, 12560
Eslava, Sebastian de, 1685-
1759, 13334
An Esmeralda of Rocky Canon, 6972
Esopus Indians - Wars, 1655-
1660, 11518
Espeio de la perfecta casada,
7032, 7033
Esperance, 10169
Esperanza, 9484
Espino Barros, Eugenio, 6691
Espinosa, Antonio, 8433
Espinosa, José D., ed., 7836
Espinosa, José María, b. 1796,
7762
Espinosa, Miguel de, 6160
Espy, Josiah Murdoch, 1771-1847,
3391
Esquisse interessant du Tableau

150

fidèle des causes qui
ont occasioné les revo-
lutions actuelles de
l'Amérique Septentrionale,
3392
Esquisse morale et politique
des États-Unis et de
l'Amérique du Nord,
4552
Essai sur la colonie de
Sainte-Lucie, 11742
Essais poétiques, 3309
Essais sur les isles
Fortunées et l'antique
Atlantide, ou... 11381
An essay concerning the
obedience to the supreme
powers, 12427
An essay for discharging
the debts of the nation,
12076
Essay on education, 2569
An essay on liberty and
slavery, 2735
An essay on organic
remains, 12272
Essay on political society,
12077
An essay on sugar, 12078
An essay on the liberty
of the press, 12756
An essay on the natural
history of Guiana, 733
An essay on the nature
and principles of public
credit, 2373
An essay on the slavery
and commerce of the human
species, 11852
An essay on the trade of
the northern colonies of
Great Britain in North
America, 12079
Essay on the warehousing
system and government
credits of the United
States, 12080
An essay on the warrant,
nature, and duties of

the office of the ruling
elder, 13433
An essay on trade and commerce,
11904
An essay on ways and means,
6712
An essay towards an improved
register of deeds, 12442
Essays on human rights and
their political guaranties,
13042
Essays on the present crisis
in the condition of the
American Indians, 12104
Essays on various subjects of
taste, morals, and national
policy, 5472
Essays, philanthropic and moral,
2968
Essays, sketches, and stories,
selected from the writings
of George Bryant Woods, 11203
Essequibo (Colony) - Hist., 1516
Essex Co., Mass., 10152
Essex institute, Salem, Mass.,
12081
Essex (Mass.) agricultural
society, 12962
Essex, Mass. - Hist., 2246
Essex, N. Y., 4726
Essex (U. S. frigate), 12841
Establishing a newspaper, 6266
Estabrooks, Henry L., 3393
Los Estados Unidos, 2706
Los Estados Unidos de América
y las repúblicas hispano-
americanas de 1810 à 1830,
8269
Estados Unidos, gran aventura
del hombre, 2499
Los Estados-Unidos (notas y
episodios de viaje) 4292
Los Estados Unidos y la América
del Sur, 4872
Estala, Pedro, 8174
Estampas de México, 7801
Estancelin, Louis, 1777-1858,
12082
Estaugh, John, 1676-1742, 12083

151

1611, 1612

Europe - Hist. - 1789-1815,
293, 11786

Europe - Hist. - 1815-1848,
2420, 12108

Europe - Hist. - Year-books,
293

Europe, Northern - Descr.
& trav., 8879

Europe - Pol. & govt.,
1819, 11324

Europe - Pol. & govt. -
1648-1789, 480

Europe - Pol. & govt. -
1789-1815, 480, 6005,
12108

Europe - Pol. & govt. -
1848-1871, 659, 12478

Europe, Southern - Descr.
& trav., 5073

European delineation of
American character, 12086

The European stranger in
America, 2200

The European traveller in
America, 2809, 12087

European war, 1914-1918 -
Addresses, sermons,
etc., 7689

The Europeans, 7120

Eustace, John Skey,
1760-1805, 12088

Eustis, William, 1753-
1825, 12364

Eva May, the foundling,
9961

Evalina's garden, 9578

Evan Dale, 10102

Evangel Wiseman, 9540

Evangelical alliance,
671, 673

The evangelist and other
peoms, 3101

Evangelistic sermons,
1687

Evangelistic work, 2922,
4469

Evans, Albert S., 6697

Evans, Caleb, 1737-1791,

12089

Evans, E. Clinton, tr., 2198

Evans, Estwick, 1787-1866,
3397, 12090, 12091

Evans, Francis A., 12092

Evans, Frederick William,
1808-1893, 12093, 12094

Evans, Sir George De Lacy,
1787-1870, 12095

Evans, Israel, 1747-1807,
12096, 12097

Evans, James, 1801-1846,
tr., 13312

Evans, John, 1814-, 3398

Evans, Jonathan, comp., 5077

Evans, Lemuel Dale, 1810-1877,
12098

Evans, Lewis, 1700?-1756, 3399

Evans, Nathaniel, 1742-1767,
12099

Evans, Oliver, 1755-1819, 12100

Evans, Thomas Wiltberger,
1823-1897, 12101

Evans, William Jones, M.R.C.S.,
12102

Evans, William Julian, 12103

Evarts family (John Evarts,
b. 1601), 5835

Evarts, Jeremiah, 1781-1831,
5452, 12104

Evarts, William Maxwell,
1818-1901, 6288, 6698

The eve of the fourth, 9567,
9570

Eveline Neville, 9487

Evelyn, the child of the
revolution, 10633

The evening book, 10147

Evening journal, Albany, N. Y.,
6288

An evening's adventure, 10163

Evenings at Donaldson manor,
10278

Evenings at Woodlawn, 9473

The eventful trip of the Midnight
Cry, 11162

Ever forgive, 8765

Everest, Robert, 3400

Everett, Alexander Hill,

1790-1847, 12105, 12106,
12107, 12108, 12109
Everett, David, 1770-1813.
Essay on the rights and
duties of nations, 413
Everett, Edward, 1794-
1865, 173, 2156, 7074,
12110, 12111, 12112,
12113, 12114, 12115,
12116, 12117, 12118
Everett, Edward Franklin,
1840-1899, 12119
Everett family (Richard
Everett, d. 1682),
12119
Everett, H., 5504
Everett, Horace, 1780-
1851, 12120
Everglades, Florida,
4056, 4633, 5731
Everheart, Lawrence,
1755-1839, 698
Evershaw, Mary, 12121
Every day, 10523
Every man his own guide
to the falls of
Niagara, 12995
Every man his own letter-
writer, 10892
Everybody's friend, 10742
The evidence that Abraham
Lincoln was not born
in lawful wedlock, 6447
The evil and the good,
9802
Evil, Non-resistance to,
2151
The evil tendencies of
corporal punishment, 1927
La evolución republicana
durante la revolución
argentina, 7943
The evolution of a life,
3126
The evolution of a state,
5223
Ewart, Frank Carman, 6699
Ewbank, Thomas, 1792-1870,
3401, 12122

Ewell, James, 1773-1832,
12123
Ewell, John D., 3402
Ewer, John, bp. of Bangor,
d. 1774, 12124
Ewer, John, bp. of Bangor,
d. 1774. A sermon preached...
February 20, 1767, 13098
Ewing, Thomas, 1789-1871, 12125
Ewing, Thomas, 1829-1896, 6700,
6701
Examen de la situación económica
de México, 5994
An examination into the conduct
of the present administration,
from the year 1774 to the
year 1778, 12126
An examination into the principles,
conduct, and designs of the
Earl of Shelburne, 12127
An examination into the pros-
pective effects of the national
banks upon the public welfare,
12128
An examination of a pamphlet,
entitled, His Catholic Majesty's
manifesto, &c, 12129
An examination of certain proceedings and principles of the
Society of Friends, 2637
An examination of the constitu-
tionality of the embargo laws,
11281
Examination of the controversy
between Georgia and the Creeks,
12130
An examination of the opinion
contained in the Report of the
Ouondaga commissioners, 12131
The examination of the President's
message, at the opening of
Congress, December 7, 1801,
12599
An examination of the rights of
the colonies, upon principles
of law, 12132
The excellencies of lying, 9486
Excelsior, The crusade of the,
6967

1817-1902, 2207

Fairfax, Wilson Miles
Cary, 12135

Fairfield, Genevieve Genevra,
1832-, 11048

Fairfield, Miss Gertrude,
11048

Fairfield, John, 1797-
1847, 187

Fairholt, Frederick William,
1814-1866, 2208

Fairy fingers, 10622

Faith, 1497, 5883

Faith and patience, 1468

Faith Campbell, 8588

The faith doctor, 9465

Faith White's letter book,
11149

A faithful account of that
singular imposition and
delusion, 12950

The faithful governess,
9194

A faithful narrative of
the remarkable revival
of religion, 1660

Faithfull, Emily, 1835-
1895, 3413

Falconbridge, Alexander,
d. 1792, 2209

Falconer, Richard, 2987

Falconer, Thomas, 1805-
1882, 3414, 3415

Fales, William R., 1820-
1850, 2210

Falk, Alfred, 3416

Falkland islands, 371,
12518, 13259

The fall of Aztalan, 144

The fall of Kilman Kon,
9273

The fall of man, 11146

The fall of Mexico, 13213

The fall of the confederacy,
12891

The fall of the Darcys,
9460

The fall of the great
republic, 9186

Fall of the Pequod, 10760

Fall River, 11170

Fall River, Mass. Citizens,
12688

Fall River, Mass. - Pol. & govt.,
11377

Falls of St. Anthony, 8991

Falls of Schuylkill, Pa. - Hist.,
12525

The falls of Taughannock, 12593

Falsehood and forgery detected
and exposed, 2211

Fama postuma del excelentísimo
e ilustrísimo señor doctor
Juan Domingo Gonzalez de la
Riguera, 1199

The fame and glory of England
vindicated, 11570

Fame's little day, 10038

A familiar conversational history
of the evangelical churches
of New York, 2212

Familiar letters to Henry Clay,
6919

Family anecdotes, 9595

The family compact, 8333

A family flight through Mexico,
6926

The family of the Fitzroyals,
9836

The family portraits, 10762

Famin, Stanislas Marie César,
1799-1853, 2213

Famous adventures and prison
escapes of the civil war, 3417

A famous battery and its
campaigns, 5201

The fanatic, 9494

Fanaticism, and its results,
2214

Fanchette, 9107

Fancies of a whimsical man, 10999

Fancourt, Charles Saint John,
2215

Fancy's show box, 9827

Fanning, David, 1756?-1825,
3418, 12136

Fanning, Edmund, 1769-1841,
12137

Fanning's illustrated
gazetteer of the United
States, 2216
Fanny Campbell, the
female pirate captain,
8670
Fanshawe, 9819
Une fantaisie américaine,
2563
Far from today, 8884
The far West, 3468
Faribault, Georges Barthé-
lemi, 1789-1866, 2217
Farley, Joseph Pearson,
1839-1912, 3419
Farm life, 9041
Farmer, Daniel Davis,
1793-1822, 2218
Farmer, John, 1789-1838,
1084, 2219, 2220, 7971,
12138
Farmer, Miles, plaintiff,
2221
The farmer refuted, 12600
The farmer's companion,
1657
The farmer's encyclopedia,
and dictionary of rural
affairs, 13234
Farming and ranching in the
Canadien North-West,
6704
Farming by inches, 8705
Farming for fun, 10792
Farmington's chapter in
the Lincoln story, 5901
Farnese, duke of Parma and
Piacenza, 1678-1727, 6366
Farnham, T. H., 10122
Farnham, Thomas Jefferson,
1804-1848, 2222, 3420, 3421
Farquhar, John, 6705
Farragut, David Glasgow,
1801-1870, 1547
Farrar, C. C. S., 2223
Farrar, Eliza Ware (Rotch)
"Mrs. John Farrar",
1791-1870, 2224
Farrar family, 2225

Farrar, Timothy, 1747-1849,
11858
Farrar, Timothy, 1788-1874,
2225, 2226
Farrington, Frank, 1872-,
6706, 6707
Farrington, Oliver Cummings,
1864-, 6708
Farrow, Henry Pattillo, 2227
Farther considerations on the
present state of affairs,
2470
A farther examination and
explanation of the South-sea
company's scheme, 2228
A farvvell sermon of Mr. Thomas
Hooker... 12882
Farewell sermons, 12882, 13243
Farwell, W. B., 2229
The fashion of this world, 8838
The fashion of this world
passeth away, 10816
Fashionable life, 9458
Fashion's analysis, 1416
Fast and loose in Dixie, 3294
Fast day sermons, 2230
Fast, Edward Gustavus, 2231
A fast life on the modern
highway, 10930
The fatal feud, 10590
The fatal gift of beauty, 4985
The fatal letter, 9815
The fatal plot, 10950
The fatal secret, 9498
The fate of a fool, 9287
The fate of blood-thirsty
oppressors, 11817
The fate of Franklin, 1376
The fate of Mansfield Humphreys,
11147
The fate of Marcel, 9738
The fate of the Union, 10826
Fate's mysteries, 9037
The father, 10762
Father Boyle, 10747
Father Drummond and his orphans,
9461
Father Ignatius in America, 3180
Father Merrill, 8976

158

Father Rowland, 10531
Father Ryan's poems, 5056
The fathers of New England,
   1755
The fathers of our republic,
   7832
The fathers of the New
   Hampshire ministry,
   11416
Fauche, Pierre François,
   2232
Faucher de Saint-Maurice,
   Narcisse Henri Édouard,
   1844-1897, 6709, 6710
Faulkner, Charles James,
   1806-1884, 6711
Faulkner, Thomas C., 2233
Fauna boreali-americana,
   4956
Fauquier, Francis, 1747-
   1768, 6712, 11621
Faust, Albert Bernhardt,
   6713, 6714
Faustino I, emperor of
   Haiti, 1789?-1867, 6583
Faux, William, ??34
Favill, Josiah Marshall,
   3422
Favorites, Royal, 12802
Fawcett, Joseph W., 3423
Fawkes, Guy, 1570-1606 -
   Fiction, 9463
The fawn of the pale faces,
   8835
Fay, Cyrus H., 2235
Fay, George Emory, 1927-,
   6715
Fay, Heman Allen, 1779-
   1865, ed., 2236
Fay, Herbert Wells, 6716
Fay, John D., jt. author,
   1897
Fay, Jonas, 1737-1818,
   jt. author, 162
A fearful responsibility,
   9943
Fearon, Henry Bradshaw,
   b. ca. 1770-, 3424
The feast of the cranberries,
10298
Featherstonhaugh, George William,
   1780-1866, 2237, 2238, 2239,
   3425, 12139
The feats and intrepidity of
   Colonel Harper, 10570
The federal government, 12254
Federal harmony, 1159
The federal judiciary, 11305
Federal law - Quebec, 11883
Federal party, 71, 88, 553,
   1349, 12693
The Federalist, 12140, 13178
The federati of Italy, 9404
Federurbian, 12936
Fedric, Francis, 3426
Fee, John Gregg, 1816-1901,
   3427
Feed-water, 11717
Feeling, 10904
Feemster, Zenas E., 1813-, 3428
Feet of clay, 8724
The feet of love, 8495
Felch, Alpheus, 1806-1896, 2240
Felipa, 11207
Félix de Jesús María, father,
   1706-1772, 6717
Felix, Elisa Rachel, 1821?-1858,
   1024
Fellowes, Gustavus, 9387
Fellows, John, 1759-1844,
   2241, 13352
The Felmeres, 3364
Felsenhart, Jacques, 1826-,
   2242
Felt, Joseph Barlow, 1789-1869,
   2243, 2244, 2245, 2246, 2247
Feltman, William, 2248
Felton, Cornelius Conway,
   1807-1862, 2249
Felton, Franklin Eliot, 2250
Feltus, Henry James, 1775-
   1828, 13289
The female poets of America,
   3699
The female prose writers of
   America, 3802
Female quixotism, 10933
The female rancher, 9295

159

The female spy, 8785
The female volunteer, 1295
Fenians (Society), 6038
Fenn, Harry, illustr., 8516
Fenning, Daniel, 3429
Fenollosa, Mrs. Mary (McNeil) 3430
Ferguson, Adam, 1782-1862, 6718
Ferguson, Fergus, 1824-1897, 3431
Ferguson, Joseph, 3432
Ferguson, Robert, 1817-1898, 3433
Ferguson, William, 3434
Ferguson's anecdotical guide to Mexico, 6719
Fergusson, D., 5539
Fern, Fanny, pseud., 10476-10479
Fern leaves from Fanny's port-folio, 10476
Fernández Cabrera, Manuel, 6720
Fernández de Castro, Manuel, 1825-1895, 12141
Fernández de Guzmán, Félix, 6354
Fernández de Liébana, Juan, 6677, 6678
Fernández de Medrano, Sebastian, 1646-1705, 6721, 6722
Fernández de Saravia, Rosa, 7910
Fernández de Velasco, Diego, duque de Frías, 1754-1811, 7959
Fernández del Corral, Francisco, 6806, 7962, 7963
Fernández Guardia, Ricardo, 6723, 6724, 8182
Fernández, José, 1617-1674, 6725
Fernández Mato, Ramón, 6726

Fernández Navarro, A., 7478
Fernando de Lemos, 3583
Fernando III, Saint, king of Castile and Leon, 1199?-1252, 8434
Fernando V el Católico, king of Spain, 1452-1516, 1200
Ferne Fleming, 5613
Fernon, Thomas Sargent, 6727
Ferree, Barr, 1862-1924, 3435
Ferrer, Leonardo, 1623-1695, 6728
Ferris, Benjamin G., 3436
Ferris, Mrs. Benjamin G., 3437
Ferris, Jacob, 12142
Ferris, Warren Angus, 1882-, 3438
Ferro Machado, Juan, 6729
Ferrocarril central mexicano, 8211
Ferrocarril mexicano, 6815
Ferrocarriles nacionales de Mexico, 6730
Ferry, Gabriel, pseud., 6065
Fessenden, Thomas Green, 1771-1837, 12143
Festival-day sermons, 6160, 7789
Fettered for life, 8811
Fetus, 535
Le Feu-follet, 9156
Fever, 459, 903, 12102, 13132
A few months in America, 4979
A few more words upon Canada, 11807
A few observations in vindication of the doctrine of the final perseverance of the saints, 4343
A few raps over the knuckles of the present age, 10714
A few words on Hudson's Bay company, 6731
A few words to begin with, 10896
Feyjos de Sosa, Miguel, 6732
Fieharty, Stephen F., 3439
Field, camp, hospital and prison in the civil war, 3966
Field, Charles D., 3440
Field, David Dudley, 1781-1867, ed., 2251

Field, Henry Martyn,
1822-1907, 3441
Field, Joseph E., 3442
Field, M. C., 3443
Field, Maunsell Bradhurst,
1822-1875, jt. author,
10009, 12502
Field, Thomas P., jt.
author, 8385
The fiend's delight, 8802
La fievre jaune à la
Habane, 1128
Fifteen days, 10581
Fifteen minutes around
New York, 9545
Fifteen years in Canada,
12749
Fifteen years in the
senior order of Shakers,
12013
Fifty years among authors,
3234
Fifty years in both hemi-
spheres, 4611
Fifty years of slavery
in the USA, 5196
Fifty years on the
Mississippi, 3654
Figg, Royall W., 3444
The fight, 9216
The fight for Canada,
8412
The fight for the Union,
2314
A fight with distances,
2570
The fight with France for
North America, 6148
The fighting Quakers,
11993
Figueroa Domenech, J.,
6733
Figueroa, Pedro Pablo,
1857-1909, 6734
The figure in the carpet,
7118, 10012
The fille de chambre,
10680
Fillmore co., Minn. -

Descr. & trav., 11278
Fillmore co., Minn. - Hist.,
11278
Fillmore, Millard, pres. U. S.,
1800-1874, 868
Filson, John, 1747?-1788, 3445,
6446
Filteau, Gérard, 6735
Finance - Confederate States of
America, 11659
Finance - Gt. Brit., 1537
Finance - Gt. Brit. - Hist.,
13499
Finance - Massachusetts, 2245,
2269
Finance - Mexico, 1217, 6756,
8423
Finance, Public - Charleston,
S. C., 11745
Finance, Public - U. S. - To 1789,
12187
Finance, Public - U. S. -
1789-1800, 12187, 12188
Finance - Puerto Rico, 7768
Finance - Spain, 5864
Finance - U. S., 2379, 7432, 11685,
11796, 12229, 13488
Finance - U. S. - Hist., 1244
Financial reform association,
Liverpool, 6736
Finch, John, fl. 1835, 3446
Finch, Marianne, 3447
Finck, Edward Bertrand, 1870-,
3448
The fine figure, 10841
Fink, Mike. See Mike Fink.
Finlason, William Francis,
1818-1895, ed., 2199
Finlay, Hugh, 3449
Finley, James Bradley, 1781-
1856, 3450, 3451, 3452,
3453
Finley, John Huston, 1863-,
6737
Finley, Robert, 1772-1817,
11563, 11565
Finn, Francis James, 1859-1928,
10675
Finney, Charles Grandison,

1792-1875, 11246
Fire-alarms, 11726
Firearms - Laws and
    regulations - Peru,
    6367
The fire-fiend, 2394
Fireplaces, 12162
The fire-screen, 8624
Fireside talk on morals
    and manners, 10147
Fire-worship, 9823
The First church in
    Providence, 100
First days amongst the
    contrabands, 2769
First families of the
    Sierras, 10352
A first family of
    Tasajara, 6968
The first flight, 9265
The first fruits, 3897
The first fruits of the
    Maine law, 10847
First general epistle of
    the first presidency
    of the Church of Jesus
    Christ of Latter-Day
    Saints, 2999
First impressions of
    America, 5606
First impressions of the
    New World on two
    travellers from the Old,
    5464
The first initiatory
    catechism, 2375
First love, 10919
The first mayor, 9582
The first of the Knicker-
    bockers, 10401
The first patient, 10978
First reflections on
    reading the President's
    message to Congress, of
    December 7, 1830, 12595
The first settlers of
    Virginia, 3189
The first Texian novel,
    9597

The first war-path, 9130
Fischer, Grete, pseud., 10713
Fish - Culture, 2409
Fish, Daniel, 1848-1924, 6738
Fish family, 12979
Fish, Joseph, 1706-1781, 12979
Fishe, John, 1842-1901, 6750
Fisher, 719
Fisher, Archibald, 7291
Fisher, Ellwood, 12144
Fisher, Fort - Expedition,
    1864-1865, 11647
Fisher, George Adams, 1835-,
    3454
Fisher, Harrison, illustr.,
    9569
Fisher, R. S., ed., 292
Fisher, Samuel Ware, 1814-1874,
    12620
Fisher, Walter Muirea, 1849-1919,
    5996
Fisher's river, N. C., 10922
Fisher's river scenes and
    characters, 10922
Fisheries - Canada, 11331
Fisheries - Nova Scotia, 6575
Fishes, 2409
Fishes - Atlantic coast, 12246
Fishes - Florida, 3839
Fishes - New York (State), 1909
Fishes - North America, 4936
Fishes - Ohio river, 4882
Fishes - Trinidad, 12247
Fishin' Jimmy, 10790
Fishing, 12257
Fishing - Adirondack mountains,
    10398
Fishing - Florida, 2495, 3094,
    3759, 5001
Fishing - New York (State),
    12630, 12631
Fishing - North America, 4216,
    4936, 7240
Fishing - South Carolina, 3369,
    5871, 12048
Fishing - U. S., 3758, 10571
Fishing - W. Va., 4157
Fisk, James Liberty, 3455, 3456,
    5535

162

Fiske, Amos Kidder, 1842-
1921, 6739
Fiske, Asa Severance,
ed., 3457
Fiske, John, 1842-1901,
6740, 6741
Fiske, Samuel Wheelock,
1828-1864, 3457
Fitch, Anna M., jt.
author, 9521
Fitch, Asa, 1809-1878,
11688
Fitch, Clyde, i.e.
William Clyde, 1865-,
10283
Fitch, John, 1743-1798.
The original steam-
boat supported, 854
Fithian, Philip Vickers,
1747-1776, 3458
Fitzgerald and Hopkins,
10376
Fitzgerald, James Edward,
6742
Fitzgerald, Oscar Penn,
bp., 1829-1911, 3459,
3460
Fitzgibbon, Mary Agnes,
1851-1915, 6743
Fitz-Gubin, 10916
Fitzhugh, Robert H., 6744
Fitz-Hugh St. Clair, the
South Carolina rebel
boy, 8970
Fitzpatrick, John Clemont,
1876-, ed., 5629
Fitz-Patrick, T., 3461
Fitzpatrick, Thomas, 3462,
3463
Fitzwilliam, N. H. -
Hist. - Civil war, 2419
Fiury, Ed K., 6745
Five acres too much, 10671
Five and twenty years ago,
9874
Five hundred days in Rebel
prisons, 3513
Five hundred dollars, 8971
Five hundred majority, 9969

"Five meals for a dollar,"
10808
Five months' fine weather
in Canada, 6330
Five months in rebeldom, 4455
Five o'clock in the morning,
9779
The five prisoners of Brandt
at the massacre of Cherry
valley, 10570
The five scalps, 3919
Five years a captive among the
Black-Feet Indians, 3112
Five years before the mast,
9829
Five years in Pennsylvania,
12121
Five years in Texas, 4616
Flack, Captain, 3464, 3465
Flaget, Benedict Joseph,
bp., 1763-1850, 5251
Flagg, Edmund, 1815-1890, 3466,
3467, 3468
Flagg, Jared Bradley, 1820-1899,
3469
Flags - U. S., 4284, 12615
Flameng, Leopold, 1831-, illustr.,
1123
Flandrau, Charles Macomb,
1871-1938, 6746
Flandreau, 9254
Flânerie parisienne aux
États- Unis, 221
Flannigan, Mrs., 397
Flash, Henry Lyndon, 3470
Flaubert, Gustave, 1821-1880,
7119
Flax, 1818
Fleeing from fate, 10394
Fleeing to Tarshish, 10250
Fleming, Sir Sandford, 1827-
1915, 6747, 6748, 6749,
7457
The Flemmings, 9414
Flesh and spirit, 9179
Fletcher, John William, 1729-
1785. American patriotism
farther confuted, 12089
Fletcher, Richard, 1788-1869,

2449
Fletcher, William Andrew,
   1839-, 3471
Fleurs d'été, 5362
The flight of Betsey Lane,
   10041
The flight of the shadow,
   9317
A flight to Mexico, 5965
A flight to the moon, 9551
Flint, Grover, 1867-1909,
   6750
Flint, James, 1779-1855,
   3479
Flint, James (Scotchman),
   3472
Flint, Thomas, 1824-1904,
   6751
Flint, Timothy, 1780-1840,
   3473, 3474, 3475, 3476,
   3477, 3478, 3479, 4715,
   5677
Flinter, George Dawson,
   2252
Flip, 9780
Flippin, John R., 6752
The flirtations of a beauty,
   10201
Flirtin' with fashion, 9888
Floods, 12239
Flora McDonald, 10172
Flora of the British West
   Indian islands, 12452
Flora virginica, 3703
Florae columbianae prodromus,
   1480
Floral home, 1352
El florecimiento de Mexico,
   8233
Florence Bardsley's story,
   9510
Florence Dalbiac, 11010
Florence de Rohan, 11188
Florence, S. C. Military
   prison, 3279, 4145, 4476
Florence, the parish orphan,
   10178
Florencia, Francisco de,
   1619-1695, 6753, 6754

Flores, José Manuel de,
   7405, 7406
Flores svmmarvm, 5870
Floriculture, 8706, 8708, 13252
Florida, 1990, 2253, 2270, 2557,
   2612, 3172, 3182, 3247, 3295,
   3482, 3813, 4962, 5146, 5690,
   5718
Florida Alexander, 10139
Florida - Antiq., 1529
Florida as a permanent home,
   4038
Florida as it is, 5146
Florida - Bibl., 11323
Florida (C. S. A. steamer), 2051
Florida - Climate, 4161, 4253
Florida. Commissioner of lands
   and immigration, 2253, 3480,
   3481, 3482, 3483
Florida. Constitution, 2254
Florida. Convention, 1861-1862,
   2254
Florida days, 3219
Florida - Descr. & trav., 2662,
   2707, 2714, 2817, 2819, 2841,
   2909, 3031, 3094, 3095, 3128,
   3138, 3180, 3251, 3348, 3360,
   3390, 3480, 3481, 3483, 3484,
   3485, 3486, 3514, 3579, 3692,
   3722, 3759, 3778, 3838, 3876,
   3979, 4018, 4038, 4135, 4146,
   4173, 4214, 4375, 4580, 4624,
   4633, 4656, 4976, 5001, 5012,
   5291, 5295, 5353, 5435, 5450,
   5572, 5625, 5689, 5747, 5762,
   11532, 12024
Florida - Descr. & trav. -
   Gazetteers, 3814
Florida - Descr. & trav. -
   Guide-books, 2802, 4239,
   4619, 4652, 4889, 4941, 5696
Florida - Econ. cond., 3674,
   3692
Florida enchantments, 3251
Florida facts both bright and
   blue, 3128
Florida - Fiction, 3656
Florida for tourists, invalids,
   and settlers, 2612

The Florida gazetteer, 3814
Florida historical society, Saint Augustine, 2205, 2255
Florida - Hist., 1529, 2206, 5572, 5718
Florida - Hist. - Bibl., 1529
Florida - Hist. - Civil war, 8940
Florida - Hist. - Colonial period to 1821, 2205, 3172, 4172
Florida - Hist. - Colonial period to 1821 - Sources, 2332
Florida - Hist. - Huguenot colony, 1562-1565, 408, 768, 4226, 7268
Florida - Hist. - Huguenot colony, 1562-1565 - Fiction, 5162
Florida - Hist. - Societies, 2255
Florida - Hist. - Spanish colony, 1565-1763, 5228
Florida - Hist. - Spanish colony, 1565-1763 - Sources, 3066
Florida. Its climate, soil and productions, 3480, 3481, 3482, 3484, 3514
Florida: its history, condition, and resources, 3295
Florida: its scenery, climate, and history, 4214
The Florida of to-day, 3182
The Florida pirate, 2256
Florida - Pol. & govt. - Civil war, 2254
The Florida railway and navigation company, 3485
The Florida reef, 9135
The Florida settler, 3483
A Florida sketch-book, 5435

Florida - Soc. cond., 3692
Florida - Soc. life & cust., 3410
Florida state historical society, 4862
Florida, the Italy of America, 3486
Florilegio medicinal de todas las enfermedades, 6694, 6695
Flour, 1032, 1615
Flour-mills, 12100
The floure of souvence, 10404
Flournoy, John Jacobus, 2257, 12146
Flower de Hundred, 9766
Flower, George, 1780-1862, 3487
The flower girl of London, 4737
A flower of France, 10687
The flower of Gala Water, 8725
Flower o' the quince, 9740
Flower, Richard, 1761?-1829, 2258, 3488
Flowers, 13252
The flowers of modern travels, 64
Flowers plucked by a traveller on the journey of life, 2075
Floyd, David Bittle, 3489
Der Flüchtling, 4497
The flush times of Alabama and Mississippi, 707
The Flying Dutchman, 10693
The flying, gray-haired Yank, 3353
The flying regiment, 12351
Flynt, Henry, 1675-1760, 2259
Foam of the sea, 8885
Fodere, M., 6755
The foe in the household, 8986
Foes in ambush, 10119
Foibles of fancy and rhymes of the times, 3280
Foiled, 9191
Foley, Daniel, 3490
Foley, Fanny, pseud., 2260
Folklore - Brazil - Paraíca,

7685
Folklore - Canada, 6892
Folklore, Indian, 2163
Folklore, Negro, 4106, 8189
Folk-songs, 4692
Folk-songs, French, 2369
Folk-songs, French Canadian, 2369
Folks next door, 6517
Follen, Eliza Lee (Cabot) "Mrs. C. T. C. Follen", 1787-1860, 2261
Following the flag, 11864
Folsom, George, 1802-1869, 3491
Folsom, James Madison, 1838-, 2262
Folsom, Montgomery M., 1857-, 3492
Folwell, Richard, 1768?-1814, jt. author, 2022
Fondation d'une colonie française, 5415
Fonerden, Clarence A., 3493
Fonseca, Fabian de, d. 1813, 6756
Fontaine family, 2263
Fontaine, Jacques, b. 1658, 2263, 3494
Fontaine, W. M., 4418
A fool of nature, 9808
The fool's opera, 2564
Foot family, 2447
Foot, George, 1800?-1867, 2264
Foot-prints of an itinerant, 3554
Footprints of the pioneers in the Ohio Valley, 5567
Foot, Samuel Augustus, 1780-1846, 11240
Foot's resolution, 1829, 11240, 12479
Foote, Andrew Hull, 1806-1863, 2265, 12147
Foote family (Nathaniel Foote, 1593?-1644), 2447
Foote, Henry Stuart,

1804-1880, 2050, 3495, 3496, 3497, 3498
Foote, Henry Wilder, 1838-1889, 2266
Foote, John Parsons, 1783-1865, 2267
Foote, Thomas Moses, 1809-1858, 2268
Foote, William Henry, 1794-1869, 3499, 3500
"For better, for worse", 10938
For honor's sake, 9275
For the major, 11206
For truth and freedom, 3644
Forbes, 6757
Forbes, Abner, 2269
Forbes, Eugene, d. 1865, 3501
Forbes, James Grant, 2270, 13000
Forbes-Lindsay, Charles Harcourt Ainslie, 1860-, 6758, 6759, 7417
Forbes, Robert Bennet, 1804-1889, 2271
A forbidden marriage, 10202
Force, Peter, 1790-1868, 2272, 2273, 11844
Force, William Quereau, 1820-1880, ed., 462
Ford, Camp, Texas, 4627
Ford, Henry Allen, 2274
Ford, Isaac Nelson, 1848-, 6760
Ford, Paul Leicester, 1865-1902, ed., 3502
Ford, Sallie (Rochester) "Mrs. S. H. Ford," 1828-, 3503, 3504, 3505, 3506, 3507
Ford, Thomas, 12148
Ford, Worthington Chauncey, 1858-1941, ed., 6761, 6762
The fore-room rug, 11162
A foregone conclusion, 9944
The Foreign enlistment act, 12230
The forest, 8380, 9975
Forest and prairie, 2675, 2676
Forest and shore, 9977
The forest bride, 10580

A forest hymn, 11592
Forest life, 10148
Forest life in Acadie, 6954
Forest life in Canada, 7528
Forest, Michael, 3508
The forest pilgrims, 1287
The forest rose, 2677
Forest scenes and incidents, 6998
A forest tragedy, 10221
Forester, Fanny, pseud., 10084
The foresters, 1082
Forestier, A., illustr., 10894
Forestiers et voyageurs, 8149
Forgiven at last, 11060
"The forgiving kiss", 10243
Formación histórica de la nacionalidad brasileña, 7640
Forman, Jacob Gilbert, 2275
Forman, Samuel S., 1765-1862, 3509
Forms (Law) - Illinois, 13302
Forms (Law) - New Hampshire, 11755
Forms (Law) - U. S., 1001
Forney, John Wien, 1817-1881, 3510
Forrest, Archibald Stevenson, illustr., 7006
Forrest House, 3914
Forrest, Michael, 3511
Forrest, Nathan Bedford, 1821-1877, 2698, 4540, 5778
Forrest, Thomas, supposed author, 926
Forrest's cavalry corps, C. S. A., 4540

Forrestal, 4004
Forry, Samuel, 1811-1844, 12149
Forster, Georg, 1754-1794, tr., 344
Forster, Johann Reinhold, 1729-1798, 7171, 7172, 12150
Forster, William Edward, 1818-1886, 2276
Forsyth, J., 7460
Fort Braddock letters, 8841
Fort Lafayette, 11197
"Fort-La-Fayette life", 2277
Fort Sumter, 8237
Fortenbaugh, Robert, 1892-, 6763
Fortier, Alcée, 1858-1914, 3512
Fortification, 834
A fortnight of folly, 5389
Fortress Monroe, 11194
The fortunate discovery, 9542
The fortune of war, 8749
The fortune teller, 10921
The fortune-teller of New Orleans, 4735
The fortunes and misfortunes of an orphan, 8701
The fortunes of an Irish girl in New York, 10271
The fortunes of Mr. Mason's successors, 10431
The fortunes of Rachel, 9679
Forty etchings, 3733
'49, the gold-seeker of the Sierras, 10353
Forty years a gambler on the Mississippi, 3240
Forty years' familiar letters of James W. Alexander, 2503
Forty years in Canada, 8106
Forty years of American life, 4603
Forty years of oratory, 5587
Forward, Walter, 2278
Fosdick, Charles, 3513
Fosgate, Blanchard, 2279
Foss, James H., 3514
Fossey, Mathieu de, comte,

169

France - Colonies - Commerce,
6643, 6650
France - Colonies - Guiana,
1831
France - Colonies -
Louisiana, 5229
France - Colonies - North
America, 4502
France - Colonies - Pol. &
govt., 8144
France - Colonies - Santo
Domingo, 19, 11235
France - Commerce, 6643
France - Commerce -
America, 11711
France - Commerce -
U. S., 2805
France - Commercial policy,
11711, 11970
France. Conseil général du
commerce, 6771
France. Constitution,
6778
France - Constitutional
law, 952
France - Descr. & trav.,
1832, 1834, 7207, 11440
France. État-major de
l'armée, 4124
France - For. rel., 5854,
11466, 11467
France - For. rel. -
Confederate States of
America, 2712
France - For. rel. - Gt.
Brit., 2183
France - For. rel. - South
America, 1588
France - For. rel. - U.S.,
1868, 1917, 1934, 2364,
5841, 6773, 6774, 11712,
11927, 12251, 12298,
12801, 13410, 13495
France - Hist., 3079,
6829
France - Hist. - 1789-
1815, 398, 3315, 11786
France - Hist. - 1789-
1815 - Fiction, 11029

France - Hist. - Louis XIV,
1643-1715 - Fiction, 6622,
9400
France - Hist. - Louis XVI,
1774-1747, 2721
France - Hist. - Louis Philip,
1830-1848, 2732
France - Hist. - Medieval
period to 1515 - Fiction, 9847
France - Hist. - Occupation
and evacuation, 1871-1873,
3895
France - Hist. - Restoration,
1814-1830, 398
France - Hist. - Revolution,
366, 5952, 6003, 6477, 6484,
6533, 8317, 9532, 11522
France - Hist. - Revolution -
1789-1791, 13441
France - Hist. - Revolution -
1789-1793, 11404
France - Hist. - Revolution -
Causes and character, 11232
France - Hist. - Revolution -
Fiction, 10365
France - Hist. - Revolution -
Personal narratives, 777,
1532, 12088
France - Hist. - Revolution -
Religious history, 6809
France - Hist. - Second empire,
1862-1870, 3895
France - Hist. - Wars of the
Huguenots, 1562-1598, 59
France in America, 8197
France. Laws, statutes, etc.,
952, 997, 1201
France. Laws, statutes, etc.,
1774-1792 (Louis XVI), 6772
France. Laws, statutes, etc.
Code civil, 388
France. Ministère de la marine,
1109
France - Navy, 1949
France - Navy - Lists of
vessels, 1757
France - Pol. & govt., 11765
France - Pol. & govt. - Revo-
lution, 1931, 12207

France. Treaties, etc.,
2183
France. Treaties, etc.,
1799-1804 (Consulate),
6773
France. Tribunat, 6774
Frances Waldeaux, 9352
Franchère, Gabriel, 3524
Francis Abbott, the
recluse of Niagara,
1331
Francis & Haley, 2310
Francis Berrian, 3473
Francis, Charles Lewis,
3525
Francis, Convers, 1795-
1863, 2309, 12157
Francis, James Bicheno,
1815-1892, 2311
Francis, John Wakefield,
1789-1861, 12158,
12159, 12160
Francis, M. C., 10448
Francis, Samuel Ward,
1835-1886, 2312, 2313
Francis, Valentine Mott,
1834-1907, 2314
Franciscans, 5885, 6775
Franciscans in Chile,
2436, 7100
Franciscans in Mexico,
5828, 5829, 5874,
7096, 7811
Franciscans in New Mexico,
1145
Franciscans in Peru,
6468, 6775
Franciscans in Spanish
America, 7918
Franciscans - Missions,
6468, 6775
Francisco, 10448
Franck, Harry Alverson,
1881-, 6776, 6777
Francklin, Thomas, 1721-
1784, 12161
Franco-German War, 1870-
1871 - Fiction, 7011
Frank Finlay, 10197

Frank Leslie's illustrated
newspaper, 6554
Frank Warrington, 9753
Franklin, A. W., ed., 2315
Franklin and Marshall college,
Lancaster, Pa., 2321, 12163
Franklin, Benjamin, 1706-1790,
28, 223, 2025, 2316, 2317,
2318, 2319, 2320, 6778, 7511,
7832, 8176, 12162, 12268,
12851, 13223
Franklin, Benjamin, 1706-1790 -
Imprints, 12083
Franklin co., Mass., 12279
Franklin co., Vt. - Hist., 5860
Franklin, Edward, 8815
Franklin, Emlen, 12163
Franklin Institute, Philadelphia,
2322, 12268
Franklin, James, 3527
Franklin, Sir John, 1786-1847,
434, 1116, 1117, 1433, 3528,
3529, 4955, 4956, 6058, 6195,
6449, 6870, 7652, 7984, 8050,
8123, 11582, 12560, 13428
Franklin, Sir John, 1786-1847 -
Fiction, 10735
Franklin, Sir John, 1786-1847 -
Poetry, 1376
Franklin, John Hope, 1915-,
6779
Franklin, pseud., 3526
Franklin, Tenn., Battle of,
1864, 3085
Frankness, 10904
Fransioli, Joseph, 1817-1890,
12164
Fraser, Charles, 1782-1860,
3530
Fraser, Eliza Anne, 12165
Fraser, John Foster, 1868-1936,
6780, 6781
Fraser, Malcolm, illustr., 4567,
5192
Fraser river mines, 7072, 7822
Frazee, Louis Jacob, 1819-1905,
3531
Frazier, Thomas Neil, d. 1887,
defendant, 2323

Freaks and kings, 9533
Freaks of fortune, 10062
Fred, and Maria, and me,
10562
Fred Douglass and his mule,
10793
Frederica, the bonnet girl,
9980
Frederick de Algeroy, the
hero of Camden plains,
9612
Frederick, Francis, 1809?-,
3532
Frederick, Gilbert, b. 1841
or 1842, 3533
Fredericks, Alfred,
illustr., 9805
Fredericksburg, Battle of,
1862, 1446
Fredericksburg, Va. -
Hist. - Civil war, 3969
Frédeux, Pierre, 1897-,
6782
The Fredoniad, 3383
Fredonian insurrection,
1826-1827, 4715
A free and impartial exam-
ination of the preliminary
articles of pacification,
2324
Free at last, 9077
The free-born subject's
inheritance, 11660
The free Britons memorial,
11334
Free collegiate education,
11595
Free Joe, 9747
Free-soil party, 2398
Free Suffrage, pseud.,
3534
Free trade and protection,
2453
Free trade and protection -
Free trade, 797, 11505,
11618
Free trade and protection -
Protection, 666, 1266,
2032, 2111, 2278, 4946,

11226, 11716, 12975
Free trade and sailors' rights,
2325
Free, yet forging their own
chains, 10658
The freebooter's foe, 8614
Freedley, Edwin Troxell,
1827-1904, jt. author, 1356
Freedman, John Joseph, 1835-
1921, 12167
Freedmen, 1890, 6582
The freedmen's book, 1890
The freedom of speech and
writing upon public affairs
considered, 11335
Freedom of the seas, 941
Freedom's early sacrifice,
10765
A Freeman, 12798
Freeman, Edward Augustus,
1823-1892, 3535
Freeman, Eugene Harrison,
3538
Freeman, Frederick, 1799-1883,
2327
Freeman, James, 1759-1835,
2328, 12168
Freeman, Mrs. Julia Deane, 3536
Freeman, Mrs. Julia Susan
(Wheelock) 1833-1900, 3537
Freeman, Samuel, 12169
Freeman, Warren Hapgood, 1844?-,
3538
Freeman's address to the North
Americans, 2326
Freemantle, Sir Arthur James
Lyon, 1835-1901, 3539
Free-masonry, 12166
Freemasons, 2241, 7230, 11664,
12181, 12425
Freemasons - Addresses, essays,
lectures, 912, 1905, 3747,
6336, 12792, 12823, 12923,
13047, 13123
Freemasons - Bibl., 2415
Freemasons - Biog., 6994
Freemasons - Boston, 12383
Freemasons - Direct., 13061, 13062
Freemasons - Fiction, 4530,

4533, 10387
Freemasons. Massachusetts. Grand lodge, 1276, 13036
Freemasons. New York (City) Holland lodge, no. 8, 717
Freemasons. New York (State) 717
Freemasons - Poetry, 4532
Freemasons. Rhode Island, 12587
Freemasons - Rituals, 11257
Freemasons. U. S. - Bibl., 900
Freemasons. U. S. - Direct., 13061
Freeport, Andrew, pseud., 6783
Freese, Jacob R., 1826-1885, 2329
Freiheit und sclaverei unter dem Sternenbanner, 3689
Freinthal, Käte, tr., 8243
Der Freischutz, 10693
Die Freistaaten von Nord-Amerika, 4310
Der freistaat von Nord-amerika in seinem neuesten zustand, 2854
Frelinghuysen, Frederick, 1753-1804, 2330
Frelinghuysen, Theodore, 1787-1862, 2331
Frémont, Jessie (Benton) 1824-1902, 12170
Frémont, John Charles, 1813-1890, 1273, 1371, 1591, 2926, 3540, 4504, 5406, 5552, 5660, 11842
Frenau, Philip Morin, 1752-1832, 474
French, Alice, 1850-1934, 8969
French arrogance, 1934
French, Benjamin Franklin, 1799-1877, 2332, 2333, 2334, 3544, 12171

French Canadians, 6769, 7525, 7841, 8129
French Canadians - Geneal. - Dictionaries, 8153
French, E., 10125
French East India company, 3552
French, Edward, 10125
French, George, 12172
French Guiana, 680
French Guiana - Descr. & trav., 870, 13358
French Guiana - Econ. cond., 870, 1831
French Guiana - Exiles, 366, 11765, 13358
French in Canada, 12350
French in Haiti, 997
French in Mississippi valley, 13501
French in North America, 6737
French in Pennsylvania, 4273
French in Texas, 5032
The French in the heart of America, 6737
French in the Mississippi Valley, 5586
French, James Strange, 1807-1886, 3545
French, Jonathan, 1740-1809, 2335
French, Justus Clement, 1587
French language - Dictionaries - Algonquian, 13143
French language - Dictionaries - Maya, 7231
French language - Dictionaries - Mohawk, 11588
The French officer, 10434
French, Parker H., 4470
French, S. G., 5547
French, Samuel Gibbs, 1818-1910, 3546
French spoliations claims, 1844, 11490
The Frenchman and the bills of exchange, 10528
A Frenchman in America, 2741
The Frenchman's story, 9618

Freneau, Philip Morin,
1752-1832, tr., 4982
Fresh leaves, 10477
Freycinet, Louis Claude
Desaulses de, 1779-
1842, 421, 422
Freytas, Nicolas de, 3547
Frick, William, 1790-1855,
2336
Friedrichsthal, Emanuel
R., d. 1842, 7917
Friend Barton's "concern",
9529
A friend of Caesar, 9366
Friend Olivia, 8726
Friend's meeting, 9683
Friends and neighbors,
8562
Friends ashore, 10040
Friends, Society of,
1151, 1154, 1155, 2637,
3001, 3246, 3340, 3516,
3694, 3905, 3941, 4954,
5077, 5106, 5139, 5293,
5318, 5727, 5744, 5768,
12152, 12434
Friends, Society of (Anti-
slavery) Indiana yearly
meeting, 4659
Friends, Society of.
Baltimore yearly meeting,
12889
Friends, Society of -
Boston, 10179, 10180
Friends, Society of -
Collected works, 2959,
5769
Friends, Society of -
Doctrinal and controver-
sial works, 681, 1650,
1652, 1735, 2285, 2636,
2773, 12563, 13006
Friends, Society of -
Epistles, 2299
Friends, Society of -
Hist., 5337
Friends, Society of -
Hist. - Revolution,
2154, 3614, 12427

Friends, Society of. Maryland,
1650
Friends, Society of. New
England, 2298
Friends, Society of. New
England yearly meeting, 4210
Friends, Society of. New York
yearly meeting, 4210
Friends, Society of. Pennsyl-
vania, 1448, 1652
Friends, Society of. Phila-
delphia monthly meeting, 5256
Friends, Society of. Phila-
delphia yearly meeting. The
testimony of the people called
Quakers, given... at Philadelphia
... 1775, 2154
Fries, John, 1764?-1825, defend-
ant, 2337, 11757
Fries rebellion, 1798-1799,
2337
Friese, Philip C., 2338
Frieze, Jacob, 2339, 2340
The frigate in the offing,
10432
Frisbie, Barnes, 2341
Fritsch, William August, 1841-,
3548
Frizon, Nicolas, d. 1737,
1189
Fröbel, Julius, 1805-1893,
3549, 6784
Frobisher, Sir Martin, 1535?-1594,
1201
Froissart ballads, 3080
A frolic among the lawyers,
10953
From a New England woman's
diary in Dixie in 1865, 2530
From Blomidon to Smoky, 6111
From Bull Run to Chancellorsville,
3144
From cliff and scaur, 5176
From clime to clime 7559
From dawn to daylight, 8767
From Dixie, 10357
From flag to flag, 4964
From fourteen to fourscore,
10044

From Glasgow to Missouri
and back, 3431
From home to home, 7046
From jest to earnest,
10646
From Liverpool to St.
Louis, 12581
From Madge to Margaret,
9284
From Manassas to Appo-
mattox, 4297
From Mexico City to the
port of Veracruz, 6372
From my youth up, 10939
From New York to Delhi,
by way of Rio de
Janeiro, Australia and
China, 13440
From New York to San
Francisco by way of
Panama Canal Zone, 6258
From North Carolina to
southern California
without a ticket, 4738
From ocean to ocean, 3550
From reveille to retreat,
9053
From sand hill to pine,
6969
From Texas to Mexico,
8170
From the depths, 10843
From the far west, 2572
From the Hudson to the
St. Johns, 4135
From the ranks, 10118
From the Rapidan to
Richmond and the
Spottsylvania campaign,
3161
From the St. Johns to the
Apalachicola, 5353
From the sublime to the
ridiculous, 9009
From Vicksburg to Raleigh,
3557
Fronde - Fiction, 9841,
10312
Frontier and pioneer life,

3452, 3731, 3955, 4951,
5412, 5460
Frontier and pioneer life -
Arkansas, 4825
Frontier and pioneer life -
Fiction, 2673, 2675, 2676,
2677, 2678, 2680, 2681, 2682,
2685, 3744, 3749, 3751, 3834,
4180, 4460, 4498, 4499, 4990,
4992, 4993, 5061, 10134
Frontier and pioneer life -
Georgia, 10772
Frontier and pioneer life -
Illinois, 5765
Frontier and pioneer life -
Illinois - Pike co., 2859
Frontier and pioneer life -
Indiana, 9705
Frontier and pioneer life -
Kansas, 12280, 12281
Frontier and pioneer life -
Kentucky, 3574, 4337, 8789
Frontier and pioneer life -
Minnesota, 1352
Frontier and pioneer life -
Mississippi Valley, 2595,
3138, 4069, 10265, 10768
Frontier and pioneer life -
New York (State), 10569,
11822
Frontier and pioneer life -
Ohio, 3352, 3450, 3954, 4367
Frontier and pioneer life -
Ohio - Richland co. -
Fiction, 10273
Frontier and pioneer life -
Ohio Valley, 2778, 2922,
3138, 3745, 4469, 5679, 12021
Frontier and pioneer life -
Ontario, 7527, 7528
Frontier and pioneer life -
Pennsylvania, 13319
Frontier and pioneer life -
Poetry, 4718
Frontier and pioneer life -
Scioto County, Ohio, 4169
Frontier and pioneer life -
Southern states, 5558
Frontier and pioneer life -

175

Fuller, Richard Frederick,
  1824-1869, 2358
Fuller, Robert, b. 1795?,
  2359
Fuller, Stephen, 13147
Fuller, Timothy, 1778-1835,
  12181
Fullerton, A. M., Dr.,
  9331
Füllner, G., tr., 1103
Fullonton, Joseph, 2360
Fulton, Alexander R.,
  1825-1891, 2361
Fulton family, 6790
Fulton, Hugh R., 6790
Fulton, James Alexander,
  12182
Fulton, John, 6790
Fulton, Robert, 1765-
  1815, 2362, 11856
Fun and earnest, 11000
Fun, frigates, and yachting,
  10916
Fun-jottings, 11177
La fundación de la república,
  5923
Fundación Eugenio Mendes,
  6794
Fundamentalism, 4937
Fundamentalism - Fiction,
  3505
The funding system of the
  United States and of
  Great Britain, 12008
The funeral march of a
  marionette, 9741
Funeral music, 7058
Funeral music for 22d
  February, 7058
A funeral oration in
  memory of Mr. Jonathan
  Lyman, 702
Funeral rites and ceremonies -
  Peru, 6519
Funeral sermons, 979,
  1645, 1851, 5856, 6378,
  6820, 7397, 8005, 8204,
  12392, 13034, 13183
Funes, Gregorio, 1749-1829,

8026
Fünf wochen im osten der
  Vereinigten Staaten und
  Kanadas, 3553
Fünfzehn jahre in Amerika,
  4252
The fur hunters of the far West,
  5018
Fur trade, 5017
Fur trade - Canada, 4362, 6228,
  7886, 8000, 8256, 13397, 13411
Fur trade - Northwest, Pacific,
  5018
Fur trade - Oregon, 3323, 4026
Fur trade - Pacific Northwest,
  5526
Fur trade - Rocky Mountains,
  2689, 2823
Fur trade - The West, 3105,
  4042, 4257
Fur trade - U. S., 5527
Fur trade - Washington (State),
  4641
Furber, George C., 6791
El Fureidîs, 9274
Furness, Henry B., 4031
Furness, William Henry, 1802-
  1896, 2363, 10521
Furney, L. A., ed., 5005
The furnished house, 9802
Furniture - New England, 2244
Further and still more important
  suppressed documents, 2364
A further consideration of the
  dangerous condition of the
  country, 13255
Fury (ship), 7696, 7697
Future glory of North America,
  8959
Future life, 11199
The future of the country,
  6792

G. S. Isham's guide to
  California, 4032
G. T. T., 9680
G. T. T. Gone to Texas, 3963
Gabb, William More, 1839-1878,

Galt, John, 1779-1839,
2387
Galt, John Minson, 1818-
1862, 2388, 12191
Galvan Rivera, Mariano,
6808
Galveston Bay and Texas
Land Company, 3566
Galveston - Descr., 3927
Gálvez, Juan de, 1750-
1807, 6809
Gálvez, Matias de, 1717-
1784, 8005
Gamage, William, 1780-
1818, 2389
Gambling, 660, 2882,
3240, 12397
Gambling unmasked! 12397
Gamboa, Federico, 1864-,
6036
Game and game birds -
North America, 4935
The gamesters, 10949
Gamio, Manuel, 1883-,
7483, 7484, 7486
Gammage, W. L., 3567
Gammell, William, 1812-
1889, 12193
Gan-Eden, 13041
Gannett, Ezra Stiles,
1801-1871, 12194
Gannett, Ezra Stiles,
1801-1871. Relation of
the North to slavery,
11918
Gannett, Henry, 1846-
1914, 6524
Gannon, Frederic Augustus,
1881-, 6810
Gano, John, 1727-1804, 3568
Gano, Stephen, 3568
Ganong, William Francis,
1864-, 6290, 6575, 7253
Gante, Pablo de, 6811
Garay, José de, 1801-1858,
2390
Garber, Mrs. Virginia
(Armistead), 6812
Garcés, Francisco Tomás

Hermenegildo, 1738-1781, 6813
Garcés, Henrique, d. 1591, tr.,
7739
García Camba, Andrés, 6814
García Cubas, Antonio, 1832-
1912, 6815, 6816, 6817, 6818,
6819, 7018
García de Escañuela, Bartholomé,
bp., d. 1684, 6820
García Figueroa, Francisco, 6604
García Gravados, Rafael, 6821
García Icazbalceta, Joaquín,
1825-1894, ed. & tr., 6388,
6389
García, José de Jesús Q., ed.,
7850
García Mérou, Martín, 1862-
1905, 3569
García y García, Aurelio, 2391
Garcilaso de la Vega, el Inca,
1539-1616, 12195
Garden, Alexander, 1757-1829,
662, 2392, 2393
The garden of dreams, 2950
The garden of the world, 3570
Gardette, Charles Desmarais,
2394
Gardiner, Abraham Sylvester,
6822
Gardiner, Sir Christopher,
fl. 1630-1632, 8468
Gardiner, David, 1784-1844,
2395
Gardiner, George A., 2396
Gardiner, Lion, 1599-1663, 2397
Gardiner, Oliver Cromwell, 2398
Gardiner, Richard, 1723-1781,
2399
Gardiner, Walter Clarke,
12196
Gardiner, William Howard,
1797-1882, 2400
Gardini, Carlo, 3571
Gardner, Charles Kitchell,
1787-1869, 2401, 2402
Gardner, Daniel, 2403, 2404
Gardner family, 12412
Gardner family (Thomas Gardner,
d. 1674), 6823

Gay, Sydney Howard,
1814-1888, 6833
Gayarré, Charles Étienne
Arthur, 1805-1895,
3582, 3583, 3584
Gayley, James Fyfe, 1818-
1894, 2418
Gaylord, William L., 2419
Gazelle, a true tale of
the great rebellion,
12201
Gazette publications, 2780
A gazetteer of the state
of Georgia, 5138
A gazetteer of the United
States, 12766
Gazophylacium divinae
dilectionis, 7449
Gaztaneta y de Iturribálzga,
Antonio, 1656-1728, 6832
Geary and Kansas, 12240
Geary, John White, 1819-
1873, 12240
Geber, a tale of the
reign of Harun al Raschid,
8792
Geer, John James, 1833-,
3585
Geijer, Erik Gustaf,
1783-1847, praeses, 439
Geist, Margarethe, 3586
Geldard, James, 12202
Gelger, John Lewis, 6834
A gem among the sea-weeds,
9712
The gem of the lake, 11219
Gemälde von Nord-Amerika
in allen beziehungen,
1560
Gemelli Careri, Giovanni
Francesco, 1651-1725,
6835
Gemidos del corazón, 7668
Gemma, Reinerus, Frisius,
1508-1555, 407
Genealogical and historical
notes on Culpepper county,
Virginia, 3680
A genealogical memoir of

the families of Lawrences,
2452
A genealogical register of the
first settlers of New England,
2219
Genealogical sketch of the
Bird family, 1330
Genealogy, 2294
Genealogy of the Everett family,
12119
Genealogy of the Henry Adams
family, 6836
Genera of North American Reptilia,
12683
The general, attacked by a
subaltern, 11239
The general character, present
and future prospects of the
people of Ohio, 539
General courses and distances
G. S. L. City to Fort Limhi,
3521
General epistle from the Council
of the twelve apostles to the
Church of Jesus Christ of
Latter Day Saints abroad, 5790
The general gazetteer, 2816
General Harrison, 10310
A general history of the British
empire in North America, 5781
General Lane's brigade in
central Mexico, 6144
The general register of politics
and literature in Europe and
America, 2420
A general survey of the present
situation of the principal
powers, 12108
A general view of the U. S.,
4489
General Washington's marquee,
10310
The general's double, 10121
Generals - U. S., 8263
Genesee consocation, 12203
Genesee region, N. Y., 1495,
3988
Genet, Edmond Charles, 1763-
1834, 12204

Geneva. American residents, 12205
Genin, Sylvester, 1822-1850, 12206
Genin, Thomas Hedges, 1796-1868, 3587, 3588
The genius and posture of America, 154, 155
The genius maker, 9331
A gentle bell, 10969
A gentle benefactress, 9079
The gentle boy, 9820, 9827
A gentle ghost, 9575
A gentleman at the bar, 12132
The gentleman from Indiana, 10923
A gentleman from South Carolina, 12289
Gentleman of America, 5229
A gentleman of Japan and a lady, 10238
A gentleman vagabond and some others, 5194
Gentry, Richard, 1788-1837, 6837
Gentry, Thomas Benton, 6837
Gentz, Friedrich Von, 1764-1832, 12207
A genuine account of earthquakes, 12208
A genuine account of the late secret expedition to Martinico and Guada-loupe, 12209
The genuine book of nulli-fication, 12635
Geografía de la República de Guatemala, 7452
Geografía de la República mexicana, 6611, 7588
Geografía de México, 7320
Geografía nacional de México, 7958
Geografía social y humana de Costa Rica, 7517
Geografía y atlas de la República mexicana, 8439

A geographical description of the state of Louisiana, 3170, 3171
Geographical distribution of animals and plants, 5291
Geographical, historical, political, philosophical and mechanical essays, 3399
Geographical memoir upon upper California, 3541
Geographical positions - Cape Breton, 11707
Geographical positions - Nova Scotia, 11707
Geographical positions - Southern states, 3360, 12024
A geographical view of the U. S., 3589
Geographie und statistik von Mexiko und Central-Amerika, 8336
Geographische gesellschaft (für Thüringen) zu Jena, 6841
Geographische wanderungen, 2540
Geography, 584, 1280, 3429, 4466, 5065, 6674, 7858
Geography - 15th-16th cent., 343
Geography - 17th-18th cent., 1515, 3683, 3722, 5066, 6294, 6525, 6526, 6721, 6722, 8254
Geography - Congresses, 6453
Geography - Dictionaries, 715, 1374, 1565, 2816
Geography, Historical, 1515
Geography - Hist., 7649, 11332
Geography, Medieval, 126
A geography of New England, 11286
The geography of South Carolina, 5159
Geography - Societies, 7654
Geography - Textbooks, 7266, 7320, 8440
Geography - Textbooks, 1800-1870, 1396
Geologie pratique de la Louisiane, 5384
Geology, 11954, 12354
Geology - Algeria, 387

182

Geology - Arctic regions, 6302
Geology - Argentine republic, 1719
Geology - Arkansas, 2238
Geology - British Columbia, 6174
Geology - California, 6913, 11283
Geology - Canada, 4685, 6218
Geology - Canada - Guidebooks, 6308
Geology - Europe, 387
Geology - Iowa, 13106
Geology - Louisiana, 5384
Geology - Massachusetts, 11956
Geology - Mexico, 2186, 6708, 6913
Geology - Minnesota, 13476
Geology - Mississippi Valley, 4664
Geology - Missouri, 2238, 4698
Geology - Montana, 3817
Geology - Nebraska, 247, 3817, 4246
Geology - Nevada, 6913
Geology - New England, 2168
Geology - New York (State) - Putnam Co., 1402
Geology - North America, 4386, 7344, 7345, 7346, 7347
Geology - North Carolina, 4486
Geology - Northwest, Canadian, 3878
Geology - Nova Scotia, 12221
The geology of the earth, 11444
Geology - Oregon, 2602
Geology - Rocky Mountains, 5524
Geology - South Carolina, 12869
Geology - Southwest, New, 5513
Geology, Stratigraphic, 12574
Geology - Tennessee, 11907
Geology - U. S., 270, 2239, 3446, 4318, 12574
Geology - Utah, 5501
George I, king of Great Britain, 1660-1727, 2304
George II, king of Great Britain, 1683-1760, 1388, 2304
George III, king of Great Britain, 1738-1820, 103
George, Alfred, 6838
George Balcombe, 5476
George Cardwell, 10383
George, Henry, 1839-1897, 6581, 8425
George, Henry, jr., 8425
George, Lake - Hist., 2093
George Mandeville's husband, 4986
George, Marian M., 6839, 6840
George Mason, the young backwoodsman, 3474
George Melville, 10800
George, Paul, 6841
George Washington's last duel, 10460
George Washington's physician, 6842
George Welding, 8998
George's mother, 9210
Georgetown, D. C. Ordinances, etc., 12210
Georgetown, D. C. St. John's church, 11648
Georgetown, S. C., 4222
Georgia, 1668, 3296
Georgia: a guide to its cities, 3236
Georgia - Antiquities, 4102, 13290
Georgia artillery. Chatham art., 1785?-1865? 4103
Georgia artillery. Howell's battery, 1863-1865, 3851
Georgia artillery. Martin's battery, 1862-1863, 3851

183

Germans in Mexico, 6917
Germans in Mexico (City),
6917
Germans in Pennsylvania,
12660
Germans in Schoharie co.,
N. Y., 11567
Germans in the U. S.,
3233, 4132, 4181, 4290,
4449, 11319, 11327
Germantown academy,
Germantown, Pa., 12216
Germantown, Battle of,
1777, 10215
Germantown, Pa., 6713
Germany - Descr. & trav.,
7806, 8877
Germany - Emig. & immig.,
1562
Germany - Hist. - Henry IV,
1056-1106 - Fiction,
10351
Gerolt, Friedrich Karl
Joseph, freiherr von,
2186
Gerrish, Theodore, 1846-,
3592
Gerritsen, Carel Victor,
1850-, 3593
Gerry, Elbridge, 1744-
1814, 560
Gerstäcker, Friedrich
Wilhelm Christian, 1816-
1872, 3594, 7272, 12217
Gerstner, Clara (von
Epplen-Härtenstein) von,
3595
Gerstner, Franz Anton,
ritter von, 1795-1840,
3595, 3596
Gertrude of Wyoming, 1824
Geschichte der englischen
kolonien in Nord-Amerika,
6843
Geschichte und handlung
der französischen
pflanzstadte in Nord-
amerika, 3597
Geschichte und Zustände

der Deutschen in Amerika,
4290
Gesner, Abraham, 1797-1864,
12218, 12219, 12220, 12221
Gesner, George Weltden, ed.,
12220
Gessner, Ludwig, 1828-1890,
12222
Getrouw verhaal van den waren
toestant der meest herderloze
gemeentens in Pennsylvanien
en aangrensende provintien,
5093
Getting under way, 9800
Gettysburg Address, 6345
Gettysburg, Battle of, 1863,
1149, 12117, 13140
Gettysburg college, 1623
Gettysburg - National cemetery,
12117
Gevers Deynoot, William
Theodorus, 6844
Ghent, Treaty of, 1814, 72, 520
Gholson, Thomas Saunders,
1809-1868, 12223
Gholson, William Yates, 1807-
1870, 12224
The ghost, 10480
The ghost in the Cap'n Brown
house, 10909
The ghost in the mill, 10909
The ghost of law, 11486
The ghost of Redbrook, 9180
A ghost of the Sierras, 9779
Ghost stories, 10693
Ghostly colloquies, 11001
Ghosts, 1474
Ghosts I have met and some
others, 8678
The ghosts of Stukeley Castle,
6965
The giant's coffin, 10783
Gibbes, George M., 12225
Gibbes, Robert Wilson, 1809-
1866, 12226
The gibbet of Regina, 6845
Gibbon, Eduardo A., 6846
Gibbon, John, 1827-1896, 3598
Gibbons, Israel, d. 1866, 12227

185

Gibbons, J. A., 3599
Gibbons, James, 12228
Gibbons, James Sloan,
  1810-1892, 12229
Gibbons, Joseph Kent,
  1840-1862, 1659
Gibbons, Thomas, 1720-
  1785, jt. ed., 1621
Gibbs family (Robert
  Gibbs, 1634?-1674?)
  12235
Gibbs, Frederick Waymouth,
  1821-, 12230, 12231
Gibbs, George, 1815-1873,
  12232, 12233, 12234
Gibbs, William, b. 1785,
  12235
Gibbs, William H., 12236
Gibson, Charles Dana,
  1867-1944, illustr.,
  8674, 9361, 9362, 9637
Gibstone, Henry, 12237
Giddings, Joshua Reed,
  1795-1864, 12238
Giddins, Edward, 12239
Gifford, John, 1758-1818,
  1932
Gift-books (Annuals, etc.),
  252
Giger, Henry Douglas, comp.,
  6847
Giguet, 366
Gihon, John H., 12248
Un Gil-Blas en Californie,
  2132
Gilbert, A., illustr.,
  4048
Gilbert, C. E., 6848
Gilbert, James Stanley,
  1855-1906, 6849
The Gilberts, 9896
Gilead, 10810
Giles, Charles, 1783-1867,
  12241
Giles, Joel, 12242
Giles, Leonidas Blanton,
  1841-, 3600
Giles Pretel, Juan de,
  6850, 6851

Giles, William Branch,
  1762-1830, 12243, 12244
Giles, William Fell, 1807-1879,
  12245
Gilfillan, Lillian, 10125
Gill, John, 1841-, 3601
Gill, Theodore Nicholas,
  1837-1914, 12246, 12247
Gilleland, J. C., 12248
Gillespie, Alexander, 12249
Gillespie, Joseph, 5933, 6852
Gillespy, Edward, comp., 12250
Gillet, Eliphalet, 1768-1848,
  12251, 12252
Gillet, Ransom Hooker, 1800-
  1876, 12253, 12254
Gillette, Charles, 12255
Gilliam, Albert M., d. 1859,
  6853, 12256
Gillies, J., ed., 5691
Gilliland, Thaddeus Stephens,
  1834-, ed., 6854
Gilliman Ogley, 10675
Gillmore, Parker, 12257
Gillmore, Robert H., 12258
Gillpatrick, Owen Wallace,
  6855, 6856
Gilman, Arthur, 1877-1909,
  12259
Gilman, Mrs. Caroline (Howard)
  1794-1888, 3602, 3603, 3604,
  3605, 3606, 3607
Gilman, Daniel Coit, 1831-1908,
  12260, 12261
Gilman family (Edward Gilman,
  1587?-1681), 12259
Gilman, Samuel, 1791-1858,
  11746, 12262
Gilmer, Elizabeth (Meriwether)
  1861-1951, 6857
Gilmer, Francis Walker, 1790-
  1826, 3608
Gilmer, George Rockingham,
  1790-1859, 12263
Gilmer, John H., 12264, 12265
Gilmor, Harry, 1838-1883, 3609
Gilmore, James Roberts,
  1822-1903, 3393, 3610, 3611,
  3612, 3613

Gilmore, Joseph Henry,
1834-, 12266
Gilmore, Patrick Sars-
field, 1829-1892, 12267
Gilpin, Henry Dilworth,
1801-1860, 12268, 12269,
12270
Gilpin, Joshua, 12271
Gilpin, Thomas, 1776-1853,
ed., 3614, 12272, 12273
Gilpin, William, 1822-1894,
3615, 3616
Ginés de Sepúlveda, Juan.
See Sepúlveda, Juan
Ginés de.
Giovanna I, queen of Naples,
d. 1382 - Fiction, 9710
The gipsey of Germantown,
9717
Gipsies, 4275
Gipsies - England, 10517
The gipsy's warning, 9449
Girard, Charles Frédéric,
1822-1895, 677, 3617
Girard college, Philadel-
phia, 438, 12276
Girard, Just [pseud. for
Just Jean Etienne Roy]
1794-1870, 3618
Girard, Stephen, 1750-
1831, 438, 12275
Girardin, Louis Hue, 1771-
1825, 11613
Girdlestone, Thomas, 1758-
1822, 12277
The girl at Cobhurst, 10888
The girl at the halfway
house, 9929
The girl of the period,
9762
The girl who died of a
broken heart, 6209
Girlhood and womanhood, 9646
Girls, 10655
Girls of a feather, 8727
The girls' sketching camp,
10163
Girod-Chantranso, Justin,
1750-1841, 4654

Girty, Simon, 1741-1818 -
Fiction, 4122, 8789
Gisborne, Lionel, 1823-1861,
12278
Gislén, Torsten, 1893-, 3619
Gist, Christopher, d. 1759,
3620
The given case, 10016
Glaciers - British Columbia,
6890
Gladden, Washington, 1836-1918,
12279
The glades of the Alleghenies,
4694
Gladstone, Thomas H., 12280, 12281
Gladys, 9329
A glance at New York, 12388
A glance backward, 3010
A glance behind the scenes,
9239
Glanmore, 9043
Glas, George, 1725-1765, tr.,
24
Glascott, Cradock, 1743?-1831,
12282
The glass, 10159
Glass, Hugh, 2675, 4262
Glasses, 7118, 10012
Glastonbury, Conn. - Geneal.,
11728
Glastonbury, Conn. - Hist.,
11728
Glazier, Lewis, 12283
Glazier, Willard, 1841-1905,
3621, 3622, 3623, 3624,
4672, 6858
Gleams of light on all sorts
of subjects, 12227
Gleanings by the way, 3013
Gleanings from real life, 9609
Gleanings from the portfolio
of the "Young 'un", 8917
Gleason, Benjamin, 1777-1847,
12284
Gleig, George Robert, 1796-
1888, 3625
Gleitsmann, William, 1840-1914,
3626
Glen, James, 3627

Glen's Creek, 9896
Glennair, 9831
The Glenns, 10263
Glezen, Levi, 1774?-1842,
  12285
Gli Stati Uniti, 3571
A glimpse at Guatemala,
  7439
A glimpse at the great
  western republic, 3143
A glimpse of paradise,
  10377
Glimpses of Mexico and
  California, 7256
Glimpses of our lake
  region in 1863, 9602
Glimpses of Texas, 2789
Glimpses of truth, 5238
Glimpses of western life,
  10149
Globe (Whaling ship),
  9090
Gloria Britannorum, 12286
Gloria Mundi, 9566
The glories of the Lord
  of Hosts, 1778
Glory, 10238
The glory of America, 137
A glossary to Say's
  Entomology, 5081
Gloucester, John, 1776 or 7-
  1822, 1840
Gloucester, Mass. - General,
  605
Gloucester, Mass. - Hist.,
  605
Glover, Livingston Maturin,
  1819-1880, 6859
Glover, Richard, 1712-1785,
  12287
Glover, Samuel Taylor,
  1813-1884, 12288
Glover, Thomas, 3628
Gloverson and his silent
  partners, 10087
Gnaw-wood, 11773
The go-between, 12289
Goadby, Mrs. Robert,
  supposed author, 4275

Gobat, Albert, 1843-1914, 3629
Gobright, Lawrence Augustus,
  1816-1879, 12290
God, 5804
God and the soul, 5239
God - Attributes, 11896
God or our country, 11437
God rest ye, merry gentlemen,
  9217
God ruling the nations for
  the most glorious end, 13033
God sometimes answers his
  people, 44
God the judge, 2304
God's culture of his vineyard,
  1925
God's judgments teaching
  righteousness, 1872
God's protecting providence,
  3247
God's ravens, 9606
"God's ways unsearchable," 13239
Godard-Lange, 12291
Goddard, Frederick Bartlett,
  1834-, 3630, 12292
Goddard, George H., 3631
Goddard, Samuel Aspinwall, 2421
Goddard, Thomas H., 2422
Goddard, William, 1740-1817,
  2423, 12293
Goddard, William Giles, 1794-
  1846, 2424, 2425
Godet, Theodore L., 2426
Godfrey, Edward K., 6860
Godfrey, Thomas, 1736-1763,
  2427
Godfrey, William C., 2428
Godley, John Robert,
  1814-1861, 3632
The godmother's gifts, 10046
Godoy Alcayaga, Lucila,
  1889-, ed., 6861
Godwin, Morgan, fl. 1685,
  1556, 2429, 12294
Godwin, Parke, 1816-1904,
  2430
Godwin, William, 1756-1836,
  2431, 2432
Goedel, C., 12295

Goethe, Mme. Louise, 2433
Gohier, Urbain Degoulet,
  called, 1862-, 3633
Going and son, 10370
Going to Shrewsbury,
  10043
Gold, 1865, 11684
Gold, A. B., 3515
Gold diggings on Salmon
  River, 3521
Gold-dust for the beauti-
  fying of lives and
  homes, 10535
Gold mines and mining,
  386, 2575, 5573
Gold mines and mining -
  Brazil, 11636
Gold mines and mining -
  California, 217, 386,
  5301
Gold mines and mining -
  Colorado, 2738, 2877,
  3715, 3717, 3987, 4594,
  4707, 4708, 5421, 5455,
  5695
Gold mines and mining -
  Fiction, 5651
Gold mines and mining -
  Kansas, 2510, 3615,
  3715, 3717, 3938, 4727,
  4845
Gold mines and mining -
  Nebraska, 2510, 3715,
  3938, 3987, 4727
Gold mines and mining -
  Nova Scotia, 12777
Gold mines and mining -
  Oregon, 4249
Gold mines and mining -
  Texas, 5648
Gold mines and mining -
  The Northwest, 862
Gold mines and mining -
  Washington, 4249, 4308
Gold mines and mining -
  Wyoming, 2877
Gold mines of the Gila,
  5648
The gold mines of Western

Kansas, 4707
The gold mines, scenery and
  climate of Georgia and the
  Carolinas, 5289
The gold placers of California,
  3515
The gold regions of Kansas and
  Nebraska, 3938
The gold seekers, 722
Gold that did not glitter, 3156
Goldberger, Ludwig Max,
  3634
The golden age, 8959
The golden book of Venice,
  11028
The golden bowl, 7121
The golden Christmas, 5160
The Golden Eagle, 9051
Golden feather, 9636
The golden fleece, 9809
The golden fleece divided into
  three parts, 13498
The golden house, 11088
The golden ladder, 11220
The golden legacy, 10374
Golden-mouthed Taylor, 10747
Golden-rod, 9764
The golden rule, 8533, 9256
A golden sorrow, 10541
Golden treasures of poetry,
  romance, and art, 9616
A golden wedding, 3562, 5311
Golder, John, comp., 12296
Goldman, Edward Alphonso,
  1873-1946, 6862
Goldsborough, Charles Washington,
  1779-1843, 12297
Goldsborough, Louis Malesherbes,
  1805-1877, 13202
Goldsborough, William Worthington,
  1831-1901, 3635
Goldschmidt, Albert, 5996
Goldsmid, Edmund Marsden, ed.,
  6925
Goldsmith, Christabel, pseud.,
  10805, 10806
Goldsmith family 12656
Goldsmith, Lewis, 1763?-1846,
  12298

189

Goldsmith, Oliver, 1794-
1861, 2434
Golovin, Ivan Gavrilovich,
b. 1816, 2435
Gómara, Francisco López de,
1510-1560? 6863, 6864
Gomery of Montgomery,
11103
Gómez de Avellaneda y
Arteaga, Gertrudio,
1814-1873, 12299
Gómez de Parada Fonseca
Enríquez, Juan María,
7321
Gomot, Hippolyte, 1837-,
7494
Goncourt, Edmond Huot de,
1822-1896, 7119
Goncourt, Jules, 1830-
1870, 7119
Gone to Texas, 9680
Gonino, J., tr., 6407
González-Blanco, Pedro,
6726
González de Agüeros, Pedro,
2436
González de Argandona,
Juana, 8145
González de la Llana,
Manuel, 6689
González de la Reguera,
Juan Domingo, abp. of
Lima, 1720-1805, 1199
González, José Antonio,
comp., 6865
González, José, conde de
Fuente González, 6657,
8278
González, Juan Vicente,
1810-1866, 6866
González Peña, Carlos,
1885-, 6867
González Suárez, Federico,
abp., 1844-1917, 6868
González y Montoya, José,
2437
Good Americans, 9767
Good company for every day
in the year, 9516

Good for the soul, 9374, 9376
Good in all and none all-good,
10279
A good investment, 9522
The good Mr. Bagglethorpe,
10235
The good-natured pendulum, 9683
Good news from Virginia, 5688
Good order established in
Pennsylvania and New Jersey,
1651
Good Samaritan, 2029
Good society, 9683
The good time coming, 8563
Good wives, 1891
Goodale, Ebenezer, defendant,
2438
Goode, William Henry,
1807-1879, 3636
Goodenow, John Milton,
1782-1838, 12300
Goodhart, Briscoe, 1845-1927,
3637
Goodhue, Josiah Fletcher,
1791-1863, 12301
Goodloe, Abbe Carter, 1867-,
3638, 3639
Goodloe, Albert Theodore, 3640
Goodloe, Daniel Reaves,
b. 1814, 2439
Goodman, John Davidson, 1794-1830.
Review of "Fauna Americana", 12686
Goodmane, W. F., 3641
Goodrich, Chauncey Enoch,
1801-1864, 12302
Goodrich, Elizur, 1734-1797,
12303
Goodrich, Frank Boott,
1826-1894, 2440
Goodrich, Frederick Elizur,
1843-1925, 6869
Goodrich, John Z., b. 1801,
2441
Goodrich, John Z., b. 1801.
Exposition of the J. D. & M.
Williams fraud, and of its
settlement, 7061
Goodrich, Samuel Griswold,
1793-1860, 2442, 2443, 3642,

12754
Goodricke, Henry, 12304
Goodsir, Robert Anstruther, 6870
Goodwin, Henry Martyn, 1820-1893, 12306
Goodwin, Hermon Camp, 1813-1891, 2444, 12307
Goodwin, Isaac, 2445
Goodwin, Nathaniel, 1782-1855, 2446, 2447, 2448
Goodwin, Thomas, 1600-1680, 12308
Gookin, Daniel, 1612?-1687, 12309
Goold, Nathan, 1846-1914, ed., 1803
A goose-chase, 9916
Gorden, Thomas Francis, 1787-1860, 12312, 12313
Gordon, Adoniram Judson, 1836-1895, 2449
Gordon, Armistead Churchill, 1855-1931, 3643, 3644
Gordon, Charles, d. 1817, 880
Gordon, Donald, 1877-, ed., 3648
Gordon, George Henry, 1825?-1886, 3645
Gordon, H. Panmure, 3646
Gordon, Harry, 3647
Gordon, J. S., illustr., 8252
Gordon, James Bentley, 1750-1819, 12310
Gordon, John, d. 1778? 13503
Gordon, John, d. 1845, defendant, 12311
Gordon, Julien, pseud., 9257-9265
Gordon, Marquis Lafayette, 1843-1900, 3648
Gordon, William, defendant, 12311
Gordon, William, 1728-1807, 12314
Gordon, William Robert,

1811-1897, 12315, 12316
Gore, Christopher, 1758-1827, 12318, 12414
Gore, Montague, 12319
The gored huntsman, 10693
Gorgas, William Crawford, 1854-1920, 7420
Gorman, Samuel, 6871
Gorrie, Peter Douglass, 1813-1884, 12320, 12321
Gorton, Samuel, 1592-1677, 12322
Göschen, Georg Joachim, 1752-1828, ed., 321
Gosnold, Bartholomew, d. 1607, 1479
The gospel-covenant, 1671
Gospel family-order, 2300
The gospel of typical servitude, 3131
Goss, Ephraim, 12323
Goss, Warren Lee, 1835-1925, 3649
Gosse, Philip Henry, 1810-1888, 3650, 12324, 12325
The gossips of Rivertown, 9801
Gostkowski, G., baron de, 6872
Gott, Elizabeth, tr., 7932
Gottheil, Gustav, 8425
Gottsberger, Francis, 6433
Gottschall, Amos H., 1854-, 3651, 3652
Götz, Karl, 1903-, 3653
Gouge, William M., 1796-1863, 12326, 12327
Gould, Augustus Addison, 1805-1866, 1404, 12328, 12329
Gould, Benjamin Apthorp, 1824-1896, 12330, 12331, 12332
Gould, Emerson W., b. 1811, 3654
Gould, Hannah Flagg, 1789-1865, 12333
Gould, Jay, 1836-1892, 12334
Gould, John Mead, 1839-, 3655

Gould, John W., 1814-1838,
10916, 12335
Gould, Nathaniel Duren,
1781-1864, 12336
Goulding, Francis Robert,
1810-1881, 3656
Goupil, E. Eugène, 6105
Goupil, René, d. 1642,
13227
Gourdin, Robert N., 11745
Gourlay, Robert Fleming,
1778-1863, 6873, 12337,
12338
Gourlie, John Hamilton,
12339
Goussencourt, chevalier de,
pseud.? 4654
Gouy-d'Arcy, Louis-Henri-
Marthe, marquis de,
1753-1794, 6874
The governess, 10350
Government and liberty
described, 620
The Governor and company
of adventurers of England,
7978
The governor's prerogative,
9582
Gowinius, Sven, 2450
Gracchus Vanderlip,
Adventures of, 4109
Grace (Theology), 2895
Grace (Theology) - Early
works to 1800, 12643
Grace Bartlett, 11187
Grace Dudley, 10510
Grace, Henry, b. 1730?
12340
Grace Morton, 10340
Grace Truman, 3505
Grace Weldon, 9980
Gracie's Alabama brigade,
5130
The gracious presence of
God, 12040
A graduate of Paris, 5258
Grady, Henry Woodfin,
1851-1889, 3657
Grafton, Mass. - Hist.,

1520
Graham, Albert Alexander,
1860-, 6875
Graham and I, 11091
Graham, Frederic Ulric, 6876
Graham, James Duncan, 3658,
5546
Graham, James J., ed., 3659
Graham, Jane Hermione, 6876
Graham, John Andrew, 1764-1841,
12341, 12342
Graham, Samuel, 1756-1831,
3659
Graham, William, 1798-1854,
12343
Grahame, 10264
Grahame, James, 1790-1842,
12344
Grammar, Comparative and general,
97
A grammatical sketch of the
Heve language, 12345
Gran Quivira, N. M., 2915
Granada (Kingdom) - Hist. -
Spanish conquest, 1476-1492,
9997
Granada (Kingdom) - Hist. -
Spanish conquest, 1476-1492 -
Fiction, 9280
Granary burial ground, Boston,
1506
Grand Alliance, War of the,
1689-1697, 1691
Grand Army Hall and Memorial
Association of Illinois, 6877
Grand Army of the Republic,
6878, 6879
The grand era of ruin to nations
from foreign influence, 363
Grand Isle County, Vt. - Hist.,
5860
Grand juries, 13089
Las grandes mentiras de nuestra
historia, 6249
Grandfather Lickshingle, 9244
A grandfather's story of the
first settlers of New England,
12806
Grandfort, Marie (Fontenay) de,

192

"Mme. Manoël de Grand-
fort," 3660, 6880
Grandfort, Marie (Fontenay)
de, "Mme. Manoël de Grand-
fort." L'autre monde,
4276
The Grandissimes, 8926
Grandpapa mouse and his
family, 10046
Grandpierre, Jean Henri,
1799-1874, 12346, 12347
Granger, Gideon, 1767-1822,
12348, 12349
Grant, Andrew, 6881
Grant, Charles, viscount de
Vaux, 12350
Grant, George Monro, 1835-
1902, 7384
Grant, Jeannette A., 6882
Grant, Joseph W., 12351
Grant, Ulysses Simpson,
pres. U. S., 1822-1885,
1531, 1547, 3661, 6569,
8374
Grant, William Robertson,
1811-1852, 535
Grantham, Sir Thomas,
fl. 1673-1711, 3662
Grases, Pedro, 1909-, 6794
Grasse-Tilly, François
Joseph Paul, marquis de,
1722-1788, 4654
Grattan, Thomas Colley,
1792-1864, 3663
Graves, John Temple, 1856-
1925, 3664
Graves, Thomas Graves,
1st baron, 1725-1802,
12352
Graves, William, 1724?-1801,
12352
Gravier, Gabriel, 1827-
1904, ed., 3724
Gravier, Jacques, 1651-1708,
3665, 3666, 12353
Gravities and gaieties,
9627
Gray, Albert Zabriskie,
1840-1889, 6883

Gray, Alonzo, 1808-1860, 12354
The gray and the blue, 10657
Gray, Andrew, 5370, 5512
Gray, Andrew B., 3667
Gray, Asa, 1810-1888, 12355
Gray, Barry, pseud., 9060
The gray champion, 9827
Gray, Edward, 1764-1810,
12356
Gray, Francis Calley, 1790-
1856, 12357, 12358
Gray, Frederick Turell,
1804-1855, 12359
Gray, Horatio, 1828-1903,
12360
Gray, Hugh, 6884
Gray, John Hamilton, b. 1814,
6183
Gray, John W., 3668
Gray, Robert, 1761-1822, 12361
Gray roses, 9740
Gray, Thomas, 1772-1847,
12362, 12363, 12364
Gray, William Cunningham,
1830-1901, 12365
Gray, William Farley, 3669,
12366
Graydon, Alexander, 1752-1818,
12367
Graydon, William Murray, 10283
Grayling, 10783
Grayson, Andrew J., 3670
Grayson, William John,
1788-1863, 3671, 3672
Graysons, Memoirs of the,
5474
Gréard, Octave, 1828-1904,
7494
The great American battle,
11677
The great and final experiment,
11164
Great awakening, 11764
Gt. Brit. - Antiq., 13225
Gt. Brit. Army - Infantry -
Prince of Wales' Leinster
regiment (Royal Canadians),
6129
Gt. Brit. - Army - Officers,

12460
Gt. Brit. - Army -
Recruiting, enlistment,
etc., 12230
Gt. Brit. - Baronetage,
758
Gt. Brit. - Biog., 223,
8177
Gt. Brit. - Biog.-bibl.,
212
Gt. Brit. - Colonies,
1514, 2450, 3249, 3388,
4853, 7913, 12825, 12378
Gt. Brit. - Colonies -
Administration, 1539,
6786, 13040
Gt. Brit. - Colonies -
Africa, South, 760
Gt. Brit. - Colonies -
America, 663, 13070,
13369, 13509
Gt. Brit. - Colonies -
America - Financial
questions, 13017
Gt. Brit. - Colonies -
Canada, 1180, 12588
Gt. Brit. - Colonies -
Econ. cond., 4176
Gt. Brit. - Colonies -
Education, 1528
Gt. Brit. - Colonies -
Law, 11809
Gt. Brit. - Colonies -
Native races, 759, 760
Gt. Brit. - Colonies -
North America, 230, 380,
519, 1071, 1709, 2242,
2288, 3737, 4502, 6434,
6435, 6843, 11258, 11656,
12132, 12304, 13040
Gt. Brit. - Colonies -
North America - Comm.,
6434, 6435
Gt. Brit. - Colonies -
North America - Financial
questions, 1509, 11617,
13211, 13494
Gt. Brit. - Colonies -
North America - Financial

questions. Pennsylvanian,
319
Gt. Brit. - Colonies -
West Indies, 500, 501,
12172, 13327
Gt. Brit. - Comm., 91
Gt. Brit. - Comm. - Hist.,
11904
Gt. Brit. - Comm. - Russia,
12192
Gt. Brit. - Comm. - South
America, 196
Gt. Brit. - Comm. - U. S.,
1329, 11713, 13477
Gt. Brit. - Comm. - West Indies,
2470, 12368
Gt. Brit. - Commercial policy,
751, 752, 1266, 12287,
13478
Gt. Brit. - Commissioners of
longitudes, 993
Gt. Brit. - Constitutional
history - Sources, 11445
Gt. Brit. - Constitutional law,
11660
Gt. Brit. Court of King's bench,
2199
Gt. Brit. - Defenses, 1706
Gt. Brit. - Descr. & trav.
3388, 3564, 3829, 4853,
4954, 5789, 10491, 11157,
11159
Gt. Brit. - Econ. cond., 112,
1537, 4487, 13113
Gt. Brit. - Econ. policy,
1539
Gt. Brit. - Emig. & immig.,
2195, 12337
Gt. Brit. - Emig. & immig. -
Hist., 7158
Gt. Brit. - Fiction, 9641
Gt. Brit. - For. rel., 1947,
6259
Gt. Brit. - For. rel. - 1760-
1789, 13364
Gt. Brit. - For. rel. - 1837-
1901, 11466, 11467
Gt. Brit. - For. rel. - Confe-
derate States of America,

4763, 12231
Gt. Brit. - For. rel. -
France, 2183
Gt. Brit. - For. rel. -
Guatemala, 8298
Gt. Brit. - For. rel. -
Netherlands, 2026
Gt. Brit. - For. rel. -
South America,
1588, 1713
Gt. Brit. - For. rel. -
Spain, 12129, 12368,
13408
Gt. Brit. - For. rel. -
Treaties, 11371
Gt. Brit. - For. rel. -
U. S., 295, 519, 520,
1142, 1948, 2183, 2416,
12199, 12231, 12378,
12797, 13405
Gt. Brit. - Historical
geography, 761
Gt. Brit. - Hist. -
Commonwealth and pro-
tectorate, 1649-1660 -
Fiction, 9843
Gt. Brit. - Hist. - To 449,
Sources, 761
Gt. Brit. - Hist. - 1066-
1687 - Fiction, 9847
Gt. Brit. - Hist. - 1714-
1837, 3662
Gt. Brit. - Hist. - 1760-
1789, 13499
Gt. Brit. - Hist. - Edward
VI and Mary, 1547-1558 -
Fiction, 10286
Gt. Brit. - Hist. - George
II, 1727-1760 - Pamphlets,
13073
Gt. Brit. - Hist. - George
III - 1760-1820, 103,
115, 1131, 1362
Gt. Brit. - Hist. - George
III, 1760-1820 - Pamphlets,
11227, 13431
Gt. Brit. - Hist. - George
IV, 1820-1830, 1131
Gt. Brit. - Hist., Naval,

185, 1540, 1690
Gt. Brit. - Hist., Naval -
18th cent., 1012, 1477, 2027
Gt. Brit. - Hist., Naval -
19th cent., 1477
Gt. Brit. - Hist., Naval -
Stuarts, 1603-1714, 1691
Gt. Brit. - Hist., Naval -
Tudors, 1485-1603, 11412
Gt. Brit. - Hist. - Puritan
revolution, 1642-1660 -
Fiction, 9842
Gt. Brit. - Hist. - Stuarts,
1603-1714 - Fiction, 9463
Gt. Brit. - Hist. - Tudors,
1485-1603, 11412
Gt. Brit. - Hist. - Wars of
the Roses, 1455-1485, 4737
Gt. Brit. - Laws, statutes,
etc., 1689-1694 (William and
Mary), 3805
Gt. Brit. - Navy, 1949
Gt. Brit. - Navy - Hist., 2096,
2187
Gt. Brit. - Navy - Lists of
vessels, 1757
Gt. Brit. - Neutrality, 1948
Gt. Brit. - Parliament, 6885,
6886, 6887
Gt. Brit. - Parliament. House
of lords, 13460
Gt. Brit. - Parliament - Reform,
11665
Gt. Brit. - Peerage, 758
Gt. Brit. - Pol. & govt., 113,
1594, 1597, 2525, 5050,
11456, 11660
Gt. Brit. - Pol. & govt. -
1727-1760, 2027, 13408
Gt. Brit. - Pol. & govt. -
1760-1789, 394, 1708, 2307,
11969, 12126, 13258, 13369,
13389, 13395, 13409
Gt. Brit. - Pol. & govt. -
1762-1765, 225
Gt. Brit. - Pol. & govt. -
1779, 95, 102
Gt. Brit. - Pol. & govt. -
1783, 11517

Gt. Brit. - Pol. & govt. -
1784, 11549
Gt. Brit. - Pol. & govt. -
1789-1820, 1932, 11616
Gt. Brit. - Pol. & govt. -
1837-1901, 5848
Gt. Brit. - Pol. & govt. -
19th cent., 1596
Gt. Brit. Privy council.
Judicial committee, 11809
Gt. Brit. - Soc. life &
cust., 8641, 10861,
2785, 12841, 13498
Gt. Brit. Sovereigns,
etc., 1649-1658,
(Oliver Cromwell), 12368
Gt. Brit. Treaties, etc.,
2183
The great Canadian north
west, 6050
The great carbuncle, 9827
The Great central route via
Nebraska City to Pike's
Peak, 3673
The great condition, 10016
The great country, 5013
The great deliverance and the
new career, 2792
The great deserts and forests
of North America, 3517
The great divorce case!
13171
The great fur land, 7886
The great good place, 10016
The great impeachment and
trial of Andrew Johnson,
13230
The great issue to be
decided in November
next! 12369
Great Lakes, 9619, 12239
Great Lakes - Comm., 940
Great Lakes - Descr. &
trav., 5103, 7454
Great Lakes - Disc. &
explor., 7008
A great love, 8914
A great man fallen! 7662
Great plains - Descr. &

trav., 1197, 4686, 5060
Great providences toward the
loyal part of this nation,
1299
The great question for the
people! 12645
The great rebellion, 11391
Great Revival of 1801, 4866
The great revolution of 1840,
7594
Great Salt Lake, 5255, 5604
Great Salt Lake - Descr. &
trav., 4281
The great secret, 10083
Great Smoky Mountains, 2997
The great south, 4173
The great southwest, 4598
The great stone of Sardis,
10889
The great surrender to the
rebels in arms, 12370
Great trans-continental tourist's
guide, 12371
The great "trunk mystery" of
New York City, 9648
The great west, 3570, 3736
The greatening of Abraham
Lincoln, 7161
Greater Britain, 3249
"The greatest of these is love",
9331
Greatness in little things,
10584
Greaves' disappearance, 9817
Grece, Charles Frederick,
12372
Greece - Colonies, 13425
Greek language - Grammar -
1500-1800, 6373
Greeley family, 9036
Greeley, Horace, 1811-1872,
3026, 3675, 6888, 11226,
11450, 12373, 12374
Greely, Allen, 1781-1866,
12375,
Green, Ashbel, 1762-1848,
12376, 12377
Green Cove Spring, Florida,
5489

Green, Duff, 1791-1875,
12378
Green family (Thomas
Green, 1606?-1667),
12400
Green, Frank William,
6889
Green, George Washington,
1811-1883, 12393, 12394,
12395
Green, H. T., 3677
Green, Jacob, 1722-1790,
12379
Green, Jasper, illustr.,
10049
Green, John, 211
Green, John, 1835-1913,
12380
Green, John Bremner,
d. 1905, 12381
Green, John Orne, 1841-,
12382
Green, John Paterson,
1845-, 3678
Green, Joseph, 1706-1780,
12383
Green, Matthew, 1696-1737,
12384
Green mountain annals,
9530
Green, Nelson Winch, 3679
Green peas, picked from the
patch of Invisible Green,
esq., 9242
Green, Raleigh Travers,
1872-, 3680
Green, Samuel, d. 1822,
12385
Green, Samuel, 1798-1834,
12386
Green, Samuel Abbott,
1530-1918, ed. and tr.,
3239
Green, Thomas Jefferson,
1801-1863, 3681
Green, Thomas Marshall,
1837-1904, 3682
Green, William, 1748-,
3683

Green, William Spotswood,
1847-, 6890
Green-back, pseud., 12387
Greenbacks, 11981, 12387
Greene, Albert Gorton,
1802-1868, ed., 2128
Greene, Asa, 1789-1838,
12388
Greene, Benjamin, 1764-1837,
12389
Greene, Charles S., lieut.-col.
61st Pa. infantry, 12390
Greene, Christopher Rhodes,
1786-1825, 12391
Greene, David, 1797?-1866,
12392
Greene, J. W., jt. author,
2269
Greene, Jerome B., 12396
Greene, John W., 3684
Greene, Jonathan Harrington,
b. 1812, 12397
Greene, Max, 3685
Greene, Nathaniel, 1742-1786,
12395
Greene, Richard Henry, 1839-,
12398
Greene, Samuel D., b. 1788,
12399
Greene, Samuel Stillman,
1810-1883, 12400
Greene, William, 1797-1883,
12401
Greene, William Batchelder,
1819-1878, 12402
Greene, William H., 12403
Greenhow, Robert, 1800-1854,
6891
Greenhow, Rose (O'Neal)
1814-1864, 12404
Greenland - Descr. & trav.,
12459, 13372
The Greenland minstrel, 1375
Greenland - Poetry, 1375
Greenleaf, A. B., 3686
Greenleaf family (Edmund
Greenleaf, 1574-1671),
12405
Greenleaf, Jonathan,

1785-1865, 12405, 12406
Greenleaf, Lawrence Nichols,
b. 1838, 12407
Greenleaf, Moses, 1777-
1834, 12408, 12409
Greenleaf, Simon, 1783-
1853, 12410
Greenough, William Parker,
1830?-1900, 6892
Greenough, William Whitwell,
d. 1899, 12411, 12412
Greenough's directory...
of Brookline, 1566
Greenwood, Andrew, 1776-
1816, 12413
Greenwood cemetery, 1855
Greenwood cemetery,
Brooklyn - Poetry, 1855
Greenwood, Francis William
Pitt, 1797-1843, 12414,
12415
Greenwood leaves, 10222
Greenwood, Thomas,
1851-1908, 3687
Gregg, Alexander, bp.,
1819-1893, 12255,
12416
Gregg, Andrew, 1755-1835,
2211
Gregg, Jarvis, 1808-1836,
12417
Gregg, Josiah, 1806-1850?
3688, 6893, 6894, 6895
Gregg, William, 1800-
1867, 12418
Grégoire, Henri-Baptiste,
constitutional bp. of
Blois, 1750-1831, 6484,
6896, 6897, 7622, 12419,
12420, 12421, 12422
Grégoire, Henri-Baptiste,
constitutional bp. of
Blois, 1750-1831.
Observations critiques,
813
Gregory, John, civil
engineer, 12423
Gregory, Olinthus Gilbert,
1774-1841, 1721

Gregory, Samuel, 6898
Greifenstein, 6495, 9224
Grenfell, Sir William Thomason,
1865-1940, 6899, 6900, 6901
Grenier, Edouard, 1819-1901,
6902
Grenville, George, 1712-1770,
12424, 13509
Greswell, William Henry Parr,
1848-1923, 6903
Greville Fane, 7126
Grey, Sir Charles Edward,
1785-1865, 12426
Grey, Isaac, 12427
Greyslaer, 3893
Grice, Julia, 9331
Grider, Henry, 1796-1866, 12428
Gridley, John, 12429
Gridley, Philo, 1796-1864,
12430
Grier, D. P., 2687
Grier, Thomas Graham, 1865-,
6904
Grierson cavalry raid, 1863,
5321
Grierson raids, 5321
Griesinger, Theodor, 1809-1884,
3689
Grieve, George, 1748-1809,
tr., 2979
Griffin, Augustus, 1767-1866,
12431
Griffin, Frederick, 12432
Griffin, Gilderoy Wells,
1840-1891, 3690, 3691
Griffin, John, 1769-1834, 12433
Griffin, Solomon Bulkey,
1852-, 6905
Griffin's journal, 12431
Griffing, Jane R., 3692
Griffis, Robert F., pub.,
1877
Griffith, James Barton, 3693
Griffith, John, 1713-1776,
3694, 12434
Griffith, Thomas Waters,
1767-1838, 12435
Griffith, William, 1766-1826,
12436, 12437, 12438

Grigsby, Hugh Blair,
1806-1881, 12439,
12440, 12441
Grigsby, Melvin, 1845-,
3695
Grile, Dod, pseud.,
8802
Grim, Charles Frederic,
12442
Grimes, Absalom Carlisle,
1834-1911, 3696
Grimes, Bryan, 1828-1880,
3697
Grimes, James Wilson,
1816-1872, 7945
Grimes, John Bryan,
1868-1923, 11515
Grimké, Frederick, 1791-
1863, 12443
Grimké, Thomas Smith,
1786-1834, ed., 2151,
12444, 12445, 12446
Grimshaw, William, 1782-
1852, 12447, 12448
Grimsley, Elizabeth Todd,
7300
Gringo, 3197, 8195
Los gringos, 8406, 8407
Grinnell expedition, 1st,
1850-1851, 13428
Grinnell expedition, 2d,
1853-1855, 2428, 13428,
Gripenberg, Alexandra,
friherrinna, 1857-
1913, 3698
Griper (ship), 7695
Griscom, John, 1774-1852,
12450
Griscom, John Hoskins,
1809-1874, 12449,
12450, 12451
Grisebach, August Heinrich
Rudolf, 1814-1879, 12452
Griswold, Alexander Viets,
bp., 1766-1843, 12453
Griswold, Mrs. Charlotte
A. (Myers), 12457
Griswold, Chauncey D.,
12454

Griswold, Hattie Tyng, 10899
Griswold, Rufus Wilmot,
1815-1857, 3699, 3700,
3701, 3702, 12455, 12456,
12457
Gritos del capvchino enfermo
a todos los predicadores del
orbe, 8008
The groans of Jamaica, 12458
Groce Camp, Texas, 4627
The grocery man, 10502
Grone, A. C. E. von, ed., 6906
Grone, Carl von, d. 1849, 6906
Gronovius, Joannes Fredericus,
1611-1671, 3703
Gronovius, Joannes Fredericus,
1690-1760. Flora virginica,
930
Groome, W., illustr., 6785
Groot, Jeldert Jansz, 12459
Gros, Jean Baptiste Louis,
baron, 1793-1870, 7903
Grose, Francis, 1731?-1791,
12460
Grose, Howard Benjamin,
1851-, 6907
Grose, William, 1812-1900,
3704
Grosó, José L., jt. author,
7769
Gross, Charles Heebner,
1838-1902, 12461
Gross, Samuel David, 1805-
1884, 3705, 3706, 3707,
3708, 12462, 12463
Gross, William, 1796-1823,
defendant, 12464
Grosscup, Ben S., jt. author,
5798
Grosvenor, Daniel, 1750-1834,
12466
Grosvenor, David Adams,
1802-1866, 12465
Grosvenor, Ebenezer, 1739-
1788, 12466
Grosvenor, Lemuel, 12467
Grotius, pseud., 12468
Groton, Mass. First parish
church. Ecclesiastical

council, 1826, 12469
Groton, Mass. - Hist.,
1766
Groton, Mass. Public
library, 12470
The group, 1901
Groussac, Paul, 1848-1929,
3709, 5849
Grout, Henry Martyn, 12471
Grout, William Wallace,
1836-1902, 12472
Groux, Daniel Edward,
12473
Grove, Joseph, d. 1764,
12474
Grover, Martin, 1811-1875,
12475
Growler's income tax,
8564
The growth of New York,
12476
Gruff, Growler, pseud.,
ed., 11933
Grund, Francis Joseph,
1805-1863, 3710,
12477, 12478
Grundy, Felix, 1777-1840,
12479
Gruner, Adelgunde, ed.,
3586
Guadalajara de Indias,
7663
Guadalajara, Jal. - Descr.,
6472, 7647
Guadalajara, Jal. - Hist.,
6070, 6846, 7907
Guadalajara, Mexico.
Catedral. Cabildo, 12480
Guadalajara, Mexico.
Santuario de Nuestra
Señora de San Juan, 6754
Guadalajara, Mexico.
Seminario conciliar,
7876
Guadalajara, Mexico -
Water-supply, 6364
Guadalupe Hidalgo, Treaty
of, 1848, 11942
Guadalupe, Nuestra Señora

de, 1786, 1787, 6160, 6269,
7013, 7789
Guadeloupe - Descr. & trav.,
1649, 4644
Guadeloupe - Hist., 2232
La Guadeloupe pittoresque,
1649
Guanajuato, Mexico (City),
7422
Guanajuato, Mexico (State),
7422
Guaraní language - Dict. -
Spanish, 7921
Guatemala, 442
Guatemala, ancient and modern,
7551
Guatemala - Antiq., 6166,
6167, 6406, 6407, 7551
Guatemala - Bound., 6803
Guatemala - Bound. - British
Honduras, 8298
Guatemala (City), 5921
Guatemala (City) Escuela normal
central para varones, 6908
Guatemala (City) Universidad
nacional. Facultad de
ciencias juridicas y sociales.
Revista, 8298
Guatemala - Civilization, 6908
Guatemala - Descr. & trav.,
5880, 5921, 6166, 6252,
6452, 6777, 6908, 6984,
7191, 7235, 7236, 7306,
7439, 7452, 7521, 7534,
7551 7552, 7648, 7655,
7686, 7893, 7917, 7961,
7996, 8075, 8164, 8182,
8183, 8282
Guatemala - Descr. & trav. -
Guide-books, 6455, 6909,
7960
Guatemala - Descr. & trav. -
Poetry, 7233, 7234, 7237,
7238
Guatemala. Dirección General
de Caminos, 6909
Guatemala - Econ. cond., 7452
Guatemala - For. rel. -
Gt. Brit., 8298

12487
Guild, Calvin, 1808-1897,
12488
Guild family (John Guild,
1616?-1682), 12488
Guild, Reuben Aldridge,
1822-1899, 12489,
12490, 12491, 12492
Guild, Samuel Eliot,
1819-1862, 12493
Guild, William, 12494,
12495
Guillemin-Tarayre, Edmond,
1832-1920, 6913, 6914
Guillermin de Montpinay,
Gilbert, 12496
Guimarães, Celso Foot,
1907-, 3716
Guinea - Descr. & trav.,
522, 6989, 8320, 8321,
13110
Guinnard, Auguste, b. 1832?
12497, 12498
Guiral Moreno, Mario,
1882-, ed., 6522
Guirey, William, 12499
Guiteras, Pedro José,
1814-1890, 12500
Guizot, François Pierre
Guillaume, 1787-1874,
12501, 12502
The Gulf coast, 5710
The Gulf-department in
'63, 12781
Gulf states, 4332
Gulf states - Descr. &
trav., 5589, 5710
Gulf states - Hist.,
13456
Gulliver Joi, 10504
Gulzar, 4923
Gun, rod, and saddle,
12257
Gunby, A. L., 6915
Gunn, Alexander, 1784-1829,
12503
Gunn, Benjamin Jesse,
1865-, 6916
Gunn, Otis Berthoude,

1828-1901, 3717
Gunnar, 8833
Gunnison, John Williams,
1812-1853, 3615, 3616,
3718, 12504
The Gunpowder Plot, 9463
Gunpowder Plot - Fiction, 9463
Gunston Hall, 7431
Günther, Erich, 6917
Gurley, Phineas Densmore,
1816-1868, 6918, 12505
Gurley, Ralph Randolph,
1792-1872, 12506, 12507,
12508
Gurney, Alfred, 1845-1898,
3719
Gurney, Joseph John, 1788-
1847, 3720, 6919
Gurowski, Adam, 1805-1866,
3721
Gustavus Vasa, the deliverer
of his country, 1564
Gutenberg, Johann, 1397?-1468,
10497
Guthrie, James, 6568
Guthrie, William, 1708-1770,
3722
Gutiérrez, Blas J., defendant,
12509
Gutiérrez, Carlos, 8096
Gutiérrez de la Arena, Diego
Martín, 6806, 7962, 7963
Gutiérrez de Quintanilla, José
Manuel, 6350
Gutiérrez, Juan María, 1809-
1878, ed., 7853, 12510,
12511
Gutiérrez Nájera, Manuel,
1859-1895, 7844
Guy Rivers, 10772
Guyer, Isaac D., 12512
Guzmán, Antonio Leocádio,
1801-1884, 12513
Guzmán de Alfarache, 5861,
5862
Gwin, William McKendree,
1805-1885, 3723
Gyles, John, 1678?-1755,
12514

The gypsies of the
Danes' dike, 10517

Haas, Elise S., 6920
Habeas corpus, 1454,
13089, 13134
Habeas corpus - U. S.,
1676, 6082, 11272,
12461, 13273
Habersham, S. E., 3724
L'habitation Saint-Ybars,
4451
Hachard, Marie Madeleine,
in religion, Sister
Saint Stanislas, 3725
Hackelton, Mrs. Marcia
W., 12515
Hacker, William, d. 1830?
5754
Hackett, Horatio Balch,
1808-1875, 12516
Hackett, James, 12517
Hackett, Karleton, ed.,
6921
Hackett, William Henry
Young, 1800-1878,
1488
Haco, Dion, pseud.,
ed., 8133
Hadfield, Joseph, 1759-
1851, 6922
Hadfield, William, 1806-
1887, 12518, 12519
Hadley, John Vestal,
1840-1915, 3726
Hadley, Mass., 12521
Hadley, Mass. - Hist.,
12571
Hadley, William Hobart,
comp., 12520
Haenke, Thaddäus, 1761-
1817, 437
Hagadorn, William, jr.,
12522
Hagar, a story of today,
8948
Hagar the martyr, 10876
Hagen, Hermann August,

1817-1893, 12523
Hagen, Hermann Bessel,
1889-, 6923
Hager, Albert David, 1817-
1888, 12524
Hager, Heinrich, 3727
Haggard, Henry Rider,
1856-, 7144
Haglee, Henry Morris,
1815-1886, 13024
Hagner, Charles Valerius,
12525
Hagner, Thomas Holme,
12526
Hague, Mrs. Parthenia
Antoinette (Vardaman)
1838-, 3728
Hague, William, 1808-1887,
12527, 12528
Haies, Edward, 1479
Haigh, Samuel, 12529
Hain, Augustus H. F.,
12530
Haines, Elijah Middlebrook,
1822-1889, ed.,
12531, 12532
Haines, William A., 12533
Haines, Zenas T., 3729
The hair-breadth escapes
and adventures of "Grizzly
Adams," 2491
A hairdresser's experience in
high life, 4835
Haiti, 6064, 6924, 7261, 11360,
11974
Haiti - Commerce, 6771, 6874,
7939, 7940, 7941
Haiti - Constitution, 7507,
11360
Haiti - Descr. & trav.,
2768, 6583, 6924, 7143,
8399, 12651, 12704
Haiti - Hist., 1993, 3237,
3829, 6064, 6477, 7261,
11568, 12704
Haiti - Hist. - To 1791,
11235
Haiti - Hist. - 1804-1844,
12496

Haiti - Hist. - Revolution, 6771
Haiti - Hist. - Revolution, 1791-1804, 11423, 11767, 11855, 12861
Haiti - Hist. - Revolution, 1791-1804 - Claims, 997
Haiti - Hist. - Revolution, 1791-1804 - Fiction, 8599
Haiti - Pol. & govt., 6924
Haiti - Pol. & govt. - To 1789, 7269, 7934, 7935, 7936, 7937, 7938, 7939, 7940
Haiti - Pol. & govt. - 1791-1804, 778
Haiti - Pol. & govt. - Revolution, 6874, 7507, 7598, 7790, 7828, 7933, 8053
Hakluyt, Richard, 1552?-1616, 6925
Hal Gilman, 3135
Halamar, 9327
Der Halbindianer, 4498
Haldeman, Samuel Stechman, 1812-1880, 5255
Haldimand, Sir Frederick, 1718-1791, 6297
Hale, B. E., 12534
Hale, Benjamin, 1797-1863, 12535
Hale, Mrs. C. L., 12536
Hale, Charles, 1831-1882, 12537
Hale, Edward Everett, 1822-1909, 2451, 6926, 8597, 12538, 12539
Hale, Enoch, 1790-1848, 11725, 12540
Hale family, 3730
Hale, John, 1800-1852, 3730
Hale, Lucretia Peabody, 1820-1900, 8597, 9688, 9693
Hale, Mercy, b. 1805, 2452

Hale, Nathan, 1755-1776, 7077
Hale, Nathan, 1755-1776 - Fiction, 10765
Hale, Nathan, 1784-1863, 2453, 2454, 8804
Hale, Salma, 1787-1866, 2455, 2456, 12541
Hale, Mrs. Sarah Josepha (Buell) 1788-1879, 2457, 2458, 2459
Hale, Susan, 1833-1910, 6926, 6927
Hales, John Groves, 12542
Haley, Michael Joachim, 1846-, jt. author, 4676
Haley, Thomas, 12543
Half a century, 5330
A half-century of the Unitarian controversy, 12053
Een half jaar in Amerika, 4197
Haliburton, Robert Grant, 12544
Haliburton, Thomas Chandler, 1796-1865, 3731, 12545, 12546, 12547, 12548
Haliburton, William, 12549
Halkett, J., 6029
Halkett, John, 1768-1852, 12550
Hall, Aaron, 1751-1814, 12551
Hall, Abraham Oakley, 1826-1898, 3732
Hall, Alfred Bates, 1875-1936, 6928
Hall, Anna Maria (Fielding) "Mrs. S. C. Hall", 1800-1881, 12552
Hall, Arethusa, 1802-1891, 12553
Hall, Basil, 1788-1844, 3733, 3734, 6929, 6930
Hall, Basil, 1788-1844. Travels in North America, 1260, 1262
Hall, Baynard Rush, 12554
Hall, Benjamin Franklin,

1814-1891, 12555,
12556, 12557
Hall, Benjamin Homer,
1830-1893, 12558,
12559
Hall, Charles Francis,
1821-1871, 12560
Hall, Charles Henry,
1820-1895, 12561
Hall, Clayton Colman,
1847-1916, ed.,
2460
Hall, David A., 11843
Hall, Daniel Weston, 1841-,
12562
Hall, David, 1683-1756,
12563
Hall, Edward Brooks,
1800-1866, 12564,
12565
Hall, Edward H., 2552
Hall, Edward Hepple, 1876,
3735, 3736, 5916, 12566,
12567
Hall, Edwin, 1802-1877,
comp., 12568
Hall, F., 3737
Hall, Fayette, 6931
Hall, Francis, d. 1833,
3738, 6932, 12569
Hall, Frederick, 1780-
1843, 3739, 12570,
12571
Hall, Gordon, 1823-1879,
6933, 12572
Hall, Harrison, 1785-1866,
ed., 12582
Hall, Henry Ware, 1839-
1864, 2302
Hall, J. B., 3740
Hall, James, 1744-1826,
3741
Hall, James, 1793-1868,
3742-3754, 5679, 12573
Hall, James, 1793-1868.
Statistics of the West,
2869
Hall, James, 1811-1878,
5255, 12574

Hall, John, 880, 2503
Hall, John, 1806-1894, 12575
Hall, John Taylor, 12576
Hall, John W., 12577
Hall, Jonathan Prescott, 1796-
1862, 12578
Hall, Joseph, 1761-1848,
12579
Hall, Marshall, 1790-1857,
3755
Hall, Nathaniel, 1805-1875,
6934
Hall, Newman, 1816-1902, 6935,
12580, 12581
The hall of fantasy, 9823
Hall, Mrs. Sarah (Ewing)
1761-1830, 12582
Hall, Sydney, illustr., 5926
Hall, Willard, 1780-1875,
12583
Hall, Rev. William A., 12584
Hall, William Henry Bullock,
1837-, 6936
Hall, Winchester, 1819-,
3756
Halleck, Fitz-Greene, 1790-
1867, 12585, 12586
Hallen, Albin, 1849-1924,
7494
Haller, Granville Owen,
1820-1897, 3757
Hallett, Benjamin Franklin,
1797-1862, ed., 12587
Halley, Edmond, 1656-1742,
11945
Halliburton, Sir Brenton,
1773-1860, 12588
Halliday, Sir Andrew,
1781-1830, 12589
Hallock, Charles, 1834-1917,
3758
Hallock, Gerard, 1800-1866,
12592
Hallock, Robert T., 12590
Hallock, William Allen,
1794-1880, 12591
Hallock, William H., 12592
Hallowell, Sarah C., 8587
Halpin, Will R., 6937

Halsey, Lewis, 1843-
1914, 12593
Halsey, William, 1765?-
1843, 12594
Halstead, Murat, 1829-
1908, 6938
A halt at dawn, 11191
Hambden, pseud., 12595
Hambleton, James Pinkney,
12596
Hambrecht, George P.,
6567
Hamburg-südamerikanische
dampfschifffahrts-
gesellschaft, 6939
Hamersly, Lewis Randolph,
1847-1910, 12597
Hamilton, Alexander,
1757-1804, 708, 1807,
2422, 7311, 7803, 8131,
9022, 12140, 12598, 12599,
12600, 12601, 12602,
12603, 12604, 13496
Hamilton, Alice King.
White lilies, 10115
Hamilton, Andrew Jackson,
1815-1875, 12605
Hamilton, Lord Archibald,
d. 1754, 12606
Hamilton, Lady Augusta,
12607
Hamilton college, Clinton,
N. Y., 616, 2268, 12619,
12620
Hamilton college, Clinton,
N. Y. Phoenix society,
12430
Hamilton college, Clinton,
N. Y. Union society,
12430
Hamilton, Dorothy, 6940
Hamilton family, 7182,
7803
Hamilton family of Charles
county, 7182
Hamilton, Frank Hastings,
1813-1886, 12608
Hamilton, Gail, pseud.,
3262

Hamilton, George, surgeon,
12609
Hamilton, Henry, d. 1796, 3760
Hamilton, Henry, pseud.,
5236, 5242
Hamilton, James, 1786-1857,
12610, 12611
Hamilton, James, 1814-1867,
12612
Hamilton, James Alexander,
1788-1878, 12613, 13178
Hamilton, James Cleland,
1836-, 6941
Hamilton, Joseph Grégoire
de Roulhac, 1878-, ed., 5148
Hamilton, Leonidas Le Cenci,
6942, 6943, 6944
Hamilton, Mass. - Hist., 2246
Hamilton, Pierce Stevens,
12614
Hamilton, Schuyler, 1822-1903,
12615
Hamilton society, New York, 392
Hamilton, Thomas, 1789-1842,
3761, 6945, 6946
Hamilton township, N. J., 8447
Hamilton, W. H. A strange
wound, 10115
Hamilton, William, 1811-1891,
12616
Hamilton, William Richard,
1777-1859, 12617
Hamilton, William T., d. 1842,
12618
The Hamiltons, 8795
Hamlin, Augustus Choate,
1829-1905, 12621
Hamlin, Hannibal, 1809-1891,
873, 6458
Hamm, Margherita Arlina,
1871-1907, 6948
Hammer, Victor, 1882-, 8190
Hammett, Samuel Adams,
1816-1865, 3762, 3763
Hammond, Charles, 1813-1878,
12622
Hammond, Jabez Delano, 1778-
1855, 12623, 12624
Hammond, James Henry,

206

1807-1864, 12625,
12626
Hammond, John, 3764
Hammond, John, fl. 1655,
12627
Hammond, Jonathan Pinkney,
d. 1884, 12628
Hammond, Marcus Claudius
Marcellus, 1814-1876,
12629
Hammond, Samuel H.,
1809-1878, 12630,
12631
Hammond versus Heamans,
3764
Hammond, Wells Stoddard,
12632
Hammond, William Alexander,
1828-1900, 12633
Hamon, Henry, 12634
Hamor, Ralph, the younger,
3765
Hampden, pseud., 12635
Hampshire and Hampden
canal company, 1906
Hampshire co., Mass. -
Descr. & trav., 2181
Hampton Heights, 10860
Hampton, John S., 3766
Hampton, N. H. Congre-
gational church, 415
Hampton, N. H. - Hist.,
415
Hampton Roads Peace
Conference, 1865,
6347, 7288
Hanaford, Jeremiah Lyford,
b. 1834, 12636
Hanaford, Mrs. Phebe Ann
(Coffin) 1829-1921,
12637, 12638
Hanckel, Thomas M.,
12046, 12639
Hancock, John, 12640,
12641
Hancock, John, 1671-1752,
12642
Hancock, John, 1702-1744,
12643, 12644

Hancock, John, 1824-1893, 12645
Hancock, Richard R., 1841?-1906,
3767
Hancock, William, emigrant,
12646
The hand but not the heart, 8565
The hand of God in American
history, 11264
The hand of God in the great
man, 925
Hand, William M., 12647
Handbook for immigrants to the
United States, 3768
A handbook of Florida, 4619
Hand-book of the state of
Mississippi, 4483
Hand-book to Kansas territory,
4910
Handbuch der geographischen
wissenschaft, 6923
Handlemann, Heinrich, 1827-
1891, 12648
A handful of lavender, 4917
Handlin, William Wallace,
b. 1830, 12649
Hands off, 9681
Handy, Isaac William Ker,
1815-1878, 12650
Haney, William Henry, 1882-,
3769
Hanford, Levi, 1759-1854,
1754
Hanks, N. C., 6949
Hanley, Mrs. May Carr, 6950
Hanna, Stewart William,
d. 1851, 12651
Hannaford, Ebenezer, 1840-,
3770
Hannah, 10377
Hannah Thurston, 10926
Hannay, J., 10916
Hannay, James, 1842-1910,
6951
Hannibal, Julius Caesar,
pseud., 10198
Hannibal's man, 10144
Hano, Juan Antonio de, 7108,
7909
Hanotaux, Gabriel, 6825

207

Hanover, Mass. - Geneal, 892
Hanover, Mass. - Hist., 892
Hans Dundermann, 9486
Hansford, 5478
Hanson, Alexander Contee, 1749-1806, 12652, 12653, 12654
Hanson, Christian, 12656
Hanson, Mrs. Elizabeth, fl. 1703-1741, 12655
Hanson, John Halloway, 1815-1854, 12656
Hanson, John Wesley, 1823-1901, 3771, 12657, 12658
Hanström, Bertil, 1891-, 3772
Hanway, Jonas, 1712-1786, 12659
The happiness of man the glory of God, 1610
Happy-go-lucky, 9754
Happy hearts make happy homes, 10086
Happy home, woman's rights, and divorce, 9010
Harbough, Henry, 1817-1867, 12660, 12661, 12662
Harben, W. H., 10125
Harben, William Nathaniel, 1858-1919, 3773, 3774, 10125
The Harbinger, 12663
Harbison, Massy (White) "Mrs. J. Harbison," 1770, 12664
Harbor and river convention. Chicago, 1847, 12665
Harby, Isaac, 1788-1828, 12666
Harcourt, Sir William George Granville Venables Vernon, 1827-1904, 12667, 12668, 12669
Harcourt, T. Arundel,

d. 1884, 5996
Hard, Abner, 3775
Harden, Edward Jenkins, 1813-1873, 12670
Harden, Jacob S., 1837-1860, 12671
Harden, Mrs. Louisa (Dorland) d. 1859, 12671
Hardenbrook, Mrs. L. E. L., 10448
Hardie, James, 1750?-1826? 12672-12676
Hardin, Benjamin, 1784-1852, 12677
Hardin co., Ky., 5953
Hardin co., Ky. - Biog., 6952
Hardin co., Ky. Historical Society, 6952
Harding, Benjamin, 12678
Harding, George Canady, 1829-1881, 6953
Harding, Stephen S., 12679
Harding, Warren Gamaliel, pres. U. S., 1865-1923, 7079
Hardinge, Sam Walde, 11455
Hardman, William, 1828-1890, 3776
Hardy, Campbell, 6954
Hardy, Iza Duffus, 3777, 3778
Hardy, John, fl. 1670-1671, 12680
Hardy, Mary (McDowell) Duffus, lady, 1825?-1891, 3779, 3780
Hardy, Robert William Hale, d. 1871, 6955
Hardy, William, defendant, 12681
Hare, Joseph Thompson, 3781
Hare, Joseph Thompson - Fiction, 9932
Hare, Robert, 1781-1858, 12682
Hargood, Sir William, 1762-1839, 186
Haring, Clarence Henry, 1885-, 6956
Harlan, James, 1820-1899, 6957
Harlan, Mary B., 3782
Harlan, Richard, 1796-1843,

12683-12686
Harland, Marion, pseud.
of Mary Virginia (Hawes)
Terhune, 1830-1922,
8167, 10163, 10934-10946
Harley, Timothy, 3783
The harlot's friend, 9011
Harlow, Louis K., illustr.,
3219
Harman, S. W., 6958
Harmar, Josiah, 1733-1813,
4096, 12687
Harmar's expedition,
1790, 12687
Harmon, Daniel Williams,
1778-1845, 3784
Harmon, Daniel Williams,
1778-1845. A journal
of voyages and travels...
6223
Harnden, Harvey, 12688
Harney, John Milton, 1789-
1825, 3785
Harney, William Shelby,
1800-1889, 12689
Harnisch, Wilhelm, i.e.
Christian Wilhelm, 1787-
1864, 5660
Harp of the South, 5582
The Harpe's head, 3743
Harper, firm, publishers,
New York. (1864,
Harper & brothers),
12486
Harper, Henry Howard, 1871-,
6959
Harper, Robert Goodloe,
1765-1825, 12133, 12690,
12691, 12692, 12693,
12694
Harper, William, 1790-1847,
12695
Harper's New York and
Erie railroad guide
book..., 12696
Harper's weekly, 6554
Harpers Ferry, W. Va. -
John Brown raid, 1859,
11389, 12779, 13386

Harpers' monthly magazine,
318
Harrington, Emilia, The
confessions of, 11184
Harrington, Timothy, 1715-
1795, 12697
Harriott, John, 1745-1817,
3786
Harris, Mrs. Caroline, 4577,
12698
Harris, Charles H., of Buffalo,
12699
Harris, Edward Doubleday,
1839-1919, 12700-12702
Harris family (Robert Harris,
fl. 1650), 12706
Harris, George, of Baltimore,
12703
Harris, George Washington,
1814-1869, 3787, 6960
Harris, Graham H., 1857-, 1875
Harris, J. Dennis, 12704
Harris, James Morrison,
1818-1898, 12705
Harris, James Sidney, 3788
Harris, Joel Chandler, 1848-
1908, 5659
Harris, Lewis Birdsall, 1816-
1893, 3789
Harris, Luther Metcalf, 1789-
1865, 12706
Harris, N. Sayre, 3790
Harris, Nathaniel Edwin, 1846-,
3791
Harris, Samuel, 1814-1899, 12707
Harris, Thaddeus Mason, 1768-
1842, 3792, 12708, 12709,
12710, 13036
Harris, Thomas, 1784-1861, 12711
Harris, W. A., 12712
Harris, William Charles, 1830-
1905, 3793
Harris, William Richard, 1847-
1923, 6961
Harris, William Tell, 3794, 12713
Harris, William Thaddeus,
1826-1854, 12714
Harrisburg, Pa. - Hist. -
Civil war, 7676

Harrison, Benjamin, pres.
U. S., 1833-1901, 3795
Harrison, C. C., 9769
Harrison, Dabney Carr,
1830-1862, 12837
Harrison, Frederic,
1831-1923, 13104
Harrison, Henry William,
12715
Harrison, Samuel Alexander,
1822-1890, 3796
Harrison, William Henry,
pres. U. S., 1773-1841,
377, 1223, 3746, 3797,
7594, 11630, 11668,
12716, 13129, 13268
Harrison, William Henry,
pres. U. S., 1773-1841 -
Poetry, 5603
Harrison, Z., 3798
Harriss, Julia Mildred,
12717
Harrisse, Henry, 1830-1910,
12718
Harrold, John, 3799
Harry Burnham, the young
Continental, 1639
Harry Henderson's history,
10906
Harsha, David Addison,
1827-1895, 12719
Hart, Adolphus M., 1813-
1879, 12720
Hart, Albert Bushnell,
1854-1943, 3800
Hart, Alfred A., 12721
Hart, Charles Henry,
1847-1918, 6962
Hart, Ephraim J., 3801
Hart, John Seely, 1810-1877,
3802, 3803
Hart, Joseph C., d. 1855,
12722
Hart, Levi, 1738-1808,
12723
Hart, Luther, 1783-1834,
12724
Hart, Oliver, 1723-1795,
12725

Hart, Seth, 1763-1832, 12726
Harte, Bret, 1836-1902, 6963-
6980
Hartford female seminary,
Hartford, Conn., 1045
Hartford. First church of
Christ, 12751
Hartford hospital, Hartford,
12728
Hartford. Public library,
12727
Harthorn, Cyrus M., 6981
Harthorn's philosophy, 6981
Hartlaub, Gustav, 1814-1900,
589
Hartley, Cecil B., 12729,
12730
Hartley, David, 1732-1813,
12731, 12732
Hartley, Thomas, 1709?-1784,
1157
Hartlib, Samuel, d. 1662,
12733, 12734, 12735
Hartpence, William Ross, 3804
The Hartwell farm, 9088
Hartwell, Henry, 3805
Harun al Raschid - Fiction,
8792
Harvard university, 10151,
12357, 12736, 12737
Harvard university - Biog.,
12737
Harvard university - Hist. -
Civil war, 12737
Harvard university. Medical
school, 12872
Harvard university. Museum
of comparative zoology, 2573
Harvard university - Registers,
12737
A harvest-day with the Pueblos,
10863
Harvey, Arthur, 1834-, 12738
Harvey, Henry, missionary to
the Shawnee Indians, 12739
Harwood, 9181
Hasbrouck, Jacob Louis, 1867-,
6982
The hasheesh eater, 10249

210

Haskel, Daniel, 1784-
1848, 3806
Haskins, William C.,
ed., 5970, 6983
Hassan Assar, caliph of
Bagdad, 10693
Hassel, Johann Georg
Heinrich, 1770-1829,
6984
Hasson, Benjamin F.,
3807
Hasted, Frederick,
b. 1793, 6985
Hastings family (Thomas
Hastings, 1605?-1685),
11609
Hastings, Mrs. Susannah
(Willard) Johnson,
1730-1810, 13078
Haswell, Anthony,
1756-1816, 4767
Hatboro, Pa. Union
library company, 12740
Hatch, William Stanley,
12741
Hatfield, Julia, 12742
Hatton, J. E., 9331
Hatton, Joseph, 1841-
1907, 3808, 3809
The haunted forest, 10693
The haunted school-house
at Newburyport, Mass.,
9799
The haunts of men, 8964
Haupt, Hermann, 1817-
1905, 12743
Haussonville, Gabriel Paul
Othemin de Cléron,
comte d', 1843-1924,
3810
Hautefeuille, Laurent
Basile, 1805-1875,
12744
Havana - Descr., 799,
4309, 4454, 4578, 4961,
7137, 8282, 12981
Havana - Siege, 1762,
570, 12500
La Havane, 4454

Haven, Gilbert, bp., 1821-
1880, 6986, 6987
Haven, Joseph, 1816-1874,
12745
Haven, Samuel Foster,
1806-1881, 12746, 12747,
12748
Havens, Palmer E., b. 1818,
6988
Haverhill, 10060
Haverhill, Mass. - Geneal, 11753
Haverhill, Mass. - Hist.,
11753, 13442
Haw, William, 12749
Hawaii - Descr. & trav.,
3047, 3619, 4196, 5445,
13165
Hawaii - Hist., 1296, 1297
Hawaii - Soc. life & cust.,
10028
Haweis, Hugh Reginald,
1839-1925, 3811
Hawes, Barbara, 12750
Hawes, Jesse, 1843-1901,
3812
Hawes, Joel, 1789-1867,
12751
Haw-ho-noo, 4216
The Hawk chief, 4024
Hawk's Nest, 8522
Hawkesworth, John, 1715?-1773.
An account of the voyages
undertaken... by Commodore
Byron, 11946
Hawkins, Armand, pub., 6785
Hawkins, Benjamin, 1754-1816,
12752
Hawkins, Christopher,
1764-1837, 12753
Hawkins, Sir John,
1532-1595, 6989, 6990
The Hawkins zouaves, 5694
Hawks, Francis Lister,
1798-1866, 2263, 12754
The Hawks of Hawk-Hollow,
1333
Hawkshaw, Sir John, 1811-
1891, 12755
Hawley, Bostwick, 1814-1910,

6991
Hawley, J. R., and
company, Cincinnati,
pub., 508
Hawley, Zerah, 1781-1856,
3815
Hawrecht, Henry, tr.,
6614
Hawthorne, Julian, 1846-
1934, 6992, 6993, 9092,
10448
Hawthorne, Una, 1844-1877,
ed., 9825
Hay, George, d. 1830,
12756
Hay, John, 1838-1905,
supposed author, 8465
Hayden, F. V., 4246
Hayden, Ferdinand Vandeveer,
1829-1887, 3816, 3817
Hayden, Sidney, 6994
Hayden, William, 1785-,
3818
Haydon, Arthur Lincoln,
1872-, 6995
Hayes, Alexander L.,
b. 1793, 2321
Haygarth, John, 1740-1827,
12757
Haygood, Atticus Greene,
bp., 1839-1896, 3819
Hayne, Paul Hamilton,
1830-1886, 3820, 3821
Hayne, William Hamilton,
1856-1886, 3822
Haynes, Dudley C., 1809-
1888, 12758
Haynes, Edwin Mortimer,
1836-, 3823
Haynes family, 6253
Haynes, Gideon, 12759
Haynes, J., 12760
Haynes, John Russell, 6253
Haynes, Lemuel, 1753-1833,
12761
Haynes, Martin A.,
1845-, 3824
Hayward, James, 1786-
1866, 12762

Hayward, John, 1781-1862,
3825, 12763, 12764, 12765,
12766, 12767, 12768
Hayward, Nicholas, 3325
Hayward's gazetteer of Maine,
12766
Haywood, John, 1762-1826,
12769, 12770
Hazard, Ebenezer, 1744-1817,
12427
Hazard, Joseph, b. 1751?
12771
A hazard of new fortunes,
9945
Hazard, Thomas Robinson,
1797-1886, defendant, 1399
Hazel, Harry, pseud., 10068-10071
Hazeltine, Silas Wood, 12773
Hazlitt, William Carew,
1834-1913, 12774
He fell in love with his wife,
10647
He knew what was due to the
court, 10465
He would have gotten a lawyer,
10465
Head, Sir Francis Bond, bart.,
1793-1875, 6996, 6997
Head, Sir George, 1782-1855,
6998
The head of a hundred, 9630
Headley, Joel Tyler, 1813-1897,
tr., 10719, 12775
The headsman, 9131
Heald, Mrs. Jean Sadler, 6999
Healing and salvation for our
country, 11306
Health and profit, 3724
Health resorts, 4039
Health resorts, watering-places,
etc., 11815
Health resorts, watering-places,
etc. - Costa Rica, 5845
Health resorts, watering-places,
etc. - Cuba, 12226
Health resorts, watering-places,
etc. - Virginia, 4605
Health resorts, watering-places,
etc. - W. Va., 4743

Health trip to the
tropics, 5730
Healy, illustr., 10520
Heamans, Roger, 3764
Heap, Gwinn Harris,
3826
Heard, Isaac V. D.,
b. 1834, 12776
Hearn, Lafcadio, 1850-
1904, 3827, 7000, 8205
Heart-histories and
life-pictures, 8566
Heart-hungry, 11128
Heart-life in song,
4394
The heart of adamant,
10747
The heart of Mabel Ware,
9834
The heart of Sam Naylor,
8723
The heart of the Alleghanies,
5798
"The heart of the Andes",
11194
The heart of the common-
wealth, 12966
The heart of the hills,
9555
The heart of the homestead,
9873
The heart of the West,
9835
The heart's highway, 9571
Heartman, Charles Frederick,
7001
Hearts and hands, 10970
The hearts of steel, 10276
Hearts unveiled, 10711
Heartsill, William Williston,
1839-, 3828
Heartt, H. G., 938
Heathcote, Charles William,
1882-, 7002
The Heathercotes, 3119
Heatherington, Alexander,
d. 1878, 12777
A heaven-kissing hill, 10301
Hebbe, Gustaf Clemens,

1804-1893, tr., 10718
Hecke, J. Valentin, 3829
Hecla (ship), 7695, 7696, 7697
Hedge, Levi, 1766-1844,
12778
Hedged in, 11073
Hedley, Fenwick Y., 3830
Heeney, Cornelius, 1754-1848,
7277
Hegewisch, Dietrich Hermann,
1746-1812, ed., 322
The heidenmauer, 9132
Heights and depths, 9868
Heikel, Karl Felix, 1844-1921,
3831
Heinrich XLIV, Count of Reuss,
b. 1753, 4960
Heinzelmann, Friedrich, 5660
The heir of Charlton, 9524
The heir of the McHulishes,
9790
The heiress, 8559
The heiress of Brandsby, 9618
The heiress of Fall Down
castle, 10746
The heiress of Greenhurst, 10867
The heiress of Redstone Hall,
3917
Heitman, Francis Bernard,
1838-1926, 7003
Helen Erskine, 10634
Helen Gardner's wedding day,
10940
Helen Halsey, 10773
Helen Harlow's vow, 11049
Helen Leeson, 9838
Helen Lincoln, 8939
Helena, Ark., Battle of,
1863, 2073
Helfenstein, Ernest, pseud.,
10804
"Hell fer Sartain", 9553, 9554,
9556
Heller, Karl Bartholomäus,
1824-1880, 7004
Heller, Louie Regina, 1870-,
ed., 7005
Hellwald, Friedrich Anton
Heller von, 1842-1892, 3832

213

Helm, Benjamin Hardin,
1830-1863, 7381
Helm, Mary (Sherwood)
Wightman, 1807-, 3833
Heloise, 10640
Helper, Hinton Rowan,
1829-1909, 12265
Heming, Arthur Henry
Howard, 1870-,
illustr., 8252
Henderson, George F.,
tr., 6037, 6815
Henderson, John, 7006
Henderson, John Brooks,
1870-1920, 7007
Henderson, Joseph F.,
3834
Henderson, Ky. - Hist.,
8217
Hendricks knew it, 10598
Hendricks, Thomas
Andrews, 6869
Henkle, Moses Montgomery,
1798-1864, 3835
Hennepin, Louis, 3836,
7008
Hennepin, Louis - Bibl.,
7008
Henningsen, Charles
Frederick, 1815-1877,
12779
Henrietta Harrison, 10194
Henriquez, Camilo, 1769-
1825, ed., 5967
Henry, Alexander, d. 1814,
7009
Henry, Alexander, 1739-
1824, 3837
Henry co., Ia. - Biog.,
7760
Henry co., Ia. - Hist.,
7760
Henry Courtland, 9042
Henry, Fort, Battle of,
1862, 2050
Henry, George, tr., 13312
Henry Howard, 9981
Henry Irving's impressions
of America, 3808

Henry, John Joseph, 1758-
1811, 12780
Henry, Patrick, 1736-1799,
5750, 8404, 13347
Henry St. John, gentleman, of
"Flower of Hundreds," 9108
Henshall, James Alexander,
1844-, 3838, 3839
Hentz, George Alfred, 1832-
1902, 7010, 7011
Hentz, Mrs. Caroline Lee
(Whiting) 1800-1856, 3840,
3841, 3842, 3843, 3844, 3845,
3846, 3847, 3848, 3849
Hepworth, George Hughes,
1833-1902, 7012, 12781
Her chance, 10088
Her er Amerika, 2842
Her first appearance, 9357,
9363
Her greatgrandmother's ghost,
10465
Her ladyship's elephant, 11120
Her sympathetic editor, 10465
Her waiting heart, 9726
A herald of the West, 2517
Heraldry - U. S., 7437, 7753
Heras, Antonio, 3850
Herbermann, Charles George,
5045
Herbert, Henry William,
1807-1858, ed., 9803
Herbert, Sidney, comp.,
12782
Herbert Wendall, 9852
Herboso, Pedro, 7013
Here and hereafter, 10524
Here and there in our own
country, 3612
Heredia y Mieses, José
Francisco, 1776-1820, 7014
La herencia de Carranza, 6268
Heres, Tomás de, 1795-1842,
7015
Heresy, 11980, 13056
Heriot, George, 1766-1844,
7016, 7017
The heritage of Dedlow Marsh,
6970

Heusken, Henry C. J.,
1832-1861, 7701
Heustis, Daniel D.,
b. 1806, 12784
Heustis, Louise L.,
illustr., 10429
Das heutige Mexiko, 8409
Hevia Bolaños, Juan de,
7042
Hewatt, Alexander, 3860
Hewett, Daniel, 3861
Hewitt, Randall Henry,
1840-, 3862
Hewlings, H. A., Dr.,
9331
Hexandria, 9330
Heyn, Piet, 7274
Heywood, John Healy,
1818-1880, 11746
Hiatt, Joel W., 4670
An Hibernian, pseud.,
9991
Hibernicus, 3863
Hibiscus moscheutos,
12968
Hickey, William, 1787?-
1875, 2461
Hickman, John, 1810-
1875, 7043
Hickory Hall, 10837
Hicks, George, 1835-,
7044
Hidalgo, Cristobal, 7045
Hidalgo de Cisneros,
Diego, 8028, 8274
The hidden mine, 2518
The hidden path, 10941
Hidden, Samuel, 1760-1837,
1988
Hidden treasure, 11101
Hiestand-Moore, E. M.,
Dr., 9331
Higbee, D., pseud. of
Mrs. Dora Higbee Deppert.
Higginson, Stephen, 1770-
1834, 52
Higginson, Thomas Wentworth,
1823-1911, 3864
A high civilization the

moral duty of Georgians,
12043
High, Edwin W., 1841-, 3865
High etiquette in Harlem,
9533
Higher than happiness, 10170
A Highland chronicle, 9407
The Highlanders of the South,
5402
Hight, John J., 1834-1886,
3866
Highway atlas, 6807
Highway law - New York (State),
11293
Highways and byways of the
Mississippi valley, 4065
Highways and byways of the
South, 4066
Higuera, Jeronimo Roman de la,
1538-1611, 400
Los hijos de Jalisco, 7876
Hildreth, Hosea, 1782-1835,
12785
Hildreth, James, 1807-1865,
3867
Hildreth, Samuel Prescott,
1783-1863, 3868, 3869, 3870
Hildt, George H., jt. author,
4353
Hill, Alexander Staveley,
1825-1905, 7046
Hill, Alonzo, 1800-1871, 12786
Hill, Alonzo F., 3871
Hill, Ambrose Powell, 1825-1865,
2073
Hill, Benjamin Harvey, 1823-
1882, 2052, 3872
Hill, Benjamin Harvey, jr.,
3872
Hill, David, d. 1810, 13241
Hill, Mrs. Emma Shepard, 7047
Hill, Frederick Trevor, 1866-,
7048
Hill, Hamilton Andrews, 1827-
1895, 12787, 12788
Hill, Isaac, 1788-1851, 936
Hill, Isaac J., 1826-, 3873
Hill, Paul T., illustr., 3316
Hill, Richard, 1795-1872,

12324
Hill, Robert Thomas,
  1858-, 7049
Hill, S. S., 7050
Hillard, Elias Brewster,
  1825-1895, 12789
Hillard, George Stillman,
  1808-1879, tr., 12501,
  12790
Hillary, William, d. 1763,
  12791
Hiller, Joseph, 12792
Hillhouse, Augustus Lucas,
  1791-1859, 640
Hillhouse, James, 1754-
  1832, 640, 12793
Hillhouse, Thomas, 1816-
  1897, 12794
Hilliard, Henry Washington,
  1808-1892, 3874, 3875
The hills of the Shatemuc,
  11095
Hilton, William, 3876
The Hilton's holiday,
  10038
Himself his worst enemy,
  8855
Hind, Henry Youle, 1823-
  1908, 3877, 3878, 3879,
  3880, 3881, 6666
Hindman, Thomas Carmichael,
  1818-1868, 2040
Hines, Thomas H., 3417
Hingham, Mass. - Hist. -
  Colonial period, 6474
Hingston, Edward Peron,
  ca. 1823-1876, jt. ed.,
  8876
Hinman, Royal Ralph,
  1785-1868, 12795
Hinman, Wilbur F., 3882
Hinton, Richard Josiah,
  1830-1901, jt. author,
  4910, 12796
Hintrager, Oscar, 1871-,
  3883
Hints and information for
  the use of emigrants
  to Pike's Peak, 3297

Hints for naval officers
  cruising in the West Indies,
  11241
Hints on emigration to Upper
  Canada, 2461
Hints on slavery, 2793
Hints to both parties, 12797
Hints to emigrants, 4300
Hints to the farmers of Rhode
  Island, 12798
The hireling and the slave,
  3671
His bad angel, 9358
His defense, and other stories,
  3344
His duty, 9580, 9581
His father's son, 10328
His fortunate grace, 8592
His friend Flanders, 10598
His Grace of Osmonde, 8904
His heart's desire, 10304
His honor, 9037
His letters, 9259
His lordship, 9768
His majesty, myself, 8655
His marriage vow, 9165
His own image, 9065
His prison bars, 9915
His second campaign, 5390
His sombre rivals, 10648
His two wives, 8532
His vanished star, 4556
His version of it, 9538
His wife's deceased sister,
  10892
Hispanic-American printing,
  8187
La Hispano-América del siglo
  XVI, 7248
Histoire de la catastrophe
  de Saint-Domingue, 11423
Histoire de la colonie française
  en Canada, 6703
Histoire de la Louisiane, 3207
Histoire et commerce des
  colonies anglaises, 2867
Histoire et description générale
  de la Nouvelle France, 2972
L'histoire notable de la

Floride, 4226

Histoire véritable et natvrelle des moevrs et prodvctions dv pays de la Novvelle France, 6126

Historia de la independencia americana, 7015

Historia general de las Indias, 6863

Historia general de los hechos de los castellanos en las islas y tierrafirme del mar oceano, 7035

Historia geografica, civil y politica de la isla de S. Juan Bautista de Puerto Rico, 3

Historia Indiae Occidentalis, 1187

Historia Indiae Orientalis, 488

The historic Lincoln car, 7051

An historical account of my own life, 1796

An historical account of some memorable actions, particularly in Virginia, 3662

An historical account of the rise and progress of the colonies of South Carolina and Georgia, 3860

Historical and legal examination, 11255

Historical and Philosophical Society of Ohio, 3561

An historical and practical essay on the culture and commerce of tobacco, 5350

Historical and revolutionary incidents of the early settlers of the U. S., 5649

Historical anecdotes, civil and military, 12799

Historical collections of Louisiana, 3544

Historical collections of Louisiana and Florida, 2332

Historical collections of Ohio, 3954

Historical collections of the great West, 3955

Historical collections of the state of New York, 785

A historical narrative and topographical description of Louisiana and West-Florida, 3979

Historical, poetical and pictorial American scenes, 786

Historical records survey, Iowa, 2865

Historical remarks on the taxation of free states, 13425

A historical sketch of the Congregational churches in Massachusetts, 11821

A historical sketch of the formation of the confederacy, 11299

Historical sketch of the Middlesex canal, 2177

Historical sketch of the third annual conquest of Florida, 8940

Historical sketch of Tomo-chi-chi, 4104

Historical sketches of North Carolina, 5683

Historical sketches of the old painters, 10186

Historical sketches of the Wabash Valley, 5687

A historical vindication of the abrogation of the plan of union by the Presbyterian church in the United States of America, 11564

Historicus, pseud., 12668, 12669

The historie of travaile into Virginia Britannia, 5296

History - Addresses, essays,

and Indian wars of
western Virginia, 3213
History of the establishment
and progress of the
Christian religion in
the islands of the South
Sea, 13479
History of the federal
government, 11494
History of the First
regt. Penn. reserve
cavalry, 4286
A history of the haunted
caverns of Magdelama,
13272
The history of the hen
fever, 1731
History of the Indian
tribes of North America,
4359
A history of the ladies'
temperance benevolent
societies, 13249
The history of the Lady
Betty Stair, 5116
History of the late war
in the Plantations,
10099
History of the late war
in the western country,
4326
History of the mission
of the United Brethren
among Indians in North
America, 13398
A history of the Negro
plot, 12911
A history of the New York
Kappa lambda conspiracy,
12805
A history of the north-
western editorial
excursion to Arkansas,
4480
The history of the Pilgrims,
12806
History of the province
of Georgia, 3208
History of the revolution

in Texas, 4592
History of the strange sounds
or rappings, heard in Rochester
and western New York, 11986
History of the town of Easton,
Mass., 2958
History of the United States,
2456, 12541
The history of the United
States for 1796, 1806
History of the United States
secret service, 693
A history of the voyages and
travels of Capt. Nathaniel
Uring, 5556
History of the war between
the United States and Mexico,
13196
History of the war between the
U. S. and the Sac and Fox
nations of Indians, 5596
History of the Wyandott mission,
3451
The history of Uncle Sam and
his boys, 10482
The history of Williamson
county, Illinois, 3389
History - Study and teaching,
11266
History, Universal, 782,
1280, 1599, 5065
History, Universal - Early
works to 1800, 584, 4466,
6525, 6526
History - Year-books, 241
History - Year-books - 1816, 294
Hitchcock, Edward, 1793-1864,
12807
Hitchcock, Enos, 1745-1803,
12808, 12809, 12810
Hitchcock, Gad, 1718?-1809,
12811
Hitchcock, Henry, 1829-1902,
3887
Hitchcock, Oscar Blakeslee,
1828-1897, 13137
Hitchcock, Reuben, 1764-1794,
12812
Hitchcock, Roswell Dwight,
1817-1887, 12813, 12814

Hither and thither, 2293
Hitherto, 11152
Hits and criticism on the
  follies of the day,
  10536
Hits and dashes, 10828
Hits at the times, 10385
Hittell, John Shertzer,
  1825-1901, 12815
Hittell, Theodore Henry,
  1830-, 3888
The hive of "the bee-
  hunter", 5412
Hiver caraïbe, 7533
Hjelm-Hansen, Paul,
  1810-1881, 3889
Ho! for the West! 12566
Hobart, Aaron, 1787-1858,
  12816
Hobart-Hampden, Hon.
  Augustus Charles, 1822-
  1886, 3890
Hobart, Harrison C., 2657
Hobart, John Henry,
  bp., 1775-1830, 12817,
  12818, 13289
Hobart, Noah, 1706-1773,
  12819
Hobbie, Hannah, 1806-
  1831, 460
Hobbs family, 12820
Hobbs, George, 1790-,
  12820
Hobby, William, 1707-1765,
  12821
Hobomok, a tale of early
  times, 8992
Hocknell, John, 1723?-
  1799, 12094
Hodge, Charles, 1797-
  1878, 12822
Hodge, Michael, 12823
Hodge, William L., 12824
Hodgenville, Ky. Herald-
  News, 7055
Hodgepodge, 10736
Hodgins, John George,
  1821-1912, 6666, 12825,
  12826

Hodgkin, Thomas, 1798-1866,
  12827
Hodgkinson, John, 1766-1805,
  12828
Hodgson, Adam, 3891
Hodgson, William Brown, b. 1800,
  12752
Hoek, Sander van, 1757-1816,
  tr., 8362
Hoeniger, Nicolaus, fl. 1573-
  1596, tr., 1186
Hoëvell, Wolter Robert,
  baron van, 1812-1879, 1126
Hofer, Andreas, 1767-1810,
  12829
Hoffer family (Matthias Hoffer,
  1718?-1803), 12829
Hoffer, Isaac, b. 1820, 12829
Hoffer, Jacob R., b. 1823,
  12829
Hoffman, Charles Fenno,
  1806-1884, 3893, 3894
Hoffman, Christian, 12830
Hoffman, Francis Suydam,
  1828-1886, 466
Hoffman, Frederick Ludwig,
  1865-, 7056
Hoffman, Mrs. Virginia Haviside
  (Hale) 1832-1856, 11902
Hoffman, Wickham, 1821-1900,
  3895
Hoffmann, Hermann, 7057
Hoffmeister, Jonathan M.,
  12831
Hogan, John, 12832
Hogan, John Sheridan, 1815?-
  1859, 12833
Hogan, William, d. 1848,
  defendant, 12834
Hoge, Jane Currie (Blaikie)
  "Mrs. A. H. Hoge", 12835
Hoge, William James,
  1821-1864, 12836, 12837
The Hohays, 10827
Hoit, C. W., 12838
Hoit, True Worthy, b. 1815,
  12839
Hølass, Odd, 3896
The Holbey family, 11169

Holbrook, Charles Warren,
1828-1888, 12840
Holbrook family (Micah
Holbrook, 1732-1817),
12840
Holbrook, Mrs. Harriott
Pinckney, ed., 4804
Holbrook, Samuel F.,
b. 1793, 12841
Holcombe, Henry, 1762-1824,
3897
Holcombe, James Philemon,
1820-1873, 3898, 12842
Holcombe, William Henry,
1825-1893, 12843
The Holcombes, 10299
Holden, Oliver, 1765-
1894, 7058
Holden with the cords,
11201
Hold-fast, Simon, pseud.,
12844
Holdich, Joseph, 1804-
1893, 12845
Holditch, Robert, 12846
Holdredge, Sterling M.,
pub., 3899
Holdsworth, Edward, 1684-
1746. Muscipula, 5264
Holgate, Jerome Bonaparte,
12847
Holiday rambles, 5711
Holiday tales, 10400
Holidays at home and abroad,
6838
Holitscher, Arthur, 1869-,
3900
Holladay, Ben, 1819-1887,
3901
Holland club, New York,
13008
Holland, John, 12848
Holland, Josiah Gilbert,
1819-1881, 7059
Holland, William M.,
12849
Hollander, Arie Nicolaas
Jan den, 3902
Hollberg, Esaias, 2462

Holley, Horace, 1781-1827,
2886
Holley, Mary Austin, 3903
Holley, Orville Luther,
1791-1861, ed., 271,
12850, 12851, 12852
Hollingsworth, Samuel L.,
12853, 12854, 12855
Hollis, N. H. - Hist., 2297
Hollister, Gideon Hiram,
1817-1881, 12856
Hollister, Hiel, 12857
Hollister, Horace, 1822-,
12858
Hollister, Ovanda James,
1834-1892, 3904, 12859
The hollow of the three hills,
9827
Holloway, Edward, illustr.,
8800
Holloway, William, jr., 8969
Holloway, William Robeson,
1836-1911, 12860
Holly and pizen, 5312
Holly, James Theodore, 1829-,
12861
Holman, Nathan, 1769-1844,
12862
Holman, William Steele,
1822-1897, 12863
Holmden, H. R., 6296
Holme, Benjamin, 1683-1749,
3905
Holmes, Abiel, 1763-1837,
12864, 12865
Holmes, Arthur, 12866
Holmes, Mrs. Charlotte
(Steevens), 7060
Holmes, Clay W., ed., 7060
Holmes, Daniel, 3906
Holmes, Elias Bellows,
1810?-1866, 12867
Holmes, Ezekiel, 1801-1865,
12868
Holmes, Francis Simmons,
1815-1882, 12869
Holmes, Frederick Lionel,
1883-1946, 3907
Holmes, Hamilton, 3908

222

Holmes, Isaac, 3909
Holmes, John, 1773-1843,
  12870, 12871
Holmes, Mrs. Mary Jane
  (Hawes) 1828-1907,
  3910-3918, 10163
Holmes, Obadiah, 1606(?)-
  1682, 7573
Holmes, Oliver Wendell,
  1809-1894, 12663,
  12872
Holmes, Reuben, 3919
Holmes, Theophilus Hunter,
  1804-1880, 2073
"Holster atlas", 5082
Holt, Edwin B., tr., 4551
Holt, Joseph, 1807-1894,
  12873
Holtrop, Willem, 1750-
  1835, pub., 1516
The holy cross and other
  tales, 9511
Holy Roman empire - Henry IV,
  1056-1106 - Fiction,
  10351
Holy water, 7957
Holyoake, George Jacob,
  1817-1906, 3920, 3921
Homans, Benjamin, ed., 11228
Home, 10190
Home again, 9696
Home and the world, 10626
A home and where to find
  one, 5062
Home as found, 9133
Home as I found it, 10003
Home ballads, 2087
The home-coming of Jim
  Wilkes, 6971, 9790
Home-heroes, saints, and
  martyrs, 8567
A home in the New World,
  3913
Home influence of religion,
  8968
Home life in Florida, 5625
Home lights and shadows,
  487
Home nook, 9420

Home scenes during the
  rebellion, 10630
Home secrets told by old
  travellers, 10516
The home side, 9331
Home stories, 9802
Homeopathy, 12884
Homer, Arthur, 1758-1806,
  supposed author, 2476
Homer, James Lloyd, 12874
Homes for Boston laborers,
  9695
Homes for the people, 3573
Homes, Henry Augustus,
  1812-1887, 12875, 12876
The homes of the New world,
  1473, 6157
Homespun, 9874
The homestead on the hillside,
  3915, 9896
Homeward bound, 9134, 10916
Homeward through America,
  3982
Homo, 3310
Homoselle, 10974
Honduras, 8096, 8280, 12877,
  13484
Honduras - Descr. & trav.,
  6402, 6777, 7974, 8280
Honduras - Descr. & trav. -
  Guide-books, 7680
Honduras - For. rel. - Guatemala,
  12877
Honduras - Hist., 8281
Honduras - Hist. - Sources,
  12877
Honduras interoceanic
  railway, 8096, 13484
Honduras - Period., 5955
Honduras - Pol. & govt., 7451
Honduras: the land of great
  depths, 6402
Hone, Philip, 1780-1851,
  12878
Honest John Vane, 9370
Honor May, 8753
El honor militar, 7719
The honor of the troop,
  10608

223

Horetzky, Charles, 6748
Horn, Hosea B., 3936
Hornaday, William Temple,
  1854-1937, 7063
Horne, Henry, 12905
Horner, Hattie, 3937
Horner, William B., 3938
Hornet, 12289
Horrall, Spillard F.,
  1829-, 3940
Horse-racing - U. S.,
  2310, 12543
Horse Shoe Robinson, 10094
A horse story, 13288
The horse thief, 9744
Horsford, Eben Norton,
  1818-1893, 12907,
  12908, 12909
Horsford, Mrs. Mary
  (Gardiner) 1824-1855,
  12910
Horsmanden, Daniel, 1694-
  1778, 12911
Horton, H. P., 12912
Horton, Joshua H., 3940
Horton, Rushmore G., 1826-,
  12913
The Hortons, 8950
Hortop, Job, fl. 1591,
  7064, 7065
Hortus Britanno-Ameri-
  canus, 1828
Hortus Elginensis, 12916
Horvel Hastings, 10432
Hosack, Alexander, 12914
Hosack, Alexander Eddy,
  1805-1871, 12915
Hosack, David, 1769-1835,
  12916, 12917, 12918
Hosie, John, ed., 8322
Hoskens, Jane Fenn,
  1694-, 3941
Hoskin, James, 3942
Hoskins, Nathan, 1795-1869,
  3943, 12919
Hosmer, Charlottes, jt.
  author, 13424
Hosmer family (Thomas
  Hosmer, 1603-1681),

12921
Hosmer, Hezekiah L., 12920
Hosmer, James Bidwell,
  1781-1878, 12921
Hosmer, James Kendall,
  1834-1927, 3944
Hosmer, Margaret (Kerr),
  1830-1897, 12922
Hosmer, Miss., 4447
Hosmer, Titus, 1736-1780, 811
Hospital pencillings, 4841
Hospital sketches, 130
Hospital transports, 13447
Hospitals, 12380
Hospitals, Military, 13304
Hospitals, Military - Mexico,
  6482
Hospitals, Naval and marine,
  944
Hossack, David, 1769-1835,
  11779
Hot and Hot Fish Club, 5871
Hot corn, 10638
Hot plowshares, 10991
Hotchkiss, Frederick William,
  1763?-1844, 12923
Hotchkiss, Jedediah, 1827-
  1899, 12924
Hotspur, 11063
Hough, Franklin Benjamin,
  1822-1885, ed., 351, 1417,
  2167, 12925-12933
Houghton association, 12935
Houghton, Edwin B., 12934
Houghton family, 12935
The hour of patriotism,
  1300
The house, 9512
A house built upon the sand,
  9764
House, E., 3945
House hunting and moving, 10820
The house in Balfour-street,
  3250
The house of Egremont, 10720
The house of the seven gables,
  9821
The house on the heath, 10921
The house surgeon and physician,

225

and Throckmorton Hall,
8949
How to be happy, 10083
How to fight the devil,
10909
How to go to Texas, 4021
How to strengthen our
army and crush the
rebellion, 11989
How Viardeau obeyed the
black abbé, 10448
How we elected Lincoln,
6597
How will it end? 9859
Howard, Alice Sturtevant,
3950
Howard, Edward, d. 1841,
12946
Howard, Frank Key, 1826-
1872, 2463
Howard, H. R., 11165
Howard, Henry, 1868-,
3950
Howard, J. H., illustr.,
10536, 10538
Howard, Katharine, 3950
Howard, McHenry, 3951
Howard, Mark, 1817-1887,
12947
Howard, Middleton, b. 1747?
12948
Howard of Glossop, Winifred
(De Lisle) 3952
Howard, Oliver Otis,
1830-1909, 12949
Howard Pinckney, 10951
Howard, Richard L., 3953
The Howards, 8704
Howay, Frederic W., 7072
Howe, Beverly Winslow,
1885-, 7073, 7074
Howe, Eber D., b. 1798,
12950
Howe, Edgar Watson, 1854-,
7075
Howe, Elias, 1819-1867,
7076
Howe, Elisha P., 12951
Howe, Henry, 1816-1893,

784, 785, 791, 3954, 3955,
7077, 12952, 12953
Howe, Joseph, 1804-1873,
12954
Howe, Mrs. Julia Ward,
1819-1910, 12955, 12956
Howe, Mark Antony Dewolfe,
1864-, ed., 3887
Howe, Richard Howe, earl,
1726-1799, 886, 2384
Howe, Samuel Gridley,
1801-1876, 12957
Howe, Thomas H., 3956
Howe, Timothy Otis, 1816-1883,
12958
Howe, William Bell White,
bp., 1823-1894, 12959
Howe, William Howe, 5th viscount,
1729-1814, 12960, 13421
Howel, Thomas, 344
Howell, George Rogers,
1833-1899, 12961
Howell, John, 1788-1863,
ed., 140
Howell, Peter, 1805-, 3957
Howells, William Dean, 1837-
1920, jt. author, 4778, 8773
Howes, Frederick, 12962
Howgate grant, 4624
Howison, John, 12963
Howitt, Emanuel, 12964
Howitt, Mary (Botham) 1799-
1888, tr., 1473, 6157, 11632
Howitt, William, 1792-1879,
12965
Howland, Henry Jenkins,
b. 1810, 12966
Howland, John, 1757-1854,
12564
Hows, John A., illustr.,
11592, 12742
Howse, Joseph, 12967
Howson, Henry, sr., 12968
Hoyne, Thomas, 1817-1883,
6415
Hoyt, David Webster,
1833-1921, 12969
Hoyt, Epaphras, 1765-1850,
12970

Hoyt family, 12969
Hoyt family (David Hoyt, 1651-1704), 12969
Hoyt family (John Hoyt, d. 1687), 12969
Hoyt, George Henry, 1837-, 12971
Hoyt, Jesse, 12972, 13412
Hoyt, Joseph Gibson, 1815-1862, 12973
Hubbard, Charles Eustis, 1842-, 3958
Hubbard, Henry, 1784-1857, 12974
Hubbard, John Milton, 3959
Hubbard, Leonidas, 1872-1903, 6671
Hubbard, Samuel Dickinson, 1799-1855, 12975
Hubbard, William, 1621-1704, 12976
Hubbard, William B., 12977
Hubbardton, Battle of, 1777, 11812
Hubbell family, 12978
Hubbell, Seth, 1759-1832, 12978
Hubbell, Stephen, 1802-1884, 12979
Hubbell, William Wheeler, 12980
Hubbub, 9281
Huber, illustr., 8458
Huber, B., attaché au Ministère des affaires étrangers, 12981
Hubert, Benjamin F., 6696
Hubert, William Henry, 13041
Hubner, Charles William, 1835-1929, 3960, 3961
Huckleberries gathered from New England hills, 9120
Hudibrastic aspects of some editions of the Emancipation Proclamation, 5836

Hudson bay, 12058
Hudson bay a free basin, 6727
Hudson, Charles, 1795-1881, 12982, 12983
Hudson, David, 12984
Hudson, Edward Maco, 12985
Hudson, Henry Norman, 1814-1886, 12986
The Hudson illustrated with pen and pencil, 12987
Hudson, N. H. - Hist., 2297
Hudson river, 9995
Hudson river - Descr. & trav., 12987
Hudson river - Descr. & trav. - Guide-books, 7748
Hudson Strait, 6303
Hudson's bay, 1924, 2604, 4626, 5057, 5950, 6302, 6670, 7808
The Hudson's Bay and Pacific territories, 7542
Hudson's Bay company, 2604, 4368, 5169, 5812, 5990, 6228, 6298, 6434, 6435, 6605, 6668, 6731, 6742, 6783, 7078, 7575, 7641, 7978, 8140, 8256, 12073
The Hudson's Bay company versus Magna Charta and the British people, 6736
Hudson's Bay - Descr., 1201, 7809, 7922, 8022
The Hudson's Bay territories and Vancouver's island, 7423
Huet, Pierre Daniel, bp., 1630-1721, 12988
Hugh Darnaby, 9344
Hugh Worthington, 3916, 9897
Hughes, Charles Evans, 1862-1948, 7079
Hughes, George Wurtz, 1806-1870, 13294
Hughes, Gerard, 3963
Hughes, Henry, 3963
Hughes, James, 1823-1873, 12989
Hughes, John, abp., 1797-1864, 12990, 12991
Hughes, John Taylor,

229

The hungry man was fed,
9357, 9363
Hunn, Anthony, 3968
Hunnewell, James Frothing-
ham, 1832-, ed., 5252
Hunnicut, James W., 1814-,
3969
Hunt, jt. author, 4845
Hunt, Benjamin Faneuil,
1792-1857, 13014
Hunt, Daniel, 1806-1869,
13015
Hunt, Edward Bissell,
1822-1863, 13016
Hunt, Isaac, 1742?-1809,
13017
Hunt, Isaac H., 13018
Hunt, James, 1833-1869,
13019
Hunt, John Warren, 1826-
1859, 13020
Hunt, Richard S., 3970
Hunt, Timothy Dwight,
1821-1895, 13021
Hunt, William, 1825-
1896, 13022
Hunt, William Gibbes,
1791?-1833, 13023
Hunt, Wilson Price,
3971
The hunted chief, 9295
Hunter, Alfred G.,
3972
The hunter and trapper
in North America, 4935
Hunter, David, 1802-1886,
13024
Hunter, John, 1728-1793,
3707
Hunter, John Dunn,
1798?-1827, 3973, 3974,
13025
Hunter, Joseph, 1783-1861,
13026, 13027
The hunter-naturalist,
5650
Hunter, William, of
Memphis, Tenn., 13028
Hunter, William Perceval,

tr., 597
A hunter's experiences in the
southern states of America,
3464
The hunter's vow, 9618
The hunters of Kentucky, 2748
The hunters of the prairie,
4024
The hunters of the Rocky
Mountains, 4993
The hunters' feast, 4924
Hunting, 423, 3852, 5650, 5656,
7063, 12257
Hunting - Adirondack mountains,
10398
Hunting - Alaska, 7369
Hunting and fishing in Florida,
3094
Hunting - British Columbia,
8074
Hunting - Canada, 6641, 6876,
6954
Hunting - Central America,
11655
The hunting flask, 4002
Hunting - Florida, 3094, 3095,
5001
Hunting - Great Plains, 4686
Hunting in Florida in 1874,
4056
Hunting - Mississippi valley,
3594
Hunting - New York (State),
12630, 12631
Hunting - North America,
4935, 9803
Hunting - South Carolina, 12048
Hunting - Southern states,
3464, 3924
Hunting - Texas, 3465
Hunting - The West, 3852, 5306,
6641
Hunting - U. S., 1197, 5054,
5060, 5983, 11585
Hunting - Yukon Territory,
7369, 8012
Huntington, Charles S.,
illustr., 13481
Huntington, Elisha, 7093

230

Huntington, Enoch,
1739-1809, 13029,
13030
Huntington, Frederic Dan,
1819-1904, 12521, 13031
Huntington, Gurdon, 1818-
1875, 13032
Huntington, Joseph, 1735-
1794, 13033
Huntington, Joseph, 1735-
1794. Letters of friend-
ship, 631
Huntington, Hon. Lucius Seth,
1827-1886, 13035
Huntington, Joshua, 1786-
1819, 13034
Huntoon, Benjamin, 1792-
1864, 13036
Huntt, Henry, 1792-
1838, 13037
Hurd, Aaron Haynes,
1813-1830, 12845
Hurd, Duane Hamilton,
ed., 7094
Hurd, John Codman,
1816-1892, 13038
Hurd, John R., 13039
Hurdis, John L., 13306
Huret, Jules, 1864-
1937, 3975
Hurlbert, Jesse Beaufort,
13040
Hurlbert, William Henry,
1827-1895, tr., 4097
Hurlbut, Elisha P.,
13042, 13043
Huron Indians - Missions,
3451
Huron, Lake - Descr. &
trav., 7135
Huron language - Glossaries,
vocabularies, etc., 7223
Huron language - Texts,
11762
Hurricanes, 2160
Hurst, John Fletcher, bp.,
1834-1903, ed., 7764
Hurst, Samuel H., 3976
Hurt-Binet, Marc Gabriel,

13045
Hurt, John, 13044
Huske, John, 1721?-1773,
13046
Husks, 5358, 10938
Hussey, H., 3977
Hussey, Josiah, 13047
Huston, J., comp., 13048
Hutchins, Cortelle, jt. author,
3978
Hutchins, Frank, 3978
Hutchins, Thomas, 1730-1789,
3979, 3980
Hutchinson family, 1856
Hutchinson, Francis, bp. of
Down and Connor, 1660-
1739, 13049
Hutchinson, John Wallace,
1821-1908, 1677, 13050
Hutchinson, Thomas, 1711-1780,
13051, 13052, 13053
Hutchinson, Thomas Joseph,
b. 1820, 13054
Hutchinson, William, b. 1586?
1856
Hutchinson, William Francis,
1868-1893, 7095
Hutchinson's Republic songster,
13050
Huth, Friedrich, 1866-, 3981
Hutson, Mrs. Mary, 1621
The hutted knoll, 9157
Hutton, Henry Dix, 1824-1907,
13104
Hutton, Lawrence, 1843-1904,
2695
Hyatt, Thaddeus, 13055
Hyde, Alvan, 1768-1833, 13056
Hyde, Mrs. Anna M., 13057
Hyde, Ezra, 1774-1849, 13058
Hyde family, 8335
Hyde, James F. C., 13059
Hyde, John, 1848-1929, 3982
Hyde, Solon, 3983
Hyde, W. H., illustr., 9637
Hyde, William Lyman, 1819-1896,
13060
Hydraulics, 2311
Hymns, Chippewa, 13312

Hymns, Creek, 1648
Hymns, English, 464,
985, 2911
Hyneman, Leon, 1805-
1879, 13061, 13062
Hyperion, 10240
The hypnotist, 9581

I. E. S., 5962
I., L. L. S. E., ed.,
13111
I. S., 1507
I go a-fishing, 10571
"I know you would like
him", 10711
I, thou and the other
one, 8729
Ibáñez, Diego, Franciscan,
7096
Ibarra, José de, 1688-
1756, 6364
Ibarreta Ribera, Pedro
Ignacio, 5803
Ichikawa, Haruko, 1896-,
3984
Ichthyologia ohiensis,
4882
The ichthyosaurus, 8756
Idaho - Descr. & trav.,
2548, 2903, 3455, 3456,
3551, 4456, 4549
Idaho - Descr. & trav. -
Guide-books, 3735
Idaho: her gold fields,
and the routes to them,
3456
Idaho - Hist., 2607
Ide, George Barton,
1804-1872, 13063
Ide, Jacob, 1785-1880,
13064
The ideal attained, 9496
Ides, Evert Ysbrandszoon,
12067
The ides of March, 13065
The idiot, 8680
The idiot at home, 8681
Idle songs and idle

sonnets, 3069
Idolatry, 9810
Idomen, 8853
Idyllic monologues, 2951
If Jesus came to Boston,
9682
Iglehart, Fanny (Chambers)
Gooch, 1851-, 7097
Ignatius, Father, 1837-1908,
3180
An ignoble martyr, 9355
Ihrie, George Percy, d. 1903,
12689
Ikin, Arthur, 3985
Illinois, 13067
Illinois and the West, 13283
Illinois artillery. 1st regt.
Battery A, 1861-1865, 4171
Illinois - Biog., 860, 8260
Illinois cavalry. 7th regt.,
1861-1865, 3335
Illinois cavalry. 8th regt.,
1861-1865, 3775
Illinois Central Railroad,
3986, 13066
Illinois. Constitutional
convention, 1862, 393
Illinois. Courts, 13302
Illinois - Descr. & trav.,
1335, 1336, 2234, 2859,
3359, 3424, 3468, 3488,
3597, 3647, 3894, 3943,
4648, 4729, 4919, 5765,
6271, 10141, 12142, 13066,
13283
Illinois - Econ. cond., 13283
Illinois - Fiction, 3754,
9207
Illinois - Hist., 4940, 6676,
6852, 7816, 8431, 11561,
12148
Illinois - Hist. - Civil war,
860, 7813
Illinois - Hist. - To 1778 -
Sources, 2523
Illinois in 1837, 13067
Illinois - Indians - Missions,
12353
Illinois infantry. 7th regt.,

232

and Republicans, 13071

An impartial statement of
the controversy, res-
pecting the decision of
late committee of can-
vassers, containing the
opinions of Edmund
Randolph... 13072

An impartial view of the
conduct of the M---ry,
13073

Impeachments - U. S.,
11269, 11757, 13317

The imperial gazetteer,
1374

El imperio del piojo
recuperado, 7516

The importance and ad-
vantage of Cape Breton,
11336

The importance of gaining
and preserving the
friendship of the Indians
to the British interest
considered, 13361

The importance of modera-
tion in civil rulers,
1963

The importance of religion
to the legal profession,
11307

The importance of the
British plantations in
America to this king-
dom, 3737

The imposter detected,
1427

Impostors and imposture,
11234

Impressions and experiences
of the West Indies and
North America in 1849,
669

Impressions de voyages et
aventures dans le
Mexique, 6065

Impressions d'une Française
en Amérique, 5570

Impressions of America,

3160, 4840, 5577

Impressions of America and
the American churches, 4268

Impressions of Kentucky, 5644

Impressions of Mexico with
brush and pen, 6016

Impressions of the West and
South, 4178

Impressment, 57, 61, 2416

Imray, James, and son, pub.,
530

In a cracker's cabin, 11198

In a crucible, 10577

In a dike shanty, 10542

In a hollow of the hills,
6971, 9782

In a pioneer restaurant, 6965

In and out of Andersonville
prison, 4322

In and out of rebel prisons,
3082

In Beaver Cove and elsewhere,
3120

In Buncombe County, 10543

In camp and battle with the
Washington artillery of New
Orleans, 4671

In changefulness of mood, 9330

In circling camps, 8524

In connection with the
De Willoughby claim, 8905

In dark New England days,
10043

In defiance of the king,
9928

In exile, 9529

In extremis, 9661

In fly-time, 9639

In "God's country", 3591

In Hampton roads, 8690

In honor bound, 9769

In Mexico with the special
trains, 5888

In mexikanischen urwäldern,
6672

In primrose time, 4782

In Sancho Panza's pit, 9276

In sight of the goddess, 9346

In Simpkinsville, 5313

234

In six months, 10342
In the Alamo, 10595
In the brush, 4795
In the Carquinez woods, 9783
In the clouds, 4557
In the cotton country, 11207
In the Cumberland Mountains, 10598
In the days of Lincoln, 8313
In the desert of waiting, 10052
In the first person, 10544
In the footsteps of Cortes, 7710
In the Gray Goth, 11075
In the heart of the Canadian rockies, 7656
In the light of today, 10605
In the "Never never country," 10122
In the new Eldorado, 10454
In the next generation, 9206
In the Okefenokee, 4746
In the order of Providence, 9749
In the palace of the king, 9225
In the pine woods, 8645
In the Quebrada, 10675
In the ranks: from the Wilderness to Appomattox courthouse, 4328
In the rapids, 9992
In the Sargasso Sea, 10026
In the sixties, 9567
In the "Stranger people's" country, 4558
In the Tennessee mountains, 4559
In the trades, the tropics, and the roaring forties, 6154
In the tropics, 9489
In the tules, 6971
In the Virginias, 2610
In the wire-grass, 4747
In war times at La Rose Blanche, 3192
Ina, 11104
An inaugural discourse... by Rev. Azel Backus, 616
The incarnation, 8766
Incas, 7964, 11330
Inchiquin, the Jesuit's letters, 13087
An incident, and other happenings, 3365
An incident at Algiers, 10919
Incidents and anecdotes of the civil war, 4829
Incidents and sketches connected with the early history and settlement of the West, 13074
Incidents in Dixie, 2725
Incidents in the life of a slave girl, 10008
Incidents of a voyage, 10310
Incidents of American camp life, 13075
Incidents of life and adventure in the Rocky Mountains, 5278
Incidents of the insurrection in the western parts of Pennsylvania, 11484
Incidents of the war, 1726
Incidents of travel in the southern states and Cuba, 5006
Incidents of travel to California, 5492
Incidents of western travel, 4791
An increased allowance, 9460
Independence preserved, 3383
Independencia americana, 7625
Independency the object of the Congress in America, 13076
Independent treasury, 2103, 2848, 13039

Independent treasury -
Speeches in Congress,
205, 12428
An index finger, 8453
Index to the Calendar of
Maryland state papers,
149
India - Descr. & trav.,
5488, 13440
India - Hist. - European
settlements, 1500-1765,
882, 2123
India rubber industry -
Peru, 8193
The India trader's directory
in purchasing the drugs
and spices of Asia and
the East Indies, 13154
Indian and Injin, 9148
Indian atrocities, 2781
Indian battles, captivities,
and adventures, 12177
Indian battles, murders,
seiges [!] and forays
in the Southwest, 13077
The Indian captive, 2756
Indian captivity, 5253,
11994
The Indian chamber, 5615
The Indian detective,
9715
The Indian hater, 3754
The Indian in his wigwam,
5097
Indian legends and other
poems, 12910
Indian narratives, 13078
Indian nullification of
the unconstitutional laws
of Massachusetts, 404
The Indian of the Connecticut,
9164
The Indian princess, 1447
The Indian reservation
sulphur springs, 13079
Indian rights and our
duties, 13007
The Indian spirit, 4460
Indian territory - Descr.

& trav., 4863
Indian wars and pioneers of
Texas, 2827
Indian wars of the northwest,
6101
Indian wars of the United
States, 2343
Indian wars of the West, 3475
Indiana artillery. 11th
battery, 1861-1865, 4663
Indiana - Biog., 13480
Indiana canal company, 13081
Indiana cavalry. 7th regt.,
1863-1865, 3044
Indiana. Constitution, 13080
Indiana - Descr. & trav.,
1230, 2943, 3314, 3472,
3714, 3739, 3943, 5147,
5375, 12142, 12554
Indiana grant, 13508
Indiana - Hist., 6423, 13480
Indiana - Hist. - Fiction,
10961
Indiana infantry. 6th regt.,
1861-1865, 2798, 3670
Indiana infantry. 12th regt.,
1861-1865, 3557
Indiana infantry. 21st regt.,
1861-1865, 6953
Indiana infantry. 27th regt.,
1861-1865, 2824
Indiana infantry. 36th regt.,
1861-1864, 3704
Indiana infantry. 42d regt.,
1861-1865, 3939
Indiana infantry. 51st regt.,
1861-1865, 3804
Indiana infantry. 57th regt.,
1861-1865, 4164
Indiana infantry. 58th regt.,
1861-1865, 3866
Indiana infantry. 68th regt.,
1862-1865, 3865
Indiana infantry. 70th regt.,
1862-1865, 4457
Indiana infantry. 72d regt.,
1862-1865, 4351
Indiana infantry. 75th regt.,
1862-1865, 3489

Indiana infantry. 81st
regt., 1862-1865, 4528
Indiana infantry. 82d
regt., 1862-1865, 3972
Indiana infantry. 99th
regt., 1862-1865, 4313
Indiana. Lincoln highway
commission, 7099
Indiana miscellany, 13480
Indiana. University -
Hist., 9705
Indianapolis - Descr.,
12860
Indianapolis - Hist.,
12860
Die Indianer Nord-
Amerikas, 1836
Indians, 1112, 1838, 7017,
7657, 11364, 11583,
11776
Indians - Antiquities,
3216, 6167
Indians - Bibl., 5996
Indians - Biog., 2443
Indians - Hist., 2442
Indians - Languages,
7305
Indians - Missions,
13297
Indians of Canada, 6731
Indians of Central
America, 5996, 7439,
8168, 11461
Indians of Central
America - Costa Rica,
8324
Indians of Central
America - Guatemala,
6789, 6908
Indians of Central
America - Panama,
13502
Indians of Mexico,
1864, 5827, 5881, 5996,
7340, 7341, 7515, 7794,
7802, 8174, 8266
Indians of Mexico -
Antiq., 6715, 7932,
11392

Indians of Mexico -
Architecture, 7414
Indians of Mexico -
Art, 7192
Indians of Mexico -
Biog., 6821, 8441
Indians of Mexico -
Hist., 1440, 1442, 7111,
11643
Indians of Mexico -
Languages, 6066, 6153
Indians of Mexico -
Religion and mythology,
6644
Indians of Mexico -
Southwest, New, 7174
Indians of North America,
9, 405, 1156, 1832, 1833,
1834, 1835, 1836, 1837,
1898, 2342, 2442, 2541,
2700, 2759, 2799, 2966,
3020, 3100, 3260, 3282,
3318, 3445, 3451, 3463,
3837, 3891, 3892, 4024,
4029, 4360, 4398, 4588,
4631, 4755, 4834, 4863,
5010, 5053, 5097, 5181,
5182, 5234, 5457, 5586,
5609, 5680, 5700, 5752,
6101, 6403, 6404, 7008,
7429, 7766, 7799, 8325,
10827, 11242, 11594, 12184,
12310, 12550, 12994, 13025,
13397, 13476, 13501
Indians of North America -
Alaska, 2231
Indians of North America -
Anecdotes, 12750
Indians of North America -
Arapahoes, 3462
Indians of North America -
Bibl., 7149, 11323
Indians of North America -
Biog., 1237
Indians of North America -
British Columbia, 4641, 7360
Indians of North America -
California - Fiction, 9068
Indians of North America -

237

Missouri Valley, 3816
Indians of North America -
Nebraska, 4025
Indians of North America -
New England, 12309,
12976, 13141
Indians of North America -
New Mexico, 1145
Indians of North America -
North Carolina, 11515
Indians of North America -
Northwest, Canadian,
4130, 11353
Indians of North America -
Northwest, Pacific,
5017, 5018
Indians of North America -
Northwestern states,
541, 542, 2784, 7009,
11681
Indians of North America -
Nova Scotia, 1558,
1559, 6575, 7268
Indians of North America -
Ohio valley, 287, 2113,
3124, 3797, 13296
Indians of North America -
Ontario, 13314
Indians of North America -
Oregon, 5183
Indians of North America -
Osage, 4924
Indians of North America -
Pacific coast, 5996
Indians of North America -
Pennsylvania, 13125,
13319
Indians of North America -
Poetry, 5693, 12910
Indians of North America -
Religion and mythology,
13169
Indians of North America -
Rhode Island, 2167
Indians of North America -
Rocky Mountains, 4257,
4701, 5180
Indians of North America -
Sioux, 13457

Indians of North America -
Soc. life & cust., 3334,
3730, 3973, 3974, 4641, 5199,
5343, 11996
Indians of North America -
Southern states, 32, 946,
2515, 2631, 2768, 5452
Indians of North America -
Southwest, Old, 4632
Indians of North America -
Tennessee, 11508, 12770,
13077
Indians of North America -
The West, 1836, 1837, 2465,
3081, 3220, 3266, 3688,
4042, 4625, 5145, 5306,
6893, 6894, 6895
Indians of North America -
Treaties, 1716, 2063, 6450
Indians of North America -
Virginia, 1231, 1232, 1249,
3189, 5204, 5252, 13301
Indians of North America -
Wars, 2343, 2554, 4942,
9585, 10570, 12177, 13078
Indians of North America -
Wars - 1600-1750, 12970,
12976
Indians of North America -
Wars - 1750-1815, 3475,
5754, 12664
Indians of North America -
Wars - 1775-1783, 12307
Indians of North America -
Wars - 1781-1795, 3232
Indians of North America -
Wars - 1815-1875, 4069,
4416
Indians of North America -
Wars - Fiction, 4460
Indians of North America -
Washington (State), 4641
Indians of South America,
592, 596, 598, 8073,
8168, 11330, 13272
Indians of South America -
Amazon valley, 31
Indians of South America -
Argentine republic,

239

Ingersoll, Lurton Dunham, 13096
Ingersoll, Samuel Bridge, 1785-1820, 13097
The Ingham papers, 9683
Ingle, Edward, 3995
Inglis, Charles, bp. of Nova Scotia, 1734-1816, 13098
Inglis, James, 1777-1820, 13099
Ingraham, Edward Duncan, 1793-1854, 13100
Ingraham, Joseph Holt, 1809-1860, 3996-4016, 8967
Ingraham, Prentiss, 1843-1904, 4017
Ingram, Mrs. Helen K., 4018
The inheritance, 10340
Inheritance and succession - Haiti, 997
An inherited debt, 10283
An initial experience, 10122
Inklings of adventure, 11178
Inland navigation, 6062
Inland navigation - Congresses, 12665
Inland navigation - Connecticut valley, 1906
Inland navigation - Pennsylvania - Hist., 8376
Inland navigation - U. S., 448, 1860, 3596, 7450, 12665, 13235, 13446
The inland sea, 9141
Inland waterway, 4941
Die innern communicationen der Vereinigten Staaten von Nord-amerika, 3596
Innes et al. vs. Roane et al., 7101
Innocent blood crying to

God from the streets of Boston, 13373
An innocent cheat, 3223
An innocent gamester, 9575
Innocent X, Pope, 1574-1655, 6383
The innocents abroad, 9027
Inorganic forces ordained to supersede human slavery, 12122
An inquiry into the causes and cost of corrupt state legislation, 13101
An inquiry into the formation of Washington's farewell address, 11270
An inquiry into the itinerancy, and conduct of the Rev. Mr. George Whitefield, 12821
An inquiry into the origin of the antiquities of America, 3216
An inquiry into the present state of the foreign relations of the Union, 13102
An inquiry into the Scriptural views of slavery, 846
Inquisition - Colombia, 5999
The inquisitor, 10678
Insane hospitals, 2388
Inscriptions on the grave stones in the grave yards of Northampton, 1504
Inscriptions, Latin, 727
Insects, 5081
Insects - Africa, 4684
Insects - North America, 4684, 5079
Inside: a chronicle of secession, 8656
Inside of rebeldom, 2907
Inside out, 1965, 9560
Inside view of slavery, 4706
The insolvent laws of Massachusetts, 11926
The instability of humane greatness, 12644
Instituciones de derecho real

Iowa and the rebellion,
13096
Iowa. Board of education,
13105
Iowa cavalry. 1st regt.,
1861-1866, 4303
Iowa cavalry. 5th regt.,
1861-1865, 4628
Iowa - Descr. & trav.,
2361, 4653, 12142,
12185
Iowa - Descr. & trav. -
Poetry, 11569
Iowa - Hist. - Civil
war, 5137, 13096
Iowa infantry. 1st regt.,
1861, 5610
Iowa infantry. 2d regt.,
1861-1865, 2665
Iowa infantry. 5th regt.,
1861-1864, 3513
Iowa infantry. 22d regt.,
1862-1865, 4121
Iowa institute of science
and arts, Dubuque,
13107
Iowa language - Grammar,
12616
Iowa. Laws, statutes,
etc., 13105
Iowa - Learned institutions
and societies, 13107
Iowa - Militia, 13096
Iowa - Pol. & govt., 7945
Iowa. State Geologist
(1866-1870), 13106
Ipsistos, 10769
Ipswich, Mass. - Hist.,
2246
Iredale, Andrew, 4022
Ireland - Biog., 10291
Ireland - Comm., 13369
Ireland - Comm. - U. S.,
11248
Ireland - Descr. & trav.,
4954, 5744
Ireland - Hist., 7257
Ireland - Hist. - Fiction,
9491

Ireland - Hist. - 18th cent. -
Fiction, 10276
Ireland - Hist. - Rebellion of
1798 - Fiction, 8544
Ireland - Poetry, 4781
Ireland - Pol. & govt. - 1760-
1820, 1113
Irene, 11048
Irigoyen, Ulises, 7105
Irisarri, Antonio José de,
1786-1868, 7106
Irish-American wit and humor,
9439
Irish, Edwin Marshall, 1848-,
7107
The Irish emigrant, 9991
An Irish garland, 4783
Irish in Massachusetts, 9602
Irish in Pennsylvania, 12880
Irish in the U. S., 6038
The Irish Ninth in bivouac
and battle, 4371
Irish publicists, 10291
The Irish refugee, 10841
Irish riflemen in America,
4242
Irish stories, 10291
An Irish wild-flower, 4784
Irish wit and humor, 10291
An Irishman, now in America,
3863
The iron furnace, 551
Iron industry and trade -
New York (State), 99
Iron industry and trade -
U. S., 2333
Iron - Metallurgy, 12905
Iron mines and mining -
Mexico, 6708
Iron ores - British Columbia,
6174
Iron ores - New York (State),
99
The iron tomb, 8831
The iron trail, 11134
Iroquois Indians, 647, 11242,
11656, 12804, 13361
Iroquois Indians - Land
transfers, 13508

243

Iroquois Indians -
Treaties, 1775, 3796
Irrigation canals and
flumes, 6122
Irrigation farming in the
kingdom of·alfalfa
Bow River Valley, 6323
Irrigation - Mexico,
6121, 6122
Irvin, Samuel Mcleary,
1812-, jt. author,
12616
Irving, Edward, fl. 1827,
ed., 7883
Irving, Henry, 3808
Irving, John Beaufain,
1800-1881, 4023
Irving, John Treat,
1812-1906, 4024, 4025
Irving, Theodore,
1809-1880, 13108
Irving, Washington,
1783-1859, 342, 656,
4026, 4027, 4028, 4029,
11591, 13109
Irwin, Richard Biddle,
1839-1892, jt. author,
11454
Irwin, Will H., jt.
author, 9509
Is a constitutional
convention a legislature?
393
Is Davis a traitor? 2736
Isaacs, Robert, 4030
Isabel, 11020
Isabel Graham, 9844
Isabel I la Católica, queen
of Spain, 1451-1504,
1200, 8083
Isabella (ship), 7912
Isabelle, 8837
Isadore Merton, 10332
Isequilla Palacio, Juan
de la, 7108
Isert, Paul Erdmann,
1757-1789, 13110
Ish-noo-ju-lut-sche, 10744
Isham, Asa Brainerd,

1844-, 4031
Isham, G. S., 4032
Island bride, 10773
The island neighbors, 8810
The island of Cuba, 189, 7086
The island of Nantucket,
6860
The island recluse, 9864
An islander, 9769
Islands of the Atlantic, 2213
The islands of the
Australasian seas, 13142
The isle of Palms, 10416
Isle of spice and palm, 5569
Israel in bondage, 9984
Israel - Ten lost tribes,
11402
Isrul's bargain, 10465
The issues of the hour, 1961
Istanbul siege, 1453 - Fiction,
11054
Isthmian tourists' guide
and business directory,
7110
Isthmiana, 8403
It came to pass, 10696
It is no crime to be a
gentleman, 8970
It is the custom, 9916
It might have been, 10275
An Italian, 799
The Italian bride, 10670
The Italian girl, 11105
The Italian sketch book, 11021
Italy - Descr. & trav.,
125, 4507, 6588, 6589,
6590, 6591, 7806, 11021
Italy - Hist. - 1492-1559 -
Fiction, 8589
Italy - Hist. - 1815-1870,
12478
Italy, Southern - Fiction,
6493
Items from Joe Miller,
10736
Ithaca, N. Y., 2444
Ithaca, N. Y. - Descr., 11838
Itinerario para parochos de
indios, 7718

Itinerarios y derroteros
de la República Mexicana,
5884
Iturbide, Agustin de,
emperor of Mexico, 1783-
1824, 1761, 6853, 7568,
12256, 13111
Iturri, Francisco, b. 1738,
13112
Ivernois, Sir Francis d',
1757-1842, 13113
Ives, Alfred Eaton,
1809-1892, 13114
Ives, Charles, 1815-1880,
13115
Ives, Joseph Christmas,
d. 1868, 5524
Ives, Levi Silliman,
1797-1867, 13116
Ixtlilxochitl, Fernando
de Alva, ca. 1568-1648,
7111, 7932
Izard, George, 1777-1828,
13119
Izard, Ralph, 1742-1804,
13117, 13118
Izlar, William Valmore,
4033

J. B. R., 13209
J. C., 401
A Jack and Jill of the
Sierras, 6969
Jack Datchett, the
clerk, 9411
Jack Harold, 10960
Jack Hilton's love-
affair, 10122
Jack Hopeton, 11031
Jack Horner, 10975
The Jack Morgan songster,
13120
Jack Tier, 9135
Jack's divorce, 10863
Jackson, Andrew, b. 1814,
13122
Jackson, Andrew, pres.
U. S., 1767-1845, 708,

1938, 5599, 5913, 7201,
8824, 10818, 11405, 11823,
13121, 13353
Jackson, Charles, 1775-1855,
13123
Jackson Co., Mich. - Biog.,
6559
Jackson Co., Mich. - Hist.,
6559
Jackson, David Prentice,
1851-, ed., 4036
Jackson, Ebenezer, 13124
Jackson, Halliday, 1771-1835,
·13125
Jackson, Helen Marie Hunt,
1831-1885, 7627
Jackson, Henry, 1798-1863,
13126
Jackson, Henry Rootes,
1820-1892, 4034, 13127
Jackson, Henry W. R., 4035,
13128
Jackson, Isaac Rand, d. 1843,
13129
Jackson, John, d. 1855,
13130
Jackson, Jonathan, 1743-1810,
13131
Jackson, Julia Newell, 7112
Jackson, La. Centenary college,
3495
Jackson, Oscar Lawrence,
1840-1920, 4036
Jackson, Robert, 1750-1827,
13132
Jackson, Samuel, 1787-1872,
13133
Jackson, Samuel Trevena,
1869-, 7113
Jackson, Tatlow, 13134, 13135
Jackson, Thomas, ed., 5672
Jackson, Thomas Jonathan,
1824-1863, 85, 3154,
4330, 8034
Jackson, W. H., 6304
Jackson, William, 1759-1828,
13136
Jackson, William Ayrault,
1832-1861, 13137

Jaco, 10310
Jacob Brown, 5259
Jacob City, 10448
Jacob, John Jeremiah,
   1758?-1839, 13138
Jacobs, Aletta H.,
   jt. author, 3593
Jacobs, Bela, 1786-1836,
   13139
Jacobs, Michael, 1808-
   1871, 13140
Jacobs, Rev. Peter,
   4037
Jacobs, Sarah Sprague,
   b. 1813, 13141
Jacobs, Thomas Jefferson,
   13142
Jacquemin, Nicolas,
   1736-1819, 13143
Jacquerie, 1358 - Fiction,
   10507
Jacques, Amédée Florent,
   1813-1865, 13144
Jacques, Daniel Harrison,
   1825-1877, 4038
Jacquess, James F., 3611
Jahnsenykes, Rev. Williamson,
   pseud., 10033
J'ai redécouvert l'Amérique,
   7217
Jalisco, Mexico. Consti-
   tution, 12480
Jalisco, Mexico - Hist.,
   7876
Jamaica, 7114
Jamaica as it is, 7786
Jamaica. Assembly, 1682,
   13145
Jamaica at Chicago, 7114
Jamaica. Commissioner
   at the World's Columbian
   exposition, Chicago,
   1893, 7114
Jamaica - Descr. & trav.,
   1035, 1246, 1272, 1425,
   5315, 5492, 6145, 6919,
   7264, 7541, 7786, 8181,
   8386, 11174, 11578
Jamaica - Econ. cond.,

1272, 11578
Jamaica. Governor, 1682-
   1684 (Sir Thomas Lynch),
   13145
Jamaica - Hist., 1499, 11371
Jamaica - Hist. - Insurrection,
   1865, 2199
Jamaica - Hist. - Maroon war
   1795-1796, 11943
Jamaica - Hist. - Sources,
   12606
Jamaica in 1850, 1272
Jamaica. Laws, statutes, etc.,
   13146, 13147
The Jamaica magistrate's and
   vestryman's assistant,
   13406
Jamaica Plain, Mass. -
   Direct., 1566
Jamaica - Pol. & govt.,
   1695, 12458, 13145
James, Bushrod Washington,
   1836-1903, 4039
James, Charles Pinckney,
   1818-1899, 13148
James, Charles Tillinghast,
   1804-1862, 13149
James, Edwin, 1797-1861, 2465,
   5343
James, George (Haffain Gelas-
   timin), 5597
James, George Payne Rainsford,
   1801?-1860, 13150
James, Henry, 1811-1882, 13151
James, Henry, 1843-1916,
   4040, 6187, 7115, 7116,
   7117, 7118, 7119, 7120,
   7121, 7122, 7123, 7124,
   7125, 7126, 7127, 7128,
   7129, 7130, 7131, 7132,
   7133
James, Horace, 1818-1875,
   13152
James, James, 13153
James, Joseph, 13154
James, Joshua, 4041
James river and Kanawha canal,
   1343
The James River tourist, 2985

246

James River, Va., 3419,
3978, 4136
James River, Va. - Descr.
& trav. - Guide-books,
2985
James, Thomas, 1782-1847,
4042
James, Thomas Horton,
4043, 7134
James, Uriah Pierson,
1811-1889, comp.,
4044
James, William, d. 1827,
13155, 13156
James, William Dobein,
13157
James's traveler's
companion, 4412
Jameson, Mrs. Anna
Brownel (Murphy),
1794-1860, 7135, 7136
Jameson, Robert Francis,
7137, 12981
The Jamesons, 9572
Jamestown, Me., 12515
Jamestown of Pemaquid,
12515
Jamestown, Va. - Hist.,
12888
Jamestown, Va. - Hist. -
Fiction, 2923, 3189
Jamie Parker, the
fugitive, 10522
Jamieson, Milton, 13158
Jan Vedder's wife, 8730
Janet Strong, 11008
Janeway, James, 1636?-
1674, 13159
Janice Meredith, 9536
Jannet, Claudio, 1844-
1894, 4045
Jansenists, 1406
Janson, Charles William,
4046
Janus, pseud., 13160
Janvier, Francis De Haes,
1817-1885, 7138, 13161
Janvier, Thomas Allibone,
7139

Japan - Descr. & trav., 4751
Japan - Fiction, 10238, 10239
Japan - Soc. life & cust.,
7610
Japanese in the Hawaiian
Islands, 7610
Japanese lady in America,
3984
Jaques, John Wesley, 13162
Jaques, Mary J., 7140
Jaquess, James Frazier,
1819-, 3611
Jaquith, James, 1781-, 4047
Jardine, L. J., 13163
Jarves, James Jackson,
1820-1888, 13164, 13165
Jarvis, Abraham, bp. 1739-
1813, 13166
Jarvis, Leonard, 1781-1854,
13167
Jarvis, Russell, 1791-1853,
13168
Jarvis, Samuel Farmar,
1786-1851, 13169, 13170,
13171
Jarvis, Sarah M'Curdy (Hart)
petitioner, 13171
Jarvis, William Charles,
d. 1836, 13172, 13173
Jason Edwards, an average man,
9604
Jasper St. Aubyn, 9842
Jay, Aimé, d. 1881, 4048
Jay, Sir James, 1732-1815,
13174
Jay, John, 1745-1829, 7141,
12140, 13175, 13176, 13177,
13178, 13179, 13180, 13181
Jay, John Clarkson, 1808-
1891, 13182
Jay, William, 1769-1853, 13183
Jay, William, 1789-1858, 2104,
13184, 13185, 13186, 13187
Jay's treaty, 1794, 295, 323,
324, 1901, 12690
Jayne, William, 1826-1916,
7142
Jean-Louis, Dulciné, 7143
Jeanne d'Arc, Saint, 1412-1431 -

Fiction, 9031
Jeannette, 11205
Jebb, John Beveridge
Gladwyn, 1841-1893,
7144
Jebb, Mrs. John
Beveridge Gladwyn,
7144
Jeff's treasure, 10653
Jefferay, William, 1591-
1675, 8610
Jefferds, Charles M.,
1837-1863?, defendant,
13188
Jefferson college,
Washington, Miss., 13189
Jefferson medical college,
Philadelphia, 2418,
13190
Jefferson medical college,
Philadelphia - Registers,
13190
Jefferson, T. H., 4049
Jefferson, Thomas, pres.
U. S., 1743-1826, 708,
1348, 1910, 2107, 2145,
4050, 7145, 7146, 7316,
7832, 8232, 11480,
12068, 12143, 13381
Jefferson, Thomas, pres.
U. S., 1743-1826 -
Fiction, 9118
Jefferson, Thomas, pres.
U. S., 1743-1826.
Memoir, correspondence,
1829, 13381
Jefferson, Thomas, pres.
U. S., 1743-1826.
Notes on the state of
Virginia, 13138
Jefferson, Thomas, pres.
U. S. - Personality,
12107
Jefferson, Thomas, pres.
U. S., 1743-1826.
The proceedings of the
government... in main-
taining the public right
to the beach of the

Mississippi, adjacent to
New Orleans... 13393
Jefferson, Thomas, pres. U. S.,
1743-1826. The writings
of Thomas Jefferson, 1853-
1854, 978
Jeffery, R., 7147
Jefferys, Thomas, 4051
Jefferys, Thomas, d. 1771, 13191,
13192
Jeffrey, Mrs. Rosa (Vertner)
1828-1894, 4052, 4053,
4054, 4055
Jeffries, Benjamin Jay,
1833-1915, tr., 11663
Jeffries, John, 1796-1876,
13193
Jenckes, Joseph, 1656-1740.
Proclamation concerning the
Rogerene episode in Norwich,
Conn. in 1725, 623
Jenings, Edmund, 13194
Jenings, Edmund. The candor of
Henry Laurens, 13374
Jenkins family, 7148
Jenkins, John, b. 1614, 7148
Jenkins, John Stilwell,
1818-1852, 13195, 13196,
13197, 13198, 13199, 13200
Jenkins, Joseph, 13201
Jenkins, Samuel, b. 1787?
13286
Jenkins, Samuel B., 7148
Jenkins, Thornton Alexander,
1811-1893, 13202
Jenkinson, Isaac, 13203
Jenks, John Whipple Potter,
4056
Jenks, William, 1778-1866,
13204
Jennings, Dudley S., 13205
Jennings, Isaac, 1816-1887,
13206
Jennings, James, 13207
Jennings, Louis John,
1836-1893, 13208
Jennings, Napoleon Augustus,
1856-1919, 4057
Jennings, Paul, b. 1799, 13209

248

Jennings, Samuel Kennedy,
1771-1854, 13210
Jenny Lind in America,
5016
Jensen, Johannes Vilhelm,
1873-1950, 4058
Jenyns, Soame, 1704-1787,
13211
Jermon, J. Wagner, 13212
Jerningham, Edward, 1737-
1812, 13213
Jerome, a poor man, 9573
Jerome, Chauncey, 13214
Jerry, 3366
Jerry's reward, 2613
Jersey (Prison-ship),
364, 1966, 2128
Jersey villas, 7126
Jervis, John Bloomfield,
1795-1885, 13215, 13216
Jessamine, 5359
The Jesuit missionary,
10297
The Jesuit relations and
allied documents, 7149
Jesuits, 6418, 7150,
7553, 7667, 8086, 12291
Jesuits - Biog., 5907
Jesuits - Fiction, 9497
Jesuits in Abyssinia,
7665
Jesuits in Canada, 11762
Jesuits in Canada -
Fiction, 10297
Jesuits in Mexico, 139,
6690, 7150, 7669
Jesuits in Mexico -
Direct., 7151
Jesuits in the United
States, 2120
Jesuits in the West
Indies, 11742
Jesuits. Letters from
missions, 2466
Jesuits. Letters from
missions (North
America), 1288, 1289,
1290, 3665, 3666, 7149
Jesuits - Missions,

1289, 1481, 1482, 1789,
2466, 3665, 7149
Jesuits. Provincia de Mexico,
7151
Jesus Christ - Biog. -
Early life, 8766
Jesus Christ - Divinity -
Sermons, 13384
Jesus Christ - Fiction,
4008, 9682
Jesus Christ - Resurrection,
9858
Jethro's advice recommended
to the inhabitants of Boston,
1496
Jets and flashes, 10253
The Jew of Milan, 9390
Jewell, Frederich Swartz,
1821-1903, 13217
Jewell, Henry, 4059
Jewell, William Ray, ed.,
4351
Jewell, Wilson, 1800-1867,
13218
The jewels, 10310
Jewels of the Third plantation,
10420
The Jewess, 10441
Jewett, Charles, 1807-1879,
13219
Jewett, Charles Coffin,
1816-1868, 13220, 13221
Jewett, Ellen, 1813-1836 -
Fiction, 11165
Jewett, Isaac Appleton,
1808-1853, 13222
Jewett, John L., 13223
Jewett, Moses, 3854
Jewett, Paul, 13224
Jewett, Mrs. Susan W., 4060
Jewitt, Llewellynn Frederick
William 1816-1886, 13225
Jews - Antiq., 13332
Jews - Hist., 13332
Jews - Hist. - Fiction,
9984, 9989
Jews - Hist. - To B. C. 586 -
Fiction, 8454
Jews - Hist. - To A. D. 70 -

Fiction, 10058, 10616
Jews - Hist. - To A. D. 70 -
  Poetry, 1902
Jews in Georgia, 11912
Jews - Legal status, laws,
  etc. - Maryland, 11480
Jews - Soc. life & cust.,
  9614
Jex-Blake, Sophia, 1840-
  1912, 13226
Jillson, Willard Rouse,
  1890-, 7152, 7153,
  7154, 7155
Jim's little woman, 10041
Jiménez Moreno, Wigberto,
  7932
Jiménez Rueda, Julio,
  1896-, ed., 6389
Jimmy's big brother
  from California, 6978
Jimty, 9916
Jinny, 9779
Joanna of Naples, 9710,
  9711
Jobson, Frederick James,
  1821-1881, 4061
Jocassee, 10769, 10783
Joe of Lahaina, 10675
Joe's pocket, 10863
Joes abenteuer im
  wilden westen, 2693
Jogues, Isaac, 1607-
  1646, 1481, 13227
John and Mary, 9665
John and the demijohn,
  11212
John Anderson and I,
  9203
John Andross, 9353
John Brent, 5748
John Bull in America,
  10485
John Delavory, 10016
John Doe and Richard
  Roe, 9632
John Eax and Mamelon,
  10992
John Godfrey's fortunes,
  10927

John Gray: a Kentucky tale
  of the olden time, 8514
John Guilderstring's sin, 10615
John Holden, unionist, 9383
John Hunter and his pupils,
  3707
John L. Stoddard's lectures,
  8114
John Law, the projector,
  118
John M. Daniel's latch-key,
  2589
John McGovern's poems, 4352
John March, southern, 8927
John Merrill's experiment in
  palmistry, 10448
The John North mystery, 9817
John Norton's vagabond, 10400
John O'Brien, 10642
John Paget, 3367
John Paul's book, 11112
John Randolph, 10953, 10310
John Ship, mariner, 10709
John Smith's funny adventures
  on a crutch, 9871
John Smith's letters, 10817
John W. Robertson, 10197
John Ward, preacher, 9375
John Worthington's name, 8777
John's alive, 10962
John's wedding suit, 10465
Johnes, Arthur James,
  1809-1871, 13228
Johnny-boy, 6963
Johns, Henry T., b. 1827 or 8,
  4062
Johns Hopkins University, 4765
Johns, Walter R., jt. author,
  2030
Johnson, Adam Rankin, 1834-,
  4063
Johnson, Alexander Bryan,
  1786-1867, 7156, 13229
Johnson, Andrew, pres. U. S.,
  1808-1875, 629, 11269,
  11868, 13230, 13231, 13232
Johnson, Andrew, pres. U. S.,
  1808-1875 - Impeachment,
  13230

Johnson, Charles Beneulyn,
1843-1928, 4064
Johnson, Charles Britten,
1788?-1835, 13233
Johnson, Clifton, 1865-
1940, 4065, 4066
Johnson, Cuthbert William,
1799-1878, 13234
Johnson, D. Vertner,
illustr., 4053
Johnson, Edwin Ferry,
1803-1872, 13235,
13236
Johnson, Ezra R., 13237
Johnson, Frederick H.,
13238
Johnson, Hannibal Augustus,
1841-, 4067
Johnson, Herrick, 1832-
1918, 13239
Johnson, James, 1777-
1845, 13240
Johnson, James, 1780-1811,
defendant, 13241
Johnson, Jeremiah, 1766-
1852, 13262
Johnson, John Barent,
1769-1803, 13242,
13243, 13244
Johnson, John Graver,
1841-1917, 13245
Johnson, Joseph, 1776-
1862, 13246
Johnson, Lorenzo Dow,
1805-1867, 13247,
13248, 13249, 13250,
13251
Johnson, Louisa, 13252
Johnson, Overton, 4068
Johnson, Reverdy, 1796-
1876, 6568, 7157,
13253, 13254, 13255,
13256
Johnson, Richard W.,
1827-1897, 4069
Johnson, Robert, fl.
1586-1626, 4070, 4071
Johnson, Robert Gibbon,
1771-1850, 13257

Johnson, Samuel, 1709-1784,
9368, 13258, 13259, 13260,
13462
Johnson, Samuel, 1709-1784.
Taxation no tyranny, 11968
Johnson, Samuel Roosevelt,
1802-1873, 13261, 13262
Johnson, Stanley Currie,
1878-, 7158
Johnson, Mrs. Thomazin Gibson
(Blanchard) 1765-1825, 13250
Johnson, Walter Rogers,
1794-1852, 13263, 13264
Johnson, Sir William, 1715-
1774, 7429
Johnson, William, 1771-1834,
13265, 13266
Johnson, William, 1771-1834.
Sketches of the life and
correspondence of Nathanael
Greene, 13380
Johnson, William Cost, 1806-
1860, 13267, 13268
Johnson, William D., 13269
Johnson, William Melanchthon,
1834-1910, 13270
Johnson's "old woman", 6965
Johnston, Charles, 1768-,
4072
Johnston, David Claypoole,
1797-1865, illustr., 10414
Johnston, Elias Schellhammer,
1834-1926, 13271
Johnston, Elizabeth Bryant,
1833-1907, 4073
Johnston, Mrs. Elizabeth
(Lichtenstein) 1764-1848,
4074
Johnston family, 4074
Johnston, Gideon, 1671 (ca.),
4075
Johnston, Sir Harry Hamilton,
1858-1927, 4076
Johnston, Henry Phelps,
1842-1923, ed., 7141
Johnston, Isaac N., 4077
Johnston, James, 13272
Johnston, James F., 13273
Johnston, James Finlay Weir,

251

Jones, James Athearn,
  1791-1854, 13303
Jones, John, 1729-1791,
  13304
Jones, John Beauchamp,
  1810-1866, 4109-4117
Jones, John G., 13305
Jones, John Matthew,
  13306
Jones, John Paul, 1747-
  1792 - Poetry,
  2191
Jones, John Wesley, 4118
Jones, John William,
  1836-, 4119
Jones, Joseph, 1833-1896,
  13307
Jones, Joseph Seawell,
  1811?-1855, 13308,
  13309
Jones, Lewis Hampton,
  7162
Jones, Lot, d. 1865,
  13310
Jones, Morris Charles,
  1819-1893, 13311
Jones, Peter, Chippera
  chief, 1802-1856,
  13312, 13313, 13314
Jones, Pleasant, pseud.,
  10861
Jones, Samuel, 13315
Jones, Samuel, 1735-1814,
  4120
Jones, Samuel, 1819-1887,
  2035
Jones, Samuel Calvin, 1828-,
  4121
Jones, Samuel W., 13316
Jones, Skelton, 11613
Jones, Thomas A., 7163
Jones, Thomas ap Thomas,
  Revolutionary soldier,
  7162
Jones, Thomas D., 1808-
  1881, 7260
Jones, Thomas Laurens,
  1819-1887, 13317
Jones, Thomas, of Nutgrove

school, Rathfarnham,
  12310
Jones, Uriah James, 1818-1864,
  4122, 13319
Jones, Walter, 1777-1861,
  13320
Jones, William, 1760-1831,
  13321, 13322
Jones, William Alfred,
  1817-1900, 13323, 13324
Jones, William D., 13325
Jones's new fin-keel, 9254
Jordan, Cornelia Jane (Matthews)
  1830-1898, 13326
Jordan, Ebenezer Stevens,
  1819-1890, 7164
Jordan, Gibbes Walker, 13327
Jordan, John, fl. 1826,
  13328
Jordan, Leonard G., 3655
Jordan, Samuel, 13329
Jörg, Eduard, 1808-1864,
  4123
Jornado del muerto, 10863
Joseph and his friend, 10928
Joseph, Henry, d. 1834,
  defendant, 13331
Joseph, pseud., 13330
Joseph Seaman Cotter, black
  poet of Kentucky, 7165
Joseph, the Jew, 10047
Joseph Wheeler, 3224
Josephine Eloise, 9725
Josephus, Flavius, 13332
Josh Billing's encyclopedia
  and proverbial philosophy
  of wit and humor, 10742
Josh Billings, hiz sayings,
  10743
Josiah Allen as a politician,
  9889
Jottings from life, 9303
Jottings of a year's sojourn
  in the South, 5558
Jottrand, Gustave, 1830-1906,
  tr., 736
Jourdanet, D., ed., 7931
Journal and letters of Col.
  John May, 4425

254

255

Katharine Walton, 10774
Katydid's poems, 4366
Kaufmann, S., tr., 4039
Kay, Charles Y., 7175
Kazakova, Liia Samuilovna,
7176
Kearney, Belle, 1863-,
4133
Kearney's expedition,
1846, 3962
Kearny, Stephen Watts,
1794-1848, 4134
Kearsarge (Man-of-war),
12003
Keasbey, Anthony Quinton,
1824-1895, 4135
Keating, William Hypolitus,
1799-1840, 13360
Kechua language, 7411
Keckley, Betsy, pseud.,
7177
Keckley, Elizabeth Hobbs.
Behind the scenes, 7177
Keef, 9047
Keefer, Thomas Coltrin,
1821-1914, 6666
Keel and saddle, 7842
Keele, William, 1781-1861,
3402
Keeling, Robert James,
1828-1909, 7178
Keene, N. H. - Hist.,
2455
Keep cool, 10408
Keese, John, 1805-1856,
ed., 12885
The Keim and allied
families in America
and Europe, 7179
Keim, De Benneville Randolph,
1841-1914, 4136, 7179
Keim family, 7179
Keith, Elbridge Gerry,
1840-1905, 7180
Keith, George, 1639?-1716,
1652, 4137
Keith, Sir William bart.,
1680-1749, 11656, 13494
Kelham, Robert, 1717-1808,

11425
Kelland, Philip, 4138
Keller, Arthur I., illustr.,
5192, 9553
Keller, George, 4139
Keller, Helen Adams, 1880-1968,
7181
Kelley, Daniel George, 4140
Kelley, Mrs. Maria Louisa
(Hamilton) 1860-, 7182
Kelley, William Darrah,
1814-1896, 4141, 8257
Kelley's Ford, Va., Battle of,
1863, 2034
Kellogg, John Azor, 1828-1883,
4142
Kellogg, John Jackson, 1837-,
4143
Kellogg, Louise Phelps,
ed., 4144
Kellogg, Robert H., 4145
Kellom, John H., 2877
Kelly, Samuel, 1784-, 4146
Kelly, William, 4147
Kelroy, 10684
Kemble, E. W., illustr.,
2741, 3192, 4091, 10896
Kemble, Frances Anne,
1809-1893, 4148, 4149, 7119
Kenan, Augustus H., 2044
Kendall, George Wilkins,
1809-1867, 4150, 4151
Kendall, John Jennings, 7183
Kendall, John Smith,
1874-, 7184
Kennaway, Sir John Henry,
baronet, 1837-1919, 4152
Kennebec river - Hist. -
Fiction, 9986
Kennebunkport, Me. - Geneal.,
11488
Kennebunkport, Me. - Hist.,
11488
Kennedy, Archibald, 1685?-
1763, 13361
Kennedy, John Pendleton,
1795-1870, 4153, 4154,
4155, 4156, 7185, 7186,
13362

Kennedy, Philip Pendleton,
1795-1870, 4157
Kennedy, William,
1799-1871, 4158
Kennedy, William,
1813-1890, 1116, 1117
Kenney, James, 1780-1849,
10736
Kent, Mrs. E. C., 4159
Kent, Edward E., jt.
author, 6538
Kent family, 6538
Kent, Richard, 6538
Kent, William, 8200
Kenton, Simon, 1755-
1836, 7376, 10953
Kenton, Simon, 1755-
1836 - Fiction, 5663,
5664
The Kentuckian in New York,
2924
Kentucky and Tennessee,
4160
Kentucky and Virginia
resolutions of 1798,
13500
Kentucky - Biog., 1359
Kentucky cavaliers in
Dixie, 4541
Kentucky cavalry. 1st
regt., 1861-1864, 5348
Kentucky cavalry (Confe-
derate) - Partisan
rangers, 1862-1864,
4063
Kentucky - Church history,
1359, 4895
A Kentucky Cinderella,
10808
Kentucky colonization
society, 1459
Kentucky (Confederate
state) Constitution,
7187
Kentucky - Descr. & trav.,
1495, 2628, 2771, 2943,
3138, 3424, 3425, 3426,
3472, 3568, 3595, 3714,
3739, 3745, 3750, 3753,

4059, 4173, 4264, 4464,
4640, 4758, 4791, 5147,
5382, 5432, 5601, 5644,
5706, 5730, 6061, 8330,
8349
Kentucky - Descr. & trav. -
Guide-books, 3798, 4160
Kentucky - Fiction, 2682,
3034, 3591, 3743, 3744,
3754, 3782, 3893, 4180,
4992, 5380, 5497, 5642,
5662, 5663, 5664, 8514,
8516, 8517, 9554, 9904,
10139, 10140, 10592
Kentucky folks and some others,
9342
Kentucky - Hist., 485, 2937,
3184, 3445, 3682, 4337,
4367, 4754, 5250, 6837,
7152, 7247, 7380, 8016,
13415
Kentucky - Hist. - To 1792,
2829, 4519, 6446
Kentucky - Hist. - Civil war,
1478, 1658, 6472, 11826
Kentucky - Hist. - Civil war -
Fiction, 2629, 8755, 9557
Kentucky - Hist. - Fiction,
4720, 8513
Kentucky in American letters,
5446
Kentucky infantry. 6th regt.,
1861-1865, 4077
Kentucky infantry. 22d regt.,
1862-1865, 5272
Kentucky. Laws, statutes,
etc., 13363
Kentucky - Pol. & govt., 3051,
4866, 7155
Kentucky - Pol. & govt. -
1792-1865, 3534, 4264, 4709,
4978
Kentucky - Pol. & govt. -
1861-1865, 7187
Kentucky - Pol. & govt. -
1865-, 13318
Kentucky - Pol. & govt. -
Civil war, 12873
A Kentucky protest against

King Philip's War, 1675-
1676, 12, 2125, 2167,
11421, 11787, 11876,
12110
King Philip's War, 1675-
1676 - Fiction, 9154,
9155, 10885, 10958
King, Richard, 4175
King Sham, 12407
King, Thomas Butler,
1804-1864, 5351, 8157
The king's jackal, 9359
The king's men, 9641
The king's ship, 11173
Kingdom, William, jr.,
4176
Kings county, N. Y. -
Registers, 11541
Kingsborough, Edward
King, viscount,
1795-1837, 7192
Kingsbury, Gaines Pease,
4177
Kingsbury sketches,
10136
Kingsford, William,
1819-1898, 4178, 7193
Kingsley, Charles,
1819-1875, 7194, 7195
Kingsley, F. M., 10448
Kingsley, Rose Georgina,
7196
The kinsmen, 10775
Kinnear, John R., 4179
Kippis, Andrew, 1725-
1795, 13364
Kirby-Smith, Edmund,
1824-1893, 2035
Kirby, William, jt.
author, 4956
Kirk, Charles D., 4180
Kirk, John Foster, 1824-
1904, ed., 7774
Kirke, Edmund, pseud.,
3610-3613, 9621-9623
Kirke, Henry, 1842-1925,
7197
Kirker, James, 1793-,
3268

Kirkham, Stanton Davis,
1868-, 7198
Kirkland, Caroline Matilda
(Stansbury) 1801-1864,
ed., 2163
Kirkwood, James Pugh,
1807-1877, 1571
Kirkwood, John, 7199
Kirsten, A., 4181
Kisch, Egon Erwin, 1885-
1948, 7200
Kismet, 10669
Kist, Leopold, 1824-1902,
4182
Kit Carson, 2581
A kitchen colonel, 9575
Kitchen, Thomas, d. 1784,
3388
Kitchen utensils, 2244
The kite trust, 10660
Kito, 10238
Kittl, Ernst Anton Leopold,
1854-, ed., 7654
Kittle, Mrs. Maria, 1721-1779,
8814
Kito, Frank Hugo, 1880-,
6306
Kitty Craig, 9892
Klamath Lake Massacre, 2920
Klausing, Anton Ernst,
1729-1803, tr., 6843
Kleen, Emil Andreas Gabriel,
1847-, 4183
Kleiber, Joseph, 4184
Klein, Félix, 1862-, 4185
Klingberg, Frank J., 4075
Klitgaard, Kaj, 4186
Klondike gold fields,
7630
Kloss, Georg Franz Burkhard,
1787-1854, 900
Knapp, J. Augustus, illustr.,
10224
Knapp, Samuel Lorenzo,
1783-1838, 13368
Knaresborough monthly-meeting,
An epistle to Friends of,
12563
Knauer, Hermann, 4187

The knave of hearts,
9642
The Knickerbocker, New
York, 1833-65, 10154
The Knickerbocker's
address to the Stuy-
vesant pear tree, 2141
The knife, 9216
A knight-errant of the
foot-hills, 6970
Knight, Henry Cogswell,
1788-1835, 4188
The knight of the
golden melice, 8468
A knight of the nets,
8731
The knight of Sheppey,
10919
Knight, Mrs. Sarah
(Kemble), 1666-1727,
13366, 13367
The knightly soldier,
5471
Knights of Columbus.
Texas state council.
Historical commission,
5368
The knights of England,
France and Scotland,
9845
Knights of Pythias,
10795
The Knights of Pythias
shown up, 10795
Knights of the golden
circle, 11209
The knights of the
seal, 9434
Knights of to-day, 8707
Knitting-work, 10754
Knobel, Fridolin Marinus,
1857-, 4189
The Knockabout club in
the Everglades, 4633
Knortz, Karl, 1841-, 4190
Knott, James Proctor,
1830-1911, 4191, 7201
Know thy neighbor, 10694
Knowles, Eric, 7715

Knowles, William, 12311
Knowlton family, 8113
Knox college, Galesburg,
Ill., 658
Knox, Henry, 1750-1806,
11497
Knox, John Armory, 1851-1906,
jt. author, 5327
Knox, Thomas Wallace,
1835-1896, 4192, 7202
Knox, William, 1732-1810,
13368, 13369, 13370
Koch, Albrecht Karl, 4193
Koch, Richert Gerhard Halfred
von, 1872-, 4194
Kohl, Johann Georg, 1808-1878,
7203
Kol, Henri Hubert van,
1852-1925, 7204
Kollonitz, Paula, gräfin,
b. 1830, 7205, 7206
Koningsmarke, the long Finne,
10486
Koppe, Carl Wilhelm, 7207,
7208
Korea - Descr. & trav., 4751
Kossuth, Lajos, 1802-1894,
954, 4865, 11309
Kotzebue, August Friedrich
Ferdinand von, 1761-1819,
1544
Kotzebue, Otto von, 7209
Kowalski, Henri, 1841-, 7210
Krantz, Camille, 1848-, 7494
Krebs, Ernst Hugo, 7211
Kreuz und quer durch Mexiko,
7821
Kriegsau, Adolf, freiherr von,
4195
Krishna Iyer, V. R., 1915-,
7212
Kroupa, B., 4196
Krzywicka-Adamowicz, Helena,
7213
Ku Klux Klan, 3678, 4796
Kultur und reiseskizzen aus
Nord und Mittel-Amerika,
4674
Kunth, Karl Sigismund,

A lady of quality, 8906
The lady of the Aroostook,
9946
The lady of the green
and blue, 8941
The lady of the isle,
10838
The lady of the rock,
11187, 11188
The lady of the West,
722
A lady of Warrenton, Va.,
10576
The lady, or the tiger?
10892
Lady Ravelgold, 11183
A lady's life in the
Rocky Mountains, 6086
A lady's second journey
round the world, 13453
Laet, Joannis de, 1593-
1649, 7221
La Fay, the pickpocket,
10310
La Fayette and the Indian
girl of Illinois,
10570
Lafayette en Amérique en
1824 et 1825, 4265
Lafayette, Fort, N. Y.,
2277, 2479
Lafayette, Marie Joseph
Paul Yves Roch Gilbert
du Motier, marquis de,
1757-1834, 77, 1408,
2346, 4200, 4265, 6428,
11703, 11924, 12029,
12113, 12417, 13473
Lafayette, Marie Joseph
Paul Roch Yves Gilbert
du Motier, marquis de,
1757-1834 - Poetry, 2843
Lafitte, Jean, c.1780-c.1825,
3036
Lafitte, Jean, c.1780-c.1825 -
Fiction, 4005
Lafitte: the pirate of the
Gulf, 4005
Lafuente y Alcantara,

Miguel, 1817-1850, ed., 1200
Lagrave, Michel, 7494
Laguna, 6910
La Harpe, Bernard de, 4201
Lahontan, Louis Armand de
Lom d'Arce, baron de, 1666-
1715? 4202, 7222, 7223,
7224, 7225
Laicus, 8449
Laicus, Philipp, pseud., 6074
Lake commerce, 940
Lake co., Ill., 12532
Lake Forest College, 8431
Lake George, 4624
Lake of the Woods, 6220
Lake poets - Hist. & crit.,
10560
Lakewood, 10429
Lalcaca, 7226
Lamar, Lucius Quintus
Cincinnatus, 1825-1893,
4426
Lamar, Mirabeau Buonaparte,
1798-1859, 13371
Lamas, Andrés, 1817-1891,
ed., 7853
Lamb, Roger, 1756-1830,
4203
Lamb's biographical dictionary
of the U. S., 7227
Lambert de Sainte-Croix,
Alexandre, 1854-, 4205, 7228
Lambert, John, 4204, 7229
Lambert Lilly, school master
[pseud.], 12754
Lamberton, James McCormick,
1856-1915, 7230
Lamprecht, Karl Gotthard,
1856-1915, 4206
Lampton, William James,
d. 1917, 4207
Lamy, Étienne Marie Victor,
1845-1919, 7525
Lanaghan, Mrs., 397
Lancaster, Ky. - Hist. -
Poetry, 4838
Lancaster, Mass. - Hist.,
12697
Lancaster, Mass. - Hist. -

266

Latin American literature -
Period., 7835
Latin language - Gender,
7728
Latin language - Grammar -
1500-1800, 7436
Latin language - Tense,
7727, 7728
Latitude, 5852
Latorre, Germán, 7248
Latour, Arsène Lacarrière,
4224
La Tour, Charles Amador
de St. Estienne, sieur
de - Fiction, 8953,
8984
Latreille, Pierre André,
1762-1833, 7092
Latrobe, Charles Joseph,
1801-1875, 4225, 7249
A latter day saint, 11132
The Latter-Day Saints'
emigrants' guide, 3027
Lauber, Almon W., 4589
Laudonnière, René Goulaine
de, 4226
Laughin' in meetin',
10909
Laughs I have taken a
pen to, 11177
Launay, Louis de, 1860-
1938, 7494
Laura Lovel, 10197
Laura Seymour, 10207
Laurens, Henry, 1724-1792,
7250, 13374
Laurens, Henry, 1724-1792.
Mr. Lauren's true state
of the case, 13194
Laval, Antoine François,
1664-1728, 4227
Lavanha, João Baptista,
1555-1624, 882
Laverdière, Charles
Honoré, 1826-1873, ed.,
6396
Laverrenz, Viktor, 1862-,
4228
Law - Addresses, essays,

lectures, 56, 12342
Law - Anecdotes, facetiae,
satire, etc., 707, 5222
Law - Canada, 11882
Law - Collected works, 8069,
8072
Law, Comparative, 952
Law - Confederate States of
America, 2054, 2055
Law - Dictionaries, 11425
Law - District of Columbia,
1686
Law - Gt. Brit. - Hist. &
crit., 1181
Law - Hist. & crit., 11253
Law - Jamaica, 13406
Law, John, 1671-1729, 3552
Law, John, 1671-1729 - Fiction,
118
Law, John, 1796-1873, 4229
Law Lane, 10037
The law of flats, 11436
Law - Oregon, 4690
The law, our school-master,
1096
Law - Period., 13338
Law reform, 554, 12065
Law reports, digests, etc. -
Gt. Brit., 12234
Law reports, digests, etc. -
Mexico, 1078
Law reports, digests, etc. -
U. S., 12234
Law - Spain, 231
Law - Spain - Collected works,
8072
Law - Spain - Colonies -
America, 5972
Law - Spanish America, 231,
7894
Law, William, 1686-1761,
1157
Lawford hall, 11101
Lawrence, Amos, 1786-1852,
12359, 12893
Lawrence, Amos Adams, 1814-
1886, 13149
Lawrence, Charles, 7602, 7603
Lawrence family, 2452

267

272

Lewis, John Henry,
  1834-, 4271
Lewis, Meriwether,
  1774-1809, 4272,
  5457, 13385
Lewis, Oscar, 5995
Lewis, Richard, tr.,
  5264
Lewis, Tayler, 1802-1877,
  110
Lewis, William, 1745?-
  1819, 1312, 11271
Leyden. English
  Dissenters' church,
  13026
Lex mercatoria americana,
  1793
The Lexington, 11010
Lexington, Battle of,
  1775, 11817, 13418
Lexington, Ky. - Descr.,
  3424
Lexington, Ky. - Hist.,
  2258, 3488, 3884,
  6457, 6459
Lexington (Steamboat),
  2352
Leyendas americanas,
  por Don José Güell y
  Renté... 12481
Leyva, Antonio de, 7273
Lezay-Marnézia, Claude
  François Adrien, marquis
  de, 1735-1800, 4273
L'Honoré Naber, Samuel
  Pierre, 1865-, ed.,
  7274
The liar, 7123
Libby, Andersonville,
  Florence, 3799
Libby life, 1845
Libby prison, 1845, 2761,
  3417, 4077, 4335, 4867,
  4970, 11706
Liber scriptorum, 8612
El Liberal, 7275
Liberia, 2457, 11783
Liberia - Hist., 503, 12147,
  12508

Libertas, pseud., 6669,
  11570
La liberté aux États-Unis,
  1862
Liberty, 325, 1862, 13038,
  13090
The liberty cap, 2261
Liberty Hall, Inc., Louisville,
  Ky., 7276
Liberty Jones' discovery,
  6972
Liberty of conscience,
  12420
Liberty of speech, 11335
Liberty of the press, 226,
  11335, 12756
Liberty of the press - U. S.,
  11987
Liberty overthrown! 10055
The liberty pole, 9977
Liberty's ordeal, 1358
Libra, 8529
The librarian's manual,
  12491
Libraries, 12491
Libraries - America, 2790
Libraries - Hist., 8186
Libraries - Kentucky, 8186
Libraries - U. S., 8186,
  13221
Library rules and regulations,
  12470
El libro de mis recuerdos,
  6819
El libro rojo del Putumayo,
  8193
Licht- und schattenbilder
  republikanischer zustände,
  4315
Lidia, 4452
Liebknecht, Wilhelm, 1816-
  1900, 4274
A lieutenant of cavalry in
  Lee's army, 2654
Lièvre, Daniel. La isla del
  Coco, 8303
Life, a poem in three books,
  1430
The life, adventures, and

4330
Life on the frontier,
2675, 2676
Life on the Indian frontier,
5772
Life on the Lakes, 9619
Life on the Mississippi,
3029
Life on the plains and
among the diggings,
3220
Life on the wave, 10789
Life scenes, 9452
Life scenes in the Old
North State, 11133
Life sketches from
common paths, 9436
Life-struggles in rebel
prisons, 3432
Life thoughts, 1058
The life, trial, and
execution of Captain
John Brown, 13386
Life without love, 9240
Life's caprices, 9669
Life's discipline, 10641
Life's lesson, 10954
Life's promise to pay,
9099
Liffith Lank, 11113
Liffy Leman, 3034
Lifting the veil, 10294
Ligan, 9431
Ligeret de Chazey,
Madame Elénore, 4276
Liggon's tobacco warehouse
prison, Richmond,
3378, 3793, 4455
Light, 10369
Light, Bianca, 4277
The light dragoon, 10069
The light keeper, 9977
A light man, 10283
Light, more light, 10091
The light of home, 9339
The light of the reef,
4004
A light sovereign, 9741
Lightcap, William Henry,

4278
Lighthall, William Douw,
1857-, 7278
The lightningrod man, 10346
Lights and lines of Indian
character, 11822
Lights and shadows of a life,
9310
Lights and shadows of American
life, 3058, 4492
Lights and shadows of domestic
life, 10207
The lights and shadows of
free-masonry, 4530
Lights and shadows of sailor
life, 11820
Lights and shadows of southern
life, 10495
Lignereux, Saint-André de,
4279
Like a gallant lady, 9019
Lilian, 9662
Lilius, A., 5872, 5873
Lily, 8828
The lily and the totem, 5162
Lima, 7050, 7411
Lima (Archdiocese), 6828
Liñ, 10420
Lincoln, A. W. B., illustr.,
9533
Lincoln, Abraham, pres. U. S.,
1809-1865, 465, 470, 627,
872, 873, 874, 1462, 1545,
3907, 5815, 5816, 5820,
5821, 5824, 5826, 5833,
5912, 5959, 5960, 5975,
5960, 5975, 5982, 6004,
6020, 6075, 6089, 6092,
6112, 6115, 6191, 6197,
6243, 6251, 6288, 6327,
6337, 6338, 6343, 6394,
6411, 6417, 6419, 6439,
6485, 6486, 6530, 6539,
6560, 6565, 6597, 6652,
6656, 6660, 6663, 6665,
6676, 6738, 6779, 6830,
6831, 6848, 6852, 6878,
6952, 6962, 6982, 6985,
7002, 7022, 7023, 7025,

Lincoln, Abraham, pres.
U. S., 1809-1865 -
Drama, 5220, 5865,
5931, 5974, 5984, 8214
Lincoln, Abraham, pres.
U. S., 1809-1865 -
Family, 5901, 5953,
6022, 6023, 6442, 6447,
6620, 6810, 6949, 7024,
7099, 7302, 7573
Lincoln, Abraham, pres.
U. S., 1809-1865 -
Fiction, 6960
Lincoln, Abraham, pres.
U. S., 1809-1865 -
Funeral and memorial
services, 7621, 7723,
8385, 8429
Lincoln, Abraham, pres.
U. S. - Funeral journey
to Springfield, 1982,
7051
Lincoln, Abraham, pres.
U. S., 1809-1865 -
Gettysburg address, 6763
Lincoln, Abraham, pres.
U. S., 1809-1865 -
Homes, 7642
Lincoln, Abraham, pres.
U. S., 1809-1865 -
Journey to Washington,
Feb. 1861, 1982, 7676
Lincoln, Abraham, pres.
U. S., 1809-1865 -
Law practice, 5823,
5887, 5935, 6006,
6018, 6019, 7614
Lincoln, Abraham, pres.
U. S., 1809-1865 -
Medals, 8435
Lincoln, Abraham, pres.
U. S., 1809-1865 -
Memorial services,
5910, 5957, 6123, 6124,
6138, 7645, 8242
Lincoln, Abraham, pres.
U. S., 1809-1865 -
Monuments, etc., 5818,
5819, 5822, 5993, 7073,

7301, 7564
Lincoln, Abraham, pres. U. S.,
1809-1865 - Museums, relics,
etc., 6033, 6034, 6035, 7038
Lincoln, Abraham, pres. U. S.,
1809-1865 - Personality,
7027
Lincoln, Abraham, pres. U. S.,
1809-1865 - Poetry, 1168,
1325, 3537, 5393, 5859,
5867, 5868, 5940, 6080,
6083, 6142, 6210, 6340,
6902, 6916, 7412, 7906,
8039, 8115, 8156, 8419,
12638, 13050, 13153
Lincoln, Abraham, pres. U. S.,
1809-1865 - Political
career before 1861, 6391,
6706, 6707, 7068, 7586,
7782
Lincoln, Abraham, pres. U. S.,
1809-1865 - Portraits,
7470, 7471, 7633
Lincoln, Abraham, pres. U. S.,
1809-1865 - Relations with
Jews, 7409
Lincoln, Abraham, pres. U. S.,
1809-1865 - Relations with
physicians, 7408
Lincoln, Abraham, pres. U. S.,
1809-1865 - Relics, 8346
Lincoln, Abraham, pres. U. S.,
1809-1865 - Religion, 5869,
5922, 6014, 6017, 6190,
6931, 7028, 7029, 7069,
7113, 7445, 7446, 7661,
7721, 7773, 7919
Lincoln, Abraham, pres. U. S.,
1809-1865 - Songs and music,
7292
Lincoln, Abraham, pres. U. S.,
1809-1865 - Songs and music -
Bibl., 8347
Lincoln, Abraham, pres. U. S.,
1809-1865 - Tomb, 6879
Lincoln, Abraham, pres. U. S.,
1809-1865 - Views on slavery,
7352, 8350
Lincoln, Abraham, pres. U. S.,

1809-1865 - Views on
temperance, 5985,
6541, 7281, 8397
Lincoln and his neighbors,
6663
Lincoln and public morality,
6779
Lincoln and the convention
of 1860, 7782
Lincoln as a politician,
7357
Lincoln cabin on Boston
Common, 6020
Lincoln campaign songster,
7292
The Lincoln catechism,
7293
Lincoln day addresses,
7142
Lincoln-Douglas debates,
1858, 6021, 6346, 6738,
7026, 7036, 7175, 7390
Lincoln, 1864 - McKinley,
1900, 7294
Lincoln family 6716, 7302
Lincoln Fellowship,
Hamilton, Ontario, 7295
Lincoln Fellowship of
Southern California,
6004
Lincoln Fellowship of
Wisconsin, 7296, 7297
Lincoln Guard of Honor,
7298
Lincoln highway, 8352
Lincoln in Pennsylvania,
7002
Lincoln in Springfield,
5816
Lincoln in the light of
his age, 7263
Lincoln in the winter of
'60-'61, 7352
Lincoln, Mary Todd, 1818-
1882, 7024, 7300
Lincoln Memorial,
Washington, D. C.,
5993, 7299
The Lincoln monument in

memory of Scottish-American
soldiers, 7301
Lincoln, Nancy (Hanks),
1782-1818, 6210, 6447
Lincoln national life foundation,
8347
Lincoln Pioneer Village,
Rockport, Ind., 6664
Lincoln sheet music, 8347
Lincoln, Solomon, 1804-1881,
7302
Lincoln, Solomon, 1828-1907,
5997
The Lincoln statue at the
University of Wisconsin,
7296
Lincoln, the man of the people,
7412
Lincoln the poet, 7287
Lincoln university, Chester Co.,
Pa., 13269
Lincoln vs. liquor, 5985
Lincoln's companions on the
trip to Antietam, 6560
Lincoln's grave, 5393
Lincoln's Italian volunteers
from New York, 7415
Lincoln's legacy, 5940
Lincoln's legacy of inspiration,
7048
Lincoln's love story, 5960
Lincoln's Negro policy, 6486
Lincoln's Springfield, 7771
The Lincolns in their old
Kentucky homes, 6022
Lind-Goldschmidt, Jenny Maria,
1820-1887, 5016, 9628
Lind, John, 1737-1781, 13387,
13388, 13389, 13390
Linda, 3843
Lindau, Martin Bernhard,
b. 1818, ed. & tr., 6893
Lindau, Paul, 1839-1919,
4280
Linden Hill, 9752
Lindsay, William Schaw,
1816-1877, 2421
Lindsey, Theophilus, 1723-
1808, 11252

Lines, Jorge A., 1891-,
ed. and tr., 8324
Linforth, James, 4281
Links in the golden
chain of brotherhood,
13061
Links of friendship, 3096
Linn, John Joseph, 1798-,
4282
Linn, William, 1752-1808.
Serious considerations...
1800, 1910
Linton, J. F., 7303
The Linton family, 8838
Linton, William James,
1812-1897, engr.,
12742
The Linwoods, 10725
The lion and the unicorn,
9360
Lionel Lincoln, 9136,
9137
Lippé, Joseph Alfred,
1865-, 7304
Lippincott, Horace Mather,
1877-, 12216
Lippincott, S. J., 10163
Liquor laws - Maine,
1916
Liquor laws - Massachusetts,
2175, 11828
Liquor problem - Gt. Brit.,
11603
Liquor problem - Maine -
Fiction, 11044
Liquor problem - Massa-
chusetts, 1487, 9879,
11828
Liquor problem - U. S.,
457
Lisle, Samuel, bp.,
1683-1749, 13391
Litchfield, Conn., 12724
Litchfield, N. H. - Hist.,
2297
Literary and historical
miscellanies, 741
Literary and historical
society of Quebec, 11449

Literary and philosophical
society of New York,
1908
Literary and philosophical
society of South Carolina,
Charleston, 13265
A literary courtship under
the auspices of Pike's Peak,
9587
Literary forgeries and
mystifications, 400
Literary life of James K.
Paulding, 4721
The literary remains of the
late Willis Gaylord Clark,
9012
Literature - Collections,
9516
Literature - Hist. & criticism,
5338
Literature, Modern - Addresses,
essays, lectures, 7119
Literature, Modern - Hist.
and criticism, 4089
Literature on foot, 10862
Littell, John Stockton,
1806-1875, ed., 12367, 13392
Little Anne's ramble, 9827
The little blind god on
rails, 9319
Little Briggs and I, 10250
Little brother, 10250
Little, C. F., 10122
A little captive maid, 10041
"Little Cuba", 8696
The little Dutch sentinel
of the Manhadoes, 10480
Little Edward, 10904
A little fool, 10546
Little French Mary, 10038
The little Frenchman and his
water lots, 10385
Little Gibraltar, 10394
Little, John, ed., 5213
A little journey to Mexico,
6839
A little journey to Mexico
and Central America, 6840
The little maid at the door,

Longfellow, Henry Wadsworth.
Song of Hiawatha -
Parodies, travesties,
etc., 5607
Longfellow, Samuel, 1819-
1892, ed., 7317
Longitude, 5852, 11707
Longstreet, Augustus Baldwin,
1790-1870, 3460, 4295,
4296
Longstreet, James, 1821-
1904, 4297
Longworth, Maria Theresa,
1832?-, 4298
Lonz Powers, 5662
Lookout mountain, Battle
of, 1863, 5352
Loose leaves, 10914
López Cordero, Fr. Antonio,
1678 or 9-1730, 7318
López de Arguleta, José,
7271
López de Avilés, José,
7319
López, Elpidio, 7320
López Herrero, Juan Antonio,
7321
López, Manuel Antonio,
b. 1803, 7322
López Valencia, Federico,
4299
López Velarde, Ramón,
1888-1921, 7323
López, Vicente Fidel,
1815-1903, ed., 7853
Lorain, John, 4300
Lord and master, 8811
Lord, George A., 1820-
1888, 2469
Lord Hope's choice, 10868
The Lord is to be praised
for the triumphs of
His power, 579
Lord, J. L., 10899
Lord, John Keast, 1818-
1872, 7324
Lord of himself, 5497
Lord, Theodore A., 7325
Lords prayer. Polyglot, 97

Lorenzana y Butrón, Francisco
Antonio, cardinal, 1722-1804,
7326, 7327
Lorette, 8825
The lorgnette, 10361
Lorimier, François Marie Thomas
Chevalier de, 1803-1839,
2202
Lorin Mooruck, 9192
Loring, Francis William,
4301
Loring, Frederick Wadsworth,
1848-1871, 9693
Loring, Nathaniel Hall,
1799-1838, 12135
Losada, Angel, ed., 8004
Loskiel, George Henry,
1740-1814, 13398
Lossing, Benson John,
1813-1891, 2481, 4302,
12901, 13399, 13400
Lost abroad, 11005
The lost cause regained,
4818
The lost child of the Delaware,
10570
The lost children, 10760
The lost daughter, 3844
The lost heir of Linlithgow,
10839
The lost hunter, 8469
The lost library, 10506
A lost life, 10373
The lost model, 9911
The lost name, 9311
The lost nationalities of
America, 11067
The lost pine mine, 10122
The lost place, 9678
The lost pleiad, 2992
A lost prima donna, 10675
The lost sealers, 9150
The lost ship, 1619
The lost tomb-stone, 10747
The lost trappers, 3105
The lost treasure found, 4948
The lost wife, 9485
Lothrop, Charles Henry,
1831-1890, 4303

Loti, Pierre, pseud. of
Viaud, Julien.
Lotos flowers, 4167
The lottery ticket,
10245
Lotz, James Robert,
comp., 7328
Loubat, Joseph Florimond,
duc de, 1831-1927,
6438
Loudoun co., Va. - Hist.,
3637
Louisa, 9575
Louisa Pallant, 7117
Louisa Williams, 9495
Louisburg - Siege,
1745, 11336
Louisburg - Siege,
1745 - Fiction, 9707
Louisburg - Siege,
1758 - Fiction, 9707
Louise Elton, 9854
Louisiana, 1561, 8907
Louisiana artillery.
Washington artillery,
1840-, 2625, 4671
Louisiana as it is, 3231
Louisiana - Bibl., 11323
Louisiana. Bureau of
immigration, 4304
Louisiana.cavalry (Confe-
derate) 1st regt.,
1861-1864, 2921
Louisiana. Citizens, 13401
Louisiana - Descr. &
trav., 1206, 2549,
2578, 2641, 2694, 2768,
2975, 3117, 3170, 3171,
3215, 3231, 3425, 3476,
3479, 3595, 3597, 3979,
4173, 4227, 4304, 4305,
4586, 4657, 4682, 4755,
4758, 4791, 5287, 5557,
7970, 8320, 8321, 13143
Louisiana - Disc. & explor.,
3329, 3836
Louisiana (District)
General assembly, 13402
Louisiana, ein heim für

deutsche ansiedler, 3215
Louisiana - Fiction, 3274,
4994, 8926, 8928, 9000
Louisiana - Geneal - Diction-
aries, 8153
Louisiana historical society,
New Orleans, 1675
Louisiana - Hist., 776, 1675,
1683, 2966, 3207, 3512,
5287, 5840
Louisiana - Hist. - Civil war,
2587, 3199, 3895, 4964
Louisiana - Hist. - Colonial
period, 2965, 3317, 3584,
3665, 3725, 4201, 4258,
5229
Louisiana - Hist. - Colonial
period - Sources, 2332,
3544, 7404
Louisiana infantry. 1st regt.,
(U.S.A.) 5195
Louisiana infantry. 2d regt.,
Native guard (colored)
1862-1863, 11326
Louisiana infantry. 3d regt.,
1861-1865, 5482
Louisiana infantry. 26th regt.,
1862-1865, 3756
Louisiana literature, 3512
Louisiana lottery, 6545
Louisiana militia, 1860-1862,
2625
Louisiana - Pol. & govt.,
13401
Louisiana - Pol. & govt. -
Civil war, 801, 9876
Louisiana purchase, 776,
1452, 1996, 5287, 5479
Louisiana Purchase Exposition,
4932
Louisiana - Sanit. affairs,
938
Louisiana - Soc. life &
cust., 3512
Louisiana state immigration
association, 4305
Louisiana state medical
society, 938
Louisiana State University,

6915
Louisiana - Statistics,
Vital, 938
Louisiana studies, 3512
Louisiana (U. S. gunboat)
2733
Louisianais [pseud.] of
Alfred Mercier.
La Louisiane ensanglantée,
2965
Louisiane - Mexique - Canada,
7970
Louisville, Ky. Congregation
Adath Israel, 7329
Louisville, Ky. - Descr.,
3755
Louisville, Ky. - Hist.,
2937, 4370
Louisville, Ky. University.
J. B. Speed memorial
museum, 7330
Louvet de Couvral, Jean
Baptiste, 1760-1797,
13403
Love a victor, 10580
The love affairs of Abraham
Lincoln, 7660
The love affairs of an
old maid, 8772
Love afloat, 10752
Love among the mistletoe,
3376
Love and loyalty, 10851
Love and principle, 3505
Love and science, 8707
Love and secession, 11197
Love and skates, 11194
Love before breakfast,
10896
Love in a cottage, 9454
Love in idleness, 9226
Love in old clothes, 8897
Love in the nineteenth
century, 10566
Love is a spirit, 9812
Love me, love my dog,
9357, 9363
The love of a lifetime,
9285

The love of country, 847
The love of Landry, 9437
Love - or a name, 9813
The love scrapes of a lifetime,
8923
The love story of Charles
Brandon and Mary Tudor,
10309
Love the light of life, 10686
Love versus law, 10904
Love with a handsome spend-
thrift, 10202
Love's cross, 9403
Love's progress, 3602
Lovejoy, Elijah Parish,
1802-1837, 1051
Lovell, John, pub., 7331
Lovell, Joseph, 1788-1836,
13360
Lovell's folly, 3845
Lovell's gazetteer of British
North America, 7331
The lovely maid of Louisiana,
4994
Loveman, Robert, 1864-1923,
4306
The lover and the tell-tale,
9216
A lover in Cuba, 3377
A lover of truth, 11138
A lover of truth and decency,
13098
Lovers and thinkers, 9013
The lover's leap, 10827,
10919
The lover's trials, 9389
The loves of the gorillas,
11146
The loves of the Lady Arabella,
5117
Lovie, Henry, illustr., 4283
Low, Alfred Maurice,
1860-1929, 4307
Low, Albert Peter, 1861-,
6302
Low, Seth, 1850-1916, 7332
The low value set upon human
life in the United States,
11308

Lowe, Charles, 1828-1874, 7333
Lowe, Nicholas, 5264
Lowell, Daniel W., & co., 4308
The Lowell factory girl, 8539
Lowell hydralic experiments, 2311
Lowell institute lectures, 1868-69, 12052, 12747
Lowell, James Russell, 1819-1891, 7119
Lowell, John, 1769-1840, 13404
Lowell, John Amory, 1798-1881, jt. author, 1577
Lowell, Mass. - Sanit. off., 11921
Lowell, Orson, illustr., 4087, 10886
Lowell, Robert Traill Spence, 1816-1891, 8597
Löwenstern, Isidor, 1815-1858, 4309, 7334, 7917
Löwig, Gustav, 4310
Lowrey, Grosvenor Porter, 7335, 13405
Lowry, Thomas, 1843-1909, 7336
Loyal Legion of the U. S. - Directories, 7500
Loyal national league of the state of New York, 2414
Loyalty, 1190, 11173
Loyalty a Christian obligation, 1190
Loyalty on the frontier, 1350
Lozada, Jesús Rodolfo, 1892-, 7337
Lubbock, Percy, ed., 7128
Lucas, C. P., jt. author, 7899
Lucas, Sir Charles Prestwood, 1853-1931,

ed., 6647
Lucas, Daniel Bedinger, 1836-1909, 4311, 4312, 7338
Lucas, Daniel R., 4313
Lucas de Ayllon, 10783
Lucas de Montigny, Gabriel, b. 1782, 13441
Luccock, John, 7339
Lucia Dare, 3273
Lucia: her problem, 9421
Lucinda, 10316
The luck of Roaring Camp, 9784
The luck of the Bogans, 10043
Lucretia and her father, 10248
Lucy Arlyn, 11016
Lucy Howard's journal, 10759
Lucy in the city, 11043
Lucy Maria, 9398
Ludecus, Eduard, 4314
Luden, Heinrich, ed., 2696
Lüders, Charles Henry, 1858-1891, 10737
Ludlow family, 12996
Ludlow, Fitz Hugh, 10899
Ludovico Sforza, il Moro, duke of Milan, 1451-1508 - Fiction, 8589
Ludvigh, Samuel Gottlieb, 1801-1869, 4315
Lujan Muñoz, Luis, jt. author, 7686
Lull, Caspar Peter, 1189
Lulu, 11064
Lumholtz, Karl [Sofus] 1851-, 7340, 7341
Lummi language - Glossaries, vocabularies, etc., 12232
Lummis, Charles Fletcher, 1859-, 7342
Lunan, John, jr., 13406
Lundy, Benjamin, 1789-1839, 4316
Lumley, illustr., 4759
The luna papers, 4862
Luna y Arellano, Tristán de, d. 1573, 4862

Lunacy, 11113
Lund. Universitet.
  Student-sångförening,
  2618
Lundy, Benjamin, ed., 2969
Lusk, William Thompson,
  1838-1897, 4317
Lutheran church in the
  U. S., 1364, 4547
Luz de verdades católicas,
  7427
Luzac, S., 7343
Lyddy: a tale of the
  old South, 8634
Lydia Hersey, of East
  Bridgewater, 9578
Lyell, Sir Charles,
  1797-1875, 4318, 4319,
  7344, 7345, 7346, 7347,
  13238
Lyford, William G., 4320
Lyman, Jonathan, 1737-1766,
  702
Lyman, Joseph, 1749-1828,
  13407
Lyman, Theodore, 1833-
  1897, 4321
Lynch, Sir Thomas,
  d. 1684? 13145
Lynchburg, Battle of,
  1864, 3324
Lynn, Mass. - Biog.,
  10420
Lynn, Mass. - Hist.,
  10420
Lynx-hunting, 9216
Lyon, Mrs. Adelia Caroline
  Duncombe, comp., 4323
The Lyon campaign in
  Missouri, 5610
Lyon, George Francis,
  1795-1832, 7348, 7349
Lyon, Matthew, 1750-1822 -
  Fiction, 5003
Lyon, William Franklin,
  1842-, 4322
Lyon, William Penn,
  1822-1913, 4323
Lyra, and other poems, 2932

Lyric touches, 4714
Lyrics, 4604, 5332
Lyrics and idyls, 2952
Lyrics of a day, 11584
Lyttelton, George Lyttelton,
  1st baron, 1709-1773,
  2470, 13408

M***, tr., 6247
M-4: a travel study tour
  through Mexico, 7098
M., G., tr., 1187
M. L. Gordon's experience
  in the civil war from his
  narrative, letters and
  diary, 3648
M., T. J., 4324
Mabel Clifton, 8844
Mabel Lee, 10971
McAdam, J. T., 7350
The macadam trail, 5746
McAfee, Nelly Marshall,
  1845-, 4325
McAfee, Robert Breckinridge,
  1784-1849, 4326
McAllister, Ward, 1827-1895,
  4327
Macaulay, Catharine (Sawbridge)
  1731-1791, 13409
M'Bride, Robert Ekin,
  1846-, 4328
McCabe, James Dabney,
  1842-1883, 4329, 4330
McCabe, William Gordon,
  4331
McCall, George Archibald,
  1802-1868, 4332, 4333,
  5545
McCalla, William Latta,
  1788-, 4334
McCallen, Robert Seth, 7351
McCamant, Wallace, 1867-,
  7352, 7353
Le Macandal, 8599
Macaria, 11185
McCarthy, Carlton, 1847-,
  ed., 5575
McCarty, Joseph Hendrickson,

288

1830-1897, 7354
MacCauley, Clay, 1843-
1925, 4335
McClellan, George Brinton,
1826-1885, 84, 5537,
6560, 7067, 7286, 7355,
8138, 12014, 12017
McClellan, Robert, 2528
McClellan, Samuel,
1787-1855, 1415
McClelland, Robert,
1807-1880, 940
McClintock, J., ed.,
4468
McCloskey, Henry, comp.,
11540
McClung, John Alexander,
1804-1859, 4336, 4337,
4338
McClung, Zarah, 4339
McClure, Alexander
Kelly, 1828-1909, 4340,
7356, 7357, 7358
McConnell, H. H., 7359
MacCorkle, William Alexander,
1857-, 7338
McCormick, Richard Cunning-
ham, 1832-1901, 4341
McCowan, Archibald, 4342
McCoy, Isaac, 1784-1846,
4343, 4344
McCrea, Jane, 1753-1777,
11688
McCulloch, Ben, 1811-
1862, 4926
McCulloch, Hugh, 1869-
1902, 4345
M'Culloh, James W., of
Baltimore, 12133
McCurtin, Daniel, 698
McCutcheon, John T.,
illustr., 8479
McDanield, H. F., 4346
McDermott, William A.,
1863-1913, 10675
McDonald, Charles James,
1793-1860, 13127
Macdonald, Duncan George
Forbes, 1823?-1884, 7360

Macdonald, Mrs. Flora
(Macdonald) 1722-1790,
13309
McDonald, John, 1775-1853,
4347
Macdonald, John Alexander,
1815-1891, 6845
The M'Donalds, 4736
M'Donnell, Alexander, 4348
McDougall, William, 7361
McDowell, Ephraim, 1771-
1830, 3708
McDowell, James, 1796-1851,
13354
M'Duffee, John, 4349
McDuffle, George, 1788-1851,
2422
McElroy, Clarence L., 1903-,
7362
McElroy, John, 1846-1929,
4350
Macfie, Matthew, 7363
McGary, Elizabeth Visère, 7364
McGee, Benjamin F., 1834-,
4351
McGee, Thomas D'Arcy,
1825-1868, 6549
Macgillivray, William,
1796-1852, 7091
McGlynn, Edward, 8425
McGovern, John, 1850-,
4352
McGowan, D., 4353
MacGowan, Robert, 7365
McGowen, M., 7366
M'Gregor, John, 1797-1857,
7367, 7368
McGuire, J. A., 7369
McGuire, Judith White
(Brockenbrough) "Mrs.
John P. McGuire," 4354
McHatton-Ripley, Elizabeth,
7370
McHenry, George, of Phila-
delphia, 1794
McIlvain, Mrs. Clara (Lovell)
1836-1881, 4355
M'Ilvaine, William, jr.,
7371

McJilton, John Nelson,
  1805-1875, ed.,
  10234
Mack, David, 1750-1845,
  11836
Mack, Mrs. R. E.,
  illustr., 12020
Mackay, Alexander,
  1808-1852, 4356
Mackay, Charles, 1814-
  1889, 4357, 7372, 7373
McKay, F. E., 10283
Mackay, James Aberigh,
  jt. tr., 10718
Mackay, Robert, 1772-,
  4358
McKean, Joseph, 1776-
  1818, 12778
McKeen, Joseph, 1757-
  1807, 13410
McKendree, William, bp.,
  1757-1835, 4679
McKenney, Thomas Lorraine,
  1785-1859, 4359, 4360
McKenney, Thomas Lorraine,
  1785-1859. Memoirs,
  official and personal,
  455
MacKenzie, Sir Alexander,
  1763-1820, 4361, 4362,
  5457, 6221, 6748, 13411
Mackenzie district -
  Descr. & trav., 8007,
  8252
Mackenzie, Eneas, 1778-
  1832, 4363
Mackenzie, George Norbury,
  1851-1919, ed., 7374
Mackenzie River, 6283
Mackenzie, William L.,
  13412
Mackey, John W., 4364
McKim, Randolph Harrison,
  1842-1920, 4365
Mackinac - Hist. - Fiction,
  8956
Mackinaw, Mich., 2080
McKinley, William, pres.
  U. S., 1843-1901, 7375

McKinney, Mrs. Kate
  (Slaughter) 1857-, 4366
McKinnie, Robert, 6164
McKnight, Charles, 1826-1881,
  4367
Mackoy, Harry Brent, 7376
Maclachlan, May A., 8210
McLagan, John Campbell,
  1838-, 7384
M'Laughlin, Charles, illustr.,
  3681
McLaughlin, James Fairfax,
  1839-1903, 7338
McLaughlin, Joseph R., 7377
Maclauries, Mr., 4361
McLean, Archibald, 7378
McLean, John, 1799-, 4368
M'Lellan's Archibald, defendant,
  8032
M'Lenan, John, illustr.,
  3004, 10922
McLeod, Alexander, 12120
MacLeod, Donald, tr., 11759
McLeod, Robert Randall, 7379
MacLeod, William, illustr.,
  12696
McMahon, John Van Lear,
  1800-1871, 13413
MacMahon, T. W., 13414
McMillan, John, 1752-1833,
  1326
McMorries, Edward Young,
  4369
McMullen, Fayette, 1810-1880,
  5270
McMurtrie, Douglas Crawford,
  1888-1944, 3994, 7029, 7380
McMurtrie, Henry, 1793-1865,
  4370
McMurtry, Robert Gerald,
  1906-, 7381, 7382, 7383
Macnamara, Michael H., 4371
McNeil, Samuel, 4372
McNemar, Richard, 1770-1839,
  4373, 4374
Macon, Ga. Military prison,
  3082
Macoun, John, 1831-1920,
  6748, 7384

M'Pherson, John, d. 1806, 1667
Macpherson, the Confederate philosopher, 9876
McQuade, James, 4375
Macrae, David, 1837-1907, 4376, 4377
McReady, John Dudley, 7385
McSherry, Richard, 1817-1885, 7386
McTeague, 10428
MacVickar, Archibald, ed., 13385
McWilliams, Carey, ed., 6278
The mad penitent of Todi, 10675
Madame Butterfly, 10238
Madame Clerc, 10283
Madame Delphine, 8928
Madame de Mauves, 10014
Madariaga, Salvador de, 1886-, 7387
Madeira - Descr. & trav., 492
Madeira - Descr. & trav. - Guide-books, 7653
Madeira - Disc. & explor., 129
Madeleine, pseud., 7388
Madelaine Darth, 9531
Madelin, Louis, 1871-, 7525
Madeline, 9898
Madelon, 9574
Madelon, The story of, 3932
Mademoiselle Blanche, 8751
Mademoiselle Joan, 9355
Mademoiselle miss, 9741
Madison, Dorothy (Payne) Todd, 1768-1849, 7389
Madison, James, pres. U. S., 1751-1836, 77, 78, 822, 1379, 2364, 6002, 6833, 7389, 12140, 12348, 12603, 13209
Madison, Wis., 2127

Madison, Wis. City council, 2127
Madog ab Owain Gwynedd, 1150-1180? 1692
The madonna of the future, 10014
A Maecenas of the Pacific slope, 6973
Maffitt, John Newland, 1794-1850, 11607
Maga stories, 10298
Magalhães, Fernão de, 1521, 7567
Magdalena, Columbia (Dept.) - Descr. & trav., 13350
Maggie, a girl of the streets, 9212
Magic, 2431, 6376
The magic dice, 10693
The magic egg, 10896
Magie, James K., b. 1827, 7390
Magill, John, 1759-1842, 7152
Magna charta, 11660
The magnetic north, 4987
Magnetism, Terrestrial, 12239
Magnetism, Terrestrial - Observations, 993
A magnificent plebeian, 10302
Magnolia leaves, 3849
Magnus Maharba, 8866, 8867
Magruder, Henry R., 7391
Mahalinda, 10176
Mahaly Sawyer, 9426
Mahoney, William D., 8319
Maid Marian and other stories, 5118
The maid of Canal street, 10196
The maid of Maiden lane, 8733
The maid of the valley, 9855
The maid's revenge, 9846
Maidee, the alchemist, 8937
The maiden and Negro, 9744
A maiden effort, 9331
The maiden's hand, 3997
Mail steamers - U. S., 2271
Main-travelled roads, 9606
Maine, 12409
Maine artillery. 7th battery,

1863-1865, 4218
Maine. Board of internal
  improvements, 12868
Maine - Bound. - New
  Brunswick, 13463
Maine cavalry. 1st regt.,
  1861-1865, 4458
Maine - Descr. & trav.,
  11194
Maine - Descr. & trav. -
  Gazetteers, 12766
Maine - Descr. & trav. -
  Guide-books, 1034
Maine - Fiction, 9657,
  9946, 10035, 10038,
  10039, 10043
Maine historical society,
  12515
Maine - Hist. - Colonial
  period, 972, 1803,
  12514
Maine - Hist. - Colonial
  period - Sources,
  12930
Maine infantry. 10th
  battalion, 1863-1864,
  3655
Maine infantry. 1st
  regt., 1861, 3655
Maine infantry. 5th
  regt., 1861-1864, 2709
Maine infantry. 10th
  regt., 1861-1863, 3655
Maine infantry. 17th
  regt., 1862-1865, 12934
Maine infantry. 20th
  regt., 1862-1865, 3592
Maine infantry. 23d
  regt., 1862-1863, 4218
Maine infantry. 29th
  regt., 1863-1866, 3655
Maine. Insane hospital,
  Augusta, 13018
The Maine law, 11044
Maine - Laws, statutes,
  etc., 745
The Maine liquor law, 1916
Maine - Pol. & govt.,
  10822

Maine - Stat., 12408
Maine - Surveys, 12868
Mair, Charles, 1838-, 7392
Maissin, Eugène, ed., 2732
Maîtres et esclaves en
  Louisiane, 4451
Maize, 910, 11863
Maize in milk, 10776
Majó Framis, Ricardo, 7393
Major Jones' courtship,
  5404
Major Jones' sketches of
  travel, 5405
Major Max, 10997
Makemie, Francis, 1658-1708,
  4378
Making an orator, 9216
Making haste to be rich, 10849
Making home happy, 8617
Making home peaceful, 8618
The making of a man, 8657
The making of Canada, 6149
Maldonado, Angel, bp.,
  1660-1728, 7860
Maldonado, Cristóbal, 6677,
  6678, 6679, 6687
Das malerische Mexiko, 6155
Malespine, A., 7394
Malet, William Wyndham, 1804-
  1885, 4379
Malezieux, Emile M., 1822-,
  4380
Mallory, illustr., 10789
Malmiztic the Toltec,
  9543
Malo de Molina y Espínola,
  Melchor, marqués de Monterrico,
  6350
Malouet, Pierre-Victor,
  baron, 1740-1814, 7395
Malte-Brun, Conrad,
  originally Malthe Conrad Bruun,
  1775-1826, 7396
Malthusianism, 2432
Malvar y Pintos, Sebastián,
  7397
Mamamtavrishvili, D. G., 7398
Mammals - North America,
  174, 678, 12684

Mammals - Paraguay,
590, 597
Mammoth, 494
Mammoth cave, Ky., 3125,
3184, 3359, 3948, 3949,
4242, 4324, 4403, 5006,
5401, 5486
Mammoth cave, Ky. -
Fiction, 2717
Mammoth cave of Kentucky,
3949
The man and the mountain,
6975
The man at the semaphore,
6972
The man from Solano, 9779
The man machine, 10487
The man of enterprise,
10852
A man of honor, 3354
The man of sorrows, 6420
The man on the beach,
9779
Man - Origin, 11146,
13228
Man proposes, 5498
A man story, 9933
The man that corrupted
Hadleyburg, 9028
The man who "hadn't
time", 8957
The man who likes Mexico,
6855
The man who worked for
Collister, 9456
The man whose life was
saved, 10899
The man whose yoke was
not easy, 9779
The man with the empty
sleeve, 10808
The man with the hoe,
7412
The man without a
country, 9684
Man's wrongs, 10155
Mañas, Uldarica, 7399
Manatee Co., Fla., 5553
Manayunk, Pa. - Hist.,

12525
Mancera, Pedro de Toledo
y Leiva, marqués de, 1585?-
1654, 6851
Manchester, N. H. First
Unitarian society, 2358
Manchester (Ship), 12637
Manchitas de color centro-
americanas, 7343
Mancisidor, José, 1894-,
ed., 7400
Mandan Indians, 5374
Mandat-Grancey, Edmond,
baron de, 1842-1911, 4381
Mandrillon, Joseph, 1743-
1794, tr., 6435
Manford, Erasmus, 4382
Mangino, Fernando Joseph,
d. 1806, 7401
The mangrove coast, 2707
The Manhattaner in New Orleans,
3732
The maniac, 10310
A manifest destiny, 10303
A manifesto of the Lord protector
of the commonwealth of
England, Scotland, Ireland,
etc., 12368
Manigault, G., 4383
Manitoba, 6234, 6769, 7384,
11353
Manitoba and the Canadian
northwest, 6621
Manitoba and the great
Northwest, 7384
Manitoba, and the Northwest
of the dominion, 8091,
8387
Manitoba - Biog., 6236
Manitoba college, Winnipeg,
6217
Manitoba - Descr. & trav.,
3200, 3878, 4361, 5674,
6233, 6299, 6531, 6941,
6943, 7988, 8078, 8091,
8240, 8241, 13360
Manitoba - Hist., 6049, 6052,
6222, 6225, 6229, 6235,
6635, 8128, 8411

Manitoba - Hist. -
  Sources, 7641
Manlius, 12318
Mann, Donald, ed., 306
Manners and customs of
  several Indian tribes
  located west of the
  Mississippi, 3973
Manning, James, 1738-1791,
  2425, 12492
Mansfield, Edward Deering,
  1801-1880, 4384
Mansfield, Lewis W.,
  jt. author, 9727
Mansfield, William Murray,
  1st earl of, 1705-1793,
  13389
Mantegazza, Vico, 1856-,
  4385
Manton, Kate, pseud.,
  10155
Manual de historia y
  cronologia de Mejico,
  482
A manual of American
  literature, 3803
Manuel Pereira, 46, 8459
Manufactures - Addresses,
  essays, lectures, 300
Manuscripts, Mexican,
  6105
Manuscripts, Mexican -
  Facsimiles, 6438, 6644
Manzano Manzano, Juan,
  ed., 5972
Map and description of
  Texas, 4510
Map and guide to the
  Kansas gold region, 4914
Map of the battle field
  of Fredericksburg, 1446
Map of the Nez Perce and
  Salmon River gold mines,
  4308
A map of Virginia, 5204
Mapleton, 9001
Maps - Bibl. - Catalogs,
  6296, 8210
Marah, 4054

Maranhão, 5809
Maranhão (State) - Hist.,
  11259
The Marbeau cousins, 3345
Marble, Manton, 1834-1917,
  7402
The marble faun, 9822
Marble - Vermont, 12524
Marbourg, Dolores, jt. author,
  9468
March hares, 9568
Marching through Georgia,
  3830
Marching with Sherman,
  3887
Marcia, 9355
Marcou, Jules, 1824-1898,
  4386
Marcus Aurelius, 5238
Marcy, Randolph Barnes,
  1812-1887, 4387, 4388,
  4703, 5532, 5537, 5547,
  5548
Mardi, 10344
Mardi gras, 11051
Marechal, Nicolas, b. 1744?
  2466
Margaret, 10075, 10076
Margaret Smith's journal,
  11154
Margaret's bridal, 10702
Margati, José, 1841-1887, 7403
Margret Howth, 9354
Margry, Pierre, 1818-1894,
  ed., 7404
Marguerite, 9899
Maria Antonia de San Joseph,
  madre, 1708-1781, 1797
María de Jesús, mother,
  1579-1637, 6717
Marian Elwood, 8887
Marian Grey, 3917
Marian Rooke, 10731
Marie, 2658
Marie de Berniere, 10776
Marin de Alfocea, Juan,
  7405, 7406
El marinero instruido en el
  arte de navegar, 6007

Marines signalling under fire at Guantanamo, 9217
Marion Darche, 6498
Marion, Francis, 1732-1795, 12729, 13157
Marion Graham, 10170
Marion-Sims, H., ed., 5170
Marion's faith, 10124
Marionettes, 9260
Mariotti, L., 3564
Mariposilla, 9306
Mariscal, Ignacio, 1829-1910, 7407
Maritime law, 812
Maritime law - Gt. Brit., 11713, 13478
Maritime law - Newfoundland, 385
Maritime law - Pennsylvania, 9918
Maritime law - U. S., 1494
Marjoribanks, Alexander, 4389
Marjorie Daw and other people, 8498
Mark Dunning's enemy, 8978
Mark Gildersleeve, 10706
Mark Heffron, 8640
Mark Rowland, 10788
Marked "personal", 10666
Markens, Edward Wasgate, 7408
Markens, Isaac, 7409, 7410
The market book, 2102
The market-place, 9569
Markham, Sir Clements Robert, 1830-1916, 7411, 7964
Markham, Edwin, 1852, 7412
Markland or Nova Scotia, 7379
Marks, Elias, 1790-1886, 4390
Marks, James Junius,

1809-1899, 4391
The marksmen of Monmouth, 9296
Marl - South Carolina, 12869
Marmaduke Wyvil, 9846
Marmier, Xavier, 1809-1892, 4392, 7413
Marmontel, Jean François, 1723-1799, 1544
The Maroon, 10776
Marquette, Jacques, 1637-1675, 4393
Marquez, Pedro [José] 1741-1820, 7414
Marr, Frances Harrison, 1835-, 4394, 4395
Marr, Janey Hope, ed., 3933
Marrant, John, 1755-, 4396
Marraro, Howard Rosario, 1897-, 7415
Marriage, 301, 7032, 7033
Marriage customs and rites, 12607
Marriage of Marie Modeste, 10135
Marriage - U. S., 11663
The marriages, 7122
Married against reason, 10290
Married by mistake, 10919
Married for a dinner, 10580
Married for both worlds, 10552
Married, not mated, 8949
"Married off", 1192
The married shrew, 10841
Marryat, Frederick, 1792-1848, 4397, 4398
Marryat, Frederick, 1792-1848. A diary in America, 11685
Marrying by lot, 10388
Marse Chan, 10461
Marseille - Comm., 11711
Marseille, Gotthold, 1852-, ed., 3270
Marsena, 9567, 9570
Marsh, Edward Sprague, 1857-, 7416

Marshall, Albert O., 4399
A marsh island, 10039
Marshall, Charles Henry,
  1792-1865, 1774
Marshall college, Mercers-
  burg, Pa. Diagnothian
  society, 1580
Marshall co., Ill. -
  Hist., 2274
Marshall, Humphrey, 1760-
  1841, 4400, 4878, 13415
Marshall, John, 1755-1835,
  1311, 1625, 13416
Marshall, John, 1783-1841,
  ed., 1565
Marshall, Logan, 7417
Marshall, Thomas Francis,
  1801-1864, 4401
The marshalship in North
  Carolina, 2439
Martha Washingtonianism,
  13249
Martha's lady, 10042
Marthas Vineyard, Mass. -
  Descr. & trav., 2101
Martí, José, 1853-1895,
  4402, 7664
Martial law, 1454, 13135
Martial law - U. S.,
  6669, 13090
Martin, Archer Evans
  Stringer, 1865-,
  6181
Martin-Chablis, illustr.,
  4381
Martín, Enrico, d. 1632,
  7418, 7419
Martin Faber, 10777
Martin, Felix, 1804-1886,
  tr., 1482
Martin, Franklin, 7420
Martin, Henri, 1810-1883,
  2414
Martin, Horace, 4403
Martin, Joseph, ed.,
  4404
Martin, Luther, 1748-1826,
  13417
Martin, Percy Falcke, 1861-,

7421, 7422
Martin, Robert Montgomery,
  1803-1868, 6742, 7423
The Martindale pastoral,
  8987
Martineau, Harriet, 1802-1876,
  7424, 7425
Martínez Caro, Ramón, 4405
Martínez de Amileta, Andrés,
  6282
Martínez de Diego, Cayetano,
  7426
Martínez de la Marcha,
  Hernando, 16th cent., 8168
Martínez de la Parra, Juan,
  1655-1701, 7427
Martínez de la Torre, Rafael,
  1828-1876, 7872
Martínez Tamayo, Francisco,
  8027
Martingale, Hawser, pseud.,
  10788
Martinique - Descr. & trav.,
  4644, 7000, 11414
Martinique - Pol. & govt. -
  Revolution, 8054
Martirologio de algunos de
  los primeros insurgentes,
  1762
Martyn, Benjamin, 1699-1763,
  4406
The martyr, 8622
The martyr-president, 2184
The martyr prince, 699
The martyrdom of Frederick,
  13032
Martyria, 12621
The martyrs, 10670
The martyrs and heroes of
  Illinois in the great
  rebellion, 860
Maruja, 9785
Marvel, Ik, pseud., 10360,
  10362
Marvin, Donald Mitchell,
  1893-, 7428
Marvin, William F., 4407
Marvin, William Theophilus
  Rogers, 1832-1913, ed., 1886

296

Mary Barker, 9218
Mary Bunyan, 3506
Mary Derwent, 10869
Mary Dyre, 10730
Mary Elmer, 11136
Mary Idyl's trials and
  triumphs, 8890
Mary Lyndon, 10422
Mary McIntire has arrived,
  10953
Mary Morland, 8701
Mary Rice, 10760
Mary Staunton, 11142
Mary V. V., pseud., 2107
Mary, Virgin, 7318, 8766
Mary, Virgin - Apparitions
  & miracles (Modern),
  6753, 6754, 7459
Mary, Virgin - Art, 1786
Maryland artillery. 1st
  battery, 1861-1864,
  12264
Maryland artillery, 1st
  regt., 1793-, 13099
Maryland - Capital and
  capitol, 12652
Maryland cavalry. 1st
  regt. Potomac home bri-
  gade, 1861-1865, 4591
Maryland - Charters,
  4929, 11748
Maryland - Church history,
  2088
Maryland. Constitution,
  1132
Maryland - Descr. & trav.,
  2515, 2646, 2771, 2773,
  2852, 2959, 3325, 3336,
  3340, 3490, 3516, 3519,
  3603, 3663, 3722, 3737,
  4173, 4682, 4929, 4930,
  4998, 5147, 5440, 5768
Maryland historical society,
  171, 12245
Maryland - Hist., 8051,
  12435
Maryland - Hist. - Civil
  war, 1849, 1850, 2479,
  3635

Maryland - Hist. - Colonial
  period, 170, 171, 769, 1603,
  2088, 3221, 3764, 4929,
  5305, 11472, 12526, 12627,
  13413
Maryland - Hist. - Colonial
  period - Fiction, 4156, 10096
Maryland - Hist. - Colonial
  period - Sources, 2460, 4378
Maryland - Hist. - Fiction,
  9003
Maryland - Hist. - Revolution,
  3336, 12245
Maryland - Hist. - Revolution -
  Sources, 698
Maryland infantry. 1st District
  of Columbia and Maryland
  regt., 1847-1848, 13320
Maryland. Laws, statutes,
  etc., 1686, 12210
Maryland. Legislature.
  Senate, 8316
Maryland - Pol. & govt.,
  13413
Maryland - Pol. & govt. -
  1775-1865, 1510
Maryland - Pol. & govt. -
  Colonial period, 11560
Maryland - Pol. & govt. -
  Revolution, 2423
Maryland toleration, 170
Marzio's crucifix, 6499,
  9227
Mashpee Indians, 404
The masked singer, 10304
Mäskōke hymns, 1648
Mason, Augustus Lynch, 7429
Mason, Emily Virginia,
  1815-1909, comp., 4408
Mason, Frank Holcomb,
  1840-1916, 4409
Mason, George, tr., 428
Mason, George, 1725-1792, 7431
Mason, John, 1586-1635, 13498
Mason, Jonathan, 1756-1831,
  4410
Mason, R. H., 7430
Mason, Robert C., 7431
Mason, Stuart, pseud., 5704

Massachusetts - Hist.,
11493, 11672
Massachusetts - Hist. -
1775-1865, 586
Massachusetts - Hist. -
Colonial period, 12052,
13422
Massachusetts - Hist. -
Colonial period -
Fiction, 8468, 8609,
8992, 10390, 10724,
11149
Massachusetts - Hist. -
Colonial period (New
Plymouth), 766, 922,
990, 991, 1513, 1755,
2018, 11824, 12806
Massachusetts - Hist. -
Fiction, 10390
Massachusetts - Hist.,
Local, 783
Massachusetts - Hist. -
War of 1812, 11799
Massachusetts infantry.
1st regt., 1861-1864,
3136
Massachusetts infantry.
2d regt., 1861-1865,
4537, 4874, 4876
Massachusetts infantry.
6th regt., 1861-1865,
3771
Massachusetts infantry,
9th regt., 1861-1864,
4371
Massachusetts infantry.
11th regt., 1861-1865,
1394
Massachusetts infantry.
12th regt., 1861-1864,
3076
Massachusetts infantry.
16th regt., 1861-1864,
2358
Massachusetts infantry.
18th regt., 1861-1864,
3186
Massachusetts infantry.
19th regt., 1861-1865,

2492
Massachusetts infantry.
20th regt., 1861-1865,
4757
Massachusetts infantry.
21st regt., 1861-1865,
5598
Massachusetts infantry.
23d regt., 1861-1865, 3381
Massachusetts infantry.
24th regt., 1861-1866, 2533
Massachusetts infantry.
25th regt., 1861-1865, 4870
Massachusetts infantry.
27th regt., 1861-1865, 3235
Massachusetts infantry.
29th regt., 1861-1865, 4661
Massachusetts infantry.
32d regt., 1862-1865, 4697
Massachusetts infantry.
33d regt., 1862-1865, 2751
Massachusetts infantry.
34th regt., 1862-1865, 1659
Massachusetts infantry.
37th regt., 1862-1865, 5490
Massachusetts infantry.
38th regt., 1862-1865, 4842
Massachusetts infantry.
43d regt., 1862-1863, 5008
Massachusetts infantry.
44th regt., 1862-1863, 3729
Massachusetts infantry.
45th regt., 1862-1863, 3958
Massachusetts infantry.
49th regt., 1862-1863, 4062
Massachusetts infantry.
52d regt., 1862-1863, 3944
Massachusetts infantry.
55th regt. (colored) 1863-
1865, 12154
Massachusetts - Manuf., 1265
Massachusetts - Militia, 1328
Massachusetts. Militia.
Courts-martial. Goodale,
1812, 2438
Massachusetts missionary
society, 4479
Massachusetts - Pol. & govt. -
1775-1865, 11913, 12537

Massachusetts - Pol. &
  govt. - Civil war,
  1785, 7592
Massachusetts - Pol. &
  govt. - Colonial
  period, 2175, 11258,
  13422, 13493
Massachusetts - Pol. &
  govt. - Revolution,
  181, 2012, 4873
Massachusetts - Population,
  1879
Massachusetts Sabbath
  school society, 644,
  12724, 13141
Massachusetts Sabbath
  school society.
  Committee of publication,
  127
Massachusetts - Sanit.
  Aff., 11921
Massachusetts - Soc. life
  & cust., 10152
Massachusetts. State
  prison, Charlestown,
  12759
Massachusetts - Stat.,
  12764
Massachusetts. Supreme
  judicial court, 580,
  856, 5997, 12681
Massachusetts. Zoological
  and botanical survey,
  12329
Masseras, E., 7432
Massey, George Valentine,
  1903-, 7433, 7434, 7435
Massey, Stephen L., 4412
Massie, James William,
  1799-1869, 4413
Master Ardick, buccaneer,
  9176
Master William Mitten,
  4295
Master of his fate, 8734
The master of magicians,
  11074
The master of Rushen, 8723
The master of silence,

8628
The master's house, 10963
Masústegui, Pedro, 7436
Matagorda, Tex. - Hist., 3833
Matanzas, Cuba (City), 153
Matanzas bay, Cuba - Capture
  of the Spanish silver-fleet,
  1628, 338
The mate of the daylight, 10040
The mate of the "Easter Bell",
  8735
Mate (Shrub), 11983
Mater Dolorosa, 9331
Mater Felix, 9331
Materia medica, 943
The materialist, 9530
Mather, Cotton, 1663-1728,
  1073
Mather, Increase, 1639-1723,
  1072, 13419
Mather, James, 4414
Mather, Moses, 1719-1806,
  supposed author, 237
Matheson, James, jt. author,
  4912
Mathews, Alfred E., 4415
Mathews, Charles, 13420
Matilda Berkely, 9595
Matilda Douglas, 10258
Matlack, Lucius C., 1243
Matrimonial infelicities,
  9060
The Matrimonial Tontine
  Benefit Association, 9639
Matthews, Albert, ed., 5216
Matthews' American armoury
  and blue book, 7437
Matthews, Brander, 1852-1929,
  2695
Matthews, Cornelius, 1817-
  1889, ed., 435
Matthews, James Muscoe, b. 1822,
  ed., 2061, 2062, 2063
Matthews, John, of London,
  ed., 7437
Matthews, John W., d. 1860,
  13188
Matto Grosso, Brazil (State),
  11384

300

Maud Elbert's love
   match, 10427
Maud Evelyn, 10016
Maud Mansfield, 9908
Maud of the Mississippi,
   2500
Maude and Miriam, 10285
Maude, John, 7438
Maudit passeport',
   2908
Maudslay, Alfred Percival,
   1850-, jt. author,
   7439
Maudslay, Anne Cary
   (Morris), 7439
Mauduit, Israel, 1708-
   1787, 13421, 13422
Mawmee Valley - Hist.,
   12920
Maurice, Caesar, ed.,
   8639
Maurice, Jacques, pseud.,
   10386
Maury, Ann, 1803-1876,
   2263, 3494
Maury, Dabney Herndon,
   1822-1900, 4416
Maury, Matthew Fontaine,
   1806-1873, 4417, 4418
Maury, Sarah Mytton
   (Hughes) "Mrs. William
   Maury", 1803-1849,
   4419, 4420
Maverick, Augustus, jt.
   author, 11520
Maverick, Augustus, jt.
   author, 11520
Max Kessler's horse-car,
   9678
Maximilian, emperor of
   Mexico, 1832-1867,
   7188, 7205, 7206, 7872,
   7944
Maxims, 793
Maximus, bp. of Saragossa,
   fl. 599-619, 400
Maxwell, Archibald Mont-
   gomery, 4421
Maxwell, William, 1784-

1857, 4422, 4423
May, Caroline, 1820(ca.)-,
   ed., 4424
May-day in New York, 10820
May, John, 1748-1812, 4425
May, Mrs. Letitia, tr., 11353
May Martin, 10959
Maya, Augustin, 7440, 7441,
   7442
Maya language - Dictionaries -
   English, 7590
Maya language - Dictionaries -
   French, 7231
Maya language - Grammar,
   1136, 7231, 7590
Mayas - Antiq., 6135, 6406,
   6407, 6408, 7231, 7439,
   7590, 8288
Mayas - Hist., 1440
Mayer, Brantz, 1809-1879,
   7443, 7444
Mayes, Edward, 1846-, 4426
The Mayflower, 10904
Mayflower (ship), 7374
Mayhew, Jonathan, 1720-1766,
   11495, 11788
Maynard, Mrs. Henrietta
   Sturdevant (Colburn)
   1841-1892, 7445, 7446
Maynard, Horace, 1814-1882,
   7447
Mayo, Amory Dwight, 1823-
   1907, 7448, 10335
Mayor des Planches, Edmondo,
   1851-1920, 4427
The Maypole of Merry Mount,
   9827
Maysville, Ky. - Hist., 8010
Mazariegos, Cristóbal, 6364
Mazyck, Arthur, 1850-, 4428
Mazzei, Filippo, 1730-1816,
   4429
Meacham, Joseph, 1742-1796,
   12094
Mead, Charles, 4430
Mead, K. C. (Hurd), Dr., 9331
Meade, George Gordon,
   1815-1872, 4321
Meade, William, bp., 1789-1862,

301

4431, 7572
Meade's headquarters,
4321
Meadow-Brook, 9900
Means and ends of
education, 5241
The mechanic, 10269
Mechanics and metals
national bank, New
York, 2182
Mechanics institutes,
12874
Mecklenburg declaration
of independence, 13309
Med kronprinsparet - for
Norge! 5092
Medals, 12875
Medals - U. S., 1750
Medford, Mass. - Geneal,
1573
Medford, Mass. - Hist.,
1573
Medford, Mass. - Hist. -
Civil war, 1572
Medical and physical
researches, 12685
Medical delusions, 12884
Medical education - U. S.,
1923
Medical geography -
Barbados, 12791
Medical geography -
Brazil, 12906
Medical geography -
Canada, 2118
Medical geography -
French Guiana, 680
Medical geography -
Jamaica, 13132
Medical geography -
Louisiana, 938
Medical geography -
South America, 1434
Medical geography -
South Carolina, 2960
Medical geography -
Uruguay, 12906
Medical geography -
West Indies, 12102

Medical literature of
Kentucky, 5784
Medical society of the county
of Cortland, Cortland, N. Y.,
11503
Medical society of the state
of New York (Founded 1807),
1415
The medical student in Europe,
3531
Medicine - Addresses, essays,
lectures, 1038, 1039,
3292, 11452
Medicine - Anecdotes, facetiae,
satire, etc., 8451
Medicine - Biography, 5170
Medicine - Biography - Kentucky,
7737, 8010, 8203
Medicine - Collected works,
12685
Medicine - Early works to 1700,
6012
Medicine - 15th-18th century,
6694, 6695
Medicine - Formulae, receipts,
prescriptions, 6694, 6695
Medicine - Hist., 1623
Medicine - Kentucky - Bibl.,
5784
Medicine - Massachusetts,
132, 913, 11433
Medicine, Popular, 12123, 12647
Medicine - Study and teaching,
3287, 3288, 3292, 3293
Medicine - Study and teaching -
Cincinnati, 11595
Medicine - U. S., 1029, 2659
Medina Avila, Juan de, 6851
Medina, L. H., 10670
Mediterranean Sea - Comm.,
692
Medley, Julius George,
1829-1884, 4432
Medley, Mat., pseud., 2564
A medley of sketches and
scraps, touching people
and things, 10828
Medoline Selwyn's work, 9080
Medrana y Vivanco, Pedro de,

302

8272
Medrano, Pedro de,
1649-1725, 7449
Medrano, Pedro Joaquín,
5807, 7013
Meehan, Thomas Francis,
5045
Meek, Alexander Beaufort,
1814-1865, 4433, 4434,
4435, 4436, 4437
Meeker, Nathan Cook,
1817-1879, 4438
Meekins' twinses, 2590
"Mces", 11198
Mees, Walter, 4439
Meese, William Augustus,
1856-, 7450
Meg, 10163
Megalithic monuments -
Gt. Brit., 13225
Meh Lady, 10462
Mehetable Roger's cran-
berry swamp, 10427
Meine reise nach Nord-
amerika im jahre 1842,
5067
Mejía Deras, Ismael,
7451
Mejía, José Victor, 7452
El Méjico de Porfirio
Diaz, 8006
Meksyk, 7213
Meléndez, Juan, 7453
Melish, John, 1771-1822,
4440, 4441, 4442, 4443,
4444, 4445, 7454
Mellen, John, 1722-1807,
13423
Mellichampe, 10778
Melville, Herman, 1819-
1891, 6782
A member of Parliament,
2324, 12126
A member of the Phila-
delphia bar, 279
Memminger, Christopher
Gustavus, 1803-1888,
2910, 4446
A memoir of Abraham

Lincoln, 6089
Memoir of Captain Frederic
Ingham, 9683
Memoir of Col. Chas. S. Todd,
3690
Memoir of Dº Escalante Fontaneda
respecting Florida, 3390
Memoir of General Graham,
3659
Memoir of John Yates Beal,
4311
Memoir of Lieut. Col. Tench
Tilghman, 3796
Memoir of the life of
Jeremiah Evarts, 5452
Memoir of the life of Richard
Henry Lee, 4241
Memoir of the northern
kingdom, 10033
Memoir of the Rev. Elias
Cornelius, 3342
A memoir of the Rev. John H.
Rice, 4422
A memoir of the Rev. William
Tennent, minister of
Freehold, 11400
Memoir of the unknown author,
10492
Memoir of William R. Grant,
M. D., 535
Mémoire sur la carte intitulée
Canada, Louisiane et terres
angloises, 2549
Mémoires d'un Américain, 11974
Mémoires de Brissot, 11522
Mémoires de M. le duc de Lauzun,
2721
Mémoires du Capitaine Landolphe,
4209
Mémoires du commandant Persat,
4758
Mémoires du comte de Moré, 4516
Mémoires historiques sur la
Louisiana, 3317
Mémoires militaires, historiques
et politiques de Rochambeau,
4997
Mémoires pour servir à
l'histoire de Cayenne, 680

303

Memorial of Lieut. Joseph
P. Burrage, 1791
Memorial of Rev. Pitt
Clark, 11845
Memorial of the late
Honorable David S. Jones,
13324
Memorial of the people of
Red River to the British
and Canadian governments,
7457
A memorial of the Pilgrim
fathers, 1641
Memorial oration in honor
of Ephraim McDowell,
3708
Memorial presented by the
inhabitants of Louisiana
to Congress of the United
States, 13401
Memorials of a century,
13206
Memorials of academic
life, 5591
Memorials of the life and
character of Stephen
I. Logan, 7458
Memorials of William
Fowler, 3518
Memorias de Gervasio
Antonio Posadas, 7762
Memorias de un Matancero,
153
Memorias de un oficial de
la legión británica, 8319
Memorias de un oficial
del Ejército español,
8009
Las memorias diplomáticas
de Mr. Foster sobre
México, 6767
Memorias historicas sobre
la legislacion y
gobierno del comercio
de los españoles con
sus colonias en las
Indias occidentales, 402
Memorias histórico-politicas,
7761

Memorias para la historia
de las armas españolas en el
Perú, 6814
Memorie della vita e delle
peregrinazioni del
Fiorentino Filippo Mazzei,
4429
Memories. A record of personal
experience and adventure
during four years of war,
2663
Memories of a grandmother,
10614
Memories of a hundred years,
12538
Memories of Canada and
Scotland, 5927
Memories of Ralph Vansittart,
6285
Memories of the southern
states, 3054
Memphis, Tenn. - Descr., 3827
Memphis, Tenn. - Direct., 1756
Men and manners in America,
3761, 6945, 6946, 6947
Men and things in America, 1086
Men and times of the revolution,
5636
Men of our day, 1546
Men, places and things, 4830
Men, women, and ghosts, 11075
Men with the bark on, 10608
Mena, Pedro de, 17th cent.,
ed., 6470
Menageries, 2491
Menard co., Ill. - Maps, 6169
Mendell, Miss., 4447
Mendell, Sarah, 13424
Mendieta, Alonso de, 6469
Mendinueta, Francisco de,
6386
Mendive y Doumy, Rafael
María, 7850
Mendon association, Mendon,
Mass., 1400
Mendoza, Antonio de, conde de
Tendilla, 1480?-1552, 4631,
5969
Mendoza, Argentine republic

(Province) Constitution,
123
Mendoza, Cristóbal, 6794
Mendoza, Gumesindo, ed.,
6644
Mendoza, Juan de, fl.
1656-1686, 7459
Menéndez de Avilés, Pedro,
1519-1574, 5228
Meningitis, Cerebrospinal,
12540
Menken, Adah Isaacs,
1835-1868, 4448
Menominee Indians, 11358
Mentoria, 10679
Menzel, Gottfried,
b. 1798, 4449
Menzies, Archibald,
1754-1842, 7460
Mera, Francisco de, 7461
Mercantile honor, 2105
Mercator [pseud.], 6668
Mercedarians. Provincia,
de el santo evangelio
de México, 6365
Mercedes, 9740
Mercer, Charles Fenton,
1778-1858, 6826
Merchant marine - Signaling,
1207
Merchant marine - U. S.,
12787
The merchant's daughter,
10919
The merchant's widow,
10710
Merchants, American,
2480
The merchants' and tourists'
guide to Mexico, 8437
Mercier, Alfred, 1816-
1894, 4450, 4451, 4452
Mercier, Honoré, 7462
Mercurio peruano, 7463,
7464
Mère Pochett, 10037
Meredith, 10277
Meredith, Sir William,
bart., d. 1790, 13425

Meredith, William Morris,
1799-1873, jt. author,
1256
Mérida, Mexico, 7465
Merino sheep, 396
The merits of Thomas W. Dorr
and George Bancroft,
11917
Meriwether, Lee, 1862-, 4453
Merlin, María de las Mercedes
(Jaruco) 1789-1852, 4454
The mermaid of Lighthouse
Point, 6978
Merrell, William Howard,
d. 1897, 4455
Merrick, Richard Thomas,
1826-1885, 7466
Merrill, D. D., 4456
Merrill, Frank T., illustr.,
9592, 12629
Merrill, Samuel, 1831-1924,
4457
Merrill, Samuel Hill,
1805-1873, 4458
Merrimac valley - Hist. -
Poetry, 11701
Merrimack, 10177
Merrimack, N. H. - Hist., 2297
Merriman family (Nathaniel
Merriman, 1613-1693), 5835
Merry, J. F., 4459
The merry maid of Arcady,
9768
The merry monomaniacs,
11065
Merry Mount, 10390
Merry tales, 9029
The merry tales of the three
wise men of Gotham, 10487
Merwin, James B., 7986
Merwin, Samuel, 1874-1936,
7467
Mes voyages en Amérique, 3856
Mesas Redondas sobre problemas
de las zonas áridas de México,
1955, 7468
Mesas Redondas sobre problemas
del tropico Mexicano, Mexico,
1955, 7469

Meserve, Arthur L.,
4460, 4461
Meserve, Frederick Hill,
1865-, 7470, 7471
Message from the President
of the United States,
11627
Il Messico, 1863
Metacomet, 13470
Metallurgy, 5998
Metallurgy - Early works
to 1800, 773
Metals, 773, 5998
Metcalf family (Michael
Metcalf, 1586-1664),
12706
Metcalfe, Grace, 5874
Meteorology - Arctic
regions, 6302
Meteorology - Falkland
islands, 11945
Meteorology - Mexico,
7969
Meteorology - Observations,
993
Meteorology - Rhode Island,
11696
Meteorology - Virginia,
11621
Methodism, 1406
Methodism - Bibl., 1847
Methodism - Collected
works, 4535
Methodist church in
Nova Scotia, 11794
Methodist church of
Canada, 13314
Methodist church -
Sermons, 2818
Methodist Episcopal church,
3256, 4061, 5672, 6387,
6423
Methodist Episcopal church -
Clergy, 490, 750
Methodist Episcopal church -
Government, 11337, 12321
Methodist Episcopal church -
Hist., 750, 12035, 12321
Methodist Episcopal church

in Mexico, 6626
Methodist Episcopal church
in New York (State), 12241
Methodist Episcopal church
in Ohio, 3554
Methodist Episcopal church
in Tennessee, 2818
Methodist Episcopal church
in the west, 3453, 3636
Methodist Episcopal church
in Virginia, 3071, 3957
Methodist Episcopal church.
Missionary society, 749
Methodist Episcopal church -
Missions, 749, 4237, 4546,
13480
Methodist Episcopal church,
South, 4679
Methodist Episcopal church,
South - Hist., 12035
Methodist Protestant church,
13210
Metropolitan sketches, 1331
The metropolites, 10694
The mettle of the pasture,
8515
Me-won-i-toc, 10639
A Mexican campaign, 10025
Mexican central railroad,
7403
Mexican central railway company,
limited, 7901
The Mexican guide, 7139
Mexican illustrations, 1018
Mexican Isthmus Land Co.,
Inc., Kansas City, Mo.,
7472
A Mexican journey, 6102
Mexican Journeys (firm, travel
agency, Austin, Tex.) 7473
Mexican letters written
during the progress of the
late war between the United
States and Mexico, 11477
Mexican literature - Period.,
7492, 7833, 7834, 7854,
7855
Mexican National Railroad,
7474, 7475

307

The Mexican papers, 6636
The Mexican patriot, 3473
Mexican periodicals, 6612,
7836
Mexican poetry, 6692
Mexican railway company,
limited, 6037, 6371,
6372
Mexican Revolution Party,
7476
Mexican scenery and
architecture, 7711
The Mexican spy, 9719
Mexican trails, 7198
Mexican typical view
album, 7477
Mexican vignettes,
6448
Mexican vistas seen
from highways and
by-ways of travel, 8018
The Mexican war and its
warriors, 12178
Mexican wit and humor,
6612
Mexicanische zustande,
7208
Mexico, 3341, 4761, 6479,
6610, 6630, 6673, 6841,
6857, 6875, 6898, 7097,
7103, 7315, 7401, 7494,
7578, 7675, 7678, 7679,
7905, 7914, 7958, 7994,
7998, 8025, 8233, 8295,
8301, 8402, 8409, 13430
Mexico: a general sketch,
7678
México a través de los
siglos, 7873
México al día, 6606
Mexico and her people,
6940
Mexico and the life of
the conqueror, 7775
Mexico and the Mexicans,
6292
Mexico - Antiq., 5875,
5881, 6046, 6105, 6153,
6167, 6185, 6406, 6407,

6438, 6544, 6644, 6715,
6865, 6914, 7092, 7192,
7414, 7483, 7484, 7486,
7491, 7569, 7570, 7589,
8251, 8288
México arqueológico, 5875
Mexico as I saw it, 8248
Mexico as it is, 6883
Mexico, Aztec, Spanish and
republican, 7444
Mexico - Bound., 7480
Mexico - Bound. - British
Honduras, 8433
Mexico - Bound. - U. S.,
2624, 3658, 5064, 5513,
5546
Mexico. Celebración del
centenario de la independencia,
1910, 6585
Mexico - Census, 7248
Mexico (City), 483, 6802,
7478, 7479
Mexico (City) - Antiq., 7490
Mexico (City) Ayuntamiento,
6802
Mexico (City) Capilla de la
Tercer orden de Santo
Domingo, 8311
Mexico (City) Cathedral.
Archicofradía del Santísimo
Sacramento, 6806, 7962,
7963
Mexico (City) Concurso Cientí-
fico y Artístico del Centenario,
7902
Mexico (City) Convento de
Jesús María, 7220
Mexico (City) - Descr. & trav.,
6388, 6389, 6883, 7403,
7725
Mexico (City) - Descr. & trav. -
Guide-books, 7769, 7869,
8279
Mexico (City) - Direct.,
6733, 7769, 8209, 8279
Mexico (City) - Hist., 1787
Mexico (City) Museo Nacional
de Artes Plásticas, 7555
Mexico (City) Universidad, 5830

7343, 7348, 7354, 7358,
7362, 7370, 7371, 7386,
7388, 7391, 7396, 7398,
7399, 7400, 7403, 7418,
7419, 7421, 7430, 7440,
7441, 7443, 7444, 7468,
7469, 7474, 7475, 7480,
7481, 7483, 7484, 7485,
7486, 7489, 7493, 7508,
7512, 7514, 7518, 7481,
7483, 7484, 7485, 7486,
7489, 7493, 7508, 7512,
7514, 7518, 7529, 7532,
7533, 7536, 7540, 7541,
7543, 7548, 7549, 7559,
7581, 7584, 7588, 7589,
7609, 7610, 7619, 7624,
7643, 7648, 7649, 7654,
7655, 7658, 7659, 7684,
7698, 7705, 7706, 7710,
7711, 7716, 7724, 7735,
7736, 7740, 7741, 7754,
7756, 7759, 7763, 7772,
7777, 7778, 7779, 7792,
7794, 7798, 7801, 7802,
7806, 7814, 7819, 7821,
7824, 7837, 7864, 7868,
7875, 7878, 7879, 7882,
7901, 7904, 7908, 7913,
7915, 7917, 7952, 7958,
7961, 7965, 7966, 7969,
7970, 7973, 7975, 7976,
7981, 7983, 7996, 7997,
8001, 8002, 8006, 8011,
8013, 8014, 8015, 8018,
8020, 8033, 8035, 8036,
8038, 8041, 8043, 8062,
8063, 8064, 8065, 8066,
8067, 8075, 8077, 8079,
8094, 8100, 8105, 8108,
8111, 8122, 8142, 8152,
8157, 8158, 8164, 8170,
8171, 8173, 8174, 8178,
8180, 8182, 8183, 8191,
8195, 8196, 8198, 8199,
8212, 8227, 8230, 8236,
8243, 8244, 8248, 8251,
8254, 8255, 8266, 8273,
8282, 8288, 8289, 8290,

8293, 8294, 8295, 8300,
8301, 8307, 8308, 8310,
8315, 8320, 8321, 8332,
8336, 8341, 8342, 8358,
8367, 8371, 8382, 8384,
8391, 8392, 8394, 8395,
8400, 8406, 8407, 8408,
8422, 8424, 8439, 8440,
8424, 8439, 8440, 11834,
12256, 13003
Mexico - Descr. & trav. -
   Bibl., 7488, 8049
Mexico - Descr. & trav. -
   Gazetteers, 6818
Mexico - Descr. & trav. -
   Guide-books, 5884, 5948,
   5949, 5962, 5980, 6291,
   6331, 6371, 6372, 6454,
   6455, 6715, 6719, 6912,
   7045, 7337, 7473, 7487,
   7653, 7677, 7679, 7707,
   7717, 7823, 7869, 7874,
   7990, 8101, 8172, 8208,
   8209, 8211, 8437
Mexico - Descr. & trav. -
   Hist., 7902
Mexico - Descr. & trav. -
   Poetry, 6448, 6646, 7233,
   7234, 7237, 7238, 7323
Mexico - Descr. & trav. -
   Views, 5851, 6155, 6156,
   6448, 6691, 6865, 6940,
   7315, 7349, 7472, 7477,
   7554, 7555, 7569, 7570,
   7612, 7903, 8107, 8339,
   8368
Mexico - Dict. & encycl.,
   6818
Mexico. Dirección de antro-
   pología, 7486
Mexico. Dirección general
   de correos, 7487
Mexico. Dirección general
   de geografía y meteorología,
   7488
Mexico - Direct., 6733, 7896
Mexico - Distances, etc.,
   6587, 7489
Mexico - Econ. cond., 5994,

6072, 6585, 6917, 6944,
7476, 7494, 7512, 7736,
7983, 8110, 8236, 8244,
8315, 8367, 8423, 8439
Mexico en conjunto, 8300
Mexico en su primer siglo
de independencia, 6585
Mexico. Estado mayor del
ejército, 7489
Mexico (Federal District),
5936
Mexico - For. rel. -
1821-1861, 13328
Mexico - For. rel. -
Argentine republic,
7792
Mexico - For. rel. -
U. S., 6636, 7532
Mexico from border to
capital, 6730
Mexico hacia el fin del
fin del virreinato
español, 8214
Mexico - Hist., 482,
1863, 3497, 4980, 5531,
6249, 6332, 6427, 6444,
6490, 6689, 6692, 6756,
6785, 6817, 6927, 7021,
7273, 7418, 7441, 7444,
7549, 7581, 7649, 7581,
7649, 7736, 7794, 7801,
7823, 7873, 7877, 8025,
8214, 8255, 13430
Mexico - Hist. - To 1519,
5881, 6644, 7546, 11392,
11643
Mexico - Hist. - To 1519 -
Sources, 1443, 6105
Mexico - Hist. - 1540-1810 -
Sources, 6518, 6604
Mexico - Hist. - To 1810,
7419
Mexico - Hist. - To 1810 -
Sources, 6821
Mexico - Hist. - 1810-,
996, 11791
Mexico - Hist. - 1810-1849,
7313
Mexico - Hist. - 1821-1861,

1104, 1758, 1760, 1825,
6043, 6045, 7568, 13111
Mexico - Hist. - 1910-1946,
7758
Mexico - Hist. - Addresses,
essays, lectures, 7663
Mexico - Hist. - Colonial
period, 7891
Mexico - Hist. - Conquest,
1519-1540, 1440, 1864,
6644, 6863, 6864, 7111,
7387, 7546, 7774, 7775,
7931, 7932, 8004, 8057,
8058, 8059, 8060, 8061,
8062, 8063, 8064, 8065,
8066, 8067, 8068, 8396,
11316, 11643, 12448
Mexico - Hist. - Conquest,
1519-1540 - Fiction,
1332, 11053
Mexico - Hist. - Conquest,
1519-1540 - Poetry, 13213
Mexico - Hist. - European
intervention, 1861-1867,
1918, 6709, 6710, 7183,
7188, 7265, 7944, 8170,
12012, 12115
Mexico - Hist., Military,
1106
Mexico - Hist. - Period.,
7492, 7854
Mexico - Hist. - Republic,
1867-, 6767
Mexico - Hist. - Revolution,
6284, 6720, 7515, 8162
Mexico - Hist. - Sources,
6604, 7663
Mexico - Hist. - Spanish
colony, 1540-1810, 5876,
5969
Mexico - Hist. - Spanish
colony, 1540-1810 - Sources,
7536, 7684
Mexico - Hist. - Wars of
independence, 1810-1821,
1104, 1106, 1294, 1759,
7568, 7756, 8213, 8342,
8441, 13111, 13430
Mexico - Hist. - Wars of

Miertsching, Johann August,
13428
Mifflin, Benjamin, 1718-,
4467
The mighty destroyer
displayed, 1152
A mighty hunter before
the Lord, 10125
Mike Fink, 2595, 2681,
2922, 2937, 3138, 3397,
3451, 3654, 3731, 3745,
3750, 3753, 3954, 3955,
4169, 4337, 4367, 4469,
4492, 4502, 4573, 4754,
4951, 5038, 5084, 5411,
5412, 5460, 5558, 5566,
5679
Mila, 3311
La milagrosa invención
de un tesoro, 6753
Milburn, William Henry,
1823-1903, 4468,
4469, 13429
A mild barbarian, 9501
Mildred's dishes, 8663
Miles, Thomas Jefferson,
7497
Miles, William, of
Carlisle, Pa., 4470
Militarism, 11333
Military art and science,
1706
Military art and science -
Addresses, essays,
lectures, 12629
Military art and science -
Period., 462, 463, 11228
Military bridges, 12743
Military control, 2405
A military genius: life
of Anna Ella Carroll,
6094
Military incapacity, and
what it costs the
country, 12017
Military journal of Major
Ebenezer Denny, 3232
Military law - Confederate
States of America, 12264

Military law - New York
(State), 12912
Military law - U. S., 1805
The military laws of the
United States, 1805
The military opinions of
General Sir John Fox
Burgoyne, 1706
Military Order of the Loyal
Legion of the United States.
Iowa Commandery, 7498
Military Order of the Loyal
Legion of the United States.
Maine Commandery, 6458
Military Order of the Loyal
Legion of the United States.
Massachusetts Commandery,
7499, 7500
Military Order of the Loyal
Legion of the United States.
Minnesota Commandery, 7501
Military Order of the Loyal
Legion of the United States.
Missouri Commandery, 7502
Military Order of the Loyal
Legion of the United States.
New York Commandery, 7503
Military Order of the Loyal
Legion of the United States.
Ohio Commandery, 7504, 8090
Military Order of the Loyal
Legion of the United States.
Pennsylvania Commandery,
7505
Military order of the medal
of honor, 8055
Military posts - U. S., 8258
Military reminiscences of
Gen. Wm. R. Boggs, 2750
Military service, Compulsory,
12794
Military service, Compulsory -
U. S., 12167
The military telegraph during
the Civil war in the U. S.,
4808
Military telegraph - U. S.,
4808
Militia immaculatae conceptionis

Virginis Mariae, 5878
Mill, Nicholas, 13430
Millbank, 9901
Miller, Andrew, 4472
Miller, Elvira Sydnor,
4473, 4474
Miller, J. R., 13431
Miller, Jacob Welsh,
1800-1862, 1538
Miller, James Ira
Deese, 4475
Miller, James Newton,
4476
Miller, John, biographer,
7506
Miller, John, 1666-1724,
13432
Miller, Joseph, 6790
Miller, Samuel, 1769-1850,
13433
Miller, O. T., 10163
Miller, Stephen Franks,
1810?-1867, 13434
Miller, William, 1795-
1861, 7506
Millet, Thomas, 7507
Milligen, George, 4477
Milliken, James, 740,
7508
A millionaire of rough-
and-ready, 9786
A millionaire of tomorrow,
9521
A millionaire's daughter,
11033
Milliroux, J. F., 4478
The mills of the gods,
11034
Mills, Samuel John,
1783-1818, 4479,
5090, 5254
Mills, T. B. & co.,
publisher, 4480
Millspaugh, Andrew Jackson,
plaintiff, 1912
Milnor, William, jr.,
1769-1848, 13435
Milton, John, 1608-1674,
12368

Milton, William Fitzwilliam,
viscount, 1839-1877, 4481
Mimic life, 10623
Mims, Stewart L., 4518
Miner, James, 7509
Miner, T. B., 13436
Mineral waters, 1089, 13079
Mineral waters - Canada,
1088, 4514
Mineral waters - New York
(State), 13079
The mineral waters of the
U. S. and Canada, 4514
Mineral waters - Queretaro,
Mexico (State), 6040
Mineral waters - U. S.,
1088, 4514
Mineral waters - Virginia,
1714, 2858
Mineral waters - West Virginia,
1714, 2858
Mineralogy, 11955
Mineralogy - California, 11282
Mineralogy - Catalogs and
collections, 11282
Mineralogy - Classification,
2185
Mineralogy - Massachusetts,
11956
Mineralogy - Nova Scotia, 12221
The mineralogy of Nova Scotia,
12944
Mineralogy - Period., 270
Miners and traveler's guide
to Oregon, Washington, Idaho,
Montana, Wyoming, and Colorado,
4549
Minerva, 7087
Mines and mineral resources,
773, 5998
Mines and mineral resources -
British Columbia, 6174, 7072,
7822
Mines and mineral resources -
California, 6913
Mines and mineral resources -
Colorado, 7868, 12859
Mines and mineral resources -
Mexico, 5888, 6913, 6914,

7082, 7084, 7085, 7087,
7088, 7090, 7246, 7262,
7422, 7596, 7868, 8340,
8342
Mines and mineral resources -
Minnesota, 13476
Mines and mineral resources -
Nevada, 6913
Mines and mineral resources -
New Mexico, 4665
Mines and mineral resources -
Nova Scotia, 12944
Mines and mineral resources -
Quebec (province), 8393
Mines and mineral resources -
U. S., 387
Mines and mining - British
Columbia, 11662
Mines and mining - Mexico,
6139, 7348, 7904
Mines, John Flavel,
1835-1891, 13437
Miniature of Dansville
village, 11816
The miniature picture,
10921
Mining industry and finance,
12063
Mining law - U. S., 4910
The minister's black veil,
9827
The minister's housekeeper,
10909
The minister's wooing, 10905
Ministers of grace, 2810
Minnesota, 11353
Minnesota and its resources,
11352
Minnesota. Constitution,
13438
Minnesota - Descr. & trav.,
1352, 3359, 3955, 4609,
5354, 11352, 11681, 12142,
13069, 13360
Minnesota - Econ. cond.,
7510
Minnesota - Hist., 1352,
4069
Minnesota. Legislature, 7510

Minnesota. Legislature.
House of Representatives.
Select Committee on the
Overland Emigration Route from
Minnesota to British Oregon,
4482
Minnesota river, 13360
Minnesota (Ter.) Constitutional
convention, 1857, 13438
Minnie Herman, 8870
Minor, John D., et al.,
plaintiffs, 13439
Minor place, 9564
Minority report of the
Committee on ways and means,
2047
The minstrel, 11998
Minto, Walter, 1753-1796,
jt. author, 1632
Minturn, Robert Bowne,
1836-1889, 13440
The minute men, a tale of,
'75, 9618
Mirabeau, Honoré-Gabriel de
Riqueti, comte de, 1749-
1791, 7511, 13441
Mirabeau, Jean Antoine Joseph
Charles Elzear Riquetti,
1717-1794, 13441
Mirabeau, Marie (de Gonnorille)
comtesse de, ed., 2588
Mirabeau, Victor de Riquetti,
marquis de, 1715-1789,
13441
Miramichi, 10708
Miranda Elliot, 10256
Miranda Fonseca, Mariano,
7512
Miranda, Francisco Antonio
Gabriel, 1756-1816, 1713
Miranda, Francisco de,
1750-1816, 5858, 6042
Miranda y los origenes de la
independencia americana,
5858
Miriam, 9711
Miriam Coffin, 9775
Miriam Monfort, 5617
Mirick, Benjamin L., 13442

316

A mirrour or looking-glasse
both for saints, and
sinners, 11846
"Mis' Elderkin's pitcher",
10909
Misantla, Relación de,
7730
Miscegenation, 206
Miscegenation endorsed
by the Republican
party, 6570
Miscellanea, 5249
Miscellaneous and patriotic
poems, 12228
Miscellaneous sketches of
occurrences during the
late American war, 9086
Miscellaneous trifles in
prose, 11661
Miscellaneous works,
prose and poetical,
10210
Miscellanies, 2543
Miscellanies selected
from the public
journals, 11605
A miscellany, 1194
Misery Landing, 11205
The mishaps of Mr.
Ezekiel Pelter, 9861
Misión diplomática y
militar, 7859
Miss Ayr of Virginia,
10304
Miss Bremer's visit to
Cooper's Landing, 9802
Miss Brooks, 11139
Miss Cherry Blossom of
Tokyo, 10239
Miss Columbia's public
school, 10579
Miss Debby's neighbors,
10040
Miss Eaton's romance,
8520
Miss Ellsabetha, 11207
Miss Esther's guest, 10041
Miss Frances Merley, 9277
Miss Gunton of Poughkeepsie,

10016
Miss Hurd, 10667
"Miss Lou", 10649
Miss Ludington's sister,
8776
Miss Madam, 4903
Miss Maria, 9376
Miss Martha Brownlow, 10612
Miss Peck's promotion,
10037
Miss Rutherford's historical
notes, 7926
Miss Slimmens' window, 11043
Miss Tempy's watchers, 10037
Miss Tiller's vegetable
garden and the money she
made by it, 11086
"Miss Träumerei", 8638
Miss Van Kortland, 8778
The Miss Vanlears, 10197
Miss Washington, of Virginia,
10378
Missent, 8489
The missing chapter in the
life of Abraham Lincoln,
6665
Mission de l'Immaculée
Conception, 12353
Mission de la Colombie, 2753
The mission of death, 11065
A mission to the Indians of
Orialla, South America,
11291
Missionaries, 4794
Missionary ridge, Battle of,
1863, 5362
The missionary sheriff, 9581
The missionary teacher,
4546
Missions, 6527, 7166
Missions - Africa, 8171, 11783
Missions - Africa, West,
11902
Missions - America, 2790
Missions - Arizona, 6813
Missions - Bermuda Islands,
1195
Missions - Canada, 1025
Missions - Chiloe, Chile

317

(Province), 2436
Missions - Cuba, 6907
Missions - Hawaiian
islands, 1296, 1297
Missions, Home, 845
Missions - Indian territory,
4863
Missions - Japan, 1789
Missions - Kentucky, 651
Missions - Mexico, 6950,
7802
Missions - Mississippi
Valley, 4479, 5090
Missions - Negroes,
1556
Missions - New Mexico,
1145
Missions - Northwest,
Canadian, 4542
Missions - Oceania, 13479
Missions - Ohio Valley,
4469
Missions - Oregon, 2508,
4237, 4546
Missions - Paraguay, 1789
Missions - Patagonia,
12612
Missions - Puerto Rico,
6907
Missions - Sermons, 654,
1007, 1196, 11407,
11651, 13391
Missions - Sonora, 6813
Missions - Southwest, Old,
5254
Missions - Spanish America,
2366, 6796, 6799, 8171
Missions - Texas,
4742, 6609
Missions - West Indies,
1993, 1995, 11866
Mississippi, 3741
Mississippi - Biog.,
6093
Mississippi cavalry. 1st
regt., 1861-1865, 4505
Mississippi - Church his-
tory, 13305
Mississippi - Descr. & trav.,

3138, 3171, 3425, 3595,
4173, 4483, 4657, 4758,
4767, 11895
Mississippi et Indiana, 3314
Mississippi-fahrten, 3859
Mississippi - Fiction,
3135, 8782, 10913
Mississippi - Hist., 1772,
3003, 8287
Mississippi. Immigration and
Agriculture Board, 4483
Mississippi - Pol. & govt.,
13205, 13402
Mississippi - Pol. & govt. -
1865-, 8344
Mississippi - Registers,
2699
Mississippi river, 337, 3029
3517, 3654, 4632, 4824,
12018, 13476
Mississippi river - Descr. &
trav., 762, 2723, 2860,
2957, 3139, 3240, 3509,
3622, 3693, 4269, 5103,
11681, 13461
Mississippi river - Disc. &
explor., 1846, 2694, 3552,
3666, 4393, 5229, 5433,
7404
Mississippi river - Fiction,
3474
Mississippi river - Navigation,
3139, 11895
Mississippi river - Sources,
1133, 1134
Mississippi scenes, 3037
Mississippi scheme, 3552
Mississippi - Soc. life &
cust., 707, 3037
Mississippi valley, 2784,
4320, 5100, 11506, 12151
Mississippi valley - Church
history, 5090
Mississippi valley - Descr.
& trav., 541, 542, 1133,
1206, 2594, 2758, 2760,
2831, 2871, 3081, 3103,
3117, 3138, 3147, 3163,
3169, 3248, 3360, 3380,

318

3397, 3468, 3479, 3647,
3859, 3988, 3990, 4065,
4126, 4258, 4472, 4479,
4653, 4696, 4717, 4729,
4755, 4919, 4951, 5090,
5099, 5112, 5773, 6271,
6403, 6404, 6529, 12024,
12573, 12678, 13143
Mississippi valley - Hist.,
3067, 4502, 4752, 5038,
5229, 6737, 7008, 9585,
12184, 13074, 13482
Mississippi valley - Hist. -
To 1803, 3547, 3748,
3988, 8401, 12720, 13461
Mississippi valley - Hist. -
To 1803 - Sources, 7404
Mississippi valley - Hist. -
Civil war, 2033, 2068,
4192, 4415, 12953
Mississippi valley - Soc.
life & cust., 10021,
10265
Mississippian scenery,
4430
Missouri, 970, 4698,
4728, 4761, 5100, 5633
Missouri as it is in
1867, 4698
Missouri cavalry. Frémont's
body guard, 1861, 12170
Missouri - Commerce -
Mexico, 5528
Missouri compromise, 11255
Missouri - Descr. & trav.,
3302, 3468, 3479, 4173,
4598, 4653, 4729, 5062,
5098, 5263, 5680, 12142
Missouri - Descr. & trav. -
Guide-books, 4699
Missouri - Fiction, 2634,
5476
The Missouri harmony,
2911
Missouri - Hist., 4573,
6837
Missouri - Hist. - Civil
war, 4192, 5610, 12170
Missouri - Hist. - Civil

war - Fiction, 10092, 11190
Missouri - Hist. - Fiction,
9202
Missouri infantry. 9th
regt., 1861-1865, 4223
Missouri river, 2779, 2784,
3578, 4272, 4625
The Missouri trapper, 4262
Missouri valley - Descr. &
trav., 2779, 3092, 3137,
4134, 4262, 4755, 4802,
5098, 5374, 5425
Missouri valley - Fiction,
3754
The mistake, 10310
Mr. Absalom Billingslea, 4081
Mr. Ambrose's letters on the
rebellion, 4155
Mr. Beverley Lee, 10385
Mr. Billy Downs and his
likes, 4082
Mr. Bilson's housekeeper,
6969
Mr. Bonaparte of Corsica,
8682
Mr. Buchanan's administration
on the eve of the rebellion,
1634
Mr. Curran, 10310
Mr. Dooley in peace and in
war, 9438
Mr. Dooley's philosophy,
9439
Mr. Dunn Browne's experiences
in the army, 3457
Mr. Dunton's invention, 9817
Mr. Durant of Salt Lake City,
10613
Mr. Fitz Foom in the country,
11043
Mr. Fortner's marital claims,
4083
Mr. Frank, the underground
mail-agent, 11046
Mr. Grantley's idea, 9110
Mr. Greeley's letters from
Texas and the lower
Mississippi, 3675
Mr. H---, 10310

A modern Mephistopheles, 8485
Modern pilgrims, 11200
The modern Psyche, 9678
Modern vengeance, 10546
The modern warning, 7117
Modes of education, 10184
Modoc Indians, 10355
Modos con que podran los christianos desagraviar a Nuestro Señor Jesu Christo Sacramentado, 6809
Moelling, Peter August, 4494
Moeran's moose, 10125
Moffat, William David, 1863-, 10283
Moffette, Joseph F., 4495
Mogul empire, 2123
Mohave Indians, 5299, 5491
Mohawk, A romance of the, 3893
Mohawk Indians, 1183, 7429, 10744, 10745, 13227
Mohawk language, 13169
Mohawk language - Dictionaries - French, 11588
Mohawk Valley, N. Y., 1183, 11657, 12928
Mohegan Indians - Language, 12004
The Mohocks, 12200
Moise, Abraham, 1799-1869, ed., 12666
Moler, Arthur Bass, 1866-, 7514
Molina Enríquez, Andrés, 7515
Molina y Saldívar, Gaspar de, marqués de Ureña, 1741-1806, 7516
Molinari, Gustave de, 1819-1912, 4496
Molleda y Clerque, Gregorio,

abp., d. 1756, 8027
Möllhausen, Balduin, 1825-1905, 4497, 4498, 4499, 4500, 4501
Mollusks, 37
Mollusks - Catalogs and collections, 12328, 12533, 13182
Mollusks - North America, 1318, 5080
Mollusks - North America - Bibl., 1317
Mollusks - Pacific coast, 11670
Mollusks - Pacific ocean, 12328
Mollusks - Panama, 36
Mollusks - Period., 259
Molly's Bible, 8979
The Moloch of decrees, 3159
Moluccas, 7567
Moluccas - Hist., 2467, 2468
Mom Bl., 9745
Momberger, illustr., 12554
Mona, the vestal, 9415
Monaldi, 2512
The monarchist, 4112
Monasteries - Mexico, 6819
Monasticism and religious orders, 584
Monckton-Dene, R., 10122
Monckton-Dene, R. The other fellow, 10115
Mondría, Ramón, tr., 6422
Mone, Franz Joseph, 1796-1871, ed., 507
Monette, John Wesley, 4502
Money, 1865, ?001, 11119
Money, and what came of it, 11125
Money - Canada, 11733
Money - Connecticut, 11535
Money, Edward, 4503
The money diggers, 10959
Money don' make 'ristercrats, 8872
Money - Massachusetts, 2245
Money - Tables, etc., 13154

Money - U. S. - Hist. -
Colonial period, 11535,
11905
The moneyless man, 5260
Monge Alfaro, Carlos,
7517
Monguagon, Mich., Battle
of, Aug. 9, 1812, 11944
The monikins, 9138
Le moniteur haitien, 6924
The monks of Monk-Hall,
10217
Monmouth's rebellion,
1685 - Fiction, 9449
Monody on the victims and
sufferers by the late
conflagration in the
city of Richmond,
Virginia, 12262
Monogenism and polygenism,
13019
Mononghahela river -
Descr., 2561
The monopoly and the
people's line, 10385
Monroe Co., Ind. - Hist.,
12899
Monroe doctrine, 7338,
11702, 12115
Monroe, James, pres. U. S.,
1758-1831, 73, 77, 78
Monroy Padilla, Salvador,
7518
Monsalve, Miguel de,
7519
Monsieur Alcibiade, 9769
Monsieur Beaucaire, 10924
Monsieur du Miroir, 9823
Monsieur Matte, 10135
Monsipi Indians, 2620
The monster and other
stories, 9213
Montagnais Indians, 7216
Montagu, Irving, illustr.,
3646
Montaignes, François des
[pseud.] 4504
Montana, 6140
Montana as it is, 5307

Montana - Descr. & trav.,
2730, 3551, 4549, 5307,
5481
Montana - Descr. & trav. -
Guide-books, 3735
The Montanas, 9730
Montanus, Arnoldus, 1625?-
1683, 7629
Montcalm-Gozon, Louis Joseph
de, marquis de Saint Véran,
1712-1759, 6397, 8414
Monte Carmelo, Fr. Juan del,
7520
Montemar, Diego Miguel
Carrillo de Albornoz,
conde de, 8277
Montemayor, Alonso de, 7096
Montemayor y Córdova de Cuenca,
Juan Francisco de, 1620-
1685, 1078, 8085
Monterey, Battle of, 1846 -
Poetry, 4407
Monterey, Mexico - Soc. life
& cust., 7364
Monterroso, Thomas de,
bp., d. 1678, 5856
Montevideo - Descr., 12518
Montezuma, the last of the
Aztecs, 10331
Montezuma, the serf, 9982
Montezuma II, emperor of
Mexico, ca.1480-1520, 7546
Montezuma II, emperor of
Mexico, ca.1480-1520 -
Fiction, 10331
Montezuma's castle, 9174
Montgomery, Cora, pseud.,
2957, 8958
Montgomery co., Pa. - Biog.,
1637
Montgomery co., Pa. - Hist.,
1637
Montgomery, Franklin Alexander,
1830-, 4505
Montgomery, George Washington,
1804-1841, 7521
Montgomery, James, 12848
Montgomery, Sir James, 7522
Montgomery, Richard, 1738-1775,

322

11482
A month in a country
parish, 10383
Monti, Luigi, 1830-1914,
7523
Montlezun, baron de,
4506
Montoto de Sedas, Santiago,
1890-, ed., 7524
Montpelier, Vt. - Hist.,
12429
Montpetit, Édouard,
1881-, 7525
Montreal after 250 years,
7278
Montreal - Descr., 7278
Montreal - Descr. -
Guide-books, 6551
Montreal Herald, 7526
Montreal. Police court,
1167
Montreal - Soc. life &
cust., 7526
Montresor family, 5111
Montresor, James Gabriel,
1709-1776, 5111
Montresor, John, 1736-
1799, 5111
The Montresor journals,
5111
Montrol, François Mongin
de, 1799-1862, 11522
Montt, Luis, ed., 7848
Montulé, Édouard de, 4507
Moodie, Susannah (Strickland)
1803-1885, 7527, 7528,
13444
Moods, 8486
Moon, 9551
Moon hoax, 10231
A moonlight boy, 9934
Moonshiners, 9246
Moore, Daniel, fl. 1800,
jt. author, 13154
Moore, Edward Alexander,
1842-, 4508
Moore, Francis, fl. 1744,
4509
Moore, Francis, jr., 4510

Moore, Frank, 1828-1904,
13232
Moore, George, 1806-1876,
4511
Moore, H. Judge, 7529
Moore, Jacob Bailey,
1797-1853, jt. author, 12138
Moore, Joseph Hampton,
1864-, 7530
Moore, Rebecca, Dr., 9331
Moore, Theophilus Wilson,
4512
Moore, Will Beno, pseud.,
5706
Moorhead, Isaac, 1828-1881,
4513
The Moorish bride, 3842
Moorman, John J. A brief
notice, 1714
Moorman, John Jennings,
1802-1885, 4514, 4515
Mora, Emilio, supposed author,
951
A moral blot, 8505
The moral significance of war,
661
Morale, 7719
Morales, Juan Bautista,
1788-1856, 7531
Morales, Vicente, 7532
The morality of the riot,
2347
The morals of freedom,
11720
Moran, Frank E., 3417
Morand, Paul, 1888-, 7533
Moravian church - Catechisms
and creeds - German, 1027
Moravian church - Hist.,
13467
Moravian church - Missions,
13467
Moravian church - North
Carolina, 4615
The Moravian Indians, 10670
Moravian Indians - Missions,
13398
Moravians, 10388, 10389
Moravians, A tale of the

primitive, 10388
More bed-time stories,
10392
Moré, Charles Albert,
chevalier de Pontgibaud,
comte de, 1758-1837,
4516
A more impartial and com-
prehensive view of the
dispute between Great
Britain and the colonies,
12600
More "Short sixes", 8898
More than she could bear,
8543
More work for the Maine
law, 9001
Moreau de Saint Méry,
Médéric Louis Elie,
1750-1819, 4518
Moreau, F. Frédéric,
4517
Morehead, Charles
Slaughter, 1802-1868,
ed., 13363
Morehead, James Turner,
1797-1854, 4519
Morelet, Arthur, 1809-,
7534
Morelia, Mexico -
Descr., 6811, 8227
Morelia, Mexico.
Ordinances, etc., 7535
Morelia, Mexico.
Universidad Michoacana de
San Nicolás de Hidalgo,
5969
Morellet, André, tr., 6778
Morelli, Jacopo, 1745-1819,
ed., 1140
Moreno de Montalvo, Jacinto,
7456
Moret, Nicolas d'Oxat,
seigneur de, 1682-1738,
11742
Morfi, Juan Agustín,
d. 1783, 7536
Morford, Henry, 1823-1881,
4520, 4521

Morford's short-trip guide
to America, 4520
Morgan, Henry James,
1842-1913, 1633, 4522
Morgan, Ike, illustr.,
4902
Morgan, John Hunt, 1825-1864,
2698, 3312, 4523
Morgan, John Hunt, 1825-1864 -
Fiction, 3507
Morgan, Julia, "Mrs. Irby
Morgan", 4523
Morgan, Mrs. Martha M.,
4524
Morgan, Matthew Somerville,
1839-1890, 7537
Morgan, William, 1774-ca.1826,
458, 4534, 10384, 11257,
11562, 12399
Morgan, William Ferdinand,
1817-1888, 7538
Morgan, William Henry,
1836-, 4525
Morgan's cavalry division
(C.S.A.) 3312
Morgan's raid, 1863, 3417,
4063, 4287
Morgan's raid, 1863 - Fiction,
9251
Morgenstierne, Wilhelm, 5092
Moriah's mourning, 5314
Morice, Adrian Gabriel,
1859-1938, 7539
Morillas Osorio, Diego de,
6677, 6678, 6679, 6687
Morillo y Morillo, Pablo,
marques de la Puerta,
1778-1837, 7897
Morineau, Auguste de, 4526
Mormon way-bill, 2881
The Mormon's wife, 10298
Mormonism unvailed, 12950
Mormons and Mormonism,
1744, 2970, 2999, 3000,
3013, 3074, 3436, 3437,
3679, 3718, 4131, 4846,
4931, 5175, 5790, 11881,
12148, 12504, 12950
Mormons and Mormonism -

Fiction, 4948, 5748, 10613, 10990
Mormons and Mormonism in Illinois, 11695
The Mormons at home, 3437
Morning mists, 9265
Morrill, Gulian Lansing, 1857-, 7540, 7541
Morris, Alexander, 7542
Morris, Charles, fl. 1749, cartographer, 7764
Morris, Eastin, 4527
Morris, George W., 4528
Morris Graeme, 4001
Morris, Harrison Smith, 1856-, 10737
Morris, Ida Dorman, "Mrs. J. E. Morris", 7543
Morris, John, pseud., 4635
Morris, Maurice O'Connor, 4529
Morris, Robert, 1818-1888, 4530
Morris, Thomas Asbury, bp., 1794-1874, 1178, 4535
Morris, William, of Swindon, Eng., 4536
Morse, Charles Fessenden, 1839-, 4537
Morse, Francis W., 4538
Morse, Horace Bassett, 1804-1825, 1740
Morse, Jedidiah, 1761-1826, 52, 1280, 4539
A mortal antipathy, 9906
Mortality, Law of, 938
The mortgage on Jeffy, 9582
Mortgages, 1254
Mortier, Michel, 7544
Morton family, 7251
Morton family (George Morton, 1585?-1624), 7251
Morton, John Watson, 4540
Morton, Levi Parsons,

1824-1920, 7251
Morton Montagu, 10389
Morton, Mrs. Sarah Wentworth (Apthorp) 1759-1846. Ouabi, 630
Morton, Thomas, 1575-1646 - Fiction, 10390
Morton's artillery, C.S.A., 4540
Morton's Hope, 10391
El Mosaico, 7545
Mosby and his men, 3114
Mosby, John Singleton, 1833-1916, 3114, 3417, 5107
Mosby, John Singleton, 1833-1916. Stuart's cavalry in the Gettysburg campaign, 4365
Mose Evans, 8658
Mose Skinner's bridal tour, 8862
Mose Skinner's great world's jubilee and humstrum convulsion, 8863
Moser, James H., illustr., 8691
Moses and Joshua, 7805
Mosgrove, George Dallas, 4541
Mosquitia, 2353
Mosquitia - Descr. & trav., 7750, 7883, 8098
Mosquito Coast, 13485
Moss-side, 10942
Mosses from an old manse, 9823
Motezuma, Diego Luis de, 1619-1699, 7546
Moth and rust, 11214
The mother's question, 9540
The mother's rule, 8572
The motley book, 10325, 10326
Mott, Valentine, 1785-1865, 2313, 12463
The moujik, 9265
Moulton, Louise Chandler, 10163, 10899
The Moultrie Co. Lincolns, 6716
Moultrie, William, 1730-1805,

325

12729
Mound-builders, 12184,
13457
Mound-builders - Manitoba,
6215
Mound-builders - Ohio,
4640
Mounds, 507, 11474
Mounds - Georgia, 13290
Mounds - Gt. Brit.,
13225
Mounds - North America,
933
Mounds - Ohio, 542
Mount Auburn cemetery,
1269
Mount Holly, N. J., 527
Mount Holyoke, Mass. -
Descr. - Guide-books,
2181
Mount Hope, 12856
Mount Vernon, 13399
Mount Vernon ladies
association of the
Union, 5629
The Mount Vernon papers,
12116
A mountain Europa, 9554
Mountain, George
Jehoshaphat, bp. of
Quebec, 1789-1863,
4542
Mountain Meadow massacre,
1857, 6335
Mountain Meadows, Utah -
Hist., 5525
The mountain mourner,
10316
The mountain muse, 2844
The mountain of the two
lovers, 10919
The mountain people of
Kentucky, 3769
Mountain sheep, 8012
Mountain whites (Southern
states), 2901, 3769
The mountaineer of the
Atlas, 10336
Mountaineering, 6890, 8126,

8372
Mountaineering - Period.,
6317
A mournful Easter, 12561
Mowat, Henry, 1734-1798,
1803
Mowatt, Anna Cora Ritchie,
10622-10625
Mowris, James A., 4543
Mowry, Sylvester, 4544, 4545
Moxon, Joseph, 7547
Moya, Rodrigo, 7440, 7441,
7442
Mudd, Samuel Alexander,
1833-1883, 1305, 6701
Mudge, Zachariah Atwell,
1813-1888, 4546
Mühlenberg, Henry Melchior,
1711-1787, 4547
Mühlenpfordt, Eduard, 7548
Muirhead, James Fullarton,
1853-1934, 4548
Mulberry, 11840
Mullan, John, 1830-1909,
4549, 4560, 5540
Müller, Johann Wilhelm von,
1824-1866, 7549
Mulligan, James Hilary,
1844-1915, 8220
Mulvany, Charles Pelham,
7550
Munchausen, baron, jr.,
pseud., 10384
Mund, August, tr., 5290
Muñoz, Joaquín, 7551, 7552
Muñoz, Juan Bautista.
Historia del Nuevo Mundo,
13112
Munsee Indians, 134
Munsell, Joel, 1808-1880,
13445
Münster, Sebastian, 1489-1552,
5920
Münsterberg, Hugo, 1863-1916,
4551
Mur, Pedro de, 13334
Murat, Achille, prince, 1801-
1847, 4552
Murch, Abel B., jt. author,

1624
Murchard, F., 17
Murder, 11963, 13241
The murder of Abraham
  Lincoln planned and
  executed by Jesuit
  priests, 7553
Murfree, Mary Noailles,
  1850-1922, 4553-4567
Murfreesboro, Battle of,
  1862-63, 2708
Murgatroyd, Matthew,
  pseud., 10061
Murrell, John A., 9931
Murillo, Gerardo, 1884-,
  7554, 7555
Murillo, marqués de,
  6386
Murphey, Claude Charles,
  4568
Murphy, D. F., 7566
Murphy, Henry Cruse,
  1810-1882, comp.,
  1568
Murphy, Lady Blanche
  Elizabeth Mary
  Annunciata (Noel)
  1845?-1881, tr.,
  3618, 5032
Murphy, Timothy, 1751-
  1818, 12334
Murray, Hon. Amelia
  Matilda, 1795-1884,
  4569
Murray, Sir Charles
  Augustus, 1806-1895,
  4570, 4571
Murray, David Christie,
  1847-, 7556
Murray family, 4572
Murray, Henry Anthony,
  1810-1865, 7557, 7558
Murray, James, 1713-1781,
  4572
Murray, Samuel, 1865-,
  7559
Murray, William, 6666
Murvale Eastman, Christian
  socialist, 10993

Muscoma, 8588
The muse of Hesperia, 4741
Museum Americanum, 12994
Music - New England, 12879
Music on the march, 4899
Music - U. S., 274
A musical reformation, 9091
Musicians - Fiction, 10307
Musick, John Roy, 1849-1901,
  4573
Musings and pastels, 3448
Muskets and medicine, 4064
Muskingum Co., Ohio - Maps,
  1068
Mustang Gray, 9021
The mute singer, 10624
Mutis, José Alestino, 1732-
  1808, 7560
Mutterings and musings of
  an invalid, 11002
My Aunt Susan, 9567, 9570
My borrowing neighbor,
  10163
My brother's keeper, 11087
My campaigns in America,
  3239
My Canadian journal, 6634
My captive, 2519
My daughter Elinor, 8780
My diary, north and south,
  7923
My double and how he undid
  me, 9686
My duty, 10956
My first book, 6963, 6971
My friend the boss, 9687
My friend the tramp, 9779
My garden walk, 4093
My grandfather's old coat,
  9798
My hero, 10553
My husband's crime, 9930
My husband's mother, 10298
My lady Pokahontas, 9111
My little love, 10943
My married life at Hillside,
  9061
My mother-in-law, 10796
My mother's gold ring, 10703

327

My native land, 5304
My new home in northern
  Michigan, 10031
My old Kentucky home,
  6061
My opinions and Betsy
  Bobbet's, 9887
My own home and fireside,
  8521
My own story, 9769
My own times, 4940
My recollections of the
  war of the rebellion,
  4218
My satchel and I, 10862
My sister Kitty, 8757
My Southern friends, 9622
My story of the war, 4284
My strange friend, 10675
My study fire, 10257
My ten-rod farm, 8708
My third book, 10393
My thirty years out of
  the Senate, 10821
My three conversations
  with Miss Chester,
  10298
My uncle Hobson and I,
  10072
My unwilling neighbor,
  10896
My visit to Sybaris,
  9695
My well and what came
  out of it, 10896
My wife and I, 10906
My winter garden, 5394
Myers, J. C., 4574
Myers, Leonard, 1827-
  1905, 7561
Mygatt, Mrs. Mary
  Stevens (Dickinson),
  6592
Myrthe, A. T., pseud.,
  9598
Myrtis, 10760
Myrtle blossoms, 9869
Myrtle lawn, 2603
The mysteries and miseries

of New York, 10080
Mysteries of city life,
  10604
The mysteries of magic,
  10693
The mysteries of Nashua,
  10402
The mysteries of the backwoods,
  5411, 10964
The mysteries of the Catskills,
  10458
The mysteries of the three
  cities, 9434
Mysteries of Washington City,
  during several months of
  session of the 28th Congress,
  11229
Mysteries, Religious, 2241
The mysterious bell, 10693
A mysterious case, 10668
The mysterious chief, 11204
The mysterious companions
  of Old John Brown, 10007
The mystery, 9249
The mystery disclosed, 10673
Mystery Evans, 8648
A mystery explained, 10713
The mystery of a Christmas
  hunt, 10125
The mystery of choice, 8965
The mystery of Mahbin Mill,
  10112
The mystery of the hacienda,
  6963, 6971
The mystery of the locks,
  9935
The mystery of the Meschianza,
  10277
The mystery of the Westervelts,
  9372
The mystery of Witch-Face
  mountain, 4561
The mystery solved, 10846
The mystic number seven in
  the life of Abraham Lincoln,
  7634
Mythology, Aztec, 7491

N. A., 3098
N., J. C., 4575
Naar Californië, 5588
Naaukeurige beschryving
  van Noord-America,
  4575
Nach Amerika im dienste
  Friedrich Schillers,
  4765
Nach Amerika in einem
  auswandererschiffe,
  5565
Nacoochee, 2994
Nadal, Bernard Harrison,
  1812-1870, 7562
Nahant, 10404
Nairne, Thomas, 4576
La naissance d'une
  nation, 6735
Nakam, a Menominee
  Indian, 11358
Nameless, 9428
A nameless nobleman, 8606
Names, Geographical -
  New York (State), 1174
Names, Geographical -
  Quebec (province), 7916
Names, Personal -
  Massachusetts - Suffolk
  Co., 11435
"Nan", 10163
Nancy Ward, 10134
Nancy Waterman, 8748
Nankivell, F. A.,
  illustr., 10998
Nantucket, Mass., 6860
Nantucket, Mass. - Descr.
  & trav., 8607
Nantucket, Mass. - Hist.,
  6860
Nantucket, Mass. - Hist. -
  Sources, 12931
Nantucket scraps, 8607
Naomi, 10179, 10180
Napier, John, 1550-1617,
  1632
The Napolead, 3587
Napoleon I - Fiction, 11029
Napoleon I - Poetry, 3587

Napoleon III, emperor of
  the French, 1808-1873,
  1125, 3617
Napoles recvperada por el
  rey don Alonso, 6118
Naron, L. H., Union scout,
  5321
The Narraganset chief, 10503
Narragansett Bay - Descr. &
  trav. - Guide-books, 764
Narragansett patent, 505
Narrative and confessions of
  Lucretia P. Cannon, 10405
Narrative of a tour from the
  state of Indiana to the
  Oregon territory, 5719
Narrative of a voyage from
  England to the United
  States of North America,
  3942
A narrative of affairs lately
  received from His Majesties
  island of Jamaica, 13145
The narrative of Arthur
  Gordon Pym, 10533
The narrative of Col. David
  Fanning, 3418
Narrative of Edmund Wright,
  11209
A narrative of events connected
  with the acceptance and
  resignation of the rectorship
  of St. Paul's church, 13170
A narrative of events in
  the south of France, 3079
A narrative of his connection
  with the Old American
  company, 12828
Narrative of James Williams,
  5717
Narrative of Johann Carl
  Buettner in the American
  revolution, 2872
A narrative of Pye and the
  highwayman, 10568
Narrative of Rosanna Hicks,
  11173
Narrative of the Arctic land
  expedition, 2585

329

A narrative of the campaigns
of the British army at
Washington and New Orleans,
3625
Narrative of the captivity
and extreme sufferings
of Mrs. Clarissa Plummer,
4577
A narrative of the dissolu-
tion of the medical
faculty of Transylvania
university, 5785
A narrative of the incidents
attending the capture,
detention, and ransom
of Charles Johnston,
4072
A narrative of the late
massacres, 2317
Narrative of the life and
adventures of Matthew
Bunn, 2855
A narrative of the pro-
ceedings of the black
people, 13284
A narrative of the pro-
ceedings of the people
of South Carolina, 5787
Narrative of the singular
adventures and captivity
of Thos. Barry, 2620
Narrative of the sufferings
of Lewis and Milton
Clark, 3014
A narrative of the
sufferings of Seth
Hubbell & family, 12978
Narrative of the travels
and adventures of
Monsieur Violet, 4398
A narrative of the visit
to the American churches,
4912
A narrative of trans-
actions in the Red River
country, 4348
Narratives from real
life, 8869
Narratives of voyages and

excursions on the east
coast, 7883
Narváez, Pánfilo de, d. 1528,
4631
Narváez, Pánfilo de, d. 1528--
Drama, 6328
Nasby in exile, 10226
Nasby on inflation, 10228
The Nasby papers, 10227
Nasby, Petroleum V., pseud.,
10226-10230
Nashua, N. H. - Hist., 2297
Nashville, N. H. - Hist.,
2297
Nashville, Tenn. - Hist. -
Civil war, 4523
Nashville. University.
Medical dept., 11453
Nason, Daniel, 4578
Nason, Elias, 1811-1887, 972,
7563
Nast, Thomas, 1840-1902,
illustr., 5460, 6591, 10579
Nat Gregory, 10738
Natalie, 9712
Natchez, Miss. - Descr., 3424
Natick, Mass. - Descr., 645
Natick, Mass. - Hist., 645, 1285
La nation haitienne, 6064
The nation's success and
gratitude, 1462
National banks - U. S.,
12128
The national "barley cake",
556
National characteristics,
2268
National characteristics,
American, 221, 1461, 5172,
5697, 12086
National characteristics,
Mexican, 8402
National editorial association
of the U. S., 8180
National equal suffrage
association, 11376
National Institute for the
promotion of science,
Washington, D. C., 21, 1475

National intelligencer, Washington, 395
The national jubilee, 3384
National Lincoln monument association, 7564
The national nest-stirring, 1470
National parks and reserves - Canada, 7173
National parks and reserves - U. S., 7173
The National party, 7870
National reconstruction, 7562
National ship-canal convention, Chicago, 1863, 2471, 13446
National songs, American, 12174, 12250
National songster, 13392
National Union Association of Ohio, 7565
National Union Convention. Baltimore, June 7-8, 1864, 7566, 7615
National virtue and national glory, 157
A national warning, 1216
Nationality, 1955
"A native author called Roe", 10653
A native of Winby, 10041
Native races, 12965
The natural and civil history of the French dominions in North and South America, 4051
Natural and statistical view, or picture of Cincinnati and the Miami country, 3289
Natural history, 12325
Natural history - Addresses, essays, lectures, 877
Natural history - Alabama, 3650
Natural history - Alaska, 5899

Natural history - Amazon valley, 961
Natural history - Arctic regions, 6058, 7911
Natural history - Atlantic states, 7172
Natural history - Bahamas, 2946
Natural history - Bermuda Islands, 13306
Natural history - British Columbia, 7324
Natural history - Canada, 6768, 6954, 7170, 7171, 7172
Natural history - Canary Islands, 11381
Natural history - Central America, 7657
Natural history - Collected works, 12685
Natural history - Colombia, 13451
Natural history - Cuba, 7007
Natural history - England, 7170
Natural history - Florida, 5012
Natural history - Hist., 11973
Natural history - Jamaica, 11578
Natural history - Labrador, 6901
Natural history - Louisiana, 5537
Natural history - Mexico, 6400, 6401, 6862, 7932
Natural history - New York (State), 1907
Natural history - North America, 6670
Natural history - North Carolina, 11515
Natural history - Northwest, Old, 6768
Natural history - Northwest Territories, Canada, 5899

Natural history - Norway,
7170
Natural history - Nova
Scotia, 6575
The natural history of
North Carolina, 2799
Natural history - Ohio,
540
Natural history - Outdoor
books, 5394, 5437
Natural history - Panama,
13502
Natural history - Paraguay,
598
Natural history - Penn-
sylvania, 931
Natural history - Pictorial
works, 2946
Natural history - Polynesia,
1172
Natural history - Pre-
Linnean works, 2946
Natural history - Societies,
etc., 2472, 12049
Natural history - South
America, 7092
Natural history - South
Carolina, 12049
Natural history - Southern
States, 2946
Natural history - Spanish
America, 5827
Natural history - Superior,
Lake, 108
Natural history - Surinam,
733, 734
Natural history - Tahiti,
3237
Natural history - Texas,
5537
Natural history - U. S.,
4193, 5700, 5701, 7170,
7171
Natural history - Utah,
5255, 5501
Natural history - West
Indies, 7657
Natural law, 13042
Natural resources - Canada,

6436
Natural resources - Northwest,
Canadian, 6062
Natural resources of the
U. S., 4716
Natural theology, 2884
A naturalist in Mexico,
5986
The naturalist on the river
Amazons, 961
Naturalization, 1955
Naturalization - U. S.,
1308, 1508, 11580
Nature, 11598
Nature (Aesthetics), 11598
The nature and danger of
heresy, 13056
Nature and human nature,
12546
Nature display'd, 5564
The nature of humiliation,
fasting and prayer
explained, 11501
Un naufrage au Texas, 5076
The naulahka, 10146
The Nautilus, 9040
Nauvoo, Ill., 11695
Nava, Pedro José de, 7768
Navajo country - Descr. &
trav., 5167
Navajo Indians - Wars, 3962
Naval art and science,
462, 463, 7995
Naval art and science -
Dictionaries, 12722
Naval art and science -
Hist., 11424
Naval art and science -
Period., 11228
Naval battles, 11424
Naval battles - Gt. Brit.,
185, 1540, 2187
Naval history, 1690
Naval hygiene, 459, 11241
Navarrete, Martín Fernández
de, 1765-1844, 7567
Navarro y Rodrigo, Carlos,
1833-1903, 7568
Navies, 1218, 1757

Navigation, 5852, 6007,
6832
Navigation - Hist., 311
Naylor, Robert Anderton,
4579
The Nazarene, 10214
Neal, John, 1793-1876,
192, 193
Near a whole city full,
10998
Near to nature's heart,
10650
Nebel, Carl, 7569, 7570
Nebraska - Descr. &
trav., 247, 2510, 2597,
2776, 3063, 3551, 3938,
3955, 4411, 4495, 4651,
4727, 5626, 5627, 5770,
12142
Nebraska - Descr. & trav.,-
Guide-books, 3735
Nebraska - Fiction, 5655
Nebraska - Gold discoveries,
2510, 4727
Nebraska in 1857, 5770
Nebraska legends and
poems, 11938
Necaxa, Mexico, 8273
Neck, S. Sanders, 4580
Necromancy in the
wilderness, 2678
Ned Myers, 9139
Nederlandsche Oost-
Indische compagnie, 348
Nederlandsche West-
Indische compagnie, 348,
1516
Nederst ved bordet, 3896
Neelmeyer-Vukassowitsch,
Heinrich, 4581
Neêrlands West-Indie in
zijne belangen, 1126
Neese, George Michael,
1839-, 4582
Negro-English dialects,
3643
The Negro in the New world,
4076
Negro literature - Hist.

& crit., 12421
Negro literature - U. S.,
7165
The negro melodist, 4044
Negro myths from the Georgia
coast told in the
vernacular, 4106
Negro race, 445, 2257, 13019
Negro songs, 4044
Negroes, 116, 703, 1823, 1890,
1929, 2165, 3819, 3896,
12421, 12422, 13237
Negroes - Baltimore, 13449
Negroes - Biog., 1890, 12421
Negroes - Civil rights,
960, 1304
Negroes - Colonization,
703, 1340, 1383, 2257
Negroes - Colonization -
Africa, 503, 639, 1340,
1459, 1699, 5039, 6429,
6486, 7513, 11563, 11565,
11783, 12506, 12508, 12618,
12692, 12827
Negroes - Education, 357,
13292
Negroes - France, 5952
Negroes - French Antilles,
6172, 6484, 6770, 6896,
6897, 7622, 7738
Negroes in Antigua, 397
Negroes in Haiti, 12861
Negroes in Jamaica, 11943,
13147
Negroes in the U. S., 3260,
3827, 3975, 4076
Negroes in the U. S. - Fiction,
2982
Negroes in the West Indies,
11235
Negroes - Legal status, laws,
etc., 13147
Negroes - Massachusetts, 1328
Negroes - Moral & soc. cond.,
4839
Negroes - New York (State),
12366
Negroes - Politics and
suffrage, 11376

333

Negroes - Religion, 646
Negroes - South Carolina,
46, 2769, 8459
Negroes - Southern states,
4813
Negroes - U. S. 8047
Negroes - West Indies,
1823
Negroes - West Indies,
British, 6339
Nehiro-iriniui aiamihe
massinahigan, 7215
Neidé, Charles A., 4583
A neighbor's landmark,
10038
Neighbours' prescriptions,
10841
Neilson, Peter, 1795-
1861, 4584
Nell' America del Nord,
5915
Nellie Norton, 11100
Nellie of Truro, 9922
Nelly Bracken, 10098
Nelson, George E. W.,
2054
Nelson, Helge Magnus
Oskar, 4585
Nelson, Henry Addison,
1820-1906, 7571
Nelson, Robert, 1656-
1715, 1556
Nelson, Robert, missionary
in China, 7572
Nelson, S., 8837
Nelson Valley railway and
transportation company,
7575
Nelson, Wilbur, 7573
Nelson, William, fl. 1720,
11660
Nemesis, 10944
Nemos, William, 1848-,
5996
Neptune (Steamship),
6302
The Nereid, 9527
Nesbitt, C. R., ed., 11457
Neshaminy, Pa. Log

college, 141
Nesterowicz, S., 4586
Nestor, pseud., 94
The nests at Washington, 4774
The net in the bay, 2536
Netherlands - Colonies -
Administration, 1127
Netherlands - Colonies -
Guiana, 1516
Netherlands - Colonies -
West Indies, 1127
Netherlands - Comm., 12988
Netherlands - Commercial
policy, 12988
Netherlands - For. rel. -
Gt. Brit., 2026
Netherlands - For. rel. -
Portugal, 104, 340
Netherlands - For. rel. -
U. S., 56
Netherlands - Hist., Naval,
1435, 7827
Nettie (Yacht), 7012
Die Neue Welt, 6557
Neuf mois aux États-Unis
d'Amérique, 13045
Neuman, Henry, 7243, 7244
"Die neuner", 5334
Neuroptera - North America,
12523
Neuroptera - South America,
12523
The neutral French, 11171
Neutrality, 1141, 1143, 1204,
11808, 12222, 12668, 13405
Nevada - Descr. & trav.,
3212, 4931, 5152, 5685,
7057
Neverfail, 4992
Never had no sleep, 10808
Nevers, Edmond de, 4587
Nevin, John Williamson,
1803-1886, 2321
Nevves from Virginia, 4947
The new Adam and Eve, 9823
The new age of gold, 10493
New Almaden quicksilver
mines, California, 1166
New America, 3259

334

The new American rational
spelling-book, 5743
A new and compleat intro-
duction to the grounds
and rules of musick,
985
A new and comprehensive
gazetteer of Virginia,
4404
A new and most exact account
of the fertile and famous
colony of Carolina, 3106
The new assistant at
Pine Clearing School,
6965
New Boston, N. H. -
Geneal, 1987
New Boston, N. H. -
Hist., 1952, 1987
New Britain, 12051
New Brunswick, 524, 6911,
12219
New Brunswick - Bound. -
Maine, 13463
New Brunswick - Descr. &
trav., 524, 4078
The new cashier, 9463
The new doctrine, 10610
New England, 11286, 11336
New England - Biog.,
12007
New England bride,
Recollections of a, 3604
New England - Church
history, 621, 13375
New England - Comm.,
751, 2009
New England - Descr. &
trav., 2959, 3595,
3991, 4574, 4998, 6517,
13366, 13367
New England - Descr. &
trav. - Guide-books,
2147, 12495
New England - Descr. &
trav. - Maps, 7764
The New England farmer,
11957
The New England farrier,

13224
New England - Fiction,
8971, 10563
New England - Geneal,
2219, 7971
New England historical and
genealogical register,
2090, 12153
New England - Hist., 53,
10854, 13419
New England - Hist. -
Colonial period, 12, 34,
1148, 1456, 1513, 2306,
11865, 12747, 12970,
12976
New England - Hist. - Colonial
period - Fiction, 767,
10958
New England - Hist. -
Chronology, 11496
New England life in a
village, 11773
New England Mississippi land
company, 1346
A New England nun, 9575
New England - Pol. & govt.,
71
New England - Pol. & govt. -
Colonial period, 1553,
13002, 13375
A New England prophet, 9578
New England - Religion,
11764
New England - Soc. life &
cust., 10, 779, 2244,
9409, 9620, 10818, 10828,
11036, 12841
New England society of San
Francisco, 13021
New England society of the
city of New York, 633,
1755, 11772, 12578, 12790
A New England tale, 10727
New England tears for old
Englands feares, 12881
New England theology,
11896
New England's chattels,
9475

335

New England's Jonas cast
up at London, 1886
New France, 6735
New France - Bibl., 2217,
7149, 12718
New France - Descr. &
trav. - Maps - Bibl.,
12718
New France - Disc. &
explor., 1289, 1481,
1482, 1827, 3666, 5433,
6396, 6403, 6404, 7008,
7149, 7197, 7268, 7404,
8401, 11715, 11762
New France - Geneal -
Dictionaries, 8153
A new gazetteer of the
U.S.A., 3173
A new geographical,
historical, and
commercial grammar,
3722
The new gold mines of
Western Kansas, 4708
The new gospel of peace,
8378, 11148
New Hampshire - Biog.,
11747
New Hampshire - Descr. &
trav., 13336
New Hampshire - Descr. &
trav. - Gazetteers,
11747, 12138, 12765
New Hampshire - Descr. &
trav. - Guide-books,
1034
New Hampshire - Fiction,
11032
New Hampshire - General
court, 11419, 11504,
11792, 12361, 12551
New Hampshire grants,
176, 13206
New Hampshire historical
society, Concord, 11418
New Hampshire - Hist.,
897, 1084, 11747, 11752
New Hampshire - Hist. -
Colonial period, 1083

New Hampshire - Hist. -
Colonial period - Sources,
11419
New Hampshire infantry. 2d
regt., 1861-1865, 3824
New Hampshire infantry. 3d
regt., 1861-1865, 3086
New Hampshire infantry. 18th
regt., 1864-1865, 4285
New Hampshire. Laws, statutes,
etc., 11755
New Hampshire - Militia -
Handbooks, 2220
New Hampshire patriot and
state gazette, 936
New Hampshire - Soc. life &
cust., 9409
New Hampshire - Stat.,
12765
New Harmony, Indiana, 4668
New Harmony, Indiana. Tornado,
1852, 11739
The new Harry and Lucy,
9688
New Haven, 5760
New Haven - Antiq., 787
New Haven - Descr. - Guide-
books, 781, 12030
New Haven - Descr. _ Views,
792
New Haven. First church of
Christ, 642
New Haven - Hist., 787, 788
A new home - who'll follow?
10149
New Homes in the West, 5276
New Indian sketches, 5182
A new invasion of the
South, 3099
New Ipswich, N. H. - Hist.,
953
New Jersey - Biog., 475
New Jersey. Constitution,
12436
New Jersey - Descr. & trav.,
784, 1651, 3446, 3568
New Jersey - Descr. & trav. -
Gazetteers, 12312
New Jersey - Descr. & trav. -

Guide-books, 12486
New Jersey - Hist.,
784, 12313
New Jersey - Hist. -
Colonial period, 1651,
7574, 13257
New Jersey - Hist.,
Local, 784
New Jersey infantry. 9th
regt., 1861-1865,
3294, 5043
New Jersey infantry. 13th
regt., 1862-1865, 5434
New Jersey. Legislature,
7574
The new life of Virginea,
4070
New London, Conn., 44
New London, Conn. -
Biog., 1842
New London, Conn. -
Hist., 1842
New map of the mining
regions of Oregon, 4249
New Mexican common life,
10863
New Mexico, 3688, 6893,
6894, 6895
New Mexico - Antiq.,
2915, 11474
New Mexico - Descr. &
trav., 1145, 2488,
2555, 2624, 3197, 3268,
3343, 3415, 3955, 4150,
4333, 4500, 4715, 4799,
4922, 5060, 5167, 5512,
5545, 5546, 5753, 6139,
6165, 8108, 8408
New Mexico - Fiction, 4497,
4925
New Mexico. Historical
society, 1150
New Mexico - Hist., 1150,
3068, 3343, 11474
New Mexico - Hist. -
War with Mexico, 1845-
1848, 3151, 3962
The new military guide,
2220

The new mirror for travellers,
10488
The new moon, 4988
The new Munchausen, 10485
New Orleans as I found it,
3327
New Orleans, Battle of,
1815, 1862, 2072, 3079,
3625, 4810
New Orleans, Battle of,
1815 - Fiction, 3036
New Orleans batture, 13393
New Orleans - Descr., 3424,
3425, 3597, 3647, 3732, 3755,
3828, 3947, 4178, 5212, 7159
New Orleans - Direct., 1756
New Orleans - Fiction,
4735, 5037, 5447
New Orleans - Hist., 3006,
3725, 4201
New Orleans - Hist. -
Civil war, 3091
The New Orleans sketch-book,
11131
New Orleans - Soc. life &
cust., 3327, 3732
New Orleans. Ursuline convent,
3725, 5453
A new parishoner, 10040
The new pastoral, 13465
New pictorial history of the
life and times of the
pioneer heroes and heroines
of America, 5460
The new Pilgrim's progress,
9027
The new purchase, 12554
The new regime, 1765-1767,
2523
New Rochelle, N. Y. -
Descr. - Guide-books, 11345
A new route from Europe to
the interior of North
America, 7575
New Salem as I knew it,
5989
New Salem, Ill. - Hist.,
5989, 7642
New Salem, Ill. - Poetry,

1741, 12911
New York (City) - Police,
852
New York (City) - Pol.
& govt., 8378, 11145,
11148, 11769
New York (City) - Popu-
lation, 12476
New York (City) - Public
works, 12338
New York (City) - Sanit.
affairs, 988
New York (City) - Soc.
life & cust., 1893,
9547, 9937, 12025,
12086, 12158, 12159,
13330
New York (City) - Stat.,
12674
New York (City) - Suburbs,
12850
New York (Colony), 1552,
12931
New York (Colony) Governor
(Benjamin Fletcher,
1692-1695), 981
New York (Colony) Provincial
congress, 1775-1776,
7577
The New York conspiracy,
12911
New York (County) Court
of general sessions,
13188
New York - Descr. & trav.,
2704, 2773, 3603, 3827,
4222, 5147, 5263
New York. Elgin botanic
garden, 12916, 12918
New York. Exhibition of
the industry of all
nations, 1853-1854,
12373
New York - Fiction, 9505
New York. Hahnemann
hospital, 9056
New York historical society,
74, 1148, 1553, 5900,
11529, 12112, 12158,

12917, 13227
New York in slices, 9546
New York infantry. 2d regt.,
1776-1783, 4589
New York infantry. 5th regt.,
1861-1863, 3177
New York infantry. 5th regt.,
1864-1865 (Veteran), 5422
New York infantry. 9th regt.,
1861-1863, 5694
New York infantry. 12th regt.,
1861-1864, 5422
New York infantry. 16th regt.,
1861-1865, 3144
New York infantry. 33d regt.,
1861-1863, 13343
New York infantry. 48th regt.,
1861-1865, 4602, 4687
New York infantry. 57th regt.,
1861-1864, 3422, 3533
New York infantry. 60th regt.,
1861-1865, 3337
New York infantry. 76th regt.,
1862-1864, 5184
New York infantry. 79th regt.,
1861-1865, 4317, 5430
New York infantry. 81st regt.,
1861-1865, 3211
New York infantry. 83d regt.,
1861-1864, 13162
New York infantry. 97th regt.,
1862-1865, 12926
New York infantry. 104th regt.,
1862-1865, 12926
New York infantry. 105th regt.,
1862-1863, 12926
New York infantry. 112th regt.,
1862-1865, 13060
New York infantry. 115th regt.,
1862-1865, 3011
New York infantry. 117th regt.,
1861-1865, 4543
New York infantry. 124th regt.,
1862-1865, 5682
New York infantry. 125th regt.,
1862-1865, 2469
New York infantry. 146th regt.,
1862-1865, 3518
New York infantry. 173d regt.,

New York. State prison,
New York, 1965, 2180
New York (State).
Secretary of state,
12930
New York (State) - Soc.
life & cust., 12241
New York (State)
University. Division
of visual instruction,
7578
New York Stock Exchange,
12634
New York. Trinity
church, 1209, 1210,
1211, 12817, 13289
New York typographical
society, 13223
New York. Union league
club, 13181
New York university,
389, 2126, 13340
New Zealand - Descr.
& trav., 7556, 7858
Newberry, John Strong,
1822-1891, 5524
Newbrough, J. B.,
supposed author, 9493
Newbury, Mass. - Hist.,
1972
Newburyport, Mass. -
Hist., 1972
Newcastle, Thomas Pelham-
Holles, 1st duke of,
1693-1768, 2028
Newcomb, Mary A., "Mrs.
H. A. W. Newcomb,"
1817-1893? 4590
Newcombe, C. F., 7460,
7579
Newcomer, Christopher
Armour, 4591
Newell, Chester, 4592
Newell, Peter, illustr.,
10889, 10896
Newell, William R., ed.,
6152
Newenham, Thomas. A view
of the natural and

commercial circumstances of
Ireland, 13113
Newfoundland, 384, 1541,
11366, 13498
Newfoundland - Descr. & trav.,
383, 2902, 6550, 6954,
7784
Newfoundland - Descr. & trav. -
Maps, 11707, 13498
Newfoundland - Hist., 383,
7197, 7784
Newfoundland in 1842, 11366
Newlin, William Henry, 4593
Newman, C. J., illustr.,
8477
Newman, Francis William,
1805-1897, 7580
Newman, John B., 7581
Newport, R. I., 5840
Newport, R. I. - Hist.,
1792
Newport, R. I. Old stone
mill, 11543
Newporte, Christopher, 4947
News from New England, by
Thomas Lechford, 13375
News from the mines! 4594
The newsboy, 10802
Newsome, Edmund, 4595
Newspaper-poetry, 11584
Newspapers, 6266
Newspapers - Direct., 1983
Newstead Abbey, 4027
Newton, Sir Isaac, 1642-
1727, 1324, 4227
Newton, Joseph, of London,
Eng., 4596
The next room, 9581
The next time, 7118, 10012
Nez Percé and Salmon River
gold mines, 4308
Nez Percé language -
Glossaries, vocabularies,
etc., 4690, 5018
Niagara Falls, 3092
Niagara Falls - Descr.,
796, 1694, 4636, 7008, 7438,
11242, 13117
Niagara Falls - Descr. -

Guide-books, 8246,
12995, 13238
Niagara Falls - Poetry,
1331, 1672
Niagara frontier -
Hist., 939
Niagara, Ont. - Hist.,
6532
Niblett, Mollie Glen,
ed., 8106
Nicaise, Auguste, 1828-,
4597
Nicaragua canal, 1124,
1125, 1897, 7338, 7751,
11654
Nicaragua - Descr. &
trav., 7750, 7883,
7917, 7974, 11461,
11655
Nicaragua - Hist., 890
Nicaragua - Hist. -
Filibuster war, 1855-
1860, 7338, 11679
Niccolls, Samuel Jack,
1838-, 7582
Nicely, Wilson, 4598
Nicholas, Francis Child,
1862-, 7583
Nicholas, George, 1755?-
1799, 4599
Nicholas, Thomas, fl.
1560-1596, tr., 6863
Nichols, Beach, 1068
Nichols, George Ward,
1837-1885, 4600,
4601
Nichols, James Moses,
1835-1886, 4602
Nichols, James Thomas,
1865-, 7584
Nichols, Thomas Low, 1815-
1901, 4603
Nicholson, Mrs. Eliza Jane
(Poitevent) 1849-1896,
4604
Nick Whiffles, the trapper
guide, 7887
Nicklin, Philip Holbrook,
1786-1842, 4605

Nicolas, John, 1761-1819,
295
Nicolette and Aucassin,
9678
Nicollet, Joseph Nicolas,
1786-, 4606
A niece of Snapshot Harry's,
6969
Nielsen, Roger, 1888-,
4607
Nieremberg, Juan Eusebio,
1595-1658, 5907
Nieuwe wereld, 5487
The night and its morning,
8870
A night at "Hays", 6965
The night before Thanksgiving,
10042
A night in Fort McHenry,
10310
A night in the sewers,
10899
A night on the divide, 9793
Night-watches, 11075
A night with the Jesuits
at Rome, 9497
A night with William of
Wykeham, 10283
The Nikkur Holl, 10693
Niles, Henry Edward, 1823-1900,
7585
Niles, Nathaniel, 1741-1828,
11688
Nina, 9669
Nine months in Rebel
prisons, 5665
Nine months in the quarter-
master's department, 4245
Nine years of Democratic
rule in Mississippi, 13205
Nineteen months a prisoner
of war in the hands of the
Rebels, 2538
Ninety years ago, June 16,
1858, 7586
Niobrara River, 4246
Niox, Gustave Léon, 1840-1921,
7494
Nisbet, James Cooper, 4608

Nitrous oxide, 11911
Nizza, Marco da,
  1510(ca.)-1570, 4631
No mistake, 12617
No news, 11075
Noachidae, 9885
Noah, and his descendants,
  9885
A noble lord, 10840
Noble, Mason, 1809-1881,
  7587
A noble woman, 10870
The nobleman's son,
  8541
Nobles, William H.,
  4609
Nobody, 11096
Nobody's husband, 9199
The No-din', 9283
Noël, François Joseph
  Michel, 1755-1841,
  tr., 5894
Noel, Theophilus, 1840-,
  4610
Nöggerath, Johann Jakob,
  1788-1877, 6254
Nolden, Arnold, pseud.,
  7741
Noll, Arthur Howard,
  1855-, ed., 4877
Nolte, Vincent Otto,
  1779-1856, 4611
The nomination of Abraham
  Lincoln, 6706
Nona Vincent, 7126
Nonantum and Natick, 13141
Nonsense, 10536
The nooning tree, 11162
Nora Brady's vow, 9415
Norah, 9892
Nord-sud, 2649
Nordamerika, die Vereinigten
  Staaten nebst einem
  Ausflug nach Mexiko,
  5980
Nordamerika, natur och
  kulturbygd, 4585
Nordamerika - Ohio, 12062
Der nordamerikanische

freistaat Texas, 5021
Nordhoff, Charles, 1830-
  1901, 4612, 8597
Norfolk district medical
  society, 132
Norfolk, Va., 4966
Noriega, Eduardo, 7588
Noriega, José Esteban de,
  7271
Norman, Benjamin Moore,
  1809-1860, 7589, 7590
Norman Leslie, 9505
Normandy - Hist., 12082
Norridgewock Indians, 198
Norridgewock, Me. - Hist.,
  198, 12657
Norris, John T., 1838-,
  6164
A Norseman's pilgrimage,
  8834
Norteamérica al dia, 3853
Norte América y los norte
  americanos, 6422
North America, 8150, 12310
North America - Antiq., 933
North America - Biog., 201, 202,
  203
North America - Climate,
  4039, 5049
North America - Descr. &
  trav., 1071, 1560, 2529,
  2540, 2541, 2549, 2667,
  2701, 3647, 4248, 4441,
  4575, 4649, 4682, 5010,
  5082, 5480, 5568, 6073,
  6167, 6797, 7225, 7266,
  7368, 8228, 8229
North America - Descr. &
  trav. - Gazetteers, 3178,
  4613
North America - Descr. &
  trav. - Guide-books, 6090
North America - Disc. &
  explor., 7629
North America - Entomology,
  4684
North America Fur Company,
  2823
The North-American and West

343

Indian gazetteer, 4613
North American pamphlet
  on South American affairs,
  11478
The North American tourist,
  4614
North and South, 10719
The North and South
  American review, 7757
North Carolina, 4615
North Carolina - Biog.,
  1169, 5684
North Carolina - Bound. -
  Virginia, 2878, 5188,
  11656
North Carolina - Descr.
  & trav., 426, 491,
  2553, 2568, 2745, 2773,
  2799, 2959, 2997, 3261,
  3340, 3403, 3425, 3516,
  3519, 3568, 3603, 3626,
  3678, 3720, 3766, 4173,
  4217, 4231, 4236, 4486,
  4588, 4646, 4682, 4790,
  4998, 5040, 5087, 5109,
  5147, 5444, 5768, 5798,
  11515, 11656
North Carolina - Descr.
  & trav. - Guide-books,
  4615
North Carolina - Fiction,
  10543, 10903, 10922,
  11133
The North Carolina guide
  and business office
  companion, 3766
North Carolina historical
  society, 13116
North Carolina - Hist.,
  1169, 3499, 5683, 5684
North Carolina - Hist. -
  Colonial period, 426,
  2553
North Carolina - Hist. -
  Revolution, 3418, 12136,
  13308
North Carolina infantry.
  30th regt., 1861-1865,
  2702

North Carolina - Pol. & govt. -
  1865-, 2439
North Carolina (Province) -
  Econ. cond., 2765
North Carolina. Trustees of
  the public libraries,
  11515
North Chelsea, Mass., 11684
North, Frederick North,
  baron, 1732-1792, 11969,
  13499
The North Georgia gazette
  and winter chronicle, 7591
North Pacific exploring
  expedition, 1853-1856,
  12328
North pole, 877, 878
North, Thomas, 4616
Northampton, Mass. - Descr. -
  Guide-books, 2181
Northampton, Mass. - Geneal,
  200
Northampton, Mass. - Hist.,
  200, 1504
Northborough, Mass. First
  Congregational Unitarian
  church, 184
Northeast boundary of the
  U. S., 519, 1421, 2377,
  6998, 10817, 12186, 12409,
  12617, 13150, 13463
Northeast passage, 11623
Northend, William Dummer,
  1823-1902, 7592
Northern and southern friends,
  11951
The northern invasion of
  October, 1780, 12928
Northern Pacific Railroad,
  8261, 13103
Northern Pacific Railroad -
  Explorations and surveys,
  4208
Northern Pacific Railway -
  Fiction, 10225
Northern railroad company
  (N. Y.), 12762
The northern route to Idaho,
  4456

344

The northern traveller,
   2147
Northrop, John Worrell,
   4617
Northup, Solomon, 1808-,
   4618
Northwest British America
   and its relation to the
   state of Minnesota,
   5354, 7510
Northwest, Canadian,
   615, 2585, 3880, 4368,
   4880, 5534, 5963, 6010,
   6048, 6050, 6059, 6238,
   6299, 6311, 6315, 6598,
   6600, 6621, 6727, 6736,
   6769, 6876, 7078, 7384,
   7510, 7542, 7550, 7591,
   7593, 7726, 7808, 7812,
   8123, 8134, 8140, 8148,
   8179, 8387, 12073
Northwest, Canadian -
   Descr. & trav., 2536,
   2604, 3200, 3528, 3529,
   3784, 3877, 3878, 3879,
   4037, 4130, 4362, 4481,
   4482, 4685, 4955, 5057,
   5169, 5354, 5674, 5925,
   5941, 5990, 6055, 6192,
   6237, 6263, 6264, 6283,
   6295, 6314, 6321, 6531,
   6549, 6605, 7009, 7046,
   7209, 7576, 7595, 7830,
   7886, 7922, 8030, 8080,
   8091, 8252, 8256, 8322,
   8428, 13411
Northwest, Canadian - Disc.
   & explor., 6221, 6886,
   6887
Northwest, Canadian - Hist.,
   6052, 6221, 6228, 6235,
   6316, 8000, 8106
Northwest, Canadian - Hist. -
   Sources, 7641
Northwest, Canadian -
   Religion, 5903
Northwest, Canadian - Soc.
   life & cust., 6731
Northwest coast of America,

2647
Northwest coast of North
   America, 6891, 8283
Northwest Company of Canada,
   4348, 6228, 6668, 7009,
   7593, 8000
North-west Fox, 2301
Northwest, Old, 3561
Northwest, Old - Biog., 12021
Northwest, Old - Descr. &
   trav., 1220, 1337, 3124,
   3163, 3359, 3943, 4472,
   4640, 5099, 5263, 5276,
   6271, 6768, 10141, 13360
Northwest, Old - Disc. &
   explor., 4144
Northwest, Old - Hist.,
   1723, 1878, 3869, 4092,
   12184
Northwest, Old - Hist. -
   Sources, 6297
Northwest, Old - Hist. -
   War of 1812, 12741, 13129
Northwest, Old - Soc. life
   & cust., 4382
Northwest, Pacific, 6143,
   6151, 6162, 8179
Northwest, Pacific - Descr.
   & trav., 2508, 2647,
   3542, 3551, 4482, 4549, 4700
Northwest, Pacific - Hist.,
   5017, 5018, 6101
Northwest, Pacific - Maps,
   5506
Northwest passage, 434, 449,
   489, 878, 1201, 1433, 1924,
   2112, 2301, 5632, 6048,
   6195, 6601, 6623, 6624,
   6670, 7109, 7547, 7695,
   7696, 7697, 7812, 7911,
   7912, 7984, 8021, 8050,
   8134, 8283, 12058
The Northwest rebellion,
   6305
Northwest territories,
   Canada - Descr. & trav.,
   8240
Northwest territories,
   Canada - Hist., 6129

Northwest Territory, 6450
Northwestern historical
association, Madison,
Wis., pub., 7455
Northwestern states, 11506
Northwestern states -
Descr. & trav., 3163,
3455, 3862, 4026, 4250,
4686, 5181, 5269, 7009,
11681, 13236
Northwestern states -
Fiction, 7887
Northwestern states -
Hist., 12184
Northwestern territories -
Canada, 6140, 6995,
7641
Northwood, 9700, 9701
Norton, Anthony Banning,
7594
Norton, Charles Ledyard,
1837-1909, 4619, 4620
Norton, Frank Henry,
1836-1921, 3449, 4621
Norton, Oliver Willcox,
4622
Norwalk, Conn. - Geneal,
12568
Norwalk, Conn. - Hist. -
Sources, 12568
Norway - Descr. & trav.,
7170
The Norwich cadets,
11141
Norwich, Conn. - Biog.,
1843
Norwich, Conn. - Descr.,
10761
Norwich, Conn. - Hist.,
623, 1843, 12260
Norwich, Conn. Second
Congregational church,
11351
Norwich university, North-
field, Vt., 13336
Norwich university, North-
field, Vt. - Fiction,
11141
Norwood, 8768

Norwood, Henry, fl. 1649,
4623
Norwood, Joseph Granville,
1807-1895, 4664
Not a hero, 10578
"Not at home", 3937
Not in it, 9089
Notaki z podróży po północnej
i środkowej Ameryce, 4586
Notas a la Recopilación
de Indias, 5972
Notas de viaje, 2894
Notas mejicanas, 6460
Notas sobre las operaciones
del Congreso del Chile,
7275
Note sur les Botecudos,
13282
Notes and letters on the
American war, 994
Notes and sketches collected
from a voyage in the
North-west, 7595
Notes by the way, 3862
Notes from Sunland, 5553
Notes in Mexico, 7265
Notes of a visit to some
parts of Haiti, 12651
Notes of a journey through
Canada, the U. S. A., and
the West Indies, 4288
Notes of a military recon-
naissance, 5516
Notes of a private, 3959
Notes of a short American
tour, 5214
Notes of a short visit to
Canada and the States,
4959
Notes of a summer trip, 5432
Notes of a tour in America,
3196, 5326
Notes of a tour in the
United States and Canada,
2862
Notes of a tour of America,
4484
Notes of fishes collected
in Florida in 1892, 3839

Notes of hospital life, 10433
Notes of travel and mementos of friendship, 5071
Notes on a journey in America, 1337
Notes on Florida, 4624
Notes on public subjects, 5458
Notes on Rio de Janeiro, 7339
Notes on Texas and the Texas and Pacific railway, 5366
Notes on the early settlement of the North-western Territory, 1723
Notes on the Missouri River, 4625
Notes on the Rebel invasion of Maryland and Pennsylvania, 13140
Notes on the slave trade, 1153
Notes on the state of Virginia, 4050
Notes on travel and life, 4447, 13424
Notes pour servir à l'histoire, 12718
Notes upon the western country, 3943
Nothing like it, 11050
Nothing morally wrong, 10195
Nothing to drink, 11215
Nothing to wear, 1775
Noticia del estableci- miento y población de las colonias inglesas en la América Septen- trional, 230
Notice sur la Rivière Rouge, 4626
Notice sur les missions du diocèse de Québec, 5227

Notices concerning Cincinnati, 3290
Noticias de los poblados de que se componen el Nuevo Reino de León, 7219
Noticias sobre que deben informar los subdelegados de jurisdicciones donde haya reales de minas, 7596
Notions of the Americans, 3083
Notizen über Mexico, 7190
Notman (William) & son, 7597
Nott, Charles Cooper, 1827-1916, 4627, 4628, 7283
Nottingham (Galley), 2089
Nouveau voyage dans les États-Unis de l'Amérique septentrionale, 2805
Nouveaux voyages de m^r le baron de Lahontan, 4202
La nouvelle Atala, 5026
Nouvelle relation de la Caroline, 4629
Nouvelle relation de la France équinoxiale, 870
Les nouvelles Amériques, 5964
Nouvelles de Saint-Domingue, 7598
Nouvelles du Scioto, 2507
Nova Britannia, 4071
Nova Lusitania, 1542
Nova Scotia, 5872, 5873, 7379, 12853, 12854
Nova Scotia - Baronetage, 758
Nova Scotia - Bound., 11331
Nova Scotia. Commissioner of public records, 7599
Nova Scotia - Descr. & trav., 4920, 6111, 6487, 6575, 6882, 6954, 8343, 11794, 12777
Nova Scotia - Descr. & trav. - Maps, 11707
Nova Scotia - Econ. cond., 12218, 12614
Nova Scotia. Executive

O I'm a good old rebel,
7804
O' pap's Flaxen, 9605
Oak, Henry Lebbeus,
1844-1905, 5996
The oak openings, 9140
The oak shade, 9486
Oakatibbe, 10783
Oakland, Md., 4694
Oakleaf, Joseph Benjamin,
1858-, 7614, 7615
Oakley, pseud., 3919
Oakridge, 10811
The oasis, 1894
Los oasis del camino,
6375
The oath a divine ordinance,
13355
Oaths - Hist., 13355
Oatman, Lorenzo D., 5299
Oatman, Olive A., 5299
Oaxaca, Mexico (City),
6276
Oaxaca, Mexico - Descr. &
trav., 6084, 7996
Oaxaca, Mexico (State) -
Hist., 1702
Ober, Frederick Albion,
1849-1913, 4633,
7616, 7617, 7618,
7619
Oberländer, Karl, 4634
Oberlin College - Hist.,
5189
The objections to taxation
of our American colonies,
13211
Objevy v Mexiku, 7200
La obra de Alexander von
Humboldt en México,
8111
Obras varias posthumas
del doctor Don Juan de
Solorzano Pereyra, 8072
Obregón Lizano, Miguel,
1861-1935, 7620
O´Brian, Matt, illustr.,
5187
O'Brien, Fitz James,

1828-1862, 8597
O'Brien, Juan Thomond,
1786-1861, 6734
Obsequies of Abraham Lincoln
in Union square, 7621
Observations d'un habitant
des colonies, 7622
Observations in the North,
4819
Observations leading to a
fair examination of the
system of government, 13382
Observations of an Illinois
boy in battle, 3335
Observations on Dr. Price's
Theory and principles of
civil liberty and government,
12304
Observations on Senator Douglas'
views of popular sovereignty,
1368
Observations on the commerce
of the American states, 13477
Observations on the fifth
article of the treaty with
America, 12190
Observations on the Florida
keys, 3579
Observations on the geology
and geography of western
Mexico, 6708
Observations on the importance
of the North American
colonies to Great Britain,
12588
Observations on the plan of
government submitted to
the Federal convention,
13459
Observations on the present
state of the waste lands
of Great Britain, 5789
Observations on the proceedings
in Parliament upon the
petitions against the
Orders in council, 12797
Observations on the reconciliation of Great-Britain,
and the colonies, 12379

Observations on the Rev.
Dr. Gannett's sermon,
11918
Observations on the river
Potomack, 4232
Observations upon the
Floridas, 5572
The Observer, 7623
Oca Nieto de Silva,
Gerónimo María, conde
de Moctezuma, 7456
O'Callaghan, B. B., 3019
O'Callaghan, Edmund
Bailey, 1797-1880,
331, 1704, 11518
Ocampo, Baltasar, 7964
The occasional writings
of Isaac Moorhead,
4513
Occidente, Maria del,
pseud., 8853
Occotlan, Virgin of,
7308
Occult sciences, 6376
The ocean monarch, 9720
An ocean special, 8457
The ocean waifs, 13468
Oceania, 7209
Oceanica, 1066, 2436
Oceanica - Descr. &
trav., 420, 13142,
13479
Oceanica - Disc. &
explor., 13200
Oceanica - Hist., 1112
Oceanus (steamer), 8237
Och, Joseph, 1725?-1773,
7624
Ockside, Knight Russ,
pseud., 11038
O'Connor d'Arlach,
Tomás, ed., 7625
O'Connor, Francisco Burdett,
1791-1871, 7625
O'Connor, John, 4635
Ocuish, Hannah, 1774-1786,
11724
Oda, que para dar principio
a un nuevo certámen de

amor compuso una colegiala,
7626
The Odd Fellow, 4007
Odd-Fellows, Independent
order of - Fiction, 4007
The odd trump, 9183
An odd volume of facts and
fictions, 1783
Oddities in southern life
and character, 5641
Odds and ends from the
knapsack of Thomas Singularity,
10434
Odds and ends of travel,
4636
An ode to Bogle, 1258
Odell, Ruth, 7627
Odes in Ohio, 4775
L'odyssée américaine d'une
famille française, 5074
Oehler, Andrew, 1781-, 4637
Oeri, Albert, 1875-, 4638
O'Ferrall, Simon Ansley, 4639
The office seeker, 9779
An officer of the army, 8619
The officers, 10197
Official correspondence
between the agents of
exchange, 2041
Official documents relating
to a "Chaplain's campaign
(not) with General Butler"
but in New York, 1765
Official letters of the military
and naval officers of the
United States, 1436
Official motorists' guide
to Mexico, 7990
Official report of the
Owyhee reconnaissance,
3299
Official reports of battles,
2068, 2069, 2070, 2071
Un officier de l'armée royale,
347
O'Gavan, Bernardo Hechavarria
y O'Gavan, marqués de,
b. 1812, 11348
Ogden, George W., 4640

350

Ogden, John Cosens,
1751-1800, 7628
Ogden, Peter Skane,
1794, 4641
Ogeechee cross-firings,
4084
Ogilby, John, 1600-1676,
7629
Ogilvie, William,
1846-1912, 7630
Ogilvie, Mrs. O. P.
(Richardson), 7630
Oglethorpe, James Edward,
1696-1785, 3989, 4172,
12709
Oglethorpe, James Edward,
1696-1785. An impartial
account of the late
expedition against
St. Augustine, 2879
O'Higgins, Bernardo,
supreme dictator of
Chile, 1778-1842,
5892, 7631
Ohio and Mississippi
Railroad, 4803
Ohio - Antiq., 542
Ohio - Bibl., 5407
Ohio - Biog., 3868
Ohio cavalry. 2d regt.,
1861-1865, 3580
Ohio - Descr. & trav.,
1014, 2853, 2943, 3138,
3147, 3148, 3408, 3472,
3479, 3745, 3750, 3753,
3792, 3815, 3943, 4472,
4640, 5147, 5382, 5383,
5789, 12062, 12142
Ohio - Descr. & trav. -
Poetry, 3562
Ohio - Fiction, 3744,
9522
Ohio - Hist., 540, 3954,
4367, 7247, 11653
Ohio - Hist. - 1757-1865,
1723
Ohio - Hist. - 1787-1865,
3792, 5602
Ohio - Hist. - Civil war,

11826
Ohio - Hist. - Period., 287
The Ohio hunter, 3352
Ohio infantry. 3d regt.,
1861-1864, 2657
Ohio infantry. 5th regt.,
1845-1848. Co. C, 13158
Ohio infantry. 6th regt.,
1861-1864, 3770
Ohio infantry. 9th regt.,
1861-1864, 5334
Ohio infantry. 11th regt.,
1861-1864, 3940
Ohio infantry. 39th regt.,
1861-1865, 1880
Ohio infantry. 42d regt.,
1861-1864, 4409
Ohio infantry. 53d regt.,
1861-1865, 3313
Ohio infantry. 55th regt.,
1861-1865, 4660
Ohio infantry. 58th regt.,
1861-1865, 5317
Ohio infantry. 63d regt.,
1861-1865, 4036
Ohio infantry. 73d regt.,
1861-1865, 3976
Ohio infantry. 78th regt.,
1861-1865, 5273
Ohio infantry. 101st regt.,
1862-1865, 2868, 3201
Ohio infantry. 105th regt.,
1862-1865, 5439
Ohio infantry. 123d regt.,
1862-1865, 4168
Ohio militia - Sherman brigade,
3882
Ohio - Pol. & govt. - Civil
war, 7565
Ohio river, 337, 4632, 12018
Ohio river - Descr. & trav.,
1133, 1134, 2465, 3124, 3139,
3472, 3509, 5103, 11895
Ohio river - Fiction, 2681,
5380
Ohio river - Navigation,
3139, 11895, 12015
Ohio river - Poetry, 5381
Ohio - Soc. cond., 539

352

The old house by the river,
10573
The old Indian chronicle,
2125
The old inn, 8713
The old Jersey captive,
364
The old judge, 12547
Old Kaskaskia, 8954
Old Madame, 10163
The old maid's secret,
10738
Old maids, 10730
The old man's bride,
8573
The old man's calendar,
2417
An old man's romance,
9070
The old manse, 9823
Old Mark Langston,
4085
The old merchants of
New York City, 2480
Old Mexico and her lost
provinces, 6088
Old neighborhoods and
new settlements, 10841
Old New-England days,
9320
The old plantation, 9971
Old Quebec, 7687
The old red house among
the mountains, 9896
The old revolutionary
soldier, 8491
Old Rube, the hunter,
3908
The old sailor's protégé,
9050
Old Saint Augustine,
4939
Old school Presbyterianism
vindicated, 11564
The old sergeant, 5733
Old song and new, 4855
The old south and the
new, 4141
The old stillhouse in the

hollow, 3556
The old stone house, 10668
Old Sue, 10465
Old theories upset, 6023
The old things, 10017
Old Tildy, 10598
Old times and new, 10714
Old times in middle Georgia,
4086
The old windmill, 10580
The old woman who dried up
and blew away, 10298
Oldfellow, Polywarp, pseud.,
10799
Oldmixon, John, 1673-1742,
4644
Oldmixon, John W., 4645
Oldroyd, Osborn Hamiline,
1842-1930, 7633, 7634, 8132
Oldtown folks, 10907
O'Leary, Daniel Florencio,
1800-1854, 7015, 7635, 7636,
7637, 8127
O'Leary, Simón Bolivar,
ed. and tr., 7635
Olin, Stephen, 1797-1851,
4646
Olinda, Brazil - Capture,
1630, 653, 8323
Oliphant, Laurence, 1829-
1888, 4647, 7638
Olivares, José de, 7639
Olive Branch (Ship), 175, 178
Olive Logan's Christmas
story, 10236
Olive, Pedro María de, tr.,
7087
Oliveira Lima, Manuel de,
1865-1928, 7640
Oliver, Edmund Henry,
1882-1935, ed., 7641
Oliver, Mordecai, 1819-1898,
5507
Oliver, William, 4648
Olliffe, Charles, 4649
Ollivant, Joseph Earle, tr.,
7205
Olmstead, Charles H., 4650
Olmstead, Samuel R., 4651

Olmstead, Victor Hugo,
1853-1925, 6524
Olmsted, Frederick Law,
1822-1903, 12280,
13447
Olney, George Washington,
1835-1916, 4652
Olshausen, Theodor,
1802-1869, 4653
Oltmanns, Jabbo, 1783-
1833, 7092
Omaha, Neb. - Hist.,
13481
Omoo, 10345
On a hill-top, 9764
On a Mexican mustang
through Texas, 5327
On and off the saddle,
8043
On both sides, 8719
On Frenchman's Bay, 9773
On horseback, 5623
On Newfound river, 10464
On picket duty, 131
On practical communication
with the Red River
district, 8141
On revisiting an exile's
grave, 10172
On Sherman's track, 4152
On southern poetry prior
to 1860, 2788
On the battery, 8663
On the beauties, harmonies,
and sublimities of
nature, 11598
On the border, 9623
On the frontier, 9788
On the Mexican highlands,
6661
On the plains, 3373
On the plantation, 9748,
10135
On the present state of
political parties in
America, 4647
On the representation of
minorities of electors
to act with in majority,

in elected assemblies,
12273
On the Suwanee River, 4905
On the trail of a Spanish
pioneer, 6813
On the training of parents,
10892
On the wing of occasions,
9749
On to Washington, 7870
On two continents, 2813
On wheels and how I came
there, 5215
Oña, Pedro de, b. ca.1570,
6469
Once more, 10304
Onderdonk, Benjamin Tredwell,
bp., 1791-1861, 979, 13179
The one fair woman, 10354
One from four, 10465
One good turn, 9689
One hundred and two essays
on the nature of men and
things, 13348
One hundred years ago,
10513
The one I knew the best of
all, 8908
The one-legged dancers,
10006
The £1,000,000 bank-note,
9030
One night's mystery, 9525
One of Bob's tramps, 10808
One of Jackson's foot cavalry,
5771
One of the elect, 11075
One of the Visconti, 2811
One of those coincidences,
10448
One pair of blue eyes,
10427
One poor girl, 10764
One short hour, 9331
One summer, 9647
One thousand smiles, 8523
One year in the civil war,
4859
Onea and Anyta, 10769

Oneida community, 2159
Oneida Indians, 12929
Oneida Indians - Missions,
  1414
Onesimus: Christ's
  freedman, 9173
Onkel Sam, 5801
Only a family party,
  9802
Only a woman's heart,
  10272
The only rose, 10038
An only son, 10040
Onondago co., N. Y. -
  Hist., 11822
Onondago Indians, 11822
Onondago language, 13169
Onstott, R. J., 7642
Ontañon, Eduardo de,
  1904, 7485, 7643
Ontario, 6873, 8048
Ontario - Biog., 12074
Ontario - Descr. & trav.,
  1025, 1095, 2461, 2814,
  3200, 3881, 5103, 6128,
  6996, 7135, 7136, 7527,
  7528, 8225, 11948, 12963
Ontario - Direct.,
  8048
Ontario - Econ. cond.,
  6873, 12337
Ontario - Hist., Local,
  8048
Ontario Lake, 12239
Ontario - Pol. & govt.,
  6997
Ontario - Stat., 6873
Ontwa, the son of the
  forest, 5692
Oonder hoofden, 11183
The open boat, 9214
An open-eyed conspiracy,
  9949
Opening a chestnut burr,
  10651
Opening of the Mississippi,
  3300
Operas - Librettos, 1447
The operations of the

French fleet under the
  Count de Grasse in 1781-2,
  4654
An operetta in profile, 9594
Opie, John Newton, 4655
Opinions on "slavery" and
  "reconstruction of the union"
  as expressed by President
  Lincoln, 7290
Opossums, 927, 929
Opportunity, 10733
Oquino, Juan, 7644
Ora, the lost wife, 10850
Oración fúnebre, 1797
Oran, the outcast, 10449
Orange, 4512
Orange blossoms, fresh and
  faded, 8574
Orange culture in Florida,
  4512
Oranges and alligators,
  3778
An oration, delivered at
  Leominster, July 4, 1815,
  3478
An oration delivered in
  commemoration of the
  festival of St. John the
  Baptist, 3747
An oration delivered in the
  Benevolent Congregational
  meeting-house, 11631
An oration: delivered on the
  occasion of the centennial
  commemoration of the battle
  of the Blue Licks, 2829
Oration on the history of the
  first discovery and settlement of the new world, 3067
An oration, on the propriety
  of introducing the science
  of jurisprudence into a
  course of classical
  education, 1502
An oration on the real nature
  and value of the American
  revolution, 2535
Orations and occasional discourses, 1226

chronicle, 10215

Origine et progrès de la mission du Kentucky, 651

Orleans, Isle of, Quebec - Hist., 11449

Ormond, 8860

Orozco y Berra, Manuel, 1816-1881, 5881, 7649, 7932

The orphan, 11223

The orphan bound-girl, 9495

The orphan of Boston, 10642

An orphan of the Old Dominion, 10914

The orphan sisters, 9883

The orphan's trials, 8788

Orr, J. W., illustr., 4403

Orr, James Lawrence, 1822-1873, 2051, 2053

Orr, Jehu Amaziah, 4657

Orr, Mrs. Lucinda (Lee), 4658

Orr, N., illustr., 4403, 4903, 4924

Orrego Luco, Augusto, 1848?-, 7650

Orrego Luco, Luis, 1866-, 7651

Orrio, Francisco Xavier Alexo de, 1715-1763?, 6160

Orser, John, defendant, 13288

Orta-undis, 4244

Ortega, Eulalio María, 7872

Ortiz de Montellano, Bernardo, ed., 6462

Osage country, 4924

Osage Indians, 3092, 5425, 12971

Osage language - Glossaries, vocabularies, etc., 2784

Osborn, Charles, 1775-1850, 4659

Osborn, Hartwell, 4660

Osborn, Sherard, 7652

Osborne, John, of the Royal mail steam packet co., 7653

Osborne of Arrochar, 9422

Osborne, William H., 4661

Osorio de Moscoso Sarmiento de Valladares, Ventura, marqués de Astorga, 7456

Osorio Mondragón, José Luis, ed., 8439, 8440

Österreichischer touristen-klub, Vienna. Sektion für naturkunde, 7654

Osuna, Joaquin, 7789

Oswald, Felix Leopold, 1845-1906, 7655

Other days, 2785

The other fellow, 10808

The other house, 10013

The other side, 2697

The other side of the question, 13394

Otia conchologica, 12328

Otis, Amos, defendant, 13331

Otis, Belle, pseud., 11202

Otis, George Alexander, 1781-1863, tr., 11390

Otis, James, 1725-1783, 11385, 13492

Otis, Joseph, 1768-1854, 11350

Oto Indians, 3281

O'Toole's mallet, 6151

Otsego co., N. Y. - Hist., 1011

Ott, Adolf, 1842-, 4662

Ottawa Indians, 5343

Otté, Elsie C., tr., 13004

Otto, Fannie (St. Jean de Crèvecoeur) 9387

Otto, John, 4663

Otto the knight, 9582

Otuquis (Dept.) Bolivia,
606
Otuquis Indians, 606
Ould, Robert, 1820-1882,
2041
Our American cousins,
2493
Our American cousins at
home, 4277
Our American neighbors,
6440
Our archery club, 10892
Our Bible-class, and the
good that came of it,
9166
Our boys, 3871
Our campaigns, 5767
Our Chatham street uncle,
11216
Our Christmas in a palace,
9690
Our country and our
Washington, 1769
Our country's mission in
history, 208
Our cousin Veronica, 10168
Our destiny, 10243
Our fire-screen, 10892
Our "first families",
10457
Our general, 10208
Our great peace festival
and pow-wow, 8864
Our homes: their cares
and duties, joys and
sorrows, 8575
Our Indian summer in the
far West, 5451
Our intellectual strength
and weakness, 6133
Our islands and their
people as seen with
camera and pencil, 7639
Our little Mexican cousin,
6262
"Our Joe", 8723
Our knowledge of California
and the North-west coast
one hundred years since,

12876
Our march to Washington,
11194
Our martyred President,
12638, 13270
Our mercies of re-ocupation,
1582
Our modern Athens, 11833
Our motherland, 2957
Our national sins, 12650
Our next-door neighbor,
6986
Our Phil, 9322
Our prospects, 10244
Our refugee household,
9004
Our regiment, 3439
Our Saturday nights,
10537
Our sister republic,
6697
Our story, 10892
Our Tolstoi Club, 10546
Our twelve months' cruise,
684
Our two lives, 11091
Our West Indian neighbors,
7618
Our western border, 4367
Our whole country, 791
Our world, 8460
Out of a pioneer's trunk,
6965
Out of her sphere, 9735
Out of his head, 8500
Out of Nazareth, 10394
Out of season, 9773
Out of the fire, 8981
Out of the foam, 9112
Out of the hurly-burly,
9006
Out of the nest, 3430
Out of the past, 9175
Out of the streets, 9611
Out of the sunset sea,
10994
Out of the wilderness, 8973
Out of town, 9062
Out West, 11380

359

Palatines in New York
(State), 1183
Palavicini, Felix F.,
1881-, 6720
Palenque, Mexico -
Antiq., 1442
Palenque, Mexico -
Descr., 6788
Paleontology - Addresses,
essays, lectures, 12272
Paleontology - California,
1404, 11283
Paleontology - Cretaceous,
2365
Paleontology - Mississippi
valley, 4664
Paleontology - North
America, 866, 11693
Paleontology - Silurian,
866, 11693
Paleontology - U. S.,
494, 2365, 4386,
12685
Palermo, 9508
Palestra historial de
virtudes, 1702
Paletto's bride, 11183
Palfrey, Francis Winthrop,
1831-1889, 4683
Palisot de Beauvois,
Ambroise Marie François
Joseph, 1752-1820, 4684
Pallio de seta, 727
Palliser, John, 1807-
1887, 4685, 4686,
6885, 6886, 6887
Palma y Freites, Luis
de la, 7674
Palmblätter und Schneef-
locken, 4499
Palmer, Abraham John,
1847-1922, 4687
Palmer, Benjamin Morgan,
1818-1902, 4688
Palmer, Donald McN., 4689
Palmer, Frederick, 1873-,
7675
Palmer, Henry Spencer,
1838-1893, 6748

Palmer, Joel, 1810-1881,
4690
Palmer, John, of Lynn, Eng.,
4691
Palmer, John Williamson,
1825-1906, ed., 4692
Palmer, Robert M., 1820-1862,
7676
Palmer, Mrs. Sarah A.,
4693
Palmetto leaves, 5295
Palmyra, N. Y. - Hist.,
12001
Palmyra, Syria - Fiction, 11084
Palos, Spain - Descr., 13109
Paltsits, Victor Hugo,
1867-, 4467, 6575, 7008,
7224
Pam, 11198
Pambrun, Pierre Chrysologne,
jt. author, 7780
Pamphlets on the Constitution
of the United States, 3502
Pan American tourist bureau,
Laredo, Texas, 7677
Pan American Union, 7678
Pan American Union. Travel
division, 7679, 7680, 7681
Pan-Americanism, 5848
Panama, 1250, 12454
Panama and the canal today,
6758
Panama canal, 1250, 1323,
5811, 5970, 6202, 6758,
6759, 6781, 6928, 6999,
7110, 7417, 7751, 7858,
7859
Panama canal - Finance, 1323
Panama canal zone, 6258
Panama canal zone - Direct.,
7110
Panama - Descr. & trav.,
4636, 5811, 5970, 6141,
6202, 6334, 6758, 6759,
6781, 6928, 6999, 7050,
7264, 7417, 7530, 7583,
7750, 7751, 8207, 8403,
9490, 11676, 13502
Panama - Descr. & trav. -

Guide-books, 6983,
7110, 7617, 7681
Panama - Descr. & trav. -
Poetry, 6849
Panama - Direct., 6983
Panama - Hist. - Period.,
7856
Panama, l'oeuvre
gigantesque, 6781
Panama patchwork, 6849
Panama railroad, 6999
Panamanian literature -
Period., 7856
Pandora (Frigate), 12609
Pangborn, Joseph Gladding,
1844-1914, 4694, 4695
Pani, Alberto J., 1878-,
7682
Panics, 13349
Panics - 1836-1837, 1511
Panics - 1857, 1511
Panola, 3274
Panoramas, 762
Pantoja, Domingo de,
pseud., 4872
Paolucci, Giuseppe,
1661-1730, ed., 1873
Papel periódico ilustrado,
7683
Papeles de Nueva España,
7684
A paper city, 10229
Paper money - Connecticut,
11535
Paper money - North
Carolina, 2765
Paper money - U. S., 754,
1457, 11342, 12327,
13487
Paper money - U. S. -
Speeches in Congress,
11262, 11355
Papers from the Canadian
archives, 6297
Papers relating to the
appointment and pro-
ceedings of the Royal
Commission, 6183
Papin, Alexander, 5503

Paraguay - Bound. - Brazil,
591, 596
Paraguay - Descr. & trav.,
592, 598, 1380, 12518
Paraguay - Hist., 1588, 6602
Paraguay - Hist. - To 1811,
592
Paraíba. Conselho estadual
de cultura, 7685
Paraíca - Hist., 7685
Paraíca - Soc. life and cust.,
7685
Parana River, 1028
Pardo, El, Treaty of, 1739,
13505
Pardo, J. Joaquin, 7686
Paris - Descr., 10520
Paris - Hist. - Commune,
1871, 3895
Paris - Hist. - Commune,
1871 - Fiction, 8966
Paris. Muséum national
d'histoire naturelle, 2472
Paris - Soc. life & cust.,
13164
Paris, Treaty of, 1783,
2324, 12190, 13364
The parish-side, 9476
Parisian sights and French
principles, seen through
American spectacles...,
13164
Parke, Daniel, 1669-1710, 11272
Parke, John Grubb, 5522
Parker, Amos Andrew, 1792-,
4696
Parker & Huyett, St. Louis,
pub., 3987
Parker, Francis Jewett,
1825-1909, 4697
Parker, Sir Gilbert,
1862-1932, 7687, 7688, 7689
Parker, Henry Elijah, 1821-
1896, 7690
Parker, Joel, 1816-1888,
7691
Parker, Nathan Howe, 4698
Parker, Samuel, 4700, 4701
Parker, Thomas H., 4702

2466
The patriarch, 10762
Patrick Henry (School-
ship), 2066
The Patriot, 4709
A patriot, pseud., 6792
Patriotic poems, 13161
Patriotism, 1121, 12516
The patriots and guerillas
of East Tennessee and
Kentucky, 1478
The patrol of the mountain,
9297
A patron of art, 9363
El patronato disputado,
6071, 6269
Patten, Edmund, 4710
Patterson, A. W., 4711
Patterson, Adoniram Judson,
1827-1909, 7699
Patterson, Edwin Hamilton
Norton, 4712
Patterson, J. B., of Rock
Island, Ill., ed.,
1366
Patterson, James Willis,
1823-1893, 7700
Patterson, John, 4713
Patterson, John Letcher,
1861-, 4714
The Patterson log cabin,
6459
Patterson, Richard S.,
7701
Patterson, Robert, 1753-
1827, 6457, 6459
Patterson, Robert Mayne,
1832-1911, 7702
Patti, Adelina, 1843-1919,
7544
Pattie, James Ohio, 1804?-,
4715
Patton, Jacob Harris,
1812-1903, 4716
Patty Cannon's times, 11004
Paul, Almarin B., 7703
Paul and Julia, 10532
Paul Ardenheim, the monk of
Wissahikon, 10216

Paul Demarisi's mortgage,
9254
Paul, John, pseud., 11112
Paul Jones and Denis Duval,
9683
Paul Fane, 11181
Paul Lynde's sketchbook, 8500
Paul Patoff, 6500
Paul Perril, the merchant's
son, 9983
Paul Ralston, 9902
Paul Redding, 10599
Paul Ulric, 10330
Paul Wilhelm, duke of Württem-
berg, 1797-1860, 4717
Paul's orange grove, 9254
Paulding, James Kirke, 1778-
1860, 4718, 4719, 4720,
4721, 8355
Paulding, John, 1753-1818,
1175, 1176, 1177
Paulding, William Irving,
1825?-1890, 4721, 10483
Pauline of the Potomac, 2501
Pauline's trial, 9185
Pauw, Cornelius de, 1739-1799.
Recherches philosophiques
sur les Américains, 11364
Pavía, Lázaro, 1844-, ed.,
7844
Pavie, Théodore-Marie,
1811-1896, 4722
Pawlet, Vt. - Geneal, 12857
Pawlet, Vt. - Hist., 12857
The pawnbroker's heir,
2670
Pawnee Indians, 4025, 4571,
5503
Pawnee Indians - Fiction,
4570
Pawnshops - Peru, 8084
Pawnshops - Spain, 8084
Pawtucket, R. I. - Hist.,
11285
Paxton boys, 2317
Paxton boys - Fiction, 9840
Paxton family 7704
Paxton, John D., 1784-1868,
4723

4740
Pefia, David, 1865-, ed.,
5961
Peg, 10863
Peirce, Thomas, 1786-
1850, 4741
Peixoto, Ernest C.,
illustr., 4565
Pelayo: a story of the
Goth, 10780
Pelayo, King of Asturias,
d, 732 - Fiction, 10780
Pelham, Henry, 1695?-
1754, 2028
Pellécer y Pilares, Juan
Antonis, 1738-1806, 399
Pellowe, William Charles
Smithson, 1890-, 7716
Pelzjäger, prärien und
präsidenten, 8410
Pemaquid, 10563
Pemaquid, Me., 12930
Pemaquid, Me. - Descr. -
Poetry, 12515
Pember, Edward Henry,
1833-1911, 13104
Pemberton, 10513
Pemberton, John Clifford,
1814-1881, 2033
Pembroke, 9576
Pemex travel club, Mexico,
7717
Pen and ink portraits,
1679
Pen and powder, 5709
Pen-pictures of the war,
11267
Peña, Domingo de la, 7108
Peña Montenegro, Alonso
de la, bp., d. 1688,
7718
Peña y Reyes, Juan Antonio
de la, 4742
Peñafiel, Antonio, ed.,
947
Peñalosa, Diego Dionisio
de, 1624-1687, 3547
Peñalosa y Zúñiga, Clemente,
7719

Pencil, Mark, pseud., 4743
Pencil sketches, 10197
Pencilled fly-leaves, 4776
Pencillings of scenes upon
the Rio Grande, 190
Pendleton, George Hunt,
1825-1889, 7720
Pendleton, John Strother,
1802-1868, 11686
Pendleton, Louis Beauregard,
1861-1939, 4744, 4745,
4746, 4747, 4748
Penelope's English experiences,
11157, 11159
Penelope's progress, 11158
Penet, Peter, d. 1789,
12929
Peninsular campaign, 1862,
47, 838, 839, 3078, 4391,
13447
The penitential tyrant, 1428
Penitentiaries (U. S.), 3115
Penmanship, 6287
Penn, William, 1644-1718,
850, 2344, 3519, 8165,
11854, 11992, 12993, 13086
Pennacook Indians, 11417
Pennell, Orrin Henry, 7721
Pennington, Edgar Legare, 7722
Pennsylvania, 7002
Pennsylvania cavalry. 1st
regt., 1861-1865, 4286
Pennsylvania cavalry. 7th
regt., 1861-1865, 3271, 5171
Pennsylvania - Charters,
11748
Pennsylvania chronicle,
12293
Pennsylvania college, Gettys-
burg. Philomathean society,
1255
Pennsylvania college, Gettys-
burg. Phrenakosmian society,
1255
Pennsylvania. Constitution,
2355
Pennsylvania. Court of
admiralty, 9918
Pennsylvania - Descr. & trav.,

1014, 1563, 1651, 2170,
2771, 2986, 3472, 3595,
3792, 4300, 4998, 5093,
5147, 7203, 11242, 11785,
11992, 12486, 13163,
13233
Pennsylvania. General
assembly. House of
representatives, 7723,
12900
Pennsylvania German
dialect, 7412
Pennsylvania. Historical
society, 450, 2130,
2248, 2410, 13093
Pennsylvania - Hist.,
6822, 11231
Pennsylvania - Hist. -
Colonial period, 444,
450, 1651, 2317, 2344,
6713
Pennsylvania - Hist. -
Fiction, 1333
Pennsylvania - Hist. -
Revolution, 466, 467
Pennsylvania - Hist. -
Revolution - Fiction,
10066
Pennsylvania infantry.
1st regt., 1776-1783,
2248
Pennsylvania infantry.
37th regt., 1861-1864,
3871
Pennsylvania infantry.
48th regt., 1861-1865,
2766
Pennsylvania infantry.
51st regt., 1861-1865,
4702
Pennsylvania infantry.
63d regt., 1861-1864,
4391
Pennsylvania infantry.
83d regt., 1861-1865,
4127, 4622
Pennsylvania infantry.
85th regt., 1861-1865,
3648

Pennsylvania infantry.
97th regt., 1861-1865, 4857
Pennsylvania infantry.
102d regt., 1861-1865, 5275
Pennsylvania infantry.
106th regt., 1861-1865, 5608
Pennsylvania infantry.
107th regt., 1862-1865, 12926
Pennsylvania infantry.
114th regt., 1862-1865, 4899
Pennsylvania infantry.
141st regt., 1862-1865, 3107
Pennsylvania - Pol. & govt.,
10317, 13101
Pennsylvania - Pol. & govt. -
1775-1865, 2211
Pennsylvania - Pol. & govt. -
Colonial period, 2318
Pennsylvania - Public works,
1458
Pennsylvania railroad company,
7724
Pennsylvania - Soc. life &
cust., 9187, 10317
Pennsylvania. University,
13174
Pennsylvania. University -
Poetry, 694
Penobscot expedition, 1779,
1803
The Pension Beaurepas, 10015
Pensions, Military - U. S.,
7101
Peonage - Peru, 8193
People I have met, 11182
The people and institutions
of the U.S.A., 3490
The people of our neighborhood,
9577
The people's book of American
history, 1598
The people's doctors, 3291
The people's keepsake, 7991
Peoria, Ill., 6653
Pepper, 1203
Pepper, George Whitfield,
1833-1899, 4749
Pepperell, Mass. Evangelical
Congregational society, 599

Pepperell, Mass. First
parish, 599
Pepperell, Mass. - Hist.,
1766
Pepys' island, 371
Pequot Indians, 405
Pequot war, 1636-1638,
2397
Peraza Sarausa, Fermín,
6523
Percival, Charles G.,
4750
Percival Mayberry, The
life and adventures of,
4006
Percival, Olive, 7725
Percival, Thomas, 1740-
1804, 12757
Percy, Algernon Heber, 7726
The Percy anecdotes, 13450
Percy, Mrs. Heber, jt.
author, 7726
Père Antoine's date palm,
8501
Père Jean, 10297
Pereda y Victoria,
Victorino, 7727, 7728
Peregrinación de Philotea
al santo templo, 7672
Pereira, Manuel, 46, 8459
Pereyra, Carlos, tr.,
7640
Pérez Bayer, Francisco,
1711-1794, 400
Pérez de Amézaga, Juan,
7729
Pérez de Arteaga, Diego,
7730
Pérez de Lara, Alfonso,
fl. 1608-1629, 7731,
7732, 7733
Pérez de Lazcano, Diego,
7734
Pérez, Felipe, 1834-,
13451
Pérez Vento, Rafael, 7779
Pérez y Hernández, José
María, ed., 7735
A perfect Adonis, 9755

The perfection of reason,
10487
The perfection of science,
10487
Périgny, Maurice de, 1877-,
4751, 7736
The peril of our ship of
state, 12315
Perils and pleasures of a
hunter's life, 3852
The perils of fast living,
8902
The perils of Pearl street,
9651
The perils of Peter Pliant,
9494
Perils of the border, 4460
Perils of the period, 9857
Periodicals - Bibl. -
Catalogs, 518
Periwinkle, 9463
Perkins, Eli, pseud., 10162
Perkins, Frederic Beecher,
1828-1899, 9693
Perkins, James Handasyd,
1810-1849, 4752
Perkins, Thomas Handasyd,
1764-1854, 13037
La perla de la America, 13350
Perley, Maie Clements, 4753
Perley, Moses Henry, 1804-1862,
6666
Permanent temperance documents,
307
Pernambuco, Brazil (State) -
Descr. & trav., 577
Perrin, William Henry,
d. 1892? 4754
Perrin du Lac, François Marie,
1766-1824, 4755
Perrine's new topographical
war map of the southern
states, 11277
Perry, J. A., 4756
Perry, John Gardner, 1840-
1926, 4757
Perry, Mrs. Martha Derby,
comp., 4757
Perry, N., 10163

Perry, Oliver Hazard,
1785-1819, 1697
Perry's saints, 4602
Perryman, James, d. ca.1882,
1648
Persat, Maurice, 1788-1858,
4758
Persecution, 2298
Perseverence of the
saints, 4343
Persia - Fiction, 4923
Personal experiences in
the war of the great
rebellion, 4538
Personal forgiveness and
public justice, 11375
Personal liberty and
martial law, 13090
Personal liberty laws,
1814
Personal memoirs and
recollections of
editorial life, 11606
Personal memories,
social, political,
and literary, with
sketches of many noted
people, 4384
Personal narrative of
travels in the U. S.
and Canada in 1826,
6576
Personal recollections of
Joan of Arc, 9031
Personal recollections of
the civil war, 3598
Personal reminiscences of
a Maryland soldier,
2762
Personals, 9857
Persons and pictures from
the histories of France
and England, 9847
Perth, Ontario, 1095
Peru, 7167
Peru - Antiq., 11330
Peru - Biog., 7770
Peru - Commerce, 5855
Peru - Descr. & trav.,

6594, 6929, 6930, 7050,
7218, 7411, 8193, 11403,
11654
Peru - Econ. cond., 6732
Peru - Hist., 5937, 6732,
6794, 7964, 8029, 8291
Peru - Hist. - To 1548, 11708
Peru - Hist. - 1548-1820,
6814
Peru - Hist. - 1548-1820 -
Period., 7463
Peru - Hist. - To 1820, 6468
Peru - Hist. - Conquest,
1522-1548, 122, 408, 1015,
12448
Peru - Hist. - Period.,
5956, 7857
Peru - Hist. - War of inde-
pendence, 1820-1829, 436,
6250, 6640, 6814, 7015,
7322, 7506, 7709, 8112
Peru - Laws, statutes, etc.,
2198
Peru. Milicias disciplinadas,
5886
Peru - Period., 6794, 7464,
7857
Peru - Pol. & govt., 6367
Peru - Soc. life & cust.,
1245
Peru (Viceroyalty) Laws,
statutes, etc., 5886,
6366, 6367, 6368, 6519
Peruvian coast pilot, 2391
Peruvian literature -
Period., 7463
The Peruvian nun, 9721
Pervana de S. María, Rosa,
7694
The pest house, 10310
The pestilence - God's
messenger and teacher,
11903
Petals plucked from sunny
climes, 2817
Pete Featherton, 3754
Peter I, the Great, emperor
of Russia, 1672-1725,
1611, 1612

369

Peter Carradine, 8987
Peter Pilgrim, 2717
Peter, Robert, 1805-
1894, 7737
Peter Rugg, the missing
man, 10693
Peter, Saint, apostle,
7449
Peter Stuyvesant's voyage
up the Hudson, 9995
Peter the parson, 11205
Peter Weaver, 11191
Peters, Absalom, 1793-
1869, ed., 261
Peters, De Witt Clinton,
d. 1876, 4759
Peters, Jeremy, pseud.,
10824
Peters, Richard, 1744-
1828, 1455
Peters, Theodore Curtis,
4760
Petersburg, Va. - Siege,
1864-1865, 4331
Petit-Thouars, Abel du,
7858
Petition nouvelle des
citoyens de couleur des
îles françoises, 7738
Petition, Right of, 76,
13268
Petitions of sundry
inhabitants of the
state of Missouri,
4761
Peto, Sir Samuel Morton,
bart., 1809-1889,
4762
Petrarca, Francesco,
1304-1374, 7739
Petroleum, 11444, 12075,
12220
Petroleum - Pennsylvania,
2030, 12699
Petroleum - Pennsylvania -
Venango Co., 2171, 12699
Petroleum - U. S., 11359
Petrolia, 2030
Pettengill, Amos, 1780-

1830, 12724
Pettes, George William, 1874
Pettit, Charles, 1736-1806,
supposed author, 13071
Le peuple de XXe siècle aux
États-Unis, 3633
"Pew 89": Lincoln and Beecher,
7039
Peyton family, 13452
Peyton, John Lewis, 1824-1896,
4763, 4764, 13452
Peyton, John Lewis, 1824-1896.
The adventures of my
grandfather, 11298
Peyton, John Lewis, 1824-1896.
The American crisis, 11298
Peyton, William Madison,
1805-1868, 13452
Pfeiffer, Ida (Reyer)
1797-1858, 13453, 13454
Pferdekamp, Wilhelm, 1901-,
7740, 7741
Pfister, Albert von, 1839-
1907, 4765
Pfleiderer, Joh. Gottlob,
4766
The phantom of the forest,
2682
The phantoms of the foot-
bridge, 4562
Pharmacy - Societies, etc.,
281
Phases of an inferior planet,
9625
Phases of life in town, 10692
Phelps, Humphrey, supposed
comp., 4768
Phelps, Matthew, 1748(ca.)-
1817, 4767
Phelps's travellers' guide
through the U. S., 4768
Phemie Frost's experiences,
10873
Phemie's temptation, 10945
Phi beta kappa addresses,
1222, 2400
Phi beta kappa. New York
Alpha. Union university,
2078

Phials of amber full
of the tears of love,
2993
Phil Scott, 9715
Philadelphia. Bank
street church, 12425
Philadelphia. Chamber
of commerce, 12080,
13322
Philadelphia. Councils,
207
Philadelphia. County
medical society.
President. Addresses,
13218
Philadelphia - Descr.,
2773, 4928, 11056,
11992, 13086
Philadelphia - Direct.,
1756, 12676
Philadelphia female
anti-slavery society,
534
Philadelphia. First
African Presbyterian
church, 1840
Philadelphia (Frigate),
11965
Philadelphia - Hist. -
Colonial period -
Fiction, 8809
Philadelphia. Mayor's
court, 12834
Philadelphia medical
society, 1923, 2021
Philadelphia. Pennsyl-
vania hall, 2363
Philadelphia - Pol. &
govt. - Civil war,
10925
Philadelphia - Riot,
1849, 10204
Philadelphia. St.
Peter's church, 11977
Philadelphia. Union
league, 7742, 7743
Philadelphia - Wharves,
1033
Philaenus, Junius, pseud.

A letter to Thomas Jefferson,
1807
Philalethes, pseud., 8816
The philanthropic results
of the war in America, 1548
A philanthropist, 10600
Phil-Ellena, Germantown, Pa.,
11667
Philip, 9304
Philip and his wife, 9377
Philip IV, 1605-1665, King
of Spain, 6277
Philip V, 1683-1746, King
of Spain, 6451
Philip, King (Metacomet)
sachem of the Wampanoags,
d. 1676, 12, 403, 12856
Philip, King (Metacomet)
sachem of the Wampanoags,
d. 1676 - Drama, 2157
Philip, King (Metacomet)
sachem of the Wampanoags,
d. 1676 - Fiction, 12856
Philip Nolan's friends,
9691
Philip Seymour, 10273
Philip Vernon, 10368
Philip Vickers Fithian,
journal and letters, 3458
Philip Winwood, 10879
Phillipia, a woman's question,
9302
Philippine Islands, 7994
Philippine Islands -
Commerce, 6161
Philippine Islands - Descr.
& trav., 7639
Philippine Islands - Hist.,
2467, 2468
Philips, George, 8228, 8229
Philips, George, Irishman,
supposed author, 5456
Phillippo, James Mursell,
1798-1879, 4769
Phillips, Mrs. Horatio G.,
1793-1864, 6457
Phillips, John M., illustr.,
7063
Phillips, Samuel, 1752-1802,

714
Phillips, Wendell, 1811-
1884, 7107, 7744
Philly and Kit, 8988
Philo-Bentham, pseud.,
1180
Philo-Jackson, pseud.,
13455
The philosophical and
political history of
the thirteen United
States of America, 3527
Philothea, 8993
Phoenixiana, 9392
Phosphate rocks of South
Carolina and the
"great Carolina marl
bed," 12869
Phosphates - South
Carolina, 12869
Phrenology, 931, 3061
Phyle, Francis Adam
Joseph, 1720(ca.)-
1778, 527
A Phyllis of the Sierras,
9789
Physical geography,
5586, 13004
Physical geography -
Canada, 7979
Physical geography -
Costa Rica, 7620
Physical geography -
Mexico, 6611, 8439
Physical geography -
Mississippi valley,
12015, 12151
Physical geography -
U. S., 3615, 8003,
13016, 13501
Physical survey of
Virginia, 4417
The physician's wife,
10848
Physicians, 2021
Physicians - Biog.,
3705, 3706
Physicians - Cincinnati,
3286

Physicians - Norfolk Co.,
Mass., 132
Physicians - U. S., 12462
Physicienne (Corvette), 421,
422
Physiognomy, 911
Phytogeography, 13426
Pianists, 3856
Piatt, John James, 1835-1917,
4770 - 4779, 4848
Piatt, Mrs. Sarah Morgan
(Bryan) 1836-1919, 4774,
4780-4788
The piazza, 10346
The piazza tales, 10346
Picard, Alfred, 1844-, 7494
Pickens, Andrew, 1739-1817,
12729
The picker and piler, 11183
Pickering, Joseph, 4789
Pickering, Timothy, 1745-
1829, 13495
Pickering, Timothy, 1745-
1829. A letter from the
Hon. Timothy Pickering, 75
The picket line and campfire
stories, 7745
Pickett, Albert James,
1810-1858, 13456
Pickett, LaSalle Corbell,
"Mrs. G. E. Pickett,"
1848-1931, 7746
Pickings from the portfolio
of the reporter of the
New Orleans "Picayune",
9167
Pickle, Peregrine, pseud.,
11040
A pic-nic at the sea-shore,
10197
Picó, Rafael, 7747
Picton, Sir Thomas,
1758-1815, 2354, 11966
A pictorial description
of the U. S., 5113
The pictorial field-book
of the revolution, 13400
Pictorial guide to the
Mammoth Cave, Ky., 4403

A pictorial history of
 Texas, 5413
Pictorial history of the
 civil war in the U.S.A.,
 4302
A picture journey through
 tropical Mexico, 7472
A picture of a picturesque
 country, 4790
Picture of Boston, 11442
The picture of Quebec
 and its vicinity, 11411
Picture-writing, Mexican,
 6105, 6153, 6438
Pictures of society and
 people of mark, 11182
Pictures from Italy,
 6588, 6589, 6591
Pictures from prison life,
 12759
Pictures of the patriarchs,
 4094
Pictures of the Virgin
 and her Son, 8766
Picturesque America,
 6214, 7173
Picturesque B. and O.,
 4695
Picturesque Mexico, 8422
Picturesque Panama, 6999
Picturesque sketches of
 American progress,
 2655
The picturesque tourist,
 7748, 12852
Pidgeon, William, 13457
A piece of red calico,
 10892
Pieces in prose and verse,
 8945
Pierce, Franklin, pres.
 U. S., 1804-1869, 11678
Pierce, George Foster,
 1811-1884, 4791
Pierce, Henry Niles, bp.,
 1820-1899, 4792
Pierce, William Leigh, 4793
Piercy, Frederick, illustr.,
 4281

Pierre, 10347
Pierre, the partisan, 9848
Pierrepont, Edwards,
 1817-1892, 7749
Pierson, Hamilton Wilcox,
 1817-1888, 4794, 4795, 4796
Pietro Ghisleri, 6501
Pike, Albert, 1809-1891,
 3065, 4797, 4798, 4799,
 4800
Pike, James, 1834-, 4801
Pike, Zebulon Montgomery,
 1779-1813, 4802
Pike's Peak, Colorado,
 3008, 3297, 3616, 3987,
 4803, 5573
Pike's Peak, Colorado -
 Poetry, 12407
Pilate and Herod, 10859
The Pilgrim, 5382
Pilgrim fathers, 922, 11824,
 12806, 13026, 13027
Pilgrim fathers - Addresses,
 commemorations, etc., 4,
 80, 219, 633, 711, 1060,
 1061, 1641, 1755, 1853, 1925,
 2150, 11731, 11925, 12306,
 12386, 12578, 12790, 12811,
 12865, 13021
Pilgrim's letters, 5031
A pilgrimage over the
 prairies, 5055
The Pilgrims of Boston and
 their descendants, 1506
A pill for Porcupine, 1945
The pillar of fire, 9984
Pills for the delegates,
 12468
The pilot, 9142
Pilot guides - Atlantic
 coast (North America),
 2526, 2527
Pilot guides - Atlantic
 ocean, 530
Pilot guides - Bahamas,
 1109
Pilot guides - Caribbean sea,
 362
Pilot guides - Haiti,

1109, 13464
Pilot guides - Massachusetts,
  11431
Pilot guides - Mexico,
  Gulf of, 362, 5012
Pilot guides - Peru, 2391
Pilot guides - Rio de la
  Plata, 11393
Pilot guides - West Indies,
  1110, 5012, 7950
Pilots and pilotage,
  6007
Pilsen, John, 13458
Pim, Bedford Clapperton
  Trevelyan, 1826-1886,
  7750, 7751
Pimentel, Francisco,
  conde de Heras, 1832-,
  947
Pimentel, Maria Josefa
  Alfonso, duquesa de
  Benavente, 7321
Pinchon, 10827
Pinckney, Charles, 1758?-
  1824, 295, 13459
Pinckney, Mrs. Eliza
  (Lucas) 1723-1793,
  4804
Pinckney, Henry Laurens,
  1794-1863, ed., 12666
The pine and the palm
  greeting, 5634
Pine knot, 2629
Pinerolo, Italy, Battle
  of, 1630, 8323
Piney Woods tavern, 3762
Pingree, Enoch M., 1816-
  1849, 4059
Pinilla, Sabino, 1851-
  1909, 7752
Pink and black, 11191
Pink Marsh, 8479
Pinkney, William, 1764-
  1822, 2364
Pinzón, Martin Alonso,
  1440?-1493, 7305
Pioneer, 12241
The pioneer bishop, 5302
The pioneer church, 10716

Pioneer history, 3870, 12307
Pioneer life in Richland
  county, Ohio, 10273
Pioneer life in the west,
  3450
Pioneer (ship), 7652
The pioneers, 9143
Pioneers of Scioto County,
  4169
The pious constancy of
  Inez de Mencia Mont-Roy,
  10338
Pious memorials, 1732
The pirate, 10310
The pirate of the Roanoke,
  8699
Pirates, 2123, 9962,
  10074, 11363
Pirates, Caribbean - Fiction,
  11195
The pirates of Cape Ann,
  8614
Pitcairn island, 884, 1554,
  10698
A pitiful surrender, 10122
Pitman, Joseph S., 12403
Pitt, William, 1st earl of
  Chatham, 1708-1778, 222,
  11227, 13460
Pittenger, William, 1840-
  1905, 3417, 4805
Pittman, Hannah (Daviess)
  1840-, ed., 7753
Pittman, Philip, 13461
Pittsburgh - Descr., 4320
Pittsburgh - Direct., 13315
Pittsburgh - Fiction, 11224
Pittsburgh - Hist., 13315
Pixley, Frank, jt. author,
  4904
Pizarro, Francisco, marqués,
  1470-1541 - Drama, 1544
A plain and friendly persuasive
  to the inhabitants of Virginia
  and Maryland for promoting
  towns and cohabitation,
  4378
Plain dealing, 13375
Plain facts, 13508

A plain state of the argument between Great-Britain and her colonies, 13462
Plain truth, 2318
The plains, being a collection of veracious memoranda, 4504
Plan of an improved system of the money concerns of the Union, 11342
Planning machines, 1008
Plantain, John, pirate, 2123
The planter, 2822
The planter's northern bride, 3846
Plants, Cultivated, 13426
P'laski's tunament, 10460
Platonic love, 9249
Platte River, 5421
Playfair, Hugo, R. N., pseud.? 4806
The Playfair papers, 4806
Playfair, Robert, 4807
A plea for a miserable world, 328
A plea for the Indians, 1070
Pleas for progress, 3819
Pleasant Waters, 9017
El pleyto de Hernán Cortés con Pánfilo de Narváez, 6328
Plodder's promotion, 10112
The plough and the sword, 10760
Plum, William Rattle, 4808
The plumb idiod, 9582
Plumero the Good, 9254
Plummer, Mrs. Clarissa, 4577, 12698
Plummer, Mary Wright,

1856-, 7754
Plymouth Co., Mass. - Descr. & trav., 9602
Pneumatic-tube transportation, 13068
Pocahontas, d. 1617, 3190, 4667, 11187, 11735
Pocahontas, d. 1617 - Drama, 1447, 4667
Pocahontas, d. 1617 - Fiction, 9111, 11187
The pocket guide to the West Indies, 5950
The pocket piece, 8633
Poe, Edgar Allan, 1809-1849, 4809
Poe, John William, 1850-1923, 7755
A poem, 816
The poem which the Committee of the town of Boston had voted unanimously to be published with the late oration, 179
Poemas de México, 6646
Poems, 3470, 3821, 4306, 4423, 4848, 5048, 5395, 5470, 5667, 5669, 5738
Poems and essays, 3960
Poems and parodies, 2933
Poems and tales, 8790
Poems by Ellis, 3374
Poems by Samuel Browning, 1604
Poems, national and patriotic, 3150
Poems of America, 4294
The poems of Duval Porter, 4831
The poems of Frank O. Ticknor, 5416
Poems of house and home, 4777
Poems of Orelia Key Bell, 2666
Poems of the Confederacy, 5261
Poems of the Mohawk valley, 11657

Poems of the prairies, 11569
Poems of the Rt. Rev. George Burgess, 1701
Poems of the war, 11325
Poems of two friends, 4778
Poems on man in the republic, 10326
Poems on several occasions, 3713
Poems, original and translated, 3152
The poet soldier, 1659
A poet's message, 6227
The poet's praise, 5242
A poetess, 9575
A poetical picture of America, 4966
A poetical rhapsody on the times, 1945
The poetical works of Elizabeth Margaret Chandler, 2969
Poetry - Collections, 4692
Poetry of places - Colorado - Pike's Peak, 12407
Poetry of places - Guatemala, 7233, 7234, 7237, 7238
Poetry of places - Iowa, 11569
Poetry of places - Italy - Pompeii, 9492
Poetry of places - Maine - Pemaquid, 12515
Poetry of places - Mexico, 6448, 6646, 7233, 7234, 7237, 7238, 7323
Poetry of places - Niagara Falls, 1331, 1672
Poetry of places - Panama, 6849
Poetry of places -

Rhode Island, 1575
The poetry of travelling in the U. S., 3603
The poets and poetry of America, 3701
The poets and poetry of Texas, 3258
The poets and poetry of the West, 3043
Poets, Canadian, 6549
Poezdka v Meksiku, 8011
Poganuc people, 10908
Poindexter, George, 1779-1853, 4810, 12972
Poinsett, Joel Roberts, 1779-1851, 7756
The point of view, 10015
Pointon, Mair, jt. author, 2980
Pokonchi language - Grammar, 2366, 6796, 6799
Poland and liberty, 10197
Polenz, Wilhelm von, 1861-1903, 4811
Poles in the U. S., 4586
Policarpo Bonilla, 7451
Police power - Quebec, 11884
Police, Traité de la, 11884
Policy, as well as honesty, forbids the use of secular force in religious affairs, 622
Política indiana, 8073
A political account of the island of Trinidad, 11966
Political ballads and songs, American, 13050
Political division - British Columbia, 6175
The political economy of slavery, 5041
The political effects of the paper system considered, 13487
Political essay on the kingdom of New Spain, 7088, 7089
Political essays, 12191
Political ethics, 1999, 6779, 9098, 12642, 13151

The political family,
13017
The political green-
house, for the year
1798, 229
Political parties -
New York (State), 13195
Political parties -
U. S., 1746, 6888,
6938, 12866, 13487
Political philosophy,
11547
Political science, 59,
60, 1181, 1606, 6579,
11547, 11781, 12077,
12443, 13042
Political science -
Addresses, essays,
lectures, 13084
Political tracts, 13258
The politician, 10492
The politicians, 10326
Politics and pen pictures
at home and abroad,
3874
Politics - Fiction, 9889
Politics for American
Christians, 1999
Politics in Ohio, 2978
Politics - Poetry, 5218
Poliuto, pseud., 5709
Polk family, 7757
Polk, J. M., 1838-, 7757
Polk, James Knox, pres.
U. S., 1795-1849,
13197
Polk, Jefferson J., 1802-,
4812
Pollard, Edward Albert,
1828-1872, 4813-4822,
5144
Pollard, Hugh Bertie
Campbell, 1888-, 7758
Pollard, The romance of,
8955
Pollen, A. H., illustr.,
8074
Polley, Joseph Benjamin,
1840-, 4823

Polly, 10466
Polly Oliver's problem,
11160
Polygamy, 12887
Polynesia, 8406, 8407
Polynesia - Descr. & trav.,
1172, 10345
Pomfret, Conn. - Hist.,
13015
Pompeii - Poetry, 9492
Ponce, Alonso, 16th cent.,
5874
Pond, Fred E., ed., 3758
Pons, François Raymond Joseph
de, 1751-1812, 2473
Pons, Jacques Samuel, tr.,
1035
Pool, Maria Louise, 1841-
1898, 8969
Poole, Mrs. Annie Sampson,
7759
Poole, T. W., 4304
Poole, William Frederick,
1821-1894, 13053
Poor Caroline, the Indiaman's
daughter, 10882
A poor fellow, 10547
Poor - Gt. Brit., 686
Poor laws, 5882
Poor laws - Gt. Brit., 12337
Poor Mr. Ponsonby, 10546
The poor rich man, and the
rich poor man, 10728
The poor scholar, 9702
The poor unhappy transported
felon's sorrowful account
of his fourteen years
transportation in Virginia,
4934
Poor whites in the South,
3902
Pope, Alexander, 1688-1744,
2917
Pope, Dunbar H., 4825
Pope, John, 4824, 5520
Pope, William F., 1814-1895,
4825
Popham colony, 12748
Popocatepetl, 2186

377

Popp, Stephan, 1755-,
4826
Popp's journal, 1777-
1783, 4826
Poppaea, 9261
Popular excitements, 780
Popular resorts, 2583
The population of the
Valley of Teotihuacan,
7483, 7484
Por las rutas del sureste,
8290
Por las tres Américas,
6561
Por los campos de México,
7235, 7236
Porcher, Francis Peyre,
1825-1895, 4827
Porcupine-Chiltat districts,
6181
Porcupine, Peter, pseud.,
5841
Porcupine's works, 1940
Port Hudson, La. -
Siege, 2587
Portalis, Albert Édouard,
1845-, 4828
Porter, David Dixon,
1813-1891, 4829
Porter, Duval, 1844-,
4830, 4831
Porter, Edward Clarke,
1836-1876, 12521
Porter, Fitz-John, 1822-
1901, 7157, 7312, 7325,
8373
Porter, Peter Augustus,
1827-1864, 11704
Porter, William Trotter,
1809-1858, ed.,
4832, 4833
The Port-folio, 4879
Port Talbot, Ont., 12074
Portland family, Leaves
from the life of a,
8508
Portland, Me. - Commerce,
13103
Portland, Me. First

parish, defendant, 856
Portland, Ore. - Descr.,
4250
The portrait, 10619
Portrait and biographical
album of Henry county,
Iowa, 7760
The portrait of a lady, 7124
A portrait of the times,
2904
Portraits of my married
friends, 11143
Portraitures of Hebrew
character, 10616
Portsmouth anti-slavery
society, 11798
Portsmouth, N. H., 137
Portsmouth, N. H. - Churches,
135
Portsmouth, N. H. - Descr.,
1488
Portsmouth, N. H. - Hist.,
1488
Portsmouth, N. H. - Soc. life
& cust., 10182
Portugal, 696, 1551
Portugal. Armada - Hist.,
1543
Portugal - Bibl., 82
Portugal - Colonies, 1551
Portugal - Colonies - Period.,
379
Portugal - Descr. & trav.,
3228, 5087, 7223, 7224
Portugal - For. rel. -
Netherlands, 104, 340
Portugal - Hist., 11397
Portugal - Hist. - Modern,
1580-, 1543
Portugal - Hist. - Period
of discoveries, 1385-1580,
882
Portuguese in India, 882
Portuguese literature -
Bibl., 82
Posada Gutiérrez, Joaquín,
1797?-1881, 7761
Posadas, Gervasio Antonio de,
1757-1832, 7762

Posie, 9053
The position of Christianity
in the United States,
2000
Posselt, Louis, 7763
The possessed, 8555
The post-mistress of
Laurel Run, 6965
Postage stamps, 6555
Postal service, 6555
Postal service - Confederate
States of America, 11873
Postal service - Rates,
959
Postal service - U. S.,
894
Postal service - U. S. -
Charlestown, Mass.,
552
Postal service - U. S. -
Hist., 2801, 3449,
5336
Postl, Karl Anton,
10717, 10718, 10719
Poston, Charles Dibrell,
1825-1902, 4834
A pot of gold, 9575
Pote, William, 1718-1755,
7764
The Potiphar papers,
9289
The Potomac and the
Rapidan, 4875
Potomac River, 4136,
4232
Potomac Valley - Descr. &
trav., 8051
Potomac Valley - Historic
houses, etc., 8051
Potter, Alonzo, 1800-
1865, bp., 2321
Potter, Eliza, 4835
Potter, William James,
1830-1893, 7765
Potter, Woodburne, 4836
Potts, Daniel T., 4837
Potts, Mrs. Eugenia
Dunlap, 4838
Pouchot, Pierre, 1712-

1767, 7766
Poultry, 1731
Pouponne et Balthazar, 3218
Le pour et le contre, 1495
Poussin, Guillaume Tell,
1794-1876, 7767
Powdermaker, Hortense, 4839
Powell family, 12996
Powell, James Augustus,
1808-1828, 12996
Powell, Lewis Thornton,
called Lewis Payne, 1845-
1865, defendant, 1305
The power of religion upon
the mind, 1732
The power of the commander-
in-chief to declare martial
law, 6669
The power of the "S.F.", 9482
Power to sell land for the
non-payment of taxes, 1377,
1378
Power, Tyrone, 1797-1841,
4840
Power's guide to Mexico
for the motorist, 7677
Powers, Elvira J., 4841
Powers, George Whitefield,
1833 or 4-1903, 4842
Powers, Stephen, 4843
Powers, William, 1765-1856,
5754
Powhatan Indians, 429
Pownall, Thomas, 1722-1805,
4844, 12432
Pozo y Honesto, José del,
7768
Practical essays on medical
education, 3292
Practical lessons under
the code duello, 9910
Practical notes made during
a tour in Canada, 6718
Practical views of Catholicity,
9881
The practice of duelling in
view of human and divine
law, 2807
Prado, Pedro, pseud., 9000

The prairie, 9144
Prairie and mountain
life, 3443
Prairie and Rocky
mountain adventures,
5561
The prairie-bird, 4570
Prairie du Chien, Wis.,
1613
Prairie du Chien, Wis. -
Descr., 3894
Prairie farming in
America, 6271
The prairie flower,
2683
A prairie infanta, 2812
Prairie Grove, 11244
The prairie province,
6941
The prairie traveler,
4388
Prairiedom, 4675
Prairies, 4027
Prantl, Adolfo, 7769
Prat de Saba, Onogre,
1733?-1810, 7770
Pratt, Harry Edward,
1901-, 7771
Pratt, John J., 4845
Pratt, Orson, 4846
Pratter, Henry, 4664
The prayer of the
presidents, 6257
Preaching, 617, 7954
Preble, William Pitt,
1783-1857, 13463
Precaution, 9145, 9146
Precious metals, 1866,
6702
El predicador, 7954
Pre-emption law - U. S.,
4910
Preface, 10338
Prejudice, 8630
Prejudices, 9702
Preliminary studies of
the Texas Catholic
historical society,
5368

The premises of Dorothea,
9376
Prentice, Archibald, 1792-,
4847
Prentice, George Denison,
1802-1870, 4848, 4849
Prenticeana, 4849
Prentis, Noble Lovely,
1839-1900, 4850, 7772
Prentiss, Charles, 1774-1820,
pub., 246
Prepost, Istvén, ed., 5783
Presas y paisajes del agro
mexicano, 6122
Presbrey, O. F., 7773
Presbury family, 6286
Presbyterian church, 13433
Presbyterian church -
Doctrinal and controversial
works, 4893
Presbyterian church - Hymns,
464
Presbyterian church in
Delaware, 2264
Presbyterian church in
New Hampshire - Clergy,
11416
Presbyterian church in the
U.S.A., 674, 853
Presbyterian church in the
U.S.A. - Biog., 141
Presbyterian church in the
U.S.A. Board of foreign
missions, 2375
Presbyterian church in the
U.S.A. Board of publication,
674
Presbyterian church in the
U.S.A. - Catechisms and
creeds - Chippewa, 2375
Presbyterian church in the
U.S.A. Executive committee
of publication, 464
Presbyterian church in the
U.S.A. General assembly,
1802, 1326
Presbyterian church in the
U.S.A. - Schism, 1837-1870,
11564

380

Presbyterian church in the
U.S.A.   (New School)
Presbytery of Phila-
delphia, Third, 13357
Presbyterian church in the
U.S.A.   (Old school),
11564
Presbyterian church in the
U.S.A. - Period., 3167
Presbyterian church in the
U.S.A.   Presbytery of
Ohio, 1326
Presbyterian church in the
U.S.A.   Synod of
Kentucky, 4851, 4852
Presbyterian church in
Wisconsin, 11857
Presbyterian church -
Kentucky, 4866
Presbyterian church -
Sermons, 848, 1063,
1065, 1216, 11317,
12507
Prescience, 5477
Prescott, William Hickling,
1796-1859, 7774, 7775
The present and future
productions of Florida,
4580
The present crisis, 2143
A present for the Whigs
of '76 & '37, 13353
The present problem,
8818
The present state of
Algiers, 1425
The present state of
Great Britain and
North America, 4487
The present state of
North America, 13046
The present state of
Nova Scotia, 12854
The present state of
the British empire in
Europe, 4853
The present state of the
country and inhabitants,
2966

The present state of
Virginia, 3805, 4108
The preservation of the
States united, 12056
President (Steamship), 1619
Presidential candidates, 902
The presidential election,
13455
Presidents - U. S., 6257
Presidents - U. S. - Biog.,
280
Presidents - U. S. - Election,
431, 1817, 8099
Presidents - U. S. - Election -
1840, 7594
Presidents - U. S. - Election -
1860, 6938
Presidents - U. S. - Powers
and duties, 937, 6669,
11361, 11914, 13083
Press congress of the world.
Regional convention,
Mexico, 1931, 6673
Press - Gt. Brit., 226
Press - Hist., 1983
Press - U. S., 1983, 11356
Pressa Carrillo, Isabel de la,
8277
Preston family (John Preston,
d. 1753), 13452
Preston, George C., 1875
Preston, Mrs. Margaret
(Junkin) 1820-1897, 4854,
4855
Preston, Walter, 2046
Preston, William Campbell,
1794-1860, 4856
Preston, William Thomas
Rochester, 1851-, 7776
Prétrel, Louis Nicolas,
1705-1765, 11742
Pretty Mrs. Gaston, 9113
The pretty sister of José,
8909
A pretty story written in
the year of our Lord 2774,
9919
Prevost, Antoine François,
called Prevost d'Exiles,

1697-1763, 211
Price, Isaiah, 1822-,
  4857
Price, Morgan Philips,
  1885-, 4858
The price of liberty,
  10489
The price of peace,
  8454, 9916
The price of the
  harness, 9217
Price, Richard, 1723-1791.
  Observations on the
  nature of civil
  liberty... 12304, 13390
Price, Sir Rose Lambart,
  bart., 1837-1899, 7777
Price, Thomas, supposed
  author, 4275
Price, Thomas W., 7778
Price, William Newton,
  1831-1905, 4859
Price, William Thompson,
  1845-1920, 4860
Price's Missouri
  expedition, 1864, 12796
Prices, 3084, 11684
Prices - Confederate
  States of America, 11871
Prichard, William, fl. 1782-
  1809, 10317
Pricilla, 9463
Prida y Arteaga, Francisco
  de la, 1850-, 7779
The pride of Britannia
  humbled, 1941
The pride of the Mercers,
  3225
Priest, Mrs. Deborah
  (Beach) b. 1768, 10569
Priest, Josiah, 1788-1851,
  11573
The priest of El Paso,
  10863
The priest of the black
  cross, 9615
Priest, William, 4861
The priest's turf-cutting
  day, 10282

Priestley, Herbert Ingram,
  1875-1944, 4862, 6863
Priestley, Joseph, 1733-
  1824, 7270
Prieto, Julio, illustr.,
  5969
The Primes and their
  neighbors, 4088
Primitive Baptists. North
  Carolina. Kehukee primitive
  Baptist association, 11619
Prince Albert (Ship),
  1116, 1117, 8050
Prince Edward island -
  Descr. & trav., 13279
Prince Edward island - Hist.,
  8337
Prince, Frederick O., 6869
The prince of darkness,
  10842
A prince of good fellows,
  10021
The prince of India, 11054
The prince of Parthia, 2427
The prince of the House of
  David, 4008
The Prince of Wales in
  Canada and the U. S.,
  8418
Prince Saroni's wife, 9814
Princess, 10262
The princess Aline, 9361
The Princess Casamassima, 7125
Princess I-would-I-wot-not,
  9916
The princess of the moon,
  10576
The Princess Sonia, 10305
Princeton (Frigate), 1768,
  11648, 12057
Princeton, Mass. Congrega-
  tional church. Mutual
  council, 732
Princeton, Mass. - Hist.,
  12636
Princeton university, 8712,
  12376
Princeton university. Alumni
  association of Nassau hall,

382

1257
A Princetonian, 8712
Principia quedā ex quibus
procedendum, 6362
The principles of civil
union and happiness
considered and recom-
mended, 12303
The principles of naval
staff rank, 1919
Principles of the
revolution, 1412
Printing, 1693
Printing - Hist. - Cuba,
611
Printing - Hist. -
Fiction, 10497
Printing - Hist. -
Kentucky, 6445,
7380, 7885
Printing - Hist. -
Louisiana, 7885
Printing - Hist. -
Spanish America, 8187
Printing, Public -
Confederate States of
America, 2054
Prinz Heinrichs Amerika-
fahrt, 4228
Priscilla, 767
Prismatics, 9196
The "Prison journal" of
Stephen F. Austin, 5968
Prison life in the
Old capitol, 5728
Prison life in the
South, 2487
Prison-life in the tobacco
warehouse at Richmond,
3793
Prison prose and poetry,
10057
The prisoner of Perote,
11023
The prisoner of war, and
how treated, 4970
A prisoner of war in
Virginia, 4867
Prisoners of conscience,

8737
The prisoners of Niagara,
9890
The prisoners of Perote,
8100
Prisoners of war and military
prisons, 4031
The prisoners' memoirs,
356
Prisons, 608, 12675, 12957
Prisons - New York (State),
2279
Prisons of air, 9101
Prisons - Pennsylvania, 2289
Prisons - U. S., 3115, 3229,
4129, 11988
Prisons without walls, 10825
Pritchard, John, 7780
Private Jones of the Eighth,
10122
The Privateer of '76, 9051
Privateering, 411, 1143,
1204, 1221, 1980, 11950
The privateers of the
revolution, 10880
The privilege of the writ of
habeas corpus under the
Constitution, 6082, 11272
The prize essay, 10415
Prize law, 12222
Prize law - France, 12298
Probate law and practice -
New Hampshire, 11755
The probe, 13348
The problem solved, 9883
Problemas de las zonas áridas
de México, 7468
Problemas del trópico mexicano,
7469
Proceedings of a board of
general officers, 354
The proceedings of a court
of enquiry, 12687
Proceedings of a general
court martial for the
trial of Major General
Arnold, 466
Proceedings of a general
court martial of the line, 467

Protestant Episcopal church.
Board of Missions, 3790
Protestant Episcopal church
in Mexico, 6883
Protestant Episcopal church
in the U.S.A., 2943, 2944,
3015, 5643, 12818
Protestant Episcopal church
in the U.S.A. - Board of
Missions, 3267
Protestant Episcopal church
in the U.S.A. Board of
Missions. Domestic
committee, 4863
Protestant Episcopal church
in the U.S.A. - Clergy,
167
Protestant Episcopal church
in the U.S.A. Eastern
diocese, 12453
Protestant Episcopal church
in the U.S.A. - Government,
11337
Protestant Episcopal church
in the U.S.A. - Hist.,
11694, 13510
Protestant Episcopal church
in the U.S.A. - Pastoral
letters and charges,
13166
Protestant Episcopal church
in the U.S.A. - Sermons,
979, 1211, 1740, 12453
Protestant Episcopal society
for the promotion of
evangelical knowledge,
New York, 358
Protestantism, 1998, 4937
Protestants in Mississippi,
13305
Provence - Descr. & trav.,
4227
Providence and government
of God, 13063
Providence. City Council,
7783, 11832
Providence. First Congre-
gational church
(Unitarian), 12565

Providence, R. I. First
Baptist church, 12528
Providence (ship), 6192
Providential escape, 11173
The province of law in
distinction from that of
truth, 11806
Provincial papers, 11419
The prowess of the Whig
club, 2423
Prowse, Daniel Woodley,
7784
Proyecto para el estableci-
miento en México, 7401
Prthibī parikramā, 6413
Prudence Palfrey, 8502
Prud'homme, Louis Arthur,
7785
Prue and I, 9290
Prussia - Descr. & trav.,
11974
Prutsman, Christian Miller,
4864
A psycho-physical study,
9331
Psychology, Religious, 1406
Public morals, 157
Public schools - South
Carolina, 218
Public schools - U.S., 795
Publishers and publishing -
U.S., 3234
El puchero, 7386
Puddleford, and its people,
10620
The Puddleford papers, 10621
Puebla, Mexico, 6077
Puebla, Mexico (Archdiocese)
7669
Puebla, Mexico (City) -
Hist., 6158
Puebla, Mexico - Descr.,
6159, 7442
Pueblo Indians, 8673
Puerto Rico, 8264
Puerto Rico - Bibl., 7305
Puerto Rico - Descr. &
trav., 3, 2252, 6595,
6907, 6948, 7049, 7639, 7747

385

Puerto Rico - Descr. &
trav. - Guide-books,
8264
Puerto Rico - Hist.,
7305
Puerto Rico - Hist. -
To 1898, 3
Puerto Rico - Hist. -
Period., 6107
Puerto Rico - Pol. &
govt., 11348
Puerto y Salgado, Nicolas
del, bp., d. 1681,
5856
Puffer Hopkins, 10326
Puget Sound, 6151
Pulaski, Kazimierz,
1748-1779, 13266
Pulaski, Kazimierz,
1748-1779 - Fiction,
13403
Pullen-Burry, Bessie,
1858-, 7786
Pulszky, Ferencz Aurelius,
1814-1897, 4865
Pulszky, Terezia (Walder),
4865
Pumping machinery - Early
works to 1800, 806
Punch, 8334
Punch, brothers, punch!
9032
Punderson, Lemuel S.,
jt. author, 788
Punishment, 7242, 12300
Punishment - Pennsylvania,
2289
The pupil, 7122
A pupil of Chestnut Ridge,
6977
The pupils of Marvel
hall, 11142
The puppet, 10674
The purification and re-
construction of the
American union, 2250
The Puritan and his
daughter, 10490
A Puritan pagan, 9262

The Puritan's daughter,
9384
Puritans, 1654, 2150,
11536, 11865
Purple eyes, 10238
The pursuit of the house-
boat, 8685
Purviance, David, 1766-1847,
4866
Purviance, Levi, 4866
Pustule, Malignant, 1085
Put to the test, 8960
Putnam co., Ill. - Hist.,
2274
Putnam co., N. Y. - Hist.,
1402
Putnam, George, 1807-1878,
7787
Putnam, George, 1807-1878.
God and our country, 11437
Putnam, George Haven, 1844-
1930, 4867, 7788
Putnam, George W., 4868
Putnam, Israel, 1718-1790,
1882, 11930, 13011
Putnam, Sallie A. (Brock)
"Mrs. Richard Putnam",
1845?-, 4869
Putnam, Samuel Henry, 4870
Putnam's magazine, 1853-1870,
10298
"Putting yourself in her
place", 9426
Putumayo River, 8193
Puységur, Antoine Hyacinte
Anne de Chastenet, comte de,
1752-1807, 13464
Pyle, Howard, 1853-1911, 9376
Pynnshurst, 10296

Qarra, N. M., 2915
Quacks and quackery, 3291
The quadroon's triumph,
4283
The quadroone, 4009
Quaife, Milo Milton, 1860-,
ed., 3696
The Quaker City, 10217

The Quaker soldier, 10066
The quality of mercy,
9951
Quarantine - Pennsylvania,
13218
The quarter loaf, 9916
A quarter past six, 10283
A quarter race in Kentucky,
4833
Quatorze mois dans l'Amé-
rique du Nord, 5484
Que ceux qui ont une
âme lisent ceci, 7790
Quebec campaign, 1759,
8412, 12474
Quebec campaign, 1759 -
Fiction, 10060
Quebec campaign, 1759 -
Poetry, 12771, 12948
Quebec (City) - Descr.,
25
Quebec (City) - Descr.
& trav. - Guide-books,
11411
Quebec (City) - Hist.,
7008, 7687
Quebec (City) - Religious
institutions and
affairs, 11254
Quebec (City) St. Louis
theatre, 5863
Quebec (City) - Siege,
1775-1776 - Drama,
11482
Quebec (City) Université
Laval, 6307
Quebec (Province), 899
Quebec (Province) - Descr.
& trav., 4204, 4691,
6128, 6214, 8393, 13117
Quebec (Province) - Descr.
& trav. - Guide-books,
1034
Quebec (Province) - Hist.,
1441
Quebec (Province). Laws,
statutes, etc., 7791
Quebec (Province). Legis-
lature. Legislative

assembly, 12426
Quebec (Province) - Pol. &
govt., 7791, 11782, 12426
Quebec (Province) Superior
court, 1167
Queechy, 11097
Queen Charlotte (Ship), 6600
Queen City, Tales and sketches
from the, 3284
Queen Krinaleen's plagues,
9075
The queen of bedlam, 10123
The queen of islands, 2957
Queen of spades, 10653
The queen of the coral cave,
8702
The queen's garden, 9350
Queen's rangers, 5153
The queen's sailors, 9663
The queen's twin, 10042
Queenie Hetherton, 9903
The queens of American
society, 12022
Queensland - Descr. & trav.,
12165
Quellenburg, Henrik van,
tr., 6798
Quentin, Karl, 4871
Quer durch Mexiko vom Atlan-
tischen zum Stillen ocean,
7975
Querbeuf, Yves Mathurin
Marie Treaudet de, 1726-1797,
2466
Quesada, Vicente Gregorio,
1830-1913, 4872, 7792
Quesne, J. S., ed., 4209
The quest for fortune, 10731
The quest of Heracles and
other poems, 4345
The quest of Mr. Teaby,
10043
The question before us,
12493
A question of honor, 10972
La question Riel, 7793, 8155
Questions and and answers -
Period., 5889
Quevedo y Zubieta, Salvador,

Railroads - Massachusetts,
1420
Railroads - Mexico, 8079,
8315
Railroads - New England,
12762
Railroads - N. J., 2407
Railroads - U. S., 1860,
3596, 5370, 11862
Railroads - U. S. -
Direct., 292
Railway economy, 4219
Raimond, C. E., pseud. of
Elizabeth Robins.
Rain and rainfall, 806
The rainbow of gold, 2520
Rainier, Peter William,
4884
Rains, George Washington,
1817-1898, 4885
Raising the wind, 10736
Raking straws, 9265
Raleigh, Walter, 1552?-
1612, 7800
Raleigh's Roanoke colonies,
1584-1590, 768, 13309
Ralph, Julian, 1853-1903,
4886
Ralphton, 8848
Ralston, Robert, 1761-
1836, 11932
The Ralstons, 6502
Ramberg, Carl August,
1873-1915, 4887
A ramble of six thousand
miles through the
U.S.A., 4639
A ramble through the
U.S., 3719
A ramble through the
U.S., Canada, and the
West Indies, 5132
The Rambler, 4888
The rambler in Mexico,
7249
The rambler in North
America, 4225
A rambler in the West,
13067

"Rambler," pseud., 4889
Rambles about Portsmouth,
1488
Rambles about the country,
3358
Rambles and reveries,
11022
Rambles and scrambles in
North and South America,
5319
Rambles by land and water,
7589
Rambles in America, past
and present, 4680
Rambles in Chile, 10574
Rambles in Mammoth Cave, 3125
Rambles in the path of the
steamhorse, 2771
Rambles in the Rocky
mountains, 4529
Rambles in the U.S. and
Canada during the year 1845,
4043, 7134
Rambles in Yucatan, 7590
The rambles of Fudge Fumble,
8923
Ramel, Jean Pierre, 1768-
1815, 366
Ramírez de Aguilar, Fernando,
1887-, 7801
Ramírez de Mendoza, Francisco,
6677, 6678, 6687
Ramírez, José Fernando, 1804-
1871, 6644, 7802
Ramírez Lavoignet, David,
ed., 7730
Ramón, the rover of Cuba,
10586
Ramona, 10005
Ramp, A. T., pseud., 3261
Ramsay, Allan, jt. author,
8480
Ramsay, David, 1749-1815,
4890
Ramsey, Hugh, 6790
Ramsey, William, 1013
Ramsing, H. U., 7803
The rancheros of the poisoned
lance, 10069

Rancho del Muerto, 10125
Ranck, George Washington,
1841-1900, 4891
Randal, Thomas, 2987
Randall, P. K., 4892
Randall, Samuel Sidwell,
1809-1881, ed., 261
Randel, Jesse F., jt.
author, 3970
Randolph, 10411
Randolph county, W. Va. -
Descr. & trav., 4157
Randolph, Innis, 7804
Randolph, John, 1773-1833,
708, 3572, 6428, 8232,
10952, 10953
Randolph, Peyton, 1721-
1775, 12468
Randolph, Thornton,
pseud., 10509
Random shots and southern
breezes, 5349
A ranger of commerce,
4725
The ranger of Ravenstream,
9298
The ranger of the Gulf,
9720
The rangers and regulators
of the Tanaha, 481
Rankin, Adam, 1755-1827,
4893, 4894, 4895
Rankin, Jeremiah Eames,
1828-1904, 7805
Ransom, H. C., illustr.,
9553
Ransom, John L., 4896
Raousset-Bourbon, Gaston
Raoux, comte de, 1817-
1854, 8308
Rape of the gamp, 10320
Raphael Inglesse, 9390
Raphaelis Landivar Rusticatio
mexicana, 7237
Rappacini's daughter,
9823
Rapport sur les missions du
diocèse de Quebec, 5227
The rapture of Hetty, 9529

A rare and new discovery,
12734
Rasgo épico, 5803
"Rasmus", 10465
Rasmussen, Vilhelm, 1869-,
4897
Raster, Hermann, 1827-1891,
7806
Der rathgeber und wegweiser
für auswanderer nach den
Vereinigten Staaten von
Nordamerika und Texas,
5755
Rattlehead's chronicles,
8924
Rattles and rhymes, 5583
Ratzel, Friedrich, 1844-
1904, 7807
Raumer, Friedrich Ludwig
George von, 1781-1873,
4898
Rauscher, Frank, 4899
Ravellings from the web of
life, 8936
Ravenia, 9435
Rawlings, Thomas, 7808, 7809
Raxworthy's treasure, 9817
Ray's recruit, 10126
Raymond family, 7810
Raymond, Grace, pseud. of
Annie Raymond Stillman,
5283
Raymond, Samuel, 7810
Raynal, Guillaume Thomas
François, 1713-1796, 4900
Raynolds, William F., 3816
Raynolds, William Franklin,
4901
Rea, Alonso de la, 7811
Read, Jesse, jt. author,
11619
Read, Oliver, d. 1803, 11173
Read, Opie Percival, 1852-
1939, 4902-4907
Readers and speakers -
1800-1870, 12936
Readers and speakers -
Geography, 6776
The reading parties, 10197

The real North America
pocket guide book, 6090
A real pirate, 10338
Real property, 1254
Real property - Arkansas,
2739
Real property - Florida,
13503
Real property - Menard co.,
Ill. - Maps, 6169
Real property - Muskingum
Co., Ohio - Maps, 1068
Real property - Sacramento,
Cal., 12838
Real property - U. S.,
12555, 12556
The real thing, 7126
The real United States
and Canada pocket
guide-book, 6091
Realities of life, 10600
Reality, 9731, 11033
Reality in romance, 8662
A realized ideal, 10306
Rear Admiral Goldsborough,
13202
Reasons to show that
there is a great pro-
bability of a navigable
passage to the western
American ocean through
Hudson's streights and
Chesterfield inlet, 7812
Reavis, Logan Uriah,
1831-1889, 7813
Rebecca, 10680
A rebel cavalryman with
Lee, Stuart, and Jackson,
4655
The rebel general's loyal
bride, 8615
The Rebel invasion of
Maryland, 13140
Rebel invasion of Missouri
and Kansas, 12796
The rebel of Dorchester,
10774
Rebel private, front and
rear, 3471

A rebel war clerk's diary
at the Confederate states
capital, 4113
A rebel's recollections,
3355
A rebellious heroine, 8686
The rebels, 8994
Rebels and tories, 10158
Rebullosa, Jaime, 7814
Receipts, 13128
Recent carnival of crime,
9035
Recent exploring expeditions
to the Pacific, 13200
The recent past from a
southern standpoint, 5734
Recherches sur leurs [Nègres]
facultées intellectuelles,
12421
Reciprocity, 12738, 12954
The reciprocity treaty,
12738
Récit d'aventures dans le
nord-ouest, 6010
Récits de voyages, 5059
Reck, Philipp Georg Friedrich
von, 1710-1798, 4908
Réclamations pour les colonies
des Antilles, 7815
Reclus, Élisée, 1830-1905,
7494
The recluse of Jamestown,
2923
The recluse of the Conewaga,
8715
Recognition (International
law), 1142, 12231
Recollections from 1860
to 1865, 4271
Recollections of a Georgia
loyalist, 4074
Recollections of a house-
keeper, 9617
Recollections of a lazy life,
8865
The recollections of a man
of the world, 11052
Recollections of a New
England bride and of a

southern matron, 3604

Recollections of a sailor
boy, 2733

Recollections of a six
years' residence in the
U.S.A., 4584

Recollections of a
southern matron, 3605

Recollections of a Virginian
in the Mexican, Indian,
and Civil wars, 4416

Recollections of an
artist, 10468

Recollections of field
service with the
Twentieth Iowa infantry
volunteers, 2615

The recollections of
Jotham Anderson, 11081

Recollections of New
York, 10310

Recollections of North
America, 5322

Recollections of our
neighborhood in the
west, 2930, 8947

Recollections of persons
and places in the West,
2778

Recollections of rambles
in the South, 5712

Recollections of seventy
years, 2224

Recollections of the
civil war, 3162, 5490

Recollections of the
early settlement of the
Wabash Valley, 3102

Recollections of the
inhabitants, localities,
superstitions, and
Kuklux outrages of the
Carolinas, 3678

Recollections of the last
ten years, 3479

Recollections of the West,
3574

Recollects - Missions,
6511, 6512

Reconciliation, 10919

La reconquista española de
Chile en 1814, 5893

Reconstruction, 361, 1585,
2250, 3155, 3546, 4818,
7290, 7562, 11868, 12265,
12958, 13329

Reconstruction - Fiction,
9383, 10467, 10992

Reconstruction - Georgia,
2124, 2227, 4796

Reconstruction - Louisiana,
11928

Reconstruction - Mississippi,
8344

Reconstruction on "my policy",
11868

Reconstruction - Speeches
in Congress, 472, 1004

Reconstruction - Tennessee,
2323

Reconstruction - Virginia,
12265

Recopilacion sumaria de todos
los autos acordados de la
Real audencia, 1078

Record of an obscure man,
10582

Record of the descendant of
Silence Holbrook, 12840

Record of the service of
the Fifty-fifth regiment of
Massachusetts volunteer
infantry, 12154

Records of a village literary
association, 9486

The records of an unfashionable
street, 10911

Records of patriotism and
love of country, 662

Records of some of the
descendants of William
Curtis, 11847

Recreations of a long
vacation, 1025

A recruit at Christmas, 9363

Recruiting and enlistment,
12230

The rector of St. Bardolph's,

10748
The rectory of Moreland,
10956
Recuerdos de Méjico, 7879
Recuerdos de un viaje
a América, 4909
Recuerdos históricos de
la guerra de la inde-
pendencia, 7322
Recuerdos y reminiscencias
del primer tercio de
la vida de Rivolba,
2754
The red box, 10197
The Red Coats, 10881
Red cross, 11451
The Red Eagle, 4434
The red republic, 8966
Red River, 4626, 6311
The Red River country,
7922
The Red River insurrection,
5813
Red River of Canada -
Descr., 7922
Red River of Louisiana,
5537
Red River of the North,
1133, 1134, 3200, 3881,
6941
Red River rebellion,
1869-1870, 6049, 6129,
6212, 6467, 6635, 7831
Red River settlement, 334,
3880, 4348, 5674, 5904,
6029, 6041, 6224, 6229,
6300, 6301, 6304, 6305,
6313, 6316, 6398, 6399,
6467, 6542, 6668, 6845,
7361, 7457, 7522, 7641,
7780, 7793, 7999, 8000,
8120, 8141, 8146, 8147,
8155, 8185, 8231, 8411
Red River settlement
(Canada) - Hist., 7462
Red Rock, 10467
The Red Rover, 9147
Red Rupert, the American
bucaneer, 8671

Red Sulphur Spring, W. Va.,
13037
Red-tape and pigeon-hole
generals, 4521
Redburn, 10348
Rede, Leman Thomas, d. 1810,
2476
The Redemption of David
Corson, 9631
The redemptioner, 9463
Reden gehalten bei der Berliner
todtenfeier für den präsidenten
Lincoln, 8125
Redfield, 9593
Redondo y Godino, Juan,
1859-1921, 4909
Redpath, James, 1833-1891,
4910, 4911
The redskins, 9148
Redwood, 10729
Redwood library and athenaeum,
Newport, R. I., 1575
Reed, Andrew, 1787-1862, 4912
Reed, Andrew, 1787-1862.
No fiction, 861
Reed, H. B., 7816
Reed, Isaac, 4913
Reed, J. W., 4914
Reed, James Armstrong, b. 1830,
7029
Reed, Joseph, 1741-1785,
739, 13245
Reed, Joseph, 1741-1785.
Remarks on a late publication
in the Independent gazetteer,
1790
Reed, Seth, 1823-, 7817
Reed, William Bradford, 1806-
1876, 7818, 13245
Reed, William Howell, 1837-,
4915
Rees, Thomas, 1850-1933,
7819
Reese family 7820
Reese, Lizette Woodworth,
1856-1935, 4916, 4917,
4918
Reese, Mary E., 7820
Reese River, 5685

Reseña histórico-descriptiva
de la ciudad de México,
6802
Reservoirs, 6121
Resistance to slavery
every man's duty, 172
Resorts - Southern
states, 4958
The resources and attractions
of the Texas Panhandle
for the home seeker,
capitalist and tourist,
5500
The resources and
prospects of America,
4762
The resources of Missouri,
5633
Resources of the southern
fields and forests, 4827
The resources of the United
States of America, 2806
Resources of West Virginia,
4418
The responsibilities of
rulers, 11420
A responsibility, 9740
Restituta, 1631
Restivo, Paulo, 1658-
1741, 7921
Resumen de la historia de
Venezuela desde el año
de 1797 hasta el de
1830, 772
Resumen de reales cedulas,
para las Indias, 8085
The retrospect, 2638
Retrospect of western
travel, 7424
Retrospections of
America, 2695
Return, 10274, 10283
The return of a private,
9606
A returned prisoner of
war, 5585
The reunion of the ghosts,
10863
Réveillaud, Eugène, 1851-,

7841
Revel, Gabriel Joachim du
Perron, comte de, 1756-
1814, 4933
Revel, James, 4934
Revelations of a life, 10422
Revenge, 10209
The revenge of Saint Nicholas,
10480
The revenge of the Adolphus,
9217
Revenge punished and
constancy rewarded, 10402
The reverberator, 7127
Revere, Joseph Warren,
1812-1880, 7842
Rev. Calvin Fairbank during
slavery times, 3412
The Reverend Washington
Ham's triumph, 9460
Reverente satisfaccion, 7843
Reveries of a bachelor, 10362
The reverse, 10760
The reverses of fortune,
10332
A review of Captain Basil Hall's
Travels in North America,
1262
Review of pamphlets on
slavery and colonization,
639
A review of the noted revival
in Kentucky, 4895
Revilla Gigedo, Juan Francisco
Guemes y Horcasitas, conde
de, 1682?-1766, 7479
Revilla Gigedo, Juan Vicente
Güémez Pacheco de Padilla
Horcasitas y Aguayo, conde
de, 1740-1799 - Poetry,
7626
Revista azul, 7844
Revista cubana, 7845
Revista de bibliografía
chilena y extranjera, 7846
Revista de Bogotá, 7847
Revista de Chile, 7848
Revista de Cuba, 7849
Revista de La Habana, 7850

Revista de Santiago,
7851, 7852
Revista del Rio de la
Plata, 7853
Revista moderna, 7854,
7855
Revista nueva, 7856
Revista peruana, 7857
Revivals, 1660, 11246
Revivals - Vermont,
1687
Révoil, Bénédict Henry,
1816-1888, 4935, 4936
The revolt of "Mother",
9575
The revolt of the Mexitili,
9982
The revolutionary officer,
10197
Revolutions, 6005
Les revolutions du Méxique,
1104
The reward of virtue,
9740
Rex Macarthy, 8723
Rey, William, 4937
Reybaud, Louis, 7858
Reyes, Alfonso, ed.,
7496
Reyes, Rafael, pres.
Colombia, 1851-1931,
7859
Reyna, Francisco de,
d. 1708, 7860
Reynal, Rafael, 4938
Reynolds, Charles Bingham,
1856-1940, 4939
Reynolds, John, 1788-1865,
4940
Reynolds, Lewis Gardner,
7861
Rhapsodies of restless
hours, 12717
Rhetoric, 11723
Rhoades, Nelson Osgood,
1869-, 7374
Rhode Island, 11168
Rhode Island - Bibl., 906
Rhode Island - Biog., 909

Rhode Island - Bound. -
Massachusetts, 505
Rhode Island - Charters,
11748
Rhode Island - Church history,
100, 1812, 13126
Rhode Island (Colony)
Commissioners to the Albany
congress, 1754, 12898
Rhode Island - Constitutional
history, 2424
Rhode Island - Descr. &
trav., 3663, 5147
Rhode Island - Descr. &
trav. - Guide-books, 764
Rhode Island. General assembly.
Committee appointed to
inquire into the charges
against masonry and masons
in Rhode Island, 12587
Rhode Island historical
society, 478, 12393
Rhode Island - Hist., 477,
13126
Rhode Island - Hist. - Colonial
period, 478, 1812, 12193, 12322
Rhode Island - Hist. - Colonial
period - Sources, 2167
Rhode Island infantry. 2d
regt., 1861-1865, 1802
Rhode Island infantry. 12th
regt., 1862-1863, 12351
Rhode Island - Pol. & govt.,
12798
Rhode Island - Pol. & govt. -
1775-1865, 2339, 2340
Rhode Island - Supreme court,
12311
Rhodes, Harrison Garfield,
1871-, 4941
Rhymes and roses, 4731
Rhys, Horton, 7862
Rialto series, 10688
Ribas family, 6866
Ribas, José Félix, 1775-
1815, 6866
Ribas, Manuel José de la,
7863
Rica's eyes, 9330

The Ricaree Indian fight,
4942
Ricaud, J. A., 4943
Rice, Cale Young,
1872-1943, 4944
Rice Corner, 9896
Rice, David, 1733-1816,
1359, 4945
Rice, John H., 7864
Rice, John Holt,
1777-1831, 4422
Rich, Isaac B.,
supposed author, 12201
The rich merchant of
Cairo, 10298
Rich, Obadiah, 1783?-
1850, 4393, 4946
Rich, R., 4947
Richard and Robin,
9639
Richard Carvel, 9003
Richard Edney and the
governor's family,
10
Richard, Edouard, 1844-
1904, 7865
Richard, Louis Claude
Marie, 1754-1821,
7092
Richards, Adolphus E.,
3417
Richards, Augustus Long,
7866
Richards, C. A. L., 13148
Richards, Robert, pseud.,
4948
Richards, Thomas Addison,
1820-1900, 4949, 5918
Richards, William Carey,
1818-1892, ed., 4950
Richardson, Mrs. Abby
(Sage), 1839-1900, ed.,
7867
Richardson, Albert Deane,
1833-1869, 4951, 4952,
7867
Richardson, Frank Herbert,
1867-, 4953
Richardson, John, 1667-

1753, 4954
Richardson, Sir John,
1787-1865, 4955, 4956
Richardson, William Alexander,
1811-1875, 87
Richardson, William H., 4957
Richardson's southern guide,
4953
Richardville, Jean Baptiste,
ca.1761-1841, 7880
Richelet, Pierre, 1631-1698,
tr., 12195
The riches of Mexico, 6630
Riches without wings, 10803
Richmond and Danville Railroad,
4958
Richmond during the war,
4869
Richmond: her glory and her
graves, 13326
Richmond, Va. - Descr.,
3015, 3401, 3755, 4128,
5794
Richmond, Va. - Descr. -
Guide-books, 2984
Richmond, Va. - Direct.,
1756
Richmond, Va. Examiner, 2589
Richmond, Va. - Hist. -
Civil war, 4113, 4869
Richmond, Va. - Siege, 1864-
1865, 6206, 7871, 11647
Richmond, Va. - Theater
disaster, 1811, 142
Richmond, Va. - Theater
disaster, 1811 - Poetry,
12262
Rickard, Thomas Arthur,
1864-, 7868
Rickman, Thomas M., 4959
Riddell, William Renwick,
1852-, ed., 7243
The riddle of Lincoln's
religion, 7661
A ride across a continent,
11461
The ride of Saint Nicholas
on New Year's eve, 10480
A ride over the Rocky

401

mountains, 3047

A ride with Kit Carson through the Great American Desert and the Rocky mountains, 2796

The riders of the plains, 6995

Riedel, Emil, 7869

Riedesel, Friederike Charlotte Luise (von Massow) friefrau von, 1746-1808, 4960

Riedesel, Friedrich Adolf, freiherr von, 1738-1800, 4960

Riel, Louis, 1844-1885, 6212, 6300, 6301, 6304, 6398, 6399, 6845, 7462, 7793, 8155, 8185, 8231

Riel rebellion, 1885, 6129, 6298

Ries, Julius, 4961

The rifle, axe, and saddle-bags, 4468

Rifle practice, 4242, 6353

Rifles, 11989

Rigby, T. C., 4962

Right and wrong in Massachusetts, 11736

The right and the wrong, 10156

Right flanker, 2277

The right of way, 9358

The right real thing, 10016

The right side of the car, 10225

The right way and the wrong way, 8572

The rights of colonies examined, 12897

The rights of the Congregational churches of Massachusetts, 12469

Riker, Carroll L., 7870

Riker, John F., 4963

Riley, James Whitcomb,

1849-1916, 10436

A rill from the town pump, 9827

Rincones mexicanos, 6544

Ringold Griffitt, 9985

Rings and love-knots, 4732

Rio de Janeiro - Comm., 691

Rio de la Plata, 13335

Rio Grande, 5513, 5549, 8255

Rio Grande del Norte, 190, 8199

Rio Grande do Sul, Brazil (State) - Descr. & trav., 578

Rio Grande do Sul, Brazil (State) - Descr. & trav. - Gazetteers, 425

Rio Grande river, 8110

Rip Van Winkle, 9995

Riparian rights - Massachusetts, 11436

Ripley, Edward H., 7871

Ripley, Mrs. Eliza Moore (Chinn) McHatton, 1832-1912, 4964

Ripley, William Putnam, 1776-1842, 1517

Risdon, F. Ray, 8354

Rising in the world, 8576

The rising village, 2434

Ritchie, Anna Cora (Ogden) Mowatt, 1870-1819, 4965

Ritson, Mrs. Anne, 4966

Riva Palacio, Mariano, 1803-1880, 7872

Riva Palacio, Vicente, 1832-1896, ed., 7873

The rival belles, 4114, 10063

The rival sisters, 9842

The rival volunteers, 9936

The rivals, 9022

The rivals of Acadia, 8984

Rivascacho, marqués de, 7405, 7406

River Plate Publishing Company, 7874

Rivera, Luis Manuel del, 7875

Rivera y Sanromán, Agustín,

402

1824-1916, 7876, 7877
Rivera y Villalón, Pedro
  de, fl. 1740, 4967, 7878
Rivero, Nicolás, 1849-,
  7879
Rivers, Pearl, pseud.,
  4604
Rives, Amélie, see
  Troubetzkoy, Amélie
  (Rives) Chanler.
Rives, Hallie Erminie,
  1876-, 4968
Rives, William Cabell,
  1825-1889, 5601
La Rivière Rouge, 4626
Rivington, Alex., 4969
Rivington, Harris, jt.
  author, 4969
Rivolba, pseud., 2754
Rix, Samuel Wilton, ed.,
  11321
Roach, Alva C., 4970
The road to Frontenac,
  7467
The road to ruin, 11275
Roads, 11293
Roads - Illinois, 5820
Roads - Mexico, 7481
Roads, Military, 4550
Roads - The West, 1184
Roads - U. S., 3163, 3861,
  4440, 4761, 5127
Roads - Virginia, 756
Roah, Sidney, 4971
Roanoke island, N. C. -
  Capture, 1862, 2049
Rob of the Bowl, 4156,
  10096
Robb, Charles, 6666
Robb, John S., 4972
The robber, 10568
The robber of Guatemala,
  10209
Robbers and outlaws,
  6164, 6958
Robert and Harold, 3656
Robert Graham, 3847
Robert Greathouse, 10917
Robert Morton, 10683

Robert Severne, his friends
  and his enemies, 9728
Robert Toombs, 5294
Roberts, Bernie K., 7880
Roberts, C. G. D., 10448
Roberts, Edwin F., 1819-1864,
  8798
Roberts, Louis A., illustr.,
  10862
Roberts, Sir Charles George
  Douglas, 1860-1943, 6318,
  7881
Roberts, Edwards, 7882
Roberts, Morley, 1857-, 4973
Roberts, Oran Milo, 1815-
  1898, 4974
Roberts, Orlando W., 7883
Roberts, Robert Richford,
  1778-1843, 12036, 12180
Roberts, Sidney, 4975
Roberts, William, fl. 1763,
  4976
Robertson, Alexander Hamilton,
  4977
Robertson, David, reporter,
  11628
Robertson, Douglas Sinclair,
  1877-, ed., 6922
Robertson, George, 1790-1874,
  4978
Robertson, James, of
  Manchester, Eng., 4979
Robertson, James Alexander,
  1873-, ed., 5469
Robertson, John Blount, 4980
Robertson, John Ross, 1841-
  1918, 8210
Robertson, Joseph Clinton,
  1788-1852, comp., 13450
Robertson, Thomas William,
  ed., 8876
Robertson, William Parish,
  4981
Robidoux, Michelle, 5503
Robin, Claude C., 1750-,
  4982
Robins, Elizabeth "Mrs. G. R.
  Parkes," 1862-, 4983, 4984,
  4985, 4986, 4987, 4988

Robinson, Charles Seymour,
1829-1899, 7884
Robinson Crusoe's money,
11119
Robinson, D., 10122
Robinson, Elrie, 7885
Robinson, Fayette, tr.,
1864
Robinson, Henry M., 7886
Robinson, Jacob S., 4989
Robinson, John Hovey,
1825-, 4990, 4991, 4992,
4993, 4994, 7887
Robinson, Joseph W., 4995
Robinson, Lewis, d. 1810,
1810, 13241
Robinson, Luther Emerson,
1867-, 7888
Robinson, Reuben D., 6423
Robinson, Richard P. -
Fiction, 11165
Robinson, Sophie Michau,
5074
Robinson, Stuart, 1814-
1881, 7889
Robinson, Thomas Hastings,
1828-1906, 7890
Robinson, William Davis,
4996
Robinsoniads - American
literature, 2664
Robles, Antonio de, 1645?-
17--, 7891
Rochambeau, Jean Baptiste
Donatien de Vimeur,
comte de, 1725-1807,
4997
Rochefort, Charles, 1605-,
4998
Rochester ladies' anti-
slavery society, 9666
Rock, James L., 4999
The Rock or the Rye, 9385
Rockefeller, John Davison,
1839-1937, 6196
Rockford, 8812
Rockford parish, 10431
The Rockies of Canada, 8383
Rockingham, Charles Watson-

Wentworth, 2d marquis of,
1730-1782, 11969
Rockport, Ind., 6662, 6664
Rockport, Ind. - Biog., 6663
Rockport, Ind. - Hist., 6665
Rockport, Mass. - Hist., 605
Rockwell, John Arnold,
1803-1861, 7892
Rockwell, William S., 5000
Rocky Mountain Indians, 4701
Rocky Mountains, 2730, 2823,
3047, 3438, 4028, 4529,
5752, 6317, 6324, 8383
Rocky Mountains, A lady's life
in the, 6086
Rocky Mountains, Canada, 7063,
7656, 8126
Rocky Mountains, Canada -
Views, 7597
Rocky Mountains - Descr. &
trav., 3455, 4500, 4705,
4837, 4951, 5007, 5018,
5053, 5060, 5098, 5180,
5183, 5561, 5772, 6342,
7196
Rocky Mountains - Fiction,
5748
Rod and gun on the west coast
of Florida, 5001
A rod for the backs of the
critics, 1932
Rod's salvation, 11018
Rode, Charles R., 1825-1865,
ed., 265
Rodgers, John Kearny,
1793-1851, 11975, 12915
Rodman the keeper, 11207
Rodney, George Brydges Rodney,
baron, 1719-1792, 4654
Rodríguez Cerna, José, 7893
Rodríguez de Almogabar, Mateo,
6348
Rodríguez de Leon Pinelo,
Antonio, d. 1660, 7894
Rodríguez de Rivas y Velasco,
Diego, bp., d. 1771, 7895
Rodríguez de San Miguel,
Juan, 7896
Rodríguez Villa, Antonio,

1843-1912, 7897
Rodway, James, 7898
Roe, Alfred Seelye,
  1844-1917, 5002
Roe, Mrs. Elizabeth A.,
  5003
Roe, Mrs. Frances Marie
  Antoinette (Mack),
  5004
Roe, Sir Thomas, 1581?-
  1644, 12067
Roebuck, 10685
Roehrig, Frederic Louis
  Otto, 1819-1908, 515
Roemer, Jacob, 1818-1896,
  5005
Roger Catron's friends, 9779
Roger Irving's ward, 9901
Roger Malvin's burial, 9823
Rogerenes, 623
Rogers, Artemas, 2218
Rogers, Carlton H., 5006
Rogers, Cornelius, 5007
Rogers, Edward H., 5008
Rogers, George, fl. 1838,
  5009
Rogers, John, 1800-1867,
  ed., 5288
Rogers, John, 1812-1882,
  11347
Rogers, John Davenport,
  1857-1914, 7899
Rogers, Joseph Morgan,
  1861-, 7900
Rogers, Robert, 1731-1795,
  5010, 5011
Rogers, Thomas L., 7901
Rogers, W. A., illustr.,
  9553
Rogers' rangers, 5011
Rojas, Isidro, 7902
Roland and Wilfred, 9200
Rolling Ridge, 9477
Romaine, Dexter, pseud.,
  10492
A Roman singer, 6503, 9227
Romance and humor of the
  road, 10823
Romance dust from the

historic places, 10338
Romance in real life, 10730
The romance in the life of
  Hefty Burke, 9358
Romance, no fiction, 2887
The romance of a Spanish nun,
  8665
Romance of a tin roof and a
  fire-escape, 10448
The romance of a western trip,
  10899
Romance of American history,
  768
The romance of American
  landscape, 13469
The romance of Beauseincourt,
  5618
The romance of certain old
  clothes, 10014
The romance of Dollard,
  6379, 8955
The romance of Guardamonte,
  9336
The romance of hunting,
  3852
The romance of Monte Beni,
  9822
The romance of natural
  history, 12325
Romance of student life
  abroad, 10104
A romance of summer seas,
  9364
The romance of the green seal,
  5619
Romance of the history of
  Louisiana, 3584
A romance of the line, 6978
Romance of the ocean, 2260
A romance of the republic,
  8995
The romance of the revolution,
  11611
A romance of the sea serpent,
  8756
The romance of the table, 9959
Romance of travel, 11183
The romance of yachting, 12722
Romance without fiction, 11025

405

Romances of New Orleans,
8598
Romanism in the United
States, 8770
Romans, Bernard, 1720(ca.)-
1784(ca.), 5012
Romantic adventures in
Northern Mexico, 4925
The Romantic historian,
10670
Romantic passages in
southwestern history,
4435
The romantic settlement
of Lord Selkirk's
colonists, 6229
A romantic tale of high
American life, 10912
A romantic young lady,
9644
Rome (City) - Soc. life
& cust., 10191
Rome - Hist. - Aurelian,
270-275 - Fiction,
11082
Rome - Hist. - Civil war,
49-48 B.C. - Fiction,
9366
Romero, Carlos A., ed.,
5937
Romero de Terreros y
Vinent, Manuel, marqués
de San Francisco,
1880-, 7903
Romero, Matías, 1837-1898,
7904, 7905
Romero Valdés, Isidro,
7321
Romig, Mrs. Edna (Davis)
1889-, 7906
Romo Celis, Guillermo,
7907
Romo de Vivar y Torres,
Joaquín, 1841-1899,
7907
Root, Elihu, 1845-, 7532
Ropes of sand, 10023
Rosa, Luis de la, d. 1856,
7908

Rosales de Velasco, José
Maximiliano, 7955
Rosanna, 10187
Rose and Elza, 9301
Rose, Aquila, 11314
The rose-bower, 4923
Rose Bradshaw, 10921
Rose Brake, 3165
Rose Clark, 10478
Rose, Edward, 3919
Rose, George, 1817-1882,
5013
Rose Mather, 3918
A rose of a hundred leaves,
8739
A rose of Glenbogie, 6963
The Rose of Ouisconsin, 5061
The Rose of Wissahikon,
10218
A rose of yesterday, 9230
Rose, Robert Hutchinson,
1776-1842, 13233
Rose, Victor M., d. 1893,
5014
Rosecrans' campaign with the
fourteenth army corps,
2708
Rosén, Maud, grevinna von,
1902-, 5015
Rosenberg, Charles G., 5016,
10508
Rosengarten, Joseph G.,
ed., 4826
Roses and thorns, 10468
Rosillo de Lara, Juan,
7909, 7910
Rosina Meadows, the village
maid, 9483
Rosine Laval, 10233
Ross, Albert, pseud., 10551
Ross, Alexander, 1783-1856,
5017, 5018
Ross, Clinton, 1861-1920,
8969
Ross, Fitzgerald, 5019
Ross, George M. von, 5020,
5021, 8408
Ross, J., 7930
Ross, Sir James Clark,

Ruins of innocence, 10949
Ruiz Canduelas, Francisco,
  d. 1696, 8292
Ruiz de la Peñuela,
  Francisco, 7920
Ruiz de Montoya, Antonio,
  1585-1652, 7921
Ruiz, Juan de Dios, 1731-
  1799, 6160
Rujub, the juggler, 7010
Rule and misrule of the
  English in America,
  12548
Rule, Lucien V., 1871-,
  5042
Rulers should be benefactors,
  12642
Rules of practice under
  the sequestration act,
  2056
Rules of the Board of
  education, 1875
The ruling and ordaining
  power of congregational
  bishops, 12156
Rumford, Sir Benjamin
  Thompson, count, 1753-
  1814, 1270
"Run to seed", 10460
Rund um die Erde, 3409
Runyan, Morris C., 5043
Rupert's land, 5903, 6311,
  6436, 7641
Rupert's land - Descr. &
  trav., 4955
Rupert's land. Northern
  dept. Council, 7641
Rural schools - U. S.,
  795
Rural sports, 4115
Rurality, 10918
Rüse, M. J., tr., 2938
Rush, Benjamin, 1745-1813,
  2478, 13245
The Rush-light, 2478
Rushville, Ill. - Hist.,
  6652
Rusling, James Fowler,
  1834-1918, 5044

Russell, Alex J., 7922
Russell, Benjamin, 1761-1845,
  989
Russell, Charles Russell,
  baron, 1832-1900, 5045
Russell, David E., 5046
Russell, George G., 5047
Russell, Irwin, 1853-1879,
  5048
Russell, John, 1773?-1795,
  11460
Russell, John Russell, 1st
  earl, 1792-1878, ed.,
  1040, 11348
Russell, Matthew, 5045
Russell, Robert, d. 1871, 5049
Russell, Robert W., 5050
Russell, Sir William Howard,
  1820-1907, 5051, 5052, 7923
Russia, 11466, 11467
Russia - Descr. & trav., 5409
Russia - For. rel. - U. S.,
  547
Russia to Abraham Lincoln,
  5947
Rust, Francis Marion, ed.,
  8330
The rustic financiers, 10957
Rusticacion mejicana, 7238
Rusticus [pseud.], 6531
La ruta de occidente, 6811
Ruth Bergen's limitations,
  10946
Ruth Emsley, the betrothed
  maiden, 8943
Ruth Hall, 10479
Ruth Whalley, 9849
Ruth's sacrifice, 10496
Rutherford, Mildred Lewis,
  1852-1928, 7924, 7925,
  7926, 7927, 7928
Rutledge, 9756
Rutledge, Ann, 1813-1835,
  5912, 5960, 5974, 6830,
  7022, 8369
Rutledge, Ann, 1813-1835 -
  Poetry, 8039
Rutledge, John, 1739-1800,
  12729

Rutt, John Towill,
1760-1841, ed., 1796
Ruy Díaz, Petronila,
7495
Ruy Díaz, Simón, 7495,
8306
Ruxton, George Frederick
Augustus, 1820-1848,
5053, 5054
Ruysdale, Philip, 5055
Ruyter, Michiel Andriaans-
zoon, 1607-1676, 1435
Rvbi (Ship), 7929
Ryan, Abram Joseph, 1838-
1886, 5056
Ryerson, John, 1799-1878,
5057

S. I., 1507
S., I. E., 5962
S., J., 10173
S., N., 11876
S. T. P., 10317
Saavedra, Alvaro, 16th
cent., 7567
Sabbath, 2990, 10904
The Sabbath breakers,
10580
Sabin, Edward, 7930
The sable cloud, 8472
Sabre, Gilbert E., 5058
Un sacerdote del obispado
de Puebla, 2011
Sachot, Octave Louis
Marie, 1824-, 5059
Sack and destruction
of the city of
Columbia, S. C., 5163
A sack of gold, 10048
The sack of Unquowa,
10881
Sackhouse, John, 1797-
1819, 12803
Saco, José Antonio, 1800?-
1879, 111
Saco, Me. Citizens, 8154
Saco, Me. First church
of Christ, 2144

Sacred dirges, hymns and
anthems, 7058
Sacred vocal music, 7058
The sacrifice of Irene,
10062
Sadlier, Anna Theresa, 1854-,
10675
Sadlier, Mary Ann (Madden)
"Mrs. James Sadlier,"
1820-1903, 10675
A safe deposit, 9692
Safe in purgatory, 10283
Safford, Clarinda (Bascom)
1804-, 12701
Sage, Rufus B., 1817-, 5060
Sagua la Grande, Cuba -
Hist., 5857
Sahagun, Bernardino de,
c. 1499-1590, 7931, 7932
A sail in sight, 11010
The sailing of King Olaf,
2820
Sailors' life and sailors'
yarns, 9055
St. Albans Confederate raid,
1864, 1167
St. Augustine - Descr., 3219
St. Augustine expedition,
1740, 2879, 3989
St. Augustine expedition,
1743, 4172
St. Augustine, Fla., 4298
St. Augustine, Fla. - Hist.,
4939
St. Catharine's eve, 10730
St. Cecilia, 10314
St. Clair, 11024
St. Clair, Arthur, 1734-1818,
4096
St. Clair flats, 11205
St. Croix, Virgin Islands
of the U. S., 5747
St. David's benevolent
society, New York, 13286
Saint-Domingue. Assemblée
Provinciale du Sud, 7933
Saint-Domingue (colony)
Chambre d'agriculture du
Cap, 7934

Saint-Domingue. Comité
colonial à Paris, 7935
Saint-Domingue. Commis-
saires, 7936, 7937
Saint-Domingue. Conseil
supérieur, 7938, 7939
Saint-Domingue. Députés
à l'Assemblée nationale,
7940
Saint-Domingue. Gouverneur-
général, 7941
Saint Dominique à la vielle
de la révolution, 8399
St. Elmo, 11186
St. Francisville, La. -
Descr., 2578
St. François de Sales.
Mission, 1288, 1290
St. George De Lisle,
10695
St. George's Hundred,
Del. First Presby-
terian church, 2264
Saint-Hilaire, Augustin
François Cesar Prouvençal
de, 1779-1853, 7092
St. John, Percy Boling-
broke, 1821-1889, 5061
St. John, Samuel, 3515
St. John's River, 4298
St. John's River society,
7942
St. John's wooing, 10261
St. Joseph's convent,
Emmitsburg, Md., 8896
St. Lawrence, Gulf of,
6575
Saint Leger, 10105
St. Louis, 12832
St. Louis, Iron Mountain
& Southern Railway
Company, 5062
St. Louis' isle, 3927
St. Louis. Louisiana
purchase exposition,
1904, 2740, 4187, 5581,
5981
St. Louis, Mo. - Descr.,
3158, 3755, 4932

St. Louis, Mo. - Hist.,
5084
St. Lucia, 11509, 11742
St. Mark's Parish, Va.,
3680
St. Michael's day, 4009
St. Nicholas society of
Nassau island, Brooklyn,
13262
St. Paul's college, Bermuda
Islands, 1195
St. Peter's at Rosendale,
10747
St. Philip's, 9757
St. Pierre (Island), 6401
St. Simon's niece, 8781
St. Twel'mo, 11114
Saint Vincent - Descr. &
trav., 6339
Saint Vincent - Hist., 574
St. Vincent, John Jervis,
earl, 1735-1823, 1476
Sala, George Augustus Henry,
1828-1895, 5063, 11455
Salado river, Sante Fé
(Province) Argentine
republic, 13054, 13144
The salamander, 10804
Salander and the dragon,
10749
Salazar Ylarregui, José,
5064
Salcedo, Gaspar de, 6348
Salcedo, José de, 6348
Saldías, Adolfo, 1850-1914,
7943
Salem female charitable
society, Salem, Mass.,
11340
Salem, Mass. City council,
1518
Salem, Mass. - Hist.,
2243
Salem, N. J. - Hist.,
13257
Salina, N. Y., 1030
Salinas y Cabrera, Diego de,
1691-1764, 8056
Salisbury, N. C. Military

prison, 2761
Sally, 9376
Sally Dows, 9791
Salm-Salm, Felix Constantin
  Alexander Johann Nepomuk,
  prinz du, 1828-1870, 7944
Salmon River, 4250
Salmon, Thomas, 1679-1767,
  5065, 5066
Salomy Jane's kiss, 6975
Salt, 1030
Salt Lake City - Descr.,
  1744, 2510, 2970
Salt of the earth, 9916
Salt water bubbles, 10789
Salted with fire, 8933
Salter, William, 1821-1910,
  7945
Saltonstall, Leverett,
  1783-1845, 1451
Salvaalegre, Juan Pio de
  Montufar y Frasco,
  marqués de, 7946
Salvador, 1129, 13484
Salvador - Descr. & trav.,
  7521, 8164
Salvatierra, García
  Sarmiento de Sotomayor
  Enríquez de Luna,
  conde de, d. 1659, 7920
Salzbacher, Joseph, 1790-
  1867, 5067
The Salzburgers and their
  descendants, 13486
Salzburgers in Georgia,
  4908
"Sam", 5652
Sam Johnson, 9044
Sam Lawson's Oldtown
  fireside stories, 10909
Sam Shirk, 9395
Sam Slick in Texas, 3762
Sam Squab, the Boston boy,
  8467
Samantha at Saratoga, 9888
Sampleton, Samuel, pseud.,
  7523
Sampson, Flem D., 7947
Sampson, William, 1764-1836,

reporter, 13241
San Alberto, José Antonio
  de, abp., 1727-1804, 7948
San Francisco - Descr., 7306
San Francisco - Fiction,
  9067
San Isidro, 9253
San Jacinto, Battle of, 1836,
  4405
San Juan Baptista (Frigate),
  8272
San Juan del Norte, Nicaragua -
  Hist., 890
San Luis Potosí, Mexico (City),
  6690
San Martín (Ship), 6352
San Martín, José de,
  1778-1850, 7949, 8112
San Martín Suárez, José de,
  7950
San Salvador. Museo Nacional
  "David J. Guzmán", 7951
The sanative influence of
  climate, 11815
Sanborn, Charles Henry,
  1822-1899, 11754
Sanborn, Helen Josephine,
  1857-1917, 7952
The sanctuary, 10421
Sánchez Espinosa, José, 7406
Sánchez, Manuel Segundo, 7637
Sánchez Pascual, Diego,
  17th cent., 8305
Sánchez Santos, Trinidad,
  1864-, jt. author, 6332
Sánchez Somoano, José, 5068
Sánchez Sorondo, Matías
  Guillermo, 1880-, 7953
Sánchez, Tomás Antonio,
  1725-1802, 399
Sánchez Valverde, Antonio,
  d. 1790, 7954
Sancho Dávila y Bermúdez,
  Antonio, 7611
Sand Creek investigation,
  2995
Sand, George, pseud. of
  Mme. Dudevant, 1804-1876,
  1104

411

Sand'n'bushes, 10545
Sandburg, Carl, 1878-1967,
  7471
Sandiel y Palacios, Mariano
  Buenaventura, 7955
Sandoval, Jerónimo de,
  7827
The Sandown victory, 9863
Sands, Frances M., 1065
Sands, Robert Charles,
  1799-1832, jt. author,
  2157
Sandys, Ed. W., 10125
Sangamon co., Ill. -
  Descr. & trav. - Maps,
  6168
Sangamon co., Ill. -
  Hist., 6847
Sangston, Lawrence, 2479
Sandwich, Edward Montagu,
  1st earl of, 1625-1672,
  tr., 773
Sanford, David, 998
Sanger, George Partridge,
  1819-1890, ed., 239
Sangster, M. E., 10163
Sanillac, 5693
Sant' Ilario, 6504
Santa Anna, Antonio López
  de, pres. Mexico, 1795-
  1876, 1758, 12256
Santa Catalina, 8291
Santa Catharina, Brazil
  (State), 11525
Santa Cruz, Andrés,
  pres. Bolivia, 1794-
  1855 - Poetry, 951
Santa Cruz, Bolivia (Dept.),
  606
Santa Fé and the far west,
  5069
Santa Fé, Conquest of,
  3068
Santa Fé Expedition, 3491,
  4989
Santa Fé, N. M., 3111, 5531
Santa Fé, N. M. - Descr.,
  5739
Santa Fé trail, 3688, 5739,

  6893, 6894, 6895, 7080
Santa Fé y Bogotá, 7956
Santa María, José de, 7957
Santa Marta, 13350
Santander, Juan de, 1145
Santangelo, Francesco Orazio
  Guiseppe de Attellis,
  1807?-1826, 13328
Santangelo, Orazio Donato
  Gideon de Attellis, b. 1774,
  13328
Santee River, 3358
Santiago de Chile. Biblioteca
  Nacional, 7275
Santiago León Garabita,
  Juan de, bp., 6754
Santibáñez, Enrique, 1869-,
  7958
Santo Domingo (French colony),
  19
Sanz de Monroy, Miguel Elias,
  7959
São Francisco river, Brazil,
  11636
Sapia Martino, Raúl, 7874,
  7960
Sapper, Carl, 7961
A Sappho of Green Springs,
  6973
Saracinesca, 6505, 9231
Saratoga, 9299, 10751
Saratoga campaign, 1777 -
  Fiction, 10510
Saratoga in 1901, 10162
Saratoga, N. Y. - Fiction,
  9949
Saratoga Springs, N. Y. -
  Descr. - Guide-books, 195
Saravia, Manuel de, 7962,
  7963
Sarfatti, Margherita Grassini,
  5070
Sargent, Angelina M., 5071
Sargent, John Osborne,
  1811-1891, 12663
Sargent, Winthrop, 1825-
  1870, ed., 5072
Sarinana y Cuenca, Isidro,
  1630?-1696, 5856

Sarmiento de Gamboa, Pedro, 7964
Sarmiento de Mendoza, Diego, 7920
Sarmiento, Domingo Faustino, pres. Argentine republic, 1811-1888, 5073, 7708
Sartorius, Christian, i.e. Carl Christian Wilhelm, 1796-1872, 7965, 7966
Saskatchewan and the Rocky Mountains, 6342, 8080
The Saskatchewan country of the northwest of the dominion of Canada, 8092
Saskatchewan - Descr. & trav., 3877, 3879
Saskatchewan - Hist., 7715, 7796
Saskatchewan river, 3878
The Saskatoon story, 7715
Satanstoe, 9149
Satin, Mark Ivor, 1946-, 7967
Satire, English, 7591
Saturday-night musings and thoughtful papers, 10538
The Saturniad, 694
Sauce for the goose, 9538
Saucier, John Baptiste, b. 1726, 5226
Saugrain de Vigni, Antoine François, 1763-1820, 5074
Saunders, Rolfe S., 7968
Saunders, William, 1823-1895, 5075
Saussure, Henri Louis Frédéric de, 1829-1905, 7969
Sauvalle, Paul Marc, 1857-, 7970
The savage beauty, 10857
Savage, James, 1784-1873, 7971

Les savanes, 5027
Savannah, Ga. - Direct., 1756
Savannah, Ga. - Hist., 6419
Savannah, Ga. - Libraries, 12045
Savannah, Ga. - Siege, 1779, 12933
Savardan, Augustin, 5076
Savery, William, 1750-1804, 5077
Savine, Albert, 8399
Sawyer, Lorenzo, 5078
Say and seal, 11098
Say, Thomas, 1787-1834, 2465, 5079, 5080, 5081, 13360
Sayer, Robert, 1725-, 5082
Sayings and doings at the Tremont House, 10791
The sayings of Dr. Bushwhacker, and other learned men, 9197
Scadding, Henry, 1813-1901, 7972
The scalp hunters, 4925
Scandinavians in the U. S., 6387
The scare-crow, 1944
Scarlet Feather, 9986
The scarlet letter, 9824
Scarritt, Winthrop Eugene, 1857-, 7973
Scattered leaves from a physician's diary, 8451
Scenery of the plains, mountains and mines, 4213
Scenery, science and art, 387
The scenery-shower, 1745
Scenes américaines, 4649
Scenes and adventures in Mexico, 10719
Scenes and adventures in the army, 3081
Scenes and adventures in theatrical life, 10376
Scenes and adventures over the Blue Ridge, 10168
Scenes and incidents illustrative of religious faith

413

and poems, 2497
Scotus Americanus, pseud.,
  5109
The scourge of the
  ocean, 8920
The scourge of the
  river, 4461
The scout, 9977
The scout and ranger,
  4801
The scout's mistake,
  10863
The scout's revenge,
  5663
The scouting expeditions
  of McCulloch's Texas
  rangers, 4926
Scoville, Joseph Alfred,
  1815-1864, 2480
Scrap book on law and
  politics, 4978
Scraps, 10260
Scraps of early Texas
  history, 3833
Scraps of song and
  Southern scenes, 3492
Scribblings and sketches,
  11109
Scribner, Benjamin
  Franklin, 1825-1900,
  5110
Scripps, John Locke,
  1818-1866, 7987
Scrofula, 726
Scrope, 10506
Scudder, Samuel Hubbard,
  1837-1911, 7988
Scull, Gideon Delaplaine,
  1824-1889, 5111, 7799
Scully, Everett Graham,
  7989
Scully, Michael, 7990
Scully, Mrs. Virginia,
  jt. author, 7990
Sculpture, Mexican, 6788
Scylla and Charybdis,
  3498
Sea and shore, 5620
Sea-gift, 9589

A sea-island romance, 8873
The sea-king, 8921
The sea lions, 9150
The sea serpent, 8702, 13010
Sea waifs, 3055
Seabrook, A. M., Dr., 9331
Seabury castle, 9913
Seabury, Samuel, 1729-1796.
  A view of the controversy,
  12600
Seacliff, 9372
Seafaring life, 4146, 9007,
  9634, 11820, 12335
Seafaring life - Fiction,
  3998, 4001, 4004, 4011,
  4014, 4015, 4016, 5157
Sealsfield, Charles, 1793-
  1864, 5112
Seamen, 9829, 11576
Search, Right of, 12222
Sears, Edward Isidore,
  1819-1876, tr., 1859
Sears, Hiram, 7991
Sears, R., 11610
Sears, Robert, 1810-1892, 5113
A season in New York, 10449
The seats of the mighty,
  7688
Seaver, Jesse Montgomery,
  1890-, 7992
Seawell, Molly Elliot,
  1860-1916, 5114, 5115,
  5116, 5117, 5118, 5119,
  5120
Sebastián de la Parra, Juan,
  1546-1622, 7993
Secession, 291, 682, 1165,
  1354, 2115, 2254, 2736,
  2840, 3370, 5943, 6586,
  7185, 10033, 11303, 11391,
  11793, 11861, 12212, 12863,
  13094, 13095
Secession and slavery,
  1354
Secession resisted, 13095
Secession unmasked, 11861
SeCheverell, John, 5121
A second appeal to the
  justice and interests... 13377

416

literature of the West,
2376, 3563
Selections from the
religious and literary
writings of John H.
Bocock, 2746
Selections from the
writings of Mrs. Sarah
C. Edgarton Mayo, 10335
Selections from the
writings of the late
Thomas Hedges Genin,
3588
Seler, Frau Caecilie
(Sachs) 1855-, 7996,
7997
Seler, Eduard, 1849-1922,
7932, 7998
Self-giving, 8646
Self-made, 11121
A self-made woman, 8890
Self-raised, 10843
Selkirk Range, 6890,
8372
Selkirk Settlement, Canada,
11352
Selkirk, Thomas Douglas,
5th earl of, 1771-1820,
6221, 6668, 7999, 8000,
8120
Selma the soprano, 10448
Selter, H. Fouré, 5074
Selwyn, Alfred Richard
Cecily, 1824-1902, 6748
Semblanza de Honduras,
8280
A semi-centenary discourse,
1840
Seminole war, 1st, 1817-
1818, 12238
Seminole war, 2d, 1835-
1842, 1990, 2617, 3046,
4332, 4836, 12238
Seminole war, 2d, 1835-
1842 - Fiction, 9410,
10589
Semmes, Raphael, 1809-1877,
5123, 8001, 8002
Semmes, Thomas Jenkins,

1824-1899, 2052
Semple, Ellen Churchill,
1863-1932, 8003
The semptress, 10904
The senator's son, 11044
Seneca co., O. - Hist.,
11653
Seneca Indians - Missions,
134
Seneca language - Glossaries,
vocabularies, etc., 13125
El Señor Root en Mexico,
7532
Señora. Cavsas ay que obligan
a romper el silencio, 6421
Sense, 10538
The sense of the past, 7128
Sentiñon, G., tr., 8025
The Septameron, 10737
September the eleventh,
1777, 10212
Septimus Felton, 9825
Sepúlveda, Juan Ginés de,
1490-1573, 6355, 8004
The sequel to Rolling Ridge,
9478
Sequestration act, Rules of
practice under the, 2056
The serenades, 10197
Sergeant Atkins, 9410
Sergeant Barnacle, 10783
Sergeant Croesus, 10114
Sergeant, John, 1710-1739,
12895
Sergeant, John, 1779-1852,
1314
The sergeant's private
madhouse, 9217
A series of essays on the
principles and policy of
free states, 13173
Sermón de honras funerales,
8005
A sermon occasioned by the
destruction of Pennsylvania
hall, 2363
A sermon on American slavery,
3303
Sermon on the life and

418

Shelby co., Kentucky -
Hist., 6199
Sheldon, Charles, 1867-
1928, 8012
Sheldon, Lionel Allen,
1831-, 8013
Sheldon, Winthrop Dudley,
1839-1931, 5135
Shells, 12328, 13022
Shelton, William Henry,
1840-, 3417
Shelvocke, George, fl.
1690-1728, 1221, 8014
Shenandoah, The valley
of the, 5474
Shenandoah Valley -
Descr. & trav., 2646,
5630
Shepard, Ashbel K., 8015
Shepard, Cyrus, 1798-1840,
4546
Shepard, Tomas, 1605-1649,
127
Shepherd, Nathaniel, 1712-
1752, 617
Shepherd, William Robert,
1871-, 8016
Sheppard, John H., 8017
Sheppard Lee, 8805
Sheppard, W. L., illustr.,
4795, 5419, 9006
Sherborn, Mass. - Hist.,
1284
Sherbrooke, Sir John
Coape, 1764-1830, 11782
Sheridan and Kotzebue,
1544
Sheridan, Emma V., 10283
Sheridan, Philip Henry,
1831-1888, 1547, 5136
Sheridan, Richard Brinsley
Butler, 1751-1816, 1544
Sheridan's ride, 13466
The sheriff of Siskyou,
6963
Sherley, Douglas, 4473
Sherman brigade, 3882
Sherman, Ernest Anderson,
1868-, 5137

Sherman, William Tecumseh,
1820-1891, 1547, 3075,
6419, 11454
Sherman's march through the
Carolinas, 3887, 4601
Sherman's march to the sea,
2787, 3075, 3546, 3830,
3887, 4601, 4749
Sherman's march to the sea -
Fiction, 4736
Sherratt, Harriott Wight,
8018
Sherwood, Adiel, 1791-1879,
5138
Shewmake, Oscar Lane, 8019
Shiftless folks, 10806
Shillitoe, Thomas, 1754-
1836, 5139
Shiloh, Battle of, 1862,
12125
Shindler, Mrs. Mary Stanley
Bunce (Palmer) Dana,
1810-1883, 5140, 5141,
5142, 5143
Shinn, Earl, 1837-1886, 5144
Ship canal from the
Mississippi to Lake
Michigan, 473
The ship-carpenter's family,
11150
Shipley, Jonathan, bp. of St.
Asaph, 1714-1788. A speech
intended to have been spoken,
2012
Shipping bounties and
subsidies - U. S., 11379
Shipping - Great Lakes, 12577
Shipping - Mexico, 11652
Shipping - Pacific coast,
1913
The shipwreck, 10434
The shipwrecked gold seekers,
9650
Shipwrecks, 199, 586, 2308,
6511, 6512, 7657, 12577
Shirley, Mass. - Hist., 1766
Shirley, Myra Bell, 1846-1889,
correct name of Belle Starr,
6958

The siege of Baltimore, 5494
The siege of Charleston, 5493, 12932
The siege of Cuautla, 7313
The siege of London, 10015
The siege of Richmond, 3078
The siege of Savannah, 12933
The siege of Vicksburg, 10054
Siege of Washington, D.C., 8461
The sieges, 3999
Sierra, Justo, 1848-1912, 5150, 8025
Sierra Nevada, 2892, 3631
Sierra O'Reilly, Justo, 1814-1861, tr., 8109
The sights and secrets of the national Capitol, 12059
Sights from a steeple, 9827
Sights in Boston and suburbs, 13427
Siglo de oro en las selvas de Erifile, 8271
The sign of the cross, 10173
The signet of King Solomon, 8551
Sikes, William Wirt, 10899
Siksika Indians, 3112
Silence, 9578
The silent partner, 11077
Silhouette, 10259
Silhouettes of American life, 9355
Silk manufacture and trade, 11840
Silkworms, 11840, 12734
Silliman, Augustus Ely, 1807-1884, 5151
Silva, J. Francisco V.,

1893-, 8026
Silva y la Vanda, Manuel de, 8027, 8028, 8029
Silver, 7734
Silver and pewter, 9964
The silver buckle, 9268
The silver cup of sparkling drops, 10548
The silver districts of Nevada, 5152
Silver-Knife, 4993
Silver lake, 9579
The silver lining, 9674
Silver mines and mining - Nevada, 2837, 3212, 5152
Silver mines and mining - The Northwest, 862
Silver mining regions of Colorado, 5695
Silver question, 7610
The silver ship of Mexico, 4010
The silver trumpets of the sanctuary, 12047
Simcoe, John Graves, 1752-1806, 5153
Siméon, Remi, ed., 7931
Simmons, Louis A., 5154
Simms, William Gilmore, 1806-1870, 5155, 5156, 5157, 5158, 5159, 5160, 5161, 5162, 5163, 5164, 5165, 5459
Simon Girty, the outlaw, 4122
Simon Kenton, 5663, 10953
Simon Suggs, 3925
Simons, M. Laird, 3332
A simple heart, 3368
Simple settings, 2623
Simplicity's defence against seven-headed policy, 12322
Simpson, Alexander, b. 1811, 5169, 8030
Simpson, Benjamin, pseud., 4830
Simpson, Sir George, 1792-1860, 5166, 6221

9646
Sketches of New England
character and manners,
10727
Sketches of Newport and
its vicinity, 1792
Sketches of North
Carolina, 3499
Sketches of scenes and
characters among the
descendants of the
Pilgrims, 10904
Sketches of society and
adventure at far-apart
times and places,
11180
Sketches of southern and
western life and
adventures, 3037
Sketches of "Stonewall
Jackson", 8034
Sketches of the naval
history of the United
States, 11831
Sketches of the South-
west, 10964
Sketches of the early
Catholic missions
of Kentucky, 5250
Sketches of the history
of literature from
the earliest period
to the revival of
letters in the fifteenth
century, 5338
Sketches of the history
of Stephenson county,
Ill., 4092
Sketches of the life
and character of
Patrick Henry, 5750
Sketches of the south
and west, 3210
Skctches of the three-
fold life of man,
10931
Sketches of the war in
northern Mexico, 8035
Sketches of the Washoe

silver mines, 3212
Sketches of travel in
Oregon and Idaho, 2548
Sketches of travel in the
Old and New world, 5716
Sketches of upper Canada,
12963
Sketches of Virginia, 3500
Sketches of western
adventures, 4337, 4338
Sketches of western
Methodism, 3453
Sketchley, Arthur, pseud.,
5013
Skillman, Isaac, 1740-1799,
supposed author, 181
Skinner, Ichabod Lord,
d. 1852, ed., 262
Skinner, John Edwin Hilary,
5174
The skipper's daughter,
10580
Skisser från en Kaliforniafärd,
3772
Skitt, pseud., 10922
Skizzen aus Amerika, 4195
Skizzen aus den Vereinigten
Staaten von Nordamerika,
4181
Skowhegan, Me. - Hist.,
12657
Slang, 12558
Slashes at life with a free
broad-axe, 10072
Slater, Med, b. 1830? 580
Slater, Nelson, 5175
Slaughter, B. R., 9331
Slaughter, Philip, 3680
The slave, 9865
Slave labor, 2019
Slave life in Virginia and
Kentucky, 3426
The slave states of America,
2850
Slave trade, 145, 522, 1153,
1403, 1512, 6643, 8052,
11563
Slave trade - Africa, 1114,
2209, 11852

427

Slavery in the U. S. -
Controversial literature -
1805, 1429
Slavery in the U. S. -
Controversial literature -
1807, 1428
Slavery in the U. S. -
Controversial literature -
1833, 639, 1881, 3132,
4723, 12783
Slavery in the U. S. -
Controversial literature -
1834, 534, 1341, 1915,
2720, 4851
Slavery in the U. S. -
Controversial literature -
1835, 563, 2257, 2719,
3131
Slavery in the U. S. -
Controversial literature -
1836, 888, 1887
Slavery in the U. S. -
Controversial literature -
1837, 325, 451, 1043,
2165, 11357
Slavery in the U. S. -
Controversial literature -
1839, 11798
Slavery in the U. S. -
Controversial literature -
1840, 3303, 5699, 6919
Slavery in the U. S. -
Controversial literature -
1841, 11853
Slavery in the U. S. -
Controversial literature -
1842, 17, 2718, 12344
Slavery in the U. S. -
Controversial literature -
1843, 721, 1722
Slavery in the U. S. -
Controversial literature -
1844, 13186
Slavery in the U. S. -
Controversial literature -
1845, 948, 3884, 12625,
13280
Slavery in the U. S. -
Controversial literature -

1846, 846, 1342
Slavery in the U. S. -
Controversial literature -
1847, 172, 11437, 13122
Slavery in the U. S. -
Controversial literature -
1848, 1214
Slavery in the U. S. -
Controversial literature -
1849, 11439
Slavery in the U. S. -
Controversial literature -
1850, 1490, 5282
Slavery in the U. S. -
Controversial literature -
1851, 1823, 2282, 2963,
3023, 12522
Slavery in the U. S. -
Controversial literature -
1852, 2474, 2475, 11740
Slavery in the U. S. -
Controversial literature -
1853, 443
Slavery in the U. S. -
Controversial literature -
1854, 387, 1381, 11918,
13260
Slavery in the U. S. -
Controversial literature -
1855, 42, 1049, 6095
Slavery in the U. S. -
Controversial literature -
1856, 2735, 12772, 13176,
13216
Slavery in the U. S. -
Controversial literature -
1857, 154, 155, 4797, 5041
Slavery in the U. S. -
Controversial literature -
1858, 98, 5281
Slavery in the U. S. -
Controversial literature -
1859, 1383, 7297
Slavery in the U. S. -
Controversial literature -
1859-1863, 1057
Slavery in the U. S. -
Controversial literature -
1860, 14, 106, 689, 1895,

10675
Smith, Joseph, 1805-1844, 8044
Smith, Joseph, 1815-1875, 8203
Smith, Joseph Warren, 1831-, 5207
Smith, Julie P., d. 1883, ed., 10805
Smith, Marcus, b. 1815, 6748
Smith, Mrs. Mary Ettie V., 3679
Smith, Philip Henry, 1842-, 8045
Smith, R. F., pub., 5208
Smith, Robert, 1757-1842, 1041
Smith, Samuel, 1759-1854, 5209
Smith, Sidney, 5210
Smith, Solomon Franklin, 1801-1869, 5211, 5212
Smith, Mrs. Susan E. D., 1817-, 5213
Smith, Truman, 1791-1884, 8046
Smith, W. F., 5547
Smith, W. F., & co., New York, 6912
Smith, W. I., jt. author, 4999
Smith, William, 5214
Smith, William, 1727-1803, ed., 267, 12099
Smith, William B., 5215
Smith, William Benjamin, 8047
Smith, William H., of Brooklyn, N. Y., comp., 11541
Smith, William Henry, of Canada, 8048
Smith, William Loughton, 1758(ca.)-1812, 5216
Smith college stories, 8635
Smith's guide to the southwest, 5208

Smithsonian institution, 675, 676, 1475, 8049, 11287
Smithsonian institution - History, 12064
Smithwick, Noah, 1808-1899, 5223
Smoked glass, 10418
The smoked Yank, 3695
The Smoky City, 11224
Smoky Hill Expedition, 3677
Smyth, Sir David William, bart., 1764-1837, 7243
Smyth, John Ferdinand Dalziel, 5224
Snake Indians, 3257
Snake Indians - Language, 5307
The snake of the cabin, 10783
Snake River Indians, 5509
Snelling, William Joseph, 1804-1848, 404
Snow-bound at Eagle's, 6974
The snow-image, 9826
Snow, W. Parker, 8050
Snowden, William H., 8051
Snyder, Adam Wilson, 1790-1842, 5225
Snyder, John Francis, 1830-, 5225, 5226
So many calls, 10904
Sociable visiting, 10197
Social destiny of man, 1530
Social fetters, 5262
Social problems, 6981, 12374
Social relations in our southern states, 3967
Social sciences - Addresses, essays, lectures, 12374
Social sciences - Study and teaching, 2287
Social silhouettes, 9502
The social war of the year 1900, 10161
Socialism, 7658, 8775
Socialism and labor and other arguments, 5245
Socialism - Fiction, 10660

Sociedad Académica de
Amantes de Lima, 7463
Sociedad de amigos del
pais, Panama, 1250
Sociedad de geografía e
historia, Guatemala,
8182
Sociedad económica de
amigos del pais, Havana,
11343
La société américaine,
3308
Société américaine de
France, Paris, 1100
Société de colonisation
européo-américaine au
Texas, Brussels, 3072
Société des amis des noirs,
Paris, 6172, 8052,
8053, 8054
Societies - Bibl. -
Catalogs, 518
Society as I have found
it, 4327
Society for propagating
the gospel among the
Indians and others in
North America, 840, 964,
2174
Society for the commemo-
ration of the landing of
William Penn, Philadel-
phia, 13086
Society for the encouragement
of the British troops
in Germany and North
America, 12659
Society for the propagation
of the faith, Quebec
(Diocese), 5227
Society for the propagation
of the gospel in foreign
parts, London, 419, 654,
1007, 11407, 11651,
12124, 13391
Society for the propagation
of the gospel in foreign
parts, London. Pro-
ceedings, 1732, 1196

A society for the special
study of political economy,
2287
Society in America, 7425
Society, manners and politics
in the United States, 1867
Society of the Army of the
Potomac, 8055
Society of the Cincinnati.
Connecticut, 2146, 2148
Society of the Cincinnati.
New Jersey, 11401
Society of the Cincinnati.
Pennsylvania, 1259, 1822
Society of the Cincinnati.
Rhode Island, 12808
Society of the Cincinnati.
South Carolina, 11448,
12391, 12445, 12611
Society of the Diffusion of
Useful Knowledge, London,
11547
Society of the friendly sons
of St. Patrick of Phila-
delphia for the relief of
emigrants from Ireland,
12880
Society of the sons of New
England of the city and
county of Philadelphia, 1456
Society of United Irishmen
of Dublin. Proceedings,
1931
Society silhouettes, 8703
The Socini-Arian detected,
3028
Socinianism, 3028
Sociology, Christian, 1998
The soft side, 10016
A sojourn in the Old Dominion,
10097
Sol veritatis, 5879
Solano, Francisco, Saint,
1549-1610, 6469, 6470
Solar system, 1696
The soldier God's minister,
2419
A soldier of Manhattan,
2521

432

A soldier of the empire, 10460

The soldier of the revolution, 9702

The soldier's aid society, 10122

The soldier's bride and other tales, 3749

The soldier's friend, 5213, 9460

The soldier's orphans, 10874

A soldier's recollections, 4365

A soldier's reminiscences in peace and war, 4069

The soldier's revenge, 9200

The soldier's story of his captivity at Andersonville, 3649

A soldier's story of the war, 2625

Soldiers, 7719

Soldiers of fortune, 9362

A solemn appeal to the church, 13289

Solís de Merás, Gonzalo, 5228

Solis Folch de Cardona, José, duque de Montellano, d. 1770, 7946

Solis Vango, Juan Próspero de, 8056

Solis y Rivadeneyra, Antonio de, 1610-1686, 8057-8068

A solitary, 9575

The solitary, 10434

Solitary rambles and adventures of a hunter in the prairies, 4686

La solitude avec Dieu, 5024

Solomon, 11205

Solorzano Pereira, Juan de, 1575-1655, 8069-8073

The solution, 7122

Some account of the fever, 2389

Some account of the life of Spencer Houghton Cone, 11870

Some adventures of Captain Simon Suggs, 3925

Some buds and blossoms of piety, 401

Some civil war letters of A. Piatt Andrew III, 2542

Some considerations on the consequences of the French settling colonies on the Mississippi, 5229

Some highways and byways of American travel, 5144

Some impressions of the United States, 3535

Some information respecting America, 3084

Some late words about Louisiana, 4304

Some little of the angel still left, 9015

Some notes on America, 2504

Some observations on a direct exportation of sugar from the British Islands, 501

Some old historic landmarks of Virginia and Maryland, 8051

Some passages in the life of Experience Borgia, 8820

Some rebel relics from the seat of war, 3640

Some religious influences which surrounded Lincoln, 7069

Some remarks on the most rational and effectual means... 13494

Some women's hearts, 10394

Somebody's neighbors, 9121

Somebody's stocking, 10236

Somerset co., Me. - Hist., 12657

Somerset, Henry Charles Somers Augustus, 8074

Something for every body, 9706

Something to do, 10024

Sommer, Johann Gottfried, 1792 or 3-1848, 8075

A son of temperance, ed., 2290

A son of the forest, 405

A son of the Old Dominion, 9770

The song of higher water, 5607

The song of Lancaster, Ky., 4838

A song of reason, 3159

Song of the rivers, 1171

Songs, American, 13420

Songs and poems of the South, 4436

Songs chiefly from the German, 5246

Songs, English, 274

Songs of a day, 5257

Songs of fair weather, 5396

Songs of the free, 11737

Songs of the heart, 4473

Songs of the soil, 5257

Um sonho! Impressões de uma viagem aos Estados Unidos, 3716

Sonora, Mexico - Descr. & trav., 2624, 2837, 4398, 4544, 4922, 6955, 7837

Sonora, Mexico - Hist., 8308

Sons and fathers, 3346

The sons of Ham, 4748

Sons of the American revolution, 8076

Sons of the American revolution. Empire State Society, 6700

The sons of the border, 10863

The soprano, 8709

Sorarte, Francisco, 8272

Sorghum, 13059

Sorondo, Xavier, 1883-, 8077

Sorrows of Don Tomás Pidal, reconcentrado, 10608

Soto, Hernando de, 1500(ca.)-1542, 5469, 7825, 12195, 13108

The soul of Ann Rutledge, 5974

The soul-sisters, 11198

Soulsby, Lucy Helen Muriel, 5230

The sources of the Susquehanna, 9143

The Souris country, 6234

The South: a tour of its battlefields and ruined cities, 5468

South Africa - Descr. & trav., 3991

The south after the war, 4152

South America, 2213, 11479, 13272

South America - Climate, 4039

South America - Comm., 492

South America - Comm. - Gt. Brit., 196

South America - Descr. & trav., 359, 1431, 2003, 4636, 6057, 6141, 6440, 6939, 7042, 7091, 7092, 7306, 7368, 7624, 7648, 7777, 8014, 8075, 8171, 8178, 8243, 8254, 8307, 11934, 11964, 13004, 13200, 13335

South America - Descr. & trav. - Guide-books, 7473, 7653

South America - Disc. & explor., 7629

South America - Hist., 3406, 6734, 11479

South America - Hist. - Wars of independence, 1806-1830, 6028, 7245, 7506, 7625, 7635, 7637, 7664, 8112, 11478

South America - Hist. - Wars of independence, 1806-1830 - Foreign participation,

3603, 4953
Southern states - Descr.
& trav. - Poetry, 4294
Southern states - Direct.,
1756
Southern states - Econ.
cond., 1997, 3902,
4141, 4475, 4611, 4673
Southern states - Fiction,
10782
Southern states - Hist.,
6000
Southern states - Hist. -
Colonial period, 12754
Southern states - Hist. -
Periodicals, 5231
Southern states - Hist. -
Revolution, 2392, 2393,
4238, 5347, 13246, 13380
Southern states - Hist. -
Revolution - Fiction,
4336
Southern states - Hist. -
War of 1812, 4224
Southern states - Pol. &
govt., 6483
Southern states - Pol. &
govt. - 1865-1900,
2124, 3226
Southern states - Soc.
cond., 2579, 3425,
3800, 5734
Southern states - Soc.
life and cust., 2834,
3262, 3967, 3995, 4013,
4133, 4719, 4835, 4886,
4888, 5320, 5349, 5558,
5641, 5799, 8634, 8926,
12841
Southern statesmen of the
old regime, 8232
A southern story, 5320
A southern view of the
invasion of the Southern
states, 5943
A Southern view of the
Negro problem, 8047
Southern war songs, 3411
The southern women of the

second American revolution,
4035
Southern writers, 2632
A southerner, 2214
A southerner among the
spirits, 5142
Southesk, James Carnegie,
earl of, 1827-1905, 8080
Southold, N. Y. - Geneal,
12431
Southward ho! 3783, 10781
The South-west, 4012, 9987
The South-west: its history,
character, and prospects,
4437
Southwest, New, 3688, 5064,
5292, 6893, 6894, 6895
Southwest, New - Descr. &
trav., 2411, 2575, 2837,
4500, 4715, 4922, 5516,
5524, 5541, 5542, 5548,
6784, 6813, 6937, 7080,
7140, 7174, 7772, 7882,
8122
Southwest, New - Descr. &
Trav. - Bibl., 7488
Southwest, New - Hist. -
Sources, 7080
Southwest, Old, 3497, 4435
Southwest, Old - Descr. &
trav., 3163, 3594, 3867,
3979, 4012, 4162, 4332,
4470, 5411, 9987, 10964
Southwest, Old - Hist.,
4437, 8016
Southwest, Old - Hist. -
Civil war, 2808, 3895
Southwest, Old - Hist. -
Revolution, 4767
Southwest, Old - Soc. life
& cust., 4012, 4795, 9987
Southwest on the turquoise
trail, 7080
Southwestern Indiana Historical
Society, Evansville, Ind.,
6665
South-western letters, 7772
Southworth, Edward, 1804-1869,
12471

Souvenir book of historic
  Springfield, Ill., 8081
Souvenir de mon voyage
  aux États-Unis et au
  Canada, 6578
Souvenir of a tour in the
  U.S.A. and Canada, 5637
Souvenirs atlantiques,
  4722
Souvenirs d'outre-mer, 6609
Souvenirs d'un diplomate,
  2588
The sovereign rule of
  South Carolina, 8459
The sovereignty of the
  people, 12402
Spaeth, Adolph, i.e.
  Philip Friedrich Adolph
  Theodore, 1839-1910,
  8082
Spain - Bio.-bibl., 399,
  400
Spain - Colonies, 2437,
  7274
Spain - Colonies - Adminis-
  tration, 6432, 8073,
  8085, 8342
Spain - Colonies - America,
  6355, 6356, 6357, 6358,
  6359, 6360, 6361, 6362,
  6363, 6432, 7657, 8073,
  12145
Spain - Colonies - America -
  Fiction, 4010
Spain - Colonies - Hist.,
  7034, 7035, 8235
Spain - Colonies - Law,
  8073, 8085
Spain - Colonies - North
  America, 4502
Spain - Colonies - South
  America, 2473
Spain - Comm., 6329
Spain - Comm. - Spanish
  America, 402
Spain - Commercial policy,
  402, 2473
Spain - Descr. & trav.,
  3228, 3555, 7842, 8212,

11811, 12722
Spain - For. rel., 5854
Spain - For. rel. - Gt. Brit.,
  12129, 12368, 13408
Spain - For. rel. - U. S.,
  8087
Spain - Hist., 8253
Spain - Hist. - Charles II,
  1665-1700, 7729
Spain - Hist. - Civil war,
  1936-1939 - Personal
  narratives, 7176
Spain - Hist. - Ferdinand
  and Isabella, 1479-1516,
  1200
Spain - Hist. - Gothic period,
  414-711 - Fiction, 10780
Spain - Hist. - Naval,
  7827
Spain - Hist. - Sources,
  1094
Spain. Junta directiva del
  cuarto centenario del
  descubrimiento de America,
  8083
Spain. Laws, statues, etc.,
  402, 5972, 8084, 8085,
  8086
Spain - Officials and
  employees, 8071
Spain - Pol. & govt., 1819,
  5864, 8069
Spain. Sovereigns, etc.,
  1700-1746 (Phillip V)
  Manifeste de Sa Majesté
  Catholique, 12129
Spain. Sovereigns, etc.,
  1788-1808 (Charles IV),
  8087
Spain's lost jewels, 7819
Spalding, Alva, 1773-1796,
  12862
Spalding, Charles C., 5233
Spalding, Henry Harmon,
  1803-1874, 4690, 5234
Spalding, John Lancaster,
  abp., 1840-1916, 5235-5248
Spalding, Martin John, abp.,
  1810-1872, 5240, 5249,

438

5250, 5251
Spangler, Edward,
  defendant, 1305
The Spanglers and Tingles,
  10063
Spaniards in Chile -
  Poetry, 6680, 6681,
  6685, 6686
Spanish America, 432,
  5827
Spanish America - Comm.,
  13383
Spanish America - Comm. -
  Spain, 402
Spanish America - Descr.
  & trav., 1, 26, 950,
  5703, 5964, 6073, 6186,
  6760, 6798, 7248, 8171,
  8289, 8307, 11367,
  11714, 13192
Spanish America - Descr.
  & trav. - Gazetteers,
  128
Spanish America - Descr.
  & trav. - Maps, 13192
Spanish America - For.
  rel. - Gt. Brit.,
  1713
Spanish America - For.
  rel. - U. S., 8269
Spanish America - Hist.,
  1, 1186, 1187, 8073,
  11367, 11523
Spanish America - Hist. -
  To 1830, 7393
Spanish America - Hist. -
  Chronology, 6430
Spanish America - Hist. -
  Sources, 7524, 7567,
  8168, 8169
Spanish America - Hist. -
  Wars of independence,
  1806-1830, 8269
Spanish America - Period.,
  7853
Spanish America - Politics,
  1713, 2437
Spanish America - Pol. &
  govt., 12145

The Spanish conspiracy, 3682
Spanish fiction - Translations
  from foreign literature,
  8223
Spanish language - Chresto-
  mathies and readers, 6699,
  6861
Spanish language - Dict. -
  Guaraní, 7921
Spanish literature - Bibl. -
  Early, 399, 400
Spanish literature - Classical
  period, 1500-1700 - Bibl.,
  399
Spanish literature - Early
  to 1500 - Bibl., 400
Spain Main, 362, 7075, 7898,
  8239, 13192
Spanish Main - Descr. &
  trav., 7095
Spanish Main - Fiction,
  4010
The Spanish pretentions
  confuted, 11523
Spanish succession, War of,
  1701-1714, 1357
Sparing to spend, 8578
Sparks, Jared, 1789-1866,
  239, 2490
Sparrow, Edward, 2044
The Sparrowgrass papers,
  9198
Spaulding, Elbridge Gerry,
  1809-1897, 8088
A speakin' ghost, 9769,
  10790
Speaking the truth for a
  day, 10832
Spear, Samuel Thayer,
  1812-1891, 8089
Spears, John R., ed., 11994
Specimens of newspaper
  literature, 1640
Specimens of the garbling
  of letters by the majority
  of the trustees of Dudley
  observatory, 12332
The spectral mortgage, 10892
The spectre lover, 10844

The spectre of the cathedral, 9716

The spectre steamer, 4011

The spectre's voyage, 10919

Speculation, 461, 10849

Speculum justitae, 10675

A speech intended to have been delivered... 13378

The speech of a Right Honourable gentleman, 12424

Speech of Cassius M. Clay, 3023, 3024, 3025

Speech of Robert Wickliffe, in reply to the Rev. R. J. Breckinridge, 5699

Speech of the Honorable James A. Bayard, 976

Speech on the slavery resolutions, 5282

Speeches and addresses, 3875

Speeches and reports in the Assembly of New York, 824

Speeches and writings of Hon. Thomas F. Marshall, 4401

Speeches of Thomas Corwin, 3093

Speed, James, 1812-1887, 8090, 8262

Speed, Joshua, 6831

Spellers, 5743, 11761

Spelman, Henry, 1595-1623, 5252

Spence, Thomas, b. 1832, 8091, 8092

Spencer, Ambrose, 1765-1848, 820

Spencer Co., Ind., 6662, 6664

Spencer Co., Ind. - Biog., 6663

Spencer Co., Ind. - Hist., 6665

Spencer, Oliver M., 1781? 5253

The spendthrift, 10172

The sphinx's children and other people's, 9122

Spicy, 10160

Spiders and rice pudding, 8694

Spindler, Charles, 9546

A spinster's story, 9518

The spinster's ward, 10860

A spirit in exile, 8688

Spirit of adventure, 2684

"The spirit of 1861", 3670

The spirit of Rhode Island history, 478

The spirit of Roger Williams, 13251

The spirit of Sweetwater, 9607

The spirit-rapper, 1607

"A spirit, yet a woman too", 9487

Spiritual manifestations, 1050

Spiritual vampirism, 5657

Spiritual visitors, 11003

The spiritual voyage, 8823

Spiritualism, 1050, 1406, 1985, 5142, 7445, 7446, 9325, 9920, 10587, 11986

The spiritualists and the detectives, 10530

Spittle (The Rev. Solomon), Diary of, 10701

The spleen, 12384

Spofford, H. P., 10163

The spoils of Poynton, 10017

Spooner, Lysander, 1808-1887, supposed author, 89

Sporting scenes and sundry sketches, 9803

Sports - Texas, 3465

Spotorno, Giovanni Battista, 1788-1844, 727

Spotswood, Alexander, 1676-1740, 6761

Spotswood family, 1820

440

Spotswood family (Alexander
   Spotswood, 1676-1740),
   1820
Spottsylvania, Battle of,
   1864, 5490
The spouse of Christ
   coming out of affliction,
   213
Sprague, Amasa, 1798-1843,
   12311
Sprague, Isaac, 1811-1895,
   illustr., 12355
Sprague, William Buell,
   1795-1876, 8093
The sprightly romance of
   Marsac, 10721
Spring, Arthur L., 8094
Spring, Gardiner, 1785-
   1873, 5254
Spring, Leverett Wilson,
   1840-, 8095
Spring notes from
   Tennessee, 5436
Springfield, Ill. Court
   House, 6847
Springfield, Ill. - Hist.,
   7771
Springfield, Ill. - Views,
   8081
Springfield, Mass. - Hist.,
   1418
Springfield, Mass. Spring-
   field cemetery, 1419
Springs, 806, 9702
Springs and mountains of
   Virginia, 4822
Springs - Virginia, 4605
Springs - W. Va., 4743
Springwinds, 9802
The spy, 9151
The spy of Osawatomie, 10007
The spy unmasked, 863
The square pew, 10747
The squarer, 9533
Squatter life and border
   warfare in the far West,
   12281
Squatter sovereignty,
   1368, 11916

Les squatters, 1108
The Squibob papers, 9393
Squier, Ephraim George,
   1821-1888, 8096, 8097, 8098
The squire of Sandal-Side,
   8742
The squirrel inn, 10895
The stability of Christ's
   church, 804
Stabler, Edward, 1794-1883,
   ed., 11585
The stage-coach, 10704
The stage in romance, and
   the stage in reality,
   10603
Stairs of sand, 2608
Stamford, Conn. - Hist.,
   233
Stamp act, 1765, 572, 2288,
   11763, 11789, 13091, 13368,
   13474
Stamp act congress, New York,
   1765, 572
Stamp duties - Peru, 6368
Standish, 9736
Standish of Standish, 8609
Standish the Puritan, 9737
Stanford University -
   Fiction, 9509
Stanhope, Philip Henry
   Stanhope, 5th earl. History
   of England from the peace of
   Utrecht to the peace of
   Versailles. v. 6, 2272
Stanley, 11052
Stanley, M. D., 10206
Stansbury, Howard, 1806-
   1863, 5255
Stanton, Benjamin, 1809-1872,
   12125
Stanton, Daniel, 1708-1770,
   5256
Stanton, Edwin McMasters,
   1814-1869, 6586, 13278
Stanton, Frank Lebby, 1857-,
   5257
Stanton, Henry Thompson,
   1834-1898, 5258, 5259,
   5260, 5261, 5262

Stanwood, Edward, 1841-
1923, 8099
Stanzas to Queen Victoria,
1711
Staples, John Summerfield,
1844-1888, 6338
Staples, William Read,
1798-1868, ed., 12322
Stapp, William Preston,
8100
The star brethren, 10769
The star corps, 2787
Star-Hunt, Jack, 8101
The star in the West,
2977, 11402
Starboard and port, 7012
Stark, James Henry, 8102
Stark's illustrated
Bermuda guide, 8102
Starks, Me. - Hist.,
12657
Starr, Belle, 1846-1889,
6958
Starr, Frank Farnsworth,
8103
The stars and bars, 10092
Stars and stripes, 2435
Stars and stripes in
maple leaves, 4439
The startled sewing
society, 9208
The starving settlers,
10957
The state, 13151
State and prospects of
religion in America,
673
The state of country,
849, 1466
A state of the province
of Georgia, 5266
State or province? 4800
State rights, 320, 11878,
12153, 12402, 12445,
12635, 12639, 13028,
13082
State, territorial, and
ocean guide book of
the Pacific, 3899

Statement of Major General
Buell, 1658
A statement of the receipts
and disbursements for the
support of the missions, 1995
The states of Central America,
8097
The statesman and the man,
188
Statesmen, American, 869, 902,
4420
Statesmen, British, 223,
11741, 12802
The states of America in
1846, 4420
A statistical account of the
U. S., 4443
A statistical and commercial
history, 13342
Statistical gazetteer of the
state of Virginia, 3351
A statistical view of the
district of Maine, 12408
Statistics of the West, 3750
Statistics - Societies, 303
The statutes at large of the
provisional government of
the Confederate States of
America, 2063
The staying power of Sir Rohan,
10896
Steam-boilers - Incrustations,
11717
Steam navigation - Hist., 854
Steam navigation - Mississippi
river, 12573
Steam navigation - Ohio
river, 12573
Steamboats, 4320
Steamboats - Kansas, 4995
Stearns, William Augustus,
1805-1876, 327
Stecher, W. F., illustr.,
2635
Steedman, I. G. W., 5628
Steel - Metallurgy, 12905
Steele, Allen, 11337
Steele, Mrs. Eliza R., 5263
Steele, James William,

442

1840-1905, 8104, 8105
Steele, Samuel Benfield,
  1849-, 8106
Steele, Zadock, 1758-
  1845, 13078
Steen, Enoch, 3257
Steevens family, 7060
Steevens, John, 7060
Steight's expedition,
  1863, 4970
Steiner, Bernard Christian,
  ed., 3077, 5264
Stella Delorme, 10081
Stella Lea, 10580
Sten, Maria, 8107
Stephen, a soldier of
  the cross, 10137
Stephen Dane, 9423
Stephen Skarridge's
  Christmas, 10896
Stephen, son of Douglas,
  pseud., 6115
Stephens, Alexander,
  1757-1821, 13352
Stephens, Alexander
  Hamilton, 1812-1883,
  3030, 4080, 8232
Stephens, Alice Barber,
  iilustr., 9577, 10896
Stephens, Charles Asbury,
  1845-1931, 8108
Stephens, Henry Louis,
  1824-1882, illustr.,
  9910, 10537
Stephens, John Lloyd,
  1805-1852, 8109
Stephens, Thomas, 5265
Stephens, William,
  1671-1753, 5266
Stephenson county, Ill. -
  Hist., 4092
The step-mother, 10683
The step-mother's recom-
  pense, 9440
Stepping heavenward, 10564
Steps to the kingdom,
  11050
Sterope: the veiled
  Pleiad, 8455

Stetson family, 891
Stetson family (Robert
  Stetson, 1613-1703?), 891
Stetson, Grace Ellery
  (Channing) 1862-1937,
  8969
Steuben, Friedrich Wilhelm
  Rudolf Gerhard Augustus von,
  1730-1794, 6714, 7866
Steuben, N. Y., 7866
Stevens, Charles Augustus,
  b. 1835, 5267
Stevens, George Thomas,
  1832-1921, 5268
Stevens, Isaac Ingalls,
  1818-1862, 5269, 5270,
  5518
Stevens, John, d. 1726,
  tr., 2468
Stevens, John Austin, 8110
Stevens, Rayfred Lionel, 8111
Stevens, Thaddeus, 1792-1868,
  1393
Stevens, Thaddeus, 1792-1868 -
  Addresses, sermons, etc.,
  7353
Stevens, Walter Barlow,
  1848-, 5271
Stevenson, Benjamin Franklin,
  5272
Stevenson, Carter Littlepage,
  1817-1888, 2073
Stevenson, Charles L.,
  jt. author, 704
Stevenson, Edward Irenaeus
  Prime, 10283
Stevenson, John White,
  1812-1886, 13318
Stevenson, Robert Louis,
  1850-1894, 8220
Stevenson, Thomas M.,
  b. 1825 or 26, 5273
Stevenson, William Bennet,
  b. 1787? 8112
Stevenson, William G.,
  5274
Stewart, Alexander Morrison,
  1814-1875, 5275
Stewart, Catherine, 5276

Stormont, Gilbert R., comp., 3866
Storrs, Augustus, 5292
Storrs, Richard Salter, 1821-1900, 8118
Story, Joseph, 1779-1845, 8119, 12410
The story of a common soldier of army life in the civil war, 5284
The story of a dream, 8842
The story of a letter, 8489
The story of a life, 9965
The story of a new parish in the West, 10716
The story of an old soul, 10304
The story of a play, 9953
The story of a pumpkin pie, 2630
The story of a recruit, 10122
The story of a regiment, 3770
The story of a summer, 9036
The story of a thousand, 5439
The story of a trooper, 47
The story of an umbrella, 10046
The story of an untold love, 9537
The story of a valentine, 9463
The story of a wall-flower, 10546
The story of Aunt Becky's army-life, 4693
The story of Avis, 11078
The story of Bryan's station, 4891
A story of Charles

Harris, 10465
The story of Christine Rochefort, 10575
The story of Don Miff, 3157
The story of Fort Frayne, 10127
The story of Judar, 10693
The story of Keedon bluffs, 4564
The story of my life, 5170
The story of old Fort Loudon, 4565
The story of Panama and the canal, 6759
The story of the Alcázar, 9529
The story of the dry leaves, 10608
The story of the great march, 4601
The story of the guard, 12170
The story of the Hessian woman in the camp of Burgoyne, 10570
The story of the seas, 8620
The story of the Sherman brigade, 3882
The story of young Gilsby, 9460
The story reader's garland, 10295
A story-teller pack, 10896
Story, Thomas, 1662-1742, 5293
Story, William Wetmore, 1819-1895, ed., 8119
The stout Miss Hopkin's bicycle, 9580
Stovall, Pleasant A., 5294
The stove, 9216
Stow, Kesiah, d. 1822, 12464
Stowe, Mrs. Harriet Elizabeth (Beecher) 1811-1896, 5295, 8766, 9693, 10163 ·
Stowe, Mrs. Harriet Elizabeth (Beecher) 1811-1896. Uncle Tom's cabin, 48, 1527

Strubberg, Friedrich Armand, 1808-1889. Amerikanische Jagd-und Reiseabenteuer, 5772

The structures on The friendly address examined, and a refutation of its principles attempted, 11239

Struggle for life, 9698, 10427

Struthers, and the comedy of the masked musicians, 9408

Struve, Gustav, 1805-1870, ed., 6186

Stryker, James, 1792-1864, ed., 2482

Stuart, Granville, 1834-1918, 5307

Stuart, James, 1775-1849, 5308

Stuart, James Ewell Brown, 1833-1864, 2034

Stuart, John, 8123

Stuart, Martinus Cohen, 5309

Stuart, Robert, 2528, 3971

Stuart, Mrs. Ruth (McEnery) 1856-1917, 5310-5314

Stuart, Villiers, 1827-, 5315

Stuart-Wortley, Emmeline Charlotte Elizabeth (Manners) 1806-1855, 5316, 8124

Stuber, Johann, 1838?-1895? 5317

Students - Language (New words, slang, etc.), 12558

Students - U. S., 12558

Studies in literature, 3691

Studies in the South and West, 5624

Studies, literary and social, 4089

Studies of the town, 10361

Study and use of ancient and modern history, 11266

A study of Mexico, 8367

Sturge, Joseph, 1793-1859, 5318

Sturz, Johann Jakob, 1800-1877, ed., 8125

Stutfield, Hugh Edward Millington, 1858-1929, 8126

Stuyvesant pear tree, 2141

A subaltern's furlough, 1992

Suburban homes, 9695

Subways - New York (City), 13068

Success (Ship), 1221

A successful man, 9263, 10356

A succinct abridgment of a voyage made within the inland parts of South America, 7218

Sucinta noticia del ramo de la cera en la isla de Cuba, 11343

The sucker's visit to the Mammoth cave, 5401

Sucre, Antonio José de, pres. Bolivia, 1795-1830, 7106, 8127

Sudbury, Mass. - Hist. - Colonial period, 11421

The sufferings of William Green, 3683

Suffolk surnames, 11435

Suffrage - Gt. Brit., 11334

Suffrage - Rhode Island, 2339, 2340

Suffrage - U. S., 12645

Sugar, 12078

Sugar-cane, 12103

Sugar growing, 576, 1080

Sugar growing - Jamaica, 1035

Sugar growing - Louisiana, 13276

Sugar - Manufacture and refining, 12103, 13345

Sugar trade - France, 11970

Sugar trade - West Indies,

500, 501, 2009, 13471
Sulgrave Manor, 5930
Sullivan co., N. H. -
  Biog., 7094
Sullivan co., N. H. -
  Hist., 7094
Sullivan, Sir Edward
  Robert, bart., 1826-
  1899, 5319
Sullivan, George, 1771-
  1838, 88
Sullivan, James, 1744-
  1805, 333, 1646
The Sullivan looking-
  glass, 10909
Sullivan, M. A., illustr.,
  5186
Sullivan, Mrs. Margaret
  Frances (Buchanan),
  jt. author, 6099
Sullivan's Indian campaign,
  1779, 1417, 12096
Sullivan's island, 3108
Sulphur (ship), 6059
Sulphur-springs, 13079
Sulte, Benjamin, 1841-
  1923, 8128, 8129
Suma de geographia, 6674
Sumichrast, Frederick
  Caesar John Martin
  Samuel Roussy de,
  1845-, 10283
A summary description of
  the lead mines in Upper
  Louisiana, 564
A summary, historical and
  political, of the first
  planting, progressive
  improvements, and present
  state of the British
  settlements in North
  America, 3276
A summary of the laws of
  commerce and navigation,
  385
A summary view of America,
  2906
Summer drift-wood for the
  winter fire, 10555

Summer gleanings, 10984
A summer in Alaska, 7982
Summer in Arcady, 8517
Summer in the winter time,
  2557
The Summer-land, 5320
The summer of 1882 among the
  health resorts of northeast
  Georgia, 4958
The summer of the pestilence,
  452
A summer on the borders of
  the Caribbean Sea, 12704
Summer rambles in the West,
  3359
Summer resorts - Canada,
  3253
Summer resorts - U. S., 3253,
  12567
A summer story, 13466
The summer tourist's pocket
  guide to American watering-
  places, 12567
Summer tours, 6322
A summer's romance at Newport,
  10201
Summerfield, John, 1770-1825,
  12848
Summerland sketches, 7655
Summers, Thomas O., ed.,
  4791
Summit Co., O. - Hist., 1263
Sumner, Charles, 1811-1874,
  6288, 8130
Sumner, Charles Allen,
  1835-1903, reporter, 1166
Sumner, William, d. 1855,
  1951
Sumner, William Graham,
  1840-1910, 8131
Sumter (Confederate cruiser),
  5123
Sumter (Confederate cruiser) -
  Fiction, 4733
Sumter, Fort, 11243, 12712
The Sun, New York, 8132
The sun of Saratoga, 2522
Sunday at home, 9827
Sunday-school Union of the

Methodist Episcopal
church, 4546
The sunny land, 10057
The sunny South, 4013
Sunnybank, 5361
Sunshine and sport in
Florida and the West
Indies, 2495
Sunshine and storm, 8812
Sunshine in storm, 8795
Sunshine in the palace
and cottage, 11041
Superannuated, 10748
Superior, Lake, 108,
984, 9619
Supernatural, 12037
Supernatural - Fiction,
10693
Supervisors - New York
(State), 12323
A supplement to the
Selection of all the
laws of the United
States, 1494
The supply at Saint
Agatha's, 11079
Sur les hauts-plateaux
mexicains, 8424
Surby, Richard W., 1832-,
5321
The surf skiff, 9988
Surgeons - New York (City),
2312
Surgery, 6801
Surgery - Congresses,
7398
Surgery - Early works to
1800, 13304
Surinam - Descr. & trav.,
733, 734
Surinam - Pol. & govt.,
2026
Surly Tim, 8910
Surrat, John Harrison,
1844-1916, 7749, 8133
Surratt, Mary E. (Jenkins)
d. 1865, defendant, 1305
Surry co., N. C. - Soc.
life & cust., 10922

Surtees, William Edward,
5322
Surveying - Hist., 6676
Les survivances françaises
au Canada, 7525
Susan's escort, 9694
Susie Rolliffe's Christmas,
10653
The suspending power and
the writ of habeas corpus,
13273
Susquehanna company, 12183
Susquehanna co., Pa. - Descr.
and trav., 13233
Susquehanna Indians, 2515
Susy, a story of the plains,
9792
Sut Lovingood, 3787
Sut Lovingood travels with
old Abe Lincoln, 6960
Sutcliff, Robert, 5323
Suther, Evelyn Greenleaf,
10127
Sutherland, Patrick, 5324
Sutherland, Peter C., 8134
Sutphen, Morris Crater,
1837-1875, 8135
Sutten's death-bed confession,
10932
Sutter, Archibald, 5325
Sutter, John Augustus, 1803-
1880, 12838
The Sutton-Dudleys of
England, 101
Sutton family, 101
Suwanee River, On the, 4905
Suzette, 10976
Svmarios de las cedvlas,
ordenes y provisiones
reales, 8085
Swain, D. L., ed., 3418
Swainson, William, jt. author,
4956
Swallow barn, 10097
Swallow, G. C., 4698
Swalue, Edelhardus Bernardus,
1806-1865, 670, 4098
The swamp outlaws, 5444
The swamp state of Conelachita,

449

10773
Swan, Lansing B.,
  1809-, 8136
Swansea, Henry Hussey
  Vivian, 1st baron,
  1821-1894, 5326
Swearing, 2990
Swedes in the U. S.,
  1364, 4585
Sweet, Alexander Edwin,
  1841-1901, 5327
Sweet bells out of
  tune, 9771
Sweet Cicely, 9889
Sweet Lake, 4837
Sweet, O. P., 5328
Sweet revenge, 10358
Sweet's amusement
  directory and
  travelers' guide, 5328
Sweetbrier and thistle-
  down, 2635
Sweethearts and wives,
  8580
Sweetser, Seth, 1807-
  1878, 8137
Swell life at sea, 10916
Swem, Earl Gregg, 1870,
  ed., 4264
Swett, Samuel, 1782-1866,
  13011
Swett, Samuel, 1782-1866.
  Historical and topogra-
  phical sketch of Bunker
  hill battle, 1882
Swett, Samuel, 1782-1866.
  Who was the commander
  at Bunker hill? 2349
Swiggett, Samuel A.,
  1834-, 5329
Swindlers and swindling,
  10736
"Swingin' round the cirkle",
  10230
Swinton, Archibald Campbell,
  1812-1890, reporter,
  13013
Swinton, William, 1833-
  1892, 8138

Swisshelm, Mrs. Jane Crey
  [Cannon] 1815-1884, 5330
The sword and gun, 3338
Sword and pen, 4672
The sword and the distaff,
  10782
Swords, Thomas, 5331
Sybaris and other homes,
  9695
Sybil Knox, 9696
Sydenham, A. H. The ebb
  tide, 10115
Sydenham, A. H. The story
  of Alcatraz, 10115
Sydenham, Alvin, 10122
Sydney Clifton, 9506
Sydnie Adriance, 9424
The sylphs of the seasons,
  2514
Sylvan lyrics and other
  verses, 3822
Sylvan secrets, 5398
Sylvester, Nathaniel Bartlett,
  1825-1894, 8139
Sylvestris, pseud., 5479
Sylvia Seabury, 10071
Sylvia's world, 8829
Symonds, William, 1556-1616?
  5204
The Symposium, 9817
Synge, Millington Henry,
  8140, 8141
Syracuse, N. Y. - Manners
  and customs, 8189
A system of exchange, 13154
Szyszlo, Vitold de, 8142

T., B., 8763
T. C., 401
Tabares de Ulloa, Francisco,
  8143
Tabb, John Bannister,
  1845-1909, 5332
Taber, I. W., illustr., 5004
Tabla chronológica de los
  descvbrimientos, 6431
Table of distances of the
  Overland daily stage line,

450

3901

Tableau de la situation actualle des colonies, 8144

Taboada e Irarrázabal, Manuel Gervasio de, 8145

Taché, Alexandre Antonin, abp., 1823-1894, 8146, 8147, 8148

Tache, Joseph Charles, 1820-1894, 8149

Tacking up the Hudson, 10798

Tacna-Arica question, 7650

Tactics, 1638, 9664

Taddei, Mario, 5333

Tadeuskund, the last king of the Lenape, 9840

Tafel, Gustav, ed., 5334

Taft, William Howard, 1857-1930, 6483

Tage in Mexico, 7388

Tagebuch einer Reise vom Mississippi nach den Küsten der Südsee, 4501

Tagebuch eines Bayreuther soldaten, 3264

Tagebuchblätter eines hessischen offiziers aus der zeit des nord-amerikanischen unab-hangigkeits-krieges, 3270

Taggart, Charles Manson, 1821-1853, 11746

Tahiti - Descr. & trav., 3977, 7858

Tailfer, Patrick, 5335

The tailor of Gotham, 5654

Taken alive, 10653

Taking chances, 9270

The taking of the Captain Ball, 10043

Talbot county, Maryland - Hist., 4017

Talbot, John, 8150

Talbot, Thomas, 1771-1853, 12074

Talbot, William, tr., 4236

Talboys, William P., 8151

A tale for the rich and poor, 8576

A tale of a lonely parish, 6506, 9232

Tale of a physician, 9335

A tale of our own times, 10723

A tale of Poland, 10760

A tale of St. Domingo, 10670

A tale of the Old Dominion, 11860

A tale of three truants, 9793

The talent in the napkin, 9533

Tales, 10188, 11173

Tales and ballads, 3606

Tales and sketches, 10172, 10730

Tales and sketches from the Queen City, 3284

Tales and souvenirs of a residence in Europe, 10627

Tales by the way, 9195

Tales for you, 10919

Tales, French-Canadian, 13048

Tales of a garrison town, 9460

Tales of a traveller, 10002

Tales of city and country life, 8934

Tales of masonic life, 4533

Tales of terror, 10693

Tales of the backwoods, 4903

Tales of the border, 3751

Tales of the Caddo, 10985

Tales of the devils, 8836

Tales of the Emerald isle, 10920

Tales of the ex-tanks, 9271

Tales of the fireside, 10921

Tales of the garden of Kosciusko, 10153

451

Tales of the good woman, 10492
Tales of the home folks in peace and war, 9751
Tales of the North American Indians, 12750
Tales of the Northwest, 10827
Tales of the Puritans, 8632
Tales of the southern border, 5653
Tales of the Spanish seas, 9850
Tales of three cities, 7129
Tales of trail and town, 9793
Talking for life, 9463
Tallack, William, 1831-1908, 5336, 5337
A Tallahassee girl, 5399
Tallmadge, Samuel, 4589
The Tallow family in America, 11043
Tallulah, 4034
Tallulah and Jocasse, 4949
Tallulah Falls, 3358
Talvi's history of the colonization of America, 13472
Tamaulipas, Mexico, 7589
Tamaulipas, Mexico - Descr. & trav., 4314, 7837
Tamayo, Antonio, 5803
Tamayo, Jorge L., 1912-, 8152
The tame seal, 10310
Tammany society, or Columbian order, 13244
Tamworth, N. H. - Hist., 1988
Taney, Roger Brooke, 1777-1864, 8250
The Tangletown letters, 10611
Tanguay, Cyprien, 1819-

1902, 8153
Tanis, the sand-digger, 5466
Tannehill, Wilkins, 1787-, 5338
Tanner, Henry Schenck, 1786-1858, 5339, 5340, 5341, 5342
Tanner, James, 1844-, 5201
Tanner, John, 1780?-1847, 5343, 6233
Tannstetter Collimitius, Georg, ed., 126
Tansill, Robert, 5344
Tans'ur, William, d. 1783. The royal melody compleat, 985
Taos, N. M., 2411
The taper, 10448
Tapley, Rufus Preston, 1823-1893, 8154
Tappan, David, 1752-1803. Christian thankfulness explained and enforced, 11501
Taquisara, 9233
A tar heel Confederate soldier, 4254
Tarahumare Indians, 7310
Tarascan Indians, 7341, 8266
Tarascan language, 947
Tarbell, J., 5345
Tardes nubladas, 7706
Tardy, Mrs. Mary T., ed., 5346
Tariff - Confederate States of America, 2060
Tariff - Confederate States of America - Law, 2064
Tariff (of 1857) made of force by act of Congress of the Confederate States of America, 2064
Tariff - Mexico, 7707
Tariff - Mexico - Law, 8209
Tariff - U. S., 291, 687, 688, 1266, 1608, 2031, 2111, 2338, 2453, 4946, 11226, 11505, 11618, 11716, 12446, 12595

Tariff - U. S. - Law,
1494
Tariff - U. S. -
Speeches in Congress,
430, 876
Tarleton, Sir Banastre,
bart., 1754-1833, 5347
Tarrant, Eastham, 5348
Tasistro, Louis Fitzgerald,
5349
Tasmania - Descr. & trav.,
12784
Tasse, Joseph, 8155
Tassin, Algernon, 10283
The taste of the age, 2564
Tatham, William, 1752-
1819, 5350
Tattle-tales of Cupid,
9538
Taughannock falls, N. Y.,
12593
La tavola di bronzo, 727
The tax-payer's manual,
11422
Tax-sales - U. S., 1377,
1378
Taxation, 6712, 13425
Taxation - Confederate
States of America,
2047, 11871
Taxation - Gt. Brit.,
6712
Taxation - Mexico - Law,
8209
Taxation of U. S. bonds,
1616
Taxation - Peru -
Colonial period, 6282
Taxation - U. S. -
Speeches in Congress,
1393
Taylor, Bayard, 1825-1878,
5351, 8156, 8157, 8158,
8597
Taylor, Benjamin Franklin,
1819-1887, 5352, 5739
Taylor, Bert Leston,
1866-1921, 6921
Taylor, Edward Burnett,

8159
Taylor, Frank Hamilton,
5353
Taylor, Henry W., 7473
Taylor, Isaac, 1759-1829,
8160
Taylor, James W., 7510
Taylor, James Wickes,
1819-1893, 5534
Taylor, John, 1753-1824,
supposed author, 5355, 13487,
13488
Taylor, John, 1779-1863,
ed., 7090
Taylor, John Glanville,
1823-1851, 8161
Taylor, Oliver Alden, 1801-
1851, 350
Taylor, Samuel, jr., jt.
author, 4210
Taylor, Mrs. Sarah Louisa
(Foote) 1809-1836, 13310
Taylor, Mrs. Susie King,
1848-, 5356
Taylor, Zachary, pres. U. S.,
1784-1850, 215, 1093,
2374, 13092
Tazewell co., Va. - Hist.,
1249
Tazewell, Littleton Waller,
1774-1860, 12439
Tea, 11368
The tea-rose, 10904
Teachings and tendencies,
10610
Teachings of patriots and
statesmen, 11751
The tear in the cup, 4906
Tears on the diadem, 9417
Tebicuary river, Paraguay,
593
Tecajic, Mexico. Nuestra
Señora de los Angeles
(Shrine), 7459
Technical education - U. S.,
12261
Technology - Period., 262, 269
Tecumseh, 2197
Tecumseh, Shawnee chief,

453

1768-1813, 3283, 12741
Tecumseh, Shawnee chief,
1768-1813 - Drama,
2197
Tehuantepec canal, 2390
Tehuantepec, Isthmus of,
1444, 1748, 2390
Tehuantepec railroad
company of New Orleans,
1748
Teja Zabre, Alfonso,
1888-, 8162
Tekel, 8840
Telegraph, 4808, 9044
Telegraph - Hist.,
11520, 13287
Telegraph - Period., 306
The tell-tale, 10516
Temperance, 1152, 2990,
7715, 9973, 10548
Temperance - Addresses,
essays, lectures, 11247,
13219
The temperance doctor, 8982
Temperance - Exercises,
recitations, etc., 10156
Temperance - Fiction,
2290, 8871, 8892, 9077,
9405, 10702, 10703
Temperance - Hist., 457,
668, 11603
Temperance - Societies,
307, 2077, 13249
Temperance tales, 8581
Temperance versus intemper-
ance, 8892
Tempest and sunshine,
9904
Tempest-tossed, 10979
The Templar's daughter,
8551
Temple, N. H. - Geneal,
11290
Temple, N. H. - Hist.,
11290
The temple of liberty,
3382
Temple, Oliver Perry,
8163

Temple, Wayne C., ed.,
6197
Tempsky, Gustav Ferdinand
von, 8164
The temptation, 10841
Ten millions, 8650
Ten months in Libby prison,
11706
Ten nights in a bar-room,
and what I saw there,
8582
Ten thousand miles in a
yacht round the West Indies
and up the Amazon, 5939
Ten thousand miles of travel,
5449
Ten thousand miles on a
bicycle, 2592
Ten years in Oregon, 2508,
4237
Ten years in Texas, 3686
Ten years in the U. S., 4485
Ten years in Washington,
2532
Ten years in Winnipeg, 6056
Ten years of a lifetime,
9927
Ten years of preacher-life,
4469, 13429
Ten years of torture, 10932
Ten years on a Georgia
plantation since the war,
4247
The tenant of Woodfell, 5721
The tenants of a lord bishop,
10339
Tennant, Charles, 1796-1873,
2483
Tennent, William, 1705-1777,
11400
The Tennessean, 5037
The Tennessean's story, 5156
Tennessee - Antiq., 12770
Tennessee. Bureau of
agriculture, statistics and
mines, 5357
Tennessee cavalry. 1st
battalion, 1861-1862, 3767
Tennessee cavalry. 7th

battalion, 1861-1862,
3767
Tennessee cavalry. 1st
regt., 1846-1847,
6791
Tennessee cavalry. 2d
regt., 1862-1865, 3767
Tennessee cavalry. 7th
regt., Co. E, 1861-1865,
3959
Tennessee - Descr. &
trav., 2745, 2752, 3089,
3261, 3342, 3425, 3739,
4173, 4217, 4559, 4646,
4758, 4791, 5382, 5436,
5601, 5706, 5723, 12770
Tennessee - Descr. &
trav. - Gazetteers, 4527
Tennessee - Descr. &
trav. - Guide-books,
3798, 4160
Tennessee, East - Descr.
& trav., 5198
Tennessee, East - Hist. -
Civil war, 1478
Tennessee, East - Soc.
life & cust., 5402
Tennessee - Econ. cond.,
2745, 5357
Tennessee - Fiction,
3366, 4553, 4554, 4555,
4556, 4557, 4558, 4560,
4561, 4562, 4563, 4564,
4565, 4566, 4567, 4907,
10592
The Tennessee gazetteer,
4527
Tennessee. General assembly.
1867. Senate, 2323
The Tennessee hand-book
and immigrant's guide, 2752
Tennessee historical
society, 2110
Tennessee - Hist.,
4527, 11508, 12769
Tennessee - Hist. -
Civil war, 1658, 2050,
2156, 3371, 3611, 4523,
11328, 11329

Tennessee - Hist. - Civil
war - Fiction, 8755
Tennessee - Hist. - Fiction,
10134
Tennessee - Hist. - Sources,
5723
Tennessee infantry. 1st
regt., Co. H., 1861-1865,
5635
Tennessee; its agricultural
& mineral wealth, 5357
Tennessee, Middle - Hist.,
11674
Tennessee - Pol. & govt. -
Civil war, 2840
The tent, 10172
The tenth of January, 11075
Teotihuacán, Mexico, 7483,
7484, 7486
Terán, Luis de, tr., 8112,
8319
Terasaki, Taro, 8165
The tercentenary history of
Canada, 8224
Tercera iglesia de Terceros
dominicos, 8311
Teresa, Saint, 1518-1582,
8166
Terhune, Albert Payson,
1872-1942, jt. author,
10937
Terhune, Mrs. Mary Virginia
(Hawes) 1830-1922, 5358,
5359, 5360, 5361, 8167,
10163
Termer, Franz. El valor
histórico, geográfico y
etnológico de los apuntes
de Cockburn, 8303
Ternaux-Compans, Henri,
1807-1864, ed., 8168, 8169
La terre chaude, 11261
Terrell, Alexander Watkins,
1827-1912, 8170
Terres mexicaines, 7262
Terrien, Ferdinand, 8171
The territories of Kansas
and Nebraska, 4495
Terror (Ship), 614

Terry rangers, 2726
Terry, Thomas Philip,
1864-, 8172, 8173
Terwecoren, Ed., ed.,
5178
The test of loyalty,
9860
Tested, 9601
The testimony of an
escaped novice from
the Sisterhood of
St. Joseph, 8896
Testut, Charles, 5362,
5363
Teverbuagh, Solomon,
jt. author, 3940
Tevis, John, 1792-1861,
5364
Tevis, Julia Ann
(Hieronymus)1799-,
5364
Texada Island, 6183
The Texas captain and
the female smuggler,
10252
The Texan emigrant, 5280
Texan Emigration and Land
Company, 5365
Texan ranch life, 7140
Texan Santa Fe expedition,
3414, 4150
The Texan virago, 5654
Texas, 2292, 2732, 2942,
3341, 3903, 4999
Texas and Mexico in
1846, 7581
Texas and Pacific
railway company, 5366
Texas and the Massachusetts
resolutions, 41
Texas and the Texans,
3497
Texas - Annexation, 12191,
12623, 13280, 13371
Texas - Annexation to the
U. S., 41
Texas - Biography, 2827
The Texas bravo, 4991
Texas brigade, 1861-

1865, 4823
Texas Catholic historical
society, 5368
Texas cavalry. 3d regt.,
1861-1865, 2619
Texas cavalry. 4th regt.,
1861-1865, 4610
Texas cavalry. 5th regt.,
1861-1865, 4610
Texas cavalry. 7th regt.,
1861-1865, 4610
Texas cavalry. 8th regt.,
1861-1865, 3600
Texas cavalry. 13th battalion,
1862-1865, 4610
Texas cavalry. McCulloch
independent company, 1845-
1848, 4926
Texas cavalry. Morgan's
battalion, 1861-1865, 3828
Texas cavalry. Ross'
brigade, 1861-1865, 5014
Texas cavalry. Sibley's
brigade, 1861-1865, 4610
Texas - Descr. & trav.,
2575, 2624, 2759, 2777,
2789, 2942, 3117, 3209,
3241, 3265, 3362, 3414,
3415, 3442, 3464, 3465,
3491, 3510, 3566, 3573.
3675, 3686, 3763, 3789,
3833, 3886, 3903, 3927,
3947, 3955, 3963, 3985,
4041, 4150, 4158, 4173,
4314, 4316, 4334, 4346,
4398, 4494, 4504, 4510,
4586, 4657, 4675, 4696,
4703, 4791, 4868, 4922,
4973, 5060, 5076, 5104,
5191, 5223, 5271, 5280,
5306, 5327, 5365, 5366,
5367, 5369, 5500, 5532,
5549, 5579, 5590, 5648,
5755, 5763, 5772, 6607,
6609, 7140, 7159, 7219,
7489, 7536, 7581, 7798,
8174, 8180, 10717
Texas - Descr. & trav. -
Guide-books, 3970, 4021

Texas - Econ. cond.,
3072, 3886, 4974,
5021
Texas - Emig. & immig.,
5365
Le Texas et sa revolution,
4233
Texas - Fiction, 4991,
8958, 9256, 10717
Texas - Hist., 2559,
2596, 2826, 2827, 3762,
4069, 4150, 4282, 5368,
5413, 5775, 6249, 7219,
7581
Texas - Hist. - To 1846,
3241, 3341, 3497, 3947,
4158, 5280, 5786, 5968,
8255
Texas - Hist. - To 1846 -
Sources, 4742
Texas - Hist. - Civil
war, 4616, 5105
Texas - Hist. - Fiction,
10372
Texas - Hist. - 1810-
1821 - Fiction, 8543
Texas - Hist. - Republic,
1836-1846, 3669, 3681
Texas - Hist. - Revolution,
1835-1836, 568, 3122,
3356, 3442, 3669, 4233,
4282, 4405, 4592, 4696
Texas - Hist. - Revolution,
1835-1836 - Fiction,
8738, 9020, 9597, 9598,
10372
Texas - Hist. - Societies,
5368
Texas im jahre 1848, 2777
Texas in 1840, 5369
Texas infantry. 1st regt.,
1861-1865, 4823
Texas infantry. 4th regt.,
1861-1865, 3195, 4823,
7757
Texas infantry. 5th regt.,
1861-1865, 3471, 4823
Texas: its history,
topography, agriculture,

commerce and general
statistics, 3985
Texas literature, 3258
Texas o Nuevas Filipinas,
8174
Texas - Pol. & govt. -
Civil war, 12605
Texas - Pol. & govt. -
1865-, 3010
A Texas ranger, 4057
Texas rangers, 4057
The Texas rifle-hunter,
3465
A Texas scrap-book, 2596
Texas - Soc. life & cust.,
4616, 4725, 8958
Texas: the home for the
emigrant from everywhere,
5367
Texas und seine revolution,
3356
Texas Western Railroad
Company, 5370
A Texian, 9598
Textbooks - U. S., 7070
Textile industry - South
Carolina, 5563
Thacher, James, 1754-1844,
5371
Thackery, William Makepeace,
1811-1863, 3133
Thames, Battle of, 1813 -
Drama, 2197
Thames, Battle of, 1813 -
Poetry, 5494
Thanet, Octave, pseud., 9581
Thankful blossom, 9794
Thanksgiving day addresses,
447, 1190, 1300, 1445,
2131, 11305, 11308, 11317,
11972, 11982, 12725
The Thanksgiving party and
its consequences, 9896
Tharin, Robert Seymour
Symmes, 1830-, 5372
That fortune, 11089
That gentleman, 10197
That Island, 9247
That lass o' Lowrie's, 8911

That new world, 4786
That same old 'coon,
10892
Thatcher, Marshall P.,
5373
Thayer, James Bradley,
1821-1902, 8175
Thayer, William Makepeace,
1820-1898, 8176, 8177
Thaxter, C. A., 10163
Thaxter, Samuel, d. 1842,
13036
Theater - Boston, 12549
Theater - Moral and
religious aspects,
6918
Theater - New Orleans,
5212
Theater - Period, 11933
Theater - Philadelphia -
Period, 11933
Theater - U. S., 2695,
5211, 5212
Theater - U. S. - Hist.,
5122, 12828
Theaters - Fires and fire
protection, 5863
The theatrical journey-
work and anecdotical
recollections of Sol.
Smith, 5211
Theatrical management in
the West and South
for thirty years, 5212
A theatrical trip for a
wager! 7862
Theatro americano, 8310
Theatro naval hydrográ-
phico, 7995
"Their children", 9014
Their pilgrimage, 11090
Their silver wedding
journey, 9954
Their uncle from
California, 9791
Thekla, 8549
Theodora, 10284
Theodore and Matilda,
10950

Theodosia Ernest, 9367
Theognis, 10986
Theology - Bibl., 349
Theology - Bibl. - Catalogs,
350
Theology - Collected works -
17th cent., 7733
Theology - Collected works -
18th cent., 1098, 2959
Theology - Collected works -
19th cent., 4535
Theology, Pastoral -
Anecdotes, facetiae, satire,
etc., 11110, 13450
A theoretical and practical
grammar of the Otchipwe
language, 771
Therapeutics, 943
They bore a hand, 10608
They met by chance, 10237
The thief in the night,
10856
Thiel, Johannes, illustr.,
2693
Thielmann, Max Franz Guido,
freiherr von, 1846-, 8178
Things as they are in
America, 2964, 11710
Things of the mind, 5247
Things seen and heard, 9854
The thinking bayonet, 9925
The third person, 10016
The third troublesome
voyage, 6989
The third violet, 9215
The thirst and the draught,
10304
Thirteen at table, 9768
Thirteen months in the Rebel
army, 5274
Thirteen years in Mexico,
6626
Thirty-six years of a
seafaring life, 8179
Thirty years in the wilderness,
3034
Thirty years' view, 1185
Thirty Years War, 1618-1648,
8323

This is the story of
  Mexico, 8173
This majestic lie,
  9217
This was Montreal in
  1814-1817, 7526
Thistle, Timothy,
  pseud., 9481
Thoburn, James M., 10333
Thomas, David, 1776-1859,
  5375
Thomas, Dr., 5374
Thomas, Ebenezer Smith,
  1775-1845, 5376
Thomas, Frederick William,
  1806-1866, 5377, 5378,
  5379, 5380, 5381
Thomas, George Henry,
  1816-1870, 1547
Thomas, Isaiah, 1749-1831,
  244
Thomas, Joseph, 1791-1835,
  5382, 5383
Thomas, Robert Horatio,
  1861-1916, ed., 8180
Thomassy, Marie-Joseph-
  Raymond, 1810-1863,
  5384
Thome, James Armstrong,
  5385, 8181
Thompson, David, 1770-
  1857, 7009
Thompson, Francis M.,
  5386
Thompson, George, gunner,
  13489
Thompson, George Alexander,
  128, 8182, 8183
Thompson, James Maurice,
  1844-1901, 5387-5400
Thompson, John Caldwell,
  1831-1904, 8184
Thompson, John Sparrow
  David, 8185
Thompson, Joseph Parrish,
  1819-1879, 313
Thompson, L., 13490
Thompson, Lawrence Sidney,
  1916-, 8186-8190

Thompson, Ralph Seymour,
  5401
Thompson, Samuel Hunter,
  1876-, 5402
Thompson, Waddy, 1798-1868,
  8191
Thompson, William Tappan,
  1812-1882, 5403, 5404,
  5405, 10861
Thomson, C. T., 8192
Thomson, James, 1700-1748,
  12368
Thomson, John, 1777-1799,
  295
Thomson, John Renshaw,
  1800-1862, 5406
Thomson, Mortimer, 1832-
  1875, jt. author, 11038
Thomson, Norman, 8193
Thomson, Peter Gibson, 5407
Thomson, William, 5408
Thornbury, George Walter,
  1828-1876, 5409
Thornton, Anthony, 6391
Thornwell, James Henley,
  1812-1862, 4688
Thorpe, 10395
Thorpe, Thomas Bangs,
  1815-1878, 5411, 5412
Those old lunes, 10783
Those orphans, 9158
Thoughts about the city of
  St. Louis, 12832
Thoughts and theories of
  life and education, 5248
Thoughts and things at
  home and abroad, 11632
Thoughts for the times, 320
Thoughts on education in
  its connexion with morals,
  1618
Thoughts on popular and
  liberal education, 2888
Thoughts on "the excitement"
  in reply to a letter to
  Hon. Edward Everett, 173
Thoughts on the increasing
  wealth and national economy
  of the United States of

461

"Tincter ov iron", 10808
Tinkling cymbals, 9503
Tippecanoe, Battle of,
  1811, 5745
Tippecanoe, Battle of,
  1811 - Poetry, 5603
Tirar y Soult, 9355, 10163
Tissandier, Albert, 1839-,
  5424
Tit for tat, 1945
Titan Agonistes, 10982
Tithes - Peru, 6828
Titus, a comrade of the
  cross, 10138
Tiverton tales, 8858
Tixier, Victor, 1815-
  1885, 5425
Tlaloc, 7491
To Cuba and back, a
  vacation voyage, 6540
To emigrants to the gold
  region, 4975
To leeward, 9234
To Mexico by palace car,
  8105
To seem and to be, 10280
To suffer and be strong,
  8952
To the electors of the
  First senatorial
  district, 802
To the freemen of Fayette,
  Woodford, and Jessamine,
  5426
To the Pacific and Mexico,
  7358
To the people of Kentucky,
  3526
To the public, 4810
To the young men of the
  states of the American
  Union, 2370
Tobacco, 1555, 2208, 3628,
  5350, 11656, 11682, 13207
Tobacco - Early works to
  1800, 11691
Tobacco manufacture &
  trade - Cordoba, Mexico,
  6481

Tobacco manufacture & trade -
  Orizaba, Mexico, 6481
Tobacco manufacture & trade -
  Virginia, 11691
Tobacco - Taxation - Peru,
  7426
Tobias Wilson, 9023
Tobler, Johannes, 5427
Toca Velasco, José Ignacio
  de, 5428
Tocqueville, Alexis Charles
  Henri Clerel de, 1805-1859,
  5429
Today, 10106
Today in America, 3809
Todd, Albert, 1854-, 8202
Todd, Charles Stewart,
  1791-1871, 3690
Todd family (Adam Todd,
  d. 1765?) 12398
Todd, Lyman Beecher, 8203
Todd, William, b. 1839 or 1840,
  5430
Toil and travel in further
  North America, 4973
Toiling and hoping, 10318
Toinette, 10996
A token for children, 13159
Tokens - New York (City),
  1752
Tokens - U. S., 1750, 11756
Told between the acts,
  11198
Told by the colonel, 8494
Told in the coffee house,
  8480
Told in the hills, 10689
Toledano, Francisco de
  Paula, 8204
Toledo, Antonio Sebastián
  de, marqués de Mancera,
  d. 1715, 7918
Toleration, 7574
Tolliver, Arthur S., 8205,
  8206
Tolliwotte's ghost, 10298
Tolmer, J., 5431
Tolstoy, L., 10448
Toluca, Mexico - Descr., 6811

trade and plantations,
1724, 501

Torrie, Hiram D., 8215

Torrijos, José María,
1791-1831, tr., 7506

The Tory of Carolina,
9433

Toscanelli, Paolo del Pozzo,
1397-1482, 1081

A toss-up for a husband,
10298

Totemwell, 10494

Totman family (Henry
Tottenham, d. 1728),
2372

Totten, Joseph Gilbert,
1788-1864, 835

Touch not, taste not,
handle not, 9877

Touched with the tar-
brush, 9460

A touchstone, 11130

Tour in America, 6241

A tour in Mexico, 7543

A tour in the states and
Canada, 3687

Tour in Virginia,
Tennessee, etc., 3089

The tour of H.R.H. the
Prince of Wales through
British America and
the U. S., 4522

A tour of the St. Louis,
3158

A tour of the prairies,
4029

A tour of the U.S.A.,
5224

A tour through part of
Virginia, 2890

A tour through the
island of Jamaica,
8386

A tour through Upper
and Lower Canada, 7628

Tourgée, Aimée, illustr.,
10944, 10995

Tourgée, Albion Winegar,
1838-1905, 3073, 5439

Tourist trade - West Indies,
6333

The tourist's guide of
Florida, 4239

Tourists' and settlers' guide
to Florida, 4018

Tourists' guide for pleasure
trips to the summer
resorts, 5440

Touro, Judah, 1775-1854,
5840

Tousey, Sinclair, 1818-1887,
8216

Toussaint Louverture, Pierre
Dominique, 1746-1803,
3237

Toutain, Paul, 1848-, 5441

Tower, Philo, 5442

Towle, George Makepeace,
1841-, 5443

Towles, Susan Starling,
8217

Town, Ithiel, 1784-1844,
2096

The town poor, 10043

Towne, Benjamin, d. 1793,
12293

Townsend, George Alfred, 5444,
8218

Townsend, Howard, 1823-1867,
11827

Townsend, John Kirk,
1809-1851, 5445

Townsend, John Wilson,
1885-1868, 5446, 8219,
8220, 8221, 8222

Townsend, Mrs. Mary Ashley
(Van Voorhis) 1832-1901,
5447, 5448

Townsend, Peter S., 11779

Townshend, Frederick Trench,
1838-1924, 5449, 5450

Townshend, Samuel Nugent,
1844-1924, 5451

Toxar, Francisco de, ed. and
tr., 8223

Tracked by blood-hounds,
3305

A tract descriptive of

464

Montana Territory, 5481
Tracy and brothers,
Claremont, N. H., pub.,
13078
Tracy, Ebenezer Carter,
1796-1862, 5452
Tracy, Frank Basil,
1866-, 8224
Tradescant, John, d. 1637?
12192
A tradesman's travels, in
the U. S. and Canada,
5408
Traditions of De-Coo-Dah,
13457
The tragedy of Abraham
Lincoln, 8215
A tragedy of the mountains,
9867
The tragic muse, 7130,
10018
Tragic scenes in the
history of Maryland and
the old French war, 769
The trail hunter, 2496
The trail of the "Bull-
dog," 4750
The trail of the lonesome
pine, 9558
Traill, Mrs. Catherine
Parr (Strickland)
1802-1899, 8225, 8226
Traite des noirs, see
Slave trade.
Traité théorique et
pratique de droit public
et administratif, 952
Traits of American humor,
3731
Traits of American Indian
life and character,
4641
Traits of American life,
2458
The tramp at home, 4453
Tramp and farmer in U.S.A.,
5096
The tramp's wedding, 10546
Tramps, 4738

Tramps and triumphs of the
Second Iowa infantry, 2665
Tranchepain de St. Augustine,
Marie, d. 1733, 3725, 5453
Trans-Pacific sketches, 3416
Transactions of the Anti-
septic club, 8452
A transatlantic holiday,
3461
Transatlantic rambles,
5454
Transatlantic tracings, 3254
Transatlantic wanderings,
4645
Transatlantisches skizzenbuch,
3935
Transcendental wild oats,
10163
The transferred ghost, 10892
La transfiguración Dominicana,
6726
The transformation, 8861
The transformation of
Buckeye Camp, 9791
Transatlantic sketches, 1852,
2502, 4138
Transportation - Canada -
Hist., 6638
Transportation - Great Lakes,
13235
Transportation - Rates, 12016
Transportation - Southwest,
New, 3113
Transportation - U. S.,
4768
Transportation - U. S. -
Hist., 6638
Transunion and Tehuantepec
route (railroad), 1748
Transvestites in fiction,
4199
Transylvania university,
Lexington, Ky., 1783-1865,
5785
Transylvania university,
Lexington, Ky., 1783-1865.
Medical Dept., 2887
The trapper's bride, 2684,
3142, 5061

465

Trappists, 7858

Tratado cōprobatorio del emperio soberano, 6363

The trauailes of Iob Hortop, 7065

Trautz, Margerete, 8227

Travaux publics des États-Unis d'Amérique en 1870, 4380

Travel and talk, 3811

Travel - Anecdotes, facetiae, satire, etc., 10930

A travel study tour through Mexico, 7098

A traveler from Altruria, 9955

The traveler's own book, 12721

The travelled spider, 10046

The traveller's and tourist's guide through the U. S. and Canada, 5726

Traveller's companion and guide westward, 4892

The traveller's directory through the U. S., 4444

The traveller's dream, 12773

The traveller's guide, 2616

The traveller's guide through the middle and northern states, 6547, 6548

Traveller's guide through the U. S., 4768

The travellers' entertainment, 8713

Travelling about over new and old ground, 2819

The travelling tin-man, 10197

Travels across the plains in 1852, 4339

Travels and adventures in Mexico, 6344

The travels and researches of Alexander von Humboldt, 7091

Travels at home and abroad, 5190

Travels by sea and land of Alithithera, 10453

Travels: comprising a journey from England to Ohio, 3408

Travels from ocean to ocean, 3652

Travels in America, 2561, 2917, 9652

Travels in Canada, and in the United States, in 1816 and 1817, 3738

Travels in Central America, 7534

Travels in Europe and America, 2755

Travels in India a hundred years ago, 5488

Travels in Mexico and California, 3018

Travels in North America, 4319, 5456, 7346, 7347, 8228, 8229

Travels in North America in the years 1827 and 1828, 3734

Travels in Peru and Mexico, 7050

Travels in search of a settler's guide book of America and Canada, 3921

Travels in some parts of North America, 5323

Travels in South and North America, 4389

Travels in the Californias, 3420

Travels in the central portions of the Mississippi valley, 5099

Travels in the great western prairies, 3421

Travels in the interior inhabited parts of North America, 6290

Travels in the interior
of Mexico, 6955
Travels in the two
hemispheres, 3304
Travels in the U.S.A.,
4445, 5147
Travels in the U. S.
and Canada in 1826,
6577
Travels of an American
owl, 10049
Travels of Anna Bishop
in Mexico, 8230
The travels of Capts.
Lewis and Clarke, 5457
Travels through America,
3508, 3511
Travels through lower
Canada, and the U.S.A.,
4204
Travels through North
and South Carolina, 2631
Travels through part of
the U. S. and Canada,
6639
Travels through the
Canadas, 7016
Travels through the
interior parts of
America, 345, 346
Travels through the
middle settlements in
North America, 2861
Travels through the states
of North America, 8363
Travels through the states
of North America, and
the provinces of Upper
and lower Canada, 5671
Travels through the
United States and Canada,
2734
Travels through the
western interior of the
U. S., 4162
Travesi, Gonzalo G., 6585
Treadmill, 12675
Treason and law, 12662
Treason in the camp, 8785

A treasure of the galleon,
6965
A treasure of the redwoods,
6969
Treaties, 7913, 11371
A treatise of church
discipline, 4120
A treatise showing the best
way to California, 4975
The tree and its fruits, 8869
The tree of knowledge, 10016
Trees - Cuba, 7693
Trees - North America, 1828
Trembley, Ernest, 8231
Tremenheere, Hugh Seymour,
1804-1893, 5458
Trent (Ship), 1818, 1067
Trent, William Peterfield,
1862-1934, 5459, 8232
Trent's trust, 6977
Trentini, Francisco, 8233
Trenton, Battle of, 1776,
12945
Trenton. First Presbyterian
church, 12575
Tres conferencias, 7399
Tressilian and his friends,
10292
Triaca producida de un
veneno, 5428
Trial and defence of First
Lieutenant James Hall, 3752
Trial: Commonwealth vs.
J. T. Buckingham... 11607
The trial, execution, and
burial of Homer Phelps,
9216
Trial of Abraham Lincoln by
the great statesmen of the
republic, 8234
The trial of Amos Broad
and his wife, 11526
The trial of Beryl, 10163
Trial of Charles M. Jefferds
for murder, 13188
The trial of genius, 10580
The trial of Henry Joseph
and Amos Otis, 13331
Trial of John Y. Beall, 1002

467

The trial of Rev. Albert
Barnes, 13357
The trial of spirits, both
in teachers and hearers,
11980
Trial of the assassins and
conspirators for the
murder of Abraham
Lincoln, 8235
Trial of the conspirators,
1305
Trial of the eleven
disciples of Christ, 9858
The trial of the Rev.
William Hogan, 12834
Trials, 1256
The trials and sufferings
of a pioneer, 9159
Trials and their uses,
10514
Trials and triumph, 9448
Trials - Canada, 334
Trials - New York (City),
12342
Trials of a housekeeper,
10904
The trials of a seamstress,
8571
The trials of a stepmother,
9158
Trials of Helen More, 10159
Trials of the heart, 8846
Trials - Quebec, 6596
Trials - U. S., 11719
A triangular society, 8508
The tribute book, 2440
A tribute for the Negro,
445
A tribute to the memory
of the Rev. George G.
Cookman, 1619
Tributes of the bar and
of the Supreme judicial
court, 5997
Tried and true, 10851
Tried for her life, 10845
Trifleton papers, 10980
Trigo, José M., 8236
Trinidad, Cuba, 7399

Trinidad - Descr. & trav.,
6028, 6339, 7194, 7195
Trinidad - Emig. & immig.,
13449
Trinidad - Pol. & govt.,
2354, 11966
Trinity, 5140, 5853
Trinity bells, 8744
A trip across the Pacific,
2486
A trip across the plains,
and life in California,
4139
A trip from Houston to
Jackson, 4657
A trip of the Porgie, 10798
The trip of the steamer Oceanus
to Fort Sumter and Charleston,
S. C., 8237
A trip to America, 3776
A trip to Florida, 2841
A trip to Manitoba, 6743, 8241
A trip to Mexico, 6046, 6757
A trip to Pike's Peak, 3008
A trip to the tropics and
home through America, 5928
A trip to the United States
in 1887, 2650
A triple entanglement, 9772
Triplett, Frank, 5460
Tripp & Morril, pub., 12485
Trippings in author-land,
10084
The triumph of music, 2954
Triumphal pompa, 7479
Triumphs of science, 5603
Trivnfo del agva bendita,
7957
Trobriand, Philippe Regis
Denis de Keredern, comis de,
1816-1897, 5461
Trois ans d'esclavage chez
les Patagons, 12498
Trollope, Anthony, 1815-1882,
5462, 8238, 8239
Trollope, Mrs. Frances (Milton)
1780-1863, 5463
A trooper Galahad, 10128
Trooper tales, 9087

Tropical America, 6760
Tropical tours to Toltec
  towns in Mexico, 7474,
  7475
Tropics, 7469
Tropics - Agriculture,
  11368
Tropics - Diseases and
  hygiene, 11578, 12791,
  13132, 13240
Tross, Edwin, 1822-1875,
  ed., 7268
Trotter, Isabella (Strange)
  1816-1878, 5464
Troubetzkoy, Amélie (Rives)
  Chanler, 1863-1945,
  5465, 5466, 5467, 11011,
  11014
The trouble brothers, 10608
A troubled heart, and how
  it was comforted at last,
  10897
The troubles of Martin
  Coy, 9749
Trout fishing, 9981
Trow, James, 1827-, 8240,
  8241
Trowbridge, John Townsend,
  1827-1916, 5468
Troy for fifty years, 1656
Troy, N. H. - Geneal,
  11700
Troy, N. H. - Hist.,
  11700
Troy, N. Y. Citizens, 8242
Troy, N. Y. - Hist., 1656
Troy - Romances, legends,
  etc., 8783
The truce of God, 10351
The True American, 3021,
  3884
A true and historical
  narrative of the colony
  of Georgia, 5335
A true copy of three
  judgements, 1652
A true declaration of the
  troublesome voyage, 6990
True Democrat, Cleveland,
11487
A true discourse of the
  present state of Virginia,
  3765
A true history of a late short
  administration, 13395
The true means of establishing
  public happiness, 2148
A true picture of emigration,
  2859
True relation of the hardships
  suffered by Governor Fernando
  de Soto, 5469
A true relation of Virginia,
  5205
The true remedy for the
  wrongs of woman, 1046
A true representation of the
  plan formed at Albany, 12898
The true state of the case,
  11855
A true story, 9035
True story of the lost
  shackle, 9305
The true story of the surrender
  of the Marquis Cornwallis,
  10465
True to him ever, 10588
True womanhood, 10413
Truesdell, Mrs. Helen, 5470
Trujillo Molina, Rafael
  Leonidas, pres. Dominican
  Republic, 1891-, 6726
Trumbull, Henry, 13078
Trumbull, Henry Clay, 1830-
  1903, 5471
Trumbull, James Hammond,
  1821-1897, ed., 13375
Trumbull, John, 1756-1843,
  6645
Trumpeter Fred, 10129
Trumps, 9291
Trusta, H., pseud., 10515
Trusty, no. 49, 9582
The truth about America,
  4503
Truth and fancy, 11188
Truth and righteousness
  triumphant, 6991

472

Uncle Phillip, 10197
Uncle Remus in Syracuse,
8189
Uncle Sam and his
country, 4681
Uncle Sam in pontifical
robes, 5848
Uncle Sam's Bible, 9098
Uncle Sam's emancipation,
10910
Uncle Sam's palace,
11118
Uncle Tim, 10904
Uncle Tom at home, 48
"Uncle Tom's cabin"
contrasted with
Buckingham hall, the
planter's home, 9245
Uncle Tom's cabin in
ruins! 1527
Under a cloud, 10899
Under currents of
Wall-street, 10107
Under fire, 10130
Under friendly eaves,
9323
Under golden skies,
10454
Under the cedars, 9797
.Under the convent wall,
9764
Under the eaves, 6978
Under the empire, 3932
Under the gridiron,
3179
Under the lion's paw,
9606
Under the man-fig, 3193
Under the palmetto in
peace and war, 8625
Under the redwoods,
6978
Under the Southern
Cross, 7095
Under the stars, 9730
Under the stars and
bars, 3016, 4099
Under the surface, 9094
Under the yoke, 11218

Underground railroad,
3042, 3412
Underhill, Updike, pseud.,
11036
Undertones, 2955
Underwood, Francis Henry,
1825-1894, 5495
The undeveloped west,
2651
The undiscovered country,
9956
The undivided household,
9005
Une année au désert, 4597
Uneffectual fire, 11018
The unequal marriage, 10710
An unexpected result,
10653, 10654
The unexpectedness of Mr.
Horace Shields, 9376
The unfathomable mystery,
10957
An unfinished story, 9363
The unfortunate Englishmen,
1958
The unfortunate shipwright,
805
The Union almanac for 1866,
8257
Union and emancipation
society, Manchester, 2276
L'union des provinces de
l'Amérique britannique
du Nord, 1841
Union down, 9343
Union foundations, 13016
Union League, Philadelphia,
7743
Union Pacific Railroad,
247, 3255, 5168, 5499,
5500
Union university, Schnectady,
N. Y. Delphian institute,
12996
Unitarian church - Sermons,
2176, 11746
Unitarianism, 2176, 11252,
11845, 12053
United brothers of temperance,

12937
United Confederate Veterans.
Georgia Division.
Confederate Survivors'
Association, Camp no.
435, 4885
United Daughters of the
Confederacy, 7924
United Press association,
2129
United States, 263, 322,
1086, 1536, 2315, 2742,
2806, 3064, 3909, 4363,
5094, 7767, 11263,
11281, 11754
U. S. Adjutant-general's
office, 8258
The United States and
Canada, as seen by two
brothers in 1858 and 1861,
8259
U. S. - Antiq., 12746
United States, appellant,
1166
U. S. - Armed Forces -
Period, 462, 11228
U. S. Army, 3757, 10601
U. S. Army - Ambulances,
11427
U. S. Army - Appropriations
and expenditures, 12940
U. S. Army - Cavalry -
History, 2783
U. S. Army - Chaplains,
3087, 12628, 12775,
13247
U. S. Army - Commissariat,
12907
U. S. Army - Corps of
engineers, 5501
U. S. Army - Corps of Topo-
graphical Engineers,
11283
U. S. Army. Courts-martial.
Arnold. 1779, 466, 467
U. S. Army. Courts-martial.
Byrne. 1859, 1782
U. S. Army. Courts-martial.
Gardner. 1815, 2401

U. S. Army. Courts-martial.
Hull. 1814, 13000
U. S. Army. Courts of inquiry.
Harmar. 1791, 12687
U. S. Army. East sub-district
of Nebraska, 5502
U. S. Army - Fiction,
10109, 10112, 10113, 10114,
10115, 10117, 10118, 10129
U. S. Army. Military
commission. Beall. 1865,
1002
U. S. Army - Military life,
3081, 4069, 4332, 5004,
7359
U. S. Army - Ohio valley,
3752
U. S. Army - Organization,
2405
U. S. Army - Recruiting,
enlistment, etc. - Civil
war, 6338, 11649, 12167,
12794
U. S. Army - Registers,
2273, 2402, 7003, 8263
U. S. artillery. Harrison's
regt., 1776-1783, 11537
The U. S. biographical
dictionary and portrait
gallery of eminent and
self-made men, 8260
U. S. - Biog., 201, 202, 203,
869, 901, 1546, 1678,
4420, 6188, 8177, 10952,
11318, 12023, 12171,
12455
U. S. - Bio-bibl., 212
U. S. - Biog. - Dictionaries,
7227
U. S. - Bound., 13016
U. S. - Bound. - Canada,
1334
U. S. - Bound. - Mexico,
2624, 3658, 5064, 5513,
5546
U. S. Bureau of refugees,
freedmen, and abandoned
lands, 11750
U. S. Cavalry, 1st regt.

dragoons, 1833-1861,
3081
U. S. Cavalry. 2d regt.,
1836, 4069
U. S. Cavalry. 3d regt.,
1846-1875, 4416
U. S. Christian Commission,
1776, 12949
U. S. Christian Commission.
Committee of Maryland,
12661
U. S. - Church history,
512, 670, 671, 672, 673
U. S. - Church history -
Colonial period, 1007
U. S. Circuit court (1st
circuit) 12403, 13331
U. S. Circuit court (4th
circuit), 11627, 11628
U. S. - Civil war -
Addresses, sermons, etc.,
12831
U. S. - Civil war -
Naval operations, 12744
U. S. - Civilization,
1461, 2556, 2925, 3061,
3663, 4129, 4279, 4587,
4811, 5565, 12118,
12818, 13085, 13087
U. S. Claims vs. France,
12111
U. S. Claims vs. Naples,
12111
U. S. Claims vs. Nether-
lands, 12111
U. S. - Climate, 4585,
11287, 11908, 12149
U. S. Coast and geodetic
survey, 245, 1920
U. S. - Comm., 692, 1019,
1020, 1424, 2007, 2008,
11796, 12016, 12079
U. S. - Comm. - Brazil,
691
U. S. - Comm. - Canada,
893, 2007, 5534, 12738,
12954
U. S. - Comm. - East
(Far East), 1913

U. S. - Comm. - France,
2805
U. S. - Comm. - Gt. Brit.,
1329, 11713, 13477
U. S. - Comm. - Hist.,
6260, 6261
U. S. - Comm. - Ireland,
11248
U. S. - Comm. - Mexico,
5527, 11652
U. S. - Comm. - West Indies,
British, 13327
U. S. Commissioner on the
boundary between the United
States and possessions of
His Catholic Majesty in
America, 12024
U. S. Congress - Chaplains,
13247
U. S. Congress. House.
Committee on commerce, 940
U. S. Congress. House.
Committee on Indian Affairs,
5503, 5504, 5505
U. S. Congress. House.
Committee on Military Affairs,
5506
U. S. Congress. House.
Committee on Naval Affairs,
13202
U. S. Congress. House.
Committee to investigate the
troubles in Kansas, 5507
U. S. Congress. Memorial
addresses, 187
U. S. Congress. Senate.
Committee on Indian
affairs, 5508
U. S. Congress. Senate -
Expulsion, 13231
U. S. Congres, 1st sess.,
1875-1876. House, 8261
U. S. 4th Cong., 1st sess.,
1795-1796, 1942
U. S. 5th Cong., 3d sess.,
1798-1799. Senate, 11296
U. S. 8th Cong., 2d sess.,
1804-1805. House, 11757,
13402

3013, 3031, 3032, 3035,
3039, 3045, 3048, 3049,
3052, 3061, 3062, 3083,
3090, 3109, 3116, 3118,
3121, 3133, 3143, 3174,
3175, 3176, 3179, 3185,
3190, 3196, 3203, 3210,
3228, 3238, 3242, 3243,
3248, 3249, 3254, 3256,
3277, 3278, 3302, 3304,
3308, 3319, 3326, 3331,
3340, 3358, 3379, 3385,
3392, 3394, 3396, 3400,
3406, 3407, 3409, 3416,
3423, 3431, 3433, 3434,
3446, 3447, 3461, 3472,
3490, 3517, 3527, 3535,
3548, 3549, 3550, 3555,
3558, 3559, 3564, 3569,
3571, 3577, 3586, 3589,
3593, 3594, 3595, 3596,
3603, 3612, 3615, 3618,
3619, 3623, 3629, 3632,
3633, 3652, 3660, 3663,
3683, 3687, 3689, 3698,
3709, 3710, 3712, 3713,
3716, 3719, 3720, 3721,
3734, 3738, 3755, 3761,
3768, 3776, 3777, 3780,
3786, 3789, 3794, 3795,
3808, 3810, 3825, 3829,
3831, 3850, 3853, 3856,
3883, 3885, 3889, 3891,
3892, 3896, 3900, 3920,
3921, 3927, 3935, 3937,
3941, 3942, 3946, 3952,
3964, 3965, 3977, 3981,
3984, 3991, 4020, 4043,
4046, 4047, 4048, 4059,
4061, 4078, 4098, 4107,
4123, 4132, 4138, 4162,
4178, 4182, 4183, 4184,
4185, 4186, 4189, 4193,
4195, 4196, 4202, 4204,
4205, 4206, 4215, 4216,
4220, 4221, 4225, 4228,
4234, 4235, 4251, 4252,
4266, 4267, 4268, 4270,
4274, 4277, 4280, 4288,

4289, 4291, 4292, 4299,
4307, 4309, 4310, 4315,
4318, 4319, 4320, 4327,
4356, 4357, 4358, 4376,
4377, 4385, 4389, 4397,
4413, 4419, 4421, 4427,
4430, 4432, 4439, 4441,
4443, 4444, 4445, 4447,
4449, 4453, 4463, 4465,
4467, 4478, 4484, 4485,
4489, 4491, 4492, 4494,
4496, 4503, 4506, 4511,
4514, 4517, 4518, 4526,
4536, 4539, 4548, 4552,
4568, 4569, 4571, 4578,
4579, 4581, 4583, 4585,
4603, 4611, 4634, 4635,
4636, 4637, 4638, 4639,
4642, 4643, 4644, 4645,
4649, 4670, 4674, 4677,
4680, 4681, 4691, 4704,
4710, 4717, 4722, 4750,
4751, 4758, 4764, 4766,
4769, 4789, 4807, 4828,
4840, 4847, 4853, 4858,
4861, 4865, 4868, 4871,
4872, 4879, 4883, 4884,
4897, 4898, 4909, 4912,
4913, 4928, 4932, 4935,
4937, 4938, 4943, 4954,
4959, 4961, 4969, 4971,
4979, 4982, 5013, 5015,
5022, 5031, 5033, 5036,
5045, 5051, 5059, 5063,
5067, 5068, 5070, 5071,
5073, 5075, 5076, 5089,
5092, 5093, 5096, 5101,
5103, 5113, 5128, 5131,
5132, 5133, 5139, 5144,
5147, 5150, 5174, 5190,
5210, 5214, 5216, 5224,
5230, 5256, 5277, 5293,
5300, 5303, 5308, 5309,
5316, 5319, 5322, 5323,
5325, 5326, 5328, 5333,
5337, 5342, 5375, 5408,
5409, 5424, 5431, 5441,
5454, 5456, 5458, 5462,
5464, 5480, 5484, 5485,

12378, 12447, 12964,
13070
U. S. - Economic policy,
11446
U. S. - Emig. & immig.,
337, 1933, 2139, 2194,
3214, 3559, 4442, 4847,
5083, 11319, 11583,
11639, 12112
U. S. - Emig. & immig. -
Hist., 7158
U. S. - Emigration,
Internal, 3630
U. S. Engineer dept.,
1404, 2238, 2239, 5514,
5515, 5516, 5517, 5518,
5519, 5520, 5521, 5522,
5523, 5524, 13322
U. S. - Exploring condi-
tions, 5255, 5516
U. S. - Exploring expe-
dition, 1838-1842, 21,
11820, 11867, 12328,
13200
U. S. - Exploring expe-
ditions, 2465, 2920,
3541, 3542, 5099, 5501,
5513, 5524, 5537, 7982,
12560, 13360
U. S. - For. rel., 1141,
6259, 6766, 11702
U. S. - For. rel. - 1789-
1797, 12603, 13495
U. S. - For. rel. - 1797-
1801, 1934, 11927,
12251, 13410
U. S. - For. rel. - 1801-
1809, 75, 974, 1019,
1020, 2364, 13088,
13102
U. S. - For. rel. - 1809-
1812, 13404
U. S. - For. rel. - 1815-
1861, 12478
U. S. - For. rel. - 1849-
1853, 11309
U. S. - For. rel. - 1851-
1865, 11466
U. S. - For. rel. - 1853-

1857, 12098
U. S. - For. rel. 1861-
1865, 547, 1142, 11467
U. S. - For. rel. - 1913-
1921, 7689
U. S. - For. rel. - Columbia,
7859, 12716
U. S. - For. rel. - Constitutional period, 1789-1809,
92, 295, 812, 818, 12230
U. S. - For. rel. - France,
1868, 1917, 1934, 2463,
5841, 6773, 6774, 11712,
11927, 12251, 12298,
12801, 13410, 13495
U. S. - For. rel. - Gt. Brit.,
295, 519, 520, 1142,
1948, 2183, 2416, 12199,
12231, 12378, 12797,
13405
U. S. - For. rel. - Japan,
7701
U. S. - For. rel. - Mexico,
6636, 7532
U. S. - For. rel. - Netherlands,
56
U. S. - For. rel. - Revolution,
58, 11959, 11960, 13118
U. S. - For. rel. - Russia,
547, 5947
U. S. - For. rel. - Spain,
5531
U. S. - For. rel. - Spanish
America, 8269
U. S. - For. rel. - Treaties,
12026, 12027
The United States gazetteer,
5108
U. S. - Geneal., 6203, 6204,
6205, 6255, 6286, 7374,
7433, 7434, 7435, 7437,
7753, 8365, 12847
U. S. - Geneal. - Sources,
7971
U. S. General directory,
5298
U. S. General land office,
4664, 11273
U. S. - Historical geography,

8003
U. S. - Hist., 9, 512,
775, 786, 790, 791,
1188, 1598, 2010, 2456,
3406, 3642, 4502, 4946,
5647, 8150, 11494,
12176, 12482, 12541,
13472
U. S. - Hist. - 1783-1809 -
Fiction, 2782
U. S. - Hist. - 1783-1865,
1960, 5376, 10952
U. S. - Hist. - 1809-1817,
294
U. S. - Hist. - 1815-1861,
241, 321, 1634, 3496,
11679, 12446
U. S. - Hist. - 1815-1861 -
Fiction, 4117
U. S. - Hist. - Addresses,
essays, lectures, 137,
447, 6393, 11264, 12538,
12725
U. S. - Hist. - Civil
war, 381, 465, 693,
725, 2116, 2598, 2900,
3187, 3202, 3498, 4311,
4808, 4814, 4815, 4820,
4869, 5052, 5759, 5988,
6094, 6419, 6915, 7239,
7989, 11244, 11597,
12913, 13128
U. S. - Hist. - Civil
war - Addresses, sermons,
etc., 65, 157, 308, 447,
453, 498, 538, 661, 844,
889, 1053, 1057, 1137,
1138, 1299, 1300, 1438,
1460, 1462, 1468, 1469,
1470, 1582, 1802, 1872,
1880, 2140, 2178, 2230,
2419, 2791, 2792, 6047,
6063, 6934, 7565, 7890,
7924, 8089, 8357, 11264,
11301, 11306, 11310,
11311, 11312, 13313,
11375, 11559, 11640,
11645, 11830, 11922,
11982, 12042, 12044,

12164, 12266, 12316,
12493, 12505, 12572,
12584, 12679, 12814,
12836, 13063, 13152
U. S. - Hist. - Civil war -
Anecdotes, 1726, 4035,
6025, 7745, 10057,
11267, 12390, 12516,
13075
U. S. - Hist. - Civil war -
Bibl., 908
U. S. - Hist. - Civil war -
Biog., 909, 1546, 6560,
11528
U. S. - Hist. - Civil war -
Blockade, 3890
U. S. - Hist. - Civil war -
Campaigns and battles,
828, 968, 1591, 1658,
1849, 1850, 2034, 2035,
2036, 2040, 2050, 2068,
2069, 2070, 2071, 2073,
2153, 2764, 2808, 2984,
3041, 3075, 3078, 3085,
3162, 3195, 3324, 3395,
3546, 3661, 3922, 4079,
4610, 4630, 4749, 5088,
5136, 5321, 5461, 6651,
7067, 8138, 11267,
11454, 11826, 11864,
12017, 13458
U. S. - Hist. - Civil war -
Cartoons, 7537
U. S. - Hist. - Civil war -
Causes, 378, 1930, 2149,
2214, 2223, 5943, 6096,
6848, 7447, 7928, 11590,
11727, 12649
U. S. - Hist. - Civil war -
Cavalry operations, 2654
U. S. - Hist. - Civil war -
Chronology, 11277
U. S. - Hist. - Civil war -
Fiction, 2500, 2501,
2516, 2565, 2774, 3097,
3192, 3507, 3610, 3918,
4199, 4329, 4733, 4736,
4746, 5186, 5187, 5715,
8524, 8603, 8615, 8752,

12781, 12986

U. S. - Hist. - Civil war -
Personal narratives -
Confederate side, 968,
1002, 2153, 2537, 2577,
2619, 2625, 2654, 2663,
2698, 2702, 2703, 2750,
2762, 2764, 2875, 2907,
2921, 2935, 2945, 2961,
2962, 2971, 3010, 3016,
3054, 3056, 3161, 3222,
3320, 3333, 3355, 3395,
3444, 3471, 3546, 3581,
3601, 3609, 3640, 3696,
3697, 3728, 3791, 3851,
3951, 3959, 4033, 4063,
4099, 4230, 4254, 4271,
4287, 4297, 4354, 4365,
4493, 4505, 4508, 4525,
4540, 4541, 4582, 4608,
4655, 4877, 4921, 4964,
5019, 5107, 5148, 5274,
5628, 5635, 5638, 5675,
5728, 5764, 5800, 6744,
7757, 9117, 10092,
11194, 13396, 13507

U. S. - Hist. - Civil war -
Personal narratives -
Union side, 3306, 3645

U. S. - Hist. - Civil war -
Pictorial works, 4302

U. S. - Hist. - Civil war -
Poetry, 1358, 1600,
2314, 2836, 11267, 11276,
11325, 11326, 11413,
12201

U. S. - Hist. - Civil war -
Poetry - Confederate,
2775, 3227, 3280, 3411,
4854, 10057, 13120,
13326

U. S. - Hist. - Civil war -
Poetraits, 7470

U. S. - Hist. - Civil war -
Prison life, 2761, 2876,
3130, 3204, 3275, 3279,
3335, 3387, 3432, 3501,
3513, 3520, 4067, 4212,
4278, 4476, 4874, 5215

5728

U. S. - Hist. - Civil war -
Prisoners and prisons,
2277, 2463, 2479, 2487,
2538, 2586, 2725, 2749,
2839, 2864, 3082, 3088,
3168, 3181, 3294, 3305,
3307, 3585, 3621, 3649,
3684, 3695, 3726, 3793,
3799, 3807, 3966, 3983,
4031, 4077, 4140, 4142,
4145, 4230, 4255, 4350,
4455, 4595, 4617, 4627,
4819, 4864, 4867, 4952,
4970, 5046, 5047, 5058,
5105, 5177, 5329, 5585,
5665, 10057, 11706,
12404, 13507

U. S. - Hist. - Civil war -
Prisoners, Exchange of,
2041

U. S. - Hist. - Civil war -
Prisons and prisoners,
6063

U. S. - Hist. - Civil war -
Regimental histories -
Ala. inf. - 1st. 4369

U. S. - Hist. - Civil war -
Regimental histories -
Ala. inf. - 60th, 5130

U. S. - Hist. - Civil war -
Regimental histories -
Arkansas infantry - 1st -
Company G, 2703

U. S. - Hist. - Civil war -
Regimental histories -
Army of Northern Virginia,
4119

U. S. - Hist. - Civil war -
Regimental histories -
Army of the Cumberland,
2708

U. S. - Hist. - Civil war -
Regimental histories -
Army of the Potomac,
839, 1394, 3050, 4097,
4521, 5461, 8055, 12014

U. S. - Hist. - Civil war -
Regimental histories -

U. S. - Hist. - Civil war -
Regimental histories -
Ill. inf. - 77th, 2687
U. S. - Hist. - Civil war -
Regimental histories -
Ill. inf. - 81st, 4595
U. S. - Hist. - Civil war -
Regimental histories -
Ill. inf. - 84th, 5154
U. S. - Hist. - Civil war -
Regimental histories -
Ill. inf. - 85th, 2567
U. S. - Hist. - Civil war -
Regimental histories -
Ill. inf. - 86th, 4179
U. S. - Hist. - Civil war -
Regimental histories -
Ill. inf. - 88th, 3525
U. S. - Hist. - Civil war -
Regimental histories -
Ill. inf. - 102d, 3439
U. S. - Hist. - Civil war -
Regimental histories -
Ill. inf. - 113th, 4143
U. S. - Hist. - Civil war -
Regimental histories -
Ill. inf. - 124th, 3953
U. S. - Hist. - Civil war -
Regimental histories -
Ind. art. - 11th
battery, 4663
U. S. - Hist. - Civil war -
Regimental histories -
Ind. cav. - 7th, 3044
U. S. - Hist. - Civil war -
Regimental histories -
Ind. inf. - 6th, 2798,
3670
U. S. - Hist. - Civil war -
Regimental histories -
Ind. inf. - 12th, 3557
U. S. - Hist. - Civil war -
Regimental histories -
Ind. inf. - 21st, 6953
U. S. - Hist. - Civil war -
Regimental histories -
Ind. inf. - 27th, 2824
U. S. - Hist. - Civil war -
Regimental histories -

Ind. inf. - 36th, 3704
U. S. - Hist. - Civil war -
Regimental histories -
Ind. inf. - 42d, 3939
U. S. - Hist. - Civil war -
Regimental histories -
Ind. inf. - 51st, 3804
U. S. - Hist. - Civil war -
Regimental histories -
Ind. inf. - 57th, 4164
U. S. - Hist. - Civil war -
Regimental histories -
Ind. inf. - 58th, 3866
U. S. - Hist. - Civil war -
Regimental histories -
Ind. inf. - 68th, 3865
U. S. - Hist. - Civil war -
Regimental histories -
Ind. inf. - 70th, 4457
U. S. - Hist. - Civil war -
Regimental histories -
Ind. inf. - 72d, 4351
U. S. - Hist. - Civil war -
Regimental histories -
Ind. inf. - 75th, 3489
U. S. - Hist. - Civil war -
Regimental histories -
Ind. inf. - 81st, 4528
U. S. - Hist. - Civil war -
Regimental histories -
Ind. inf. - 82d, 3972
U. S. - Hist. - Civil war -
Regimental histories -
Ind. inf. - 99th, 4313
U. S. - Hist. - Civil war -
Regimental histories -
Ia., 13096
U. S. - Hist. - Civil war -
Regimental histories -
Ia. cav. - 1st, 4303
U. S. - Hist. - Civil war -
Regimental histories -
Ia. inf. - 1st, 5610
U. S. - Hist. - Civil war -
Regimental histories -
Ia. inf. - 2d, 2665
U. S. - Hist. - Civil war -
Regimental histories -
Ia. inf. - 6th, 5774

U. S. - Hist. - Civil war -
Regimental histories -
Ia. inf. - 20th, 2615
U. S. - Hist. - Civil war -
Regimental histories -
Ia. inf. - 22d, 4121
U. S. - Hist. - Civil war -
Regimental histories -
Ia. inf. - 36th, 5329
U. S. - Hist. - Civil war -
Regimental histories -
Irish brigade, 3087
U. S. - Hist. - Civil war -
Regimental histories -
Iron brigade, 3145
U. S. - Hist. - Civil war -
Regimental histories -
Kan. cav. - 7th, 3523
U. S. - Hist. - Civil war -
Regimental histories -
Ky. cav. - 1st, 5348
U. S. - Hist. - Civil war -
Regimental histories -
Ky. cav. (Confederate) -
Partisan rangers, 4063
U. S. - Hist. - Civil war -
Regimental histories -
Ky. inf. - 8th, 5777
U. S. - Hist. - Civil war -
Regimental histories -
La., 2625
U. S. - Hist. - Civil war -
Regimental histories -
La. art. - Washington
art., 2625, 4671
U. S. - Hist. - Civil war -
Regimental histories -
La. cav. (Confederate) -
1st, 2921
U. S. - Hist. - Civil war -
Regimental histories -
La. inf. - 3d, 5482
U. S. - Hist. - Civil war -
Regimental histories -
La. inf. - 26th, 3756
U. S. - Hist. - Civil war -
Regimental histories -
Me. art. - 7th battery,
4218

U. S. - Hist. - Civil war -
Regimental histories -
Me. cav. - 1st, 4458
U. S. - Hist. - Civil war -
Regimental histories -
Me. inf. - 1st, 3655
U. S. - Hist. - Civil war -
Regimental histories -
Me. inf. - 5th, 2709
U. S. - Hist. - Civil war -
Regimental histories -
Me. inf. - 10th, 3655
U. S. - Hist. - Civil war -
Regimental histories -
Me. inf. - 17th, 12934
U. S. - Hist. - Civil war -
Regimental histories -
Me. inf. - 20th, 3592
U. S. - Hist. - Civil war -
Regimental histories -
Me. inf. - 23d, 4218
U. S. - Hist. - Civil war -
Regimental histories -
Me. inf. - 29th, 3655
U. S. - Hist. - Civil war -
Regimental histories -
Md. (C.S.A.), 3635
U. S. - Hist. - Civil war -
Regimental histories -
Md. cav. - 1st - Potomac
home brigade, 4591
U. S. - Hist. - Civil war -
Regimental histories -
Mass. art. - 1st battery,
2669
U. S. - Hist. - Civil war -
Regimental histories -
Mass. art. - 10th battery,
2715
U. S. - Hist. - Civil war -
Regimental histories -
Mass. cav. - 1st, 11430
U. S. - Hist. - Civil war -
Regimental histories -
Mass. inf. - 1st, 3136
U. S. - Hist. - Civil war -
Regimental histories -
Mass. inf. - 2d, 4537, 4876
U. S. - Hist. - Civil war -

Regimental histories -
Mass. inf. - 6th, 3771
U. S. - Hist. - Civil war -
Regimental histories -
Mass. inf. - 9th, 4371
U. S. - Hist. - Civil war -
Regimental histories -
Mass. inf. - 12th, 3076
U. S. - Hist. - Civil war -
Regimental histories -
Mass. inf. - 18th, 3186
U. S. - Hist. - Civil war -
Regimental histories -
Mass. inf. - 19th, 2492
U. S. - Hist. - Civil war -
Regimental histories -
Mass. inf. - 21st, 5598
U. S. - Hist. - Civil war -
Regimental histories -
Mass. inf. - 23d, 3381
U. S. - Hist. - Civil war -
Regimental histories -
Mass. inf. - 25th, 4870
U. S. - Hist. - Civil war -
Regimental histories -
Mass. inf. - 27th, 3235
U. S. - Hist. - Civil war -
Regimental histories -
Mass. inf. - 29th, 4661
U. S. - Hist. - Civil war -
Regimental histories -
Mass. inf. - 32d, 4697
U. S. - Hist. - Civil war -
Regimental histories -
Mass. inf. - 33d, 2751
U. S. - Hist. - Civil war -
Regimental histories -
Mass. inf. - 38th, 4842
U. S. - Hist. - Civil war -
Regimental histories -
Mass. inf. - 43d, 5008
U. S. - Hist. - Civil war -
Regimental histories -
Mass. inf. - 44th, 3729
U. S. - Hist. - Civil war -
Regimental histories -
Mass. inf. - 45th, 3958
U. S. - Hist. - Civil war -
Regimental histories -

Mass. inf. - 49th, 4062
U. S. - Hist. - Civil war -
Regimental histories -
Mass. inf. - 52d, 3944
U. S. - Hist. - Civil war -
Regimental histories -
Mass. inf. - 55th (colored),
12154
U. S. - Hist. - Civil war -
Regimental histories -
Mich. cav. - 2d, 5373
U. S. - Hist. - Civil war -
Regimental histories -
Mich. cav. brigade, 4170
U. S. - Hist. - Civil war -
Regimental histories -
Mich. inf. - 24th, 3145
U. S. - Hist. - Civil war -
Regimental histories -
Mo. (C.S.A.) - 1st brigade,
2537
U. S. - Hist. - Civil war -
Regimental histories -
Mo. cav. - Frémont's body
guard, 12170
U. S. - Hist. - Civil war -
Regimental histories -
Mo. inf. - 9th, 4223
U. S. - Hist. - Civil war -
Regimental histories -
Morgan's cavalry division
(C.S.A.) 3312
U. S. - Hist. - Civil war -
Regimental histories -
Morton's artillery (C.S.A.),
4540
U. S. - Hist. - Civil war -
Regimental histories -
N. H. inf. - 2d, 3824
U. S. - Hist. - Civil war -
Regimental histories -
N. J. inf. - 9th, 5043
U. S. - Hist. - Civil war -
Regimental histories -
N. J. inf. - 13th, 5434
U. S. - Hist. - Civil war -
Regimental histories -
New York, 12926
U. S. - Hist. - Civil war -

Regimental histories -
N. Y. art. - 9th, 5002
U. S. - Hist. - Civil war -
Regimental histories -
N. Y. art. - 34th battery,
5005
U. S. - Hist. - Civil war -
Regimental histories -
N. Y. art. - Independent
battery - 4th, 5201
U. S. - Hist. - Civil war -
Regimental histories -
N. Y. inf. - 5th, 3177
U. S. - Hist. - Civil war -
Regimental histories -
N. Y. inf. - 9th, 5694
U. S. - Hist. - Civil war -
Regimental histories -
N. Y. inf. - 16th, 3144
U. S. - Hist. - Civil war -
Regimental histories -
N. Y. inf. - 33d, 13343
U. S. - Hist. - Civil war -
Regimental histories -
N. Y. inf. - 48th,
4602, 4687
U. S. - Hist. - Civil war -
Regimental histories -
N. Y. inf. - 57th, 3533
U. S. - Hist. - Civil war -
Regimental histories -
N. Y. inf. - 60th, 3337
U. S. - Hist. - Civil war -
Regimental histories -
N. Y. inf. - 76th, 5184
U. S. - Hist. - Civil war -
Regimental histories -
N. Y. inf. - 79th, 5430
U. S. - Hist. - Civil war -
Regimental histories -
N. Y. inf. - 81st,
3211
U. S. - Hist. - Civil war -
Regimental histories -
N. Y. inf. - 83d, 13162
U. S. - Hist. - Civil war -
Regimental histories -
N. Y. inf. - 112th, 13060
U. S. - Hist. - Civil war -

Regimental histories -
N. Y. inf. - 115th, 3011
U. S. - Hist. - Civil war -
Regimental histories -
N. Y. inf. - 117th, 4543
U. S. - Hist. - Civil war -
Regimental histories -
N. Y. inf. - 124th, 5682
U. S. - Hist. - Civil war -
Regimental histories -
N. C. inf. - 7th, 3567,
3788
U. S. - Hist. - Civil war -
Regimental histories -
O., 3882
U. S. - Hist. - Civil war -
Regimental histories -
O. inf. - 3d, 2657
U. S. - Hist. - Civil war -
Regimental histories -
O. inf. - 6th, 3770
U. S. - Hist. - Civil war -
Regimental histories -
O. inf. - 7th, 5756
U. S. - Hist. - Civil war -
Regimental histories -
O. inf. - 9th, 5334
U. S. - Hist. - Civil war -
Regimental histories -
O. inf. - 11th, 3940
U. S. - Hist. - Civil war -
Regimental histories -
O. inf. - 29th, 5121
U. S. - Hist. - Civil war -
Regimental histories -
O. inf. - 39th, 1880
U. S. - Hist. - Civil war -
Regimental histories -
O. inf. - 42d, 4409
U. S. - Hist. - Civil war -
Regimental histories -
O. inf. - 53d, 3313
U. S. - Hist. - Civil war -
Regimental histories -
O. inf. - 55th, 4660
U. S. - Hist. - Civil war -
Regimental histories -
O. inf. - 58th, 5317
U. S. - Hist. - Civil war -

Regimental histories -
O. inf. - 63d, 4036
U. S. - Hist. - Civil war -
Regimental histories -
O. inf. - 73d, 3976
U. S. - Hist. - Civil war -
Regimental histories -
O. inf. - 78th, 5273
U. S. - Hist. - Civil war -
Regimental histories -
O. inf. - 101st, 2868,
3201
U. S. - Hist. - Civil war -
Regimental histories -
O. inf. - 105th, 5439
U. S. - Hist. - Civil war -
Regimental histories -
O. inf. - 123d, 4168
U. S. - Hist. - Civil war -
Regimental histories -
Pa. cav. - 1st, 4286
U. S. - Hist. - Civil war -
Regimental histories -
Pa. cav. - 7th, 3271,
5171
U. S. - Hist. - Civil war -
Regimental histories -
Pa. inf. - 31st, 5767
U. S. - Hist. - Civil war -
Regimental histories -
Pa. inf. - 37th, 3871
U. S. - Hist. - Civil war -
Regimental histories -
Pa. inf. - 48th, 2766
U. S. - Hist. - Civil war -
Regimental histories -
Pa. inf. - 51st, 4702
U. S. - Hist. - Civil war -
Regimental histories -
Pa. inf. - 83d, 4127
U. S. - Hist. - Civil war -
Regimental histories -
Pa. inf. - 97th, 4857
U. S. - Hist. - Civil war -
Regimental histories -
Pa. inf. - 102d, 5275
U. S. - Hist. - Civil war -
Regimental histories -
Pa. inf. - 106th, 5608

U. S. - Hist. - Civil war -
Regimental histories -
Pa. inf. - 107th, 12926
U. S. - Hist. - Civil war -
Regimental histories -
Pa. inf. - 114th, 4899
U. S. - Hist. - Civil war -
Regimental histories -
Pa. inf. - 141st, 3107
U. S. - Hist. - Civil war -
Regimental histories -
R. I. inf. - 1st, 5761
U. S. - Hist. - Civil war -
Regimental histories -
R. I. inf. - 12th, 12351
U. S. - Hist. - Civil war -
Regimental histories -
Sibley's brigade, 4610
U. S. - Hist. - Civil war -
Regimental histories -
S. C. inf., 2889
U. S. - Hist. - Civil war -
Regimental histories -
S. C. inf. - Edisto rifles,
4033
U. S. - Hist. - Civil war -
Regimental histories -
S. C. inf. - 4th, 4921
U. S. - Hist. - Civil war -
Regimental histories -
S. C. inf. - Kershaw's
brigade, 3244
U. S. - Hist. - Civil war -
Regimental histories -
Stonewall brigade, 2935
U. S. - Hist. - Civil war -
Regimental histories -
Tenn. cav. - 1st battalion,
3767
U. S. - Hist. - Civil war -
Regimental histories -
Tenn. cav. - 2d, 3767
U. S. - Hist. - Civil war -
Regimental histories -
Tenn. cav. - 7th battalion,
3767
U. S. - Hist. - Civil war -
Regimental histories -
Tenn. inf. - 1st - Co. H,

488

5635
U. S. - Hist. - Civil war -
Regimental histories -
Texas brigade, 4823
U. S. - Hist. - Civil war -
Regimental histories -
Texas cav. - 3d, 2619
U. S. - Hist. - Civil war -
Regimental histories -
Texas cav. - 8th, 2726,
3600
U. S. - Hist. - Civil war -
Regimental histories -
Texas cav. - Morgan's
battalion, 1861-1865,
3828
U. S. - Hist. - Civil war -
Regimental histories -
Tex. cav. - Ross'
brigade, 5014
U. S. - Hist. - Civil war -
Regimental histories -
Tex. cav. - Sibley's
brigade, 4610
U. S. - Hist. - Civil war -
Regimental histories -
Texas inf. - 4th, 3195
U. S. - Hist. - Civil war -
Regimental histories -
U. S. inf. - 8th, 5105
U. S. - Hist. - Civil war -
Regimental histories -
U. S. inf. - 33d, 3864,
5356
U. S. - Hist. - Civil war -
Regimental histories -
U. S. inf. - 1st sharp-
shooters, 5267
U. S. - Hist. - Civil war -
Regimental histories -
U. S. inf. - 2d sharp-
shooters, 5267
U. S. - Hist. - Civil war -
Regimental histories -
Vt., 1149, 5600
U. S. - Hist. - Civil war -
Regimental histories -
Vt. inf. - 10th, 3823
U. S. - Hist. - Civil war -

Regimental histories -
Va. - Richmond howitzers,
3166
U. S. - Hist. - Civil war -
Regimental histories -
Va. art. - Carpenter's
battery, 3493
U. S. - Hist. - Civil war -
Regimental histories -
Va. art. - Parker
battery, 3444
U. S. - Hist. - Civil war -
Regimental histories -
Va. art. - Richmond
howitzers, 5575
U. S. - Hist. - Civil war -
Regimental histories -
Va. art. - Surry light
artillery, 1861-1865,
4099
U. S. - Hist. - Civil war -
Regimental histories -
Va. cav. - 9th, 2656
U. S. - Hist. - Civil war -
Regimental histories -
Va. cav. - 43d battalion,
3114
U. S. - Hist. - Civil war -
Regimental histories -
Va. cav. (Union) -
Loudoun rangers, 3637
U. S. - Hist. - Civil war -
Regimental histories -
Va. inf. - 11th, 4525
U. S. - Hist. - Civil war -
Regimental histories -
Va. inf. - 17th, 5751
U. S. - Hist. - Civil war -
Regimental histories -
Va. inf. - 21st, 5771
U. S. - Hist. - Civil war -
Regimental histories -
Va. inf. - 33d, 2935
U. S. - Hist. - Civil war -
Regimental histories -
Walker's Texas division
(C.S.A.), 2737
U. S. - Hist. - Civil war -
Regimental histories -

12070, 13009
U. S. - Hist. - Revolution -
Prison life, 1753, 1754,
1966
U. S. - Hist. - Revolution -
Prisoners and prisons,
161, 163, 164, 165, 166,
364, 2128, 2367, 11284,
12070, 12753
U. S. - Hist. - Revolution -
Prisoners, Exchange of,
571
U. S. - Hist. - Revolution -
Regimental histories -
American loyalist, 5153
U. S. - Hist. - Revolution -
Regimental histories -
Md., 698
U. S. - Hist. - Revolution -
Regimental histories -
U. S. artillery -
Harrison's regt., 11537
U. S. - Hist. - Revolution -
Registers, lists, etc.,
1370, 7003
U. S. - Hist. - Revolution -
Societies, 8076
U. S. - Hist. - Revolution -
Sources, 250, 698, 4589,
13369, 13473
U. S. - Hist. - Revolution -
Welsh participation, 13286
U. S. - Hist. - Seminole
war - Fiction, 10589
U. S. - Hist. - Societies,
255
U. S. - Hist. - Study and
teaching, 2117
U. S. - Hist. - Tripolitan
war, 1801-1805, 256,
2172, 11965
U. S. - Hist. - War of 1812,
548, 665, 1937, 1941,
1978, 6617, 7613, 8804,
9507, 11475, 11574,
12248, 13129
U. S. - Hist. - War of 1812 -
Addresses, sermons, etc.,
114, 363, 416, 562, 566,

11249, 11557, 11810, 11911,
12870, 13099
U. S. - Hist. - War of 1812 -
Biog., 656
U. S. - Hist. - War of 1812 -
Campaigns and battles, 1436,
2236, 3625, 4224, 4326,
11458, 11574, 11575, 12741,
12999, 13100, 13119
U. S. - Hist. - War of 1812 -
Causes, 57, 11771, 13404
U. S. - Hist. - War of 1812 -
Claims, 11799
U. S. - Hist. - War of 1812 -
Fiction, 2517, 3997, 9636,
10432, 11204
U. S. - Hist. - War of 1812 -
Naval operations, 1980,
2325, 12841, 13155
U. S. - Hist. - War of 1812 -
Naval operations - Fiction,
9388
U. S. - Hist. - War of 1812 -
Period, 316
U. S. - Hist. - War of 1812 -
Personal narratives, 1682,
11575
U. S. - Hist. - War of 1812 -
Poetry, 1379, 2136, 3188,
3383, 12250
U. S. - Hist. - War of 1812 -
Prisoners and prisons, 11107
U. S. - Hist. - War of 1812 -
Songs and music, 12250
U. S. - Hist. - War of 1812 -
Sources, 316, 1436, 2236,
13119
U. S. - Hist. - War of 1898 -
Campaigns and battles,
8265, 8379
U. S. - Hist. - War with
Algeria, 1815, 12841
U. S. - Hist. - War with
France, 1798-1800, 182
U. S. - Hist. - War with
Mexico, 1845-1848, 992,
1579, 1763, 3546, 4980,
6785, 6791, 8002, 12178,
13185, 13196

U. S. - Hist. - War with
Mexico, 1845-1848 -
Addresses, sermons,
etc., 1688, 12194
U. S. - Hist. - War with
Mexico, 1845-1848 -
Campaigns and battles,
1666, 4151, 4926, 6144,
7386, 7529, 8001, 8035
U. S. - Hist. - War with
Mexico, 1845-1848 -
Causes, 1215
U. S. - Hist. - War with
Mexico, 1845-1848 -
Fiction, 9020, 9295,
9649, 9716, 9718, 9719,
10069, 10213
U. S. - Hist. - War with
Mexico, 1845-1848 -
Personal narratives,
190, 2605, 3661, 4332,
4416, 4957, 6344, 6614,
6615, 6791, 6906,
13158
U. S. - Hist. - War with
Mexico, 1845-1848 -
Prisoners and prisons,
6614, 6615
U. S. - Hist. - War with
Mexico, 1845-1848 -
Regimental histories -
Army of Chihuahua, 1666
U. S. - Hist. - War with
Mexico, 1845-1848 -
Regimental histories -
Lane's brigade, 6144
U. S. - Hist. - War with
Mexico, 1845-1848 -
Regimental histories -
O. inf. - 5th - Co. C,
13158
U. S. - Hist. - War with
Mexico, 1845-1848 -
Regimental histories -
Tex. cav. - McCulloch's
independent company,
4926
U. S. - History, Comic,
satirical, etc., 9507

U. S. - Industry - Hist.,
1356
U. S. infantry. 1st regt.
Sharpshooters, 1861-1865,
5267
U. S. infantry. 2d regt.
Sharpshooters, 1861-1865,
5267
U. S. infantry. 6th regt.,
3081
U. S. infantry. 8th regt.,
1838-, 5105
U. S. infantry. 8th regt.,
colored, 1863-1866, 4622
U. S. infantry. 33d colored
regt., 1862-1866, 3864,
5356
U. S. - Insular possessions,
7639
U. S. - Intellectual life,
12502
U. S. labor greenback song book,
5143
U. S. Laws, statutes, etc.,
1494, 1686, 11422, 12085,
12210, 13302
U. S. lessons, 12936
U. S. - Life & cust., 2588
U. S. - Mail, 5757
U. S. - Manners and customs,
4478
U. S. - Manuf. - Hist.,
1356
U. S. - Maps, 2913, 3399,
5082
U. S. - Marine corps - Biog.,
12597
U. S. - Marine corps -
Registers, 2402
The U. S. marshalship in
North Carolina, 2439
U. S. Military academy,
West Point, 557, 836,
2481, 11470, 12135
U. S. Military academy,
West Point - Fiction,
9664, 10111
U. S. Military academy,
West Point - Registers,

11889
U. S. Military secretary's dept., 8263
U. S. - Militia, 2402
U. S. Mint, 2173
U. S. - Moral cond., 4129, 11308
U. S. - Nationality, 13016
The U. S. naval chronicle, 12297
U. S. Naval observatory, 2160
U. S. Naval shipward, Boston, 12997
U. S. Naval station, New London, Conn., 1432
U. S. Navy, 2142, 6576, 6577, 7842, 13264
U. S. Navy - Appointments and retirements, 13202
U. S. Navy - Appropriations and expenditures, 13167
U. S. Navy - Biog., 656, 12597
U. S. Navy - Chaplain corps, 13247
U. S. Navy. Courts-martial. Barron, 1808, 880
U. S. Navy. Courts of inquiry. Hull, 1822, 12997
U. S. Navy - Hist., 182, 11831, 12174, 12297
U. S. Navy - Hist. - Civil war, 11469
U. S. Navy - Hist. - War with Mexico, 1845-1848, 8002
U. S. Navy - Officers, 1919
U. S. Navy - Registers, 2273, 2402
U. S. Office commissioner for exchange, 2041
U. S. Office of Indian affairs. The Cherokee question, 1866, 11775

U. S. Office of internal revenue, 11422, 12085
U. S. - Officials and employees, 12871
U. S. - Officials and employees - Appointment, qualifications, tenure, etc., 937, 11489
U. S. - Officials and employees - Salaries, allowances, etc., 2106
U. S. Patent office, 1032
U. S. - Pol. & govt., 113, 133, 280, 705, 776, 859, 1020, 1021, 1022, 1244, 1606, 1630, 1867, 1914, 1999, 2149, 2326, 2404, 2525, 2988, 3051, 3664, 3872, 4261, 4526, 4551, 4898, 5050, 5355, 5429, 5462, 5609, 7425, 7913, 8099, 8238, 8329, 9098, 11324, 11494, 11759, 12029, 12077, 12101, 12253, 12254, 12290, 12447, 12557, 12866, 12951, 13173, 13208, 13325
U. S. - Pol. & govt. - 1783-1789, 74, 332, 10317, 13131
U. S. - Pol. & govt. - 1783-1800, 7141
U. S. - Pol. & govt. - 1783-1809, 2780, 4599, 11299, 11671, 12367, 13381
U. S. - Pol. & govt. - 1783-1865, 63, 279, 1403, 7005, 8249, 11751, 11878
U. S. - Pol. & govt. - 1789-1797, 1931, 1932, 1942, 1945, 5890, 11500, 11501, 12318, 12603, 13244
U. S. - Pol. & govt. - 1797-1801, 57, 58, 229, 556, 1344, 1345, 1387, 1808, 1910, 2478, 11768,

11770, 12068, 12693
U. S. - Pol. & govt. -
1801-1809, 94, 519,
712, 1019, 1347, 1348,
1996, 2192, 12204,
12289, 12348, 12349,
12599, 12654, 12844,
13506
U. S. - Pol. & govt. -
1809-1817, 78, 9552,
12243
U. S. - Pol. & govt. -
1815-1860, 12592
U. S. - Pol. & govt. -
1815-1861, 1185, 2963,
3093, 3301, 3663, 3874,
4384, 4401, 7186, 11391,
11447, 12624, 12871
U. S. - Pol. & govt. -
1817-1825, 78
U. S. - Pol. & govt. -
1825-1829, 935
U. S. - Pol. & govt. -
1829-1837, 1592, 8824,
12002, 12106, 12444,
12479, 12677
U. S. - Pol. & govt. -
1837-1841, 1592, 7594,
13353
U. S. - Pol. & govt. -
1841-1845, 41, 67,
1605, 8249, 11897,
12623, 13280
U. S. - Pol. & govt. -
1845-1849, 1647,
4296, 13197
U. S. - Pol. & govt. -
1845-1861, 3875,
6592, 11740
U. S. - Pol. & govt. -
1848-1861, 5831,
12144
U. S. - Pol. & govt. -
1849-1853, 1655,
5477, 6711, 11303,
12191
U. S. - Pol. & govt. -
1849-1861, 2643, 6888
U. S. - Pol. & govt. -

1849-1877, 3022, 7945
U. S. - Pol. & govt. -
1853-1857, 895, 1161,
2430, 11678, 11890,
11931, 12772, 13216
U. S. - Pol. & govt. -
1857-1861, 412, 601, 682,
1160, 1163, 1165, 1282,
1438, 1463, 1718, 1727,
1953, 1997, 2233, 3898,
4154, 4920, 6586, 6938,
7283, 7284, 11313, 11389,
12010, 12056, 12315, 12650,
13065, 13212
U. S. - Pol. & govt. -
1865-1869, 849, 1409,
2032, 2129, 2188, 4647,
7592, 8216, 8378, 11669,
11793, 11868, 13181,
13254, 13255
U. S. - Pol. & govt. -
1865-1869 - Fiction,
10418
U. S. - Pol. & govt. -
1865-1873, 11233
U. S. - Pol. & govt. -
1865-1898, 4830
U. S. - Pol. & govt. -
1869-1877, 9798, 10228,
10579
U. S. - Pol. & govt. -
1885-1889, 4402, 5848,
6433
U. S. - Pol. & govt. -
1893-1897, 6981, 7870
U. S. - Pol. & govt. -
1897-1901, 7351, 7377
U. S. - Pol. & govt. -
Addresses, essays,
lectures, 1412, 4414, 5587,
11622
U. S. - Pol. & govt. -
Civil war, 87, 121, 209,
248, 299, 320, 381, 469,
470, 471, 551, 602, 638,
706, 801, 827, 999, 1003,
1053, 1055, 1057, 1121,
1122, 1251, 1281, 1302,
1303, 1313, 1354, 1355,

Vangrifter, Zachary Philemon,
pseud., 10791
Vanquished, 9870
The vanquished life-dream,
9752
Van Rensselaer, Stephen,
1765-1839, 821
Vans, William, b. 1763,
1884
Van Sinderen, Adrian,
1887-, 8288
Van Texas naar Florida,
5589
Van Tramp, John C.,
5561
Van Vorst, Bessie (McGinnis)
"Mrs. John Van Vorst,"
1873-1928, 5562, 5563
Van Vorst, Marie, jt.
author, 5563
Van Wart, Isaac, 1760-
1828, 1175, 1176, 1177
Van Wert Co., O. - Biog.,
6854
Van Wert Co., O. - Hist.,
6854
Vaquero, pseud., 8289
Vargas, Elvira, 8290
Varias relaciones del
Perú y Chile y conquista
de la isla de Santa
Catalina, 8291
The varieties of love,
9795
Varlo, Charles, 1725-
1796? 5564
Varnhagen, Francisco
Adolpho de, visconde de
Porto Seguro, 1816-
1878, 582
Varon de deseos, 7673
Varona y Pera, Enrique
José, 1849-, ed.,
7845
Varones ilvstres en
santidad, 5907
Vashington, ou La liberté
du nouveau monde, 1293
Vázquez de Velasco, Pedro,

8292
Vassal, William, d. 1655,
1886
Vassall family, 12702
Vassall family (William
Vassall, 1590?-1655),
12702
Vassall Morton, 10475
Vater, Johann Severin,
1771-1826, ed., 97
Vaughan, Benjamin, 8017
Vaughan family, 8017
Vaughan, John Champion,
11487
Vaughan, Mary C., jt. author,
11528
Vaughn, C. R., 2746
Vay, Péter, gróf, 1864-,
5565
Vázquez de Coronado, Francisco,
1510-1549, 8293, 8294
Vázquez, Jesús María, 7872
Veer, Theo de, 8295
Vega, Alonso de la, 17th cent.,
8296
Vega Bazán, Juan de, 7827
Vega y Mendoza, Francisco
José de la, 8297
Vegetable gardening,
8705, 8706, 11086
Vegetable gardening - U. S.,
11629
Vegetables - Varieties,
11629
The veiled doctor, 9365
Vela, David, 8298
Velasco, Diego del, d. 1648,
8299
Velasco, Juan de, 1727-1819,
8168
Velasco y Pérez, Carlos de,
1884-1923, ed., 6522
Velásquez, César Vicente,
8300
Velloso, José Mariano da
Conceição, 1742-1811,
1128
Venable, William Henry,
1831-1920, 5566, 5567

Vendors and purchasers,
1254
Venereal diseases, 726
A Venetian June, 9588
The Venetian marriage,
13213
A Venetian study in
black and white, 8718
Venezuela, 2473
Venezuela - Descr. &
trav., 5319, 6028,
6471, 6545, 7204, 7530,
8299, 8319, 12755
Venezuela - Hist., 772
Venezuela - Hist. -
To 1810, 6629
Venezuela - Hist. -
To 1810 - Sources,
6793
Venezuela - Hist. -
Miranda's expedition,
1806, 1278, 1279, 1713,
6042
Venezuela - Hist. -
War of independence,
1810-1813, 2396, 6629,
7014, 7635, 7637, 7664,
7897, 8009, 8268, 12517
Hist. - Hist. -
War of independence,
1810-1823 - Sources,
6476, 6793
Venezuela. Ministerio
de relaciones exteriores,
11514
Venezuela - Pol. & govt.,
11514, 12088
Venezuela - Pol. & govt. -
Period., 6476
Venezuela - Pol. & govt. -
Sources, 6793
Venice - Hist. -
Fiction, 11028
Venice - Hist. -
697-1508, 1139, 1140
Venice - Hist. -
1508-1797 - Fiction,
11028
Venus (planet), Transit

of - 1769, 6400, 6401
Vera, pseud., 4277
Vera Cruz - Descr. & trav.,
6171
Vera Cruz, Mexico (City) -
Hospitals, 6482
Vera Cruz, Mexico (State),
7589
Vera Cruz, Mexico (State) -
Descr. & trav., 6959
Verbrugghe, Georges, jt.
author, 5568
Verbrugghe, Louis, 5568
La verdad, y la justicia,
6584
Verdadera idea de la primera
campaña de Tejas, 4405
Verdadera medicina, cirurgía,
y astrología, 6012
Verdadera relacion: de lo
sussedido en los Reynos
e provincias del Peru,
122
Verdugo, Pomposo, 12509
Die Vereinigten Staaten von
Amerika, 4581
Die Vereinigten Staaten von
Nordamerika, 2873
Die Vereinigten Staaten von
Nordamerika im Jahre 1852,
4653
Verissimo, Erico, 1905-, 8301
La vérité sur la révolution
actuelle au Méxique, 1825
Vermejo River, 437
Vermont, 162
Vermont - Descr. & trav.,
12341
Vermont - Descr. & trav. -
Gazetteers, 12767
Vermont historical society,
1770
Vermont - Hist., 1036, 1770,
11673, 11752, 12919
Vermont - Hist. - Civil war,
1149, 12472
Vermont - Hist. - To 1791,
162, 175, 176, 177, 178,
12559

Vermont infantry. 10th
regt., 1862-1865,
3823
Vermont infantry. Vt.
brigade, 1861-1865,
5600
Vernon, Edward, 1684-
1757, 573
Vernon, Edward, 1684-
1757. Original papers
relating to the expe-
dition to the island
of Cuba, 1829
Vernon in the vale, 9842
Vernon, Ruth, pseud.,
10585
Verplanck, Gulian Crommelin,
1786-1870, 1904, 10697
Verrill, Alpheus Hyatt,
1871-, 5569, 8302
Vers le coeur de
l'Amérique, 5594
Versailles, Ky. - Hist. -
Fiction, 9904
Verses of a life time,
3607
Versuch einer getreuen
schilderung der
republik Mejico, 7548
Versuch über den politischen
zustand der Vereinigten
Staaten von Nord-Amerika,
5094
Vertebrates, Fossil,
4246
Vespucci, Amerigo, 1451-
1512, 582, 7567
Vesty of the basins, 9657
The veteran of the Grand
army, 9049
Veterinary colleges -
U. S., 1622
Veterinary medicine -
Early works to 1800,
13224
Vi titta på Amerika, 5015
Via crucis, 9235
Viage a Méjico, 6765
Viagem ao Mexico, 6475

Viaggio negli Stati Uniti
dell'America Settentrionale,
2940
Viaje a Yucatán, 8109
Viaje de indios y diario del
Nuevo México, 7536
Viaje por los Estados Unidos
del Norte, 4938
El viajero en México, 8279
Los viajes de Cockburn y
Lièvre por Costa Rica, 8303
Viajes de vacaciones, 5949
Viajes en Europa, Africa i
America, 5073
Viajes y estancias en América
del Sur, 7264
Vianzone, Thérèse, 5570
Viaud, Julien, 1850-1923,
7119
The vice president's daughter,
11048
Vicissitudes exemplified,
3278
Viccisitudes in both hemispheres,
9506
The vicissitudes of life, 8891
Vicksburg - Siege, 1863,
2033, 4143
Vicksburg - Siege, 1863 -
Fiction, 10054
The victim of excitement,
3848
The victim of intrigue,
10929
The victims of gaming, 11042
The victims of revenge, 10670
Victor, Benjamin, d. 1778,
supposed author, 2986
Victor La Tourette, 11102
Victor, Orville James,
1827-1910, 8304
Victoria, Paulo de, 8305
The victorious, 6083
A victorious defeat, 8666
Victory (ship), 7911
Victory turned into mourning,
13114
Vicuña Cifuentes, Julio,
1865-1936, 5967

502

1829-30, 12441
The Virginia convention
of 1829-30, 12441
Virginia - Court of
Appeals, 7101
A Virginia cousin, 9773
Virginia - Descr. &
trav., 1198, 2646,
2771, 2773, 2852, 2890,
2959, 2983, 2985, 3071,
3089, 3325, 3340, 3342,
3404, 3425, 3426, 3446,
3490, 3516, 3519, 3568,
3603, 3614, 3628, 3663,
3720, 3722, 3737, 4071,
4108, 4137, 4173, 4217,
4236, 4417, 4513, 4596,
4605, 4646, 4682, 4719,
4822, 4998, 5147, 5173,
5204, 5232, 5473, 5601,
5623, 5630, 5632, 5688,
5712, 5749, 5768, 6463,
8360, 8363, 11656,
13301
Virginia - Descr. &
trav. - Gazetters,
3351, 4404
Virginia - Descr. &
trav. - Maps, 5204
Virginia - Econ. cond.,
2852
Virginia - Fiction,
5476, 8758, 8759, 9766,
9770, 9894, 10686,
10807
Virginia. Governor,
8316
Virginia, her past and
her future, 2601
Virginia historical
society, Richmond,
12441
Virginia - Hist., 486,
2601, 3500, 7146, 7247,
8019, 8051, 11985
Virginia - Hist. - Civil
war, 1849, 1850, 2727,
3969
Virginia - Hist. - Colonial

period, 768, 1198, 1231,
1232, 2242, 3221, 3494,
3727, 3765, 4070, 4623,
4934, 4947, 5204, 5205,
5252, 5296, 5632, 6761,
9917, 11613, 12627
Virginia - Hist. - Colonial
period - Fiction, 2923,
3189, 8943, 9111, 9630
Virginia - Hist. - Colonial
period - Sources, 4378
Virginia - Hist. - Fiction,
8903, 9571
Virginia - Hist. - Revolution,
3659, 11613
Virginia - Hist. - Revolution -
Fiction, 9104
Virginia impartially examined,
2852
Virginia infantry. 5th
regt., 1861-1865, 4655
Virginia infantry. 6th
regt., 1861-1865, 2961
Virginia infantry. 8th
regt., 1861-1865, 5148
Virginia infantry. 11th
regt., 1861-1865, 4525
Virginia infantry. 12th
regt., 1861-1865, 2830
Virginia infantry. 33d
regt., 1861-1865, 2935
Virginia infantry. 56th
regt., 1861-1865, 12837
Virginia. Laws, statutes,
etc., 1686
Virginia of Virginia, 5467
Virginia - Pol. & govt.,
5906, 5913, 5914, 7838,
12441
Virginia - Pol. & govt. -
1775-1865, 12596, 13452
Virginia - Pol. & govt. -
Colonial period, 3805
Virginia - Pol. & govt. -
Revolution, 1955, 12440
Virginia - Public lands,
7985
A Virginia raid in 1906,
5988

Virginia - Soc. life
  & cust., 660, 2785,
  3957, 4658, 5023
Virginia - Soc. life
  & cust. - Colonial
  period, 4966
Virginia - Soc. life
  & cust. - Fiction,
  9116
Virginia - Stat., 3351
Virginia, Tennessee and
  Georgia air line, 5576
Virginia, the new
  dominion, 5023
The Virginia tourist,
  4822
Virginia. University.
  Society of alumni,
  11638
Virginia White Surphur
  Springs, 4515
A Virginian, now a
  citizen of New York,
  12366
A Virginian, pseud., 315
The Virginians in Texas,
  8660
Virginius (steamer), 8328
Virgo triumphans, 5713
Virtue and vice contrasted,
  10068
Virtue in war, 9217
A virtuoso's collection,
  9823
Visão panoramica dos
  Estados Unidos, 2918
Viscardo y Guzman, Juan
  Pablo, 1713
Visconti-Venosta, Enrico,
  marchese, 1883-, 5577
The vision, and other
  poems, 11457
The vision of All souls'
  hospital, 10810
The vision of Columbus,
  819
The vision of judgment,
  13353
The vision of Randalthus,

9551
A vision of the fountain,
  6978, 9827
Visit Honduras, 7680
The visit of the merchants
  and manufacturers of
  Philadelphia to "The
  World's exposition" at
  New Orleans, 5578
Visit Panama, 7681
A visit to Canada and the
  U.S.A., 3555
A visit to Cincinnati, 10310
A visit to Louisville, 10310
A visit to Mexico, 4981
A visit to Mount Vernon,
  10310
A visit to New-Orleans and
  the battle ground, 10310
A visit to North America and
  the English settlements
  in Illinois, 5668
A visit to St. Louis, 10310
A visit to Texas, 5579
A visit to the States, 5580
A visit to the U. S. in
  1841, 5318
Visit to the vineyard, 10310
A visit to the wounded
  English officers, 10310
Visitations, Ecclesiastical -
  Maryland, 1448
Visiting the sin, 10592
Visits to Brunswick, Georgia,
  and travels south, 5207
Visscher, William Lightfoot,
  1842-1924, 5581, 5582,
  5583
Viva Mexico! 6746
Vive l'empereur, 2547
Vivian of Virginia, 9592
Vivian, Sir Arthur Pendarves,
  1834-, 5584
Vivisection, 6031
Voeu patriotoqie d'un
  américain, 8317
A voice from Kentucky, 412
A voice from Rebel prisons,
  5585

506

11749
Voyages and travels -
Collections, 64
Voyages and travels -
Collections - Bibl.,
495
Voyages around the
world, 421, 422, 423,
1221, 1967, 2838, 3249,
4678, 5166, 6059, 6527,
6600, 8014, 8283, 12609,
13453, 13454
Voyages chez différentes
nations sauvages de
l'Amérique Septentrio-
nale, 13397
Voyages dans les parties
intérieures de
l'Amérique, 347, 5895
The voyages, dangerous
adventures and imminent
escapes of Captain
Richard Falconer, 2987
Voyages du baron de
Lahontan dans l'Amérique
Septentrionale, 7225
Voyages du Capitaine
Robert Lade, 4198
Voyages du r. p. Emanuel
Crespel, 6512
Voyages d'un François,
3325
Voyages et aventures du
chevalier de ***, 8321
Voyages from Montreal,
4362
Voyages, Imaginary,
2986, 9551, 10735
Voyages to the Pacific
coast, 4524, 5125,
5351, 8157, 8158, 8406,
8407
Voyages, travels and
discoveries of Tilly
Buttrick, jr., 2874
Le voyageur américain,
6435
Vries, Hugo de, 1848-
1935, 5588, 5589

Vue de la colonie espagnole
du Mississippi, 1206
Vues d'Amérique, 2489
Vues et souvenirs de
l'Amérique du Nord, 2939
Vues pittoresques de la
Jamaïque, 1035

W. G., 11876
The Wabash, 1220
Wabash Valley - Hist.,
3102, 5687
Wabshutt, Robert, fl. 1754-
1758, 805
Wachtmeister, Hans, greve,
1828-1905, 5590
Wachusetts (U. S. steamer),
2051
Wacousta, 10670
Waddel, John Newton,
1812-1895, 5591
Waddle, Angus L., 1826?-,
5592
Wade, Benjamin Franklin,
1800-1878, 6288
Wade, Mark Sweeten, 8322
Wade, Mrs. May A. (Thompson)
ed., 10962
Wadsworth, James Samuel,
1807-1864, 11704
Wadsworth, Samuel, 1630?-
1676, 11421
Wadsworth's map of Cariboo,
Saskatchewan, Nez Percés
and Salmon River gold
fields, 5593
Waerdenburgh, Dirk van,
8323
Wager of battle, 9851
Wages or the whip, 2019
Wages - U. S., 2338
Waggerics and vagaries,
1747
Wagnalls, M., 10448
Wagner, Charles, 1852-1918,
5594
Wagner, Henry Raup, 5739
Wagner, Moritz, 1813-1887,

Walton, William, d. 1668,
12006
Walton, William, 1784-
1857, tr., 1020
Walworth, Reuben H.,
8335
Wamesit Indians, 197
The wanderer in America,
8390
The wanderers of the west,
4990
Wandering Jew, 11054
The wandering Jew in
America, 9071
The wandering philan-
thropist, 9552
Wanderings in Mexico,
6856
Wanderings in the western
land, 5584
Wanderings north and
south, 11329
Wanderings of a vagabond,
4635
Wanderings of an artist
among the Indians of
North America, 4130
Wander jahre in Mexiko,
7232
Wanderungen durch die
mittelamerikanischen
Freistaaten Nicaragua,
Honduras and San
Salvador, 7974
Wanderungen durch die
prairien und das
nordliche Mexiko,
6895
Wanderungen eines jungen
norddeutschen durch
Portugal, Spanien und
Nord-Amerika, 3228
Wanderungen in Mexico,
7169
Wanderungen zwischen Hudson
und Mississippi, 2866
Wanted: a chaperon, 9762
Wanted - a match maker,
9539

Wanton, Mrs. Abigail,
1735?-1771, 1360
Wappäus, Johann Eduard,
1812-1879, 8336
Wappinger Indians - Wars,
1655-1660, 11518
War, 1037, 1277, 2151, 11370,
12072, 13130, 13187
War and peace: the evils of
the first, and a plan for
preserving the last,
13187
The war and slavery and their
relations to each other,
889
The war between the U. S.
and Mexico, 4151
A war correspondent's field
notebook, 6750
War, Cost of, 1949
A war debt, 10038
War diary of Rodney W.
Torrey, 5438
The war dreams, 10608
War experiences and the
story of the Vicksburg
campaign, 4143
The war in Florida, 4836
The war in Kansas, 11512
War letters of a disbanded
volunteer, 8693
War letters of William
Thompson Lusk, 4317
War, Maritime (International
law), 941, 12744
War memories, 9217
War of races, 12265
War of the metals, 7610
War of the rebellion,
3498
War pictures from the South,
3395
War-ships, 1218
War stories and school-day
incidents for the
children, 5800
The war-time journal of a
Georgia girl, 1864-1865,
2544

510

A war-time wooing, 10131
The war widow, 9567,
9570
Warbler, Forest, pseud.,
10267
Warburton, Alexander
Bannerman, 1852-1929,
8337
Warburton, George Drought,
1816-1857, 8338
Ward, Anna Bell, 1897-,
jt. author, 7551
Ward, Charles James,
7114
Ward, Emily Elizabeth
(Swinburne) lady, 8339
Ward, George Atkinson,
ed., 11923
Ward, Herbert Dickinson,
1861-, jt. author,
11069, 11074
Ward, Sir Henry George,
1797-1860, 8340,
8341, 8342
Ward, J. H. H., 8381
Ward, James Warner,
1817?-1897, 5607
Ward, Joseph Ripley
Chandler, 1845-,
5608
Ward, Mary Augusta
("Mrs. Humphry Ward"),
1851-1920, 7119
A ward of Colonel Star-
bottle's, 6977
A ward of the Golden
Gate, 6980
Warden, David Baillie,
1772-1845, 5609,
12422
Warden, David Baillie,
1778-1845. A statis-
tical, political, and
historical account
of the United States,
13156
Warden refuted, 13156
The wardman's wooing,
9533

The wards of Mount Vernon,
10814
Ware, Eugene Fitch, 1841-1911,
5610
Warehouses, 1608
Warehouses - Law and legis-
lation - Confederate States
of America, 2060
Warehouses - U. S., 12080
Warfield, Mrs. Catherine Ann
(Ware) 1816-1877, 5611-5621
Warfield, Ethelbert Dudley,
1861-1936, 5622
Warhaffte Nachricht, 3727
Warhafftige Historien einer
wunderbaren Schiffart,
7977
Waring's peril, 10132
Warner, Anna Bartlett,
1820-1915, jt. author,
11098, 11099
Warner, C. D., ed., 5459
Warner, Charles Dudley,
1829-1900, 5623, 5624,
8343
Warner, Helen Garnie, 1846,
5625
A warning to lovers, 9538
Warren, Edward, 5279
Warren, Fort, 2479
Warren, Gouverneur Kemble,
1830-1882, 4246, 5514,
5515, 5626, 5627
Warren, Henry Waterman,
1838-, 8344
Warren, John, 1753-1815,
915
Warren, Joseph, 1741-1775,
11571
Warren, Joseph, 1741-1775 -
Drama, 1707
Warren, Louis Austin, 1885-,
8345-8351
Warren, Mrs. Mercy (Otis),
1728-1814, supposed author,
1423
Warrick county Lincoln route
association, 8352
Warwick, 11067

511

7676, 11279, 11300,
11315, 11492, 11608,
11633, 11835, 11891,
11898, 11906, 11971,
12252, 12285, 12358,
12438, 12499, 12594,
12708, 12710, 12723,
12809, 13030, 13242,
13473
Washington, George, pres.
U. S., 1732-1799 - Bibl.,
12925
Washington, George, pres.
U. S., 1732-1799 - Drama,
1293
Washington, George, pres.
U. S., 1732-1799 -
Farewell address, 12270
Washington, George, pres.
U. S., 1732-1799 -
Funeral and memorial
services, 12413
Washington, George, pres.
U. S., 1732-1799 -
Music, 7058
Washington, George, pres.
U. S., 1732-1799 -
Poetry, 228, 649, 1799,
5868
Washington, George, pres.
U. S., 1732-1799 -
Portraits, 2296
Washington, George, pres.
U. S., 1732-1799 -
Religion, 12661
The Washington guide, 12033
Washington, John, 13452
Washington, John M., 5167
The Washington Manor House,
5930
Washington - Maps, 4249
Washington, Martha (Dan-
dridge) Custis, 1732-
1802, 2083
Washington, Mary (Ball)
1708-1789, 2083, 8167
Washington, Mt., N. H.,
718
Washington society. Charles-

ton, S. C., 13014
Washington Square, 7132
Washington (State), 5837,
6013
Washington (State) - Descr. &
trav., 2408, 3551, 3955,
4549, 5270, 8403
Washington (State) - Descr. &
trav. - Guide-books, 3735
Washington, Treaty of, 1842,
1595, 2265, 6259
Washington-Virginia Railway,
8051
A Washington winter, 9313
Washington's Expedition to the
Ohio, 1st, 1753-1754, 5631
Washington's first battle,
or Braddock's defeat, 10338
Washington's words to intending
emigrants to America, 2863
Washoe co., Nev., 8878
Washoe silver mines, Sketches
of the, 3212
Wasserburg, Philipp, 1827-,
tr., 6074
Wastelands - Gt. Brit., 5789
The watchman, 9529
Water-drops, 10763
The water ghost and others,
8689
Waterbury, Conn., 12724
Waterhouse, Edward, fl. 1622,
5632
Waterhouse, Sylvester, 1830-
1902, 5633
Waterloo, 10310
A water-logged town, 10808
The water-spirit's bride
and other poems, 2648
Watering places, etc. - America,
4039
Waters, Mrs. Abigail (Dawes)
1721-1816, 13034
The waters of Caney Fork, 4907
Waters, Thomas H., 3884
Waters, Wilburn, 1812-, 3033
Watertown, Mass. - Hist., 2309
Watkins, Floyd C., 8355
Watkins, N. J., ed., 5634

513

Watkins, Samuel R.,
5635
Watkins, Tobias, 1780-
1855, 192, 193
Watmough, Edward Coxe,
1821-1848, supposed
author, 11109
Watrous, John Charles,
1806-1874, 12939
Watson, Edmund Henry
Lacon, 1865-, 8356
Watson, Elkanah, 1758-
1842, 5636, 11961
Watson family (George
Watson, 1603?-1689),
11961
Watson, John, of Glas-
gow, 6737
Watson, William, of
Skelmorlie, Scotland,
5638
Watson, William J.,
5639
Watson, Winston Cossoul,
1803, ed., 5636
Watterson, Henry, 1840-
1921, 5640, 5641
Watts, William Courtney,
1830-1897, 5642
Wau-bun, the "early day"
in the Northwest, 10141
Wauna, the witch-maiden,
10122
The way it all ended,
10030
The way it came, 7118,
10012
The way of the world and
other ways, 9100
Way sketches, 5078
A wayfaring couple, 9575
Waylen, Edward, 5643
Wayman, James, 5644
Wayne, Anthony, 1745-
1796, 6464
Ways and means, 10609
The ways of the hour,
9153
Wayside courtships, 9608

A wayside episode, 9355
Way-side glimpses, north and
south, 2286
Way-side violets, 10584
We and our neighbors, 10911
We four villagers, 9541
Wealth and wine, 8983
Wearing of the gray, 9117
Wearing out the carpet, 10598
Wearithorne, 10605
Webb, Charles Henry, 1834-
1905, ed., 9026
Webb, Edwin Bonaparte,
1820-1901, 8357
Webb, J. Watson, ed., 5278,
5645
Webb, Thomas Hopkins, 1801-
1866, 5646
Webb, William Bensing, 1825-
1896, 6514
Webber, Charles Henry,
5647
Webber, Charles Wilkins,
1819-1856, 5648-5657
Webber, Horace Hervey, 11344
Webster, Daniel, 1782-1852,
207, 763, 925, 1680, 8202,
11304, 12745, 12813, 13193
Webster, Daniel, 1782-1852.
Speech on the subject of the
northeastern boundary,
April 15, 1843, 12186
Webster, Noah, 1758-1843, 266,
328, 5658
Wedded bliss, 9533
Wedderburn, John Walter,
13306
A wedding, 9265
The wedding and the funeral,
9702
The wedding days of former
times, 9973
The wedding guest: a friend of
the bride and bridegroom,
8586
The wedding knell, 9827
Weed, Thurlow, 1797-1882,
360
Weeden, Miss Howard, 1847-1905,

514

5659

Weedon, George, 1730?-
1790, 698

A week in Wall street,
10004

Weenokhenchah Wandeeteekoh,
10827

Wehe, Trude (Petersen)
1888-, 8358

Weichardt, Karl, ed.,
5660

Weichmann, Herbert, 5661

Wein, Paul, supposed
author, 2018

Weinman, Adolph Alexander,
1870-, 7296

Weir, Harrison William,
1824-1906, illustr.,
3594

Weir, James, 1821-1906,
5662, 5663, 5664

Weiser, George, 5665

Weishampel, John F.,
comp., 5666

Weiss, Mrs. Susan Archer
(Talley) 5667

Welby, Adlard, 5668

Welby, Amelia Ball
(Coppuck) 1819-1852,
5669

The Welch Indians, 1692

Weld, Charles Richard,
1813-1869, 5670

Weld, Isaac, 1794-1856,
5671, 8359, 8360, 8361,
8362, 8363, 8364

Well! Well! 11055

Welles, Albert, 8365

Welles, Alonzo Merritt,
8366

Wells, David Ames, 1828-
1898, 8367

Wells, John Doane, d. 1830,
1896

Wells, William, d. 1812,
6617

Wells, William Charles,
1757-1817, 2622

Welsh in the U. S., 13286

Welshmen and their descendants
of the American revolution,
13286

Wender, Ernesto J., tr.,
8324

Wenham, Mass. - Hist., 191

Wensley, 10583

Went to Kansas, 3059

Wentworth, Thomas, f. 1741,
573

The wept of Wish-ton-wish,
9154, 9155

Wesley, Charles, 1707-1788,
5672

Wesley, John, 1703-1791, 5673

Wesleyan Methodist church
in the West Indies, 1993

Wesleyan Methodist church
mission, 4037

Wesleyan Methodist church -
Missions, 1995

The Wesleyan student, 12845

Wesleyan university, 4646

West, Benjamin, 1738-1820,
2387

The west coast of Florida,
2707

The West - Descr. & trav.,
2465, 2486, 2488, 2498,
2499, 2528, 2572, 2581,
2597, 2607, 2616, 2621,
2651, 2652, 2653, 2668,
2689, 2710, 2756, 2772,
2783, 2796, 2823, 2845,
2846, 2881, 2891, 2892,
2916, 2926, 2936, 3005,
3017, 3047, 3081, 3100,
3105, 3111, 3117, 3129,
3169, 3179, 3220, 3257,
3266, 3268, 3299, 3321,
3349, 3380, 3414, 3421,
3438, 3444, 3462, 3521,
3524, 3540, 3543, 3551,
3570, 3578, 3630, 3636,
3651, 3658, 3676, 3723,
3790, 3795, 3826, 3837,
3862, 3888, 3901, 3923,
3955, 3982, 3992, 3993,
4026, 4027, 4028, 4030,

515

trav., 11382
West Indies, Dutch - Pol.
& govt., 1127
West Indies, French -
Descr. & trav., 4227
West Indies, French -
Hist., 12209
The West Indies: the natural
and physical history of
the Windward and Leeward
colonies, 12589
The West; its commerce
and navigation, 3753
West, John, chaplain to
the Hudson's Bay company,
5674
West, John Camden, 1834-,
5675
The West - Maps, 4353
West, Mary Eliza, 5682
West Newbury, Mass. -
Hist., 1972
West Point, N. Y. -
Hist., 11470
West Roxbury, Mass. -
Direct., 1566
The West - Statistics,
5233
West Virginia - Descr.
& trav., 3104, 3206,
3613, 3977, 4173, 4418,
5173
The West Virginia hand-
book and immigrant's
guide, 3206
West Virginia - Hist.,
3213, 5754
West Virginia - Hist. -
Civil war, 3670
West Virginia infantry.
4th regt., 1861-1864,
2627
Westbrook parsonage, 10287
Westchester Co., N. Y. -
Geneal, 11346
Westchester Co., N. Y. -
Hist., 11346
The western address
directory, 4320

The western Avernus, 4973
Western Baptist educational
association, 13139
Western border life, 11126
Western characters, 10265
Western clearings, 10150
Western country, Sketches of
a tour to the, 3138
The western gazetteer, 2831
The western Ginevra, 9678
A western journey with
Mr. Emerson, 8175
Western Kentucky, above ground
and below, 4324
Western lands and western
waters, 12217
The western merchant, 4116
The Western monthly review,
5677
Western museum society,
Cincinnati, 3285
The western navigator, 6529
Western North Carolina as a
health resort, 3626
The western pilot, 11895
Western, pseud., 5676
Western railroad, 12494
The Western railroad corporation,
1420
The Western review and
miscellaneous magazine, 5678
The Western sanitary
commission, 2275
The western sketch-book, 9596
The Western souvenir, 5679
Western windows, 4779
The western world, 4356
Westman, Georgius A., 2484
Westminster, Mass. Anti-
slavery picnic. 1843, 721
Westminster, Mass. - Hist.,
12983
Weston, Theodore, 1571
The Westover manuscripts,
2878
Westward Ho! 4720
Wet days at Edgewood: with
old farmers, old gardeners,
and old pastorals, 13443

The Wetherel affair, 9373
Wetherell, Elizabeth, pseud.,
11097
Wetmore, Alphonso, 1793-
1849, 4761, 5680
Wetmore, Prosper Montgomery,
1798-1876, 10403
Wette, Ludwig de, 5681
Weyer's cave, Va., 4100
Weygant, Charles H., 1839-
1909, 5682
Weymouth, Mass. North
church, 2193
The whale-fishermen, 9775
Whaling, 2838, 11576
Wharf property, 11436
Wharton, Charles Henry,
1748-1833, 12438
Wharton, Edward Clifton,
1827-1891, tr., 6880
Wharton, Joseph, 8368
Wharton, Thomas, 1731-
1783? 12293
What a farmer can do,
9042
What answer? 9399
What are you going to
do about it? 8534
What can she do? 10655
What constitutes the
state? 13151
What dreams may come,
8594
What Fanny Hunter saw
and heard in Kansas
and Missouri, 11126
What happened at the
fonda, 6969
What I did in "the long",
2626
What I did with my fifty
million,s 8639
What I saw and suffered
in rebel prisons, 4140
What I saw in California,
2846
What I saw in Dixie,
2876
What I saw in Texas, 3510

What I think of you, 9471
What is best? 10427
What is gentility, 10813
What "Jeems Pipes, of Pipesville"
saw and did, 10321
What Maisie knew, 7133, 10019
What may have been, 9304
What not, 9391
What shall we do with the
Hudson's Bay territory,
7809
What the world made them,
10050
What the years brought,
9797
What think ye of the Congress
now? 11722
What was the matter? 11075
What was thought of Amberglow,
8369
What would the world think,
9045
Whates, Harry Richmond,
d. 1923, 8370
Wheat, 1032, 1615
Wheat, Marvin, 8371
Wheat and tares, 9018
Wheaton and the panther,
10570
The wheel of time, 10020
Wheeler, Arthur O., 8372
Wheeler, George Bomford,
1805-1877, ed., 1794
Wheeler, John H., ed., 3418
Wheeler, John Hill, 1806-
1882, 5683, 5684
Wheeler, Joseph, 1836-1906,
3224, 6651, 8373
Wheeling - Bridges, 12019
Wheelock, Harrison, 5685
Wheelock, John, 1754-1817.
Sketches of the history of
Dartmouth college, 2134
Wheelock, Mrs. Julia Susan,
3537
Wheelock, Thompson B., 5686
Wheelwright, John T., jt.
author, 9641
Whelpley, James Davenport,

White-jacket, 10349
White, Jonah H., 5689
White, Joseph W., 5690
White, Josiah, 1781-1850,
8376
White Marie, 3774
The white mask, 11061
White, Matthew, jr., 10283
White Mountains, 718, 1271
White Mountains - Descr. &
trav. - Guide-books,
1034, 12485, 12495
White Plains, N. Y.
Bloomingdale hospital,
2152
White, Pliny Holton,
1822-1869, 8377
White, red, black, 4865
White, Richard Grant,
1821-1885, 8378
The White Rocks, 9867
The white rose road,
10043
The white rover, 4994
White, Samuel, of Adams
Co., Pa., 8379
The white slave, 9866
White slavery, 1746
The white snake, 2956
White, Stewart Edward,
1873-, 8380
White Sulphur papers,
4743
White Surphur Springs -
Fiction, 11187
White Sulphur Springs,
W. Va., 4515, 4743
White Sulphur Springs,
W. Va. - Soc. life
& cust., 11187
A white umbrella in
Mexico, 8041
White's guide to Florida
and her famous resorts,
5690
Whitefield, George, 1714-
1770, 1074, 5124, 5691,
11764, 12821
Whitfield, James M., 13237

Whither curiosity led, 11198
Whiting, Henry, 1788-1851,
5692, 5693
Whiting, Samuel, pub., 3892
Whiting, William Henry Chase,
5547
Whitman, Elizabeth, 1752-
1788 - Fiction, 9549, 9550
Whitney, Adeline Dutton
(Train) 1824-1906, 9693
Whitney, J. H. E., 5694
Whitney, Joel Parker, 5695
Whitney, John Prescott, 5696
Whitney, William Dwight,
1899-, 5697
Whitney's Florida pathfinder,
5696
Whittaker, James, 1751-1787,
12094
Whittelsey, Charles, 1723 or 4-
1764, 11953
Whittier, John Greenleaf,
1807-1892, 76, 13442
Whittlesey, Charles, 1808-
1886, 4664
Whitworth, Miles, 2089
Who are the Americans, 5697
Who did it? 10442
Who goes there? 8791, 11318
Who is free? 10207
Who is the captain? 9981
Who is to blame? 12344
Who was he? 11045
Who was my quiet friend?
9779
Who was the first governor
of Massachusetts? 2247
Who was who in Hardin county,
6952
Who were the early settlers
of Maryland, 171
Who would have thought it?
8918
The whole story in few words,
12995
Whose wife was she? 10006
Why and what am I, 10029
Why are we still at war?
2017

Why Constantinople fell,
11054
Why I am a Republican,
6134
Why I am a temperance
man, 8871
Why I married Eleanor,
10546
Why Mrs. Radnor fainted,
10899
Why the Confederacy
failed, 9749
Wickliffe, Robert, 1775-
1859, 1467, 2794,
5698, 5699
Wickliffe, Robert, 1775-
1859. Speech... 10th...
of August, 1840, 1465
Wide Awake Central
committee, 8381
Widow Guthrie, 4091
A widow of the Santa
Ana Valley, 6978
The widow Rugby's
husband, 3926
Widow Spriggins, 11136
The widow's bandbox,
10909
The widow's cruise,
10896
Wie lebt und arbeitet
man in den Vereinigten
Staaten? 3883
Wied-Neuwied, Maximilian
Alexander Philipp, prinz
von, 1782-1867, 5700,
5701
Wieland, 8861
Wieliczka salt-mines, 8877
Wiesse, María, 1894-, 8382
The wife of his youth,
2982
The wife of Leon, 5621
The wife of Lothario,
11191
The wife of two husbands,
11048
The wife's messengers,
9923

The wife's secret, 10875
Wightman, Elias R., 3833
The wigwam and the cabin,
10783
Wilberforce, Samuel, successively
bp. of Oxford and of
Winchester, 1805-1873.
A history of the Protestant
Episcopal church in America,
1214
Wilbur, Charles Edwin, 1833-
1896, reporter, 13188
Wilcox, E. W., 10163
Wilcox, the counterfeiter,
10310
Wilcox, Walter Dwight,
1869-, 8383
Wild, Ebenezer, 1758-1794,
5702
Wild flowers, 3961
The wild girl of the
Nebraska, 5655
Wild Jack, 3849
Wild life in Florida, 5450
Wild life in the interior
of Central America, 11655
The wild north land,
6264, 6265
Wild oats sowings, 3146
The wild riders of the
First Kentucky cavalry,
5348
Wild scenes and wild
hunters, 5650
Wild scenes and wild
hunters of the world,
5656
Wild scenes on the frontiers,
2685
Wild shrubs of Alabama,
12717
Wild southern scenes,
4117
Wild sports in the far West,
3594
Wild Nell, the White
Mountain girl, 10375
The wild rose of Cherokee,
10134

521

Wild western scenes,
10064
Wilda, Johannes, 1852-,
5703
Wildash, 4014
Wilde, Oscar Fingall
O'Flahertie Wills,
1856-1900, 5704
Wilde, Richard Henry,
1789-1847, 5705
The wilderness and the
war path, 3754
The wilderness of the
upper Yukon, 8012
Wildfire the wanderer,
9718
Wildmoor, 8900
Wildwood, Will, pseud.,
3758
Wilhelm, Honor Lupfer,
1870-, 5706
Wilhelmina, 11205
Wilkes, George, 1820-
1885, 5705
Wilkes, John, 1727-
1797, 11406, 12424
Wilkeson, Frank,
1845-, 5708
Wilkie, Franc Bangs,
1832-1892, 5709
Wilkins, James Hepburn,
8384
Wilkins Wylder, 10356
Wilkinson, James, 1757-
1825, 3682, 8016
Wilkinson, Jemima, 1752-
1819, 12984
Wilkinson, R. A., 5710
Wilkinson, Thomas Read,
5711
The will, 10085
A will and a way, 10580
Will it blow over? 10579
Will she succeed, 9447
Willamette Valley, Ore.,
4690
Willard, Archibald M.,
illustr., 2630
Willard, Conrad Brown,

1775-1826, 4715
Willcox, Giles Buckingham,
1826-1922, 8385
Willcox, Orlando Bolivar,
1823-, 3417
Willett, Edward, 1830-,
10445
William III, king of Great
Britain, 165--1702,
663
William and Mary College -
Fiction, 9118
William and Mary College.
Licivyronean society, 1959
William and Mary College,
Williamsburg, Va., 4124
William (Brigantine), 11281
William, Father, pseud., 5712
William Forbes, 9702
William Gilmore Simms, 5459
William Morgan, 458, 4534
William Penn et la paix,
8165
William Russell, Autobiography
of, 5377
William Wirt, 10953
Williams, Anna Vernon (Dorsey),
8969
Williams, C. D., illustr.,
10924
Williams, Cynric R., 8386
Williams, David, 1754-1831,
1175, 1176, 1177
Williams, Edward, fl. 1650,
5713
Williams, Edward Peet,
5714
Williams, Ezekiel, fl. 1807-
1827, 3105
Williams, Francis Howard, 1844-
1922, 10737
Williams, George Forrester,
1837-, 5715
Williams, George W., 5716
Williams (J. D. & M.) Boston,
2441
Williams, James, 1805-, 5717
Williams, John Aug., 4366
Williams, John Lee, 5718

Williams, John S., ed.,
287
Williams, John Sharp,
7263
Williams, Joseph, 5719
Williams, Mrs. Martha
McCulloch, 5720,
5721, 5722
Williams, Richard,
1815-1851, 12612
Williams, Roger, 1604?-
1683, 12193, 13251
Williams, Roger, 1604?-
1683 - Bibl., 12489
Williams, Samuel Cole,
1864-, ed., 5723
Williams, Thomas, 50
Williams, Thomas, 1815-
1862, 2587
Williams, W. H., 8387
Williams, Wellington,
5724, 5725, 5726,
8388, 8389
Williams, William, 1763-,
5727
Williamsburg, Battle of,
1862, 11625
Williamsom, Caleb, 8103
Williamson county, Ill. -
Hist., 3389
Williamson family, 8103
Williamson, James Joseph,
1834-1915, 5728
Williamson, Mary Cobb,
8103
Willie Baker's good
sense, 9254
Willis, Nathaniel Parker,
1806-1867, 5729, 5730
Willis, Simeon, 1879-,
7153
Willoughby, Sir Hugh,
d. 1554, 12192
Willoughby, Hugh Laussat,
1856-, 5731
Wills, Charles Wright,
1840-1883, 5732
Willson, Forceythe, 1837-
1867, 5733

Wilmer, Richard Hooker,
bp., 1816-1910, 5734
Wilmere, Alice, tr., 11714
Wilmot proviso, 1846, 1214,
4296
Wilson, A. E., 10163
Wilson, Alexander, 1766-
1812, 5735
Wilson, Charles Henry, of
Northallerton, 8390
Wilson, ---, commissary of
General Amherst's army,
1759, 331
Wilson, Henry, 1812-1875,
6288
Wilson, Herbert Michael,
8391
The Wilson House, 10197
Wilson, James, 1739 or 60-1814,
12433
Wilson, James A., 8392
Wilson, Jane Adeline, 5736
Wilson, John Alfred, 1832-,
5737
Wilson, John Lyde, 1784-
1849, 9910
Wilson, Lawrence, Maurice,
1896-1963, 7526, 8393
Wilson, Lizzie, 1835-1858,
5738
Wilson, Richard Lush, 5739
Wilson, Robert Anderson,
1812-1872, 8394, 8395,
8396
Wilson, Robert Burns,
1850-1916, 5740, 5741
Wilson, Samuel, fl. 1678-1682,
5742
Wilson, Samuel (of Kentucky)
5743
Wilson, Samuel (writer on
temperance) 8397
Wilson, Thomas, 1655?-1725,
5744
Wilson, William, the whistling
shoemaker, 10849
Wilson, William Thomas,
1834-1890, 8398
Wilstach, John Augustine,

Woman's faith triumphant, 8748
Woman's foibles, 10155
A woman's inheritance, 9425
A woman's journey round the world, 13454
Woman's medical college of Pennsylvania, Philadelphia, 9331
A woman's poems, 4788
A woman's reason, 9957
Woman's record, 2459
Woman's relation to education, labor, and law, 11939
A woman's right, 8531
The woman's story, 10163
A woman's wanderings in the western world, 1557
A woman's way through unknown Labrador, 6671
Woman's work in the civil war, 11528
Woman's wrongs, 9970
Women, 10300
Women as authors, 2334
Women - Biog., 12023
Women in America, 1102, 11545
Women in New York (City), 9732, 12025
Women in the Confederate States of America, 4035
Women in the U. S., 1044, 11663
Women in the U. S. - Biog., 12022
Women of the South distinguished in literature, 3536
Won by a bicycle, 9976
Wonder tales of early American history, 2870
The wonder-worker of Padua, 10898

The wonderful adventures of a Pullman, 9680
The wonderful adventures of Captain Priest, 9724
The wonderful preservation of Mrs. Moore, when a prisoner among the Indians, 10570
Wonders of the great Mammoth Cave of Kentucky, 5486
Wontus, 10682
The wood demon, 10919
Wood, Fernando, 1812-1881, 7286
Wood, George L., 1837 or 8-, 5756
Wood, J. C., 5757
Wood, John, 5758
Wood, John, 1775?-1822. A correct state of the various sources from which the History of the administration of John Adams was compiled, 11768
Wood, John Taylor, 3417
Wood, Louis Aubrey, 1883-, 8411
Wood notes wild, 2582
Wood, Robert Crooke, 5759
Wood, S., 5760
Wood, William Charles Henry, 1864-, 8412, 8413, 8414
Woodbridge, Hensley C., ed. & tr., 7089
Woodburn, 4055
Woodbury, Augustus, 1825-1895, 5761, 8415, 8416
Woodbury, John H., 5762
Woodcliff, 10288
Woodcraft, 10782
Woodland lays, legends and charades, 12536
Woodlawn cemetery. Maiden, Mass., 2356
Woodley, William J., 8417
Woodman, David, jr., 5763
Woodman family (Edward Woodman, fl. 1635), 1971
Woodreve manor, 9418

Woodruff, William Edward,
   1831-, 5764
Woods, John, 5765, 5766
Woods, Nicholas Augustus,
   8418
Woodstock, Conn. First
   Congregational church,
   12467
Woodville, 10983
Woodward, Evan Morrison,
   5767
Woodward, William H.,
   2226
Woodworth, Samuel,
   1785-1842, 9649
Wooing and warrning in
   the wilderness, 4180
Wool-gathering, 3262
Wool, John Ellis,
   1784-1869, 992
Wooldridge, John, 6514
Woolen and worsted
   manufacture, 4019
Woolman, John, 1720-
   1772, 5768, 5769
Woolson, A. G., 10163
Woolworth, Aaron, 1763-
   1821, 1661
Woolworth, James, 5770
Worcester as it is,
   12966
Worcester central
   conference of Congre-
   gational churches, 172
Worcester, Joseph
   Emerson, 1784-1865, ed.,
   239
Worcester, Mass. -
   Cemeteries, 945
Worcester, Mass. First
   church, 636
Worcester, Mass. First
   Unitarian church, 731
Worcester, Mass. - Hist.,
   12966
Word for word and letter
   for letter, 8800
Worden, A. T., jt.
   author, 8546

Words in affliction, 8419
Words that burn, 8881
Work: a story of experience,
   8487
Work, John, 8420
The workingman's paradise,
   3613
The works of God declared
   by one generation to another,
   2283
The works of Jeremy Peters,
   10824
World history, 12175
The world in a man-of-war,
   10349
The World, New York, 7402
The world of chance, 9958
A world of green hills, 5437
World politics, 1947
World politics - Period., 7275
The world to blame, 10518
World's masonic register,
   13062
The world's progress, 12396
Worm, A. W. van den, tr., 670
Wormeley, Elizabeth, see
   Latimer, Elizabeth Wormeley,
   10167, 10168
Wormsloe quartos, 3208
Worrosquoyacke, 9768
Worsham, John H., 5771
The worst enemy conquered,
   1073
Worthies of old Red river,
   6236
Worthington, William G. D.,
   11480
Wounded in the house of a
   friend, 8561
Wounds in the rain, 9217
Wounds - Treatment, 13304
Wraxall, Sir Frederick Charles
   Lascelles, 3d bart., 1828-
   1865, tr., 2496, 5772
The wreath of Eglantine, 4312
A wreath of Virginia bay
   leaves, 3933
The wreck on the Indian Ocean,
   8669

Wrecked, but not lost,
8692
The wrecker's daughter,
9977
The wreckers of St.
Agnes, 10693
Wrede, Friedrich W. von,
5773
Wright, Henry H., 1840-
1905, 5774
Wright, Irene A., jt.
ed., 7274, 8421
Wright, John, 5775
Wright, John W., 5776
Wright, Lucy, 1760-1821,
12094
Wright, Mrs. Marie
(Robinson) 1866-1914, 8422
Wright, Silas, 1795-1847,
12269, 12624, 13198
Wright, Thomas J.,
captain 8th Kentucky
infantry, 5777
Wrightstown township,
Pa. - Geneal, 1636
Wrightstown township,
Pa. - Hist., 1636
Writers' program. Puerto
Rico, 8264
Writing - Hist., 2351
The writing on the wall,
9358
Writings, 4243
Writings: including
speeches and addresses,
3026
Writs - Illinois, 13302
Written in red, 10371
The wrong of slavery, 4669
Wrottesley, George, 1827-
1909, ed., 1706
Wunnissoo, 204
The Wyandot's story,
9618, 10919
Wyandotté, 9157
Wyandott Mission, 3451
Wych Hazel, 11099
Wyeth, John Allan,
1845-1922, 5778

Wyeth, John B., 5779
Wylie, Andrew, 1789-1851,
5780
Wyllie, Robert Crichton,
1798-1865, 8423
Wynne, John Huddlestone,
1743-1788, 5781
Wynne, Thomas Hicks,
d. 1875, ed., 11656, 12136
Wyoming - Descr. & trav.,
2877, 4549
Wyoming - Hist., 8318
Wyoming massacre, 1778, 10569
Wyoming Valley, Pa. - Hist.,
1824, 11734
Wyse, Francis, 5782
Wyse, Sir Thomas, 1791-1862.
Education reform, 2280
Wyss-Dunant, Édouard, 8424
Wythe, George, 1726-1806,
8019

The XY company, 6228
Xántus, János, 1825-, 5783
Xariffa's poems, 5448
Ximénez, Andrés, fl. 1643,
6469, 6470
Xuarez, Fernan, tr., 122
The yacht "Alice", 3950
Yachts and yachting, 7012,
12722
Yale university, 2371, 11800,
11801, 11802, 12819
Yale university. Amasa Stone
Mather memorial publication
fund, 3887
Yale university - Hist., 701
Yamoyden, 2157
Yanacocha, Battle of, 1835 -
Poetry, 951
Yancey, William Lowndes,
1814-1863, 3301
Yandell, Lunsford Pitts,
1805-1878, 5784, 5785
The Yankee, 10760
A Yankee among the nullifiers,
9653, 9654
Yankee chronology, 2136

10059
Young Abraham Lincoln
and Log College, 7070
A young American in England,
10310
Young, Arthur, 5789
Young, Bennett Henderson,
1843-1919, 1167
Young, Brigham, 1801-1877,
3679, 5790, 10613
The young captive prince,
9459
The young Carolinian of
1776, 8848
The young chief of the
Abenaquies, 9986
A young Christian's
choice, 10389
The young citizen's
catechism, 12951
The young disciple, 9008
Young, Edward, 1814-1909,
jt. author, 1356
Young, Edward James,
1829-1906, 8427
Young, Egerton Ryerson,
1840-1909, 8428
The young emigrants,
8226
The young franc-tireurs
and their adventures
in the Franco-Prussian
War, 7011
A young girl's wooing,
10656
Young Goodman Brown, 9823
Young Greer of Kentucky,
10140
Young, Jacob, 1776-1859,
5791
Young Jo, attributed author,
12087
Young, John Clarke,
1803-1857, 4851
Young knighthood, 10471
A young lady of the state
of New York, 9542
The young lady's friend,
10679

The young marooners on the
Florida Coast, 3656
Young men, 957
Young Men's Christian
Association, Chicago, 8429
Young men's Democratic club,
Philadelphia, 12269
Young Men's Republican Union,
New York, 8430
The young mill-wright & miller's
guide, 12100
Young Miss Giddy, 10551
The young mountaineers,
4567
The young pilot of the
Belle Creole, 3843
Young Robin Gray, 6963
Young, Thomas M., 5792
Young, W. A., 5793
Young, William Henry, 5794
The youngest prospector in
Calaveras, 9793
Yount, Charles Allen, 8431
Yourtree, Samuel L., d. 1880,
8432
Youth and manhood, 10264
The youth of Jefferson, 9118
Yucatan, 6612, 7836, 7998,
8433
Yucatan - Antiq., 1830, 5932,
6404, 6407, 7590
Yucatan - Descr. & trav.,
3491, 5932, 5986, 7590,
8109
Yucatan - Hist., 2215, 5825,
7231, 7465
Yucatan - Pol. & govt.,
7465
Yukon river and valley -
Descr. & trav., 7982
Yukon river and valley -
Hist., 7630
Yukon territory, 7630
Yukon territory - Bibl., 7328
Yukon territory - Descr. &
trav., 7369, 8012
Yurami, Antonio Miguel, 8434
Yusef, 8880

Zabel, Eugen, 1851-,
5795
Zabriskie, Andrew Christian,
1853-, 8435
Zacatecas, Mexico (City) -
Festivals, etc., 6160
Zacatecas, Mexico (City)
Santo Domingo (church),
5803
Zadoc Pine, 8899
Zamora Castellanos, Pedro,
jt. author, 7686
Zamorano, Rodrigo, b. ca.
1542, 8436
Zannini, Alessandro, conte,
5796
Zanzibar - Descr. & trav.,
11576
Zapapán, Mexico. Santuario
de Nuestra Señora, 6754
Zaragoza, Justo, d. 1896,
ed., 6789
Zárate, Julio, 1844-1917,
7873
Zarco, João Gonçalves,
ca. 1400-ca. 1465, 129
Zaremba, Charles W.,
8437
Zavala, Lorenzo de, 1788-
1836, 5797
Zehntausend meilen im
sattel vom kreuz des
südens zum polarstern,
8243
Zeigler, Wilbur Gleason,
5798
Zelayeta, Martin de,
d. 1756, 8145
Zelotes, pseud., 5799
Zenaida, 8536
Zenana missions, 8852
Zenkovich, Vsevolod Pavlovich,
1910-, 8348
Zepeda Rincón, Tomas,
8439, 8440
Zerecero, Anastasio, 1799-
1875, 8441
Zes maanden in Amerika,
5309

Zetina Infante, Juan Pablo,
6269
Zettler, Berrien McPherson,
1842-, 5800
De zevende haven, 7159
Ziegler, Eustace Paul,
illustr., 4568
A zigzag journey in the
sunny South, 2870
Zigzag journeys on the
Mississippi, 2871
Zigzag, Zelotes, pseud., 5799
Zimmermann, Karl, 5801
Zincke, Foster Barham, 1817-
1893, 5802
Zinzendorf, Nicolaus Ludwig,
grav von, 1700-1760,
jt. ed., 1027
Zoë, 4283
Zoology - Arctic regions, 4956
Zoology - Argentine republic,
1719
Zoology - Classification, 107
Zoology - French Guiana, 680
Zoology - Massachusetts, 12329
Zoology - Mexico, 7549
Zoology - North America, 12150
Zoology - Oregon, 5445
Zoology - South America, 7092
Zoology - Southwest, New, 5513
Zoology - U. S., 107
Zoroaster, 6509, 9237
Zuloaga, Joaquín de, 6386
Zuni River, 5517
Zúñiga Montúfar, Tobías, 8442
Zürich. Comité zur unterstützung
der befreiten farbigen, 12295
Zurita, Fernando, 8443
Zyx and his fairy, 8868

531

ILLUSTRATORS